CONTINUITY & CHANGE IN MARRIAGE & FAMILY

CONTINUITY & CHANGE IN MARRIAGE & FAMILY

Jean E. Veevers

Professor of Sociology
University of Victoria

HARCOURT
BRACE
CANADA

HARCOURT BRACE & COMPANY, CANADA
TORONTO   MONTREAL   FORT WORTH   NEW YORK   ORLANDO
PHILADELPHIA   SAN DIEGO   LONDON   SYDNEY   TOKYO

Canadian Cataloguing in Publication Data

Main entry under title:
Continuity and change in marriage and family

ISBN 0–03–922658–1

1. Family - Canada. 2. Marriage - Canada.
I. Veevers, J.E.

HQ560.C6 1991   306.8′0971   C89–094996–4

Acquisitions Editor: Heather McWhinney
Developmental Editor: Graeme Whitley
Managing Editor: Liz Radojkovic
Editorial Assistant: Robert Gordon
Copy Editor: Yvonne Bondarchuk
Cover and Interior Design: Angela Vaculik
Typesetting and Assembly: True to Type Inc.
Printing and Binding: Webcom Limited

∞ This book was printed in Canada on acid-free paper.

2 3 4 5   95 94

To the Memory of
EDITH LILIAN CARMICHAEL GRATZ
1908–1987

Preface

The present anthology is intended to supplement a variety of contemporary theoretical approaches to the study of the family. After teaching the sociology of marriage and the family for 20 years — at Queen's, at the University of Western Ontario, and most recently at the University of Victoria — I have found no shortage of family textbooks. There has been, however, a dearth of competent empirical works specifically applicable to the task of describing and understanding Canadian family life. This collection brings together the works of a wide variety of scholars, all of whom address issues directly relevant to the study of marriage and family in Canada. All of the works selected were originally published in recognized referred journals, and so have been subjected to rigorous and anonymous peer review. In compiling this anthology, I am indebted to the 53 authors who graciously consented to have their works reprinted, and to the several anonymous reviewers who offered constructive suggestions.

Some of the articles that appear in this volume have been lightly edited. All of the changes have been approved by the authors of the articles. In addition, Harcourt Brace & Company, Canada has made every effort to standardize the style of documentation in this volume to comply with the guidelines published in the *MLA Handbook for Writers of Research Papers*, 3rd ed. These changes have been made to aid the student in any further research.

This project has benefited greatly from the assistance of two graduate students in the Sociology Department at the University of Victoria. I wish to thank Mr. Michael Bergob for his diligent and meticulous library research, and Ms. Shelley Eisler for her compilation of the companion *Instructor's Manual*.

My work on this and other projects has benefited substantively and stylistically from insights shared with me by my colleague Ms. Sue Dier of the University of Victoria, and by my long-term collaborator, Dr. Ellen M. Gee of Simon Fraser University. I appreciate their singular perspectives and value their friendship.

Throughout it all, I have appreciated the support and *bonhomie* of my covivant, Ron Whitmarsh, who suffered with good grace the tribulations of the anthologist.

J.E.V.
Victoria, British Columbia
April 1990

Publisher's Note to Instructors and Students

This textbook is a key component of your course. If you are the instructor of this course, you undoubtedly considered a number of texts carefully before choosing this as the one that will work best for your students and you. The authors and publishers of this book spent considerable time and money to ensure its high quality, and we appreciate your rec-·ognition of this effort and accomplishment.

If you are a student, we are confident that this text will help you to meet the objectives of your course. You will also find it helpful after the course is finished, as a valuable addition to your personal library. So hold on to it.

As well, please don't forget that photocopying copyright work means the authors lose royalties that are rightfully theirs. This loss will discourage them from writing another edition of this text or other books, because doing so will simply not be worth their time and effort. If this happens, we all lose — students, instructors, authors, and publishers.

And since we want to hear what you think about this book, please be sure to send us the stamped reply card at the end of the text. This will help us to continue publishing high-quality books for your courses.

Contents

Part Six

PROCREATION AND PARENTHOOD

Part Seven

FAMILY ISSUES OF THE MIDDLE-AGED AND THE ELDERLY

Part Eight

SERIAL MONOGAMY: DIVORCE AND REMARRIAGE

Part Nine

FAMILIES, SOCIAL POLICIES, AND THE STATE

Part Ten

EVOLUTION, REVOLUTION, AND THE FUTURE OF THE FAMILY

HOW TO READ RESEARCH ABOUT MARRIAGE AND FAMILY

Keith Melville

Ours is an age of science and statistics, in which one of the most common ploys in persuasion is to introduce key claims with such phrases as "Experts agree that" or "Studies indicate that." So toothpaste is sold and arguments won with such statements as "Three out of four dentists surveyed recommend Bronzo as the most effective toothpaste." Very often, such phrases serve only as a magic wand to be waved over dubious opinions to make them sound more convincing, more scientific.

How, then, can you judge for yourself the reliability of any observation or generalization? By reading social-science research carefully, you can learn to detect exaggerated or erroneous claims. Like well-informed consumers who read labels before making purchases, sceptical readers look for certain clues to determine whether they are getting reliable information or misinformation.

Social-science research provides several observational techniques, or methodologies, that allow you to see important facts or relationships more clearly than you could by casual observation or intuition. However, the language of social-science research may at first seem difficult to comprehend. The following suggestions should help you to read social-science research about the family.

• *Remember to distinguish between facts and personal opinions.* Like well-coached witnesses in a courtroom, social scientists are trained to stick to the facts and to avoid personal

opinion. You should learn to distinguish between the two. To be sure, there is nothing wrong when a writer argues a case and tries to persuade you to share an opinion. As novelist and essayist Larry McMurtry said in his introduction to *In a Narrow Grave: Essays on Texas* (1971, vi), "I haven't spent thirty years in Texas just to be objective about the place." But, you should always be aware of whether the author's intention is to report certain facts or to convince you of his or her opinion.

• *The facts don't, as the saying goes, speak for themselves.* Most articles and books consist mainly of inferences or interpretations based on a relatively small number of facts. Research data can often be used to support quite different conclusions. For example, two authors might begin with the same statistics on divorce. If one intended to show how alarmingly high the divorce rate is and the other wanted to argue that many marriages remain intact, they would present the same facts from different perspectives. Told that a glass is half full, you are likely to perceive it one way; told that it is half empty, you may see it quite differently.

• *Pay close attention to the words that researchers use.* In social-science research, words often have a slightly different meaning from their everyday sense. When you read about studies of marital adjustment, for example, the words don't necessarily mean the same thing that they do in normal usage. Get into the habit of asking whether such terms refer to some specific behaviour that the investigator might observe or measure.

• *Examine the size and nature of the sample from which a generalization is drawn.* One dif-

Source: *Marriage and Family Today* (New York: Random House, 1988), 26–28. Reprinted with permission.

ference between popular journalism and social-science research is that popular accounts are often based on nothing more than interesting anecdotes or colourful quotes. In contrast, social scientists are concerned with studying a representative sample to reach a more valid generalization. But, even in the writings of social scientists, some generalizations are based largely on impressions and insights from clinical observations. These can be valuable. You should be aware, however, that such cases may not be representative. Remember to ask whether the population that was studied is representative of the people to whom the conclusions are applied. Scientists, like others, sometimes make the mistake of reaching for the overly ambitious generalization that cannot be supported by evidence from a small or nonrepresentative sample.

• *Learn to distinguish valid generalizations from stereotypes.* Certain generalizations made by sociologists — the statement that black people have a higher rate of separation and divorce than white people, for example — sound very much like bigoted stereotyping — in this example, an insistence that black men run out on their families. What is the difference between a valid generalization and a stereotype? The most important difference is that the sociologist begins with a careful observation of a representative sample of the population to which the generalization applies. Social-science explanations are generally an expression of statistical correlation. This means simply that two factors are associated more frequently than we would expect on a chance basis. Social scientists speak in the language of probability — certain things are more likely to happen than others — rather than in the more reassuring language of predictability or certainty.

• *One "fugitive from the law of averages" does not disprove a generalization.* One of the puzzling things about the language of social research is that you often encounter generalizations to which you can immediately think of an exception. For example, you may read that teenage marriages are more likely to end in divorce than are marriages between individuals who are a few years older. But, you may know several couples who married at an early age and are still happily married 25 years later. Is the generalization wrong? No, because generalizations are statistical in nature. Sociologists are concerned not with individual cases, but with the relation between certain factors for the population as a whole. If a connection is discovered, the existence of some kind of causal pattern may be assumed, even though it cannot be demonstrated in every case.

It has been well established, for example, that smoking cigarettes may cause cancer. The most convincing evidence that led the Surgeon General to require the warning that appears on every package of cigarettes was statistical: individuals who smoke cigarettes are much more likely to be victims of lung cancer. The fact that there are many individuals who have been smoking two packs a day for 70 years does not disprove the generalization. There are, to use a phrase from one of Bill Mauldin's cartoons, certain "fugitives from the law of averages." Smokers are, however, much more likely to contract cancer. This is the sort of probability statement that social researchers offer.

• *Social-science research, like bread on a grocer's shelves, does not stay fresh forever.* Rapid social change creates problems for social researchers. Some studies that were conducted no more than a few years ago are already outdated. They may be useful as social history, to help us understand who we were, but they no longer illuminate who we are. You should get into the habit of looking at the date when research studies were conducted. However, older studies may still be valid, and their findings should not automatically be dismissed.

• *Learn to recognize ethnocentric attitudes, in which the standards of one's own group are used to judge another.* Much of what is written about marriage and family behaviour still betrays middle-class bias. It is quite common, as sociologist Hyman Rodman points out, to view any household arrangement or intimate bond that does not correspond to middle-class norms as a problem rather than as a practical solution. He asks,

> Are "illegitimacy," "desertion," and "common law" unions problems of the lower class or are they solutions of the lower class to more basic problems? Do we take the fact that there are few interracial marriages and few full-time career women [see the item above on outdated studies!] to indicate that these matters are somehow against human nature and therefore best to avoid? Or do we take these as indicative of cultural obstacles that should be removed? (Rodman 1965, 450)

• *Learn how to use statistics and to beware of their misuses.* Statistics can help us to think clearly and precisely about social phenomena. But they are frequently misapplied, as Mark Twain observed when he referred to the man who used statistics "like a drunk uses a lamp-post — not for light, but for support." You sometimes see articles or books in which the statistics march right across the page, like soldiers on parade. But don't be too impressed. Get into the habit of asking about the source of statistics. Figures may be quoted to the third decimal place and still be useless if they come from an unreliable source. Be especially wary of an isolated statistic in an imprecise context.

• *Remember that social-science research cannot provide an answer to moral questions.* Although individuals who wish to act responsibly have to be aware of the likely consequences of their actions, social-science research cannot tell you what to do. In many instances, however, it can help you to anticipate consequences. The mere fact that a majority shares a certain belief does not prove that it is morally right.

Works Cited

Rodman, Hyman. 1965. "The Textbook World of Family Sociology." *Social Problems* 12: 445–56.

McMurtry, Larry. 1971. *In a Narrow Grave: Essays on Texas.* Albuquerque, NM: University of New Mexico Press.

Introduction

MAJOR TRENDS IN THE CHANGING CANADIAN FAMILY

• • •

The only person sure of himself is the man who wishes to leave things as they are, and he dreams of an impossibility.

George M. Wrong, *Canadian Historical Review* (1921)

The family is an institution of major importance in Canadian society. It reflects the complex components of our intellectual and cultural traditions, structures many of the major events in our lives, and will ultimately play a major part in determining the nature of our society in the future.

Because the changes that have occurred in the Canadian family since the turn of the century are both pervasive and amorphous, they are difficult to document in any systematic way. To provide a convenient springboard for discussion, we have identified eight major trends that characterize changes in the Canadian family over the past several decades:

1. a modification of gender roles;
2. an increase in sexual freedom and a consequent decline in the double standard;
3. an increase in freedom in mate selection;
4. an increase in the visibility and prominence of unmarried persons, including an increase in awareness of the homosexual presence;
5. an increase in divorce and remarriage;
6. an increase of women in the work force, with subsequent problems of double workloads on the job and at home;
7. a marked decline in fertility; and
8. an increase in the visibility and prominence of elderly persons.

In choosing these eight changes for discussion, we have tried to focus on trends that touch the lives of *all* Canadians. The total population of Canada is now about 26 million. Within that population, there are, of course, real and important divisions in terms of regional differences, as well as religious and ethnic polarities. More detailed analysis would doubtless find that families in the western provinces are in some ways different from those in central Canada or those in the Atlantic region (Veevers 1990a). French Catholic families are in some ways different from English Protestant families, just as families of the middle class are different from those of the working class. Our purpose here is not to deny or to minimize these differences, but rather to stress the features that all Canadian families have in common, and to describe the general context in which particular subcultures operate.

The study of the Canadian family can draw from a vast array of historical sources. Because the plethora of materials available for study is initially confusing and can be overwhelming, we have concentrated only on trends between 1921 and the present, and only on data collected during the seven intervening census years. Accordingly, although we have sacrificed some of the available information, we have highlighted the major trends. Individual articles in this text explore in greater detail the richness and complexity of available data.

The reader of this overview should keep two major limitations in mind. First, identifying a set of eight trends is an arbitrary way of classifying events. One might as easily come up with a minimum of five megatrends or a selection of twenty. Second, and more important, it must be remembered that in reality these trends do not occur in isolation. A continuous interaction changes and modifies each of the trends in terms of all of the others. Although, for the purposes of discussion, we can separate issues and consider each one separately, in fact, each of the observed changes continually affects all of the others.

Modifying Gender Roles: Words and Deeds

Male domination has had some very unfortunate effects. It made the most intimate of human relations, that of marriage, one of master and slave, instead of between equal partners.
Bertrand Russell, *Marriage and Morals* (1929)

Marriages and families begin with the complimentary roles of wife and husband, mother and son, father and daughter, and sister and brother. Changes in family relationships are inevitably and inextricably affected by changes in the more comprehensive social roles of woman and man, girl and boy. Conversely, changes in the cross-sex arrangements made within families will have ramifications for male–female roles in other institutions.

The roles of men and women are determined and defined by both biological and social factors. In discussing them, it is useful to differentiate *sex roles* from *gender roles*. Sex roles involve differences that can be attributed entirely or mostly to biological differences. Implicit in the discussion of sex roles is the idea that, because they have a physiological basis, they are difficult or impossible to change. In contrast, gender roles involve differences that are to be attributed entirely or mostly to social differences. By implication, if gender roles are a product of social learning, they are potentially variable and malleable.

The systematic study of gender roles, and of these roles in a family context, has been undertaken from a number of perspectives. For our purposes, it is useful to consider simultaneously at least three major dimensions. The first, and perhaps the most obvious, is the *normative* component, which includes the values people hold about how family life ought to be, and the attitudes they have about how individuals should behave. These normative expectations may or may not be reflected in the second component, which is the legal context that regulates various aspects of family life. The *de jure* facets of family life — that is, those sanctioned by law — may or may not be reflected in a third component, which is the *de facto* component, or how persons actually act. When we study the normative aspects, we pose a series of questions about opinions, expectations, values, and ideals; when we study the *de facto* family, we pose questions about what persons actually do. Sometimes, the opinions that Canadians hold about gender roles and family life coincide both with how they act and with the existing legal framework. In many instances, however, the scope and pace of social change have been such that the three components are not synchronized, and contain implicit or explicit contradictions.

Talking Equal: The Decline of Blatant Sexism

The social reformations of the 1960s initially focussed on *consciousness raising*. Gender-role programming can be so pervasive and subtle that the constraints and obligations it imposes are effective even when they are below the level of awareness. Betty Friedan's best-selling book *The Feminine Mystique* (1963) spawned widespread interest and focussed conversations on "the problem that has no name." Many people of both sexes became aware of the existence of sexism, and came to define it, like racism, as outmoded and socially unacceptable.

In Canada, in the 1960s, the mores of polite society came to require ritualized recognition of equality between men and women, at least among members of the educated middle class, and at least while in mixed company. Dirty jokes, discriminatory policies, or provocative advertisements came to be seen as "sexist," and therefore subject to umbrage and outrage. Similarly, the use of the term "chauvinist" to describe a person of either sex became derogatory, whether it referred to male chauvinist pigs or female chauvinist sows. Blatant sexists, like blatant racists, became a source of embarrassment to their families and associates, and were chided to contain their disrespect.

Thinking Equal: The Persistence of Sexist Attitudes

The social construction of gender-role awareness is a complex and pervasive process that begins in earliest childhood, is elaborated in adolescence, and is continually reinforced in adulthood. The components of this socialization range from the public education system to the structure of language, the symbolic messages of the mass media, and the micropolitics of everyday life (Greenglass 1982; Mackie 1983, 1987). Although the implicit assumptions that become part of the taken-for-granted reality can, of course, be changed, they are notoriously resistant to change. The creation and acceptance of an alternative world view requires not only consciousness raising but also the internalization of a new lexicon for describing the social world, and a new basis of support for sustaining it.

Modern sexism may be less blatant than before, but may still involve subtle and covert discrimination on many levels (Benokraitis and Feagin 1986). Advocates of sex-role equality have been largely successful in modifying what people think they should *say* about gender roles: they have not been nearly

as successful in modifying what people actually *think*. An appropriate parallel can be drawn from the field of race relations. One level of social change may prevent bigots from acting in discriminatory ways, at least in public. Quite another level of social change is required to stop them from feeling prejudiced. As one disillusioned civil-rights advocate proclaimed in discouragement: "The most progress we have made is to teach them not to say *nigger* in public." While this may overstate the case with regard to changes in both racism and sexism, it remains true that changes in the open expression of disparaging attitudes are much easier to effect than are fundamental changes in the attitudes themselves.

Acting Equal: Changes in the Law

The extent to which there have been normative changes in gender-roles is difficult to assess and remains a focus of debate and speculation. The extent to which *de jure* changes have occurred is more readily apparent.

At the turn of the century, a married woman had no legal status as a person, other than as an extension of her husband. She was pledged to obey her husband, and was in many ways "civilly dead" (Schmid 1976, 3). The gradual evolution of legal and social reforms was brought into focus in 1970, when the Royal Commission on the Status of Women was instructed to inquire into the status of women and make recommendations "to ensure for women equal opportunities with men in all aspects of Canadian society" (Bird 1970, ix). Ten years later, 96 of the commission's 122 specific recommendations within the jurisdiction of the federal government have been implemented or partly implemented (Anderson 1979). Another official endorsement of equality was the establishment in 1983 of the Canadian Advisory Council on the Status of Women.

General concern with issues of justice and equality led to the enactment, in 1982, of the Canadian Charter of Rights and Freedoms. Section 15 of the Charter, which came into effect in April 1985, asserts that: "Every individual is equal before and under the law and has the right to the equal protection and equal benefit of the law without discrimination and, in particular, without discrimination based on . . . sex" (Boyer 1985). Following this perspective, the Parliamentary Committee on Equality Rights has considered the specifics of *Equality for All* (Boyer 1985), and specified a number of interventions that would equalize the roles of Canadian men and women.

But Some Are More Equal Than Others

The formal acceptance of the ideology of equality and its symbolic manifestation in pronouncements and laws does not mean that opportunities for men and women are, in fact, equal. For example, theoretically, Canadian men and women have equal access to education; in practice, they do not. In the 1920s, of all undergraduate degrees, about one in five was granted to a woman. Since then, the ratio has increased to half and half, clearly a step in the direction of equality. However, this equality does not extend to advanced degrees, which are granted to three times as many males as females (Prentice et al. 1988, 428).

To take another example: one of the earliest and usually least controversial rights to be granted was the right to vote and to hold public office. From 1920 to 1970, women made up only 2.4 percent of candidates for the House of Commons, and only 0.8 percent of those elected. By 1984, these rates had increased, but only to 14.8 percent of the candidates and 9.6 percent of those elected (Wilson 1986, 136). Alternatively, we might observe that nine out of ten members of the House are male, a balance that is a far cry from half and half.

Finally, let us look briefly at the nitty-gritty issue of money. Most Canadians now endorse the normative principle of "equal pay for work of equal value," meaning that men and women performing comparable jobs should receive comparable wages. In fact, however, Canadian men and women are still far from

equal economically. In 1987, women who worked full-time earned only 65.9 percent of the income of men who worked full-time (Statistics Canada 1989b). Apparently we believe that women should be paid equally, and we have introduced legislation to facilitate that goal, but, in fact, men still earn substantially more.

These brief examples are offered to illustrate three important points, which should be kept in mind throughout this chapter and throughout all of the readings. First, the move toward gender equality has resulted, sometimes, in a situation of *less inequality* than existed a generation or two ago. Second, however a man and woman may feel about each other when they enter into a relationship, marital or otherwise, they rarely approach each other from equally advantageous positions. Third, the move toward gender equality is not part of an inexorable and inevitable trend. The changes that have been observed may continue in the same vein, may remain stable, or may even be reversed.

The changing role of women, a subject of extensive controversy for at least a century, cannot exist independent of a comparable changing role of men. The women's liberation movement may be amorphous and fragmented, but its existence is a matter of record and has been effectively articulated. Although not all of the movement's diverse objectives have been achieved, some modifications of women's roles have occurred within the past several generations, and indeed have become manifest within living memory. The men's liberation movement is still nascent, and is just emerging as a theme in the public consciousness. Whatever "progress" may be made by either side will doubtless meet with resistance from some men and some women, and enjoy support from others. Choosing sides in this ongoing renegotiation of the arrangement between the sexes will continue to depend on the experiences of individuals, their awareness of their experiences, and the social contexts that make it possible to define change as feasible and the costs of change as acceptable.

repessed asceticism   *single/double standard of abstinance*

Sexual Freedom: The Decline of the Double Standard

Liberated sex means an end to the double standard about who can enjoy sex and who can't, and how much, and who can initiate sex and who can't. . . . It means an end to "nice girls don't" and "real men must."
Charlotte Hold Clinebell, *Meet Me in the Middle* (1973)

At the turn of the century, the Judaeo-Christian tradition formed the cultural basis for much of the thinking of the Western world. The attitude toward sex and sexuality that it endorsed was basically one of *repressive asceticism.* Sex was defined primarily as a negative force to be controlled and contained. The expression of sexuality was, at best, considered a necessary evil, to be tolerated in marriage for the purpose of having children, and prevented, or at least minimized, in all other contexts. Although this puritan view was obviously not shared by all Victorians, it was essentially the official view of the meaning of sex in society, and provided the basis for structuring premarital, marital, and extra-marital sexual relations.

Since about 1900, sexual attitudes in the countries of the developed Western world have generally shifted away from a value on sexual repression to a value on sexual expression. Whether this shift in orientation is rapid enough or dramatic enough to be termed a revolution is debatable, but it has certainly led to marked differences in the acceptance of many kinds of sexuality, and in the numbers and kinds of persons who are sexually active. Pioneer researchers such as Sigmund Freud and Havelock Ellis began an intellectual tradition in which research concerning sexuality was respectable; survey researchers such as Alfred Kinsey brought discussions of sexuality to the general public; and modern researchers such as William Masters and Virginia Johnson instructed a generation in the possibilities of human sexual response (Schulz 1988, 49–67).

Premarital Sexual Standards

Reiss (1980) observes that there are four distinct sets of standards of behaviour concerning premarital sexuality. The most conventional is the *single standard of abstinence,* based on the belief that premarital sexual activity is undesirable and unacceptable for either men or women. Such a belief may be based on religious prohibitions, or may stem from pragmatic concerns regarding pregnancy, sexually transmitted diseases (STDs), and other potential problems.

The *double standard* is based on the premise that men and women are intrinsically and importantly different, and that there should therefore be two normative standards for evaluating them. Premarital sexual expression is considered acceptable for men, or at least tolerable, but is not acceptable for women. The logistical dilemma posed by this paradox is resolved by an implicit assumption that there are two kinds of women: "respectable" women who are chaste, and therefore suitable persons to be sweethearts and wives; and "disreputable" women who are sexually active, and therefore not the kind of girls men should marry.

The double standard usually applies to sexual behaviour, but may be applied to any behaviours that have moral overtones. Women are supposed to be more moral than men, and are judged more harshly if they behave in inappropriate ways. Examples of the operation of a double standard of morality are ubiquitous in our culture, ranging from expectations regarding alcohol use to the acceptability of swearing or of being rude. In this context, it is important to note that a double standard may be endorsed by both men and women. Men judge women more harshly than they judge themselves; women may also judge themselves and other women more harshly than they do men. The gender-role expectations for women are still different from those for men: the double standard has declined, but certainly still exists.   *double*

[handwritten margin notes: men vs women / - permissiveness with affection / - permissiveness with or without]

Another standard is that of *permissiveness with affection*. Under this standard, premarital sexuality is acceptable in the context of an ongoing affectionate relationship. Finally, there is a standard of *permissiveness with or without affection*. Those who uphold this standard maintain that sexual expression by unmarried persons is acceptable regardless of whether they are also emotionally involved. All four of these standards have found supporters in our society. What appears to have changed with the so-called sexual revolution is the proportion of persons who endorse each one.

Increasing Sexual Permissiveness

The revolution in sexuality in the Western world began somewhere about the time of World War I. A major contributing factor was the introduction of some forms of contraception (however unreliable) that reduced the possibility of accidental pregnancy. A second factor was the shift in values that occurred with the emergence of the counter-culture in the 1960s. Helen Gurley Brown's book *Sex and the Single Girl* (1962) was one of the first popular works that openly advocated recreational sex for "nice" young women. Since that time, increasing numbers of Canadians, young and old, have come to believe that sexual expression is acceptable and even desirable whether or not one is married.

In Canada, research on attitudes toward premarital sex has not been extensive, but the data that are available show a clear trend. For example, in 1968, Hobart's study of anglophone students showed that 31 percent of males and 52 percent of females endorsed traditional standards of abstinence. By 1977, the proportions had declined sharply, to only 12 percent of males and 22 percent of females (Hobart 1984, 240–41).

In 1984, Bibby surveyed 3600 Canadian teenagers aged 15 to 19. He found that 84 percent of males and 77 percent of females

agreed with the statement: "Sex before marriage is all right when people love each other." The standard of permissiveness with or without affection is apparent in that half of the teenagers felt that intercourse was appropriate on the first date or after a few dates (Bibby and Posterski 1985, 76).

Regardless of a trend toward more permissive attitudes, how many persons are actually sexually active? Are there more or fewer than there were in the past? In the United States, the Kinsey Institute for Sex Research provided base-line data on the sexual behaviours of both males (Kinsey, Pomeroy, and Martin 1948) and females (Kinsey et al. 1953). In California, a recent study comparing white women aged 18–36 with women studied by Kinsey in the 1940s found that

> shifts in sexual behaviour were dramatic. As compared to women in the Kinsey sample, the newer subjects began intercourse earlier, were less likely to have a fiancé or husband as their first sex partner, reported a higher number of sexual partners, and participated in a broader range of sexual behaviours. (Wyatt, Peters, and Guthrie 1988, 201)

Unfortunately for students of the family, there has never been a Canadian equivalent to the Kinsey Institute to provide reliable base lines for comparisons. It seems most likely, however, that similar trends are occurring in Canada (Barrett 1980). Herold (1984, 13) reviews twelve surveys done on Canadian university students. Although the samples involved are small, the implications for a declining double standard and increased sexual permissiveness are clear.

An indirect indicator of levels of sexual activity among the unmarried is in their need for birth control. In 1984, more than half of all never-married women aged 18–49 were using contraceptives. Among women aged 25–34, two-thirds were protected, most by contraceptive pills (Balakrishnan, Krotki, and Lapierre-Adamcyk 1985, 213).

Sexual Freedom: The Right to Say No

One aspect of the sexual revolution that often goes unremarked is that the social atmosphere of sexual permissiveness can sometimes create an atmosphere of sexual obligation. Sexual freedom is not really accomplished unless freedom *for* sex is accompanied by freedom *from* sex. The sexual excesses of the late 1960s and 1970s led to a backlash of conservative sexual attitudes. Arguments in favour of *The New Celibacy* (Brown 1980) emphasized other sensual pleasures and nonsexual relationships.

The freedom to say no has also been the basis for a growing awareness of the inappropriateness of any kind of compulsory sex. Violent rape has always been considered a serious criminal offence. Concern with rape victims has led to comparable concern with statutory rape of children, date rape, marital rape, and many other lesser forms of sexual harassment. Lindemann (1983) even makes a convincing case for the right of some married persons to opt for celibacy. Key components of the new attitudes toward sexual freedom are that acceptable sexuality must involve only adults, in circumstances in which consent is freely given.

Living Together Unmarried

Further evidence of the increase in sexual permissiveness can be seen in the changing attitudes and behaviours concerning cohabitation. The Gallup poll posed the question: "If they can, do you think that a couple should live together for a time before deciding to get married or not to get married?" In 1971, only 22 percent of persons said yes; by 1986, 51 percent agreed. Among young persons aged 18–29, 40 percent agreed in 1971, compared with 66 percent in 1986 (Gallup Canada 1986c).

In 1961 and 1971, fewer than 3 percent of all households were estimated to involve common law unions (Hobart 1983, 48). Beginning in 1981, the Canadian census began counting marriage-like unions. At that time, of all cohabiting heterosexual couples, 6.4 percent were in common law relationships. By 1986, this had increased to 8.3 percent (see Table 1). The concentration of common law couples among the younger segments shows marked changes in behaviour. Among young couples in the 20–34 age group, one couple in six is a common law couple. In certain parts of the country, the incidence of cohabitation

Table 1
Incidence of Cohabitation: Canada 1981 and 1986

Age Group	Common Law Couples As % of All Couples		Common Law Persons As % of All Single Persons[a]	
	1981	1986	1981	1986
15–19	49.5	59.6	1.9	1.4
20–34	12.0	16.6	18.3	20.5
35–49	4.1	6.1	19.7	25.0
50–64	1.9	2.7	6.9	9.5
65 and over	1.0	1.5	1.3	1.9
All ages	6.4	8.3	9.1	11.3

Source: Adapted from Turcotte (1988, 38)
[a]Single persons include all persons "eligible" to live common law: the never-married, separated, divorced, and widowed.

is much higher. For example, in the Mont Royal Plateau in Montreal, a 1984 survey found that, of all young French Quebecker couples aged 20–29, 64 percent were not married (Laplante, cited by Mishra-Bouchez and Emond 1987, 383).

Counting persons who are currently living common law tends to underestimate the actual social significance of cohabitation, because it ignores those persons who were in common law unions but who have since moved on to other arrangements. In 1984, among women aged 18–49, 29 percent had been in a common law relationship at some time; for women aged 25–29, the proportion rose to 43 percent (Balakrishnan, Krotki, and Lapierre-Adamcyk 1985).

The Future of Permissiveness

If we could have surveyed Canadians in the 1920s, we would doubtless have found some individuals who endorsed each of the four premarital sexual standards. We would also have found some persons who were chaste, some who were sexually experienced, and some who were *very* sexually experienced. The same range of attitudes and behaviours would be found in Canada today, but the proportions of persons in each of the categories would be markedly different. Public opinion has shifted dramatically in the direction of increased permissiveness, with a substantial majority of both men and women accepting permissiveness with affection as inoffensive behaviour.

A decade ago, family sociologists would confidently have predicted that the norms of sexual permissiveness established in the 1970s would continue to flourish, and would come to be endorsed by increasing proportions of the population. A substantial part of the social import of virginity was related to the perennial threat of illicit pregnancy. This consideration, which was a major bulwark of

the traditional double standard, became increasingly obsolete with the introduction of effective contraception.

Today, however, expectations about the future of sexuality must take into account the spectre of acquired immunodeficiency syndrome (AIDS), which requires us to make drastic changes in those liberal projections. With the potential spread of AIDS to the heterosexual community, virginity may again emerge as a socially significant characteristic. Moreover, since AIDS is an "equal opportunity disease," virginity may come to be considered as important for males as for females. The permissive approach to sexuality that has increasingly characterized North American society has been predicated upon effective control of conception and of various STDs. The prospect of STDs that cannot be controlled or treated may substantially affect the trend toward permissiveness, and again make lifelong monogamy an option to be seriously considered.

Free Trade in the Marriage Market

As a general thing, people marry most happily with their own kind. The trouble lies in the fact that people usually marry at an age where they do not really know what their own kind is.
Robertson Davies, A Voice from the Attic
(1960)

A marriage is not only a union of a man and a woman; it is also a union of his family and kin group with her family and kin group. Consequently, many people other than the bride and groom have a vested interest in the question of who marries whom. Relationships between in-laws and the sharing of grandchildren strengthen or weaken the cohesion of the community as a whole. Although mate-selection norms vary widely from one society to the next, they always begin with the explicit or implicit definition of a field of eligibles; that is, of a group of persons any one of whom would be socially and psychologically acceptable as a mate.

① endogamous; given group
↑
homogamous; like themselves.

② exogamous; not members of a given group.
heterogamous; not like themselves.

Defining the Field of Eligibles

Marriage norms are basically *endogamous*, in that the field of eligible persons is defined as those within a given group. Taboos against *exogamous* marriages — that is, those between persons who are not members of a given group — are strongest when they involve interracial or interfaith marriages. Other kinds of mixed marriages, such as those across lines of ethnicity or social class, may also be subject to some disapproval.

The field of eligible mates is defined by personal as well as by social characteristics. Generally, individuals prefer to enter into a *homogamous* union, that is, a union with someone who is like themselves in important ways. Other things being equal, the usual choice is for a husband or wife who is the same race and religion, who is about the same age, and who has about the same education, income, and social standing. Persons who are getting married for the first time tend to seek others getting married for the first time, much as divorced women seem to prefer divorced men, and widows widowers. Marriages between persons who do not share similar social or personal characteristics are termed *heterogamous*.

The Mating Gradient

Within a field of eligibles who are generally defined as suitable, most married couples exhibit a pattern of *hypergamy*, in which the bride chooses a groom who is, in a number of important ways, of higher status than herself. The opposite of this pattern is *hypogamy*, which occurs when the bride is the person who is of higher status. In Canada and in the rest of the Western world, hypergamy is consistently more common and more acceptable than hypogamy. From childhood, we have a model of Cinderella who makes a "good" marriage to a passing prince; the model of the grocery boy who makes a "good" mar-

riage to his boss's daughter is not considered to be as laudable.

The principle of hypergamy applies to many dimensions of mate selection. For example, men tend to marry women who are as tall as themselves *or shorter*; women tend to marry men who are as tall as themselves *or taller*. Similarly, men select women who have as much education as themselves *or less*; women select men who have as much education as themselves *or more*. This further restriction on eligible mates leaves two kinds of persons who are disadvantaged in the marriage market: low-status males who find few women of even lower status, and high-status females who find few men of even higher status.

Many of these patterns have minimal social impact. However, one area that does have wide-ranging consequences is the norm concerning age. Theoretically, any single man could be an eligible groom for any single woman. Beyond the minimal requirements that brides and grooms be old enough to be considered adults, there are no formal legal or religious restrictions in terms of age. In practice, however, for most males the actual pool of eligible mates is restricted to women about their own age *or younger*; for most females, the pool is restricted to men about their own age *or older*.

Canadian norms and practices concerning mate selection have been gradually changing to allow individuals a wider choice of marriage partners. Two specific trends are worth noting: the changes in religious heterogamy and the changes in age-discrepant marriages.

Interfaith Marriages

When marriages are homogamous in terms of social characteristics, the offspring of these unions are more likely to be similar in many ways to *both* their parents. Such marriages are therefore a conservative force; they tend to perpetuate the social system as it is. Conversely, heterogamous unions may produce offspring who are not exactly like either their

hypergamy — ♂ ↑ gher
hypogamy — ♀ ↑ gher

miscegenation; marriage across racial lines

mother or their father. For example, Goldstein and Segall (1985) have shown that children of ethnic intermarriages have a reduced sense of ethnic identity compared with the children of homogamous couples. Because children who are different are potentially a force of change, persons and groups with a conservative attitude toward family change generally resist mixed marriages.

For most persons, the most important endogamous prohibitions involve *miscegenation*, or marriage across racial lines. Historically, interracial marriages have been rare. In the United States, black–white unions constitute less than one in one thousand marriages (Porterfield 1982, 18). In Canada, the incidence of these unions is also extremely low, but the sensitivity concerning questions of racial origin is such that no official data are available to document how often they do occur.

Gallup polls in Canada have asked: "In general, do you approve of marriages between whites and blacks?" In 1968, only 29 percent of English Canadians approved; by 1983, this had increased to 66 percent. Approval among French Canadians was even higher. In 1968,

46 percent of Québécois approved; by 1983, 86 percent of them did so (Lambert and Curtis 1984, 34). The Gallup polls also asked Canadians: "In general, do you approve of marriages between Catholics and Protestants? What about marriages between Jews and non-Jews?" In 1968, about 60 percent approved of Catholic–Protestant marriages, and about 50 percent approved of Jewish–Gentile marriages. By 1983, these proportions had increased to about 85 percent and 79 percent, respectively (p. 35). Careful analysis of these data, with appropriate controls, confirms that the increase in positive attitudes toward religious intermarriages is both real and substantial (p. 41). Acceptance of religious heterogamy is inversely correlated with age, with younger people being consistently and notably more permissive.

Analysis of interfaith marriages in Canada has shown a consistent upward trend since records were first kept in the 1920s (Heer and Hubay 1975). However, the changes from 1921 to 1961 were gradual, whereas the disparity between 1961 and 1971 is quite pronounced (see Table 2).

Table 2

Proportions of Brides in Religiously Homogamous Marriages: Canada, Selected Years, 1921–1985

Year	Catholics with Catholic Groom	Jews with Jewish Groom	Protestants with Groom not RC/Jew	Protestants with Groom in Same Denomination[a]
1921	83.7	98.1	95.9	60.0
1951	87.9	97.2	91.6	54.7
1961	87.1	95.6	89.1	52.3
1971	78.5	88.7	82.0	41.7
1981	54.9	74.6	78.3	39.5
1985	58.6	78.9	75.7	40.0

Source: *Vital Statistics, Vol. II: Marriages and Divorces.* 1986 and preceding years. Catalogue 84–205.

[a] Based on brides with grooms in the same Protestant group for Anglicans, Baptists, Greek Orthodox, Lutheran, Mennonite, Pentecostal, Presbyterian, Salvation Army, and (from 1951) United Church. Excluded are minor Protestant denominations that were not consistently reported over the 60-year period and/or were too small for analysis. In 1985, the data presented include 85.5 percent of the 105 028 marriages performed.

Norms of religious endogamy are clearly stronger among Jews than among members of any other group. In Canada, in 1921, 98.1 percent of Jewish brides married Jewish husbands. In 1961, this trend was still very common (95.6 percent), but it declined to 88.7 percent by 1971, and to 78.9 percent by 1985. Intermarriage of Catholics with non-Catholics also increased markedly during the 1960s. In 1921, 83.7 percent of Catholic brides made endogamous choices: by 1961, 87.1 percent of them still did so. However, by 1971, the rate was down to 78.5 percent, and by 1985 it was only 58.6 percent.

Assessment of Protestant heterogamy over time is more difficult. The degree of difference between two Protestant groups may be very pronounced (as, for example, Hutterites compared with Unitarians) or quite minimal. It is not exactly clear which interfaith marriages should be counted as "really" mixed in the social as well as the theological sense. Marriages between Protestants and Jews, or between Protestants and Catholics, are clearly heterogamous. Marriages between persons of different Protestant denominations are usually less controversial, and the norms forbidding them are substantially weaker.

If we consider the marriages of Protestant brides to non-Protestant grooms, the rate of endogamy has declined from 95.9 percent in 1921 to 75.5 percent in 1985. If we take a more stringent measure, and consider inter-denominational marriages to be mixed as well, the rate of endogamy among Protestant brides is now only 40 percent (see Table 2).

The decline in endogamous norms that require people to marry persons like themselves does not mean that most marriages will not still be homogamous — that is, will involve people of similar social characteristics. It does mean, however, that homogamous mating will likely be a result of ethnocentric preference rather than of religious or moral restraints. The more freedom is allowed in mate selection, the more we can expect to have a wide variety of mixed marriages.

Age-Discrepant Marriages

If both parties are of age, intergenerational marriage is considered to be an unusual psychological preference and/or an unusual economic arrangement, but it is not usually considered an immoral act. Nevertheless, in spite of this apparent permissiveness, age norms of hypergamy are followed with great uniformity in the developed world (Veevers 1987).

The mate-selection norm requiring the husband to be older than his wife reinforces within the microcosm of the family the traditional roles of male dominance and female submission. This may be especially true when the husband is substantially older than his wife. Under these circumstances, the husband is likely to have not only the advantages that accrue from his gender but also a number of other advantages (such as greater affluence, higher education, and wider experience) that further exaggerate his power and prestige in relation to his younger wife.

Marriage data available in British Columbia for the past 60 years reveal two dominant trends (see Table 3). First, there is a marked decline in the incidence of couples where the husband is ten or more years older than his wife. In 1921, such couples constituted nearly one in five; now they are less than one in ten. Second, there is a trend for more and more couples to be coevals, give or take a year. Equal-age marriages increased from 21.0 percent in 1921 to 28.6 percent in 1979.

In Canada, age-discrepant couples are now about one in ten of all couples, with husbands who are ten years older being about twice as common as wives who are five years older. Where these trends will lead is still unclear. On the one hand, because age discrepancies are more common in second than in first marriages, they may be expected to increase with the increases in longevity and the divorce rate. On the other hand, if the status of women does become closer to the status of men, there may be fewer husband-ascendant marriages and more that are wife-ascendant.

Table 3
Distribution of Marriages by Age Discrepancy of Bride and Groom: British Columbia 1921–1979 and Canada 1981[a]

Year	Groom Older (in Years)				Coevals	Bride Older (in Years)			
	10+	5–9	3–4	2	+/– 1	2	3–4	5+	Total
British Columbia									
1921	19.1	28.4	15.3	8.3	21.0	2.7	2.8	2.6	100.1
1931	18.0	26.9	16.6	8.8	21.9	2.3	2.7	2.6	99.9
1941	13.9	24.7	18.0	9.7	24.3	3.4	3.4	2.7	100.1
1951	11.3	22.1	18.5	11.0	26.0	3.2	3.8	4.2	100.1
1961	9.4	23.0	21.7	12.2	24.1	2.5	3.0	4.2	100.1
1971	8.1	19.1	21.4	13.6	29.1	3.2	3.5	4.5	100.0
1979	9.5	20.8	17.9	12.0	28.6	3.2	3.5	4.5	100.0
Canada									
1981[a]	7.2	18.3	18.8	12.9	31.5	3.6	3.8	3.9	100.0

Source: Province of British Columbia (1979 and preceding years).
[a]Adapted from Veevers (1985). Totals vary from 100 because of rounding.

Unmarried Lifestyles: Choice and Chance

Marriage may be compared to a cage: the birds outside despair to get in and those within despair to get out.
Montaigne, Essays III (1595)

Almost every child in our society is taught to expect that, once a person is grown up, he or she will almost inevitably fall in love, get married, and have children. Demographers have focussed attention on the *pronatalist* pressures that encourage people to become parents, but have often neglected the comparable *pronuptualist* pressures that encourage people to marry. Almost everyone marries, but not everyone does so; possibly almost everyone *wants* to marry, but not everyone does so. In fact, several indicators point to the increased visibility and significance of the unmarried segment of the adult population.

Marital Status

At any one time, among persons who can more or less be considered to be adults — that is, among persons over the age of 15 — about two-thirds are married. This proportion increased from about 57 percent in 1921–41 to a high of about 65 percent in 1951–61. Since that time, it has decreased to about 60 percent (see Table 4). In looking at these trends over time, it is noteworthy that, although the proportion of the population who is widowed — roughly one adult out of 17 — has remained quite constant, the proportions of persons who are divorced or separated has increased, especially since 1971, until they now constitute as large a group as the widowed. Altogether, the formerly married represent 12.4 percent of the population — one in eight of the adult population. This is a substantial increase from one in sixteen in 1921.

The unmarried segment of the population is a diverse group, and has not been studied systematically. Stein (1981) differentiates at

Table 4

Population Aged 15 and Over by Marital Status: Canada, Selected Years 1921–1986

Year	Single	Married	Separated[a]	Widowed	Divorced	
1921	35.8	57.9	NA	6.2	0.1	100.0
1931	37.7	56.1	NA	6.2	0.1	100.1
1941	36.5	57.0	NA	6.3	0.2	100.0
1951	28.9	64.2	NA	6.6	0.3	100.0
1961	26.5	66.6	NA	6.5	0.4	100.0
1971	28.3	61.9	2.4	6.2	1.1	99.9
1981	27.9	60.9	2.5	6.1	2.7	100.1
1986	27.2	60.4	2.6	6.3	3.5	100.0

Source: 1986 Census of Canada, Catalogue 93–101, Table 1.

[a] Before 1971, data on married persons included separated persons. Totals vary because of rounding.

least four kinds of single adults. Some un-married persons would like to be married but have not been able to find a suitable mate. This group can be divided into those who consider being single a temporary state and who are actively looking for someone to marry, versus those who are not actively look-ing, and for whom being single is probably permanent. Other unmarried persons are sin-gle by choice. Some of these are postponing getting married, but others, the confirmed bachelors, are intrinsically opposed to the idea of marriage, at least for themselves. An individual's experience and satisfaction with single status will be quite different, depending on which of these circumstances prevail. At present, there are no data to suggest how the single population is distributed among these categories, much less to compare and evaluate them.

Declining Marriage Rates

One barometer of the changing meaning of marriage is the marriage rate. Marriage rates were low during the Depression, and in-creased after World War II; since the 1950s, they have declined for both men and women (see Tables 5 and 6). The average age at first

Table 5

Marriage Rates[a] for Males by Age: Canada, Selected Years 1931–1985

Year	15+[b]	15–19	20–24	25–29
1931	18.4	3.1	50.9	52.3
1941	29.4	5.4	80.0	84.5
1951	28.2	12.5	101.6	62.9
1961	25.0	12.0	103.5	51.1
1971	26.2	12.7	107.0	51.1
1981	20.4	5.7	65.7	49.5
1985	18.7	3.1	49.4	50.9

Source: Nagnur and Adams 1987–3.

[a] Rate per 1000 women.

[b] Standardized to 1981 population.

Table 6
Marriage Rates[a] for Females by Age: Canada, Selected Years 1931–1985

Year	15+[b]	15–19	20–24	25–29
1931	18.1	29.8	65.1	32.7
1941	28.5	42.5	101.8	56.5
1951	27.4	60.5	100.1	36.0
1961	23.6	57.8	91.5	24.7
1971	24.4	50.3	97.7	27.5
1981	19.8	25.1	75.7	34.1
1985	18.6	16.1	67.6	38.9

Source: Nagnur and Adams 1987, 3.

[a] Rate per 1000 women.

[b] Standardized to 1981 population.

marriage in 1985 was 26.7 for men and 24.6 for women, an increase of about two years from the early 1970s (Nagnur and Adams 1987, 5). The trends are especially apparent when we consider the precipitous decline in teenage marriages. In 1985, rates of teenage marriages for either sex are about one-third of what they were in the 1950s and 1960s. Rates for women aged 20–24 show a marked decline, while rates for women aged 25–29 show a slight increase, reflecting the trend toward postponing first marriage.

Living Alone

The increasing proportion of persons who live alone indicates the emergence of a single lifestyle. In Canada, in 1951, only about 3 percent of persons over the age of 15 lived alone: by 1986, that rate had tripled to nearly 10 percent (see Table 7). Since living alone is more common for the elderly than for the young, part of this increase is attributable to the increase in the proportion of the population over age 65, especially the increase in

Table 7
Persons Living Alone: Canada,[a] Selected Years 1951–1986

Year	% of Persons Age 15+	% of Persons Age 65+	One-Person Households As a % of All Households[c]
1951	2.6	9.2	7.4
1961	3.5	12.4	9.3
1971	5.3	18.4	13.4
1981	8.9	24.0[b]	20.3
1986	9.7	25.2	21.5

Sources: Peron and Strohmenger (1985,65–232); 1986 Census of Canada; *The Daily*, 11–001E, July 9, 1987,13.

[a] Excludes Yukon and Northwest Territories.

[b] 13.0 percent of men and 32.2 percent of women.

[c] Statistics Canada, Catalogue Nos. 93–809, Census of Canada, *Private Households by Marital Status, Sex and Age of Head*; 92–903, Census of Canada. *Occupied Dwellings, Type and Tenure*; and *The Daily*, 11–001E, July 9, 1987,13.

the female elderly. However, significant changes are also happening among younger persons. Put somewhat differently: in 1951, only 7.4 percent of all households contained only one person, compared with 21.5 percent of all households in 1986 (see Table 7).

Premarital Pregnancy

As more adolescents and young adults become sexually active, there is an increased awareness and concern with the problem of premarital pregnancy, especially among teenagers. There has been increased awareness of the negative long-term economic consequences of adolescent childbearing (Grindstaff 1988), and increased attention to prevention programs. For example, among adolescents in Ontario in 1976, the pregnancy rate was 44.9 per 1000, and about one-third of these ended in abortion; by 1983, the rate was down to 36.4 percent, and about half of these ended in abortion (Orton and Rosenblatt, 1986, 154). Premarital pregnancy has generally been considered a problem of teenage girls. Recent research has expanded this view to include attention to the role and rights of adolescent fathers as well, and to the family context in which unwanted pregnancies occur (Redmond 1985).

Illegitimacy

If premarital sex and/or cohabitation is a taken-for-granted option, and if antinuptial values are questioning the necessity of marriage, it is not surprising that there should be an increase in the proportion of persons who opt for parenthood without marriage. Increasing tolerance of premarital relationships has lead to an increasing tolerance of illegitimacy. Obviously, the unmarried woman who has a child was sexually active, but in most segments of society that fact per se is no longer stigmatic. Accidental pregnancies out of wedlock may be considered to reflect bad luck,

and deliberate pregnancies out of wedlock may be considered to reflect bad judgement, but in most instances they are no longer condemned as reflecting immorality.

The more both mother and father are socially valued as parents, the less the fact of illegitimacy will constitute a problem of social placement. The unwed mother can give her child her own name. If the parents are cohabitating, the child is legally illegitimate, in that it was born to parents not married to each other, but it is socially in a situation comparable to that of children born to parents who are formally married. Alternatively, the out-of-wedlock child is not necessarily a child without a known father. The man in question may acknowledge the paternity of the child, and establish a father–child relationship with it, without being married to the mother.

British common law made elaborate distinctions between the rights of legitimate and illegitimate offspring. Now, the Law Reform commissions federally and provincially have generally recommended eliminating the distinction. Illegitimacy has been abolished as a legal status in four provinces (Quebec, Ontario, Manitoba, and New Brunswick) (Nett 1988, 147).

Until the 1960s, illegitimate births in Canada were rare: for every 100 babies born, fewer than five were born out of wedlock. Since that time, however, the rate has increased markedly. In 1986, for every 100 babies born, there were 19 born out of wedlock. Some of those were the result of accidental pregnancies with unknown or undeclared fathers; others, however, were the result of deliberate pregnancies, some of which involved couples who chose to become parents but did not choose to marry.

When illegitimacy was a significant stigma, the problems it occasioned were most frequently "solved" by placing the bastard child for adoption. If an unwanted premarital pregnancy could not be aborted, and if the mother did not have a "forced" wedding, the most likely outcome was the surrender of the child.

As illegitimacy becomes commonplace, however, and the attendant stigma is reduced, there is an increased tendency for unwed mothers to keep their children. Recent studies suggest that as many as eight out of ten unwed mothers now decide to keep their child (Adler, Congdon, and Scrambler 1980; Orton and Rosenblatt 1986, 112).

Lone-Parent Families

Being unmarried, by chance or by choice, does not necessarily mean that one lives alone, or that one forgoes having children. In 1961, of all families, only 8.4 percent involved only one parent (Statistics Canada 1984). This proportion has been increasing steadily until, in 1986, 13 percent of all families involved only one parent (Moore 1989). This rate seems high relative to the recent past; however, it is actually about the same as it was in the 1930s. What has changed is the cause of being a lone parent. In the past, most lone parents were widows; now, they are often single or divorced women.

Most lone-parent families, about eight out of ten, are headed by women. On average, mothers who are on their own stay in that status for about five years before they marry or their children leave home (Moore 1989). Changing gender roles might be expected to make it more acceptable and more likely for lone-parent families to be headed by men. However, such changes have not occurred. In 1976, of all lone-parent families, 16.9 percent involved fathers and their children; in 1986, 17.8 percent of them did so (Wargon 1987).

The Homosexual Lifestyle

Another element of the unmarried population involves persons who choose to stay single because they are homosexual. There are no valid data available to estimate the number of Canadians who would identify themselves as being *homophiles*, that is, persons who have a special liking for or attraction to persons of the same sex. Consequently, no one knows whether the proportion of the population that is gay has increased, decreased, or remained constant in recent years. What is clear is that the visibility of both male and female gay communities has increased markedly.

In 1973, the American Psychological Association recognized that homosexuality is not a disease or a neurosis, but simply a lifestyle preference. This enlightened view was not as readily adopted by all academics and professionals, or by the general public, but it has been gaining increasing acceptance. A 1988 Gallup poll found that 80 percent of respondents felt that homosexuals, as a group, are now more accepted by society than they were 25 years ago (Gallup Canada 1988c). However, being "more" accepted is not yet the equivalent of having a public that regards sexual orientation as simply a matter of personal preference. Many persons still exhibit varying degrees of *homophobia* — that is, fear of homosexuality and homosexuals.

As the homosexual lifestyle becomes more visible and more acceptable, more attention must be paid to the new family forms that are evolving. Professionals in the mental-health fields need to recognize that same-sex couples face problems of adjustment and of intimacy comparable to those of husband and wife, and need to respond to such couples in a nonjudgmental and accepting manner (Stein 1988). Some lesbians and some homosexual men are parents, and some have retained custody of their children. In raising them, either as lone parents or in homosexual families, persons of either sex may assume the roles of "mother" and of "father" (Agbayewa 1984).

Although the homosexual lifestyle is not yet fully accepted by most Canadians, there is evidence that attitudes toward this alternative are becoming more permissive and accepting. For example, the 1988 Gallup poll found that 35 percent of young persons aged 18–29 thought that homosexuals should be allowed to adopt children (Gallup Canada 1988c). About half of respondents felt that a homosexual should be entitled to employment as a high school teacher, a clergyman, or a Member of Parliament. Generally, permissive attitudes were more characteristic of persons under 30 than of the older populations (Gallup Canada 1988c). While this may seem permissive in relation to the attitudes of several decades ago, we must point out that about half of respondents did *not* feel that gays were qualified to hold responsible jobs. The Canadian Human Rights Act now prohibits discrimination on the grounds of sexual orientation (Boyer 1985, 30). Therefore, a substantive trend in the Canadian family system in the next few decades will, we suggest, be an increased awareness of the gay lifestyle and an increased acceptance of it as one variety of intimate relationship and one dimension of family life.

Serial Monogamy: Marriage, Divorce, and Remarriage

If you still want marriage to mean anything at all, you must open the door to divorce equally wide.
Frederick P. Grove, *A Search for America* **(1927)**

The nature and meaning of marriage is always defined, in part, by attitudes and expectations concerning divorce. Changes in marriage may precipitate changes in divorce and, conversely, any major reconstruction of the parameters of divorce colours the perceptions that husbands and wives have of their options and of each other. The past several decades have been characterized by dramatic changes in all aspects of the divorce process. The changes in Canadian laws and practices closely parallel changes in the divorce process in the United States and in other countries in the developed Western world.

Rising Divorce Rates

The upswing in the divorce rate is not news, but it is interesting to note just how sharp that upswing has been. In 1961, the divorce rate was 164 per 100 000 married women;

by 1985, the rate was 1004 per 100 000, a *sixfold* increase. In other words, in Canada in the 1980s, in any given year, about 1 percent of all wives obtained a divorce. Wives in their late twenties have the highest risk of divorce; in any given year, about 2 percent of them obtain a divorce (Adams and Nagnur 1988, 72). Put somewhat differently: in Canada in 1982, of all young couples in their early twenties, approximately one in three could expect to be divorced at least once before age 85 (pp. 47–52).

While recognizing that Canadian divorce rates seem to be both high and rising, it is important to keep in mind that they seem so only in comparison with our very low rates in the past. In 1985, the American rate was 2170 per million, more than twice as high as the Canadian rate (National Center for Health Statistics 1989).

The ubiquity of the divorce experience has meant that divorce has become a "normal" experience that touches virtually all families directly or indirectly. A generation ago, getting a divorce was accompanied by the psychological strain of being involved in a "deviant" and stigmatized activity. Today, except in some atypical subcultures such as fundamentalist religious groups, getting a divorce is not considered an unusual occurrence, nor it is necessarily a source of stigma and shame. In the 1950s, persons who had ever been divorced were a deviant minority, and they were faced with restricted options; in the 1980s, persons who have never been divorced constitute a substantial and growing minority, and they enjoy a proliferation of interpersonal, vocational, and social options.

The Liberalization of Divorce Laws

Before 1968, divorce law in Canada was modelled directly on British common law, and had remained essentially unchanged since the 1880s. The only grounds for divorce was adultery, and in the provinces of Newfoundland and Quebec, divorces were granted not by the courts but by acts of Parliament. Under such circumstances, divorce rates were understandably low (Pike 1975).

In 1968, the passage of the Canadian Divorce Act provided one national divorce law that was uniformly applicable in all provinces. The updated legislation included two major changes. First, it extended the number of matrimonial faults that could be considered as adequate grounds for divorce to include not only adultery but also homosexuality, alcohol or drug addiction, and physical or mental cruelty. Second, the act made provision for matrimonial breakdown as a basis for divorce. Marital breakdown was defined as a situation in which there was "no reasonable hope of reconciliation." This could be demonstrated by the simple expedient of the couple living separate and apart for several years. A divorce action could be brought after a period of three years if the petitioner had been deserted by his or her spouse, and after five years if the petitioner was the one who initiated the separation.

Before the 1968 Divorce Act, marriage was defined as a legal contract between a person and the state: hence, if a married person sought a divorce, it was necessary to show cause to the state why the marital contract should be terminated. The 1968 Divorce Act was revolutionary in that it introduced the definition of marriage as a legal contract between a person *and another person*. Under this radically different orientation, a marital partnership had the same legal status as any other kind of partnership, and could be dissolved at will, whether or not the state considered that the partners had just cause to do so. The introduction of marital breakdown as a basis for divorce had two major and far-reaching implications for the legal and social meanings of marriage. First, it provided a means whereby a couple could, in effect, have *divorce on demand*, provided that they were willing to wait to have their demands met. In essence, the act provided Canadians with freedom from "compulsory marriage." It was no longer necessary to consider whether one's spouse would "give" one a divorce: if one was willing to wait five years, one had the right

to a divorce, with or without the consent of the spouse.

The second important social implication of no-fault divorce legislation was that, for the first time, it was possible for a couple to obtain a divorce on "respectable" grounds. Rather than having to face an open court and admit to or prove adultery, homosexuality, cruelty, or other socially disapproved behaviours, a couple could divorce without giving anyone any explanation as to why they wanted to do so. The reason could be something morally reprehensible; however, it could also be something as simply and as morally acceptable as a change of heart.

The move toward divorce reform continued with the passage of another divorce act in July 1986. This new legislation continues the reform begun almost two decades earlier. It retains the idea of divorce for cause, but simplifies it to include adultery as well as physical or mental cruelty, defined as behaviour "which would render future cohabitation intolerable." The recognition of divorce by reason of marriage breakdown is also retained, but the period of time needed to establish it is reduced to only one year. Moreover, during that year, couples must be encouraged to seek mediation, and have up to 90 days to attempt reconciliation without it affecting their divorce case.

The divorce process, which establishes a person's marital status and conveys the right to remarry, is only one aspect of the complex process of disbanding a marital union. The 1986 Divorce Act also made provision for major changes in three other facets of the divorce process: support, property, and custody.

Phasing Out Alimony

British common law could require a husband to pay alimony to his wife, provided that she was the innocent party in the divorce. The amount of alimony was determined by the financial resources of the husband and, once granted, it was theoretically payable to her for her lifetime or until she remarried. The new Canadian law makes two major breaks with this tradition. First, it incorporates the idea of the mutual-support obligations of spouses, making it possible for wives to be required to support husbands as well as the other way around. Second, the basis of claiming support is no longer determined by the guilt or innocence of the wife or the husband, but rather by his or her demonstrated need for financial aid. Except in unusual circumstances, as for example with a handicapped person, support is expected to be granted not for a lifetime but only until such time as the dependent spouse can learn to be financially self-sufficient. It is interesting to note in passing that these reforms, which presumably were intended to improve the lot of women, have on occasion had the opposite effect. In the 1950s, an abandoned wife who did not remarry would have been entitled to alimony for life; in the 1980s, she may only be entitled to a few years of support while she goes back to school.

The Rise of Communal Property

Under the common law, persons owned the property they had bought and paid for. Since in most families only the husband was earning money in the paid labour force, that usually meant that all of the family assets belonged to him. The inequity of this situation was brought to light in the 1975 case of *Murdoch v. Murdoch* ([1975] 1 S.C.R. 423), in which the Supreme Court of Canada ruled that a farm wife had, in law, no right to the farm property she had worked on for many years. In the late 1970s, all of the provinces introduced family-law reform legislation that provided for a more or less equal division of family assets between husband and wife. Public opinion seems to support this new policy. In 1986, a Gallup poll asked: "Do you or do you not believe that when a couple is divorced, all assets accumulated by them during their marriage should be divided equally between the spouses?" In response, 73 percent

of men and 76 percent of women believed assets should be shared (Gallup Canada 1986b).

The home in which a couple have lived together is now almost always considered to be shared property. Beyond that, the exact definition of what is to be considered individual property, and what is to be considered family property that must be shared, varies from province to province, and is open to a variety of interpretations by the various divorce courts. At the point of a marital separation, neither husband nor wife can be certain which assets will have to be shared with the other, or in what proportion. Awareness of this uncertainty is leading many persons to write their own domestic contracts, which provide guidelines for the courts but are not always legally binding.

The Best Interests of the Child

Under British common law, children were the property of their father. This presumption was modified by British family law in the early 1900s by the emergence of the "doctrine of tender years." Children under the age of seven were presumed to be better off with their mother than with their father, and the mother was therefore most often granted custody. In the 1970s, legal opinion again shifted to incorporate the concept that custody should be awarded "in the best interest of the child." Theoretically, this provision could grant custody to either the mother or the father, depending on the circumstances. In practice, 75 percent of awards are made to the mother, a proportion that has remained stable since the early 1970s (Eichler 1988, 244).

The increased involvement of fathers in child care has led to an increased demand for joint custody, in which parents agree to share the physical custody of the child on a regular basis, and both retain the legal rights and responsibilities of a parent. In the United States, joint custody is rapidly becoming the preferred custody arrangement. Although Canadian legislation does not specifically refer to this option, the courts have occasionally sanctioned the concept and are likely to make greater use of this option in the future (Irving, Benjamin, and Trocme 1984).

The increased desire of fathers to maintain access to their children, and/or to have custody of them, tends to increase the potential for litigation between divorcing parents. An adversarial approach, with an emphasis on the rights of one parent at the expense of the other, has proven to be particularly difficult for the children caught in the middle. The confrontation in the court often furthers the negative feelings implicit in the divorce, and renders a decision that is difficult or impossible to enforce. An alternative that has become increasingly attractive is that of mediation, which is nonadversarial and that can often provide an equitable solution with a minimum of distress. Mediation services were first offered in Canada in the 1970s. Since then, they have been encouraged by provincial statutes concerned with children, and by the requirement in the 1986 Divorce Act that all lawyers discuss mediation with their clients (Devlin and Ryan 1986, 100).

Mediation is a method of dispute resolution in which an impartial professional, the mediator, helps the parents to reach a cooperative and voluntary resolution between themselves (Landau 1988). Under the best of circumstances, it enables the child to maintain a good relationship with both parents, and reduces tension and improves communication between the parents. In addition, because the agreement reached is a voluntary one, mediated solutions are more likely to be honoured than are those imposed by the courts.

Serial Monogamy

The increase in divorce rates does not indicate a movement away from marriage, or an evolution of new marriage forms. Rather, it seems indicative of a trend toward serial monogamy. A man or woman still lives a lifestyle in which he or she has only one spouse at a time, but there is no longer the automatic assumption that one's full-time mate will necessarily also be one's lifelong mate. Of all persons getting married, an increasing proportion of them have been married and divorced previously.

The increase in the remarriage of divorced persons means that the overall incidence of

Table 8
Distribution of Marriages by Marital Status of Bride and Groom: Canada, Selected Years 1921–1985

Year	Primary Marriages[a]	Divorced Groom[b]	Divorced Bride[b]	Both Divorced	Other[c]
1921[d]	83.0	0.7	0.7	0.1	15.4
1961	87.2	2.8	2.9	1.0	6.0
1971	83.4	5.0	4.4	3.1	4.1
1981	72.5	9.2	7.7	7.9	2.8
1985	70.3	9.8	8.3	9.1	2.5

Source: *Canada Year Book 1922–1923; Vital Statistics Volume II. Marriages and Divorces, 1985* and preceding years (Statistics Canada, Catalogue 84–205 Annual).

[a] Primary marriages are between a never-married bride and a never-married groom.

[b] Married to someone either never-married or widowed.

[c] Includes marriages of widows and widowers to singles and marriages of widows and widowers to each other.

[d] Cross-tabulations of brides and grooms by marital status are not available for the years 1931, 1941, and 1951.

primary marriages — that is, first-time marriages for both bride and groom — has declined. Early in the century, nine out of ten weddings were first-time affairs for all concerned; by 1985, more than a quarter of them involved at least one divorced person, and one in ten involved two divorced persons (see Table 8). In British Columbia, where divorce rates are consistently and substantially higher than in the rest of the country, only 58 percent of all marriages were primary. Four out of ten (39 percent) of all marriages involved at least one divorced person, and nearly one in six (15 percent) involved two divorced persons (Province of British Columbia 1986).

The pattern of serial monogamy seems to signal a move of the Canadian family toward a situation of *permanent availability* for marriage (Farber 1964). Increasingly, we behave as if every adult were permanently available as a marriage mate for every other cross-sex adult, excluding members of the nuclear family precluded by the incest taboo. (This situation is less characteristic of a conservative society, such as Ireland, than it is of a more liberal and permissive one, such as California [Veevers 1990b].) The patterns of change in the Canadian family system seem to be moving us toward a future that will increasingly be characterized by permanent availability for marriage, and in which a pattern of marriage–divorce–remarriage will be the norm rather than the exception (Veevers 1990b).

The Double Shift: Working Wives and Working Mothers

The superwoman who knits marriage, career, and motherhood into a satisfying life without dropping a stitch is as oppressive a role model as the airbrushed Bunny in the Playboy *centerfold.*
    Sylvia Rabiner, *Village Voice* (1976)

A century ago, a working wife was not normally accepted by society unless her employment was a dire necessity (Chekki 1976, 207). If she entered the labour force at all,

it was usually in response to some misfortune: an unemployed husband, an early widowhood, or the disgrace of being divorced for just cause and hence deprived of alimony. In the middle and upper classes, and to a lesser extent in the lower classes, a wife was expected to be totally dependent on her husband for all her financial resources. The marriage proposal was not only a proposition, it was also a job offer.

Working Wives

Attitudes toward working wives have become increasingly accepting. The Gallup poll asked Canadians: "Do you think that married women should take a job outside the home if they have no young children?" In 1960, two-thirds of persons said yes; by 1987, nine out of ten approved of this option (Gallup Canada 1987).

In Canada, in 1931, about one in five adult women were in the labour force: however, very few of these women were also wives. Since then, the labour-force participation rate of wives has increased markedly and steadily until, in 1988, nearly two-thirds are working. More noteworthy, the discrepancy between labour-force participation rates for wives compared with those for all other women has virtually disappeared.

Working Mothers

In the early decades of this century, the primary goals of the family system still revolved around having and raising children, often a large number of children. The paid employment of women who were also mothers was considered especially inappropriate. Attitudes toward this have also changed precipitously. The Gallup poll asked Canadians: "Do you think that married women should take a job outside the home if they have young children?" In 1960, only 5 percent said yes; by 1987, 47 percent of all persons agreed (Gallup

Table 9
Labour-Force Participation Rates for Women by Age of Youngest Child: Canada, Selected Years 1975–1983

| Year | All Women with Children Under 16 | Age of Youngest Child | | |
		Less Than 3 Years	3–5 Years	6–15 Years
1975	41.6	31.2	40.0	48.2
1977	44.9	34.0	42.5	51.9
1979	49.4	39.4	47.8	55.6
1981	54.5	44.5	52.4	61.1
1983	56.8	48.9	55.6	62.0

Source: Lindsay and Belliveau (1985,18).

Canada 1987). Although the trend is toward increasing permissiveness, there is still a residue of ambivalence concerning working mothers. The Gallup poll also asked: "There are more married women with families in the working world than ever before. Do you think this has a harmful effect on family life or not?" In 1973, 59 percent thought it was harmful; by 1988, the proportion had decreased, but a third of persons under 30 still felt it was harmful (Gallup Canada 1988a).

In the recent past, there were considerable disparities in labour-force participation rates for wives as compared with mothers, and further disparities for mothers who had children under 15 compared with those who did not. In 1961, of wives who had children under the age of 15, only 17.0 percent were in the labour force, compared with 33.1 percent of those without them. By 1971, one third of women (32.9 percent) with children under 15 were also working, compared with about half (47.6 percent) of those without them (Veevers 1977, 22). This trend accelerated through the 1970s and 1980s. By 1986, *62 percent of all wives with children under six years of age were working outside the home* (Statistics Canada 1989b, vii).

In addition to this general trend, the age at which children are perceived no longer to need a full-time mother living at home is becoming younger and younger. In 1975, one-third of women with children under age three were in the labour force; by 1983, half of them were working (see Table 9).

Child Care

If mothers, including those with young children, are going to work, then there is an obvious need for other child-care arrangements. A survey of child-care arrangements for children under the age of six showed that, in 1981, only about half were cared for exclusively by their own parents in their own homes (Lindsay and Belliveau 1985, 20). The rest were in day-care centres or nursery schools, or taken care of by private arrangements. In 1988, a majority of Canadians (57 percent) were in favour of increased tax spending for subsidized government day-care centres for preschool children (Gallup Canada 1988b).

Symmetrical Families

Although some women may not want to relinquish responsibilities in the household, most sources show increasing support for the sentiment that the sharing between husbands and wives in wage earning ought to be accompanied by sharing in housework. For example, the Gallup poll asked respondents: "In your opinion, should husbands be expected to share in the general housework or not?" In 1976, 57 percent of men and women agreed that husbands should share the housework; by 1986, 81 percent of them did so (Gallup Canada 1986a).

Verbal agreements that husbands *ought* to share responsibility for housework do not ensure that they actually will do so. When the Gallup poll asked: "Would you say that your husband helps with the housework fairly regularly, occasionally, or not at all?" only 42 percent of wives reported regular help and 43 percent reported occasional help (Gallup Canada 1986a). In many instances, the husband–father's contribution to housework and child care is consistently and substantially lower than the wife–mother's and it is often only a token gesture. The result is what has been accurately termed the problem of the "double shift": many wives and mothers are employed for a full eight-hour shift in the labour market, and then come home to many more hours of housework and child care. The result can be cumulative stress that causes an increased risk to women's health: there are too many physical and emotional demands to meet, too many hours of work, and a continuous struggle to reconcile the demands of the two work settings (de Koninck 1984, 28).

Men Earn More: The Persistent Gender Gap

Women who are in the labour force earn about half as much as men who are in the labour force. This disparity, which has been termed "the gender gap", has been subjected to intense analysis by a number of researchers (e.g., Armstrong 1984; Hunter 1986; and Wilson 1986). Part of the discrepancy is accounted for by the fact that women are more likely than men to work part-time. However, even when comparisons are restricted only to persons who work full-time for a full year, the discrepancy is large and consistent. Moreover, this is one area in which there has been remarkably little change. In 1970, women who worked full-time for a full year earned 59.2 percent as much as men working the same way; in 1980, this had increased to 63.7 percent; by 1986, the proportion had increased, but *full-time women workers still earned only two-thirds as much (65.9 percent) as full-time male workers* (Statistics Canada 1989b, 31). This ratio is comparable with the gender gap for full-year full-time workers in the United States (Benokraitis and Feagin 1986, 55).

There is still every indication that more and more Canadian women will seek to enter the paid labour force until, eventually, their patterns of labour-force participation will not be markedly different from those of men, and will not be markedly different for single women compared with wives, or for mothers compared with the childless. As discussed above, many working women now assume what amounts to a double shift of paid work in the labour force and unpaid work in the home, a burden that is not equally shared by their mates. This circumstance may be modified by an increased awareness of gender-based inequities, but it is unlikely to be eliminated until women not only work as many hours as do men, but also receive equal pay for their work.

Baby Boom to Baby Bust: The Birth-Control Revolution

Women of the working class, especially wage workers, should not have more than two children at most. The average working man can support no more and the average working woman can take care of no more in decent fashion.
  Margaret Sanger, *Family Limitations* (1917)

A century ago, the Canadian family was based on the pronatalist assumption that having children was an obligation to God and to one's religious community. Beginning about the 1950s, the social meaning of parenthood began to be defined as a privilege rather than an obligation. Decisions about childbearing were determined by the ability of would-be parents to care for their offspring in a way acceptable to themselves and to others. Couples were expected to have as many children as they could afford, but not more, depending on their physical, financial, and psychological resources. Since the 1970s, the meaning of parenthood has again shifted to something that is a lifestyle option. Couples can decide if and when to have children, depending on their personal preferences and on their anticipation that children will augment their quality of life, or will detract from it.

The Two-Child Ideal

A social climate that defines parenthood as an option rather than an obligation and that makes effective family planning possible can still accommodate some couples who continue to opt for large families. Today, however, very few do so. In 1945, in response to the Gallup poll question "What do you think is the ideal number of children for a family to have?" only 17 percent of Canadians said two or fewer, and 60 percent said four or more. By 1988, most people, 58 percent, thought the ideal was two or fewer, and only 13 percent thought four or more (Gallup Canada 1988d).

When the trend toward small families is taken to its logical extreme, couples may decide that their life chances will be enhanced by forgoing parenthood entirely. The choice of childlessness meets with disapproval in some groups, but in many communities such a decision is not necessarily seen as either immoral or unwise. An increasing proportion of couples elects to remain childless (Veevers 1980).

Women's Control of Fertility

None of the changes in opinion about parenthood and childbearing would have been effective in inducing social change had there not also evolved, more or less simultaneously, effective and available methods of controlling conception. In Canada, in 1984, of all wives who were not pregnant or trying to get pregnant, only 6 percent were not using any method of contraception. More noteworthy, wives had very low risk of conceiving accidentally. Of all wives aged 18–49 who were not pregnant or trying to get pregnant, 95 percent had virtually no risk of accidental pregnancy, in that they were sterile, had been sterilized, had sterilized husbands, or were on the pill (Balakrishnan, Krotki, and Lapierre-Adamcyk 1985, 213).

Even good access to contraception does not provide freedom from "the tyranny of pregnancy" unless there is also access to therapeutic abortion as a back-up. In 1953, the Canadian Criminal Code made abortions illegal. This position was liberalized in 1969, by a provision that made abortions possible with the consent of formal abortion committees at approved hospitals (Veevers 1971). Systematic data on the incidence of therapeutic abortion have been available through the 1970s. The increase in abortion rates has been substantial: the rate of abortions per 100 live births doubled from 8.5 in 1971 to 17.0 in 1981 (Statistics Canada 1986).

In 1988, the Supreme Court ruled that hospital abortion committees were illegal, thereby making it possible to consider abortion a private medical decision between doctor and patient. Public opinion on this issue remains divided. A recent Gallup poll found that 13 percent of persons feel that all abortions should be illegal and 20 percent feel that all should be legal regardless of circumstances (Gallup Canada 1988g). Increased controversy in the United States suggests that acceptance of the principle of a woman's access to abortion cannot be taken for granted.

Canada was without an abortion law for some time following the 1988 Supreme Court ruling. In November 1989, Prime Minister Brian Mulroney and Justice Minister Douglas Lewis proposed a compromise abortion bill that continued to include abortion in the Criminal Code, but permitted a woman to terminate a pregnancy on the advice of her doctor (Delacourt 1989). Parliament approved the bill in May 1990. Pro-abortion (or pro-choice) forces are displeased that there is a need for any law at all; anti-abortion (or pro-life) forces are displeased that, with judicious choice of doctor, the law could amount to abortion on demand.

Precipitous Fertility Decline

When couples use no birth control at all, and when their standard of living is relatively high, they have exceedingly large families. For example, families in the Hutterite colonies of western Canada have averaged as many as ten to twelve children (Eaton and Mayer 1953). In Canada, in 1851, the average family consisted of seven children (Beaujot and McQuillan 1986, 58). When parenthood becomes discretionary, and when effective birth control is available, the almost universal tendency is toward small families. The result is a dramatic decline in fertility.

The Canadian baby-bust, which began in the 1960s, parallels similar declines in the rest of the developed Western world. Over the period from 1951 to the present, the Canadian crude birth rate has been approximately halved, from 27.2 births per 1000 persons to 14.8 births per 1000 (Ramu 1989, 94). In Canada, in 1981, the overall fertility level is appreciably below the replacement threshold of 2.1 children per woman (Dumas 1987, 96).

The Perpetuation of Low Fertility

During the 1960s, concern with population growth led to active programs to combat pronatalism and to encourage zero population growth. In the 1980s, the excessive decline of fertility has become problematic. Persons concerned with social policy are now involved in developing pronatalist incentives to encourage people to have more children. For example, concern with falling fertility has led the government of Quebec to consider paying

parents to have children. Although the majority of persons in Quebec (53 percent) are in favour of this scheme, only 29 percent of all Canadians are in favour and, in British Columbia, the proportion endorsing the plan drops to only 15 percent (Gallup Canada 1988e). Indeed, in spite of the strategies of pronatalists, low fertility is so closely tied to attitudes and behaviours involving gender roles, marriage, birth control, and paid employment that it seems clear that low fertility is indeed here to stay.

Seniors Boom: The Emergent Elderly

Each generation imagines itself to be more intelligent than the one that went before it, and wiser than the one that comes after it.
      George Orwell, *Animal Farm* (1945)

The ageing of the population is one of the most important developments in Canadian society during the past several decades. In 1921, about one person in twenty was a senior citizen over the age of 65; by 1986, that proportion had doubled to about one person in ten (see Table 10). The emergence of the elderly as a increasing minority has a wide range of consequences for the society as a whole, and for the family in particular.

Increased Vitality: Chronological Versus Biological Age

Several decades ago, a person at the age of 65 was likely ready to retire from active life. In contrast, today's elderly have had the advantage of better nutrition and better medical care, with the result that a person at the age of 65 is likely to be stronger, healthier, and generally more viable than his or her grandparents were at the same point in life. The elderly are emerging as a social force not only because there are more of them but also because they are more socially active than they were before.

Table 10
Proportion of Elderly Persons in the Population by Age and Sex: Canada, Selected Years 1921–1986

	The Elderly		The Frail Elderly	
Year	% of All Persons Who Are 65+	Females per 100 Males	% of All Persons 65+ Who Are 85+	Females per 100 Males
1921	4.7	95.5	4.9	119.4
1931	5.6	95.6	4.4	125.7
1941	6.6	96.4	4.7	124.2
1951	7.8	97.0	4.8	131.0
1961	7.6	106.4	5.8	130.1
1971	8.1	123.1	7.9	151.8
1981	9.7	133.6	8.2	204.5
1986	10.7	138.0	8.4	229.1

Source: 1986 Census of Canada, Catalogue 93–101, Table 1.

Longer Marriages with Empty Nests

When Maurice Chevalier sings "I'm So Glad I'm Not Young Anymore," one point he makes is that: "Even if love comes in the door, the kind that will last forever more, for-ever more is shorter than before." From the other perspective, young persons who are fall-ing in love today are probably going to live longer than their parents or their grandpar-ents. In that sense, "forever more is *longer* than before," and the open-ended commit-ment of husbands and wives to one another is substantially longer than it was in the past. To take a not-entirely-frivolous example: if a young woman of 20 marries, and if she can expect to live until she is 80, she has com-mitted herself to a "date" for every Saturday night for 60 years, which is 3120 consecutive dates.

When fertility rates were high, a woman often continued in the role of mother until she was close to retirement age. When fertility rates decline and fewer children are born, the "empty nest" period when the children are gone starts earlier in life and, because of in-creased life expectancy, it lasts longer. Women born in 1930 could expect to live an average of 21 years in the empty-nest phase; women born in 1960 can expect it to last 30 years (Gee 1987). Whether or not par-enthood is considered to be a full-time oc-cupation, it certainly cannot be a lifelong one.

Decreasing Sex Ratios

Biological predispositions and cultural pat-terns combine to determine that, in the de-veloped Western world, women will, on the average, live significantly longer than men. Moreover, the discrepancy is generally in-creasing. In 1931, it was only about two years; by 1981, it was about seven years; by the year 2001, the projected life-expectancy figures are 73.9 for men and 82.2 for women, a differ-ence of 8.3 years (Marshall 1987, 560).

Sex differences in mortality have resulted in a marked and increasing imbalance between the number of elderly men in relation to the number of elderly women. From 1921 to 1951, there were slightly more elderly men than elderly women, but the sex ratio was ap-proximately equal (see Table 10). Since that time, death rates for all of the elderly have declined systematically and dramatically. However, the decline for elderly women has been much more precipitous than the decline for elderly men, with the result that the sex ratio in old age becomes increasingly distorted. In 1986, of all elderly persons over the age of 65, there were 138 women for every 100 men (see Table 10).

A Winnowing of Widows

When the biological fact that women live longer than men is combined with the social fact that women typically marry men older than themselves, the ubiquity of widowhood is inevitable. From the 1920s to the 1940s, mortality rates for both men and women were relatively high. Among persons age 65 and older, about a quarter of all men and about half of all women were widowed (Connidis 1989, 9). Since then, two factors have combined to increase the preponderance of widows: compared with married men, married women are much more likely to be bereaved; once bereaved, they are much less likely to remarry. In 1986, of persons over age 65, 13 percent of men were widowed, compared with 48 percent of women (p. 9).

The Frail Elderly

The elderly are not a homogeneous group. Among the old, it is also important to consider the "oldest old" who are the frail elderly, usually considered to be those persons over the age of 80 or 85. Demographically, this group is different from the other elderly in two important ways. First, its growth in the population has been especially dramatic. The elderly in general have increased twofold since 1921; the frail elderly have increased more than fourfold, from 0.2 percent of the population to 0.9 percent. Second, the sex ratio among the very old is especially distorted. In 1921, among persons aged 85 and older, there were 119.4 old women for every 100 old men; now, that ratio has increased to a ratio of 229.1 to 100. Demographic projections suggest that the imbalance between the sexes will stabilize at about 135 females

to every 100 males for persons aged 65–79, but will continue to increase for the frail elderly (Novak 1988, 68).

The Crisis in Home Care

The task of caring for the elderly is certain to increase dramatically in the near future. Not only will their numbers increase, but also the proportions of the elderly needing special care will increase. From 1921 to 1951, only about 5 percent of all elderly persons were among the "oldest old"; by 1986, that proportion had increased to 8.4 percent, and is likely to continue to rise (see Table 10). These persons will require more personal and medical attention than the other elderly. Gee and Kimball (1987, 31–33) note that persons over 70 report having significantly more health problems than do other elderly persons, exhibit more sick role behaviour, and are disproportionately involved in health-care utilization.

The Dearth of Daughters

When considering the problem of care of the elderly, the focus of attention is usually on the choice between at-home care and care in an institutional setting. What is often overlooked is that the role of primary caregiver in the home is, almost always, filled by a woman. Family care of the elderly translates into care by daughters, or by daughters-in-law (Aronson 1985). It has been established that as much as 80 percent of the work of caring for the elderly is done by women (Chappell, Strain, and Blandford 1986). In the past, when much larger families were the norm, an elderly couple could expect to have several daughters and/or daughters-in-law to share the task of caring for them. Now, with reduced fertility and small families of origin, many have only one or two. The crisis in home care is compounded by three simultaneous trends: an increase in the numbers of elderly in the population; an increase in the proportion of them who are frail elderly and who therefore need extensive care; and a decrease in the numbers of adult daughters available to provide home help or home care.

Another factor to be taken into account is that daughters and daughters-in-law are less and less likely to be full-time homemakers. Helping one's mother or mother-in-law, or even caring for her completely, is a different level of task if the caregiver is a homemaker than if she is employed full-time. For some, the needs of the elderly make up yet one more component of the double shift. As the burden increases, some kind of relief for this burden must be found, either by increased participation on the part of sons and sons-in-law, or by institutional alternatives.

Income Inequalities: Old and Poor

Elderly persons over age 65 are more likely than others to be poor, but their situation has improved since 1980. In 1986, among the elderly, one in eight of the men lived below the poverty line, compared with nearly one in four of the women. The rates for unattached are notable higher: about one-third of the men and nearly one-half of the women (National Council of Welfare 1988, 40–43).

Although poverty is a real problem for many of the elderly, it must be remembered that not all of the elderly are poor. The distribution of incomes among the elderly is less equitable that for the rest of the population. A minority have savings and pension plans to enjoy comfortable incomes while the majority get by on modest or low incomes. "Four percent of the aged enjoy more than 40 percent of the investment income" (National Council of Welfare 1984, 55).

Elderly persons are becoming an economic force in Canada. They spend a disproportionate amount of discretionary income on travel, recreation, and other luxuries, all of which contribute to their social and political clout (Dychtwald and Flower 1989). Also, because of their increasing numbers and viability, they are becoming more and more a political force to be taken into account. In 1961, persons over age 65 made up 12.9 percent of the voters; by 1981, they made up 13.3 percent of voters; and by 2001 they will be 16.2 percent (Novak 1988, 324). In the next few decades, the presence of elderly persons will become an increasingly prominent feature of the social landscape.

Letting Many Flowers Bloom

Man desires to be free not in order to be spared tribulation — this is more liable to increase in proportion to the degree of self-determination attained — but in order to grow.
Count Hermann Keyserling, *The Book of Marriage* (1927)

The family structure that we have shown to be evolving in Canadian society is very fluid and contains many options for groups and for individuals. The family as it is now defined is a voluntary organization. Individuals may or may not decide to get married. That decision is independent of whether or not they decide to become sexually active, and whether or not they decide to cohabit with someone. If they are sexually active and/or cohabiting, they may be with someone of the opposite sex or of the same sex. Decisions about assuming the role of parent, or continuing in the role of parent, can be made independently from choice of sexual preference, marital status, sexual activity, or cohabitation. Once these decisions are made, they are often reversible. Cohabitants can split up, engagements can be broken, marriages can end in divorce.

An important part of voluntarism is not only the right to decide what one wants to do, but also *the right to quit*. Persons still make decisions about family relationships, but those decisions are increasingly reversible. The permissiveness concerning movement in and out of commitments is itself a marked change from the recent past.

The right to quit is not only important in itself — giving a person greater control of his own life. Even more important is its effect in giving a person a crucial bargaining element in his relationships with . . . those with whom he has kinship ties. . . . The very fact that one has the right to quit and *is in a realistic position to exercise that right* will in itself greatly improve one's bargaining position in relation to those who have some control over one. The improved bargaining position in turn gives one greater control over one's own life choices, enables one to fashion one's place in an . . . interpersonal relationship more to one's liking, and thus makes one's membership in the . . . relationship more desirable. Thus an effective operational right to quit will often have the effect of reducing the desire to quit. (Roth 1973, 395)

The end result is a pluralistic family system, with an emphasis on the self-actualization of the individual; a system in which the goals of stability and security have been ranked as less important than the goals of freedom and personal growth. We do not view the individual as existing for the family, but rather the family as existing for the individual. Under these circumstances, many different family forms are needed. What emerges is a pluralistic model that supports and celebrates a diversity of lifestyles — that is, a tolerant system in which it is indeed possible to let many flowers bloom.

Works Cited

Adams, O.B., and D.N. Nagnur.1988. *Marriage, Divorce and Mortality: A Life Table Analysis.* Catalogue 84-536E. Ottawa: Statistics Canada, Minister of Supply and Services.

Adler, Cathy, Shirley Congdon, and Nancy R. Scrambler. 1980. *An Overview of Teenage Pregnancy and Parenthood in British Columbia.* Vancouver: Social Planning and Review Council of British Columbia.

Agbayewa, M. Oluwafemi. 1984. "Fathers in the Newer Family Forms: Male or Female?" *Canadian Journal of Psychiatry* 29: 402-5.

Beaujot, Roderic P., and Kevin McQuillan. ~~~ "The Social Effects of Demographic Change: Canada 1851-1981." *Journal of Canadian Studies* 21: 57-69.

Benokraitis, Nijole V., and Joe R. Feagin. 1986. *Modern Sexism: Blatant, Subtle, and Covert Discrimination.* Englewood Cliffs, NJ: Prentice-Hall.

Bibby, Reginald W. 1983. "The Moral Mosaic: Sexuality in the Canadian 1980s." *Social Indicators Research* 13: 171-84.

Bibby, Reginald W., and Donald C. Posterski. 1985. *The Emerging Generation: An Inside Look at Canada's Teenagers.* Toronto: Irwin.

Bird, Florence (Chairman). 1970. *Report of the Royal Commission on the Status of Women in Canada.* Ottawa: Information Canada.

Boyer, J. Patrick. 1985. *Equality for All: Report on the Parliamentary Committee on Equality Rights.* Ottawa: Queen's Printer.

Brown, Gabrielle. 1980. *The New Celibacy.* New York: McGraw-Hill.

Brown, Helen Gurley. 1962. *Sex and the Single Girl.* New York: Bernard Geis.

Chekki, Dan A. 1976. "The Changing Roles of Women in Canada." *Sociologia Internationalis* 14: 201-19.

Chappell, N.L., L.A. Strain, and A.A. Blandford. 1986. *Aging and Health Care: A Social Perspective.* Toronto: Holt, Rinehart and Winston.

Connidis, Ingrid Arnet. 1989. *Family Ties and Aging.* Toronto: Butterworths.

de Koninck, Maria. 1984. "Double Work and Women's Health." *Canada's Mental Health.* 32: 28-31.

Delacourt, Susan. 1989. "Compromise Abortion Bill Unveiled Today." *Globe and Mail.* November 3.

Devlin, Audrey, and Judith P. R... Mediation in Canada: Pas... Development." *Internati... vorce Mediation Quart...

Dumas, Jean. 1987. ...uation in Canada... tawa: Minister...

Dychtwald, K... Los Ange...

Eaton, Jo... Soci...

H...

yan. 1986. "Family ..., Present and Future ...nal Developments in Di-...rly 11: 93–108.

...eport on the Demographic Sit- ...1986. Catalogue 91–209E. Ot- ...of Supply and Services.

...n, and Joe Flower. 1989. Age Wave. ...es: J.P. Tarcher.

...seph W., and Albert J. Mayer. 1953. "The ...l Biology of Very High Fertility Among the ...utterites: The Demography of a Unique Population." Human Biology 25: 206–64.

Eichler, Margrit. 1988. Families in Canada Today: Recent Changes and Their Policy Consequences. Toronto: Gage.

Farber, Bernard. 1964. Family Organization and Interaction. San Francisco: Chandler.

Friedan, Betty. 1963. The Feminine Mystique. New York: Norton.

Gallup Canada, Inc. 1986a. "4 in 5 Feel Men Should Share General Housework." The Gallup Report. March 10.

———. 1986b. "75% Endorse Equal Sharing If Couple Should Divorce." The Gallup Report. May 22.

———. 1986c. "More Canadians Approve than Disapprove of Trial Marriage." The Gallup Report. June 9.

———. 1987. "Approval Up for Working Mothers of Young Children." The Gallup Report. March 23.

———. 1988a. "Opinion Split on Family Life of Working Wives." The Gallup Report. February 4.

———. 1988b. "Majority Supports Increased Spending for Day Care." The Gallup Report. March 3.

———. 1988c. "Opinion Split on Gay Clergymen." The Gallup Report. April 18.

———. 1988d. "Two Child Family the Ideal of Most." The Gallup Report. June 4.

———. 1988e. "Majority of Quebeckers Favor Payments for Bearing Children." The Gallup Report. July 7.

———. 1988f. "Many Canadians Concerned About Possible AIDS Epidemic." The Gallup Report. August 25.

———. 1988g. "Fewer Canadians Favor Unrestricted Access to Abortion." The Gallup Report. September 29.

Gee, Ellen M. 1987. "Historical Change in the Family Life Course of Canadian Men and Women." Aging in Canada: Social Perspectives. Ed. Victor W. Marshall. Markham, ON: Fitzhenry and Whiteside, 265–87.

Gee, Ellen M., and Meredith M. Kimball. 1987. Women and Aging. Toronto: Butterworths.

Goldstein, Jay, and Alexander Segall. 1985. "Ethnic Intermarriage and Ethnic Identity." Canadian Ethnic Studies 17: 60–71.

Greenglass, Esther R. 1982. A World of Difference: Gender Roles in Perspective. Toronto: Wiley.

Grindstaff, Carl F. 1988. "Adolescent Marriage and Childbearing: The Long Term Economic Outcome, Canada in the 1980s." Adolescence 33: 45–58.

Heer, David M., and Charles A. Hubay, Jr. 1975. "The Trend in Interfaith Marriages in Canada: 1922–1972." Marriage, Family and Society: Canadian Perspectives. Ed. S. Parvez Wakil. Toronto: Butterworths. 85–96.

Herold, E.S. 1984. Sexual Behaviour of Canadian Young People. Markham, ON: Fitzhenry and Whiteside.

Hobart, Charles W. 1983. "Marriage or Cohabitation." Marriage and Divorce in Canada. Ed. K. Ishwaran. Agincourt, ON: Methuen. 47–69.

———. 1984. "Changing Profession and Practice of Sexual Standards: A Study of Young Anglophone and Francophone Canadians." Journal of Comparative Family Studies 15: 231–55.

Hunter, Alfred A. 1986. Class Tells: On Social Inequality in Canada. Toronto: Butterworths.

Irving, Howard H., Michael Benjamin, and Nicholas Trocme. 1984. "Shared Patenting: An Empirical Analysis Utilizing a Large Data Base." Family Process 23: 561–69.

Kinsey, A., W. Pomeroy, and C. Martin. 1948. Sexual Behavior in the Human Male. Philadelphia: W.B. Saunders.

Kinsey, A., W. Pomeroy, C. Martin, and P. Bebhard. 1953. Sexual Behavior in the Human Female. Philadelphia: W.B. Saunders.

Lambert, Ronald D., and James E. Curtis. 1984. "Québécois and English Canadian Opposition to Racial and Religious Intermarriage, 1968–1983." Canadian Ethnic Studies 16: 30–46.

Landau, Barbara. 1988. "Mediation: An Option for Divorcing Families." Advocate's Quarterly 9: 1–21.

Lindemann, Constance. 1983. "Sexual Freedom: The Right To Say No." Social Casework 64: 609–17.

Lindsay, Colin, and Jo Anne Belliveau. 1985. Women in Canada: A Statistical Report. Catalogue 89–503E. Ottawa: Statistics Canada, Social and

Economic Studies Division.

Marshall, Victor W. 1987. *Aging in Canada: Social Perspectives.* Markham, ON: Fitzhenry and Whiteside.

Mishra-Bouchez, Therese, and Eise Emond. 1987. "The Marital Status of Gatineau Mothers Between 1976 and 1984 or the Rapid and Deep Change of a Society." *Canadian Journal of Public Health* 78: 381–84.

Moore, Maureen. 1989. "How Long Alone? The Duration of Female Lone Parenthood in Canada." *Transition* March: 4–5.

Nagnur, Dhruva, and Owen Adams. 1987. "Tying the Knot: An Overview of Marriage Rates in Canada." *Canadian Social Trends*: 2–6.

National Center for Health Statistics. 1989. "Advance Report of Final Divorce Statistics 1986." *Monthly Vital Statistics Report* 38 (June 6).

National Council of Welfare. 1984. *Sixty-Five and Older: A Report by the National Council of Welfare on the Incomes of the Aged.* Catalogue H68–11–1984E. Ottawa: Ministry of Supply and Services.

———. 1988. *Poverty Profile 1988.* Catalogue H67–1/4–1988E. Ottawa: Ministry of Supply and Services.

Nett, Emily M. 1988. *Canadian Families: Past and Present.* Toronto: Butterworths.

Novak, Mark. 1988. *Aging and Society: A Canadian Perspective.* Scarborough, ON: Nelson Canada.

Orton, Maureen Jessop, and Ellen Rosenblatt. 1986. *Adolescent Pregnancy in Ontario: Progress in Prevention.* Hamilton: School of Social Work, McMaster University.

Peron, Yves, and Claude Strohmenger. 1985. *Demographic and Health Indicators: Presentation and Interpretation.* Catalogue 82–543E. Ottawa: Statistics Canada.

Pike, Robert. 1975. "Legal Access and the Incidence of Divorce in Canada: A Socio-Historical Analysis." *Canadian Review of Sociology and Anthropology* 12: 115–33.

Porterfield, Ernest. 1982. "Black-American Intermarriage in the United States." *Marriage and Family Review* 5: 17–34.

Prentice, Alison, et al. 1988. *Canadian Women: A History.* Toronto: Harcourt Brace Jovanovich.

Province of British Columbia. 1986 (and preceding years). *Vital Statistics of the Province of British Columbia.* Victoria: Queen's Printer for British Columbia.

Ramu, G.N. 1989. "Profiles of Marriage and the Family." *Marriage and the Family in Canada Today.* Ed. G.N. Ramu. Scarborough, ON:

Prentice-Hall. 77–99.

Redmond, Marcia A. 1985. "Attitudes of Adolescent Males Toward Adolescent Pregnancy and Fatherhood." *Family Relations* 34: 337–42.

Reiss, Ira. 1980. *Family Systems in America.* New York: Holt, Rinehart and Winston.

Roth, 1973. "The Right to Quit." *Sociological Review* 21: 381–96.

Schlesinger, Ben, ed. 1974. *Family Planning in Canada: A Source Book.* Toronto: University of Toronto Press.

Schmid, Carol. 1976. "The Changing Status of Women in the United States and Canada: An Overview." *Sociological Symposium* 15: 1–27.

Schulz, David A. 1988. *Human Sexuality.* Englewood Cliffs, NJ: Prentice-Hall.

Statistics Canada. 1984. *Canada's Lone-Parent Families.* Catalogue 99–933. Ottawa: Ministry of Supply and Services.

———. 1986. *Therapeutic Abortions, Canada, 1986.* Catalogue 82–546. Ottawa: Ministry of Supply and Services.

———. 1989a. *The Nation, Families, Part 2.* Catalogue 93–107. Ottawa: Queen's Printer.

———. 1989b. "Social Indicators." *Canadian Social Trends* (Winter): 31.

Stein, Peter J. 1981. "Understanding Single Adulthood." *Single Life: Unmarried Adults in Social Context.* Ed. Peter J. Stein. New York: St. Martin's. 9–21.

Stein, Terry S. 1988. "Homosexuality and the New Family Forms: Issues in Psychotherapy." *Psychiatric Annals* 18: 12–20.

Turcotte, Pierre. 1988. "Common-Law Unions." *Canadian Social Trends* (Autumn): 35–39.

Veevers, Jean E. 1971. "The Liberalization of Canadian Abortion Laws." *Critical Issues in Canadian Society.* Eds. Craig Boydell, Carl Grindstaff, and Paul Whitehead. Toronto: Holt, Rinehart and Winston. 33–39.

———. 1977. *The Family in Canada.* Catalogue 99–725. Ottawa: Census of Canada Profile Study, Statistics Canada.

———. 1980. *Childless by Choice.* Toronto: Butterworths.

———. 1984. "Age-Discrepant Marriages: Cross-National Comparisons of Canadian-American Trends." *Social Biology* 31: 18–27.

———. 1985. "Age-Discrepant Marriages in Canada: An Analysis of Incidence and Trends." Paper presented to the Canadian Sociology and Anthropology Association, Montreal.

———. 1987. "Age-Discrepant Marriages: Some International Comparisons of Incidence and

Trends." Paper presented to the Canadian Sociology and Anthropology Association, Hamilton.

———. 1990a. "The Wayward West: Regional Variation in Deviance in Canada." Forthcoming.

———. 1990b. "Permanent Availability for Marriage: Considerations of the Canadian Case." Paper presented to the Committee for Family Research at the 12th World Congress of Sociology, Madrid.

Wargon, Sylvia. 1987. *Canada's Lone-Parent Families.* Catalogue 99-933. Ottawa: Department of Supply and Services. Statistics Canada.

Wilson, Susannah Jane Foster. 1986. *Women, the Family and the Economy.* Toronto: McGraw-Hill Ryerson.

Wyatt, Gail Elizabeth, Stefanie Doyle Peters, and Donald Guthrie. 1988. "Kinsey Revisited Part I: Comparisons of the Sexual Socialization and Sexual Behaviour of White Women over 33 Years." *Archives of Sexual Behavior* 17: 201-39.

Part One

THE CANADIAN FAMILY IN HISTORICAL PERSPECTIVE

• • •

Actual social change is never so great as is apparent change. Ways of belief, of expectation, of judgment and attendant emotion, dispositions of like and dislike, are not easily modified once they are in place. Political and legal institutions may be altered, even abolished, but the bulk of popular thought which has been shaped to their pattern persists.

John Dewey, *Human Nature and Conduct*
(1930)

An understanding of contemporary Canadian families is enhanced by some understanding of what Canadian families were like in the past. Sweeping demographic changes are both a reflection of family change and, eventually, a cause of further modifications in family patterns. Some changes reflect basic societal changes, such as urbanization and an increase in standard of living. Other changes in Canadian families have been ideologically based; that is, they have come about because of fundamental modifications of how people think about the world, and what they believe to be right. Still other changes occur in response to technological innovations, such as the introduction of reliable birth control. All of these factors combine to produce families that differ from families earlier in the century.

The historical background of the Canadian family draws from the patriarchal family system that flourished in the Victorian era. The presumption of male dominance was explicitly supported by biblical teachings, and was entrenched in both laws and customs. The domination of the husband–father characteristic of that system has not been eliminated, but it has been substantially eroded. Changes in the Canadian scene closely parallel changes in other developed Western nations, such as the United States, Australia, New Zealand, and many countries in northern Europe. None of these nations has achieved true equality of the sexes; however, they have evolved gender systems in which male supremacy is no longer taken for granted, and in which the roles of both men and woman are considered to be malleable and therefore negotiable.

The public articulation of feminist ideas first began in Canada before the turn of the century, and focussed on the issues of missionary work, temperance, and enfranchisement. The first wave of the women's movement as a political and social force was manifested by the suffragettes and came into full expression in the 1920s. The visibility and political import of feminism waned somewhat through the Depression and World War II, but was revitalized with the second wave of feminism that had its roots in the counter-culture and the sexual revolution of the 1960s.

Under British common law, which was the basis for Canadian law, a woman did not have the legal status of personhood. The reforms in the early part of this century corrected the situation, but only in part and only gradually. Between 1916 and 1922, most Canadian provinces gave women the vote. However, women in Quebec did not get the right to vote or to hold public office until 1940. If suffrage seems to be an issue of historical interest only, consider that there are still women in Quebec who can remember being grown up enough to marry and have babies but not grown up enough to vote.

About the Articles

For most persons, family life now provides the main opportunity for emotional and psychological intimacy. Kersten and Kersten point out that, in the recent past, traditional family roles were not especially conducive to the development of real intimacy; this situation, however, has been somewhat modified by changes in the roles of both men and women. As a result, in many marriages there is both a greater capacity for emotional sharing and a heightened expectation that husbands and wives can and should provide for each other's emotional needs.

The tenuous and troubled course of changes in women's roles is outlined by Schmid, who traces the development of the feminist movement from the early days of suffrage and temperance to the current concern with equality of employment and legal personhood.

While we are focussing on the changes in the family, it is also prudent to keep in mind the French observation: "*Plus ça change, plus c'est la même chose*" (The more it changes, the

more it remains the same). Cutler's article focusses on such familiar problems as the breakdown of monogamous marriage, declining fertility, the changing status of women, the instability of the family, and the plight of children in divorce. Although the terminology may be slightly strange, you need to look twice to notice that this article, which in many ways is very modern in tone, was in fact written more than 70 years ago.

Further Readings

Anderson, Michael. 1983. "How Much Has the Family Changed?" *New Society* 66: 143–46.

Chekki, Dan A. 1976. "The Changing Roles of Women in Canada." *Sociologia Internationalis* 14: 201–20.

Gee, Ellen M. 1986. "The Life Course of Canadian Women: A Historical and Demographic Analysis." *Social Indicators Research* 18: 263–360.

Nett, Emily M. 1981. "Canadian Families in Social-Historical Perspective." *Canadian Journal of Sociology* 6: 239–60.

Prentice, Alison, et al. 1988. *Canadian Women: A History.* Toronto: Harcourt Brace Jovanovich.

Strong-Boag, Veronica. 1988. *The New Day Recalled: Lives of Girls and Women in English Canada, 1919–1939.* Toronto: Copp Clark.

Strong-Boag, Veronica, and Anita Clair Fellman, eds. 1986. *Rethinking Canada: The Promise of Women's History.* Toronto: Copp Clark.

A HISTORICAL PERSPECTIVE ON INTIMATE RELATIONSHIPS

Karen K. Kersten
Lawrence K. Kersten

Emotional intimacy is one of the primary functions of marriage today. This paper focusses on the major social changes in North America that have resulted in the marital unit becoming a more important source of intimacy. Factors that enhance or discourage the development of marital intimacy are discussed.

Human beings have always had a desire for some degree of emotional closeness. However, at various times in history and in various places of the world, cultural norms have either encouraged or discouraged the seeking of human intimacy. Norms not only regulated how close people should be to each other but also to whom, in particular, they could be close. The expectations were often different for men and women.

We define intimacy as a close emotional bond between two human beings, involving sensitive self-disclosure, emotional support, physical contact, and companionship. Intimacy development is a process, but intimacy itself can be viewed as an outcome that can vary in degree. Our use of the concept of intimacy does not coincide with the popular usage of the term, which implies primarily sexual behaviour. Our view is much broader and stresses a more emotional than physical bond.

Source: *In Praise of Fifty Years: The Groves Conference on the Conservation of Marriage and the Family* (Lake Mills, IA: Graphic Publishing Company, 1986) 8–18. Reprinted with permission from Paula W. Dail and Ruth H. Jewson (editors).

Nineteenth Century to World War I

The Good-Provider Role

Sociologist Jessie Bernard (1981) has described the growth and decline of the male breadwinning role or the good-provider role. This male role seems to have arisen when men moved out of the home into the world of work — a move accelerated by the industrial revolution. It emerged around the 1830s and it had wide ramifications. Bernard says it marked the beginning of a new type of marriage and it did not have good effects on women.

Since women were discouraged from participating in the outside labour force, they were deprived of opportunities to achieve power and competence. Women were not allowed to acquire productive skills and they were not reimbursed for their contribution to the family. Women "dedicated themselves instead to winning a good provider, who would take care of them. The wife of a more successful provider became for all intents and purposes a parasite, with little to do except indulge or pamper herself" (Bernard 1981, 2).

The new industrial order fixed the site of the work that the two sexes engaged in. Each sex had its own turf. This resulted in "the identification of gender with work site as well as with work itself" (Bernard 1981, 3). The spatial separation of the work site reduced the amount of time available for personal interaction, spontaneous emotional give-and-take, and intimacy within the family. In contrast, in the premodern period — when men and women worked in an economy based in the home — frequent opportunities for interaction were available. Bernard writes:

> When men and women are in close proximity, there is always the possibility of reassuring glances, the comfort of simple physical presence. But when the division of labor removes the man from the family dwelling for most of the day, intimate relationships become less feasible. (p. 3)

Certainly the spatial separation of the sexes did nothing to help men become emotionally expressive. What was important to men was their new "enormous drive for achievement, for success, for 'making it'" (Bernard 1981, 3). A real man was not only a provider, but a *good* provider. Bernard says "success in the good-provider role came in time to define masculinity itself. The good provider had to achieve, to win, to succeed, to dominate. He was a bread-*winner*" (p. 4). A man's family became a display case for his success as a good provider. One person took on the responsibility for the whole family's support. In the middle class, if a wife worked, the man was humiliated — it admitted to everybody that the husband was a failure as a good provider. Without the wife working, the man maintained the power of the right to decide about expenditures (Bernard 1981).

A man was usually so busy that he had little time even to talk to his wife or children.

> Emotional expressivity was not included in the good-provider role. . . . [But,] if in addition to being a good provider, a man was kind, gentle, generous, and not a heavy drinker or gambler, that was all frosting on the cake. Loving attention and emotional involvement in the family were not part of woman's implicit bargain with a good provider. (Bernard 1981, 3)

To be sure, some men disliked the role that was forced upon them. Some took it out on

their families and punished them for the heavy burden they had to carry. Some considered that the money they earned belonged to them — members of the family often had to beg for money. Other men knew how to show love only by buying expensive gifts — "the fur coat became more important than the affectionate hug" (Bernard 1981, 5).

Bernard argues that the good-provider role lasted a century and a half, until the 1980 census, in which a man was no longer considered automatically to be the head of the household (1981, 1). In reality, however, much of the good-provider role still exists in the lower class and, to a lesser degree, in the middle class.

Sexuality in the Victorian Period (1880–1920)

Toward the end of the last century, sexual desire was regarded as exclusively male. Women were supposed to be passionless — literally devoid of sexual feelings. There was general agreement that male sexuality could not be repressed; this was evidenced by the growth in prostitution during this period. Usually men were allowed to "indulge their 'lowest' instincts with women from the lowest social class" (Demos 1974, 437). But, as much as women tried to depress their sexual urges, they must have had them anyway, because the demand for the surgical procedure of clitoridectomy was "astonishing." "Evidently this was the last resort of women who, contrary to expectation, found themselves afflicted with 'sensual' wishes" (p. 437).

Given all of these limitations, Demos argues that it is hard to imagine that many married couples were either emotionally or physically close. Sexuality merely reflected the pattern that existed in the entire relationship. Nineteenth-century society was one based on same-sex companionship. Membership in the increasing number of "voluntary associations" was restricted to one sex or the other. Such companionship seemed preferable to what was available between husband and wife at home. "The growth of these organizations was, then, another sign of a deficit in family life, and particularly in the relationships of men and women" (Demos 1974, 438).

Intimacy Between Women

Apparently — at least until World War I — husbands and wives did not experience much intimacy in their marriages. But, it appears that there was indeed some meaningful emotional closeness, in that women formed deep ties with other women. Apparently, strong patterns of friendships existed between women but not between men in the nineteenth century. Historian Carroll Smith-Rosenberg (1978) describes the significance of numerous diaries and thousands of letters that women wrote to each other from adolescence to old age.

For most of these women, their affection for each other remained strong throughout their entire lives. This affection was accentuated by their loneliness and by their desire to spend time together. Female friendship was the only real option for an emotionally close relationship between equals. The single-sex or homosocial networks were facilitated and supported by severe social restrictions on intimacy between men and women generally, and particularly between young men and women. The distinctly male and female spheres in the world were assumed to be determined by the laws of God and nature. Contacts between men and women were usually formal and stiff (Smith-Rosenberg 1978).

Middle- and upper-class women of the nineteenth century lived within a world "bounded by home, church and the institution of visiting — that endless trooping of women to each other's homes for social purposes" (Smith-Rosenberg 1978, 340). This world was encompassed by children and other women. "Women helped each other with domestic chores and in times of sickness, sorrow, or trouble" (p. 340). Women at suppers huddled together, sharing and comparing the letters received from other close women friends. Secrets were exchanged and cherished. Women held communities and kin systems together. They exchanged news letters with almost any female extended kin and such letters gradually formed deeply loving and dependent ties. Smith-Rosenberg writes:

> Especially when families became geographically mobile, women's long visits to each other and their frequent letters filled with discussions of marriages and births, illnesses and deaths, descriptions of growing children, and reminiscences of times and people past provided an important sense of continuity in a rapidly changing society. (p. 340)

Within this close-knit female world, sorrows, anxieties, and joys could be shared by women who were confident that other women had experienced similar feelings. Women gave each other inner security and self-esteem. Talking helped to relieve troubles — troubles that apparently no man could understand. The woman's world was an emotional one to which men had little access (Smith-Rosenberg 1978). Nineteenth-century society did not place taboos on close female relationships but, rather, recognized them as a valuable form of human contact throughout a woman's life. Lower-class wives, of necessity, often had to work outside the home and they did not have the extensive leisure that middle- and upper-class wives had. However, lower-class women still sought emotional support from other women, instead of from their own husbands.

Marriage resulted in a major problem of adjustment. Much of the emotional stiffness and distance that is associated with the Victorian marriage is a consequence of gender-role differentiation. "With marriage both women and men had to adjust to life with a person who was, in essence, a member of an alien group" (Smith-Rosenberg 1978, 350).

Between the World Wars

In 1920, the United States officially became an urban nation with 51 percent of the total population living in cities. Women now had the right to vote for the first time in history. Yet, there continued to be a sharp division of gender roles in the family. In the 1920s and 1930s, sociologists Robert and Helen Lynd found a similar pattern to that of the previous 100 years in their family study of "Middletown," a small midwestern community (Muncie, Indiana). The husband's responsibility was still to be a good provider, and the wife was primarily responsible for keeping the house and raising the children.

But there were some meaningful rumblings of change — in part brought about by the crisis of World War I — that challenged the traditional gender-role pattern. The percentage of working-class wives who worked full-time outside the house had increased to 25 percent in 1920. In addition, some husbands of working wives "were beginning to help clean the house, cook the meals, shop for groceries, do the laundry and care for the children" (Caplow et al. 1982, 112). Nevertheless, the role of the full-time homemaker and mother was still the ideal and the most highly respected role for women (Caplow et al. 1982).

Marriage

According to the Lynds' account, the typical marriage in the 1920s was a dreary one, particularly for the working class. For most families the primary concern was economic survival. Happy marriages were rare and the majority of couples appeared to lead a depressing existence. Most married partners were pressured to remain together by community values discouraging divorce. "Married life was disappointing, but the prospect of a divorce was even more painful" (Caplow et al. 1982, 117). "Love" continued to be the only valid basis for marriage. Even though Middletowners could not define what love was, it was still considered to be the mystical force that guided two people together.

Marriages involved very limited companionship. Social and recreational activities were usually separated by gender; men talked about business, sports, and politics, and women discussed children, dress styles, and local gossip. The widely held view that the two sexes were quite different species encouraged the separation of men and women. "Women were seen as emotional, illogical and incapable of sustained thought, and as being morally superior to men" (Lynd and Lynd 1929, 118).

Working-class families in particular had little time, energy, or money to spend on family leisure. But even when couples spent time at home together there was little pleasant or stimulating conversation. When they were not "bickering" over family problems, they often lapsed into "apathetic silence." Many of the wives were so lonely that they did not want the Middletown researchers' interviews with them to end.

"I wish you could come more often. I never have anyone to talk to," or "My husband never goes anyplace and never does anything. In the evenings he comes home and sits down and says nothing. I like to talk and be sociable, but I can hardly ever get anything out of him." (Lynd and Lynd 1929, 120)

Their sexual relations also were troubled. Lack of knowledge about birth control, and religious beliefs opposing its use, made babies the inevitable consequence of physical closeness. Another child was often an unwanted burden. Women were so emotionally separated from their husbands that they felt they could not ask the men in their lives what they thought about birth control, let alone how they felt about practising it. The fear and worry of having unwanted children often made wives resentful — they felt that their husbands were selfish and insensitive. Other women just "kept away" from their husbands; certainly this did nothing to strengthen their marriages (Caplow et al. 1982).

Husbands, on the other hand, felt rejected by their wives' avoidance of sexual activity, which was the only form of closeness they knew. The fact that prostitution flourished in

Middletown during the 1920s may be attributed to the limited marital sex. In any case, husband–wife relationships were neither physically nor emotionally close. This is demonstrated by the responses of working-class wives to the question "What are the thoughts and plans that give you courage to go on when thoroughly discouraged?" Not a single wife mentioned her husband as a source of emotional support!

Wives of businessmen, in addition to "making a home" for their husbands and children, played a more active and meaningful social role in the world. Besides having traditional skills, these women were expected to be physically attractive and well-dressed. In general, "brains" were not regarded as important in a wife. The key skill that girls were expected to learn from high school was the ability to pick a good provider.

The depression of the 1930s did not really change marriages very much, except perhaps to make life harder. While husbands and wives did spend more time together — partly because outside activities were unaffordable — the quality of their interaction was still poor. Norms discouraging open self-disclosure continued to exist; spouses were not supposed to be frank with each other, particularly regarding emotional matters. The partners did a lot of mutual tearing down, with wives blaming their husbands for failing to "bring home the bacon" and with the husbands defending their wounded egos by lashing out at their wives and children. "Despite these mounting tensions, the typical marital relationship during the depression was similar to that of the 1920s" (Lynd and Lynd 1937, 145). However, the Depression seemed to have more devastating effects on men than on women. A number of men who "lost everything" in the Depression, and therefore failed in the good-provider responsibility, committed suicide.

The divorce rate actually decreased in the 1930s and early 1940s. Marriages were not really better but many couples were forced to stay together out of poverty. Many did not have the $60 needed to pay for a divorce.

However, the economic upheaval of the 1930s hit the working class the hardest; this was reflected in the large number of desertions that took place.

Sexual Behaviour and Dating

The period of 1920–45 was generally one of uncomfortableness with sexual activity. People in Middletown tried to "keep the subject out of sight and out of mind as much as possible" (Lynd and Lynd 1937, 169). But, in comparison to the Victorian standards that existed up until World War I, the 1920s were a transitional period for sexual behaviour — possibly the most significant period of change in the twentieth century.

Most meaningful was the change from a pattern of courtship to a lesser committed pattern of "dating" encouraged by the growing popularity of the automobile. The automobile freed young people from the watchful eyes of their parents and greatly enhanced opportunities for sexual activity.

Feminine clothing was now utilized in an erotic way to show off the body instead of concealing it. Illicit sex became a common theme in popular literature and in the movies. Petting became popular, beginning in the 1920s. It emerged as a compromise between the new opportunities to engage in sexual intercourse and old internalized values that indicated that such behaviour was wrong. "Although petting included most of the sexual activities that often precede intercourse, it stopped short of actual intercourse" (Caplow et al. 1982, 165). It allowed sexually active girls to preserve their "technical" virginity while "petting to orgasm" (Hunt 1974). This sexual pattern persisted through the 1950s.

The amount of sexual intercourse also increased in the roaring '20s, even though it was much less common than petting. Birth control devices such as condoms and diaphragms were now generally available. "Twice as many young men as young women reported having premarital sexual intercourse. Working-class men reported having more premarital intercourse and less petting than business-class men" (Caplow et al. 1982, 166). Many young men were involved in sexual behaviour with prostitutes. Masturbation continued to be a secret activity with almost as much shame and guilt as in the Victorian period. The first marriage manuals that viewed sexual activity positively appeared in the 1920s and, in them, the female orgasm was "discovered" (Clanton 1984).

In the 1920s and 1930s, dating became the accepted method of checking out possible mates. This practice gave young people more freedom than ever before in their search for a marriage partner. But dating served additional functions for many individuals. Dating also became an end in itself — just a way of having a good time, a way of gaining status and prestige, and a way of learning about different types of human beings.

The sharing of true feelings and open communication were not common during the couple's dating. Dating appeared, at least among college students, to involve more play acting than the honest sharing of emotions. Sociologist Willard Waller, who studied dating patterns during the 1930s and 1940s, described the concept of "light love," which involved little vulnerability or emotional dependence among young people. A lot of game playing was involved in dating, and Waller argued that this was a way of avoiding emotional hurt (1937).

The bargain being struck in the search for a marriage partner was a practical, economic one for women — a desire to have a good provider. The man, in turn, focussed on the search for a "beautiful object." An attractive woman was regularly looked upon as a symbol of a successful man. In general, the search for intimacy was not a prime concern of couples during this period between the two world wars.

1945–1965

The Rush to Marry and Have Children

Norms in the postwar period were strongly family-centred and young people rushed into marriage to legitimize their sexuality. Marriage, in fact, became a duty or an obligation, and there were few other options. However, marriages continued to be governed by rigid gender roles. Men were primarily concerned with job success and making money. After the poverty of the 1930s and the sacrifices demanded by war, people became oriented toward the accumulation of material rewards in this period of prosperity (Schnall 1981).

The key to upward mobility for females was to marry up in social class, or at least better than their mothers. A woman's self-esteem and self-worth were obtained vicariously through her husband's success. Women were attracted to men who gave the appearance of being the best of the good providers. Dating continued to be a rather formal process of going somewhere and "making out" afterward. Mutual in-depth self-disclosure and the sharing of real feelings continued to be rare during the courtship and marriage. Couples generally had children soon after they were married (Schnall 1981).

Most of the women who worked during World War II gave up their jobs and returned to the world of children. Parenting was considered in such a positive light in this period that, in a study conducted by Gurin, Veroff, and Feld (1960), parents seldom responded negatively to the parenting experience. "It was apparently not possible in the normative climate of that time for a parent to say he/she was dissatisfied or unhappy with her/his experience of parenthood" (Veroff, Douvan, and Kulka 1981, 203). Seldom did couples carry out activities together, apart from their children.

Women in the 1945–65 period were expected to be completely fulfilled through marriage and childrearing. But, more often than not, particularly in the isolation of suburbia, this idealistic view of domestic life was found lacking. Wives usually found that their husbands did not have much sympathy or understanding for the loneliness they were experiencing. Men escaped by focussing on their work. In reality, husbands were seldom available physically or emotionally (Schnall 1981).

Financial security was considered to be much more important than emotional closeness; loving was shown through material things. Advice from professionals also contributed to what came to be called a "period of family renaissance." Social workers, psychologists, and other professionals "were preaching the virtues of domesticity to their female clients: The good mother, it was maintained, stayed at home and devoted herself full time to the tasks of child rearing" (Berger and Berger 1983, 37). If women resisted their role "psychologists were ready to treat this reluctance as a neurotic ailment" (p. 15).

The majority of Americans in 1957 thought that people who didn't marry were sick, immoral, selfish, or too neurotic to marry (Gurin, Veroff, and Feld 1960). These attitudes reflect the very powerful norm favouring marriage that operated at that time. A negative view of nonmarriers was even taken by the majority of people who had themselves not married and by respondents who had had previous marriages end in divorce. In fact, individuals who had never married expressed the most positive views of the institution (Veroff, Douvan, and Kulka 1981).

In general, women in 1957 were always more negative about marriage than were men. "Only among those who had never been married were women *more positive* about marriage than men. And they were extraordinarily positive — more so than married women, and more than any group except widowed men" (Veroff, Douvan, and Kulka 1981, 148). Single women idealized marriage because they wanted to achieve it. In this era, marriage was often seen as the only legitimate status for a woman. But women were more likely to report problems in their marriages. They seemed to demand more of their husbands than men demanded of their wives. What they appeared to be demanding was intimacy, but this was seldom obtained (Veroff, Douvan, and Kulka 1981).

A random sample of wives in the early 1950s, in a study conducted by sociologists Blood and Wolfe (1960), was asked to choose the most important aspect of marriage. The largest percentage chose "companionship in doing things together with the husband." This suggests that women in general desired to share activities closely with their husbands. Couples that were most egalitarian had the highest level of companionship and couples where one partner had much more power over the other had the least.

Two key elements of intimacy mentioned by Blood and Wolfe were "understanding and emotional well-being." They saw these elements as the primary emerging function of marriage. These authors were among the first to argue that emotional security is not just something that parents give to children but, in addition, is an element needed in the exchange between the husband and wife. Adults also have emotional needs: "needs for acceptance as a person, for a sense of belonging, for knowing someone understands how they feel, and for sympathy and empathy" (1960, 176). These needs can be met through "intimate others" (Blood and Wolfe 1960).

Marriages had traditionally provided limited opportunities for such emotional support. The dominant male was expected to depend on his own competencies. The traditional husband was not really expected to rely upon his wife for emotional sustenance, even though he covertly did. "A real he-man does not depend on petticoat encouragement. He gets it — to be sure — but only because it is his due, not because he needs it" (Blood and Wolfe 1960, 178). A good provider is not supposed to have problems; he even denies their existence. To turn to the "weaker sex" for help in time of trouble would be disgraceful and admitting to defeat. This pattern was particularly true of lower-class men.

However, Blood and Wolfe argue that tradition has also discouraged the wife from relying on her husband for help with emotional problems.

Her right to have problems was fully accepted — for the weaker sex by definition is subject to limitations. To cry was an acceptable symbol of her inability to cope with difficulties, and the appropriate place for crying was on her husband's brawny shoulder. Yet the difference between a good wife and a troublesome wife was whether she "bothered her husband." (1960, 179)

In reality, the "ideal woman" was a mother who could cope with the problems of the children on her own, without giving her mate undue worry about her sphere of things. After all, he was much too busy to be bothered with such matters.

Indeed, very few wives in the 1950s reported that they sought emotional support from their husbands. Only 8 percent of the city wives and 3 percent of the farm wives specifically mentioned their spouses as a source of help when they were tense, upset, or just having a bad day. On the other hand, the husbands were often the target of the wives' growing anger or aggression, and the husband was even less likely to respond sensitively and empathically after being attacked (Blood and Wolfe 1960).

Blue-Collar Marriages

The greatest separation of the sexes and the least intimacy is found among blue-collar husbands and wives (Komarovsky 1962). From early in life, working-class children are taught to distinguish between men's and women's roles. A common complaint of the women in Komarovsky's research was that their husbands did not talk enough. Most of the men felt that there really was nothing to say. They found their jobs monotonous and felt that there was little to elaborate about their work. They wanted merely to come home and rest. Some men felt that their jobs were too technical for women to understand. Also, the men felt that talking about the job carried the connotation of "griping," which was thought to be unmanly. It was considered masculine not to bring one's job home. The working-class male's view was that work and home should be kept separate. Not only did men not want to share their daily experiences, they also did

not want to hear about their wives' days. The working-class situation stands in sharp contrast to the frequently reported involvement of the "corporation wife" in her husband's career (Komarovsky 1962).

A major trait found among blue-collar men is a "trained incapacity to share." "The ideal of masculinity into which they were socialized inhibits expressiveness both directly, with its emphasis on reserve, and indirectly, by identifying personal interchange with the feminine role" (Komarovsky 1962, 156). Of the 23 qualities of a good husband that women were asked to rank, "speaks his mind when something is worrying him" came out second most important (p. 157). This reflects the desire of women to know their husbands and to share in their lives. But the ideal of masculinity accepted by the men is a key factor in their meagre disclosure of stressful feelings.

The working-class wives of the 1945–65 era ended up seeking emotional closeness — just as women did in the nineteenth century — from other women. Two-thirds of the wives had "at least one person apart from their husbands in whom they confided deeply personal experiences" (Komarovsky 1962, 208). In most cases they shared significant segments of their lives *more fully* with female confidantes than with their husbands.

1965–1975

The Modern Women's Movement

A key stimulus to the feminist movement was the publication of Betty Friedan's book *The Feminine Mystique* in 1963, but the full impact of the book was not evident until years later. "This book was an indictment of the middle-class housewife's imprisonment in domesticity" (Berger and Berger 1983, 24). The problem was that women had been told throughout the years after World War II that their only dream should be to be perfect wives and mothers, and that their highest ambition should be to have four or five children and a beautiful house. "Occupation: housewife" was something women should be proud to announce (Friedan 1963).

Women throughout the 1945–65 period increasingly complained of not being happy. They knew something was missing from their lives but most couldn't put their finger on what. They went to doctors by the thousands and were given tranquillizers. The bottom line of this "housewife syndrome" was that women wanted something more than a husband, children, and a home in suburbia. Starting in the mid-1960s, the popular literature became focussed on the plight of the trapped housewife (Friedan 1963).

The solution, according to Friedan, was clear: women should get out of the household and into the world of work, in which they could create a new, positive self-image of themselves. They, like slaves, were to be set free. This freedom, above all else, meant freedom from the family. In the 1960s, women were entering the work force in record numbers, with mothers of young children making up the bulk of the rise. Because many women encountered discrimination, by the late 1960s a new feminist ideology emerged, asserting that women are "the most oppressed of all people" (Berger and Berger 1983, 24–25). The modern feminist movement was largely a middle-class movement. Lower-class women have typically always had to work outside the home to survive.

The Personal-Fulfilment Movement

Values of "personal fulfilment," "self-realization," "self-actualization," and "human potential" became the ultimate goals for some people in the period from 1965 to 1975. With an emphasis on "self," in-depth commitments and close relationships took a back seat. In fact, some individuals went to great lengths to avoid attachments.

There was an enthusiasm, almost a mania, for "new experiences." People challenged each other to try different patterns of behaviour. Single people were pressured to experiment with various drugs and to try almost

anything sexually. Simply experiencing homosexuality, a one-night stand, group sex, group living, and nonmarital cohabitation was considered to be an important form of "growth." Having an open marriage, a variety of sexual partners, multiple orgasms, a marriage contract, or even a divorce (to get back into the singles action) was considered to be "where it was at."

The 1965–75 decade saw people struggling to achieve a measure of autonomy and independence away from restricted and traditional gender roles, even at the cost of isolation. A proliferation of self-help books instructed people how to find happiness. Weekend marathons — dressed or nude — promised to remake personalities and provide "instant intimacy." Books were even written to teach people how to exploit other human beings without guilt.

Watching out for yourself or "number one" was the ethic of the times. Self-proclaimed gurus emerged to become prophets to thousands of unhappy individuals. Encounter groups, T-groups, sensitivity training, Est, psychodrama, and primal-scream therapies were focussed on the personal self. Whatever else, the personal-fulfilment movement gave people the right to focus on themselves and to seek individual happiness. In addition, the movement helped to contribute to the greater intimacy found in marriages of the later 1970s.

Sexual Behaviour

The 1965–75 decade saw dramatic changes in sexual behaviour. There was a shift toward liberal sexual attitudes, ideas, and behaviour. Total nudity made its mass-circulation debut in the January 1972 issue of *Playboy*. Abortion was made legal by the U.S. Supreme Court in 1973. Two-thirds of the population now saw premarital sexual intercourse as acceptable behaviour. About 50 percent of both men and women did not see homosexuality as wrong. The vast majority of both sexes did not see oral sex as wrong. Only a little over a quarter of all men and women saw anal intercourse between a man and a woman as wrong (Hunt 1974).

There is ample evidence to describe this time period as the most sexually permissive decade in North American history. The traditional, committed, monogamous marriage coexisted along with sexual activity without commitment, open marriages, adultery, high rates of divorce, high rates of remarriage, significant numbers of unmarried couples living together, and many married couples living separately.

A major shift that occurred in the 1965–75 era was the growing acceptance of nonmarital sex when there was mutual affection. This value change had been evolving since the 1920s but was helped along by the extensive use of the birth-control pill. "The partners, especially the woman, no longer need to assume that they will ultimately marry this lover to justify the sexual relationship" (Bardwick 1979, 87–88). While the number of virgins was still considerable in this era — 30 percent at the time they left college — the trend was to define sexual activity as morally acceptable outside of marriage if the partners are in a continuing relationship (p. 88). There was considerably less guilt about sexual activity as well as less effort to hide it from family and friends.

1975–Present

Marriage

Despite all of the media attention given to "self-fulfilment," the human-potential movement, and alternative lifestyles during the 1970s, marriage was still of central importance to the vast majority of people. This importance was now based more on the interpersonal support that marriage provided. In a study done in 1976, family relationships (marital and parental) were almost uniformly rated higher than either work or leisure activities in fulfilling personal values for both men and women. This seems to suggest that these relationships are really at the core of

a meaningful life. In addition, comparing the 1976 respondents to an earlier sample interviewed in 1957, there was an increase in reported marital happiness. Two factors, "frequency of chatting" and "physical affection," were highly correlated with marital happiness (Veroff, Douvan, and Kulka 1981).

The greater marital happiness in the 1970s is partly accounted for by a very high divorce rate. People who were really unhappy in the 1970s were much less likely to stay in their marriages than had been the case in the 1950s. Thus, the modern institution of divorce may not be a force weakening marriage but may ultimately be strengthening marriages. Also in 1976 — compared to the 1950s — most people thought that an unmarried person could have a happy life. Marriage, by 1976, had come to be seen as only one potential mechanism for increasing happiness.

Veroff, Douvan, and Kulka (1981) found that people in 1976 were more open about the negative, as well as the positive aspects of marriage. Individuals in the 1970s were more likely to say that marriage both enlarges *and* restricts life and they were more likely to see both sides of the decision to marry or not to marry. Marriages in 1976, as compared to 1957, were more likely to involve an intimate, interpersonal relationship between partners than an institutional arrangement of interacting roles.

The growth of female power and the greater concern for personal feelings in our culture help to account for this trend. When Veroff, Douvan, and Kulka (1981) restricted their analysis to those factors that specifically have to do with intimacy — e.g., thoughtfulness, sensitivity, responsiveness to the spouse — a change from 1957 to 1976 was definitely apparent. Moreover, people *want* even more closeness in their marriages. The majority of individuals interviewed in the 1976 study indicated that they "often" or "sometimes" wished that their spouse understood them better.

The results from the 1976 study clearly show that women see more problems in marriage than men do. Women wished that their husbands would talk more about their thoughts and feelings. "In marriage, then, women talk and want verbal responsiveness of the kind they have had with other women, but their men are often silent partners, unable to respond in kind" (Veroff, Douvan, and Kulka 1981, 178).

Caplow's 1978 replicated study of Middletown revealed major changes in the style of communication between husbands and wives from that of the 1920s and 1930s. Contributing to these changes in the late 1960s and 1970s were assertiveness-training programs, and the women's rights movement. These events helped contribute to the possibility of "more equal marriage relationships in which the needs and wishes of the wives are considered to be at least as important as those of the husbands" (Caplow et al. 1982, 124).

Caplow found that not only were husbands and wives talking more to each other, but they were also engaging in more leisure activity together. Overall, the study indicates a very high level of marital satisfaciton and much improvement over marriages 50 years earlier. More wives reported their husbands as a source of strength and comfort in 1978 than had in 1929. Caplow concludes that "the marital relationship has deepened since the 1920s and that husbands and wives share each other's burdens and provide emotional support to a greater degree now than then" (1982, 128). Indeed, interpersonal intimacy had become much more of a "vehicle for personal fulfilment" and emotional well-being in contemporary society (Veroff, Douvan, and Kulka 1981).

The War Over the Family

From 1975 to the present, a controversy begun in the early 1970s regarding the state of health of the American family has continued. An enlightening summary of the deep divisions in the United States regarding the family is Brigitte and Peter Berger's book *The War Over the Family* (1983). The major groups — the family liberals and conserva-

tives — continue to war over the family in the 1980s. There are many subgroups within each of these two camps but they easily lean toward one or the other major orientation.

The conservatives, who began to join together in the late 1970s, came to be known as the "pro-family" group. Among the people involved were anti-feminists, anti-Equal Rights Amendment (ERA) people, people who were concerned about homosexuality and pornography, those opposed to sexual "permissiveness," people concerned with growing secularism in American life, and (most significantly) the "pro-life" anti-abortionists. These various groups developed a remarkably strong working relationship and exerted powerful political pressure in the national elections in 1980 and 1984. The Moral Majority, led by Jerry Falwell, came to be a meaningful force on these issues (Berger and Berger 1983). "People in this camp are *for* the traditional family and traditional roles within the family" (p. 31). Many people feel so intensely about these matters that they see themselves as engaged in a moral battle with pagans. But the family conservatives stand in opposition to a pluralistic society. They want "a public affirmation of moral values which, however widespread, are no longer *generally* held" (p. 31).

The original stimulus for the conservatives came with the 1973 U.S. Supreme Court decision that allowed abortions during the first three months of pregnancy. Fuel was added to the fire in 1976 when the Supreme Court further decided that abortion was a right solely of women, over which neither a husband nor a parent had a veto. This decision was viewed as challenging the very basis of the family as a group entity over and beyond individual interests.

The family liberals are also a diverse group. The biggest challenge to traditional norms came from feminism and its allies in the other liberationist movements. Although changes in family-role patterns in favour of more equality were stressed, emotional moral issues such as abortion were central. Feminists wanted women to be able to get out of the household and into the world of work. Women's freedom, to the greatest extent, meant the choice to be free from family obligations. What has remained into the 1980s among the militant feminists is the theme of total liberation and "a view of the family as the major obstacle to this liberation" (Berger and Berger 1983, 25). New bonds of "sisterhood" are called upon to provide for intimacy needs, replacing the "confining" bonds of the family. But, most of all, the family was seen as interfering with women's search for self-fulfilment (Berger and Berger 1983).

The family conservatives want to uphold the traditional image of the family. It is this nostalgic image of the harmonious and stable nuclear family that the conservatives are determined to bring back. And although, in reality, these idealistic families never existed or could exist, the *image* of them has extraordinary influence on people and their expectations (Skolnick 1979). Hence, the conservatives continue to believe that a woman's place is in the home — "that's where she's the happiest." Women's fulfilment, it is said, lies in taking care of the personal and emotional needs of their husbands and children.

The 1980s find the family liberals and family conservatives in a political deadlock. The liberals and conservatives agree that family life has undergone tremendous change from what it was in the past. But the conservatives believe these changes will bring about a steep demise of the family and its values that will be harmful both to the individual and to society. The changes are negative and are considered to be leading to decadence (Berger and Berger 1983).

The liberals, in contrast, see the decline, or even the disappearance, of the family as it was in the past to be a good thing because of the harmful effects of the traditional nuclear family. In between these opposite stances is a more moderate view, which is probably held by the majority of the population. This perspective says "that social changes have had a massive impact on the family, which has shown itself to be a remarkably robust and adaptable institution but which is nevertheless in a state of crisis" (Berger and Berger 1983, 86).

Conclusion

A historical analysis of interpersonal relationships offers an insightful look into those societal and cultural dynamics that affect psychological intimacy. In terms of building emotional closeness between husbands and wives, it appears that the "good old days" were not as good as we sometimes think. There are several reasons for the greater potential for marital intimacy in the 1980s than existed in the past.

First, life-cycle changes have resulted in married couples spending more years together without the presence of children. In addition, having fewer children allows the couple more time to focus on and cultivate their own relationship. Getting married at a later age means that individuals will have more opportunity to experience various types of potential partners and possibly to make a better choice in a compatible partner. Furthermore, a longer life expectancy means that marriage partners will spend more time as a couple alone. The "Golden Years," after the children have left and work accomplishments have been achieved, may have the greatest potential for couples to achieve marital intimacy.

Second, changes in gender roles have had probably the most significant impact on marital intimacy. One thread running throughout the historical overview is that, when gender roles are such that one gender is dominant and the other subordinate, intimacy is less likely to flourish. Because women are gaining more power and opportunities in society, feeling more respect for themselves, and improving their self-esteem, they can now function as equal partners in marriage. The husband can no longer unilaterally make decisions or rule the household when the wife is less dependent on him economically and is self-sufficient enough to leave the marriage. She is no longer powerless in the relationship and is demanding the same respect she gives him.

There is an increased willingness for men to give up total control in a marriage and to be more flexible in their gender-role orientation. In addition, there is a growing societal expectation that a husband should provide for a wife's emotional needs. The separation of the sexes is diminishing; male and female worlds are no longer separated as in previous historical periods. The extent to which family conservatives are successful in bringing about a return to a more patriarchal structure in the marital relationship will inhibit the potential for intimacy development.

Third, there is a growing expectation for marriage to provide personal fulfilment, a goal stimulated by the 1970s human-potential movement. This movement encouraged people to "get in touch" with the more feeling or expressive side of themselves. Marital-enrichment programs have been springing up across the country, attracting thousands of couples seeking to "breathe new life" into their marriages. Marital therapy is increasingly becoming an acceptable recourse for couples who are dissatisfied with their marriages.

The growing acceptance of divorce and easy access to it allow couples who cannot attain happiness together to dissolve their marriages and seek it elsewhere. Spouses no longer must feel "stuck" or trapped in "empty-shell" or distressed marriages.

Finally, the "sexual revolution" has given people broader permission to be sexual. The relaxation of binding proscriptions on sexual behaviour are contributing to the greater quantity and quality of sexual satisfaction and, indirectly, to psychological closeness between husband and wife.

Works Cited

Bardwick, J. 1979. In Transition. New York: Holt, Rinehart and Winston.

Berger, B., and P. Berger. 1983. The War Over the Family. Garden City, NY: Anchor.

Bernard, J. 1981. "The Good-Provider Role: Its Rise and Fall." American Psychologist 36: 1–12.

Blood, R., and D. Wolfe, 1960. Husbands and Wives. New York: Free Press.

Caplow, T., et al. 1982. Middletow neapolis: University of Minnesota

Clanton, G. 1984. "Social Forces and th Family." Marriage and the Family in 2020. Eds. Lester A. Kirkendall and Art Grovatt. Buffalo, NY: Prometheus.

Demos, J. 1974. "The American Family in Pa Time." American Scholar 43: 422–46.

Friedan, B. 1963. The Feminine Mystique. New York: Dell.

Gurin, G., J. Veroff, and S. Feld, 1960. Americans View Their Mental Health. New York: Basic Books.

Hunt, M. 1974. Sexual Behaviour in the 1970s. Chicago: Playboy.

Komarovsky, M. 1962. Blue-collar Marriage. New York: Random House.

Lynd, R., and H. Lynd, 1929. Middletown. New York: Harcourt, Brace and Co.

———. 1937. Middletown in Transition. New York: Harcourt, Brace and Co.

Schnall, M. 1981. A Search for New Values. New York: Potter.

Skolnick, A. 1979. "Public Images, Private Realities: The American Family in Popular Culture and Social Science." Changing Images of the Family. Eds. V. Tufte and B. Myerholf. New Haven: Yale University Press: 297–315.

Veroff, J., E. Douvan, and K. Kulka, 1981. The Inner American. New York: Basic.

Waller, W. 1937. "The Rating and Dating Complex." American Sociological Review 2: 727–34.

Families. Min-
Press.
Changing
the Year
ur E.

ING STATUS OF WOMEN IN
STATES AND CANADA: AN

The term "status of women" has come to mean almost anything having to do with women. As Jessie Bernard (1968, 4) has so aptly commented, it is a term that "refuses to sit still for its portrait; it is one of those evocative expressions which have no precise referent but which everyone understands." Although there is perhaps no exact referent in discussing the status of women, there can be little doubt that it is profoundly influenced by many factors. This paper presents an overview of the development of women's rights in the United States and primarily the English-speaking part of Canada during the past 150 years. The discussion focusses on three of the more important elements that determine women's position in North America today — legislative reform, values and attitudes, and demographic change.

The Early Status of Women

The first settlers brought to North America as invisible baggage the philosophy, traditions, and customs of the country from which they came. These included their attitudes toward women, which had already developed in Europe. In general, their traditions emphasized the subordination of women to men. Under English common law, a woman's independent existence was terminated by marriage when her husband assumed control of her person, all her property, and her earnings.

This principle of common law was expounded by the English jurist Sir William Blackstone (1922, 422) 200 years ago: "The husband and wife are one and that one is the husband. . . . Even the disabilities that the wife lies under are for the most part intended for her protection and benefit."

In the United States, the founding fathers eloquently proclaimed in the Declaration of Independence "that all men are created equal with certain inalienable rights." They did not, however, envisage within that concept that black men, native people, or women were endowed with inalienable rights equal to those of white men. Although the Declaration of Independence marked a milestone in granting freedom to more than a small privileged class, it cannot be regarded as a charter of freedom for women.

Almost 100 years after the signing of the Declaration of Independence, the English and French settlers in the provinces of Canada passed a resolution that established a single Canadian confederation. Provisions concerning the rights and liberties of the citizens were not incorporated in that resolution or in the British North America Act. This act, subsequently passed by the British Parliament in 1867, would serve as the Canadian constitution. Because civil rights were deemed to be of a local nature, they came under the jurisdiction of the provinces. However, it is questionable whether the inclusion in the British North America Act of guarantees for individual rights would have had any substantial effect on the status of women in Canada (Gelber 1973, 5).

Source: *Sociological Symposium* 15 (1976): 1-27. Reprinted with permission.

In the pioneer conditions that were typical of most of North America during the nineteenth century, women were respected as individuals for their usefulness in family, church, and community life. In the rural ambience of family farms and enterprises, husbands, wives, and offspring were economically interdependent. Before the coming of the machine, women were needed in the home to produce food and clothing for their families. The great majority of men and women were co-workers on the land and in the home. However, whatever the status of women might have been in pioneer society, it was not accurately reflected in legal and political rights. Margaret MacLellan (1971, 1) notes that

> though their voice might be listened to in private, it could not be heard at the polls or in the law courts. In accordance with the social and religious mores that pioneer men upheld and pioneer women accepted, the security of a married woman was vested by law in her husband. She had no right to property in her own name. Her only basic legal right was the right to support by her husband with the necessities of life according to his means.

Although individual women undoubtedly protested against this one-sided liberty, the first organized feminist movement did not appear until 1848 in the United States. The feminists who gathered at Seneca Falls, New York, were far removed from the mainstream of American life. Many, such as Lucretia Mott and Elizabeth Cady Stanton (Heckler 1971, 157–58), had participated in the abolitionist struggle. The feminists, led by Elizabeth Cady Stanton, addressed themselves to the injustices of the law of the land and to the assumptions underlying it. They also made the first formal demand for female suffrage. The Declaration of Sentiments that was adopted exhibits the temper of the convention. Beginning with the assertion that "all men and women are created equal," the declaration proceeded to indict mankind for its "history of repeated injuries and usurpations" toward women. The delegates charged that men had denied them political representation, made them "civilly dead," refused them the right to their own property, and "oppressed them on all sides." In marriage, a wife was compelled to pledge obedience and to give her husband "power to deprive her of all liberty." In business, men "monopolized nearly all the profitable employments." And in morals, women suffered from an iniquitous double standard dictated by men who claimed it their right to "assign for her a sphere of action, when that belongs to her conscience and to her God" (qtd. in Hole and Levine 1971, 6). This document was too radical to be accepted by the majority of the American public. Most Americans reacted to the feminists with a large measure of hostility. The American public believed that the feminists were criticizing the nuclear family and marriage, institutions to which most people were deeply devoted.

Considering the popular attitudes that were espoused by the courts of law, from the pulpit, and in popular magazines at the end of the nineteenth century by both men and women, it is hardly surprising that the feminists and their goals were rejected. The following ruling of the Wisconsin Supreme Court in 1875 that denied the petition of a woman for admission to the bar is probably typical of the prevailing attitude toward women:

> The law of nature destines and qualifies the female sex for the bearing and nurture of the children of our race and for the custody of the homes of the world. . . . All life-long callings of women, inconsistent with these radical and sacred duties of their sex . . . are, when voluntary, treason against it.
>
> The cruel chances of life sometimes leave [some] women free from the peculiar duties of their sex. These may need employment, and should be welcome to any not derogatory to their sex and its proprieties or inconsistent with the good order of society.
>
> It is public policy to provide for the sex, not for the superfluous members, and not to tempt women from the proper duties of their sex by opening to them duties peculiar to ours. (qtd. in Smuts 1971, 110)

Although the Court was shortly overruled by the legislature, few North Americans challenged this view of women for several decades thereafter. A great many Americans believed that no girl or woman should work unless compelled to by the absence of a male breadwinner. Only a very small minority believed that a woman should be free to pursue the career of her choice.

In the decades before and after the turn of the century, the employment of women was a major issue. Many Americans viewed work as improper for women. Most of the arguments advanced to support this position were based on a common conception of the nature and role of women. This view emphasized sexual differences in temperament, and a sexual division of labour. As the home was woman's sphere, so the work place was man's. Man was seen as deficient in the feminine ideals of "tenderness, compassion . . . beauty and the harmonies of grace essential to the creation of a true home, but abundantly endowed with the masculine qualities of energy, daring and forcible possession necessary in the world of business, government and war" (Howe 1887, 9).

Judith Blake (1974, 138) has suggested that, by the full bloom of the Victorian era, industrializing societies capitalized into a virtue what appeared to be a necessity.

Before the industrial revolution, women played a very active part in the economic life of society. Their two roles, raising a family and doing economically productive work, were fused into one way of life, work at home. When industrialization and the accompanying demographic transition forced these two roles to be separated, all kinds of rationalizations and legitimations for the wrenching changes in the position of women were elaborated. For example, the idea that the female body was an extremely delicate mechanism remained an important element in the prevailing picture of women until the end of the nineteenth century. It was commonly believed that the female organs were readily damaged by the pursuit of any unwomanly activity. A physician, Edward Clarke, in a classic elaboration of this viewpoint in his book *Sex in Education*, wrote in 1874:

> Woman in the interest of the race is dowered with a set of organs peculiar to herself whose complexity, delicacy, sympathies and force are among the marvels of creation. If properly nurtured and cared for, they are a source of strength and power to her. If neglected and mismanaged, they retaliate on their possessor with weakness and disease as well of the mind as of the body. (p. 33)

Clarke and his follower Anzel Ames, who espoused similar ideas, were eminent doctors whose opinions were taken seriously. Clarke was a professor of medicine at Harvard University for seventeen years. Although by the end of the century it was generally acknowledged that women were much stronger than Ames and Clarke had imagined, their opinions were cited into the twentieth century.

The contention that women possessed distinctive attributes requiring special attention constituted the principal rationale for protective legislation. In the United States, the well-known Supreme Court case of *Muller v. Oregon* in 1908 employed this rationale. Louis Brandeis stated that the

> two sexes differ in structure of body, in the function to be performed by each, in the amount of physical strength [and] in the capacity for long continued labour. . . . Differentiated by these matters from the other sex, she is properly placed in a class by herself, and legislation designed for her protection may be sustained, even when like legislation is not necessary for men, and could not be sustained. (qtd. in Hole and Levine 1971, 38)

According to the Court, this type of labour restriction could not be imposed on men because it would violate men's constitutional rights of personal liberty and the liberty of contract. This was not, however, held to be true for women. On the basis of *Muller v. Oregon*, sex became a valid basis for legal distinctions.

Even after extreme views of women's physical weakness were discredited, psychological arguments continued to be cited to oppose women's employment. Industrial employment was viewed as dangerous because it supposedly produced an "unfeminine" woman. Even professions such as medicine, law, and journalism were unfit for ladies. The Wisconsin judge whose opinion has already been cited wrote:

It would be . . . shocking to man's reverence for womanhood and faith in woman, on which hinge all the better affections and humanities of life, that woman should be permitted to mix professionally in all the nastiness of the world which finds its ways into courts of justice; all the unclean issues, all the collateral questions of sodomy, incest, rape, seduction, fornication, adultery, pregnancy, bastardy, legitimacy, prostitution, lascivious cohabitation, abortion, infanticide, obscene publications, libel and slander of sex, impotence, divorce. (qtd. in Smuts 1971, 116)

Purity, modesty, and lack of passion were among the most valued of the qualities generally attributed to women. Often the rather crude, uncouth working woman was contrasted with the "ennobling spectacle of the pure and tender mother, carefully nurtured from childhood to fulfil her position in the centre of her brood of happy children." This picture of the passive, feminine woman, however, was more of an ideal than a reality. As more and more women worked, the notion that women were physically and emotionally unfit for work was countered and weakened. As Degler (1964, 656) notes, "it was difficult to argue that women as a sex were vessels of spirituality when thousands of them could be seen trudging to work in the early hours of the day in any city of the nation."

Women could fit the "ideal" pattern that idealized the nonworking woman only as long as those who did not marry, or were widowed, divorced, or deserted, could be absorbed into the kinship structure and be attached to fathers, brothers, uncles, or other male relatives. As family enterprises disappeared and family ties became weakened by demographic changes, unattached women were forced to seek outside employment. They were thrown into a work world for which they were often unprepared and in which their opportunities for employment were drastically restricted. Such women were available for employers seeking cheap labour.

Although it was assumed that, in the "normal" course of events, a woman would have a man fend for her, in actual fact the proportion of women without husbands was substantial in North America around the turn of the century. Peter Uhlenberg has shown that among 1000 white women born between 1890 and 1894 in the United States who survived to age 50, 100 never married, 225 were childless, 165 had fertile marriages that broke up (owing to separation, divorce, death, or desertion), and only 510 — slightly more than half — experienced the "normal" pattern for a woman of having a fertile marriage that had not dissolved by the time she was middle-aged (cf. Blake 1974, 139).

Increasingly, self-sufficient city residents tended to go their own ways. The traditional family with several generations under one roof broke up. At the same time, the number of children per family was shrinking steadily. Therefore, paradoxically, many of the same forces that denuded women's status of economic functions were motivating couples to want fewer births, and the decline in infant and childhood mortality reinforced that motivation. Thus, while the ideology of women's dependence gained momentum, the workload in the home was drastically reduced. Women's entire lifetime status was geared to a function — reproduction — at a time when these demands were diminishing in scope.

Given the incongruities between women's prescribed status in the home and the realities of the changing situation in North America, it is hardly surprising that the "woman issue" flared up periodically on different fronts. Women were fighting for much more than the right to work in occupations of their choice. They insisted upon admission to colleges, universities, and professional schools. They argued in the courts and lobbies of the legislatures to expand the narrow rights of married women and widows under common law. They rallied behind the temperance crusade and the suffrage movement.

Women Become Citizens

Some of the earliest efforts to extend opportunities to women were made in the field of education. In 1833, Oberlin became the first college in the United States to open its doors to both men and women. Female education at Oberlin was regarded as necessary to ensure the development of good and proper wives and mothers. Lucy Stone, who was later to become one of the outstanding feminists and orators of the day, noted:

> Oberlin's attitude was that women's high calling was to be the mothers of the race and that they should stay within that special sphere in order that future generations should not suffer from the want of devoted and undistracted mother care. If women become lawyers, ministers, physicians, lecturers, politicians or any sort of "public character" the home would suffer from neglect. . . . Washing the men's clothes, caring for their rooms, serving them at table, listening to their orations, but themselves remaining respectfully silent in public assemblages, the Oberlin "co-eds" were being prepared for intelligent motherhood and a properly subservient wifehood. (qtd. in Flexner 1959, 30)

Despite its traditional orientation, the open admission policy of Oberlin paved the way for the founding of other schools. Mount Holyoke was opened in 1837 as a seminary. It became not only the first women's college but also the first place of higher education that was not geared to the concept that women needed an improved education only to carry out their housewife or teaching duties. It opened the way for other women's college: Vassar, 1865; Smith and Wellesley,

1875; Radcliffe, 1879; and Bryn Mawr, 1885. Much of the groundbreaking work in education was done by Emma Willard, who had campaigned vigorously for educational facilities for women, beginning in the early 1820s. Francis Wright, one of the first agitators for women's rights in the United States, was also a strong advocate of education for women. She adopted many of the views of Mary Wollstonecraft and argued that men were themselves degraded by the inferiority imposed on women (cf. Wollstonecraft 1967). "Until women assume the place in society which good sense and good feeling alike assign to them, human improvement must advance but feebly" (qtd. in Flexner 1959, 27). Central to her discussion of the inequalities between the sexes was a particular concern with the need for equal access to education for women.

In Canada, equal opportunity — especially unrestricted admission to institutions of higher education — came relatively later than in the United States. Although Mount Allison University in Sackville, New Brunswick, admitted women to classes as early as 1858, it was not until 1875 that it granted the first university degree to a woman. (Interestingly, it was also the first university degree granted to a woman in the British Empire.) Colleges in Nova Scotia followed closely on the heels of Mount Allison in granting degrees to women: King's College, Halifax, 1879; Acadia, 1884; and Dalhousie, 1885 (MacLellan 1971, 6).

Views on the education of women were more liberal in the universities in Nova Scotia and New Brunswick than in Ontario and Quebec. Queen's University in Kingston was Ontario's first university to admit women in 1869. However, it was another ten years before women were admitted to all classes and another five before the first woman graduated. In Quebec, the resistance to women in higher education was even greater. Most Québécois believed that "the daughters of the middle class needed no knowledge beyond an elementary grasp of catechism, grammar, literature, elementary mathematics and above all, the polite arts and social graces" (Johnson

1971, 26). Given the alternatives of providing women with an opportunity to pursue their higher education or having them enrol at McGill University or a nonsectarian French-language lycée, the Catholic Commission of the Public School Commission authorized the first classical college for women in 1908.

Discrimination against married women in the field of property rights was also gradually reduced in the United States and Canada. New York was the first state, in 1848, to emancipate the wife completely and give her full control of her own property. Ontario, undoubtedly influenced by the Married Woman's Property Act, enacted in 1870 in England, granted this right to women in 1872. Quebec, under the influence of French civil law, took much longer to grant this right to women. Even today, however, in the United States and Canada, outside the influence of the Napoleonic Code, married women are still not treated as their husbands' equals under the property laws.

The injustice of this unequal status, stemming from nineteenth-century property laws, has recently been demonstrated in Canada. Irene Murdoch, wife of an Alberta rancher, was awarded only $200 a month but no interest in the property when her marriage broke up after 25 years, although she had worked as a partner on the farm.

Her appeal was rejected by the Supreme Court of Canada by a four-to-one margin because the majority agreed with the Alberta judge who had ruled that Mrs. Murdoch had made "only a normal contribution as wife to the matrimonial regime." A similar case in Saskatchewan produced the same result: Helen Rathwell was denied a half-interest in the farm that she and her husband had worked for 23 years, even though she had provided the down payment on the first piece of land they bought (*Canada and the World* 1974, 4-5).

Increased educational and employment opportunities encouraged requests by women for more legal rights. After several decades of a multi-issued campaign for women's equality, the suffrage became the single focus of the "movement." Although Canadian women received full enfranchisement before American women did, the Canadian movement had many roots in the United States. It may, therefore, be helpful, first, to survey the events in that country.

In large part because of the hostile political climate that was experienced by the feminists after the Seneca Convention, the "conservative" American Women's Suffrage Association led by Lucy Stone (which was concerned almost exclusively with the more "respectable" issue of women's suffrage) and the "liberal" National Women's Suffrage Association led by Susan B. Anthony and Elizabeth Cady Stanton (which was committed to more far-reaching institutional change) reunited in 1890 after splitting in 1869 over ideological and tactical questions. As long as feminists focussed on women's right to be free of social restraints, they invited association of their movement with such issues as divorce and free love. The new organization, therefore, evolved a set of tactics to minimize controversy. Very gradually, the women's movement accepted the opposition's premise on the sanctity of the home and pursued the fight for the vote within the context of conventional ideas on women's place (Chafe 1972, 10–13). As the campaign for women's suffrage became respectable in the eyes of society, it attracted more and more sympathizers.

During this same period of reform, a strong temperance movement had also emerged. Large numbers of women, including some suffragists, became actively involved in the temperance cause. Flexner (1959, 181) notes that

> women reformers had been concerned with the temperance movement since the 1840s, not merely out of sympathy with an abstract idea, but because the law placed married women so much at the mercy of their husbands. What might be a moral injustice if the latter was a sober citizen became sheer tragedy if he were a heavy drinker who consumed not only his own earnings but his wife's also and reduced her and her children to destitution.

Susan B. Anthony, Anna Howard Shaw, Jane Addams, and other prominent leaders became temperance crusaders, espousing the cause of women's rights as such. For these women, suffrage and the cause of social welfare were inextricably tied together. This connection was to be carried over into the Canadian campaign for women's suffrage.

Shortly after the turn of the century, the second generation of women suffragists came of age, and new leaders replaced the old. Carrie Chapman, who succeeded Susan B. Anthony as president of the National American Suffrage Association, devised a plan based on the concept that state and federal efforts should reinforce each other. For every victory won on a local level, she reasoned, additional congressmen and senators should be persuaded to vote for a suffrage amendment (Flexner 1959, 279, 367). Her strategy of compromise, together with that of Alice Paul, a militant suffragist, were instrumental in finally getting the vote for women. In April 1913, Alice Paul formed a small radical group known as the Congressional Union to work exclusively on a campaign for a federal women's suffrage amendment. Her group organized mass demonstrations, parades, and hunger strikes. Although her organization offended many of the more conservative suffragists, the energy, excitement, and publicity played a key role in focussing renewed attention on the necessity for a national constitutional amendment (Chafe 1972, 19; O'Neill 1969, 166–68). The women's suffrage amendment, introduced into every session of Congress from 1879 on, was finally ratified on August 26, 1920.

Demands for political equality came later in Canada than in the United States. Even at a time when the suffrage movements in Britain and the United States were going strong, Canadian women remained largely silent. The Canadian movement, concentrated in the last quarter of the nineteenth century and the first quarter of the twentieth century, borrowed inspiration from suffragists in both these countries. A direct influence can be traced in the lectures given by Susan B. Anthony and Anna Shaw in Toronto in 1889, which were enthusiastically attended by Canadian women (MacLellan 1971, 13; Gelber 1973, 7).

The first female suffrage organization in Canada was formed in Toronto by Dr. Emily Howard Stone, after she had attended a meeting of the American Society for the Advancement of Women in 1876. Refused entry to the University of Toronto on the grounds of her sex, she enrolled in the New York Medical College for Women. This background made her sensitive both to women's rights and to health and general welfare. In 1889, she was elected president of the Dominion Women's Enfranchisement Association, a post she held until her death in 1903.

The arguments in opposition to female suffrage were similar in the United States and Canada. They often centred around the differences in physical strength, stamina, and mental ability between men and women and in the concern for femininity. According to this argument, women were too weak to withstand the vigours of election and lacked the mental capacity to comprehend political problems. Furthermore, it was argued, allowing women to vote or run for office would diminish their femininity and destroy the harmony of the home. Could not women exert just as much power through "loving persuasion" as through the ballot?

Despite rigorous protest against enfranchisement, the suffrage movement had its lighter moments. Nellie McClung, probably the most diligent member of the Political Equality League of Manitoba, used humour to weaken antisuffragist arguments. MacLellan (1971, 17) relates that

in 1914 her mockery was turned on Manitoba Premier Sir Rodmond Roblin, an adamant opponent of female suffrage. He countered a delegation led by Mrs. McClung with a long argument to the effect that women's place was in the home and added that his wife agreed with him. "When I come home at night," he said, "I don't want a hyena in petticoats talking politics to me, I want a sweet gentle creature to bring me my slippers." The next night the Political Equality League hired the Walker Theater and staged a burlesque skit in which an all-women Parliament debated whether to give men the vote. Premier McClung, in a wickedly witty parody of Roblin, declared, "Politics unsettles men and unsettled men mean unsettled bills, broken furniture, broken vows and divorce. Man's place is on the farm."

On January 28, 1916, largely as a result of Nellie McClung's efforts, Manitoba passed the first woman suffrage act in Canada. The prairie provinces and the frontier states in the United States, where women in the pioneer communities shouldered a proportionately heavier burden, were the first to receive the suffrage. The territory of Wyoming, which had granted full political equality in 1869, became the first state to enter the Union with full suffrage for women in 1890. Colorado, Utah, and Idaho also granted women the right to vote before the turn of the century. In Canada, Saskatchewan and Alberta granted suffrage and eligibility to hold office to women in 1916, followed by British Columbia in 1917. Women in active military service were the first to be granted the right to vote in Dominion elections in 1917 under the Military Voters Act and the War-Time Act (Cervantes 1965, 356). The federal franchise was granted to Canadian women in 1918. Women gained the right to sit in Parliament in 1919.

The majority of women in Canada and the United States, as well as the public at large, assumed that, when women gained the vote, their equality was assured. The progress that had taken place since 1848, when American feminists first met in Seneca Falls, provided some justification for the conviction that extending the franchise would demolish one of the last barriers to equality. Common law restrictions had largely been removed, educational opportunity was available in many universities and professional schools, and during World War I thousands of women moved into jobs formerly held by men.

The "Persons" Case in Canada

After suffrage was enacted, unprecedented provincial appointments of women to public offices followed. In Edmonton, the first woman was appointed as a police magistrate; this was followed by a similar appointment in Calgary. It was in connection with these appointments that trouble started to brew. Enraged by what he considered to be an unduly harsh sentence imposed on his client by a woman magistrate, an Alberta lawyer challenged her right to hold court. He claimed that as a woman she did not qualify to be a magistrate because she was not a "person" in the sense used in the British North America Act. Although the Alberta Supreme Court ruled in 1917 that there was no legal disqualification from holding public office arising from any distinction of sex, the case did not rest there. One of the magistrates, not completely satisfied with the outcome, sought to determine how the federal government interpreted the British North America Act in relation to the word "person." After the Federation of Women's Institutes passed a resolution suggesting that the prime minister summon a woman to the Senate, the matter was referred to the law officers of the Crown. They advised the prime minister that the nomination of a woman to the Senate was impossible because the British North America Act limited such nominations to "qualified persons." The law officers did not consider women to be so qualified (Cleverson 1950, 141–55).

After a long-drawn-out judicial process, the case finally went to the British Privy Council for decision. Before this happened, however, five women from the west petitioned and obtained from the government an order-in-council directing the Supreme Court of Canada to make an interpretation of the term "qualified persons" in the British North America Act. In April 1928, the chief justice and four other justices unanimously decided that women were not "qualified persons" and, therefore, were not capable of being called for appointment to the Senate of Canada. The judges reasoned that it was the duty of the Court to resort to the state of the law at the time it was enacted. Of course, in 1867, when the British North America Act was adopted, women's legal capacity had been severely restricted. The following year, an appeal was made to the Judicial Committee of the Imperial Council of the House of Lords of England. The Privy Council unanimously turned aside the judgement of the Supreme Court of Canada, stating "[we] do not think it right to apply rigidly to the Canada of today the decisions and the reasons therefore which commended themselves, probably rightly, to those who had to apply the law in different circumstances, in different centuries, to countries in different stages of development" (qtd. in Gelber 1973, 17).

This judgement appeared to remove the remaining obstacles standing in the way of the full participation of Canadian women as citizens, at least within the federal sphere. Feminist leaders in both Canada and the United States predicted that their newly won rights would help to establish women's emancipation in the economic arena. This expectation was, however, only partially fulfilled in the succeeding decades.

Women and Social and Economic Equality: 1920–1940

Social commentators disagree on the significance for women of the decades between the two world wars, particularly in the world of work. Some historians in the United States have characterized the decade of the 1920s as one of unparalleled economic emancipation for women (cf. Mowry 1965, 159–60; Commager and Morison 1942, 659; Degler 1964, 657). Degler, for instance, notes that the most dramatic alteration in the image of women came after World War I, when there was a new upsurge in women's employment. Although there was an increase in the number of women holding jobs immediately before and during World War I, many women dropped out of the labour force soon after the conflict was over. The type of work performed by women underwent substantial change with the increased importance of the service sector; white-collar work and especially clerical jobs became important outlets for middle-class girls. However, assertions of new economic independence overlooked the fact that the majority of women workers still toiled because of economic necessity. According to Chafe (1972, 51):

> Historians have overstated the amount of economic change that occurred during the 1920s. There is no evidence that a revolution took place in women's economic role after World War I, nor can it be said that the 1920s represented a water-shed in the history of women at work. . . . Aspiring career women were still limited to positions traditionally set aside for females. . . . The overwhelming majority of American women continued to toil at menial occupations for inadequate pay; and the drive to abolish economic discrimination enlisted little popular support.

In Canada, as in the United States, the war produced only short-lived opportunities. Munitions factories closed after the war, and farm labourers came back from the trenches to the fields of western Canada. With the end of the war, women returned to jobs they had worked in before the war, as secretaries, telephone operators, factory girls, and sales clerks, and in jobs that had been theirs before the turn of the century, as seamstresses, teachers, nurses, and domestic servants (Davitt et al. 1974, 139).

Although opinions were divided about the amount of economic change, most social observers agree that the 1920s was an era of greater personal freedom for women. Within a short time, many social taboos were shed. For the first time, women began publicly to smoke and drink. Many popular magazines characterized this "new woman" as a flapper who enjoyed many of the same privileges men did. Smuts (1971, 144) observes that the flapper, often portrayed as a "co-ed," was one sign of the growing acceptance of higher education for women. More physical freedom of dress was also acquired during the 1920s. Women threw out the corset and the numerous petticoats in favour of light undergarments, short skirts, and bobbed hair (Degler 1964, 667). Women also gained more sexual freedom. Knowledge and approval of birth-control methods spread, especially among the middle classes. In sum, the decade after World War I witnessed a many-sided equalization of both the public and the private status of women; these developments, however, were only partially carried over to the work world.

The depression of the 1930s intensified the feeling that working women took jobs away from men. Many state, provincial, and municipal governments revived old bans on the employment of women in teaching and other public jobs. A Canadian feminist, Dorothy Johnson (1943, 353), wrote that, as late as July 1941, she could not get employment in substitute teaching as a married woman unless she could prove she was destitute. "I had a husband and he was there to support me. The idea that I might be a good teacher was of no importance."

In spite of the scarcity of jobs, the female labour force increased between 1930 and 1940 in both the United States and Canada. A great many women who would not have thought of working during normal circumstances took whatever jobs they could get, while millions of unemployed men were forced to stay at home with the children. Both American and Canadian observers have suggested that this situation brought about a certain amount of equality by putting many women in the factory and men in the house and by breaking the justification for masculine dominance based on economic support (cf. Sinclair 1965, 347; Hobart 1973, 138–39). When the Depression gave way to war, jobs again became more plentiful.

World War II and Its Impact

Within five years, World War II had radically transformed the economic outlook of women. The eruption of hostilities generated an unprecedented demand for new workers. In the United States, more than six million women took jobs, increasing the size of the female work force by over 50 percent (Chafe 1972, 135). In Canada, at the outbreak of the war, only 144 000 women were engaged in factories and industrial work, whereas, by 1943, 255 000, or over 10 percent, of the women between 18 and 45 were engaged either directly or indirectly in war work, not counting those employed in nonessential industries (Morin 1943, 352).

At first, employers resisted hiring women, particularly for jobs traditionally filled by men. However, as the need for labour grew more severe, both industry and government abandoned their reluctance to use females in war industries. Almost overnight, Mary Anderson observed in the United States, "women were reclassified from a marginal to basic labour supply for munitions making" (qtd. in Chafe 1972, 137). Women were found operating "bolt and nut threaders, lathes, buffers, and milling machines, armature winders and a hundred and one other occupations throughout the industrial fabric" (Sutherland 1940, 17).

The ability with which women assumed their new jobs challenged many of the conventional stereotypes of women's work. As one Canadian employer put it: "All these girls know their jobs and are efficient, just as efficient as men, and perhaps more so on certain tasks that call for a special touch. . . . There is hardly an employer who does not speak highly of his girl employees" (Sutherland 1940, 17). In the midst of the wartime emergency, sex labels lost some of their meaning, both in the type of jobs assigned and in the attitudes of employers toward women.

The attitudes of the general society regarding the employment of married women also changed. At the height of the Depression, over 80 percent of the American people strongly opposed work by married women. By 1942, in contrast, 60 percent believed that wives should be employed in war industries (only 13 percent were opposed), and 71 percent asserted that there was a need for married women to take jobs (Chafe 1972, 148).

A very significant change brought by the war involved the age and marital status of the new recruits to the labour force. Previously, the young and single had always predominated in the female labour force. However, by the end of the war, in the United States, it was just as likely for a wife over 40 as a single woman under 25 to be employed. The proportion of all married women working jumped from 15.2 percent in 1940 to more than 24 percent by the end of 1945.

In Canada, perhaps because the social mores were more restrictive and the war effort less encompassing, married women did not assume their importance in the labour force for at least another decade. Canada did, however, witness an increase in the proportion of middle-aged women working. Between 1941 and 1951, the proportion of women 35–44 years old in the labour force had risen from 18 to 22 percent, and the percentage between 45 and 54 years old had jumped from 15 to 21 percent (Ostry 1968, 3). For the first time, older women were playing an important part in the economic process of their country.

The war by its very nature had disrupted the established order. Women substituted for men in many fields of endeavour. Restrictions against the employment of middle-aged and married women were loosened. Also important was the change in the public's attitude toward woman's work. At least temporarily, it switched from outright condemnation to tolerant sanction.

Revival of Feminism

After 40 years of dormancy there was an upsurge of feminism during the 1960s. Alice Rossi sees the dramatic changes in women's role in the economic system as the chief factor in the renascence of the women's rights movement. In fact, she says:

> I would argue that it was the changed shape of the female labour force during the period beginning with 1940 that gradually provided the momentum that led to such events as the Kennedy Commission on the Status of Women, and eventually to the formation of new women's rights organizations like the National Organization for Women. So long as women worked largely before marriage while they were single, or after marriage only until a first pregnancy, or lived within city limits where there was a diversity of activities to engage them, there were feeble grounds for any significant movement among women focused on economic rights, since their motivation in employment was short-lived and their expectations were to withdraw when they became established in family roles. It was the gradual and dramatic change in the profile of the female labour force from unmarried women to a majority of older married women that set in motion a vigorous women's rights movement. It is only among women who either expect or who find themselves relatively permanent members of the work force whose daily experience forced awareness of economic inequalities on the grounds of sex. (qtd. in Murray 1971, 239–40)

Job discrimination and the concentration of women in a few jobs are also important factors that have contributed to the growing protest. The occupations in which many women engage are remarkably similar to those held by women historically. The majority of women are employed in jobs in which they predominate. Almost a third of the female labour force in Canada and the United States work as stenographers, typists, and secretaries. These job categories first became prominent as "women's place" more than seven decades ago.

Partially in response to the increased employment of women and the growing protest of a minority of vocal women during the 1960s, more concern for the legal status of women has been demonstrated than at any time since the adoption of suffrage. The President's Commission on the Status of Women was established in the United States in 1961, and the Royal Commission on the Status of Women was set up in 1967.

In 1960, Canada passed the Canadian Bill of Rights, which ,among other things, guaranteed equality before the law within the area of federal jurisdiction without distinction on grounds of sex. In the United States, the Fair Labor Standards Act was amended by the Equal Pay Act of 1963 to provide equal pay for equal work without discrimination on the basis of sex. To date, this is the only federal law that deals with sex. Sex was included with race, colour, religion, and national origin under Title VII of the equal employment opportunity provision of the Civil Rights Act of 1964. This section guarantees the right to equal opportunity in employment.

Until well into the twentieth century, the term "status of women" referred primarily to the political and legal status of women. Many rights in these areas have now been achieved. The more difficult task, however, of changing traditional attitudes toward "women's place" remains. It is precisely in this area that feminists face their greatest challenge and their greatest opportunity in coming decades. No one can claim that equality between the sexes has been achieved, in spite of the vast changes that have occurred in the status of women. But, it may be that a new foundation for seeking equality has been established. As North Americans move into the last quarter of the century, no aspect of contemporary life exhibits greater flux than relations between the sexes.

Works Cited

Bernard, Jessie. 1968. "The Status of Women in Modern Patterns of Culture." *Annals of the American Academy of Political and Social Science* 375: 3–14.

Blackstone, Sir William. 1922. *Commentaries on the Laws in England*. 2 vols. Ed. W.D. Lewis. Philadelphia: Geo. T. Bisel.

Blake, Judith. 1974. "The Changing Status of Women in Developed Countries." *Scientific American* 231: 136–47.

Canada and the World. 1974. "Women's Rights: Rewrite the Law?" May: 4–5.

Cervantes, Lucius. 1965. "Women's Changing Role in Society." *Thought* 40: 325–68.

bridge: Belknap.

Gelber, Sylvia M. 1973. "The Rights of Man and the Status of Women." Hugh C. Arrell Memorial Lecture, delivered November 15, 1973, at McMaster University.

Heckler, Eugene A. 1971. *A Short History of Women's Rights*. Westport, CT: Greenwood.

Hobart, Charles. 1973. "Equalitarianism After Marriage." *Women in Canada*. Ed. Marylee Stevenson. Toronto: New Press. 138–56.

Hole, Judith, and Ellen Levine. 1971. *Rebirth of Feminism*. New York: Quadrangle.

Howe, Julia Ward. 1887. "Opening Address." Papers, Association for Advancement of Women, 15th Congress. New York, October 9.

Johnson, Dorothy. 1943. "Feminism, 1943." *Canadian Forum* 22 (March): 352–53.

Johnson, Micheline D. 1971. "History of the Status of Women in the Province of Quebec." *Cultural Tradition and Political History of Women in Canada*. No. 8. Studies of the Royal Commission on the Status of Women in Canada. Ottawa: Information Canada.

MacLellan, Margaret E. 1971. "History of Women's Rights in Canada." *Cultural Tradition and Political History of Women in Canada*. No. 8. Studies of the Royal Commission on the Status of Women in Canada. Ottawa: Information Canada.

Morin, Rene. 1943. "Canadian Women in War Industry." *Canadian Forum* 22 (March): 352–53.

Mowry, George. 1965. *The Urban Nation*. New York: Hill and Wang.

Murray, Pauli. 1971. "Economic and Educational Inequality Based on Sex." *Valparaiso University Law Review* 5: 237–80.

O'Neill, William. 1969. *Everyone* cago: Quadrangle.

Ostry, Sylvia. 1968. *The Fem* 1961 Census Monogr minion Bureau of Sta

Sinclair, Andrew. 19

Harper and Ro

Smuts, Robert. New York:

Sutherland *Saturd*

Urqu

Was Brave. Chi-

ale Worker in Canada.
ph Series. Ottawa: Do-
tistics.

5. _The Better Half._ New York:

1971. _Women and Work in America._
Schocken.

, Harold. 1940. "Beauty in Overalls."
ay Night 55 (May): 17.

art, M.C., and K.A.H. Buckley, eds. 1965.
istorical Statistics of Canada. Toronto:
Macmillan.

Wollstonecraft, Mary. 1967. _Vindication of the Rights of Women._ New York: Norton.

DURABLE MONOGAMOUS WEDLO

J.E. Cutler

Observations on the high divorce rate, and on the tendency of the population to commit "race suicide" prompt this author to reflect on the future of the family, with special attention to the dwellings in which families are housed, and to the new status of women. The folkways and the terminology have changed in the 70 years since this paper was written, but the central themes and concerns are remarkably similar.

Anachronisms in the American Home

A pessimistic view of monogamous wedlock is now current, and it receives confirmation from what appears to be an obvious interpretation of pertinent facts. It is true that the divorce rate in this country is presumably very nearly, if not quite, the highest shown by any people. It is also true that the average number of persons per family has been steadily declining decade by decade during the last 50 years, even though exceptionally large families have been added to the population in recent years through the fecundity of the foreign-born women. This large number of divorces and the rapid increase in the divorce rate, together with the noteworthy tendency in the native element in the population to commit "race suicide," seem, obviously enough, to warrant not a little misgiving as to the durability and permanence of monogamous wedlock.

But do these facts, and others of a similar nature that are now available, tell the whole story? It may be that we shall find on exam-

ination that erroneous inferences have been drawn from detailed facts seen out of perspective. It may be that we are concentrating our attention upon symptoms and overlooking the seat of the difficulty. Perhaps our interest in individuals and their tribulations blinds us to great social and industrial changes now in progress of which these individuals are unwilling and, for the most part, unwitting victims. Surely, it is a time when, if ever, serious consideration should be given to the history of human marriage and to the factors that determine the nature of the family as a social institution.

It is our purpose in the first section of this article to examine the general assumption, inherent in all of the pessimistic interpretations, that the permanence of monogamy rests upon the perpetuation of a particular type of home and of family life; and in the second section, dealing with the new status of women, we shall consider what basis there is for the stability of the modern family as a societal unit.

In discussing the vicissitudes of the modern family, speakers and publicists commonly separate themselves into two groups. One group is concerned with the home as the dwelling-place of the family and urges "the housing question" as the vital issue in community welfare. The centre of concern for this group is the complete disappearance of the single-family residence in the older sections of our great cities. The other group is concerned with the interrelations and the mutual responsibilities of the members of the family unit. The centre of interest for this group is the rising divorce rate and the tendency toward "race suicide." It is perhaps unfortunate that these two groups are so sharply differentiated, assuming themselves to have nothing

Source: *American Journal of Sociology* 32(1916): 226–51. Reprinted with permission from The University of Chicago Press.

in common, when both evidently have what is essentially a common interest — namely, the perpetuation of the advantages that are believed to inhere in monogamous wedlock.

For our present purposes, however, it is convenient to follow this line of demarcation and to distinguish two components of the home: the family and the dwelling. Both are undergoing marked change and modification at the present time and both are involved in the question of the durability of our standard form of the marriage institution.

Our traditional idea of what constitutes a home is rarely a topic of conversation nowadays and we are quite unconscious of the fact that it produces a bias in our minds. No doubt, to most American citizens, home still means a house occupied more or less permanently by a single family (husband, wife, and children), with an adjoining plot of ground at the disposal of the residents. It depends on the economic and social status of the individual whether this single-family dwelling be conceived of as a mansion, or as a cottage or bungalow, and whether the area of land surrounding the dwelling be large or small. But, there is agreement that this single-family dwelling constituting a home is, or ought to be, owned by the family occupying it and that the adjacent land may furnish supplies for the family.

Such a household serves as an economic and social centre. Economically it is largely self-supporting and self-sufficient. Food supplies and raw products are obtained from the land, and the members of the family carry on the necessary processes of manufacture and exchange, both sexes sharing in the work. This household is also a social unit. It serves as a meeting place for neighbourhood gatherings; it is the place where the young people meet socially and where courtship may happily proceed under parental supervision.

But, we find that an increasing proportion of the population is coming to live under urban conditions, and that in the cities the single-family dwelling is becoming surprisingly rare. For perfectly obvious and valid reasons, it is being replaced by terraces, double houses, flats, apartment houses, tenements, and lodgings. Many families — there is reason to believe that they will soon be a majority — are now living in these multiple dwellings, owning no residence and possessing no land. They have a right to use a balcony, a porch, or part of a veranda, some stairs and a hall, a section of the basement, or the attic — and the public streets. There is no place for the children to play without disturbing the neighbours or obstructing the traffic on the streets.

There is little chance for peaceful domesticity in these multiple dwellings. The streets are noisy. Some of the neighbours keep unreasonable hours and have vociferous pets. Others are amateur musicians. Vacations are necessary to avoid nervous breakdowns, and these vacations must be spent away from home. Sundays and holidays must be spent in an automobile or on a trolley car. Isolated security, rest, and recuperation are not to be found at home. All must go away when they are in search of pleasure and recreation.

The domestic arts are now largely factory processes. There is almost no sex division of labour in the household, for there are left to it none but the "sweated trades." To contribute to the support of the family, it is necessary for both sexes to work away from home and become wage-earners. No longer is the household a self-sufficient unit, either socially or economically.

The proper care of sick family members is impossible in these modern dwellings. We are obliged, therefore, to take an interest in hospitals and their management. We discover that the modern hospital has a new and peculiar function, a community service, which was foreign to the work of the old-time hospital.

In brief, although we move slowly because of our failure to discern the anachronisms in some of our cherished standards and ideals, we are learning that all the advantages of multiple dwellings are not to be secured at their maximum value without intelligent and persistent community action. We are learning, too, that there is such a thing as public health and that it bears a vital relation to the health and welfare of the members of the individual household.

Thus, the new types of dwellings modify our traditional views of domestic life. Equally important changes are to be noted in the organization of the household and of the family itself.

In the Colonial type of home, the family formed a fairly stable unit. The relations and mutual responsibilities of husband, wife, and children were well understood. The family was patriarchal in organization, its headship being vested in the husband, who bore without protest the duties and the responsibilities of that position. Children were, both economically and socially, an asset, and they enjoyed all the advantages of being an asset instead of a liability. The school merely supplemented the home in the education of the children. There was a well-established sex division of labour. The women did practically all the spinning, dyeing, weaving, and sewing. They had general charge of the preparation of the food supplies and did much of the brewing and baking. The status of women was not questioned; it was in harmony with the customs and traditions of the time. The wife was subservient, in a gladsome, womanly way, to the head of the family. Only the spinster occupied uncertain status, attested to by the fact that she has been popularly called an old maid.

In the modern family all of this has been changed; the relations of husband, wife, and children are no longer so completely patriarchal in character. The wife is much less subservient to the husband; not infrequently, the bride stipulates that the word "obey" shall be omitted from the pledge in the marriage ceremony. A new order of things has altered the relation of woman to the institution of marriage.

In the marriage institution, we really have a case of antagonistic co-operation. Neither party wants to enter such a permanent relationship unless there are distinct advantages to be gained. New ways of earning a living, therefore, make necessary a readjustment in the relations of the two parties. At present,

a revolutionary readjustment is in progress. A new alignment for the sex division of labour is being worked out. The entrance of women into wage-earning occupations gives them a stronger economic position, and hence the terms of the marriage relation are being revised.

It cannot be doubted that, as time goes on, a larger and larger proportion of women must necessarily work for wages in factories, stores, and offices. And they are, as a matter of fact, now entering practically all the branches of the modern factory system and the business world. They are also establishing businesses of their own and they are entering the professions. The spinster is happily no longer the traditional old maid; she is achieving an assured status as a business and professional woman.

What is new about this situation is not that women are working. Women have always worked. The new fact is that women are working for wages; they are becoming wage-earners. It was not so very long ago that men began to work for wages. Some important consequences followed that change. Now women are working for wages and still more important consequences are, at length, beginning to be recognized. It is becoming apparent that a new type of home and of family life is necessary. The old is no longer possible.

All that may be involved in the development of a new type of family life cannot be determined in advance, and opinions differ considerably at present regarding the possible advantages to be gained. There can be no question, however, that current tendencies warrant certain inferences.

If the married women go out from the home to work for wages, that seems to mean less care of the home, less care of the young children. No substitute has been found for a mother's care of her young children, but it is becoming clear that the educational agencies and curricula must be much more closely related to the needs of the members of the family. The boys cannot work with the father. The girls cannot work with the mother. Neither the boys nor the girls have any adequate means, directly through the family relationship, of choosing or of learning a useful occupation. It is incumbent on the educational leaders to provide practical and effective vocational education and training in the schools, along with a considerable amount of vocational guidance. It is urged that emphasis needs to be placed on the education of boys as homebuilders and income-earners, while girls should be educated as homemakers and income-spenders. There are strong reasons, some of which have here been referred to by implication, for insisting on the education of girls as income-earners. And it is evident, even to the casual observer, that both boys and girls might profit from instruction and training as income-spenders.

The modern home seems, on the whole, not to be giving to children the very valuable moral training that was possible in the Colonial home. Agencies outside the home must, therefore, assume a larger measure of responsibility for this essential moral training, at any rate until the family as a societal unit becomes much more stable than it is at present. Both the church and the school are now, with some deliberation and insight, undertaking this task, and there is the promise of gratifying results, although, here again, the failure to discern anachronisms is a serious handicap.

If girls and young women go out from the home to work for wages, they tend to be bound less closely to the home and to their parents. They come to feel more or less independent and their social life no longer centres in the home. Instead, it centres in dance halls, moving-picture shows, theatres, and parks — public places of amusement. Hence, it is necessary to exercise supervision over public places of amusement. In this matter of recreation, we are facing a serious community problem, particularly serious because so few people as yet recognize the fact that it is a community problem. To seek fun is a perfectly normal and wholesome human experience. In our dance halls and pleasure resorts, young people are seeking the fun that is not easily obtainable in their homes as now constituted, and they are being exploited for gain,

often to their utter ruin and the desolation of future homes.

In general, the woman has had more to gain from wedlock than has the man. It is not surprising, therefore, that the woman has usually got the worse of the bargain. She has, for various reasons, been the weaker party, and hence not in a position to dictate terms; she has generally accepted the larger measure of the disadvantages. Our existing laws on domestic relations represent a measurable attempt to safeguard the woman, in recognition of her weaker position and her handicaps. As she gains a position of economic independence, she has less need of statutory guardianship in the domestic relation, and the basic terms of wedlock must be altered somewhat in her favour. Chivalrous attention and care are no longer the full measure of compensation for the burden of childbearing that falls more heavily on her. She is insisting that she shall determine whether and how often she shall assume that burden.

The family as a societal unit is now in a period of transition, a period of essential and thoroughgoing adjustment. Most people are, at present, giving their attention to the symptoms of this transition. They are studying desertions and divorces, when they ought to be studying the marriage institution and the family. They are seeking a remedy for divorce and for the social evil, when they might much more profitably be seeking a new basis for the stability of the family in accord with a higher status for the woman and be devoting themselves to the initiation and perfection of measures of community action that are essential to the maintenance of a modern home that will give to all its members a maximum of satisfaction. Wedlock must yield a profit in satisfaction of interests of the parties concerned, and there must be mutual advantages for the two sexes in order that the marriage institution shall be stable.

Durable monogamous wedlock is not dependent on the perpetuation of the Colonial type of home; nor is pair-marriage for life conditioned on the maintenance of the patriarchal form of the family. A study of the history of human marriage shows that this institution has, in the past, undergone many changes and modifications. Just now, another notable change is in progress. Monogamous wedlock is not threatened with extinction, nor is its durability fatally impaired; but it is undergoing an essential and wide-reaching adaptation to new life conditions. Prominent as a factor in this adaptation, perhaps the most prominent factor of all, is the change in the status of women. In the next section, we shall consider the bearing of the new status of women on the stability of the modern family.

The New Status of Women

In general, the status of women has been controlled, in all civilization up to the highest, by their power to help in the work of life. Where women have had important functions they have been valued; where they have needed protection and support, and have not been able to contribute much, they have been treated with contempt. If the economic situation is strong, so that each man can pay a good price for a wife, girls are valuable; in the contrary case female infanticide arises. If the women's contribution to the food supply is essential, women are well treated; while if the men are warlike meat-eaters [their own providers, therefore], they treat women as drudges, tempering the treatment with respect for them as necessary mothers of warriors. Among nomads the status of women is low, and women, children, and the aged are regarded as burdens. The two former are necessary, but all are treated capriciously. Under agriculture women win a position of independent co-operation. When towns are built women incur dangers on the streets and complications arise; their position in rural life is then far more free than in towns. Public security in the latter once more changes the case. When women are valued for grace and beauty and are objects of affection, not means of gain, they win, as compared with earlier stages.

Thus did the late Professor W.G. Sumner cogently summarize the history of the status of women. With his usual sagacity and insight he also, at the same time, indicated the boundary lines within which the new status of women is to be achieved. Perhaps, the time is not propitious for a full characterization of the new status; perhaps, we are as yet too closely involved in the complicated phenomena that surround its achievement; but, in certain innovations and observable tendencies, there are foreshadowings, at least, of a different and somewhat more responsible status than women have hitherto known.

The fact that society propagates itself by the co-operation of two sexes is of tremendous sociological importance. To treat the *socius* as the centre or nucleus of societal relations is to deal with an absurd abstraction. There are two sexes, separate and distinct, in human society, and the dividing line between them is one that is never crossed. Men and women have never thoroughly understood each other and they do not today. The two sexes can never look at the problems of life in precisely the same way; the difference of sex gives them two diverse viewpoints. A common viewpoint is as impossible for them as a common gender.

The status of women at any given time is the result of an adaptation between the two sexes, reached by an adjustment of the prevailing sex mores to the life conditions. If the life conditions are altered at any time, a new adjustment is necessary, and the part that the woman can take under the new life conditions will largely determine her status. Woman has always been limited and handicapped in the struggle for existence by her child. To win subsistence has been no easier for her than for the man, and, in addition, her infant has claimed a portion of her time and labour. It has been to her interest to develop a plan of co-operation with the man through a marriage institution. But this marriage institution has also been of great advantage to the man, as well as to the woman, because it permitted a division of labour in the struggle for existence — a method of co-operative effort that has, in the last 50 years, so effectively demonstrated its utility in all branches of industry.

The facts of human history make us exceedingly cautious about saying that there are some kinds of work women are not fitted to do. Every considerable change in life conditions in the past has resulted in a change in the sex division of labour. The nineteenth-century change in life conditions, which we call the industrial revolution, is now producing a new sex division of labour and is thus altering the status of women. Some 100 years ago, the economic effects of the industrial revolution became noticeable, and students began to be interested in the new science of economics. Somewhat later, the more circuitous but equally positive societal effects and consequences became evident, and people awoke to an interest in *social* problems. This interest gave point and significance to the development of another new science, that of sociology or the science of society. We are now discovering not only that there has been an unprecedented increase in the rate of production of wealth, with all the problems connected therewith, but also that the system of wage or monetary payment for labour has been introduced and established, not for one sex alone, but for both sexes.

The absorption of the domestic arts by the factory system of production has left the "waiting women of romance" in a somewhat precarious position, and so far they are by no means clear in their own minds as to what course they should pursue. It is not even clear to all of them that they face the alternatives of remaining at home with little or nothing to do or of accepting the opportunity to work for wages outside the home. Furthermore, their fathers and mothers seem often to be in even greater perplexity. The situation in which the woman college graduate not infrequently finds herself would be amusing if it were not so full of tragedy. After four years of self-reliant effort away from her parents, she is expected to be idly contented in a well-appointed home in the management of which her mother needs no assistance; and she dis-

covers, perhaps, that her parents fail to understand in any measure why she should wish to do anything other than grace the home with her presence until she finds a man to marry — or until an acceptable man finds her.

Attention was directed in the preceding section to an indication that a change in the status of women is in progress — namely, that, at present, some women are income-earners and some are not.

Many of the women occupying the better grade of family residences and apartments are living under conditions that do not permit them to work, i.e., to contribute to the family income. These women are not permitted to work at anything that is remunerative, on account of the attitude of their parents and husbands and of the prevailing social standards. They are occupying, perhaps we may say, the position of ornamental fixtures in the home. Their function in the household is apparently to make themselves indispensable luxuries and thus keep the family together.

From 1900 to 1910, there was a considerable increase in the proportion of women engaged in gainful occupations, i.e., working for wages or on a salary. In 1900, one woman in every five was engaged in a gainful occupation; in 1910, nearly one out of every four was a gainful worker.

These facts are not to be interpreted as meaning that women are becoming more industrious and ambitious, or that they are becoming less womanly and virtuous; they mean merely that the women are entering occupations outside the home under a system of wage payment for labour. It has been well said that

woman is no larger factor in industrial life than she has always been, but the form of industry has changed. It draws her into great groups, and those groups collect in cities and manufacturing towns. We see her oftener than we did when she canned and wove and sewed in small isolated groups. She is more obvious. She marries, makes her home, bears her children. That which disconcerts those who observe her . . . is mainly that she talks, thinks, and wants things that apparently never interested her before.

The change in life conditions is altering her status.

Illustrations are at hand that clearly foreshadow the nature and extent of the altered status of women. A new code of conduct, corresponding to the new status, is already taking shape.

The mixed and unsettled state of street-car ethics offers one illustration. At the present time we have conflicting ideas as to what constitutes proper treatment of women in street cars. Should a man keep his seat while any woman in the car is standing and hanging on to a strap? In many cities, it is customary now for men to keep their seats, unless there are exceptional circumstances. Suppose an employer gets on a crowded car along with a number of his women office employees or clerks. If they were men, they would, of course, expect him to take a seat, if he could get one, and keep it. That corresponds also to their relationship in the office or store. In the case of women, however, if he treats them as women used to be treated, he offers his seat. That means a reversal of the relationship that exists in the office or store. There they must do his bidding, run errands for him, write his letters, sell his goods for him. There he must have absolute obedience and quick compliance with his orders. A certain amount of work must be done. If one girl is too tired or too weak to do the work, he must get someone else. He must consider the woman worker as no different from the male employee. The question arises whether he should maintain this attitude outside the office, store, or shop. Of course, many employers avoid this question entirely by riding in automobiles.

But even if the street-car difficulty can be avoided, there is still the question of recognizing women employees on the streets. There is a difference in social standing. The old standard of conduct was for the woman to speak if she regarded the man as of the same social standing and if there had been a proper introduction. May the woman employee continue to exercise this prerogative? The question arises: Is business acquaintance and relationship a sufficient introduction and does it constitute a basis for a measure of social recognition?

Then there is the woman's side of the question. Suppose she pleases her employer, suppose she does her work so well that he wishes to show her some special courtesy or favour and he presents her with gifts — flowers, a box of candy, or theatre tickets. That was the old way for a gentleman to show courtesy or favour to a lady. Should the woman employee insist upon no courtesies or favours that have any social significance? Should she insist upon nothing else than more wages, a higher salary, as a return for particularly efficient work or for a satisfactory performance of her duties?

There is no generally recognized standard in regard to these matters at present. Women's entrance into wage-earning occupations requires some new ethics concerning the relationship between the sexes in society.

Individuals whose status is rapidly changing (as is true of women today) are ordinarily affected disadvantageously and suffer many hardships — and no exception has been made in this case in favour of women.

It has been said that those who have benefited most by the innovation of women as wage-earners are the large employers of labour who offer wages that men would spurn. Women workers are no doubt being extensively and shamelessly exploited; it cannot very well be otherwise when they are obliged to pass at once from the position of adornments in the home, with no adequate preparation and training for their new kind of work. They are sadly in need of education as income-earners, but this education is difficult to obtain when many occupations that they are entering have not yet received, for them, the stamp of social approval. Even our census authorities say that one of the factors influencing the proportion of women among gainful workers is the existence of industries that furnish "suitable employment for females." In taking up new occupations, the women are obliged to combat the current notion that these occupations are not *suitable* for women. One of the handicaps that women have, at present, in business, particularly if they are dealing chiefly with women, is that they must "chat awhile." The tendency is still strong among young women not to accept the life of a wage-earner as a final fact but as a mere interval between school and marriage. In some cases, married women have shown themselves more independent and disinclined to accept low wages when offered and more disposed to grumbling and making complaints to employers, with the result that many employers prefer those who are unmarried.

There is substantial evidence, however, that women are slowly winning their way, not only as industrial wage-earners, but also in the business and professional world. Their presence as income-earners is regarded less and less in the light of an innovation and they are coming to occupy a position of recognized independence and competence. They are developing self-reliance and common standards as to hours and conditions of work and rate of pay. They are becoming direct contributory factors once more in the struggle for existence and are thereby gaining a higher status and avoiding the degeneracy that follows luxurious idleness, as well as the fretfulness, depression, and morbidity that attend insufficient employment of brain and body. Common observation gives a measure of general application and credibility to the remark of an elderly gentleman who said to a friend: "While my wife was having babies, she was quite contented and happy, and found full employment. Now that the children have grown up, she is capricious, dissatisfied with life, and full of worries."

The self-possession and worldly wisdom that women gain in remunerative occupation outside their own homes are giving them far better protection than an abject reliance on the chivalry of men. Nor are they any the less womanly because they have ceased to occupy a merely adventitious position as connubial parasites, and are maintaining their self-

respect as income-earners and actual participants in the work of life, with a keener perception, gained by having worked for it, of the value of money.

The economic equality of men and women has thus far perhaps become more fully established on the stage than in any other profession or in the fields of industry and business. The difference of sex does not now operate in the acting profession against the women and in favour of the men in determining the amount of their remuneration. Actors marry actresses, and both husband and wife continue to support themselves, assuming a joint responsibility for the maintenance and care of the children.

"Woman," it has been said, "has been deified as the Mother of God, worshipped as queen, revered as priestess, honoured as teacher, respected and protected for her maternal function." It is now an open question whether she will achieve the full status of a wife. The notion of a woman as a *wife* is a very late one in the history of the human race and of the marriage institution. Woman has been a sharer in the primitive struggle for existence; among nomads, a servant and a drudge; with the growth of the idea of property, woman became such, occupying the status of a chattel or a slave; in the marriage relation, woman has become a *mother*, not merely a slave or property. Her sex function has been socially recognized and she has been given a higher status on account of it. Chivalry well illustrates this conception of woman, which persists to this day. Many men argue that woman's function is limited to that of rearing children, as that is the noblest work to which she can aspire. The present emperor of Germany has said that woman's function is "Kinder, Kirche und Küchen." Although many women complacently accept this as their position at present, women in increasing numbers are not content to remain in a status prescribed by social standards that grew out of the life conditions of the past.

No doubt many women are more interested in the rights and privileges of the new status than in the duties and additional responsibilities that it imposes. Many do not see that there are any new responsibilities to be assumed. When a census-taker asked a women in New York City for the name of the head of the house, she replied promptly and emphatically: "I am." When she was confronted with the question about the nature of her business, in a tone of utter contempt she naïvely replied: "Why should I have a business? Haven't I a husband?"

Woman as a *wife* is a conception not yet fully attained by everybody. It really is a very modern notion. Although the word "wife" seems to connote a high status, a position of large responsibility in the household, it has, in fact, been interpreted as meaning a position with restricted authority. The wife is more or less a *silent* partner; she may act as a representative of the firm up to a certain point and no farther. Clearly, it is an issue at present whether the wife will be given, and whether she will intelligently and capably accept, complete joint partnership in the family. Many women are refusing to be *silent partners* any longer. They are breaking the silence and the result is the modern-woman movement.

It may safely be said that the new status will place women in a freer, but at the same time, more responsible position. They will contribute as income-earners to the maintenance of the family and, as income-earners along with men, they will receive equal pay for equal work. The property right in women will at length cease to prevail and their general legal status will be modified in their favour as individuals, while the law of domestic relations will have to be largely revised. The relationship of chivalry between the sexes will be less prominent, but in its place will be a much larger measure of mutual respect and confidence. The position of unmarried young women will be less adventitious in character, unrestricted to the one trade of pleasing men and becoming a wife (now said to be "a matter about which a nice girl does well to know nothing"), while they will win in the marriage relation the rank of competent membership in the family copartnership and the full status of a wife.

The present instability of monogamous wedlock results from an imperfect adaptation to modern social and industrial conditions. The family is not functioning effectively as an industrial and societal unit, and an adjustment is necessary in its basic relationships. This adjustment involves the entrance of women into wage-earning occupations and their participation once more in the support and maintenance of the family through a new sex division of labour. It is not too much to say that, wherever and whenever the family has functioned effectively as an industrial unit through an accepted sex division of labour, it has been stable and has brought satisfaction to all the parties concerned.

The growing conception of the modern home as a domestic unit much larger and more inclusive than that cherished in our traditions, together with the fact that women in increasing numbers are entering wage-earning occupations and effecting a new sex division of labour that is rapidly gaining general recognition, may reasonably be expected to contribute to the durability and the permanence of monogamous wedlock. The current symptoms of instability in the institution of marriage may be regarded as characterizing a notable transition period that will culminate in a better adaptation to new life conditions and a new status for women. This change in the status of women is not likely to be generally mischievous in its effects; on the contrary, it will materially strengthen the coherence and the stability of the modern family.

Part Two

DEMOGRAPHIC ASPECTS OF FAMILY CHANGE

• • •

It is my observation that the disadvantages of a larger population are seen most vividly by those who were born in an earlier era. Often the current inhabitants see nothing wrong with many of the changes that the older citizens decry.

Ansley J. Coale, Speech to the Population Association of America (1968)

When we think about the family life of a particular couple, one of the first characteristics that comes to mind is their status as parents or as nonparents. The decisions that a husband and wife make about birth control and family planning seem to be issues reflecting individual whims and circumstances — or, in some cases, the random happenstance of accidentally conceiving or not conceiving. In reality, however, the apparently private nature of the number and the timing of births is a clearly patterned phenomenon that can be successfully and precisely predicted at the group level. The implications of the ultimate outcomes of childbearing decisions are widespread. One of the major social consequences of the family system is the way it influences which kinds of people will become parents, how many children they will have, and when they will decide to have them.

Societies that do not have a very high level of industrial development usually have very low rates of population growth. Their birth rates are typically very high. However, because of poor sanitary conditions and a relatively low standard of living, high birth rates tend to be counterbalanced with relatively high death rates; as a result, there is little increase in population. When health standards improve with increasing industrialization and development, mortality rates drop sharply and a period of rapid population growth ensues.

In the 1960s, demographers became increasingly concerned with the explosive increase in world population, which became a problem of global concern. The perception of excess fertility as a social problem leads to a need for smaller families, and an acceptance of contraception to reduce birth rates. In the more developed nations, such as Canada, the United States, northern Europe, and Japan, the birth rates fell rapidly. These nations have now completed what is called the *demographic transition* — that is, they have changed from a society characterized by high birth rates and high death rates to a society characterized by low birth rates and low death rates. The result is very low population growth or, sometimes, no growth at all.

Paradoxically, the same social scientists and policy makers in the developed world who used to be concerned with the "problem" of too many babies must now be concerned with the "problem" of too few. In either circumstance, the implicit social policies that encourage either large families or small ones have a pervasive impact on the meaning of parenthood and on the nature and functioning of the family unit.

About the Articles

Beaujot and McQuillan trace the demographic patterns of Canadian society through the transition to its current circumstance of low mortality and low fertility, a situation that has markedly changed the family life cycle and led to an ageing population. Their creation of a hypothetical representative village of 1000 persons in the year 1851 makes it easy to visualize the social implications of the documented demographic changes.

The future of marriage and fertility, as viewed by Westoff, includes not only the demographic changes we have discussed but also an increase in cohabitation and illegitimacy. The move toward informal marriage and parenthood signals a real change in the normative structure of marriage, and suggests that family-life patterns can no longer be adequately described by reliance on data concerning only "official" marital status.

Recognition of the master trend toward secularization ought not to obscure the fact that religious affiliation continues to influence decisions about marriage and the family. Heaton presents detailed census data concerning patterns of fertility, income, and divorce among 19 denominations.

The demographic transition that has been experienced in all of Canada has been especially manifest in Quebec. As a result, the issue of population policy has come to have a wide range of political implications for the future of the French minority. Caldwell and Fournier outline the history of population dynamics in Quebec, and note the many implications of Quebec's dramatically low birth rates.

Further Readings

Dumas, Jean. 1987. *Current Demographic Analysis: Report on the Demographic Situation in Canada, 1986*. Catalogue 91–209E. Ottawa: Statistics Canada.

Grindstaff, Carl F. 1985. "The Baby Bust Revisited: Canada's Continuing Pattern of Low Fertility." *Canadian Studies in Population* 12: 103–10.

Guttentag, Marcia, and Paul F. Secord. 1983. *Too Many Women? The Sex Ratios Question*. Beverly Hills, CA: Sage.

McLaren, Arlene. 1986. *The Bedroom and the State: The Changing Practices and Politics of Contraception and Abortion in Canada, 1880–1980*. Toronto: McClelland and Stewart.

Ram, Bali. 1987. "Reproduction: The Canadian Family in Transition." *Journal of Biosocial Science* 20: 19–30.

Romaniuc, A. 1984. *Current Demographic Analysis: Fertility in Canada: From Baby-Boom to Baby-Bust*. Catalogue 91–524E. Ottawa: Statistics Canada.

THE SOCIAL EFFECTS OF DEMOGRA
CHANGE: CANADA, 1851–1981

Roderic P. Beaujot
Kevin McQuillan

The wide-ranging effects of the postwar baby boom on Canadian society have focussed attention on the significance of demographic change. However, most of this attention has centred on relatively short-term fluctuations in demographic patterns while ignoring equally important long-term trends. In this paper, we describe the transformation in Canadian population patterns since the mid-nineteenth century and briefly consider some of the more important social and economic consequences of these trends. Some of the implications of a continuation of present trends for the future of Canadian society are also discussed.

Few people realize how much the framework of their lives has been shaped by demographic changes. The postwar baby boom and its attendant consequences have focussed attention on the wide-ranging impact of demographic factors on social life. Yet, these effects are even more dramatic when we extend the time horizon for comparison and examine the role of demography in helping to shape social patterns in Canada since the mid-nineteenth century. In this paper, we will compare three different periods in Canadian history, first looking at differences in demographic patterns, and then commenting on the implications for society of the shifts that have occurred.

Source: *Journal of Canadian Studies* 21. no. I (1986): 57–69. Reprinted with permission.

Canada's Demographic Transition

Demographers claim that Canada, like all industrialized countries, has passed through a three-stage transition in demographic patterns. Up until the early nineteenth century, Canada experienced high birth and death rates. After this point, both birth and death rates began to fall, but the drop in the death rate was sharper than the decline in the birth rate. In recent times, the two rates have come back toward a rough equilibrium, and the prospects for the near future are for a slow rate of population growth.

To examine the consequences of these changes, we have selected three years that illustrate markedly different demographic patterns: 1851, 1921, and 1981. While the selection of particular dates is arbitrary, and determined, in part, by the availability of data, these years provide good vantage points for examining changes in population patterns. Birth rates were high and relatively stable in the mid-nineteenth century (Gee 1981; McInnis 1977) and, although the death rate had declined somewhat by this point, the rate of decrease accelerated in the following decades (Legare and Desjardins 1976). The year 1921 marks a good midway point for our analysis. Increases in life expectancy have been much slower since that date, while declines in fertility have been much sharper (Beaujot and McQuillan 1982). Moreover, 1921 marks the beginning of Canada's national system of vital registration. In looking at these three dates, we will consider the nature of the demographic changes themselves as well as the social, economic, and psychological consequences that flow from these changes in population.

Since we wish to focus on the demographic transition, we will consider the effects of changes in fertility and mortality. In so doing, we will ignore the third component of demographic change: migration. That is not to say that migration has not in itself had important consequences on Canadian society. This importance can be highlighted by the fact that, since Confederation, about 17 percent of population growth was due to net immigration and that, in 1971, more than one-third of the population were either foreign born or had at least one foreign-born parent (Beaujot and McQuillan 1982, ch. 4). As important as immigration and emigration have been for Canadian society, we have chosen to focus here on the factors of natural increase, fertility, and mortality.

Childbearing

A major problem with many demographic measures is that they do not communicate to nonspecialists the real nature of demographic change. Thus, to note that the crude birth rate declined from 46 per 1000 in 1851 to 15 per 1000 in 1981 gives us only a vague sense of the dimensions of this change for society and for individuals. More useful is the total fertility rate that measures the number of children a woman would have if she experienced the age-specific rates for a given year. This measure suggests that, in 1851, a woman would have borne slightly more than seven children by the end of her childbearing years. This figure declined by roughly 50 percent by 1921 and was cut in half again between 1921 and the present, to the level of 1.7 births per woman, on average.

A different way to look at this issue involves comparing the number of small children to the number of women of childbearing age. As the figures in Table 1 indicate, there were more children in Canada under the age of five in 1851 than there were women aged 20–44. By contrast, in 1981, there were only about four small children for every ten women in this age group. One direct result

Table I
Measures of Fertility and Mortality: Canada, 1851, 1921, 1981

	1851	1921	1981
Fertility			
Births per 1000 Population	46.2	29.3	15.3
Births per Woman (TFR)	7.02	3.54	1.7
Children 0–4 per 100 Women Aged 20–44	120.3	68.7	37.5
Mortality			
Deaths per 1000 Population	22.2	11.6	7.0
Infant Mortality Rate	184.1	102.1	9.6
Life Expectancy at Birth			
Male	40.0	55.0	71.9
Female	42.1	58.4	79.0
Life Expectancy at Age 20			
Male	39.6	45.1	53.4
Female	41.4	47.5	60.1
Life Expectancy at Age 65			
Male	10.6	11.7	14.6
Female	11.4	12.8	18.9

Sources: Henripin (1972, 30, 366); Urquhart and Buckley (1965, 16); Statistics Canada (1981a, 2, 9); *1921 Census of Canada,* III: 7; *1981 Census of Canada,* 92–901: Table 1; Bourbeau and Legare (1982, 79, 86); Statistics Canada (1984, 16–19).

of this decline in fertility has been a shortening of the period in a woman's life devoted to childbearing and childrearing. The century since 1851 has seen the virtual elimination of childbearing among women over 35. And, while there has been some move toward childbearing among some groups of older women in recent years, their childbearing experiences are limited to a short part of the life cycle. Indeed, one of the most remarkable changes in recent years has been the steady increase in the proportion of first births occurring to women over 30 years of age. This suggests that women who begin their childbearing early finish early; those who begin later also restrict the period of childbearing to a small number of years.

Along with the decline in the birth rate has come a marked change in the distribution of Canadian families by size. The change, however, is not precisely what one might have expected. Obviously, there has been a large decline in the number of families with four or more children. But, in the years from 1921 to the 1970s, there has also been a large decline in the proportion of women who are childless or who have only one child. Put differently: there has been increasing adherence to the norm of the two-child family. Whether this will continue to be the case in the future is debatable. There are some indications that rates of childlessness may again be on the increase. Nevertheless, the data for the recent past demonstrate that the relationship between declining fertility and family size is not as simple as we might have predicted.

Death

The decline in death rates has been as dramatic as the decline in fertility. The crude death rate has declined from 22 per 1000 in 1851 to 12 per 1000 in 1921 and to 7 per 1000 in 1981. However, because it is affected by the age composition of the population, the crude death rate is not a particularly good indicator of changes in mortality. Several other figures are more illuminating. Expectation of life at birth, for example, has increased

from approximately 40 years for males living in 1851 to 72 years for males living in 1981. For females, the gains have been even larger, with life expectancy rising from 42 years in 1851 to 79 years in 1981.

It is particularly important, when examining changes in mortality, to identify the groups in the population that have benefited the most from changes in the overall patterns. Doing this, we note that the most significant change concerns the drop in infant mortality. The infant mortality rate, which measures the proportion of children who do not survive the first year of life, declined from 184 per 1000 in 1851 to 102 per 1000 in 1921. Thus, while considerable progress was made during this period, the rate remained very high. In the more recent period, however, infant mortality has fallen precipitously. In 1981, only about 10 of every 1000 live-born children failed to celebrate their first birthday. Stated differently: almost 1 in 5 children did not survive their first year in 1851, compared to 1 in 100 in 1981. It is this decline that has helped to boost life expectancy so dramatically. As the figures in Table 1 indicate, the gains in life expectancy for those who reach their 65th birthday have been relatively small. These data show that the most important consequence of falling mortality rates has been that the vast majority of the population now reach retirement age. The proportion of persons living to age 65 has increased from 32 percent in 1851 to 80 percent in 1981.

As another way of demonstrating the salience of these figures, let us assume that at each year we could look at a "representative village" of 1000 people whose age structure and mortality pattern by age reflected that of the entire country. In 1851, the village of 1000 people would experience a death of a child under one year of age every month and a half, while, in 1981, one would occur every seven years. Similarly, at ages one to four years, a death occurs every 2.5 months under 1851 conditions but every 33 years under 1981 conditions. One can say that deaths of children aged one to four years are now virtually nonexistent. Let us take the point of view of a doctor who is the general practitioner for this village. If we assume a professional life of 35 years, the doctor would experience 465 deaths of children before their fifth birthday under 1851 conditions, but only six such deaths under 1981 conditions. At later stages of life, deaths of older people are now more frequent. In a village of 1000 people, there would be one death of a person over age 80 every 15 months in 1851 but every six months in 1981. The greater frequency of deaths of older people is not because their death rates have increased — in fact the rates have decreased — but because there is a higher proportion of older people in the population.

Life expectancy at age 20 gives a picture of the proportion of adult life that might be spent in retirement. In 1851, having reached age 20, an average person could expect to live another 40 years. If we consider retirement to be after age 65, this means that, on average, people could not expect to retire. In fact, retirement as we know it now was nonexistent. In 1921, people could expect at age 20 to spend 3 percent of their adult life in retirement, while, in 1981, it would be 21 percent. Stated differently: in 1921, having reached age 20, one could expect to work an average of 34.6 years for each year of retirement, but, by 1981, it would be 3.8 years of work for each year of retirement.

These changes in demography have had far-reaching effects on the Canadian community and, no doubt, on the attitudes of Canadians toward a number of important issues. The family, perhaps more than any other institution, has been transformed by the decline in mortality. The orphan was a significant figure in much nineteenth-century literature, and the regular appearance of such characters reflected the frequency of the status in society. Under conditions of life expectancy similar to those experienced in Canada in 1851, 11 percent of children would have been maternal orphans by the age of ten, while, under 1981 conditions, such would be the case for only 1 percent of children (Burch 1965). More generally, under high mortality conditions, a large amount of chance and variability are injected

into human affairs (Ryder 1975). For instance, it is estimated that, in seventeenth-century New France, half of couples would have lost a child before their sixth wedding anniversary, while, now, in only 10 percent of cases would a child die or leave the family by the fifteenth wedding anniversary (Lapierre-Adamcyk 1984; Peron and Lapierre-Adamcyk 1984). It can be argued that the greater role played in the past by relatives outside the nuclear unit was a response to the greater likelihood of family disruption as a result of mortality. As death rates have fallen, the need for this form of insurance has declined as well.

Other social and psychological consequences of falling mortality rates, although no less important, are harder to measure. It seems almost certain, for example, that our increasing ability to relegate death to the older ages of life has profoundly affected attitudes toward and customs surrounding death. Philippe Ariès (1974) has traced the evolution of customs associated with death in Western societies and has argued that modern societies attempt to banish death from sight so as not to be constantly reminded of the inevitability of dying. The dead and dying are increasingly removed from public view in order to limit contact between the living and the dead. There can be little doubt that the decline in death rates and the increasing concentration of deaths among a restricted group of the population, a group whose participation in society is generally limited, has facilitated the development of these practices. The increasing predictability of death has allowed us to handle it in a more businesslike and orderly fashion. Blauner has argued that "the disengagement of the aged in modern societies enhances the continuous functioning of social institutions" (1966). That is, companies, bureaucracies, and other institutions can suffer from the sudden disappearance of a given person in the structure. By setting old people aside, institutions are less subject to this disruption. The problem, of course, is that, while the disengagement of the aged may be beneficial to the social structure, older people themselves bear the social costs of this isolation.

The fall in mortality has also revolutionized relationships between parents and children. A number of authors have pointed to the poor quality of care accorded to small children in premodern societies (Shorter 1975; Stone 1977). Much of this can be traced to the generally low standard of living in such societies, but it can be argued that the high infant mortality rates also discouraged the development of strong emotional bonds between parents and children. Parents resisted making large emotional investments in their children until they demonstrated their ability to survive. The delay in naming infants, and giving the name of a child who had died to a subsequent child, are cited as practices that demonstrate this relative lack of attachment (Shorter 1975). Thus, a situation of high infant mortality is, in a sense, a vicious circle, with children valued less because they are less likely to survive, and with the lower emotional investment in children reducing their survival chances.

Children's views of parents must also have been transformed by changing mortality experiences. Not only can most children expect that their parents will live until they (the children) achieve adult status, but a large proportion can expect to interact with their parents as adults for as long or longer than they did as children. Indeed, for many, at least one parent may be dependent on them for as long as they themselves were dependent on their parents during childhood. These changing roles of parents and children are likely to affect both family relationships and the decisions of young couples to have children.

Another consequence of the increased length of life is that the various parts of the life cycle have become more differentiated and more strictly tied to age. For instance, the boundaries between middle age and old age have been sharpened. In addition, as we will see in the next section, new stages of life have emerged, especially the empty-nest period, retirement, and a long period of widowhood.

Marriage and the Family

Marital patterns have changed radically in some ways in the period since 1851, although not always in the manner one might have expected. For example, as Table 2 indicates, average age at first marriage has fluctuated somewhat, but the overall trend has been downward since 1851 (Rodgers and Witney 1981). Contrary to what is sometimes thought, marriage did not occur at a particularly young age in the nineteenth century. But, while age at marriage has changed very little, the potential length of marital life has been altered considerably. If all marriages are assumed to end in the death of one partner, the average duration of marriage will have increased from 28 years in 1851 to 47 years in 1981. In the mid-nineteenth century, only 6 percent of couples would have celebrated their fiftieth wedding anniversary, compared to 39 percent under 1981 conditions. When romantic love was introduced into Western civilization as the basis for marriage, the promise to "love each other for life" had a vastly different time horizon. When young lovers make a lifetime promise, they probably do not realize that it is for almost 50 years. This change in the average length of marriage has given new meaning to the phrase "till death do us part." An unhappy marriage is probably more likely to be broken when one has the horizon of a long life to "endure." The longer life provides the opportunity for a "new" life, including the possibility of a new spouse. In fact, it can be argued that the longer married life and the sharpening of boundaries between the various stages of life are an additional strain on marriage, as not all couples can successfully adapt to the successive sets of new roles that are implied (Stub 1982).

Thus, the instability in family life caused by death is gradually being replaced by instability caused by voluntary dissolution. Whereas 98 percent of marital dissolutions in 1921 were caused by the death of one partner, death was responsible for only 55 percent of dissolutions in 1981 (Basavara-

Table 2

Measures of the Marital Life Cycle: Canada, 1851, 1931, 1981

	1851	1931	1981
Singulate Mean Age at First Marriage:			
Wife	23.8	24.6	23.1
Husband	26.8	27.7	25.2
Mean Age of Mother at:			
All Births	30.7	29.9	26.6
Birth of First Child	25.4[a]	26.6[a]	24.8
Birth of Last Child	35.9[a]	34.9[a]	31.1[a]
Marriage of Last Child	63.0	58.3	55.3
Mean Age at Death of One Spouse:			
Wife	51.7	62.8	69.7
Husband	54.7	65.9	71.8
Mean Years Between Marriage and First Birth	1.6	2.0	1.7
Mean Years of Childbearing	10.5	8.3	6.3
Mean Years of Empty Nest (Marriage of Last Child to Death of One Spouse)	NIL	4.5	14.4
Mean Years of Marriage	27.9	38.2	46.6
Percent Reaching 50th Wedding Anniversary	6.1	16.6	39.4
Percent Never Married at Age 50:			
Females	7.7	10.4	5.9
Males	8.0	13.6	7.7
Percent of 15+ Married	54.8	56.0	63.3

Sources: Basavarajappa (1978, 62); Bourbeau and Legare; Dominion Bureau of Statistics (1967, 16); Statistics Canada (1984); Statistics Canada (1981a, 6, 17); *1981 Census of Canada*, 92–901, Table 5; *1931 Census of Canada*, III: Table 12; *1851–52 Census of Canada*, I: nos. 5 and 6; Henripin (1972, 378).

Note: For procedure used in calculation of mean age at death of one spouse, see Shryock and Siegel (1973, 311). In calculating mean age at marriage of last child, we used singulate mean age at first marriage for 1881, 1956, and 1981, respectively.

[a]Very approximate estimates were derived using U.S. data on average intervals between marriage and birth of first and last child, from Glick (1977, 6).

jappa 1979; Statistics Canada 1981a, 48; 1981b, 14). And, of course, in the younger age groups, the importance of divorce as the source of family breakup is even greater.

It is significant to note that the difference between typical ages of men and women at marriage has also decreased, by one year, or one-third of the earlier difference. While this decrease is not particularly large, we would argue that it has considerable social significance. The younger person in a marriage is likely to have less education, to be less experienced at taking responsibility and leadership, and generally to have a lower status. The decrease in the typical age difference at mar-

riage is thus probably associated with an increase in the relative status of wives in marriages and of women in society.

One other consequence of changing demographic patterns for marriage and the family deserves attention. The combination of declining fertility and mortality has served to create new stages in the marital life cycle that did not previously exist for most couples. The emergence of the empty-nest stage between the marriage of the last child and the death of one of the spouses has become an important feature of contemporary marriages. This stage did not exist for the typical couple living in the mid-nineteenth century, but, by 1981, the average couple could expect to live together for 14 years beyond the marriage of their last child. And interestingly, research on marital satisfaction suggests that many couples view this stage as among the happiest in their marital life (Rollins and Feldman 1970; Lupri and Frideres 1981).

In general, compared to the mid-nineteenth century, couples now have five fewer children, they end childbearing five years earlier, and they have 14 more years of married life after the last child marries. In other words, there is a longer family lifetime. The family life cycle is longer even if divorce is included in the calculations. Under 1976 conditions, it was estimated that the average duration of marriage was 31.5 years (Adams and Nagnur 1981). Women spent an average of 9.5 years as widows and 3.5 years as divorced; for men the figures were 2.0 years as widowers and 1.7 years as divorced.

Age Structure

Much attention has been focussed recently on the ageing of the Canadian population. The reasons for this phenomenon are not well understood, however, nor have many of the consequences been fully explored. Again, it is a problem better analyzed by looking at long-term changes rather than by restricting our view to the post–World War II period, as is often the case.

The age structure of the population is a function of the level of fertility and mortality and migration. But, contrary to popular beliefs, the fertility rate is by far the most important determinant. The population ageing that Canada is now experiencing is the result of the continuing decline in fertility since the end of the baby boom and is only marginally a product of increases in life expectation. Immigration has tended to moderate slightly the ageing of the Canadian population, but, over the more recent period, its impact on the age distribution has been "almost imperceptible" (Foot 1984, 13). The ageing of the population is thus a long-term process that parallels the decline of fertility since the mid-nineteenth century. Although it was common during the 1960s to emphasize the youthful nature of the population, in fact, nineteenth-century Canadian society was far younger. As Table 3 shows, the median age of the population has risen from 17.2 in 1851 to 29.6 in 1981. And this figure is projected to increase to 41.0 by the year 2026 (Statistics Canada 1979, 468). The changes can be highlighted by comparing the relative predominance of older and younger persons in the population. In 1851, there were five persons aged 65 and over for every 100 persons aged 0–19, while, in 1981, there were 30, and in 2026 there will be 82 older persons for every 100 younger persons. In 1921, there were ten persons of retirement age (65 and over) for every 100 persons at working ages (20–64). In 1981, there were 17

Table 3
Measures of Age Structure: Canada, 1851, 1921, 1981

	1851	1921	1981
Percent Aged 0–19	56.3	43.6	32.0
20–64	41.0	51.5	58.3
65+	2.7	4.9	9.7
Persons 65+ per 100 Persons Aged 20–64	6.6	9.5	16.6
Median Age	17.2	24.0	29.6

Sources: Urquhart and Buckley (1965, 16); Norland (1976, 22); *1981 Census of Canada*, 92–901: Table 1.

retirement age persons for every 100 working-age persons, but this figure will double to 32 by 2026.

The ageing of the population is a complex phenomenon. Most of the attention given to this question has centred on the increase of the aged population and the potential difficulties facing governments charged with providing social services to this group. And, indeed, problems are likely to emerge in the near future in this regard. Retirement funds such as the Canada Pension Plan, which are funded by the contributions of current workers, are destined to encounter severe problems in the future (Asimakopulos 1984). Given the disproportionate use of medical facilities by the elderly population, health costs are also likely to rise (Foot 1982; Lefebvre, Zigmund, and Devereaux 1979; Stone and Maclean 1979). These trends suggest the need for a rearrangement of procedures for the organization and funding of many forms of social services. Patterns with respect to retirement itself may also need to change. An increase in employment rates among senior citizens would counter part of the transfer-payment burden that will be associated with population ageing after the turn of the century.

It is worth noting that the funding of retirement through year-by-year transfers from the working to the retired population is an attractive scheme when each generation is larger than the one before, but is considerably less attractive when the relative size of working-age cohorts is decreasing. Stated differently: cohorts that give birth to many children will be more easily taken care of in their old age than those with few children. Thus, after the turn of the century, the baby-boom cohorts will be at a disadvantage because the smaller baby-bust cohorts that follow will be hard pressed to make contributions necessary to support their elders. One frequently hears the argument that pretransition fertility was high partly because parents needed their children as a source of support in old age. While providing for the elderly no longer occurs through family relationships, the argument that large families are useful for support in old age may still be true at the level of a total society.

Important as these issues are, however, they have deflected attention from other consequences of shifts in age structure, some of which benefit Canadian society. As Richard Easterlin has pointed out in his analysis of American society, a decline in the proportion of the population in the young age groups can yield major benefits for the members of those groups and for society as a whole (1978). The rapid growth of the Canadian labour force during the last half of the 1960s and throughout the 1970s exacerbated the problem of unemployment. While increases in female participation rates contributed to this phenomenon, the major factor was the entrance into the labour force of the baby-boom cohorts (Foot 1982, 191–94). The recent slowdown in fertility will contribute to a slower rate of growth in the labour force and may well ease the problem of providing jobs for new entrants.

Shifts in age structure can have other beneficial effects. Since certain age groups are primarily responsible for certain forms of behaviour, changes in the relative weight of age groups within the population can produce important changes in the prevalence of certain types of activity. Crime is a particularly good example. Young males are responsible for a disproportionate share of most major crimes, particularly violent crimes. Thus, the ageing of the population will bring about a decline in numbers in these high-risk groups in the population and, other things being equal, lead to a decline in crime rates (Easterlin 1978; Wellford 1973). Similar arguments can be extended to other issues such as traffic fatalities (Irwin 1975; Waldron and Eyer 1975).

One final consequence of shifts in age structures should be noted. While being a member of a relatively large cohort can have disadvantages, it can also yield a number of advantages to the members of such a group. Thus, a society such as Canada's in 1851, in which the median age of the population was quite young, may accord to the young more power and privileges than would be the case in older societies. In this regard, it is interesting to note how young many Canadian political leaders were when they began their careers. Both Sir John A. Macdonald and Sir Wilfrid Laurier were first elected to public office by the age of thirty (Wallace 1978, 444, 495). Indeed, young people generally assumed positions of importance at an earlier age in nineteenth-century societies.

One might expect that the current ageing of the Canadian population will have analogous effects. While the elderly may well suffer certain disadvantages, they may also find that their power and influence as a group are increasing. The potential for such change can be seen clearly if we look at the proportion of the voting population 65 years of age and over. In 1981, 13.5 percent of voters belonged to this age category; by 2026, the proportion will rise to approximately 23.3 percent (Statistics Canada 1979). Combined with the fact that elderly people are more likely to turn out to the polls, these trends suggest that senior citizens will be able to wield increasing political power in the future.

Implications for the Future

The effects of demographic change have received considerable attention recently in both popular and professional journals. The effect of a declining birth rate on school enrolment and the continuing growth of the elderly population are now widely known and efforts are being made to come to terms with some of the problems created by these developments. However, in focussing on these particular issues, attention has been directed away from long-term trends that have had profound and far-reaching effects on Canadian society. From this perspective, the postwar baby boom is best seen as a deviation from the trend of declining fertility that stretches back to the mid-nineteenth century. Understanding the impact of demographic forces on social

behaviour will require that more attention be paid to these less obvious but not less important long-term changes.

Projections of future demographic developments envision further small improvements in mortality rates and continued low fertility. If true, Canada will experience further changes in the age composition of the population; we may expect that, in the early decades of the next century, close to one in five Canadians will be over the age of 65. However, while assuming a continuation of present trends is the easiest strategy to follow when making projections, there is no guarantee that it is the most accurate. Preparing for the future demands that we examine the possible consequences of at least two other plausible paths of development. The first would entail a cyclical pattern of growth based on alternating periods of relatively high and relatively low fertility. Such a pattern would exacerbate problems of social planning, particularly in sectors such as education that are directly affected by population changes. The second alternative would see further declines in fertility and the prospect of population decline. This route would also necessitate major rearrangements in the structure of Canadian society (Lux 1983). Given the profound effects that past demographic changes have had, it is essential that demographers and social planners pay more attention to the potential effects of future changes in population patterns.

W

Ad

Ari

Asi

Henrip
tility in
Irwin, A.C.
Deaths." C
457–60.
Lapierre-Adamcyk,
de la vie familiale au
XVIIe–XXe siècles.'
Démographie 13(1): 59–7

Basavarajappa, K.G. 1978. *Marital Status and Nuptility in Canada*. Catalogue 99–704. Ottawa: Statistics Canada.

———. 1979. "Incidence of Divorce and the Relative Importance of Death and Divorce in the Dissolution of Marriage in Canada, 1921–1976." Paper presented at the meetings of the Canadian Population Society, Saskatoon.

Beaujot, Roderic, and Kevin McQuillan. 1982. *Growth and Dualism: The Demographic Development of Canadian Society*. Toronto: Gage.

Blauner, Robert. 1966. "Death and Social Structure." *Psychiatry* 29(4): 378–94.

Bourbeau, Robert, and Jacques Legare. 1982. *Evolution de la mortalité au Canada et au Québec, 1831–1931*. Montreal: Presses de l'Université de Montréal.

———. *Essai sur la mortalité par génération au Canada et au Québec, 1831–1931*. Document de travaille no. 11. Montreal: Université de Montréal, Départemente de démographie.

Burch, Thomas K. 1965. "Some Social Implications of Varying Mortality." United Nations World Population Conference, Belgrade.

Dominion Bureau of Statistics. 1967. *Life Expectancy Trends: 1930–32 to 1960–62*. Catalogue 84–518. Ottawa: Dominion Bureau of Statistics.

Easterlin, Richard. 1978. "What Will 1984 Be Like? Some Socioeconomic Implications of Recent Twists in Age Structure." *Demography* 15(4): 397–432.

Foot, David K. 1982. *Canada's Population Outlook: Demographic Factors and Economic Challenges*. Toronto: James Lorimer.

———. 1984. "Immigration and Future Population." Paper prepared for Policy and Program Analysis Branch, Employment and Immigration Canada.

Gee, Ellen M. Thomas. 1981. "Early Canadian Fertility Transition: A Components Analysis of Census Data." *Canadian Studies in Population* 6: 23–32.

Glick, Paul. 1976. "Updating the Life Cycle of the Family." *Journal of Marriage and the Family* 39: 13.

——n, Jacques. 1972. *Trends and Factors of Fertility in Canada*. Ottawa: Statistics Canada.

——. 1975. "A New Look at Accidental ——nadian Journal of Public Health 66:

——Evelyne, et al. 1984. "Le cycle ——Québec vues comparatives, ——Cahiers Québécois de

Lefebvre, L.A., Z. Zigmund, and M.S. Devereaux. 1979. *A Prognosis for Hospitals*. Catalogue 83–250. Ottawa: Statistics Canada.

Legare, Jacques, and Bertrand Desjardins. 1976. "La situation des personnes âgées au Canada." *Canadian Review of Sociology and Anthropology* 13(3): 321–36.

Lupri, Eugen, and James Frideres. 1981. "The Quality of Marriage and the Passage of Time: Marital Satisfaction Over the Life Cycle." *Canadian Journal of Sociology* 6: 283–305.

Lux, André. 1983. "Un Québec qui vieillit: Perspectives pour le XXIe siècle." *Recherches Sociographiques* 24: 326–77.

McInnis, R. Marvin. 1977. "Childbearing and Land Availability: Some Evidence from Individual Household Data." *Population Patterns in the Past*. Ed. Ronald Demos Lee. New York: Academic. 201–28.

Norland, Joseph A. 1976. *The Age-Sex Structure of Canada's Population*. Catalogue 99–703. Ottawa: Statistics Canada.

Peron, Yves, and Evelyne Lapierre-Adamcyk. 1984. "Les répercussions des nouveaux comportements sur la vie familiale: la situation canadienne." Paper presented to the Conference on the Family and Population, Hanasaari, Expoo, Finland.

Rodgers, Roy H., and Gail Witney. 1981. "The Family Cycle in Twentieth Century Canada." *Journal of Marriage and the Family* 43: 727–40.

Rollins, Boyd C., and Harold Feldman. 1970. "Marital Satisfaction over the Family Life Cycle." *Journal of Marriage and the Family* 32: 20–28.

Ryder, Norman B. 1975. "Reproductive Behaviour and the Family Life Cycle." *The Population Debate: Dimensions and Perspectives*, Vol. III. New York: The United Nations. 278–88.

Shorter, Edward. 1975. *The Making of the Modern Family*. New York: Basic.

Shryock, Henry S., and Joseph S. Siegal. 1973. *The Methods and Materials of Demography*. Washington, DC: Government Printing Office.

Statistics Canada. 1979. *Population Projections for Canada and the Provinces*. Catalogue 91–520. Ottawa: Statistics Canada.

———. 1981a. *Vital Statistics. Vol. 1: Births and Deaths*. Catalogue 84–204. Ottawa: Statistics Canada.

———. 1981b. *Vital Statistics. Vol. 2: Marriages and Divorces*. Catalogue 84–205. Ottawa: Statistics Canada.

———. 1984. *Life Tables, Canada and Provinces,*

1980–1982. Catalogue 84–532. Ottawa: Statistics Canada.

Stone, Lawrence, 1977. *The Family, Sex and Marriage in England 1500–1800*. New York: Harper and Row.

Stone, Leroy O., and Michael J. Maclean. 1979. *Future Income Prospects for Canada's Senior Citizens*. Montreal: Institute for Research on Public Policy.

Stub, Holger R. 1982. *The Social Consequences of Long Life*. Springfield, IL: Charles C. Thomas.

Urquhart, M.C., and K.A.H. Buckley, eds. 1965. *Historical Statistics of Canada*. Toronto: Macmillan of Canada.

Waldron, I., and J. Eyer. 1975. "Socioeconomic Causes for the Recent Rise in Death Rates for 15–24 Year Olds." *Social Science and Medicine* 9: 383–96.

Wallace, W. Stewart, ed. *The Macmillan Dictionary of Canadian Biography*. 4th ed. 1978. Toronto: Macmillan.

Wellford, C.F. 1973. "Age Composition and the Increase in Recorded Crime." *Criminology* May: 61–71.

SOME SPECULATIONS ON THE FUTURE OF MARRIAGE AND FERTILITY

Charles F. Westoff

Twenty-six of the world's 33 industrialized countries — including the United States — are currently experiencing extremely low fertility, and some are rapidly approaching zero population growth. In at least five (Austria, the United Kingdom, East and West Germany, and Luxembourg), there are already more deaths than births. If we project current trends (Bourgeois-Pichat 1977), these five countries are likely to be joined, in about 1980, by Belgium, Denmark, Czechoslovakia, Hungary, Norway, and Sweden. By 1990, negative population growth should also occur in Bulgaria, Finland, Greece, Italy, and Switzerland; by the year 2000, France and the Netherlands should be added to the list. The populations of the remaining countries in Europe should begin to decline in subsequent decades. Collectively, the population of Europe and the Soviet Union should begin to decline around the year 2000. Deaths should outstrip births in the United States by about 2020, when the population should reach about 250 million.

This projected decline implies a total fertility rate of 1.5 births per woman over her reproductive lifetime. Although such low fertility has never existed for an actual cohort of women (the lowest on record is 1.8 for women born in 1907 in England and Wales), an argument can be made that, because of the development of modern contraceptive technology and the increasing availability of legal

abortion, such a low level is quite possible over sustained periods of time.

The question of obvious policy significance is what really will happen in the future. Fertility in the United States is already very low. The birthrate is 15.3 per 1000 population, and the death rate is 8.8. The total fertility rate is below 1.9 births per woman (projected from current rates to a lifetime total). Were it not for a net legal immigration of about 400 000 per year, the growth rate would be 6.5 per 1000 population. With immigration included, it is about 8.5 per 1000 population. Even with continued immigration at that volume, such below-replacement fertility means that the population will stop growing in about 50 years, at about 250 million, and will then begin to decline. If the current rate continues, a total of 245 million in the year 2000 may be expected, a far cry from the 300 million anticipated by the president in a message to Congress only eight years ago. But such projections assume the continuation of this rate of fertility. Is fertility likely to rise or decline? The honest answer is that nobody knows; only more or less plausible speculations can be advanced. Back in the late 1930s, there was also a very low fertility level, and some expressions of apprehension about the prospect of impending decline were heard. Such concerns disappeared rapidly with the war and the ensuing baby boom. How do we know that another baby boom is not in store? Not long ago, some demographers were talking about a second baby boom, a kind of echo effect of the first one. They believed that a large number of babies could be expected as

Source: Charles F. Westoff, "Some Speculations on the Future of Marriage and Fertility," *Family Planning Perspectives* 10, no. 2, (March/April 1978): 79–83. ©The Alan Guttmacher Institute.

the products of the first baby boom reached the age of parenthood (Brass 1974; Easterlin 1962; Lee 1976; see also Keyfitz [1972], who suggests a great amount of variability around replacement). This has not yet occurred because the extremely low fertility rates have outweighed the increase in the numbers of young people.

Predictions of another baby boom have also come from some economist-demographers who believe that, as the children born during the recent years of declining birthrates come of age and enter the labour force, they will enjoy a competitive advantage and brighter prospects because of their smaller numbers (Lee 1976). They are, therefore, expected to marry earlier and have more children because their incomes will be relatively higher and their futures more promising. The empirical evidence for this hypothesis is essentially the relationship observed between previous increases in the number of births over time and declining cohort fertility. The small cohorts of the 1930s experienced high fertility in the 1950s, whereas those born during the baby boom of the 1950s are experiencing low fertility in the 1970s. If the cycle is repeated, those born in the 1970s will produce another baby boom toward the end of the century.

Although attractive because of its theoretical grounding, this method of forecasting leads to an expectation of cyclical patterns for which there are only two historical examples. What is more, no similar evidence has yet been adduced for other countries. Even for the United States, this theory ignores what appears to be a massive postponement of marriage. A steady decline since 1960 in the proportion of women marrying at ages 20–24 may be the unrecognized beginning of a radical change in the family as we know it. Even more important, perhaps, the theory does not take into account the changing status and role of women in our society. The assumption that the future increase in the demand for labour resulting from smaller cohorts entering the labour force will automatically translate into higher fertility ignores the very real changes in women's attitudes toward work (the supply of labour includes female labour), marriage, and childbearing.

There is also a seemingly irreversible change: the technology of fertility control has improved tremendously in the past 15 years and is widely diffused throughout the population. Virtually all American married couples use contraception if they are not pregnant, trying to get pregnant, or sterile. Among those currently using contraception in 1975, three out of four had either been sterilized or were using the pill or the IUD (Westoff and Jones 1977). Abortion is now widely available, and further technological developments in fertility control (e.g., to enable the predetermination of sex of offspring) are on the horizon. We are fast approaching the perfect contraceptive society in which unwanted births among adults will become nonexistent, although teenage childbearing will still be a major social problem.

Another sustained baby boom does not seem likely when these social changes are taken into account. But what fertility can we expect? For one thing, annual fertility rates should become more volatile, more responsive to short-term fluctuations in the economy. Perfect control of fertility does not imply that couples will *want* no more than one or two children; in theory, they could just as easily opt for twice that number. But larger family size in the future does not seem likely. The historical trends all point in the downward direction. The one exception, the baby boom, was not created by a return to the large families of the nineteenth century, but by a movement away from spinsterhood, childless marriage, and the one-child family, and by a bunching together of births at early ages. Only a minor part of the baby boom can be attributed to increases in the proportions having three or more births. The decline in births that occurred in the 1960s was almost entirely attributable to a decrease in the number of unplanned births (Westoff 1976). The accelerated decline since 1970 no doubt continues this trend, but includes a reduction in the number of planned births as well. Some observers argue that the low fertility of recent years reflects primarily the postponement of births, and that the postponed births will be made up in the next few years (Sklar and Berkov 1975). The decline in total expected family size (the number of children that women in surveys say they expect to have) does not substantiate this view. There has been some postponement, and modest increases in fertility during 1977 suggest that some of this postponement is now being made up. However, there is now increasing evidence to support the view that "later means fewer," and low fertility at one level or another seems here to stay.

Marriage and the Family

If we look closely at current social trends and their demographic outcomes, we see signs that the institution of marriage may be changing in still new ways that will cause fertility to decline to new lows. The theory that the historical demographic transition will terminate in a magical balance of births and deaths at low levels may be more aesthetic than realistic. The current evidence from the United States and from two Scandinavian countries that historically seem to be in the avant-garde of social change in the developed world reveals a significant constellation of social and demographic changes:

• *Marriage.* Radical changes in marriage patterns are both the cause and the consequence of declining fertility. In the United States, the proportion not married by ages 20–24 increased from 28 percent in 1960 to 43 percent by 1976 (Glick 1978). In Denmark, this figure rose between 1970 and 1975 from 44 to 59 percent (Roussel 1977). In Sweden, the number of marriages declined by 30 percent between 1966 and 1975 (Prioux-Marchal 1974; Bourgeois-Pichat 1977, 64).

• *Cohabitation.* It is estimated that, in the United States, nearly one million unmarried couples were living together in 1976 — about 2 percent of *all* couples living together. This proportion will undoubtedly increase (Glick

1978). In Denmark, about one-quarter of *all* women 18–25 are living with a man to whom they are not married. The number of such relationships increased by half between 1974 and 1976, from 200 000 to 300 000 couples (Roussel 1977). In Sweden recently, about 12 percent of all couples living together (ages 16–70) were not married (Prioux-Marchal 1974). The intriguing question is whether we are witnessing a postponement of marriage with an institutionalization of trial marriage or a more basic change that will eventually alter the institution itself.

• *Divorce.* It is abundantly clear from our very high divorce rate that the traditional concept of one partner forever has disappeared for growing segments of our society. A recent estimate indicates that one-third of all U.S. children will spend a significant amount of time with a divorced or separated parent (Glick 1978).

• *Remarriage.* Since such a high proportion of divorced persons remarry, there seems little reason to think of divorce as a reflection on the institution of marriage itself. But we also see signs of change here. In the United States, the remarriage rate, which has steadily increased over recent decades, has started to decline. (In Sweden, it has declined by about 50 percent since 1965.) A higher proportion of second marriages now seem headed for divorce. Cohabitation is not limited to the young premarital state; one is increasingly aware of middle-aged and even older divorced persons living together without the formality of marriage. There are more and more "nonfamily" households consisting of individuals either living alone or sharing quarters with one or more unrelated persons. Such nonfamily households accounted for nearly one-half of the entire increase in the number of households between 1970 and 1976 (Glick 1978).

• *Illegitimacy.* In the United States, there was a record high proportion of out-of-wedlock births (14.2 percent of all births) in 1975 (National Center for Health Statistics 1975). In Denmark, the proportion of births out of wedlock doubled in a decade — to 18.8 percent in 1974 (Roussel 1977); in Sweden, the number tripled, so that out-of-wedlock births now comprise about one-third of all births (Prioux-Marchal 1974).

One could argue that all of these changes simply mean that formal marriage in the sense of a legal contract is just going out of style, at least in the early stages of "coupling," and that the rate of living together in monogamous unions is basically not changing. Indeed, research in Denmark suggests that cohabitation is for some an institutionalization of experimental or trial marriage. In a sample survey of unmarried Danish couples, about one-third said that they regarded living together as a period of experimentation, and about one-seventh indicated that it was economically advantageous; but one-quarter simply rejected the idea of the necessity of the legal formality (Roussel 1977). At any rate, it seems reasonable to infer that such informal arrangements will hardly contribute to increasing fertility, and that there will probably be less stability in the early (more fertile) years of marriage than in past generations. As an observer of the Danish scene concludes, these changes "make marriage a less 'weighty' commitment than formerly" (Roussel 1977).

Women's Status

All of these trends that seem to be depressing reproduction, separating sex from reproduction, and weakening the permanence of marriage are tied in one way or another to the growing economic independence of women as well as to the diminishing influence of religion in our lives. There has been a substantial increase in the proportion of women employed outside the home. The proportion of U.S. women in the prime childbearing years (20–34) who are working has increased from less than two-fifths in 1960 to about three-fifths in 1976; and it is projected to reach about two-thirds by 1990 (U.S. Bureau of Labor Statistics 1976). The International Labour Organization projects that three-fifths of European women of reproductive age will be participating in the labour force by the year 2000 (Bourgeois-Pichat 1977).

There is a considerable body of research literature on the relationship between fertility and women's work. Much of it is ambiguous about the causal sequences involved and there are certainly institutional child-care arrangements that facilitate a mother's working. Nevertheless, there is little doubt that women's work and fertility are negatively related on the whole, and that the future will probably see increasing proportions working.

The increasing equality of the sexes, however, still has a long way to go in the economic sphere. Although educational differences between the sexes have greatly diminished and more and more women are working, there is still a wide gap in economic status between men and women. Women are concentrated disproportionately in less remunerative jobs and are paid less in the same jobs. Among year-round full-time U.S. workers who received income in 1975, the earnings of women 20–44 years of age were 61 percent those of men (U.S. Bureau of the Census 1977a). (Significantly, that ratio remains unchanged at different levels of education.)

Nonetheless, the future trend of women's economic status seems fairly clear. Increasing proportions of women will have the option of financial independence, although genuine economic equality is probably generations away. (Indeed, such equality may never materialize, although it may be approximated to some significant degree.) But imagine the consequences for marriage and fertility of a society in which men and women are economically equal and independent!

The institution of marriage will lose yet another part of its sociological foundation. For centuries, men have exchanged some of the financial rewards, social status, and security associated with their employment and income for the sexual, companionate, and maternal services of women. This is hardly a romantic view of the relationship, but it does go a long way toward explaining the universality and historical persistence of marriage. But consider a social system in which just as many women as men are engineers, bank presidents, corporation executives, doctors, lawyers, and salespersons. What exactly will be the motivation of women to enter the legal partnership of marriage? Sex and companionship are certainly available without the commitment implied by marriage. Given the ease of divorce and the growing acceptability of simply living together, does it not seem probable that traditional forms of marriage will diminish even further than they have already?

One of the remaining sociological rationales for marriage is the bearing and raising of children, but with the retreat from parenthood that seems to be in process, even this age-old function seems shaky. If current first-order birth rates were to continue, about 30 percent of women would never have any children — an unprecedented but not totally implausible development. There is now evidence that childlessness within marriage is increasing. The proportions of ever-married women aged 25–29 who had not yet given birth increased from 12 percent in 1965 to 22 percent by 1976 (U.S. Bureau of the Census 1977b). Moreover, if the large increase in out-of-wedlock births that has occurred in Sweden in recent years as a consequence of unmarried couples' living together is any indication of a diminishing taboo on having children out of wedlock, then even this function of marriage may be weakening. It seems significant that, in the United States, in 1975, the greatest increase in out-of-wedlock births occurred among white women 20–29 years old. At the same time, the birth rate reached a new low (National Center for Health Statistics 1976).

Thus, demographic trends, more particularly the decline of fertility, can be regarded as both a cause and a consequence of changes in the family. The decline of childbearing can be construed as freeing women for economic equality with men, which in turn makes marriage and childbearing less of an automatic social response. The future seems less and less compatible with long-term traditional marriage.

Future Growth

If this is a reasonable interpretation of the evidence and if this diagnosis is even approximately correct, then fertility in the United States and other developed countries seems destined to fall to very low levels, probably below replacement. Several countries such as France and some East European nations already seem very uncomfortable with this trend. How, then, is society going to sustain the level of reproduction necessary to replace one generation with the next? Such questions are not new; they were raised more than 40 years ago during the depths of the Depression, when birth rates had fallen sharply and an impending decline in population was projected. At that time, there was speculation by at least one serious sociologist that society would develop professional breeders, that reproduction would become the specialized function of a category of women who would be paid for their childbearing services (Davis 1937). The products of such specialists would be raised in special child-care institutions in the absence of conventional family arrangements.

This all has a ring of science fiction about it, and, of course, World War II and the subsequent scramble to the suburbs, universal marriage, and the baby boom made the whole speculation seem ludicrous in retrospect. Yet, given current trends, it is not difficult to visualize a society in which perhaps one-third of women never have any children; this would mean that the remaining two-thirds would have to reproduce at an average rate of three births per woman to maintain replacement. Under such circumstances, there is little doubt that some types of financial incentives to encourage childbearing will have to be implemented, as they already have been, in mild form, in many European countries. And my guess is that there will have to be considerable public investment in underwriting such incentive systems. There is no clear evidence that the trivial baby bonuses, maternity-care benefits, and various employment benefits that have been legislated in European countries have had any appreciable impact on the birth rate. It is difficult to imagine well-paid women with little interest in childbearing being attracted by a few hundred dollars' worth of miscellaneous benefits. There may very well have to be a serious investment in child-care institutions and a willingness to subsidize reproduction on a large scale.

There is an alternative to subsidizing reproduction to meet the consequences of negative natural increase, and that is immigration. Assuming that our economy can remain strong enough to attract immigrants, the desired rate of population increase could be achieved through the manipulation of immigration quotas, a practice not unknown in our past. Since the supply of potential immigrants to the United States typically exceeds existing quotas, the qualifications for immigration could be set fairly high to bring in persons with training in skills in short supply in our economy. This concept already exists in our immigration law. From the economic point of view, such a practice would be highly rewarding, since the capital costs of education and training would have been borne by other countries. From the social point of view, however, to depend entirely on importing our population deficit would have many of the problems that we associate with the assimilation of immigrants in our past — e.g., different customs and languages, additional minority-group problems, and hostility of many native citizens (50 percent of the public in 1971 thought that immigration should be reduced) (Wolman 1972). It is instructive that other countries confronted with such questions have opted primarily for programs to raise the fertility of their native populations. The recent labour migrations in Europe, and the resulting difficulty of accommodating large numbers of foreign workers in countries with labour shortages, have been an experience that the receiving countries are not likely to forget if it comes to the more basic question of supplementing population growth.

Also, it seems unlikely that the current volume of illegal immigration (whatever its magnitude may actually be) will be permitted to continue indefinitely, and in any event, it could hardly be rationalized as a substitute for native fertility.

Thus, immigration does not seem to be a basic long-term solution if the rate of natural increase falls and remains radically below replacement. If current fertility rates were to continue beyond the time when zero population growth was reached, our net legal immigration volume would have to be about double to avoid population decline.

This whole discussion is predicated on the assumption that governments will not look kindly on negative population growth or, for that matter, even on a sustained period of below-replacement fertility before zero population growth. It is obvious that negative population growth cannot be sustained indefinitely, although some of our citizens appear not to be averse to returning to a population about half our current size, which was the level experienced around 1920. We know very little about the short-run consequences of negative population growth; the long-run consequences are clear.

Conclusions

So what does it all add up to? Americans are having fewer children than ever before, and there do not seem to be any forces in view that will reverse this trend. Better contraception is available and is being used, and abortion is more or less available. The demographic result is a declining rate of population growth and an expectation that zero population growth may be reached in 50 years, if not sooner. Estimates for a total population as low as 250 million are now in vogue. The age composition will change significantly with an increase in the proportions of individuals of working age and aged 65 and older, and with a decrease in youth.

In general, as we have explained elsewhere, the social, economic, environmental, and political consequences of these demographic changes seem desirable (Commission on Population Growth 1972). There are some concerns about the implications of an older population, but sooner or later such change is inevitable as the population growth slows. At any rate, the reduction of growth means less pressure on the environment and resources and an opportunity to invest economic growth in improving the quality of life. From the standpoint of the economy, there will be more workers and fewer dependents, and per-capita income will be higher. From the standpoint of government, there will be an opportunity to invest public resources in better education and to improve the level of government services generally.

The future of marriage and the family is less clear. The divorce rate continues at a high level, the marriage rate is low, and there seems to be a massive postponement of marriage in the making. Increasingly, young men and women are living together without the added commitment of marriage; illegitimacy rates will probably continue to increase. Whether increasing proportions will never marry or will just marry at a later age is unknown. Although it seems ironic, if not ludicrous — in view of our concerns about growth of only a few years ago — to be thinking about the possible need in the near future to *maintain* replacement fertility, there are reasons to believe that some subsidization of reproduction may eventually become necessary. The problem has already arisen in more than one European country, and the social trends apparent in the United States today all seem to point in that direction.

Works Cited

Bourgeois-Pichat, I.J. 1977. "The Economic and Social Implications of Demographic Trends in Europe up to and Beyond 2000." *Population Bulletin of the United Nations* 8: 34.

Brass, W. 1974. "Perspectives in Population Prediction: Illustrated by the Statistics of England and Wales." *Journal of the Royal Statistical Society* 137:532.

Commission on Population Growth and the American Future. 1972. *Population and the American Future.* Stock no. 5258–0002. Washington, DC: Government Printing Office.

Davis, K. 1937. "Reproductive Institutions and the Pressure for Population." *The Sociological Review* 29: 289.

Easterlin, R.A. 1962. *The American Baby Boom in Historical Perspective.* New York: National Bureau of Economic Research.

Glick, P.C. 1978. "Social Change and the American Family." National Conference on Social Welfare. *Social Welfare Forum, 1977.* New York: Columbia University Press.

Keyfitz, N. 1972. "On Future Population." *Journal of the American Statistical Association* 67: 361.

Lee, R. 1976. "Demographic Forecasting and the Easterlin Hypothesis." *Population and Development Review* 2: 459.

National Center for Health Statistics. 1976. "Advance Report: Final Natality Statistics 1975." *Monthly Vital Statistics Report* 24 (10): Supplement.

Prioux-Marchal, F. 1974. "Le mariage en Suède." *Population* 29: 824.

Roussel, L. 1977. "Démographie et mode de vie conjugale en Danemark." *Population* 32: 339.

Sklar, J., and B. Berkov. 1975. "The American Birth Rate: Evidence of a Coming Rise." *Science* 189: 693.

U.S. Bureau of the Census. 1977a. "Characteristics of the Population Below the Poverty Level: 1975." *Current Population Reports.* Series P–60, No. 106.

———. 1977b. "Fertility of American Women: June 1976." *Current Population Reports.* Series P–20, No. 308: Table 19.

U.S. Bureau of Labor Statistics. 1976. "New Labor Force Projections to 1990." *Special Labor Force Reports.* Report no. 197. Washington, DC: U.S. Bureau of Labor Statistics.

Westoff, C.F. 1976. "The Decline of Unplanned Births in the United States." *Science* 191: 38.

Westoff, C.F., and E.F. Jones. 1977. "Contraception and Sterilization in the United States 1965–1975." *Family Planning Perspectives* 9: 153.

Wolman, D.M. 1972. "Findings of the Commission's National Public Opinion Survey." Commission on Population Growth and the American Future. *Aspects of of Population Growth Policy.* Eds. R. Parke Jr. and C.F. Westoff. Vol. VI of Commission Research Reports. Washington, DC: U.S. Government Printing Office. 491.

SOCIODEMOGRAPHIC CHARACTERISTICS OF RELIGIOUS GROUPS IN CANADA

Tim B. Heaton

Religious differences in socioeconomic and family characteristics have been the topic of numerous studies. Since most analyses of religious groups rely on sample data, most of our information applies to relatively large aggregations; we know little about smaller denominations. By utilizing special tabulations from the 1981 Canadian Census, this paper compares 19 religious groups in terms of several socioeconomic and family characteristics. Standardized distributions also are presented that adjust for age, sex, and regional differences between religious groups. Correlations and covariance analysis of these variables indicate a high degree of association between socioeconomic and family characteristics. Religions characterized by low socioeconomic status exhibit more traditional family behaviour; and high SES religions have lower rates of marriage and fertility, but higher divorce rates.

The relationship between religious affiliation and other social characteristics has provided the basis for a long history of demographic and sociological research. Religion has been viewed both as a determinant (Lenski 1961) and as a consequence (Stark 1972) of socioeconomic status. In demographic analysis, religion is more often treated as an independent variable that influences factors such as fertility, marriage, and divorce (Bouvier and Rao 1975; Westoff and Jones 1979; Mosher and

Hendershot 1984; Heaton and Goodman 1985). One of the major shortcomings of much of this research is that sample sizes require aggregation of Protestant denominations into one or two conglomerate groups. Studies that have made distinctions between denominations have often found significant differences. The first goal of this research will be to provide a more complete comparison of religious differences for socioeconomic and family variables.

The second goal is to examine the relationship between these two sets of characteristics. Most previous research treats the individual as the unit of analysis so that association among characteristics of religious groups cannot be directly evaluated. Here we examine the aggregate characteristics of religious groups. Without denying the importance of individual-level analysis, there are several advantages to comparisons of groups. At the individual level, a variety of other attributes obscures the tendencies for persons with differing socioeconomic and family characteristics to belong to different religious groups. The within-religion variation masks the importance of between-group differences. In considering religions and denominations as organizational units of society, the aggregate characteristics of membership are important to consider. By taking religious groups as a unit of analysis, we can examine the way in which people are sorted into membership groups on a variety of variables, and provide a description of the relationships among these variables.

Source: *Sociological Analysis* 47 (1986): 54–64. Reprinted with permission.

In order to describe religious groups and evaluate the interrelatedness of their characteristics, six characteristics have been selected. Education, occupation, and income are included as measures of socioeconomic status, and traditional family behaviour is measured by the percentage of adults who have ever been married, the percentage of ever-married people who are separated or divorced, and the number of children per 1000 women. Religious differentials on these characteristics have received considerable attention from social scientists, but the comparative rankings of religious groups on these characteristics have not been adequately examined. Two questions need to be answered. First, do religious groups rank consistently on socioeconomic and on family characteristics when each set of variables is considered separately? Second, is socioeconomic status correlated with family status?

Methods

Most sample surveys are too small to provide detailed information about specific religious groups. To provide larger sample sizes, we have obtained special tabulations from the 1981 Canadian Census. Canada is one of the few countries to include religion on the Census. The Census includes both the socioeconomic (i.e., educational attainment, occupation, and income) and family variables (i.e., fertility and marital status) of interest.

Religions differ substantially in terms of age, sex, and regional distributions. These factors need to be controlled when we examine socioeconomic and family characteristics. To purge socioeconomic and family variables of differences that might arise as a result of age, sex, and region, demographic standardization will be used to adjust the values on these variables. These standardized values indicate what each religion would be like if its membership had the same age, sex, and regional distribution as the total population. That is, the values reflect the aggregate of religious differences within each age–sex–region group.

To explore the patterns of religious-group ranking, we will examine the interrelationships within and between family and socioeconomic variables. We have hypothesized a model in which family structure and socioeconomic status are underlying constructs, each having three indicators. The effect that these constructs have on the measures of family structure or socioeconomic status indicate the degree to which each indicator taps an underlying dimension of religious groups. Association between the two constructs is examined by estimating the correlation between the two unmeasured variables.

LISREL will be utilized to evaluate this model (Long 1983a, 1983b). Indicators of the socioeconomic-status construct include the percentage with postsecondary education, the percentage with professional occupations, and average income. The percentage over age 15 who have ever married, the percentage of ever-marrieds who are divorced or separated, and average number of children born are the indicators of family status. LISREL simultaneously estimates the factor-analytic model for each construct, and the correlation between the two constructs. This simultaneous estimation procedure does not differ greatly from the more traditional approach of estimating each factor model separately, computing constructs based on factor scores, and then correlating the constructs; but it does provide a more efficient solution to the entire model.

Results

The absolute and relative sizes of the various religious groups are reported in Table 1. Nearly half of the Canadian population is Roman Catholic. The United Church of Canada and the Anglican Church are substantial, each containing more than 10 percent of the population. The next-largest group has no religious preference. Other groups containing more than 1 percent of the population are Presbyterians, Baptists, Lutherans, Pentecostals, Eastern Orthodox, Jews, and a residual Protestant category. All other groups consti-

Table I
Absolute and Relative Size of Religious Groups

Religion	Number (1000s)	% of Total Population
Roman Catholic	11 210	46.5
Ukrainian Catholic	191	0.8
Polish Catholic	2	0
Anglican	2 436	10.1
Baptist	697	2.9
Jehovah's Witness	143	0.6
Latter Day Saints (Mormon)	82	0.3
Lutheran	703	2.9
Mennonite	189	0.8
Hutterite	17	0.1
Pentecostal	339	1.4
Presbyterian	812	3.4
Reformed Bodies	104	0.4
Salvation Army	125	0.5
United Church of Canada	3 758	15.6
Other Protestant	501	2.1
Eastern Orthodox	362	1.5
Jewish	296	1.2
All Other Religions	19	0
No Religion	1 748	7.4
Total Population	24 083	—

Source: 1981 Census of Canada, Special Tabulation.

tute a small minority. In fact, there are too few Polish National Catholics for detailed analysis, so this group will be deleted from subsequent tables.

The percent ever married and the percent of marrieds who are currently divorced or separated (for the population aged 15 and over) are presented in Table 2. Focussing on the percentage married, Jehovah's Witnesses are the most married denomination, with 78.4 percent. At the other extreme, only 56.9 percent of the Hutterites are married. This low percentage is not merely a function of late marriage; even in the 46–60 age group, Hutterites have a lower percentage ever married than does the country as a whole.[1] Some other groups deviate from the national pattern by at least 4 percent. For example, Lutherans and the Eastern Orthodox tend to be above

average, while those with no preference lie below the average. Mainline Protestants in general tend to be above average and Roman Catholics are somewhat below the national norm. When adjusted percentages are compared, most groups lie closer to the national average, indicating that some variation is the result of age, sex, and regional distributions. Still, the major outliers have adjusted rates that are consistent with the unadjusted rates. Only Ukrainian Catholics, Reformed Bodies, and Jews have adjusted rates that are substantially different from unadjusted rates.

Hutterites, Mennonites, and Reformed Bodies have divorce percentages well below the national average. In contrast, the residual Protestant groups and the unchurched have divorce rates well above the national average. The Latter Day Saints church also has a di-

Table 2

Percent of Those Age 15+ Who Have Ever Married and Percent of All Ever-Married (Nonwidowed) Who Are Divorced or Separated

Religion	Percent Ever Married	Percent of Ever-married, Nonwidowed Who Are Currently Divorced or Separated	Adjusted	
			Percent Ever Married	Percent of Ever-married, Nonwidowed Who Are Currently Divorced or Separated
Roman Catholic	69.7	7.2	71.8	7.4
Ukrainian Catholic	75.0	6.8	68.5	7.9
Anglican	75.6	8.5	72.0	8.7
Baptist	74.6	8.2	73.0	8.7
Jehovah's Witness	73.4	7.2	77.2	7.1
Mormon	74.2	9.1	73.9	10.5
Lutheran	76.2	7.3	71.8	7.7
Mennonite	71.7	3.3	74.2	5.6
Hutterite	56.9	0.2	55.7	a
Pentecostal	72.7	8.2	74.5	8.8
Presbyterian	76.0	8.2	71.5	8.7
Reformed Bodies	69.1	1.9	74.7	2.6
Salvation Army	74.7	8.6	73.8	10.9
United Church of Canada	76.1	7.3	72.8	7.7
Other Protestant	73.4	8.3	71.9	8.5
Eastern Orthodox	76.5	6.7	72.3	6.7
Jewish	75.6	7.5	68.4	8.0
All Other Religions	70.8	17.0	69.1	16.0
No Religion	67.3	12.0	69.9	13.0
Total Population	72.2	7.7	72.2	7.7

Source: 1981 Census of Canada, Special Tabulation.

[a] Cell sizes too small for adjustment.

vorce rate somewhat above the national average. The adjusted rates here are similar to the unadjusted rates, and the major deviations from the average still stand out.

Fertility rates (children ever born per number of females) show substantial variation (see Table 3). Here we focus on adjusted rates, since age structure can dramatically affect fertility; the adjusted rates are generally larger than the unadjusted rates. Ukrainian Catholics, Lutherans, Presbyterians, Jews, and those with no religious preference have rates about one-half child lower than the national average. Anglicans, the United Church of Canada, and the Eastern Orthodox also have rates substantially below the national average. At the other extreme, Hutterites have nearly three more children than average. Conservative Protestants, including the Latter Day Saints, Mennonites, Pentecostals, and Reformed Bodies, have rates well above average. Roman Catholics are also somewhat above average. In sum, there appears to be a rough continuum with conservative Protestants at the top, followed by Roman Catholics and the liberal Protestants, with Jews and the unchurched falling at the bottom of the distribution.

Socioeconomic Status

Levels of educational attainment for each group are documented in Table 4. Jews, the unchurched, and the residual group are clearly above average in education. The mainline Protestants and the Mormons tend to fall near or somewhat above the national average and Catholics fall below average. More conservative Protestants are below average, with Hutterites having by far the lowest educational attainment. In most cases, standardization for age, sex, and regional differences reduces the variability in educational attainment, but the differences described above still persist.

Occupation follows a pattern similar to that for education (see Table 5). Jews have by far the highest percentage in professional and managerial occupations, followed by the residual category and those with no preference. The adjusted rates also show Ukrainian Catholics, Anglicans, Lutherans, Presbyterians, the Reformed Bodies, the United Church of Canada, and the residual Protestant group to lie somewhat above average in professional employment. Blue-collar or agricultural employment is more predominant among Jehovah's Witnesses, Mennonites, Pentecostals, and Hutterites. A large majority of Hutterites are employed in agriculture.

Income differentials parallel, but are not identical to, those for occupation and education. Jews clearly have the highest incomes. Anglicans, Presbyterians, the United Church

Table 3
Children Ever Born per 1000 Women

Religion	Children/1000 Women	Adjusted for Age and Region Children/1000 Women
Roman Catholic	2.702	2.765
Ukrainian Catholic	2.468	1.979
Anglican	2.330	2.260
Baptist	2.504	2.454
Jehovah's Witness	2.733	2.765
Mormon	3.044	3.001
Lutheran	2.268	1.990
Mennonite	3.308	3.065
Hutterite	5.281	a
Pentecostal	2.799	2.866
Presbyterian	2.195	2.112
Reformed Bodies	3.368	3.251
Salvation Army	2.999	2.608
United Church of Canada	2.313	2.242
Other Protestant	2.457	2.484
Eastern Orthodox	2.314	2.170
Jewish	1.970	1.837
All Other Religions	2.207	2.504
No Religion	1.845	2.117
Total Population	2.493	2.493

Source: 1981 Census of Canada, Special Tabulation.
[a]Cell sizes too small for adjustment.

of Canada, and those with no preference are also substantially above average (see Table 6). Conservative Protestants generally have below-average incomes, and Catholics are somewhat below average. In sum, all three status indicators reveal a hierarchy, with Jews at the top, followed by liberal Protestants and the unchurched. Catholics follow, with conservative Protestants at the bottom of the scale.

Model Evaluation

Correlations among variables are shown in Table 7. In order to give each group an impact commensurate with its size, the size of each group was used to weight the analysis. Measures of socioeconomic status are highly intercorrelated. The percent married and children ever born are also positively related, and each is negatively related to divorce. Also, the percent divorced is positively correlated with socioeconomic variables.

A more concise picture of the relationships among these variables is obtained by evaluating the proposed model. Results of this analysis are presented in Figure 1. Each socioeconomic indicator loads highly on the socioeconomic variable. The percent divorced and children ever born also load highly on the family variable, but the percent married does not do quite so well. These loadings indicate that religious groups are consistently ranked on socioeconomic characteristics. Moreover, religions that are more traditional

Table 4
Level of Education

Religion	Unadjusted			Adjusted		
	Post Secondary	11–13	Less than Grade 11	Post Secondary	12–13	Less than Grade 11
Roman Catholic	35.9	25.0	39.1	36.0	24.4	39.6
Ukrainian Catholic	32.8	20.8	46.4	43.2	22.3	34.5
Anglican	41.4	27.2	31.5	42.8	26.3	30.9
Baptist	37.5	24.7	37.8	39.5	24.7	35.8
Jehovah's Witness	26.8	29.1	44.1	27.2	28.2	44.5
Mormon	48.3	27.9	23.8	44.1	24.7	31.2
Lutheran	40.4	24.5	35.1	47.2	23.8	29.0
Mennonite	31.8	19.3	48.9	36.5	21.2	42.3
Hutterite	1.1	1.4	97.5	12.2	0.6	87.2
Pentecostal	32.1	23.8	44.1	32.6	22.3	45.1
Presbyterian	39.5	28.7	31.9	43.2	27.5	29.3
Reformed Bodies	40.6	26.6	32.8	49.9	20.8	29.4
Salvation Army	26.2	21.1	52.7	30.9	24.7	44.4
United Church of Canada	40.7	27.7	31.6	41.3	26.9	31.9
Other Protestant	46.6	24.3	29.2	45.8	23.5	30.7
Eastern Orthodox	32.0	20.6	47.4	33.7	22.0	44.3
Jewish	55.6	22.3	22.1	61.0	21.7	17.3
All Other Religions	59.7	18.8	21.5	54.6	19.4	26.0
No Religion	50.8	25.2	23.9	49.0	22.7	28.2
Total Population	39.1	25.5	35.4			

Source: 1981 Census of Canada, Special Tabulation.

Table 5
Occupational Distribution

| | | | | Adjusted | | |
Religion	Professional	Clerical–Sales Service	Blue-Collar Farm	Professional	Clerical–Sales Service	Blue-Collar Farm
Roman Catholic	22.4	40.2	37.5	21.8	39.9	38.3
Ukrainian Catholic	22.9	38.8	38.3	28.2	41.3	30.5
Anglican	27.1	42.1	30.8	28.1	41.2	30.7
Baptist	22.4	40.4	37.2	23.2	39.5	37.3
Jehovah's Witness	11.9	45.4	42.7	12.3	45.9	41.8
Mormon	24.4	41.5	34.1	24.4	43.0	32.6
Lutheran	22.3	37.8	39.9	25.8	38.0	36.2
Mennonite	21.0	29.5	49.5	24.9	33.1	42.0
Hutterite	10.4	1.4	88.2	15.5	7.0	77.5
Pentecostal	17.7	40.4	41.9	18.6	40.2	41.2
Presbyterian	24.4	41.6	34.0	26.1	41.5	32.4
Reformed Bodies	21.6	30.7	47.7	30.5	31.3	38.2
Salvation Army	17.3	39.0	43.7	19.5	43.3	37.2
United Church of Canada	25.6	40.4	34.0	26.1	39.6	34.2
Other Protestant	27.8	37.8	34.4	27.8	37.7	34.5
Eastern Orthodox	18.9	44.5	36.6	18.5	48.1	33.3
Jewish	45.6	43.4	10.9	45.5	43.4	11.0
All Other Religions	36.2	36.1	27.7	34.5	39.4	26.0
No Religion	30.4	35.2	34.3	34.0	36.9	29.1
Total Population	24.4	39.9	35.7			

Source: 1981 Census of Canada, Special Tabulation.

on one measure of family structures are generally more traditional on other characteristics — low divorce, larger families, and, to a lesser degree, high rates of marriage tend to go together.

Perhaps the most interesting aspect of the model is the strong relationship between the two unobserved variables, socioeconomic status and family structure. Groups that have high socioeconomic status have less traditional family patterns; the magnitude of the correlation indicates that this is a nearly one-to-one correspondence. In short, the parameters of this model indicate a high degree of consolidation of socioeconomic and family characteristics. Religious groups are consistently ranked on a variety of variables.

A few other aspects of the model deserve mention. In order to improve the fit between correlations implied by the model and the observed correlation matrix, it was necessary to include a correlation between income and divorce. This relationship suggests that income is lower where divorce is high, presumably because of the poor financial status of divorced households. There is also a possibility that other indicators are correlated (e.g., fertility and education), but further elaboration would make statistical evaluation more intractable. Overall, the model does provide a reasonable fit.

Statisticians generally recommend that the covariance matrix rather than the correlation matrix be used to estimate models. Accordingly, this analysis was repeated using the covariance matrix, yielding similar results. The Chi-square test, t-values, and the correlation between unobserved variables are virtually

Table 6
Average Income for Those Reporting Income

Religion	Average Income of Persons with Income	Adjusted Average Income of Persons with Income
Roman Catholic	12 293	12 452
Ukrainian Catholic	12 421	13 271
Anglican	13 661	14 000
Baptist	11 740	12 230
Jehovah's Witness	10 309	10 347
Mormon	12 412	11 827
Lutheran	13 303	13 322
Mennonite	11 809	11 468
Hutterite	11 392	[a]
Pentecostal	10 782	10 909
Presbyterian	13 334	13 815
Reformed Bodies	12 306	12 678
Salvation Army	10 317	10 866
United Church of Canada	13 693	13 839
Other Protestant	12 586	12 471
Eastern Orthodox	12 395	11 749
Jewish	19 529	19 329
All Other Religions	12 734	12 384
No Religion	14 854	13 903
Total Population	12 993	12 993

Source: 1981 Census of Canada, Special Tabulation.
[a]Cell sizes too small for adjustment.

Table 7
Correlations Among Indicators of Socioeconomic and Family Status for Canadian Religions ($N = 19$)[a]

	1	2	3	4	5	6
1 Percent with Post-Secondary Education	1.000					
2 Percent in Professional and Managerial Occupations	.956	1.000				
3 Average Income	.823	.865	1.000			
4 Percent Over Age 30 Ever Married	−.419	−.518	−.421	1.000		
5 Percent of Marrieds Ever Divorced	.589	.634	.314	−.412	1.000	
6 Children Ever Born	−.796	−.724	−.736	.187	−.525	1.000

Source: 1981 Census of Canada, Special Tabulation.
[a]Weighted by size of the religion.

Figure 1
Path Model of the Relationship Between Socioeconomic Status and Traditional Family Behaviour for Religions of Canada (N = 19)

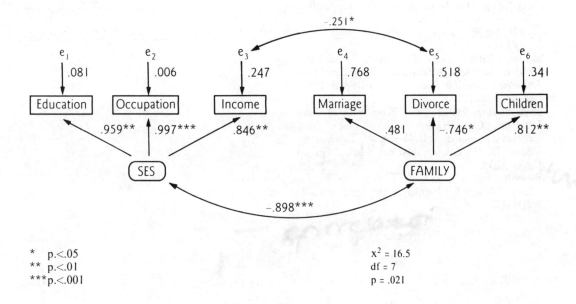

* p.<.05
** p.<.01
***p.<.001

x^2 = 16.5
df = 7
p = .021

identical if the covariance matrix is used. We have opted for the correlation matrix to facilitate interpretation, but this comparison indicates that we would have reached the same conclusions with covariances.

Summary

This paper has examined the relationships among various socioeconomic and family attributes, with religious groups as the units of analysis. Analysis indicates that religious groups that are high on one measure of socioeconomic status are also high on other measures, that religious groups that are more traditional on one measure of family structure are more traditional on other measures, and that there is a near-perfect negative relationship between socioeconomic status and traditional family structure. In short, religions evidence a high degree of consolidation of socioeconomic and family characteristics.

Notes

1. This low marriage rate is inconsistent with traditional Hutterite marriage patterns. Although the census data may be in error, other census results match the public image of Hutterites. For example, census data indicate low divorce, high fertility, heavy concentration in the prairie region, low educational attainment, and high percentages in agriculture. Unfortunately, there are no additional current data sources to corroborate or refute this finding. In any event, Hutterite numbers are small enough that they have little impact on the overall result.

Works Cit

Bouvier, Lec
   Socioreligiou
   bridge, MA
Heaton, Tim
   "Religion a
   ligious Rese

Lenski, Gerhard. 1961. *The Religious Factor: A Sociological Study of Religion's Impact on Politics, Economics, and Family Life*. Garden City, NY: Doubleday.

Long, J. Scott. 1983a. *Confirmatory Factor Analysis*. Beverly Hills, CA: Sage.

———. 1983b. *Covariance Structure Models*. Beverly Hills, CA: Sage.

Mosher, William D., and Gerry E. Hendershot. 1984. "Religious Affiliation and the Fertility of Married Couples." *Journal of Marriage and Family* 46: 671–77.

Stark, Rodney. 1972. "The Economics of Piety: Religious Commitment and Social Class." *Issues in Social Inequality*. Eds. Gerald W. Thielbar and Saul D. Feldman. Boston: Little, Brown. 483–503.

Westoff, Charles F., and Elise F. Jones. 1979. "The End of 'Catholic' Fertility." *Demography* 16(2): 209–17.

THE QUEBEC QUESTION: A MATTER OF POPULATION

Gary Caldwell
Daniel Fournier

After an introduction in which they situate the importance of demographic issues in Quebec, the authors review the contemporary demographic evolution of Quebec society. They first consider population growth in Quebec and the respective contributions of natural increase and migration to the present rate of growth. They then turn to the issues of linguistic composition, language assimilation, and the volume and composition of immigration to Quebec. Nuptiality, fertility, and divorce are all touched upon inasmuch as they bear upon procreation. Lastly, attention is drawn to the ageing of the Quebec population. Having characterized the major demographic trends, the authors go on to discuss the major political, economic, and social consequences of these trends.

Introduction

For as long as there has been a Quebec, the overriding issue has been one, not (as in the case of Poland, another "impossible" society) of political independence, but of population. Indeed, the issue emerged as early as the seventeenth century. At that time, it took the form of getting population numbers up to a critical level that would ensure the simple biological perpetuation of the resident population. Until the native-born population, which was adapted to the new environment, was sufficiently numerous that it outnumbered the more volatile immigrant population, French colonial administrators continued to be con-

Source: *The Canadian Journal of Sociology* 12 (1987): 16–41. Reprinted with permission.

cerned (Langlois 1934). In the subsequent race with the English for control of the continent that had been largely discovered and explored by the French, the insufficient size of the French population has been judged to be the decisive factor in their defeat.

After the final military defeat in 1759 and the containment of French North America to, essentially, Lower Canada (the Quebec and Constitution acts), the issue became one of establishing a French demographic hegemony in Lower Canada at a period when the St. Lawrence River had become a funnel for English and Irish immigration to British North America. As a result of this immigration, both Quebec City and Montreal became English cities as French society ruralized in a retreat to the land (Garigue 1956). Soon after, at the time of the controversy over the creation of the Union in 1840, the demographic gauntlet was thrown down again as French Quebec was faced with the prospect of becoming a minority in a united Canada. Subsequent failure of the Union and the advent of Confederation in 1867 provided a certain respite. The French population was by then firmly established as the majority in Lower Canada, which was to become the new province of Quebec. This period (the mid-nineteenth century) was one of super-fertility — relative to the surrounding population — that lasted a century. This demographic investment alone ensured the survival of French society in geographical Quebec as we know it today, despite political and economic subjugation.

But demographic superiority was only a limited consolation, because French Quebec was now part of a larger political entity, the new Dominion of Canada, which was expanding to the west. The dream of Quebec nationalists (such as Henri Bourassa) at the time was to establish Quebec's land-hungry progeny on the fertile plains of the new frontier. Debates on who would people the west constituted a major public issue of the day. As fate — or rather politics — would have it, the battle for the settlement of the west was lost by Quebec[1] as her sons and daughters (for whom the cost of going west was higher than it was for East European immigrants) poured over the close-by international border into the demographic vortex of the new republic, never to be seen again as a distinct national group. From this point on, any hope of influencing the Canadian demolinguistic equilibrium in favour of French was lost. Had it not been for the dividends reaped in the early half of the twentieth century from the great demographic investment of the nineteenth, as well as massive emigration from western Canada to the United States, the one-third/two-thirds linguistic balance would not have held as it did for a century.

However, the post–World War II economic boom, the consummation of the industrialization of Canadian society, massive immigration from Europe, and the modernization of Quebec society opened up two cracks in this precarious equilibrium. First, it became apparent that the French-speaking population outside Quebec was destined to melt away under the hot sun of language assimilation (Maheu 1970). Quebec nationalists finally abandoned the dream of a Canada of two nations from coast to coast. The *Report on Bilingualism and Biculturalism* was the last gasp. The French nation was, ineluctably, fading away outside Quebec, except perhaps in northwestern New Brunswick. Indeed, even in the part of the bilingual belt (Joy 1972) that is in Quebec, the outcome appeared dubious (Lachapelle and Henripin 1980).

Hence, the "French Canadian" question had become, for French speakers, the "Quebec" question, and French-speaking non-Quebeckers were abandoned to their fate.

However, as soon as these losses had been cut — ideologically speaking — and a new line drawn (the provincial political boundary), it was discovered in the 1960s that within bastion Quebec was a demographic Trojan horse. Differential linguistic assimilation of immigrants into the English sector was such in Montreal that, had trends then current continued uninterrupted, there would have been more students in English than in French schools today (Charbonneau, Henripin, and Légaré 1970). Differential linguistic assimilation to English was not new: what *was* new was francophone out-migration and a decline in francophone fertility, which, when combined, left the French population exposed to the consequences of language assimilation.

Incidentally, it is now *de bon ton* in English-Canadian journalistic and academic circles (*Saturday Night* 1985) to demonstrate that this perception of a threat to the demographic predominance of French in the Quebec metropolis was an alarmist scare that did not come to pass. This is an error: the situation that existed in the 1960s has not changed. What *did* change was the political climate, which generated action to reverse certain trends. We repeat, there has been no systematic demographic demonstration that, in the light of conditions prevailing at the time, the analysis of the 1960s was error. Indeed, as a consequence of political action that stemmed from an ideological *crise de conscience* with regard to the demographic threat, a lowered level of immigration, increased out-migration of anglophones from Quebec, as well as the constraint of language laws, have averted the feared outcome.

Nevertheless, Quebec is again faced with the issue of the early seventeenth century: that of a level of fertility insufficient to assure the biological perpetuation of its existing population base. For over a decade now Quebeckers, as a population, have not been reproducing themselves: with the lowest fertility rate in the industrialized world, with the exception of Denmark and West Germany, the prospect of a declining population within 15 years now faces Quebec (Quebec 1982). Once again, in its simplest form, the Quebec question has become one of numbers. Having put into place a quasi state, which assured the role of French in public life and insured itself against being swamped by immigrants, the inhabitants thus protected are fading away.

The importance of demographics as the dialectic of the Quebec question is reflected in the importance of the discipline of demography in contemporary Quebec. The "Association des démographes du Québec" has almost 200 members and these members have probably been more effective in reading, empirically, the changing social reality of Quebec society than have been all other social scientists put together. The demographers, and the demographic writers who were their precursors, have now defined the Quebec issue for over a quarter of a century. The vitality and productiveness of the discipline is reflected in the fact that Quebec demography is the only Quebec social science that has attracted international recognition for its scientific production.

Furthermore, although individual historians and sociologists may have played a role in shaping a national consciousness in contemporary Quebec, only demography has directly inspired political action. This happened in the late 1960s and early 1970s when concern over the consequence of language assimilation of both immigrants and francophones led to language legislation, particularly Bill 101. The latter created a situation of reduced immigration, of increased out-migration of anglophones, and the channelling of immigrant children into French schools. The legislation indeed changed the course of events insofar as the linguistic composition of Quebec society is concerned.

Why have demographic issues been so critical throughout the history of Quebec? Before we attempt to address this question, a preliminary remark is in order: although there is a highly developed demographic tradition on such issues as immigration, language assimilation, fertility, and ethnic studies (Caldwell 1983), there is a very limited contemporary literature on the role of demographic

factors as a causal variable in the long-term determination of the nature of Quebec society. Cultural or economic factors are more likely to be cast as the key to Quebec's survival. Indeed, the classical thesis is that if Quebec cultural consciousness and economic expansion continues, Quebec will retain and expand its population, and thus persevere.

We contend that this has not been adequately demonstrated, despite the conventional wisdom; on the contrary, both the longer view of Quebec history and a more detailed analysis of the postwar period (Caldwell and Czarnocki 1977) suggest that economic growth in Quebec is a consequence of demographic expansion. In other words, in Quebec history the most successful societal investments have been demographic rather than economic. The obverse demonstration of this is the economic consequences (Mathews 1984) of the contemporary demographic disinvestment.

However, this thesis — growth in Quebec is population driven — has neither been convincingly argued in the social science literature, nor is it, to say the least, the object of a consensus of opinion. However, if, as one of us has suggested (Caldwell and Czarnocki 1977), this thesis is valid, why may it be so?

Quebec society is, and historically has been, subject to at least three conditions or geopolitical constraints that limit its ability to use either the state or the economy as levers of development. First, Quebec is, and always has been, a truncated political entity; second, it is, and always has been, an integral part of a metropolitan economy (French, English, and now American) that it responds to but does not determine; and finally, Quebec has, and always has had (albeit for different reasons) an open boundary for those wishing to leave. Because of these three geopolitical constraints — political truncation, economic dependence, and unrestricted emigration — the only effective lever that Quebec possesses to make its influence felt is sheer numbers, and from those numbers all else follows. We will first examine the contemporary numbers and how they are evolving; second, we will briefly consider the political, economic, and social consequences of these numbers.

Contemporary Evolution of the Population

Decline in Growth Rate

In terms of the volume of its population and its rate of growth, Quebec, like the rest of Canada, has experienced a declining growth rate since the 1950s. Quebec has, however, distinguished itself since the 1960s with a growth rate that has been declining faster than that of the rest of Canada. Relative to the period between the two wars (1921–41), when Quebec was growing faster than the rest of Canada, the tables have been turned.

At the beginning of the 60-year period depicted in Table 1, Quebec was growing considerably faster than Canada as a whole. Halfway through the period the rates were equal, whereas, by the end, Quebec was growing at a rate half that of Canada as a whole.

Looking more closely at the second half (1951–81) of the more than half-century under consideration (see Table 2), we can see that the turning point was, indeed, the mid-1960s. Up until that time, Quebec's growth rate, for whatever reasons, was essentially equal to Canada's, although already less than Ontario's. Rather suddenly, in the five-

Table 2
Population Growth by Five-Year Periods: Canada, Quebec, and Ontario, 1951–1981 (Percentage)

	Canada	Quebec	Ontario
1951–56	14.8	14.1	17.6
1956–61	13.4	13.6	15.4
1961–66	9.7	9.9	11.6
1966–71	7.8	4.3	10.7
1971–76	6.6	3.4	7.3
1976–81	5.9	3.3	4.4

Source: Canadian Census, 1921 to 1981.

year period from 1966 to 1971, Quebec's growth rate weakened dramatically and fell to half that of Ontario and 45 percent that of Canada. Although Canada's and Ontario's growth rates have continued to decline, Quebec's has remained lower.

Migratory Movements

However, the single most important factor in the relative (to the rest of Canada) deterioration in the growth rate of Quebec's population between 1951 and 1981 was not, as is often assumed, the relative decline in natural increase. Although the natural growth rate in Quebec in the 1950s and early 1960s

Table 1
Population Growth by Ten-Year Periods: Canada and Quebec, 1921–1981 (Percentage)

	Canada	Quebec
1921–31	18.1	21.8
1931–41	10.9	15.8
1941–51	21.8	21.7
1951–61	30.2	29.7
1961–71	18.3	14.6
1971–81	12.9	6.8

Source: Canadian Census, 1921 to 1981.

Table 3
Rate of Natural Increase by Five-Year Periods, Quebec and Ontario, 1950–1980 (Percentage)

	Quebec	Ontario
1951–55	22.0	14.7
1956–60	21.4	17.9
1961–65	17.1	15.4
1966–70	10.1	10.2
1971–75	7.5	8.4
1976–80	8.5	7.2

Source: Canada 1980–85, Quebec 1980–85.

Table 4

Components of Demographic Growth in Quebec, 1951–1981

Periods	Natural Increase	Residual Migratory Balance	Total Increase
1951–56	488 991	83 706	572 697
1956–61	533 564	97 269	630 833
1961–66	471 190	50 444	521 634
1966–71	307 778	–60 859	246 919
1971–76	246 027	–39 346	206 681
1976–81	272 855	–68 895	203 960

Source: Quebec, 1985a: 35.

declined more than in Ontario, since the mid-1960s (see Table 3) the rates of natural increase in Quebec and Ontario have been almost identical. Consequently, the cause of the relative deterioration of the Quebec growth rate is to be found elsewhere: the answer lies in the nature of migratory movement, as Table 4 clearly indicates.

Again, the late 1960s, the period 1966–71, was the turning point (see Table 4): from this period on, the migratory balance (obtained by subtracting natural increase from actual increase) became negative. The loss reached a peak of almost 70 000 for the five-year period from 1976 to 1981. However, according to a recent estimate of Statistics Canada (as reflected in Table 5, section b), Quebec's migratory balance began to improve in the early 1980s and, in 1985, became positive once more.

Table 5, by revealing the evolution in migratory currents, is very instructive and allows us to draw a number of conclusions. First, it is apparent that the negative migratory balances experienced by Quebec during the 1960s and 1970s were a consequence of its disproportionate net losses to the other provinces, losses constantly higher in volume than the net international migratory gain. Second, since 1983 the hemorrhage has been stemmed; furthermore, it appears that, since 1985, Quebec has been experiencing a positive net migratory balance. Third, and a consequence of our first conclusion above, this turnaround is due to a decline in out-migration to other provinces. Finally, notwithstanding the decline in interprovincial

Table 5

Quebec's Migratory Balances, Interprovincial, International, and Overall, 1967 to 1985

	International Migration	Interprovincial	Balance
a) 1967 to 1984			
1967–71 (Average)	+3 686	–25 627	–21 941
1972–76 (Average)	+10 937	–15 439	–4 502
1977–81 (Average)	+10 892	–30 815	–19 923
1982	+13 749	–28 169	–14 420
1983	+8 641	–20 473	–11 852
1984	+6 897	–12 345	–5 448
b) First Nine Months months 1982 to 1985			
1982	+10 912	–19 809	–8 897
1983	+7 051	–12 841	–5 790
1984	+5 704	–8 125	–2 421
1985	+4 987	–2 404	+2 585

Source: Canada, 1985.

Table 6

The Relative Importance of Quebec's Population Within Canada, 1951 to 1981

Census Year	Population of Canada (000s)	Population of Quebec (000s)	Quebec/Canada (%)
1951	14 009	4 056	29.0
1961	18 238	5 259	28.8
1971	21 568	6 028	28.0
1981	24 343	6 438	26.5

Source: Canada, Census 1951 to 1981.

out-migration, there has been a marked decline in international immigration to Quebec.

At this point in our description of the contemporary evolution of Quebec's population, we can characterize what has happened to Quebec demographically thus: as in the case of most Western societies, the growth rate of Quebec's population has slowed since the 1950s. As has generally been the case in industrialized societies, in Quebec the origin of this population-growth slowdown has been a decline in natural increase. In Quebec's case, however, the decline has been more marked than in the rest of Canada, especially when compared with the neighbouring province of Ontario, which shares a similar geographic and industrialization history. More precisely, Quebec began to lag seriously with respect to the other provinces in the mid-1960s; and, it was precisely at this time that Quebec's net migratory balance became negative, owing largely to heavy net losses to the other provinces. These two tendencies — dramatic decline in natural increase compounded by negative net migratory balances — led to a reduction of Quebec's relative demographic weight within the Canadian confederation (see Table 6).

Linguistic Composition of the Population

One of the outcomes of the recent demographic evolution of Quebec has been — all the recent consciousness of immigrant communities notwithstanding — an incipient homogenization of the population around the French linguistic pole. Although the proportion of those whose mother tongue is French declined from 81.2 percent to 80.7 percent between 1961 and 1971, the proportion climbed back up to 81.1 percent in 1976 and to 82.4 percent by 1981. Meanwhile, the size of the English mother-tongue population had been declining in relative terms since 1961, from 13.3 to 12.8 percent in 1976. In the course of the five-year period from 1976 to 1981, the decline accelerated, with the result that, by 1981, the English mother-tongue population constituted only 11.0 percent of the total Quebec population (see Table 7). We have here, as far as the English mother-tongue population is concerned, not only a relative but (between 1976 and 1981) an absolute decline.

Table 7

French and English Mother-Tongue Proportions of the Quebec Population, 1961 to 1981 (Percentage)

Census Year	French	English	Other
1961	81.2	13.3	5.6
1971	80.7	13.1	6.2
1976	81.1	12.8	6.1
1981	82.4	11.0	6.6

Source: Canada, Census 1961 to 1981.

The beginning of the period of absolute decline of the English mother-tongue population coincides, as history would have it, with the ascension to political power of the Parti Québécois; this coincidence allows us to speculate on the demographic effect of this exceptional political event. To highlight the change at issue — the reversal of English demographic fortunes — it is sufficient to say that, while the English mother-tongue population grew by 1 percent between 1971 and 1976, it declined by a full 11 percent in the succeeding five years. It would appear then that the *péquiste* victory had an important impact on the out-migration of anglophones.

Yet, in historical terms, the heavy out-migration of anglophones in the period from 1976 to 1981 was an amplification, albeit intense, of a long-term trend of disproportionate anglophone out-migration from Quebec: even in contemporary times, this trend has been evident, as confirmed by Table 8.

Hence, in the period from 1966 to 1971, the interprovincial migratory balance of the English mother-tongue population of Quebec already amounted to a deficit of 52 000 persons; this represents, in absolute terms, 4 times the French mother-tongue deficit, and 23 times in relative terms, taking into account the proportionate size of each language group in the Quebec population. In the subsequent five-year period, 1971–76, the English losses remained at the same level, while the French and Other mother-tongue losses declined considerably. Then, between 1976 and 1981 — the *péquiste* period — the English losses doubled compared to the two preceding five-

year periods; this, however, was matched by losses to the Other mother-tongue population. The French losses to the other provinces also rose substantially.

Indeed, at least insofar as interprovincial population movements are concerned, the net migratory deficit of Quebec since 1966 has been largely at the expense of the English population. This trend, already evident — in fact, dating back to Confederation (Rudin 1985, 29) — was amplified by the political events of the 1970s. On the other hand, the Other mother-tongue population, thanks to important gains from immigration, experienced positive balances. (Here, reference should be made to the ephemeral nature of immigration currents; for example, there is reason to believe that more Greeks are now leaving Quebec then are arriving.) As for the French mother-tongue population, it appears that an equilibrium has been reached between out- and in-migration. This was indeed true of the decade 1971–81. Even English out-migration appears to have moderated considerably (Maheu 1980).

The increasingly francophone character of immigration to Quebec has, as we shall now see, contributed to this situation. This becomes apparent when one examines the complex of population movements that produced the 1971–81 migratory balance equilibrium. Effectively, the variation in the size of the French mother-tongue population of Quebec corresponds to what would have been expected from the effect of natural increase alone. Put rather simply: for the ten years from 1971 to 1981, 85 percent of the natural

Table 8
Quebec Interprovincial Migratory Balances by Mother Tongue, 1966 to 1981

Period	French	English	Other
1966–71	–13 500	–52 200	–9 800
1971–76	–4 100	–52 200	–5 700
1976–81	–18 100	–106 300	–17 300

Source: Quebec, 1985.

increase of the Quebec population has been French mother-tongue: more precisely, 441 000 of a total of 519 000. As it happens, this 441 000 added to the 1971 French mother-tongue population of 4 866 000 gives us 5 307 000, exactly the 1981 French mother-tongue census population.

Yet, we just saw that, on balance, more francophones (4100 from 1971–76 and 18 000 from 1976–81) left Quebec for the other provinces than arrived from the same provinces (see Table 9). But, during the same ten-year period, between 35 000 and 40 000 French mother-tongue immigrants came to Quebec — notably 22 000 Haitians and a further 10 000 from France. These facts allow us to conjecture that between 13 000 and 18 000 French mother-tongue Quebeckers left Canada: more than 1000 a year but fewer than 2000 — rather few, given that the size of the French mother-tongue population is over 5 million.

Given the above, we can conclude that the recent relative decline in the demographic growth of Quebec — relative to that in the rest of Canada — is, above all, attributable to the departure of members of the English population.

Language Assimilation

Up to this point, we have touched on the evolution of population size, on natural increase and migration as factors determining this evolution, and (what is crucial in the Quebec context) on the *ethnic* composition (using mother tongue as a surrogate for ethnicity) of this population. What we have not touched on is the question of language use, as opposed to mother tongue.

The issue of language use and change in language use — language assimilation — provoked a heated debate, leading, as we mentioned in the introduction, to political action. Language assimilation became an issue 15 years ago, when it became generally appreciated that the number of people using English in their homes was substantially greater than those whose mother tongue was English.

And as, on the other hand, the number using French was only marginally greater than the number of those whose mother tongue was French, the issue was posed in terms of the relative power of attraction of the two languages and what was seen as, inevitably, a long-term deterioration of the status of the French language. The issue was, how many francophones were assimilating to English, and, of even more import, would other linguistic groups continue to opt massively for English?

A large body of research arose around these questions, inspired in particular by the work of Maheu, Castonguay, and Paille. This research and subsequent censuses have permitted a clearer picture of the phenomenon of language assimilation (or language "transfers," as they are called in the Quebec literature) in Quebec. The 1981 census data, as revised by Castonguay (1985), demonstrates that the initial published but "controlled" data was deceptive, the "controlling" process having created, for instance, 40 920 transfers from English mother tongue to French as the language of use in the home. After elimination of the multiple answers (the correction of which gave rise to the problems), the outcome of language-assimilation movements as reflected in the 1981 census is as depicted in Table 9.

As can be seen from the net transfers in section a of the table, English still has a superior power of attraction, having attracted 33 000 net from French; the breakdown by age group indicates no letup in this superiority, rather the contrary. However, the total of those that have assimilated from French to English is relatively small, 1.4 percent of the present French mother-tongue population; whereas those who have assimilated from English to French represent 6.5 percent of the present English mother-tongue population of Quebec. As for the Other mother-tongue population, English has attracted almost three times more individuals than has French. Section b in Table 9 analyzes the overall assimilation balances among Quebeckers as of 1981. In round figures, English has

Table 9

Intragenerational Language Assimilation in Quebec, 1981

a) Net Intragenerational Assimilation		
Direction of Assimilation		
French to English	Other to English	Other to French
33 305	74 865	24 475
b) Overall Assimilation Balances		
English	French	Other
108 170	–8 560	–99 610

Source: Reproduced from Castonguay 1985.

gained 108 000, French has lost 9000 and the Other mother-tongue population has lost 100 000.

Most of the gains to English are from the Other mother-tongue population rather than from French. As we pointed out earlier, three times as many Other mother-tongue language transfers are to English as opposed to French. Obviously, there are reasons, arising from the North American cultural and economic context, for this language behaviour. This is not the place to elaborate on or to try to fathom these reasons: suffice it to say that such a phenomenon is of great demographic consequence for Quebec society. Bill 101, with its measures for the francization of the work place and French-language schooling for immigrant children has been implemented precisely with this phenomenon in mind. The question now becomes whether Bill 101 has in fact been successful in terms of the issue it addressed.

Bill 101 did make French the predominant language of work in Quebec (Amyot 1985) and created a situation whereby the children of new immigrants found themselves in French-language schools (Paille 1985). As a result of these two developments, by the early 1980s there began to emerge what might be called a French-language public culture. Nevertheless, subsequent developments — the

referendum defeat, the triumph of neo-conservatism, the effects of the recession, and stagnating population growth have created a climate in which the French-language public culture has become extremely fragile. Indeed, the speed with which the population at large, French and English, is reverting to pre–Bill 101 patterns of linguistic behaviour is disconcerting. The moroseness that has overcome the nationalist movement in Quebec and the victory of the Liberal party in December 1985 have both contributed to this new climate.

Bill 101 itself generated, with its intended legal coercive effects, unintended effects that also contributed to the emergence of a French-language public culture. One of these effects was the selective nature of out-migration from Quebec in the late 1970s. As already mentioned, considerable numbers of anglophones chose to leave Quebec. Another effect made itself felt in both the volume and the linguistic composition of immigration. The negative, and largely undeserved, publicity that Bill 101 gave Quebec in the other provinces and internationally resulted in a decline in immigration; and of those who did come, a higher proportion than in the past were francophone. This brings us to a consideration of recent immigration streams to Quebec, their volume and their linguistic and ethnic composition.

Immigration

With regard to recent immigration, we begin by noting, as presaged in the above remarks, that recent immigration has had in its ranks a higher proportion of persons susceptible to assimilating to French: this is true, for instance of both the Haitians and the Indo-Chinese. Simultaneously, anglophone immigration currents, such as those originating in the former British Caribbean and to a lesser extent in the United States, have dried up since 1976. In this respect, it is worth noting that immigration to postwar Quebec has been made up of successive and ethnically different waves, and that the period of arrival as well as cultural affinities has had much to do with subsequent linguistic choices. From 1946 to 1955, the major waves were Italians (46 000) and Slavs (Poland 27 000; USSR 17 000), as well as 25 000 British immigrants, 11 000 French and 9000 Germans. From 1956 to 1965, the Italian wave crested (65 000), while 19 000 Greeks and 9000 Portuguese made their presence felt in Montreal, reflecting the newfound predominance of southern European immigration over that of the more traditional northern European groups (12 000 from the British Isles and 14 000 from France) and Eastern European groups (Poland 5000; Hungary 7000; USSR 1000). During the next ten years, 1966-75, Italy remained the major source of immigrants (21 000), but its importance diminished as the diversity of immigration increased. Along with substantial contingents from Greece (13 000), France (16 000), and Portugal (15 000), a host of immigrants from other countries made their presence felt in Quebec: Haitians (16 000); Egyptians (8000); Moroccans (16 000); Indians (6000); and Jamaicans and Trinidadians (8000). After 1976, Haitians predominated (13 000 from 1976 to 1981), while Vietnam (8000), France (6000), Lebanon (5000), and the United States (6000) were all well represented (Quebec 1986a). The figures for the period 1982-84 in Table 10 confirm this diversification trend.

In Table 11 we have provided a list of the ten most important groups of non-Canadian-born national groups in Quebec in 1981: the sediment of over half a century of international immigration and interprovincial migration. In this balance sheet, there are perhaps two surprises: the relative importance of Americans (almost as many as there are of British birth) and of Egyptians.

A similar table for 1986 would mark the appearance of the Vietnamese in the top ten and place Haiti in a higher position. Yet, these most recent developments only serve to confirm the increasingly diversified — and, as argued above, susceptible to making a French linguistic choice — nature of immigration to

Table 10
Immigrants to Quebec, 1982 to 1984: Ten Most Important Contingents, by Country of Origin

1.	Haiti	7 824
2.	Vietnam	4 231
3.	France	3 119
4.	Poland	2 263
5.	El Salvador	2 175
6.	Kampuchea	1 893
7.	United States	1 837
8.	Libya	1 428
9.	Morocco	1 291
10.	China	1 138

Source: Quebec 1982–84.

Table 11
Foreign-Born Living in Quebec, 1981: Ten Most Important Contingents, by Country of Origin

1.	Italy	88 000
2.	British Isles	42 000
3.	United States	38 000
4.	France	36 000
5.	Greece	28 000
6.	Haiti	26 000
7.	Portugal	21 000
8.	Poland	20 000
9.	Germany	15 000
10.	Egypt	14 000

Source: Quebec 1984.

Table 12
Concentration in Quebec of Ten Selected
Canadian Immigrant Populations, by Mother
Tongue, 1981

High Concentration	(%)
French	84.9
Cambodian	71.7
American	53.9
Yiddish	37.8
Greek	35.6
Low Concentration	
Swedish	3.2
Punjabian	2.0
Finnish	2.3
Dutch	3.0
Danish	3.0

Source: Quebec 1984.

Quebec. The present specificity of immigration to Quebec — relative to the rest of Canada — is reflected in Table 12, which lists
ten Canadian immigrant populations in terms
of their high (five groups) and low (five
groups) concentration in Quebec in 1981.

Procreation

Despite the changes that have taken place in
Quebec's demographic history with regard to
domestic and international migration, the
most fundamental changes have been at the
level of procreation. Moreover, changes at
this level — reflecting themselves in a lowered
natural increase — have put the problems of
out-migration and language assimilation into
relief and made issues out of phenomena that
are not at all new. We will review the procreation revolution in terms of changes in
marriage and fertility, beginning with the
former.[2]

Like other industrialized populations in the
Western world, Quebec has recently experienced a new pluralism with regard to the marital status of the adult population. The most
sensitive indicator, that of the number of marriages per 1000 population (see Table 13),

Table 13
Marital Behaviour in Quebec, 1969 to 1983

Year	Nuptiality Rate per 1000 Population	Total Divorce Rate per 100 Marriages
1969	7.9	8.7
1971	8.2	14.5
1973	8.6	22.0
1975	8.4	36.5
1977	7.7	35.5
1979	7.3	34.1
1981	6.4	44.3
1983	5.5	39.1

Source: Quebec 1985a.

reveals a continuing decline since the middle
of the 1970s. Yet, the total marriage rates of
the never-married, that is, the cumulative
marriage rates of all age groups under 50, reveal an even more precipitous decline (Quebec 1986). In the case of men, the rates passed
from 906 per 1000 in 1971, to 571 in 1981,
to 493 in 1984; whereas in the case of women
the rates for the same dates are 863, 579, and
514, respectively. This means, quite simply,
that if present trends continue to prevail, one
in two Quebeckers will not marry. Table 14
reveals that this is, in Western terms, a rather
exceptional performance.

The transition to this new state of affairs
was a steady progression, with no remarkable

Table 14
Rate of Total Nuptiality of the Never-Married,
Quebec, Canada, and Four Western European
Countries

Country	Year	Men	Women
Quebec	1983	.491	.502
Canada	1982	.656	.663
West Germany	1982	.609	.662
Denmark	1983	.496	.525
France	1983	.601	.627
Sweden	1981	.493	.516

Source: Quebec 1985a.

discontinuities, during the period 1971–83. However, the decline in nuptiality was arrested — for the first time in 12 years — in 1984, as the combined male and female rate bounced back from the floor of 500 per thousand population, moving up from 493 to 514. But it is too early to tell if the trend of the last 12 years has been reversed. As for the divorces of those who do marry, the number has varied considerably over the past 15 years. Following the liberalization of the divorce law in 1969, the number rose from 2947 in 1969 to 15 186 in 1976, falling back to 13 899 in 1980, only to climb again to 19 931 in 1981 (a gain of 38 percent in one year), levelling off at 16 845 in 1984 (Quebec 1985). Quebec is close to a situation whereby only half of the population marries, and of that half, between a quarter and a half divorces (Festy 1986, 42).

It is widely believed in Quebec that one consequence of this state of affairs has been a spectacular increase in the number of common law unions. Yet the census figures do not bear this out. In 1981, after the change in marriage behaviour described above was well underway, only 4.8 percent of the Quebec population 15 and over admitted to living common law, as opposed to 30.2 percent who were single, 56.5 percent married, 5.8 percent widowed, and 2.6 percent divorced (Canada Census 1981). Nonetheless, this was five years ago, and the proportion of the population living common law or divorced has certainly increased (Gautron 1986). As for the tendency of the divorced to remarry, it has declined from 603 per thousand divorced in the case of men and 521 in the case of women to 325 and 282, respectively, in 1983. What is in fact happening is that an increasingly important part of the population is living alone. This state is reflected in the ever-declining average size of households to 2.8 persons in 1984 as compared to 4.6 in 1953 (Canada 1986).

Yet, the dramatic decline in nuptiality notwithstanding, the precipitous drop in the fertility rate constitutes the most remarkable demographic development in Quebec since the great out-migration of 1850 to 1920 (Lavoie 1979). In the late 1950s (1955–60), Quebec still had one of the highest fertility rates in the industrialized world. Today it finds itself at the bottom of the list, with a rate similar to or lower than that of the Germanic and Scandinavian countries.

The phenomenon of fertility decline began to make itself felt in the late 1950s. It accelerated shortly thereafter and became precipitous in the late 1960s, with a fall of 28 percent in the three years from 1964 to 1967. A slippage in the fertility rate of this amplitude is rather extraordinary. It did, however, coincide with what is recognized as the watershed years in terms of fertility decline in Western Europe and North America generally. By 1969–70, the total fertility rate fell below the critical level of 2.1 children per woman required for replacement. Thereafter, it appeared to stabilize at around 1.8 between 1977 and 1979. This level (well below replacement) provoked much concern at the time. Yet, after 1979, the rate began to decline again, heading for a new floor just under 1.5 (1.454 in 1983 and 1.447 in 1984). Preliminary 1985 figures indicate a stabilization at just under 1.5, a far cry from the 4.0 of 1954.

However, the birth rate (births per thousand population; see Table 15) itself did not decline as rapidly in the 1970s as did the total fertility rate. In fact, the arrival of the baby-

---

Table 15

Total Fertility and Birth Rates, Quebec, 1954–1984

Year	Total Fertility	Birth Rate
1954	4.038	31.0
1959	3.988	28.8
1964	3.411	24.0
1969	2.186	16.6
1974	1.786	14.9
1979	1.752	15.8
1984	1.447	13.4

Source: Quebec 1985a.

boom generation at the age of maximum pro-creation (25–34 years) temporarily compensated for the decline in the number of births per woman. This effect was such that the birth rate, which was 14.6 in 1972, rose to 15.8 in 1979. Subsequently, however, the collapse of fertility was such that even this favourable evolution in the age structure of the female population was insufficient to compensate for the missing births per woman. Consequently, in 1984–85, the birth rate was in the range of 13 to 14 per thousand. What does the future hold in terms of the natural increase of the Quebec population? After 1986, the age structure of the female population will cease to favour more births; in fact, it will begin to move in the opposite direction. As for mortality, the rate has been vacillating between 6.7 and 7.0 per thousand population since 1960 but will begin to rise as soon as the population ages; we shall address this situation in the next section. Inexorably, given present trends, natural increase in Quebec will be negative by the turn of the century.

The Age Structure

As a consequence of the fertility decline, the population of Quebec is ageing (Lux 1983) faster than populations elsewhere in the industrialized world, although the imminence of this reality is being temporarily camouflaged by the baby-boom echo (births to baby-boomers). The Quebec Bureau of Statistics published a series of three population projections based on three different migration and fertility scenarios. These projections cast some light on the future in terms of the age-structure of the population (Quebec 1985a).

We have retained for our purposes the middle projection, leaving aside the lowest and the highest in terms of the population volumes they predict. This middle projection supposes that the number of children born per woman between 1986 and 1991 will be 1.6 per woman. This is considerably above the present number of 1.45. To better illustrate (see Table 16) the demographic future that this projection holds out for Quebec, we have listed the change in the proportion of the total population represented by four age groups, two at the bottom of the age pyramid (0–14 years and 15–29 years) and two overlapping age groups at the top end of the pyramid (50 years old and over, and 60 and over).

The ageing process is already well under way as the 0–14 group indicates, having passed from a total of 35 percent of the population in 1961 to 22 percent in 1981. Although the ageing process has yet to strike the active population, it will do so in the next 20 years. The age groups of those over 50 and those over 60 have, however, represented a steadily increasing proportion of the population since 1961. By the end of the period envisaged here, the year 2041, the proportion

Table 16
Evolution in Percentage of Certain Age Groups of the Quebec Population, 1961 to 2041

Year	0–14 Years	15–29 Years	50 and Over	60 and Over
1961	35	23	17	9
1981	22	29	23	13
2001	18	19	30	17
2021	16	17	41	27
2041	15	17	42	29

Source: Quebec 1985a.

in these four age groups will stabilize, by ascending age order, at 15, 17, 42, and 29 percent, respectively. In other words, half the population will be over 45!

Projections such as those represented by Table 16 have less and less credibility as the time to which they refer becomes more distant. Nonetheless, we can be sure of what will become of the adult population (20 years and over) in the course of the next 20 years, because these people are already born. Between 1954 and 1963 — the era of the last and most prolific decade of the baby boom — a groundswell was produced at the bottom of the age pyramid. This cohort, now in their 20s, is more numerous than that which preceded it or that which followed it: in 1984 it represented 1.25 million persons (aged 21–30) against 1.05 million persons 31–40 years old, who came before and 1.01 million persons 11–20 years old, who came after. These three cohorts represent 19, 16, and 15 percent of the population, respectively.

As the wave of those born between 1954 and 1963 — the prominence of which contrasts sharply with the 1966-to-1973 desert — works its way through the Quebec population age pyramid, it will have given the pyramid the form of a coniferous tree in 1980, that of a maple leaf in 2000, and the silhouette of a weeping willow in 2020, before disappearing between 2030 and 2040. The crest of this generation, those who were 24 to 29 years old in 1986, are those who have, since 1982, been experiencing the youth unemployment crisis — hence the somewhat conjunctural nature of this crisis. This same cohort will be the most prominent of all ten-year age groups for the next 35 to 40 years. It will make its presence felt continuously before coming to depend for its sustenance, after it reaches 65 years of age, on the meagre cohorts that succeed it. Furthermore, it is precisely this cohort that produced the lowest marriage and fertility rates, as well as a suicide rate higher than that of the rest of Canada, the United States, and most of Western Europe (Charron 1981).

Overall, the contemporary demography of Quebec is singular, not by virtue of the trends that have manifested themselves — trends in fact common to other industrial countries — but rather by the amplitude of these same trends that, in Quebec, have attained extremes unknown except in very rare instances in most "modern" industrial democracies. The fact that this extreme evolution has occurred with respect to several demographic phenomena points to something more than a chance or ephemeral circumstance. From the highest to the lowest fertility, from a traditional extended family-based society to a state of extreme fragility of marriage itself, low nuptiality and high divorce rates; the accompanying changes in values reflect, directly, the rather surprising ideological, electoral, and economic volatility of this same population. Since the 1950s, the most revealing aspect of change has been the velocity of these same changes. A dramatic manifestation of this velocity is the rapidity of recourse to female sterilization by tubal ligation in the early 1970s: in the short space of *two* years, the annual rate of sterilization by tubal ligation of women of childbearing age quadrupled, increasing from 4.2 percent in 1971 to 17.1 percent in 1973 (Lapierre-Adamcyck and Marcil-Gratton 1981, 11).[3]

A contributing but not sufficient factor in generating this velocity has been, we submit, the small Quebec population, made up of 5.5 million francophones in an anglophone continent. In the small states of Europe such as Switzerland, the Scandinavian countries, Holland, and Belgium — for the same reasons — one finds the same tendencies. Although there are, no doubt, other and perhaps more important factors behind the amplitude and velocity of the changes, the consequence of size alone merits consideration.

Returning to the very concrete and very present consequences of current demographic trends on the fabric of Quebec society, the decisive rupture — the beginning of the fertility collapse — took place at the beginning of the Quiet Revolution. Whereas it was 15 years later, at a time when the fall in fertility appeared to have been arrested between 1973 and 1979, that the marriage and divorce graphics began to take a strange turn. These interdependent changes — the fading of children from the social stage, and marriage instability — resulted in a decline in procreation that constitutes a world record. No sooner had Quebeckers come to grips with the fact that their society was no longer biologically perpetuating itself than they saw, on a not-too-distant horizon, the spectre of a rather brutal ageing of the whole society.

Political, Economic, and Social Consequences

In the previous section, we found a population that is about to stop growing and is ageing rapidly. Moreover, this population, which threatens to become more, rather than less, ethnically homogenous, is, at the same time, undergoing a process of atomization that is reflected in the ever-smaller families and average household size. Paradoxically, the same population, in terms of the people making it up, is more stable than it has been for a long time: fewer and fewer people are leaving Quebec and fewer and fewer are arriving. Incidentally, we also suspect that, despite the available figures on population distribution (Quebec 1986, 30–36) that Quebec is experiencing an increasing concentration of an almost constant population around the existing urban poles, and a reduction of population density in the rest of the inhabited territory. What, then, are the political, economic, and social consequences of these changes?

Political and Economic

Geopolitcally, the most obvious consequence of the present situation is a weakening of Quebec's political weight within the Canadian federation. As we pointed out earlier, Quebec has — for a variety of demographic reasons

— been able to maintain its three-tenths position in the Canadian demographic balance for over 125 years. This remarkable demolinguistic equilibrium (Lachapelle and Henripin 1980, 14–16) is now seriously threatened with the size of the Quebec population in the federation down to 28 percent in 1981, and even lower in 1986 (see also Paille 1986).

A second less obvious geopolitical consequence lies within Quebec's own territory: it is the potential threat to cultural, and eventually political, sovereignty represented by a failure to occupy adequately its territory. This potential problem presents itself in the peripheral areas, many of which are contiguous with other more demographically dynamic jurisdictions, such as Ontario and a number of American states. The lure of almost unoccupied territory in the Eastern Townships, the upper Ottawa valley, and the lower Gaspé regions may prove irresistible to those for whom the "open" border may seem a temporary obstacle.

The decline in the population of municipalities outside the shadow of the three metropolitan areas (Montreal, Quebec, and Hull) and the dozen or so regional urban centres will further reinforce the centralization process already underway, despite rhetoric to the contrary. Communities facing population decline, onerous debts, and a scarcity of available talent will not have the means or the will to oppose the logic of efficiency that presages further centralization.[4]

Economically,[5] the major consequences of the present demographic state of Quebec society will be the burdens of an ageing population and increased costs per person of the social infrastructure. George Mathews has dramatized the first consequence in his book *Le choc démographique* (1984). He points out that the short-term and immediate social-cost relief of the fertility decline is inversely related to the weight of the burden that will be occasioned by the implacable outcome of lowered fertility — an aged population.

As for the second consequence, increased costs per person of the social infrastructure, this is already upon us. Part of the legacy of the Quiet Revolution was an infrastructure built on the premise of a growing population, and the debt that goes with it. Population growth has since declined from 2.5 percent annually to 0.5 percent or less, whereas the accompanying debt has continued to grow (10 percent in the last year).

In fact, as the "French" Commission pointed out (Quebec 1986), Quebec is facing the prospect of a reverse investment dynamic. When investors and government foresee growth they undertake capital expenditures — production plant, housing, highways, hospitals, schools, etc. — to be paid for by a greater number of consumers or users in the future. The economic activity generated by these capital expenditures itself contributes to stimulating the banked-upon growth. When non-growth is foreseen, the opposite happens: no investments are made; and in some cases even already existing investments are not maintained or replaced; this amounts to disinvestment.

This process of decapitalization has clearly taken place in, for instance, Quebec's health-services sector, where hospitals and equipment are not being capitalized at a rate sufficient to maintain or replace them (Backley 1984, 38).

Although at present there is a flurry of construction activity in Quebec in residential and commercial facilities such as shopping centres and office buildings, there is no corresponding investment in industrial (Canada 1986) or social infrastructure. In fact, the consumer-oriented investment — housing, shopping centres, and office space for service-oriented companies — that is now taking place is being fuelled by the arrival in the market of the baby-boomers, the "groundswell" cohort born between 1953 and 1964. However, behind them there is no followup; within a decade, housing and commercial capacity will be so plentiful that there will be little need even to replace existing but obsolete facilities; hence, disinvestment in the consumer-oriented sector is also likely. Should this come to pass (as it will unless present demographic trends change), there will be (as Mathews points out) few jobs in construction, the activity that has been the mainstay of the Quebec economy since the war (Caldwell and Czarnocki 1977).

A striking example of overcapitalization relative to the effective market demand, and the subsequent decapitalization with the havoc that such a situation creates in terms of those stuck with the debts, is Quebec agriculture. Having increased, in real terms, capitalization by two and a half times in the ten-year period 1971 to 1981 (Caldwell 1986, 28), and now faced with declining demand, a productive capacity premised on growth has become superflous. As a result, the number of farmers in Quebec will probably decline by half in the last 20 years of the century as those saddled with too much debt abandon land and equipment at fire-sale prices to the high-equity-to-debt-ratio farmers who can afford to weather the crises. Those who leave the land will go to the regional urban poles, or in some cases to Ontario or the United States.

We conclude these brief remarks on the economic consequences of the contemporary demographic evolution of Quebec by remarking that the processes invoked here are the obverse confirmation of the thesis that in Quebec economic expansion is population-fuelled, and not vice versa, as conventional wisdom would have it. In answer to those who point out that income per capita in Quebec has been maintained or even improved relative to that of Ontario, we recall that, in 1950, the Quebec population was 89 percent of Ontario's and today it is less than three-quarters (74 percent).

Social

The difficulties faced in maintaining a social capital that was put into place in an investment perspective provide an example of the social consequences of Quebec's present demographic state. The stagnation, even decline, in the social infrastructure is reflected in the personnel of the public-administration establishment — which, when one includes all levels of government, includes over 40 percent of all employment — in which there is no expansion. No expansion — contraction, rather, is the rule — results in few openings and few promotions. Were the same situation to prevail in the private sector, one would get what Lise Bissonnette calls *une société bloquée*. Those who are securely installed in the bureaucratic apparatus, public or private, hesitate to venture elsewhere, knowing that opportunities are limited and that there is no coming back. Everyone stays put and new talent does not get beyond the door. A striking example of this is the CEGEP (junior college) establishment where, of 10 000 teachers, half would like to get out but do not dare (Gregoire et al. 1985).

In a blocked society that is moving toward greater ethnic homogeneity, the objectives of democratization and pluralism become more difficult to achieve. Democratization is easiest when "system" social mobility is possible: that is, when everyone moves up in terms of socioeconomic status because the system itself is expanding. This, in fact, happened in Quebec in the 1950s and 1960s. An expanding population, an expanding economy, and — more particularly in the case of Quebec's francophone population — an expanding public sector meant better jobs for all and intergenerational mobility was high. But there was also a political will to ensure democratization, particularly in health services, and to provide for equality of opportunity through an enlargement of the educational establishment.

In a context of system expansion, democratization as a political *leitmotif* was in everyone's interest. In a context of non-expansion, it is a different story. Every social formation, class or otherwise, looks after its own — if it did not it would cease to be an effective social force. In Quebec, the rough waters being encountered by democratization (the ideological and institutional bases to which the society committed so much energy and financial resources in the 1960s and 1970s)

are reflected in the flight from the public school. The private-school sector in Quebec is the fastest-growing private educational sector in Canada, having doubled its enrolment in a period in which public-school enrolments actually fell (Quebec 1985b). The institutionalization of the "pure science" route in high school and CEGEP as the elite corridor is another instance. Effectively, the pure-science option, beginning with the third year of high school, has replaced Greek and Latin as an elite screening process to the extent that it has become the best route of entry to even nonscience fields. Indeed, any middle-class child who can manage it would have to be very much of a maverick not to take the pure-science option (Bélanger 1979).

Pluralism and democratization are interdependent, the latter facilitating the former. Ideologically, Quebec society has, in the last 20 years, committed itself heavily to pluralism. Yet, a blocked society (at least as far as the public sector is concerned) and the decline of immigration lead to a different reality. A rather dramatic instance of this was the fate of the Quebec government's announced objective of increasing the presence of ethnic minorities in the public service (Quebec 1981): instead of rising from 5 to 9 percent between 1976 and 1985, the percentage actually declined (Quebec 1983). We have here an example of how corporate self-interest — the Quebec francophone civil service — in a period of contraction produces defensive postures that do not augur well for pluralism, be it ethnic or otherwise. In a small society, particularly in a period of contraction, it is difficult to countenance the same degree of value plurality that is possible in a larger society.

Indeed, the relationship that exists between the size of a society and its potential for pluralism is crucial. Inasmuch as pluralism is both a condition of and a driving force within a modern society, the demographic stagnation of Quebec is a threat to its continued existence. The rapid evolution of Western civilization in the last 20 years has led to a splitting apart of populations into heterogenous cultural fragments, distinguished by increasingly subtle criteria of taste, lifestyle, and economic priorities. This centrifugal process is underway in Quebec as elsewhere, albeit temporarily masked by the ephemeral preeminence of certain culturally innovative groups (yesterday the technocrats of the public sector, today the "Yuppies"). The process is not endogenous, but is accelerated by the confluence in Montreal of two poles of cultural diffusion, those of the United States and of France.

The risk to a small society in such a context is that none of the new cultural groups that emerge from an already limited population base will attain the threshold at which the number of adepts will be sufficient to generate a subculture rich and dense enough to play an integrating and innovative role. If it fails to attain the critical threshold, a subcultural group runs the risk of being stillborn, its members overcome by social atomization and psychic depression. The diversification of cultural affinities, implacable corollary of modernism, leads in a population of limited size to disintegration.

Quebec is then, we advance, condemned to confronting the following dilemma: either arrest cultural dispersion by putting up barriers to foreign cultural influences, or expand its population, especially in as far as the younger half of the age pyramid is concerned. This dilemma is all the more cruel for Quebec in that it is precisely the essence of modernity — the cultural force of our time emanating from New York — that leads to a fall in fertility and undermines the demographic rampart of peripheral societies. The ideological plurality, ethnic and cultural, of the great metropolitan centres, which is the manifest sign of their vigour, thus constitutes a mortal threat for the unsuspecting hinterland. Or, allegorically, the fire from the centre illuminates the hearth but scorches the forest, destroying by its very vigour the exterior and ultimate sources of its own regeneration. When the process is complete, there will be no more Jack Kerouacs to wander America, sparking a beat culture and a cultural revolution while

haunted until his death by his French-Canadian origins. He did not speak English until he was 14 (Waddel 1984).

The drama of contemporary Quebec is that, in achieving the much-sought-after modernism, it has effectively liquidated the essential spring of its survival as a society, its demographic dynamism. Worse yet, the comforting thought that by economic development it may regain the vitality necessary to survive in a modern world will prove to have been a cruel illusion when the present consumer-oriented mini-boom dries up for want of consumers; and when, because of a crippling debt burden on the shoulders of a constant or declining population, public sector- or government-stimulated investment in construction projects ("mega" or "mini") will no longer be possible. Such an outcome might have been averted had the tertiarization of the Quebec economy been turned around by the state-as-lever economics of the Quiet Revolution, but such was not to be, for reasons too complex to be invoked here. The only lever that remains — having used up the collective financial credit — is, as has always been the case, demographic; and, in the short term, this can only mean more (not less) immigration. Such a prospect is not very likely, given the present rather defensive and corporatist posture. This is rather a shame. It makes good economic sense to capitalize on an overdeveloped infrastructure and surplus human capital in the social services, health, and educational sectors, as well as on better-than-ever protective cultural legislation.

Unfortunately, there is no looking back from modernism, as George Grant in his *Lament for a Nation* (in which he foresees the inevitable modernization and subsequent demise of Quebec society) so eloquently pointed out. Yet, there lies in another essential spring of Quebec society — that is, its capacity for collective mobilization (itself a heritage of its premodern social structure and which, if the velocity and monolithic character of recent demographic change is any indication, still persists) — the key to averting the inevitable.

Notes

1. The enshrined ruins of the cathedral of St. Boniface in Winnipeg are a very dramatic symbolic representation of their defeat. Inside the ruins, a very much smaller cathedral was built.

2. Within the confines of this article, we shall not enter into the reasons for these changes; nor the question as to what extent the cross-sectional indicators (annual rates) reflect, or do not reflect, the longitudinal (behaviour of real cohorts) picture. In this respect and in so far as procreation in Quebec is concerned, compare Festy (1986).

3. The rate, of course, stabilized later at a lower level; nonetheless, 70 percent of Quebec women born in 1942 will be sterilized by 45 years of age (Festy 1986, 48), Furthermore, in 1981, half of tubal ligations were on women younger than 32 (Lapierre-Adamcyck and Marcil-Gratton 1981, iii).

4. For a demonstration of this, see the unpublished work of Charles Côté, Conseil de la famille, Government of Quebec.

5. For an insightful and precocious survey of the economic consequences of slowed growth in Quebec, see the study directed by Hervé Gauthier, particularly the conclusion (Quebec 1980).

Works Cited

Amyot, Michel. 1985. "La planification linguistique québécoise, bilan et orientation." *Le Conseil de la langue française, Québec.*

Backley, W. Alan. 1984. "Capital Expenditures for Hospitals." *Health Management Forums.* Summer: 36–42.

Bélanger, P.W. 1979. *Le rapport du comité d'évaluation pédagogique du college de Limoilou.* Quebec: Conseil d'administration, CEGEP Limoilou.

Caldwell, Gary. 1983. *Les études ethniques au Québec: bilan et perspectives.* Quebec: Institut québécois de recherche sur la culture.

———. 1986. *English Farmers in Quebec.* Research report. Quebec: Institut québécois de recherche sur la culture.

Caldwell, Gary, and Dan Czarnocki. 1977. "Un rattrapage noté, II. La variation à Court terme." *Recherches Sociographiques* 18(1): 9–58.

Canada. 1921–51. Census of Canada.

———. 1980–85. Yearbooks.

———. 1986. "Households." Series 64-202; "Investments in manufacturing." Series 61-205. Ottawa: Statistics Canada.

Castonguay, Charles. 1980. "Sur quelques indices de propension à l'exogamie et au transfert linguistique." *Cahier québécois de démographie* 9(3): 53–70.

———. 1985. "Transferts et semi-transferts linguistiques au Québec d'après les recensements de 1981." *Cahier québécois de démographie* 14(1): 59–85.

Charbonneau, Hubert, Jacques Henripin, and Jacques Légaré. 1970. "Avenir démographique des francophones à Québec et à Montréal en l'absence de politiques adequates." *Revue de géographie de Montréal* 24(2): 199–202.

Charron, Marie-France. 1981. *Le suicide au Québec.* Quebec: Ministères des affaires sociales.

Festy, Patrick. 1986. "Conjoncture démographique et rythmes familiaux: quelques illustrations québécoises." *Population* 1: 37–58.

Garigue, Philippe. 1956. "French-Canadian Kinship and Lubon Life." *American Anthropologist* 58(6): 1090–1101.

Gautron, Helene. 1986. "L'évolution démographique des personnes vivant seules au Québec, de 1966 à 1981." Paper presented at l'Association Canadienne Française pour Avancement des Sciences, Montreal.

———. 1964. "Folk society." *French-Canadian Society.* Eds. Marcel Rioux and Yves Martin. Toronto: McClelland and Stewart.

Gregoire, Reginald, et al. 1985. *Etude de la pratique professionnelle des enseignants et des enseignantes du Cegep: ou l'autre Cegep.* Quebec: Conseil des collèges.

Joy, Richard. 1972. *Languages in Conflict: The Canadian Experience.* Toronto: McClelland and Stewart.

Lachapelle, Réjean, and Jacques Henripin. 1980. *La situation démolinguistique au Canada: évolution passée et prospective.* Montreal: The Institute of Research on Public Policy.

Langlois, Georges. 1934. *Histoire de la population canadienne-française.* Montreal: Editions Albert Levesque.

Lapierre-Adamcyck, Evelyne, and Nicole Marcil-Gratton. 1981. *La sterilisation au Québec, 1971-1979.* Montreal: Departemente de démographie, Université de Montréal.

Lavoie, Yolande. 1979. *L'immigration des Québécois aux Etats-Unis de 1840 à 1930.* Quebec: Conseil de la langue française.

Lux, André. 1983. "Un Québec qui vieillit. Perspectives pour le XXIe siècle." *Recherches sociographiques* 24(3).

Maheu, Robert. 1980. *Les francophones du Canada: 1941-1971.* Montreal: Editions Parti Pris.

Mathews, George. 1984. *Le choc démographique: le déclin du Québec est-il inevitable?* Montreal: Boréal Express.

Paille, Michel. 1986. *Consequences des politiques linguistiques québécoises sur les effectifs scolaires selon la langue d'enseignement.* Quebec: Conseil de la langue française.

Quebec. 1980–85. *Annuares statistiques du Québec.*

———. 1981. *Autant de façon d'être Québécois.* Quebec: Ministère du développement culturel et scientifique.

———. 1982. *La démographie québécoise: passé, présent, perspectives.* Quebec: Office de planification et de développement du Québec.

———. 1982–84. *L'immigration du Québec: Bulletin Statistique.* Annual. Quebec: Ministère des communautés culturelles et de l'immigration.

———. 1983. *Comité d'implantation du plan d'action à l'intention des communautés culturelles: rapport annuel 1981–1982.*

———. 1984. *Quelques caractéristiques ethnoculturelles de la population du Québec.* Cahier II by Mireille Baillargeon and Gisele Ste-Marie. Quebec: Ministère des communautés culturelles et de l'immigration.

———. 1985a. *Etude de l'impact culturel, social et économique des tendances démographiques actuelles du Québec, comme société distincte.* Quebec: Assemblée nationale. Commission parlementaire permanente sur la culture. [The "French" commission in honour of its president, the deputy Richard French.]

———. 1985b. *L'avenir démographique du Québec.* Quebec: Bureau de Statistique du Québec.

———. 1985c. *Statistiques de l'enseignement.* Quebec: Ministère l'education du Québec.

———. 1986. *La situation démographique du Québec.* Quebec: Bureau de Statistique du Québec.

Rudin, Ronald. 1985. *The Forgotten Quebecers: A History of English-Speaking Quebecers, 1759–1980.* Quebec: Institut québécois de recherche sur la culture.

Saturday Night. 1985. June: 20.

Waddel, Eric. 1984. Symposium on Jack Kerouac, Quebec City.

Part Three

DATING, MATING, AND MATE SELECTION

• • •

When one thinks of how many people there are that one does not in the least want to marry, and how many there are that do not in the least want to marry one, and how small one's social circle really is, any marriage at all seems a miracle.

Barry Pain, *Readers Digest* (1952)

Canadians almost universally endorse the idea that the selection of a marriage mate is, and should be, a matter of individual preference. Unlike people in many other countries, we believe in the right of brides and grooms to make their own choice of partner, rather than having their liaisons arranged for them by parents or by marriage brokers. This endorsement of "free" mate selection does not mean that the mate-selection process is a random one that is left to chance and circumstance. It merely means that the social forces that encourage some marriages while discouraging others are so culturally pervasive that their influence is indirect, subtle, and perhaps even below the level of awareness. If asked, most individuals would say that they decide to get married because they fall in love. However, they are not always aware that a wide range of influences determines the kind of person they will consider attractive enough that they will "choose" to fall in love and want to marry.

In thinking about mate selection, it is important to make a distinction between dating and courtship. The purpose of dating is primarily to have fun. It is intrinsically rewarding as an end in itself. The ideal date, therefore, is someone who is interpersonally appealing in some way, for at least a short period of time. In contrast, the purpose of courtship is to select and woo a future husband or wife. Courting may also be intrinsically rewarding, but it has the extrinsic purpose of husband-shopping or wife-shopping. The ideal mate is someone who is not only appealing for a short period of time, but will be a satisfactory life partner and (for many) an adequate mother or father. None of those ideals necessarily has much to do with being a good dancer or driving an expensive car. However, it is the dating filter, based on rather frivolous criteria, that defines the actual pool of eligibles from which husbands and wives are selected.

Another major factor in the mate-selection process is the factor of *propinquity* or nearness. To see how these components work in practice, let us consider the mate-selection process of a young Catholic woman of 25, who has never been married, and who is a university student in Montreal. Theoretically, this woman might marry any unmarried adult male. Most likely, however, she will marry someone close to her own age. Of all marriages that took place in Canada in 1981, 70.6 percent involved a bride and groom who were four years or less apart in age (see Table 3, p. 00). Her prospective groom could, therefore, be a man of any age, but most likely will be in his twenties. He will also likely be someone who is Catholic, who has never been married before, and who has at least some university education. These few simple parameters markedly reduce the effective pool of prospective husbands from all single Canadian males to only a select few. If our young woman living in Montreal does not travel to other cities, her effective pool of eligible men is Catholic, university-educated, unmarried men in their twenties *who live in Montreal.* More precisely still, it involves those eligible men in Montreal *whom she can meet.* More precisely still, it really involves those eligible men in Montreal whom she can meet *and whom she can date at least once.* One seems to select one's mate from a vast array of choices: in fact, one selects one's mate from the relatively small number of persons who are dating partners. Increasing recognition of the restrictive nature of the dating filter is leading to a number of innovations in mate selection, such as the use of personal advertisements or of introduction services.

About the Articles

Falling in love involves not only a feeling state but also a shift in the balance of power between persons. Zetterberg's speculative but provocative article offers some insights into the dynamics of how such changes happen, and of the potential for exploitation that they evoke. The theme of power is further elaborated by McCormick and Jesser, who point out that contemporary courtship has changed from a goal-oriented encounter ending in marriage to a process-oriented encounter that may or may not relate to mate selection. Increased sexual permissiveness and a decline of the double standard have led to marked

changes in the rituals and dialogues associated with seduction and rejection.

Mate selection today involves not only young persons considering a first liaison and/or marriage but also formerly married persons, most of them divorced, who form a new singles subculture. Veevers documents how women in midlife and older are subjected to a real "marriage squeeze" because of the increasingly pronounced imbalance in sex ratios among the unmarried population. This reality has many implications, including the emergence of a demographic double standard that augments the traditional double standard.

Endogamous norms concerning ethnicity tend to perpetuate ethnic identity from one generation to the next. Goldstein and Segall present data to show how interethnic marriages affect the retention of ethnic identity among persons in Winnipeg.

Further Readings

Bibby, Reginal W., and Donald C. Posterski. 1985. *The Emerging Generation: An Inside Look at Canada's Teenagers.* Toronto: Irwin.

Harold, Edward S. 1984. *Sexual Behaviour of Canadian Young People.* Markham, ON: Fitzhenry and Whiteside.

Jansen, Clifford. 1982. "Inter-Ethnic Marriages." *International Journal of Comparative Sociology* 23: 3–4.

Lambert, Ronald D., and James E. Curtis. 1984. "Québécois and English Canadian Opposition to Racial and Religious Intermarriage, 1968–1983." *Canadian Ethnic Studies* 16: 30–46.

Redmond, Marcia A. 1985. "Attitudes of Adolescent Males Towards Adolescent Pregnancy and Fatherhood." *Family Relations* 34: 337–42.

Travato, Frank. 1988. "A Macrosociological Analysis of Change in the Marriage Rate: Canadian Women, 1921–25 to 1981–85." *Journal of Marriage and the Family* 50: 507–21.

THE SECRET RANKING

Hans L. Zetterberg

After all, what is marriage? . . . It completely regulates the life of passion . . . and closes the horizon.

Durkheim

In a business enterprise, the president wanted to fire his obvious crown prince. The board of directors objected, because they liked the up-and-coming man, had invested company funds in his training, and had gladly met the offers he had received from competitors by paying him a very high salary; in fact, they had done all this at the suggestion of the present who now wanted him fired. A look into the situation showed that the president's private secretary had fallen in love with the young man. As far as one could tell, it was a purely emotional surrender and involved no sexual relations nor any proven attempts by the young man to get access to information that should remain confidential with the secretary and her boss. Nor was there any indication that the president and the secretary were or had been lovers. Yet the behaviour of the parties resembled the triangle of a love story in which an older rival attempted, with aggressive unreason, to remove a younger one. After a consultation with a sociologist, the problem was readily solved at modest cost to the corporation by removing the secretary instead of the young man. She was helped to a better job with another company; a storm in an office teapot had been averted and a company had been saved the high cost of replacing an executive.

This incident is trivial enough and, on the surface, hardly worth much attention from

Source: *Journal of Marriage and the Family* 28 (1966): 134–42. Reprinted with permission.

the consulting sociologist. However, conceptualizing a problem like this one to gain a basis for a recommendation is not simple. The ready-made sociological view of the above problem conceives of the young man as a charismatic leader who, by the personal loyalties he can command, disturbs the formal authority of other offices and upsets the work flow in the organization (Etzioni 1961). Given this diagnosis, the alternative solutions to the problem, with the most preferable one last, would be to remove or isolate the young executive, keep him where he is but neutralize his charisma, or let him assume a formal authority within the organization that matches his charismatic authority so that his charisma works for organizational rather than personal aims.

In the above instance, this sophisticated model appeared less relevant. Psychodynamic as well as commonsense talk about love and jealousy seemed as close to the truth as theories of routinization of charisma, although neither seemed entirely relevant. The sociological consultant had hit on a helpful solution for his client, but he did not really know why it was helpful. The process of applying social theory to a practical problem had revealed a hole in his theoretical knowledge.

Wading through some similar problems, one eventually stumbles on ideas for a new theory that allows a diagnosis more sensitive to the facts involved. In helping a board of directors to tackle problems such as major reorganizations or firing the big executive, there is always a need to know the actual hierarchy and communication flow within the organization. Because the organizational chart is too rough an approximation of these patterns, a consultant pursues other ways to establish who has power and prestige and who can talk effectively with whom. In the course of establishing the real hierarchy and the real communication pattern, the consultant repeatedly encounters a latent but significant rank order that, for want of a better term, might be called the *erotic ranking*. The young man in our illustration had bypassed his boss in the erotic ranking within the company. The reaction of the boss is understandable from the dynamics of interaction in hierarchies, and the solution recommended by the consultant is one of several that are compatible with well-known theories of relations between ranks. The missing link in our theoretical knowledge turns out to be the concept of erotic ranking.

Therefore, we will now present a theory of erotic ranking. The evidence backing the theory is admittedly anecdotal. Nevertheless, a concept of erotic ranking can claim a status in science as a hypothetical entity that may be used to explain some findings, familiar events, and common sayings in stories about love. Today, such a concept is justified only as a theoretical construct — like the electron in early atomic theory — that forms necessary conceptual bridges between a variety of theory fragments. At some future date, researchers may actually have found a way to measure it objectively and study it directly.

Overcomeness and Secrecy

Erotic rankings enter into the "rating-dating complex" observed on some American campuses (Walter 1937) as well as in other patterns of courtship. Their operation, however, is usually intermingled with and obscured by other more conventional rankings. The hero of the football field, the owner of the flashy sports car, the president of the fraternity, and the senior student are ranking persons on campus not primarily because of their position in an erotic stratification, but because of their position in the hierarchies of athletics, publicity, consumption, power, and occasionally education. The rating-dating complex is highly visible; one advertises one's rank by being seen with a ranking figure in public. The point of the rating-dating game is to catch a high-ranking partner and be seen together. By contrast, the erotic ranking is incognito.

The secrecy of the erotic hierarchy, as we know it, may be reinforced by the puritan culture in which it is encountered. Yet the private nature of the erotic hierarchy is best seen as a part of its definition; the emotional "overcomeness" we here deal with thrives only in privacy. It stands to reason that the one who has surrendered emotionally is unwilling to have this fact advertised; but one may go further — although hesitantly — to say that to show this kind of overcomeness openly is to change its very nature. To preserve it, all parties must keep it from open inspection by others. The erotic hierarchy, as well as love, belong in "the hidden society." The erotic rank is one of the secrets of love. "Love is sacred in that its secrets are essential and must remain secrets if the phenomenon is not to change character," says Aubert (1965, 209). An erotic rank may also be one of the aspects of a profound sexual union and as such resist public analysis. What Doris Lessing in her *Golden Notebook* says about the difficulty in writing about sex for women applies particularly to the emotional overcomeness that defines erotic rank: "Sex is best when not thought about, not analysed. Women deliberately choose not to think about technical sex. They get irritable when men talk technically, it's out of self-preservation: they want to preserve the spontaneous emotion that is essential for their satisfaction."

The private aspect of the erotic ranking makes it an elusive topic of study. Novelists have, of course, dealt with it. In the classical erotic literature, one may single out *Les liaisons dangereuses* (Laclos 1782) as exposing erotic stratification and describing the ascents and descents of its ladder. The steps up and down are not necessarily signalled in the form of sexual relations between the principals — such instances, although plentiful, are rather trivial from the point of view of a person's placement in the erotic hierarchy — but as events when someone no longer is the master over his or her feelings. The critical events are the emotional surrenders, not the sexual conquests as such.

Throughout its long existence *Les liaisons dangereuses* has been considered viciously immoral and pornographic. Although it lacks a close-up view of sexual acts, like pornography it violates a privacy taboo, the private quality of emotional surrender. The naked struggle for erotic hegemony — the pursuit of erotic success rather than erotic pleasure — among the characters in Laclos's book so affects the readers that they respond by putting the book into the pornographic category. It is precisely this strong reaction against making the erotic ranking public that suggests an element of privacy in its definition.

To sum up: a person's erotic ranking is the secretly kept probability that he or she can induce an emotional overcomeness among persons of the opposite sex. It is not altogether the same as love, for "love is a many-splendoured thing"; but it enters as an element of love.

A rank in the erotic hierarchy can presumably be assigned to an individual, but it is discernible only in the individual's interaction with others. For a man and woman, we get two measures — one, her surrender to him; the other, his surrender to her. For larger groups, the establishment of erotic ranks becomes more complicated because we obtain more measures than there are persons. The problem in quantifying the ranks is not likely to get out of hand because of the requirement of privacy, which tends to keep the groups small. Probably the mathematics used to calculate sociometric ranks from friendship choices can be adapted to calculate erotic ranks. For sexual minorities, such as homosexuals, the measures must relate to the object of their choice, regardless of its gender.

In searching for the erotic hierarchy, one cannot expect to find it equally pronounced everywhere. In the lowest classes of society, this hierarchy might be more salient than elsewhere. Because the poor, powerless, and uneducated have bottom positions in all other respects, they may turn more to the rewards offered by erotic ranks. Erotic rankings are particularly significant among teenagers, who have not yet grown into the ordinary community ranks that dominate adult life. Probably teenagers will forever remain puzzling unless we learn to understand interaction in erotic hierarchies. It also makes sense to assume that the erotic hierarchy is more salient in co-educational organizations, such as hospitals, laboratories, and offices, than in settings where one sex prevails. (The common conception of army life as preoccupied with erotic ranks may not be entirely correct.) Nevertheless, the question as to in what settings this ranking becomes dominant remains puzzling. In some occupational communities (such as filmdom and advertising), the erotic hierarchy is part of the folklore, but in others (as in publishing and banking) it is not. Variations also seem great between otherwise similar organizational structures. In one university department, the erotic stratification may be so emphasized that the female graduate student who is offered an assistantship does not know whether her academic or erotic competence has brought her the job. In the same university, there may be other departments in which academic competence rules supreme. An easy — perhaps too easy — explanation for these differences is that the leaders of an occupational community or the heads of divisions and departments set personal examples that eventually spread among their subordinates.

Since erotic hierarchies are made up of secret ranks, everything we know about secrets, ranks, and stratifications should apply to them. Therefore, we turn our attention to existing theories of these phenomena.

Secret Societies

A secret group has several features. The political conspiracy, the guerrilla, the insiders trying to corner the stock market, the spy network — all engage in activities that, if revealed to the general public or its law-enforcement agencies, would cause failure and disaster to the group. Common to all these, therefore, as shown by Georg Simmel (1908, ch. 5) are several societal devices to protect the secret.

When an erotic hierarchy is made public to the participants and their environment, an unusual amount of disgust and sense of degradation seems to spread among them. This may again be mostly a result of our puritan culture, or, as previously suggested, this may be the nature of the beast. The erotic hierarchy never seems the same after it has been publicized, and making it visible generally leads to reorganization of social relations. Hence, the erotic hierarchy is a secret to be preserved. Around it forms a group with the characteristic norm of secret societies — thou shall not squeal. The continued social relations of the group depend on the observance of this norm.

The preservation of the secrecy of erotic ranks is further guaranteed if the participants are also involved in other activities that require privacy. Lawrence Durrell concludes correctly, in his *Alexandria Quartet*, that love reinforced by conspiracy is the most unbreakable kind.

The instability of love is otherwise proverbial. This may be attributable to the fact that the stability of a secret rank is not a simple average of the stability of secrets and the stability of ranks. Secrets can be very stable; some family skeletons in the closet undoubtedly count their age in decades. Ranks can also be very stable; some count their age in centuries. But the chemistry of social life does not guarantee, any more than does the chemistry of matter, that a compound formed by two stable elements will also be stable. Among the unstable sociological compounds, we count the secret ranks; for ranks do not naturally stay incognito but need public recognition, and secrets about glorious things urge to be told and thus lose their secrecy. Here, then, is a possible explanation for the fleeting quality of love — yesterday it was with us; today we are uncertain about it; and tomorrow it is gone.

The most heinous crime in a secret society is to inform outsiders. The informer threatens the very existence of his group, and therefore gets the most despised status in the group. The outside world may give the informer some compensation for loss of status in the in-group, as long as he or she keeps informing. (Hence, the pressure on the informer to fabricate evidence about the in-group.) In the end, however, the out-group distrusts the informer.

Those who gossip about erotic ranks and give them away are treated very much like informers, wreckers of something worthwhile. Even the person who takes a problem involving an erotic ranking to a marriage counsellor or psychiatrist may be given the stigma of an informer, and, as such, is never really welcome back into the group whose secret was revealed.

The norm against informing applies with equal force to an offended party who has lost his or her erotic rank. Smarting under jealousy and the pain of having been replaced, bypassed, or abandoned, those who complain publicly about their degradation will not readily be reinstated to their former rank. Thus, the old advice "grin and bear it" applies to all such degraded persons who want to keep a realistic possibility of regaining a lost love.

The norm against informing applies to those who have gained erotic rank. One must not brag about this rank if it is to be kept. If a person illicitly has made an advance, and guilt feelings have accompanied his or her climb in the erotic hierarchy, clinical practice allows the person to talk about it. While a confession may help in coping with guilt, it may destroy the person's standing with the loved one and lower his or her erotic rank. Thus, the usual ideology of clinical counselling with its "let's-talk-about-it" and "tell-it-all" rules is not necessarily appropriate here.

Visibility of Erotic Ranks

A general rule about the way in which we perceive hierarchies, first used by Max Weber (1922, I), may be formulated in this way: if a given dimension of ranking becomes less-visible, associates tend to assume that a person's position on this less-visible dimension is commensurate with his or her ranks on the visible dimensions. When, for example, Calvinist theology made a person's religious standing invisible — no one but God knew who belonged among the elect or the damned — the ordinary Calvinist parishioners began to use their visible stratification criteria as a symptom of their religious standing. Economic success, in particular, was thought to be an indicator of religious standing. A rank held on the visible dimensions thus suggested the rank on the invisible one.

This proposition is obviously relevant for erotic hierarchies, since, by definition, they are private. We all have seen instances in which students fall for their teachers, airline stewardesses for their pilots, theatre-going gentlemen for a ballerina or actress, men for the rich belle at the ball, nurses for their doctors, secretaries for their bosses, teenagers for a pop idol, laboratory assistants for a scientist, the females in the congregation for the minister, and so on. In these instances, they may be attracted to an assumed high erotic rank: ranks in the world of money, power, academic competence, sacredness, and artistic taste provide cues for assumed erotic ranks. Of course, the high community rank need not be real; to start this process, it is enough if it appears high.

Many novels describe a seduction process that makes use of the likelihood of falling for visible ranks. The plot may show an ambitious but poor family banding together in an attempt to appear blue-blooded and honourable. They sacrifice to dress up one of the daughters to attract desired suitors. The prospect falls for the visible and is then stuck with the privately kept truth. This may help explain why someone with a low erotic rank can be a little Casanova. A man who has many conquests but who nevertheless lacks a commanding erotic rank can, with the help of this process, seduce his ladies by emphasizing his visible rank, be it real or faked. Often enough, such men give an appearance of riches that is not backed by a careful credit investigation,

or academic honours not backed by a check of school or university records, or a noble background that is faked. The philanderer is called "false," and this may be true in more than one sense.

If a surrender to visible status is pursued into the private world of the object of infatuation, the actual erotic rank may end up being very different from the one inferred from visible status characteristics: for example, the famous doctor may turn out to be a narrow-minded bore, the rich girl a drab lover, and the celebrated actor or popular singer an insecure mother's boy. That "disappointment in love" should be a prevailing theme is thus quite predictable.

The constellation of a high visible rank in the larger community but a modest erotic rank leads to a pattern in which people attract partners but soon find that they are dissatisfied. Either they leave, or they hang on for reasons other than erotic ones. Persons with this constellation of ranks thus change partners quite often. One mistakenly speaks of their "high sex drive" or their "nymphomania" or "philandering." The truth probably is that they cut a painfully modest erotic rank. Perhaps the most stable relation or marriage they can have is with a "gigolo," that is, a person who uses and comforts the unhappy, lowly erotic state of another in return for money or the other advantages of the victim's high community rank.

The frequent failure of marriages formed after brief courtships may also be seen in this context. Both lay and professional marriage counselling holds that one should not make lasting commitments on the basis of a first love-impulse. We can perhaps refine this and say that love is fine as a basis for immediate commitment, but since it consists of rather private qualities, invisible to the outside, it takes time to cut through the visible, misleading paraphernalia. "Love is blind," one says. Its blindness can be of two entirely different kinds: one can fail to see things that are there, and one can see things that are not there. The person who is falling in love is usually blind in the second sense: the presence of visible desired attributes leads us to believe that the less-visible desired quality is there. Great love can be blind in the other sense: our erotic rank exalts us so that no other consideration matters; concern over worldly station and the pursuit of ordinary goals become totally unimportant by comparison. As Antony said to Cleopatra, "We have kissed away kingdoms and provinces."

The Psychodynamics of Erotic Ranks

Like other ranks, the erotic rank is accorded a person by others. It cannot simply be taken, but must be granted. Those who speak and act as if they were generals, kings, or physicians without being certified by others as occupants of such ranks are treated as fools or psychiatric cases. Erotic ranks are accorded by others; but the private, small groups in which this takes place make the process more personal. Thus, love is said to be not a right but "a gift." Those who lay claim to erotic ranks that are not theirs, given them freely, are the fools of love.

We know from the theory of the looking-glass self (Cooley 1902, 193-95) that a person's rank is reflected in his self-evaluation. Low-ranking strata of the population have a lower conception of their own worth than have the established high strata. Thus, we also expect a high self-esteem among persons who are superiors in the erotic hierarchy.

The dynamics of interaction in hierarchies are linked to the psychodynamics of the self-image. The topic is too complicated to cover here; but it should be pointed out that the direct relation between a person's downward move in the erotic hierarchy and threats to his or her self-esteem allows us to pursue a number of psychodynamic mechanisms described in the clinical literature. The erotic downgrading leads to the whole web of aggression, projections, reaction-formations, regressions, distortions, and rationalizations that fill the psychiatric and clinical dialogues.

A comfortable self-esteem is an asset in most social relations; it allows a person to have greater tolerance for ambiguity, depart with greater ease from conventional ways, assume more readily the tasks of leadership, and be less anxious in new situations. To the extent that we need such persons to fill particular positions in society and organizations, we must also pay attention to their place in the erotic hierarchy. Commonsense considerations about the importance of "virility" in a man and "poise" in a woman when they are judged for a job can in this way receive a theoretical rationale.

The pressure to equalize erotic rank with other ranks can also be observed. We have, in other words, a new application of the Rank Equalization Theorem (Benoit-Smullyan 1944). A person who gets his self-esteem built up by community ranks signifying money, power, or knowledge will not tolerate a low erotic rank that hurts his self-conception. Throughout history, the high and the mighty have usually extracted a tribute from the opposite sex and considered it their fair due. Public opinion has usually accepted that the strong deserve the beautiful. On the other hand, someone without high community rank who is firmly established in a high erotic rank can lay claim to power, money, and other kinds of status. Public opinion, as it is captured in fairy tales, rationalizes this tendency — he who wins the princess's heart gets half the kingdom, while the rivals who lose leave the court and the land to seek their fortune elsewhere. Whether some comings and goings of executives, politicians, white-collar workers, and professionals in the real world follow parallel principles is an open question.

However, among the norms that govern interactions in all hierarchies are always some that reduce the risk of capricious downgrading in rank. Arbitrary demotions lead to more than personal agonies for the degraded; they confuse the communication system and destroy morale among those who remain in the ranks — hence, the pressure for tenure or other safeguards.

The Justice Proposition in theoretical sociology, formulated by George Homans (1961, ch. 12), says that resentments are generated among those who see others obtain high ranks without commensurate effort. Bitterness particularly besets those who, in spite of committed strivings, fail to advance and are left by the wayside. It is conceivable that this applies also along the erotic hierarchy. For the erotically high might be envied much like the very rich or the very powerful. Some lows may conceivably band together against someone high and plot his or her downfall. A high may behave like a typical snob and contemptuously ignore the lows; or, if someone is on the rise in an erotic hierarchy, an established high may put all kinds of blocks in his or her way. All this may be observed in adolescent society.

However, nowhere in history have we seen recorded an outright erotic class struggle. The reason for this is presumably the secret nature of the erotic ranking. What we do not know cannot be a basis for class consciousness. An individual or a small coalition of individuals can protest on the basis of indignation at their erotic ranks; but nothing can be observed on the level of the total society.

Hugh Duncan (1962, ch. 24) has made a good case for the proposition that equals in rank have a broader spectrum of communication and also enjoy being together more than those who talk and meet as superiors and inferiors. While experimental support for this contention is largely missing, we may assume that equals in erotic rank get along best. They surrender to each other in equal shares and seem to have a wide range of conversation and fun. The matchmaker is probably most successful when pairing off equals. Yet minor asymmetries in erotic ranks are as common as in other kinds of status; one person usually outranks another, and one usually surrenders more than the other. When the asymmetries are large, the problems may be great; there is immeasurable agony in loving without being loved in return. However, even small rank differences can have large emotional con-

sequences. Baudelaire, in his *Intimate Journals*, pinpoints the torture these differences may bring.

> For even when two lovers love passionately and are full of mutual desire, one of the two will always be cooler or less self-abandoned than the other. He or she is the surgeon or executioner; the other, the patient or victim. Do you hear these sighs — preludes to a shameful tragedy — these groans, these screams, these rattling gasps? . . . A terrible pastime, in which one of the players must forfeit possession of himself.

The adviser in matters of the heart has to deal with interaction in hierarchies, although his or her work is not usually perceived in these terms. Marriage counselling may have much to learn from the general study of interaction in hierarchies, conducted on the level of organizations, markets, and communities. And the experience of marriage counsellors may benefit those who consult with large complex organizations. We must lift our thinking to a theoretical level with enough informative value to apply to all hierarchies.

Achievement and Ascription in Erotic Stratification ✗

The motivation to hold one's rank in the erotic hierarchy may be considered universal. However, the motivation to achieve higher ranks is something that develops only under special circumstances, if we are to assume that it follows the pattern of other varieties of achievement motivation. The circumstances that give rise to achievement motivation include a person's encounters with those who use more demanding scales of status symbols to gauge the person's standing than the ones to which he or she is accustomed. When the person takes over these more demanding standards of self-evaluation, he or she simply must do better. Since status symbols change according to a dynamic of their own, the individual has little control over the process. For example, in an expanding economy an individual must achieve to keep up with the Joneses, to maintain standing.

Applied to our problem, this means that, the more invidious comparisons of erotic ranks are made, the more pronounced becomes the desire to climb the erotic ladder. By keeping the erotic hierarchy secret, society discourages a large-scale emergence of erotic achievers.

The question of ascription, that is, the measures taken to keep persons in a given position, applies to all hierarchies, including the erotic one. In our culture, the social norms allow a person to achieve along the erotic hierarchy during courtship, but frown on efforts to make others surrender after he or she is married. Marriage thus follows the pattern of academic achievement; one is free to aim high, and, once the chosen degree is achieved, no one is allowed to remove it. What is gained through achievement becomes ascribed. A wedding in Western culture is like a college commencement ceremony, transforming an achieved status into an ascribed one to last for better or worse until death does the parting. The difficulties in upholding this pattern are apparent in the divorce statistics.

The secrecy of the erotic hierarchy keeps opportunities hidden from view, so that they do not generate temptations to pursue further heights of the hierarchy. That erotic achievement would stop, for all practical purposes, at the cutting of the wedding cake seems problematic, because the rest of society nowadays is arranged so that opportunities for erotic advancement are present in virtually every setting, particularly in the white-collar city. Love stories as well as pornography aid the process of breaking down secrecy, making it a less efficient check. The literature on love is not merely a more or less idle pursuit of more or less artistic value with more or less beneficial effects on the sexual imagination. It also helps to remove ascription from the erotic hierarchy. Since secrecy about the erotic ranking aids a conservative view of marriage, it is understandable that conservatives — although they do not usually know why — are against Kinsey-type research and favour censorship of books on love and sex.

Anomie in Erotic Ranks

The most interesting insights into the concept of the erotic hierarchy come from its confrontation with the theory of anomie. Anomie (as Durkheim [1906] used the term) is what prevails outside our customary range of ranks. A sudden loss of all one's money removes a person from accustomed rewards. Likewise, to quickly come into a huge amount of money places a person outside the security of the familiar range. Such sudden changes up or down leave the individual without bearings and are dangerous; in extreme cases, they may result in suicide.

The secret nature of the erotic hierarchy implies that people in general have a very limited accustomed range of erotic scale. Breakouts into anomic territories are therefore possible for most. Feelings of "Where have I been? I never knew anything like it," are therefore predictable as new experiences are encountered. In love, one discovers letters before *a* and others after *z*, and life translates into new languages. The sudden great falls into anomie, where the comfort of the familiar no longer embraces us, may, of course, be desperate. To be totally bereaved of erotic rank causes despair and, in extreme cases, suicide. A sudden gain in rank beyond all imagination is also frightening; in extreme cases, as we have heard, the great lovers seek death together.

Anomie, here as elsewhere, is countered by norms and social controls. Durkheim noted this in one of his striking insights into the sociology of marriage: "It [marriage] completely regulates the life of passion, and monogamic marriage more strictly than any other. For by forcing man to attach himself forever to the same woman it assigns a strictly definite object to the need for love, and closes the horizon" (1897, 270).

The horizon of the erotic hierarchy closes, restricting people to whatever have become their customary ranges. This Durkheim sees as a gain.

> Thus we reach a conclusion quite different from the current idea of marriage and its role. It is supposed to have originated for the wife to protect her weakness against masculine caprice. Monogamy, especially, is often represented as a sacrifice made by man of his polygamous instincts, to raise and improve woman's condition in marriage. Actually, whatever historical causes may have made him accept this restriction, he benefits more by it. The liberty he thus renounces could only be a source of torment to him. (pp. 273–74)

Durkheim's argument that the restriction to a customary range is beneficial becomes more eloquent in an article written several years later.

> In assigning a certain object to desires, definite and unvariable, it prevents men from exasperating themselves in the pursuit of the ever new, the ever changing. . . . It prevents the heart from becoming agitated and from tormenting itself in a vain search for happiness . . . it renders more easily peace of heart, that inner equilibrium which is an essential condition for mental health and happiness. (1906, 552)

The phrase that "marriage kills love" can now be appreciated as an important half-truth: marriage restricts the pursuit of erotic rank to a customary range. Upon marriage, the spouses become members of castes, be they high or low, and are prohibited from leaving their accustomed territories.

Durkheim presumably was writing about the Frenchman who settles down after having established a fairly wide accustomed range. From his theory, one may also argue that the premature closure of the range to which a person gets accustomed is equally inappropriate, since it leaves that person vulnerable to any erotically ranking person who may cross his or her path. To be rigidly confined to one narrow ascribed range was called "fatalism" by Durkheim and was illustrated by the hopeless condition of a slave.

The Social Norms of Sex

All this talk of an erotic hierarchy may have led some learned colleagues to visualize a sociometric ranking of who sleeps with whom within a community. Of course, every co-educational office, hospital, laboratory, or college has more or less appealing men and women, and the issue of who has access to whose bed is not an idle one. However, as we have seen, what is at stake in the erotic hierarchy (namely, emotional overcomeness) is different from sexual intercourse. This emotional surrender may, of course, lead to, be achieved with, or be confirmed in sexual intercourse. But the latter is not necessarily involved; and, as is well known, there are many sexual relations that do not involve the emotional surrender of either party. The connection we may have between the sexual sociometry and the erotic hierarchy must be specified by hypotheses and not taken as true by definition.

A person's place in an erotic hierarchy may be confirmed through a variety of activities, but some, such as flirtation and dancing, may place a person more readily than others. Sexual intercourse seems to produce an erotic rank for a person more easily than anything else. The fact that sexual intercourse can produce not only children but also erotic ranks is of the greatest importance to an understanding of the norms that govern it. One of the more interesting aspects of the theory of erotic hierarchies is the predictions it allows about the content of sexual norms.

Sexual norms range from conducive requests to coercive commands. The former are numerous and varied and seem to depend so much on accidents of tradition and situation as to escape systematic prediction. At any rate, we must here forgo the attempt to explain the sexual norms that might be called the etiquette of seduction. We have to restrict ourselves to the ones having a more coercive quality — that is, to fundamental sexual morality.

It is clear that society wants to regulate something that produces its new members, particularly since human offspring need so much care and training before they can fend for themselves. Traditional sex norms served, among other things, to restrict unregulated conceptions and births. Some of these norms are being replaced in our generation by norms requiring the use of contraceptives. Here, indeed, we notice a big change. However, the planned children that result from this pattern must still be cared for. The norms around "procreational" sex relations ensure that parenthood is established, responsibility for the offspring assigned, and the offspring placed in the proper stratum of society. These norms have not changed much, except that they now tend to be phrased not in terms of "When and with whom may one have sexual intercourse?" but rather "When and with whom may one have sexual intercouse without using contraceptives?" The question that is currently much debated is entirely different. It is whether sexual activity not involving parenthood — "recreational" sex — should be pursued freely, in the sense that one should be free from social controls that go beyond the prescription to use contraceptives.

The argument for erotic hierarchies that we have sketched gives us an answer. It is known that society regulates whatever places persons in any one of its strata. In all societies, norms govern the acquisition and assignment of economic, political, academic, and religious ranks. It seems entirely reasonable to assume that norms emerge to govern erotic ranks as well. If sexual relations produce ranks, that fact in itself will generate a set of social norms.

If our theory is correct, the norms of love must be those of a secret society and of hierarchy. From the theory of the secret societies, we trace the norms of privacy surrounding the sexual relation. From the theory of interaction in hierarchies, we trace the norms

protecting the individual from capricious erotic degradation.

Such considerations lead us, first, to an explanation of the incest taboo. From the varying and sometimes fantastic explanations offered for this set of norms, we can now select the one that implicitly assumes an erotic hierarchy as the one deserving special attention. In other words, we follow Kingsley Davis.

> Suppose that brothers and sisters were allowed to violate the incest taboos. Consider first the effect of the sexual rivalry which would develop between brothers and between sisters. If, for example, there were two brothers and only one sister in the family, sexual jealousy would probably destroy the brotherly attitudes. . . . Moreover, since the number and sex distribution of the siblings in different families is impossible to control, no standard institutional pattern could be worked out so that jealousy would be a support rather than a menace. . . . If sexual relations between parent and child were permitted, sexual rivalry between mother and daughter and between father and son would almost surely arise, and this rivalry would be incompatible with the sentiments necessary between the two. (1949, 402–3)

The family is only one of the primary groups in which insurance against erotic degradation emerges. Other groups in which we are much involved, such as friendships, neighbourhoods, and work groups, develop similar prohibitions. A social norm that, in addition to the ordinary incest taboo, is irremovable from any society is, therefore, a prohibition against stealing a friend's, workmate's, or neighbour's spouse. In other words, the minimum sexual morality is an extension of the incest taboo to cover not only close relatives, but friends of the family, workmates, and neighbours. Sexual licence in groups in which people are intimately engaged makes for shifts in erotic hierarchies that cause too much agony to be tolerated.

The person who violates the incest taboo is certain to be abhorred in every society; the person who violates the extended taboo that puts a spouse beyond the sexual access of immediate friends, colleagues, and neighbours is also likely to be despised. This is true even where all other restrictions on sexual relations are dropped; friends, colleagues, or neighbours in prostitution consider it immoral to sleep with one anothers' pimps. Thus, there is always a minimum code of honour for sexual behaviour. Free love, in the sense of sex unregulated by any social norms, is a sociological anomaly. The sexual revolution of our times that abolished conventional morality will predictably stop in front of an extended incest taboo covering all primary relations, not merely immediate blood relatives. Those in the current debate who formulate and teach the abolition of conventional sexual morality in return for an extension of the incest taboo may well be judged as the wisest.

Caveat

New theoretical ideas require special care. On the one hand, one must not believe in them and act as if they were true; for they have not yet met the test of research. On the other hand, one must show them much confidence and attention and help them grow strong before they are hit by tough formal logic and hard research data. Thus, there is an emotional ambivalence in the nursing of a new theoretical idea. It is not unlike the parental hypocrisy that calls the same child "a big boy" in the morning when he manages to get dressed by himself and "a little boy" in the evening when it is bedtime. This theory is presented in the happy morning hour when standards are generous. We have taken key ideas from sociological theory as developed by Durkheim, Simmel, Weber, and others and applied them to a new field. A theorist is supposed to gather ideas and propositions from various fields into a parsimonious bundle that is handed over to the researchers, who guide

further investigation, and to the practitioners, who make use of it in their recommendations to clients. What they say about it at the end of their working day must now be awaited.

Works Cited

Aubert, Vilhelm. 1965. *The Hidden Society*. Totawa, NJ: Bedminster.

Benoit-Smullyan, Emile. 1944. "Status, Status Types, and Status Interrelations." *The American Sociological Review* 9: 151–61.

Cooley, Charles H. 1902. *Human Nature and Social Order*. New York: Charles Scribner's Sons.

Davis, Kingsley. 1949. *Human Society*. New York: Crowell-Collier and Macmillan.

Duncan, Hugh D. 1962. *Communication and Social Order*. Totawa, NJ: Bedminster.

Durkheim, Emile. 1897. *Suicide*. Trans. 1951. New York: Free Press.

———. 1906. "Le divorce par consentement mutuel." *La Revue Bleue* 5: 552.

Durrell, Lawrence. 1960. *The Alexandria Quartet: Justine, Balthazar, Mountolive, Clea*. London: Faber and Faber.

Etzioni, Amitai. 1961. *A Comparative Study of Complex Organizations*. New York: Free Press.

Homans, George C. 1961. *Social Behavior: Its Elementary Forms*. New York: Harcourt, Brace and World.

Lessing, Doris. 1962. *The Golden Notebook*. London: Michael Joseph.

Simmel, Georg. 1908. *Soziologie*. Leipzig: Dunker und Humbolt.

Waller, Willard. 1937. "The Rating and Dating Complex." *The American Sociological Review* 2: 727–34.

Weber, Max. 1922. *Gesammelte Aufsätze zur Religionssoziologie*. Tübingen: J.C.B. Mohr.

THE COURTSHIP GAME: POWER IN THE SEXUAL ENCOUNTER

Naomi B. McCormick
Clinton J. Jesser

The boundaries of heterosexual courtship — the institutional way that men and women become acquainted before marriage — have changed dramatically since a physician (Robinson 1929, 262) offered the following warning:

> Fortunate are you, my young girl friend, if you come from a well-sheltered home. . . . But if you have lost your mother at an early age, or if your mother is not the right sort . . . if you have to shift for yourself, if you have to work in a shop, in an office, and particularly if you live alone and not with your parents, then temptations in the shape of men, young and old, will encounter you at every step; they will swarm about you like flies about a lump of sugar; they will stick to you like bees to a bunch of honeysuckle.

In the 1800s and at the beginning of this century, courtship among middle-class North Americans was a sober process that strongly emphasized the end goal of marriage. Almost everyone, including feminists, valued sexual self-control (Hersch 1980). Unmarried people were severely restricted as to *whom* they might court and *what* went on during courtship (Gordon 1980). Because the respectable unmarried woman was constantly supervised by older adults, sexual experience with her courtship partner was unlikely (Kinsey et al. 1953).

Source: *Changing Boundaries: Gender Roles and Sexual Behaviour* (Mountain View, CA: Mayfield Publishing Company, 1983), 150–72. Reprinted with permission from Elizabeth Rice Allgeier and Naomi B. McCormick (editors).

Power — the ability to influence another person's attitudes or behaviour — is an essential component of courtship. As societies become increasingly industrialized and urbanized, family and kin exercise less power over the young. "The world, as a whole, seems to be moving toward the idea of free choice in marriage" (Murstein 1980, 778). The absence of parental power does not imply that courtship has become a free-for-all. Now, unmarried people have most of the power in determining the course of their own courtship.

To some extent, the sexual revolution is the result of this shift in power. As premarital sex has gained peer acceptance, increasing numbers of youthful North Americans, especially women, have sexual intercourse before marriage (Zelnick and Kantner 1977, 1979, 1980). Sex and intimacy, not always leading to marriage, may be the new end goals of courtship.

In this paper, we look at the ways people use power in courtship. Given the limited research in the area, some of our discussion is more relevant to never-married, heterosexual, middle-class youth than to other groups. We examine gender differences in using and responding to power, and explore all levels of courtship, from meeting someone to having sex. In this paper, we focus predominantly on new dating relationships (such as how people flirt and ask dates out). We ask who holds most of the power in a dating relationship, the man or the woman. After this inquiry, we subject the sexual encounter itself to rigorous power analysis. We view sexual expression in political terms. And we inquire how and why people use particular strategies for having and avoiding sex and prefer some coital positions over others.

Power and Courtship

Power is one person's ability to impose wishes on another more than that other can impose his or her wishes (Weber 1964, 152). The exercise of power is effective when one person succeeds in changing another person's thoughts, attitudes, or behaviour (Raven 1965, 1971). People acquire power and dominance in many ways. Sometimes they acquire and use power in a heavy-handed way. They use physical strength, social position in organizations and politics, and control over land and money, and often take unfair advantage of an influencee, or target (Collins and Raven 1968; French and Raven 1959).

Rape occurs when an influencing agent uses physical strength or the threat of violence to influence a victim (influencee) to have sex. Using superior wealth or the authority one has acquired as the boss or leader to convince a less-than-willing influencee to have sex is also heavy-handed. In the very least, such a use of power is sexual harassment. At its most extreme, it is rape.

Students sometimes balk when we suggest that nice people, not just sadists, use power during courtship. "If both the man and the woman like each other or want sex," they argue, "then power is irrelevant." According to these romantic students, lovers just happen to meet, just happen to get carried away and have sex. Characteristic of this attitude, some California college students are unable to relate to the assignment "Assuming you are very desirous of sexual intercourse . . . describe how you would try to influence your date to have sex" (McCormick 1976b):

I don't think I would try to influence my date to have sex. If it's time and everything is right, sex will follow in its own pattern.

I would not try. In time we would make it.

It must come about naturally. No persuasion should be necessary. Otherwise, lovemaking is not a sign of affection but rather a disgusting sexual act.

Not everyone sees dating and mating in the same romantic light as these three students. Many, ourselves included, speculate that people are able to plan strategies carefully for attracting and seducing sexual partners. Power, the potential to influence another person's attitudes or behaviour, may be an essential component of any romantic attraction or sexual relationship.

As we said before, there is more than one way to acquire and use power. The development of skills and knowledge, being perceived as attractive and likeable, and even acting helpless or "needy" can all be used to influence someone else (Collins and Raven 1968; French and Raven 1959). Often, these less obvious kinds of power are more effective because they avoid hitting the influencee over the head.

People often assume that their behaviour is self-motivated when they receive relatively little feedback indicating that they are being influenced by someone else (Bem 1972). For this reason, the effective strategies for influencing courtship tend to be subtle enough to convince a partner that he or she wanted what happened as much as the influencing agent wanted it. Flirtation in bars is an excellent example:

We begin with a woman entering the bar. She is nicely dressed, and perhaps she expects to meet someone. As she enters, she characteristically stops, and nearly always adjusts some item of clothing, an accessory, or her hair. Then she looks around the bar, a deliberate scan, not a casual glance. . . . Then, she goes to the bar itself, walking directly to it and ends up standing next to some man. . . . If he fails to look at her, or if he turns away, the interaction is likely to cease immediately. But we assume that he moves slightly, perhaps looking at her briefly, perhaps just shifting his weight. His seeming trivial action is essential, since it has communicated to her that she has been noticed. . . . If things go further, he may well believe that *he* picked up *her*. (Perper and Fox 1980a, 12)

Men as Pursuers, Women as Pursued

Sex and the broader conditions of life cannot be separated. This fact is especially important today with the changing circumstances and opportunities in men's and women's lives. Because societies vary greatly, it is difficult to generalize about the relationship between sex and power.

Where or under what conditions do women have the most control over their sexual lives? Generally speaking, in five specific situations women have greater say over whom they have sex with and how they have sex (see Hacker 1975, 212–14). First, women enjoy more sexual freedom where there is little or no emphasis on warfare and militarism. Second, women control their own sexuality more where men participate in childrearing or where child-care services are available. Third, women have greater power in their sexual relationships when they have political representation. Fourth, women enjoy greater sexual freedom where they have helped mold the mythology, religious beliefs, and world view of their groups. Finally, women are more sexually emancipated where they have economically productive roles such as control over tools, land, produce, and products.

In most societies, women's sexuality is more restricted than that of men (Safilios-Rothschild 1977). A *double standard* — the expectation that premarital and extramarital sex is more permissible for men — has been employed. The cultural conditions just cited modify the extent to which the double standard is enforced. On the other hand, cultures that emphasize male dominance in society as a whole severely penalize premarital sex by women (Safilios-Rothschild 1977). For example, in some Arab societies, women who

break sexual conventions may be executed, sometimes by their brothers or fathers (Critchfield 1980, 67).

Fortunately, not all societies oppress the sexual choices of women. The more power women have in society as a whole, the weaker the double standard is. The double standard is weak or absent in matrilineal societies, where descent and inheritance occur through the mother and land is owned or controlled by women (see Jesser 1972, 248–49). The double standard is also on the wane in societies that reward women for bearing children by encouraging them to be sexually permissive, as in Polynesia. Finally, the double standard dies in societies that have an overabundance of men. For example, in the Marquesa Islands, where men greatly outnumbered women at one time, men did all the work, including housework and child care. In contrast, Marquesan women spent their time attracting and pleasing sexual partners. In glaring contrast to North American culture, Marquesan men catered to women's whims, women were viewed as hypersexual, and sex started only after the woman gave the signal (Leibowitz 1978).

Intriguing as they were, the Marquesans were unusual. Most societies are politically controlled by men. Consequently, sexual access to women is part of the property system (see Stephens 1963, 240–59). In societies in which women are regarded as property, men try to "enrich" themselves by having sex as frequently and with as many women as possible. Correspondingly, women try to keep themselves "precious" by staying beautiful or desirable while they refuse to give themselves to any but the "right" men — their present or future husbands (Safilios-Rothschild 1977).

Male-dominated societies seem to permit men to use power to have sex with women, while women are allowed to exercise power only to avoid sex with unsuitable partners. In these societies, a woman who uses power to seduce a man openly is regarded as "bad" and possibly dangerous. A man who uses power to avoid sex with a "turned-on" woman is

regarded as "religious" at best, and inept, stu-
pid, and unmanly at worst. This paper explores the extent to which this value system
about power in sexual encounters survives in
North American society.

Politics of Courtship in North America

It would be difficult to describe adequately
the conditions of North American society that
have affected the status of women and, consequently, their sexual relations with men. Essentially, the industrial system has become so
successful during the past 70 years that men's
and women's spheres of work have separated.
Except for lower-class women and during
times of war, many women were eliminated
from the expanding work force. Place of work
and place of residence separated under industrialization, and for the "secure and successful" work force, a man's paycheque became
adequate for the support of the family (see
Deckard 1975, 199–375). A "cult of domesticity" emerged (Degler 1980), supposedly
reigned over by women. This involved the attempt on the part of the middle class to up-
grade (professionalize) full-time housework.

Such developments were not without
strains, which have become especially noticeable within the past 25 years. Middle-class
women became dissatisfied with the "gilded
cage" — the house — in the midst of their
declining and unrewarded domestic functions. More educated than ever before and
trying their best to manage while the family's
income was eaten away by inflation, housewives did not find their lot easy. As a more
companionate marriage of equality became
the ideal, middle-class homemakers became
even more sharply aware of their unhappiness.

Divorce, when it did break the trap, sometimes resulted in more difficulties than it
solved. Outside employment or going back
to college also posed dilemmas for women.
Domestic duties could be reduced but not
completely   eliminated   (Davidson   and
Kramer-Gordon 1979); instead of having one

job, working and student mothers now had
two. Eager to pacify insecure husbands, employed women retained major responsibility
for child care and housework (Berkove 1979;
Hooper 1979; Pleck 1979).

Just as the balance of power between the
genders influences sexual relations in other
cultures, North American women's subordinate economic and political status severely
limits their sexual freedom. It should come
as no surprise that the "battle of the sexes"
in the living room spills over into the
bedroom.

Although it is less severe in North America
than in the Third World, a double standard
— unfavourable to women's premarital and
extramarital sexual expression, while favourable to such expression by men — has prevailed. Admittedly, this standard is looser
than in the past (Hopkins 1977; Komarovsky
1976; Peplau, Rubin, and Hill 1977). Also,
it is important to remember that the double
standard is stronger among white, lower-
middle-class people. It is rare among certain
ethnic or racial groups, including working-
class U.S. blacks, who do not stigmatize children who are born out of wedlock (Broderick
1979; Scanzoni and Scanzoni 1976). Here,
too, women's relative power outside sexual
relationships is important. Although economically oppressed in their own right, lower-class
black women are less dependent on men for
their livelihood than are white women. Consequently, they may enjoy sex for its own sake
rather than expecting it to be an economic
bargaining tool (Coleman 1966).

Unlike their lower-class black counterparts,
middle-class white women use sex as a bargaining tool with some hazard to themselves
because of the lingering double standard. Specifically, they are tacitly expected to exchange
sexual and emotional companionship for economic support from men (Scanzoni 1970,
4–25). The sexual revolution has not changed
matters much. Instead of waiting until she
marries the "right man" before having sex,
today's middle-class woman waits until she
finds the "right man" to have *premarital* sex
(Hunt 1974).

For some, the goal of courtship continues to be finding the right man to marry. Such arrangements give women veto power over sex and thus a bargaining lever for other things for which sex might be exchanged. The extent to which this veto power operates successfully, or even the desirability of that kind of power in the first place (as compared to true independence and initiative power), can be questioned (Gillespie 1971, 448). Nevertheless, current researchers continue to find that women are less interested in having sex than are men (Mancini and Orthner 1978; Mercer and Kohn 1979) and have greater power than men when a couple makes the decision to abstain from sexual intercourse (Peplau, Rubin and Hill 1977). If men are really more enthusiastic about sex, it is likely that the traditional pattern of bargaining continues.

Changing Boundaries of Courtship

Not all North American women view sex as a bargaining tool for finding men who will take care of them. Courtship patterns are changing and these changes could alter the balance of power between the genders. The decrease in the number of people marrying early and staying married weakens the once close connection between successful courtship and marriage. Courtship now occurs for a variety of other purposes, such as for having "a good time," for sexual release only, and for proving one's competence and status. Nevertheless, these changes in themselves may not lead to substantial social change.

The sexual politics of courtship may be especially resistant to change because couples beginning to court often engage in posing — the tendency to fall back on those gender roles that are stereotypically appropriate or safe (Heiss 1968, 82). For example, even if such stereotyped behavior is uncharacteristic, a woman might be careful to appear as sweet and unassertive as possible on the first date so as to make a good impression.

In the next two major sections of this paper, we question the extent to which "posing" continues in sexual encounters (in bars, bedrooms, or the back seats of cars). The following types of questions arise:

- Do men and women desire (seek) different types of benefits, satisfactions, and goals in the courtship process, and if so, what are they, and who actually achieves them?
- Who may touch whom, and how or where?
- When sex and sexual signalling occur, to what extent do the values of the society and the gender roles disadvantage one or the other party in the form, content, timing of the acts, or in the benefits to be derived?

Dynamics of Dating

Despite some speculation that the traditional date is disappearing (Murstein 1980, 780), dating remains a crucial part of courtship for many young people (Bell 1979, 49), although now, with more mixed gender places available and more casualness as the norm, people do not date as much, or they just call it "going out." Dating enables courting partners to get away from their parents and have the opportunity to know each other better. However, there is more to dating than just being alone together. Dating is also a bargaining process in which the man provides certain goods and services in exchange for others provided by the woman. In other words, dating is similar to marriage because it requires negotiations to take place. Perhaps this point will be much clearer if we analyze how the genders use power on the typical date. The best and most enjoyable way to do this is to imagine a traditional date.

When we imagine the classic North American date, the following narration comes to mind. On Tuesday, Herbert Dumple makes the first move. He calls Mildred Smedly, doing his best to sound sophisticated and desirable over the telephone. Herbert asks Mildred out for the following Saturday.

Mildred accepts, especially impressed that he phoned a few days in advance. She assesses that this means that Herbert *values* her. She might have refused, even if she had nothing to do but wash her hair, if he phoned only one day before.

On Saturday, Herbert arrives at Mildred's home promptly at 7.00 P.M. He is neatly attired in a sports jacket and dress slacks. His neat appearance brings home the fact that he values Mildred (jogging shoes and old jeans would be a "putdown") and that he himself is valuable. Herbert's middle-class status or aspirations are clear from his respectable appearance. In other words, he looks like a "good catch."

Mildred is not ready yet, accidentally on purpose. Consequently, Herbert has about ten minutes to chat with her family. He sits on the loveseat, somewhat anxious about making a good impression, and tries to sound intelligent and responsible. Meanwhile, Mildred's Mom and Dad look him over. The assessment process is so critical that the family has turned off the television set and is even checking out Herbert's manners, asking, "Would you like a snack while you wait?"

Mildred finally comes down to the living room at 7:10 P.M. However, perhaps we are jumping the gun. Before we describe her entrance, it might be useful to speculate about her reasons for being late. Actually, Mildred has two reasons for taking her time, both of which are relevant to our previous discussion of courtship as a bargaining process. First, by being late, she has more time to make herself attractive (put on makeup, fix her hair, make sure she has chosen the right outfit). Second, by being late, she is telling Herbert that she is a valuable person, a woman *worth* waiting for.

At last, Mildred comes down the stairs from her room. She looks "beautiful," at least according to Herbert and her father. Some parent–child negotiations take place concerning where the couple is going and when Mildred can be expected home. "Oh, Mom!" she says, "Can't you trust me?" Finally, the

awkward process is over, and Herbert escorts Mildred to his car. He opens the door for her, an excellent example of the posing we described earlier.

Mildred is relieved that Herbert has a car. This increases his marketability. Apparently, he might have some money. She dislikes dating men who expect her to travel on the bus. After all, dates are potential husbands, and it is important to find a good provider.

Mildred and Herbert go to dinner. Again, Herbert provides evidence of his potential as a good provider by taking her somewhere expensive and paying for their meal. Furthermore, he shows that he is appropriately masculine (posing again) by ordering their meals and taking responsibility for assessing the quality of the wine.

During dinner, Mildred tries her best to be a good conversationalist. This means that she asks Herbert about school or his job, focussing on *his* interests and trying her best to sound enthusiastic. Mildred's selfless concern for Herbert's interests is not accidental. After all, she wants to present herself as a valuable person, a potential spouse. She has already established that she is attractive ("beautiful"); her market value could only increase if she also seems empathic and emotionally supportive.

After dinner, the couple goes to Herbert's apartment. He has carefully made sure that his roommates are out so that the two of them can be alone. Mildred and Herbert smoke a couple of joints and share a small bottle of imported wine. Then, Herbert begins to make some sexual moves. Now, Mildred must make a choice. It is up to Mildred (the woman) to decide "how far to go" (Peplau, Rubin, and Hill 1977).

Back in the 1950s, Mildred would probably have gone along with Herbert until they engaged in heavy petting. She would have been unlikely to have had sexual intercourse. In those days, many women remained "technical virgins" until marriage because coital experience would have "cheapened them" or decreased their market value for marriage.

The values of the 1950s are over, however. These are the 1980s. More and more women, including young adolescents, are having sex before marriage. Today, a woman's market value might be increased by being a good lover (provided, of course, that she has sex with only one man at a time in a relationship). There are still strong prejudices against women who have many partners.

If Mildred really likes Herbert (she may convince herself she loves him), she will probably have sex. However, she will let Herbert make most of the moves. Although it is acceptable for today's woman to have sex, it is still risqué for her to ask for it.

Mildred and Herbert do have sex. Before they straighten out their hair and clothing, trying to look innocent for the benefit of parents, it is appropriate to analyze the power implications behind Mildred's decision to have sex. Mildred's potential power during her sexual encounter depends heavily on her age. If she is a young adolescent, she is probably trading off sex for Herbert's esteem. Indeed, if this is the case, Mildred may have traditional gender-role attitudes and be looking toward Herbert to fulfil multiple dependency and status needs (Scanzoni and Fox 1980). Young adolescent women who wait until they are older before having sex often have higher self-esteem and more pro-feminist attitudes than their more coitally experienced peers (Cvetkovich et al. 1978; Larkin 1979; Scanzoni and Fox 1980).

Putting on your Sherlock Holmes hats, you may be confused at this point. How could Mildred be a young teenager? Was she not able to order wine at the restaurant? Well, if Mildred was not "passing" as an older woman, you have a good point. More importantly, the power implications of having sex are completely different for older, college-age women. If Mildred is a college student, having sex suggests that she feels good about herself. In contrast with younger women, sexually active college women are more independent, autonomous, assertive, and pro-feminist than their less sexually active peers (Scanzoni and Fox 1980).

Dating, Power, and Equity

Our description of Herbert and Mildred's date provides some insight into how men's and women's different interests are reflected in their experience of power during courtship. Equity theory, which predicts that people prefer relationships in which each party receives equal relative gains (Hatfield and Traupmann 1980), is useful at this point. Will Mildred and Herbert become a couple? Will they feel secure enough about each other to have sex again? Will Herbert and Mildred eventually have a long-term relationship?

According to equity theory, people in inequitable (or "unfair") relationships (both those receiving too little and those receiving too much) become distressed enough either to balance or end the relationship. According to equity theory, then, Herbert and Mildred will be likely to seek a balanced or fair relationship, especially if they have already made a heavy investment in one another (Walster, Walster, and Berscheid 1978, 6).

As their dating relationship develops, if either Herbert or Mildred feels that he or she is getting a "raw" deal, the injured party will use power ploys to achieve a better position. For example, if Herbert "cheats" on Mildred by sleeping with another woman, she will let him have it during an argument. Mildred will continue to feel distressed until Herbert makes it up to her for cheating, perhaps by being especially considerate or even by purchasing an engagement ring. Such actions would help balance the relationship and would lead to greater happiness for both members of the couple (Hatfield and Traupmann 1980).

Suppose, however, that Mildred's power ploys have failed. Despite her entreaties, Herbert goes out with even more women. Her friends tell her that he is sleeping around with everyone. Moreover, Herbert is into drugs quite heavily and appears to have become an insensitive lout. Unless she can convince herself that she deserves such treatment (alas, some women do this and stay around), Mildred may end or withdraw from what has become an unsatisfactory relationship. Inequitable relationships are unstable. Both the overbenefited, cheating Herbert and the underbenefited, jealous Mildred are not satisfied with the way things are going (Hatfield and Traupmann 1980). Motivated by anger and guilt, such people would be more likely than equitable couples to use power ploys or attempt to end their relationships (see Walster, Walster, and Traupmann 1978).

Another important issue for Herbert and Mildred is their evaluation of each other's value or marketability with different dating partners. As described earlier, Herbert and Mildred are constantly assessing each other and themselves. Early on, even Mildred's parents get into the act. This evaluation process continues throughout their relationship. Herbert and Mildred are more likely to stay together if they are well-matched in age, intelligence, educational plans, and good looks (Hill, Rubin, and Peplau 1976).

Finally, equity theory is relevant to the quality of Herbert and Mildred's sex life together. They are more likely to continue having sex if neither partner feels "ripped off" or overbenefited. Actually, having sex in the first place suggests that this couple feels they are a good match. Couples in inequitable relationships are more likely to stop before "going all the way" (Walster, Walster, and Traupmann 1978, 89). Even more relevant to power during sexual encounters, Mildred and Herbert will have very different feelings about *why* they had sex, depending on whether their relationship is equitable or unfair. If Herbert and Mildred truly make up after their argument about Herbert's affair, they will say that they had sex because *both* wanted to, citing reasons such as "mutual physical desire" and "enjoyment" (Walster, Walster, and Traupmann 1978, 89). On the other hand, if their sexual relationship continues, despite the fact that Mildred still feels she is getting the short end of the stick, sex too would be seen as unfair. Herbert, for example, might feel that Mildred obliged him to make love to her to apologize for his indiscretion. In contrast, if Herbert wanted sex more than Mildred, she

might blame him for taking advantage of her here, too.

Strategies for Initiating New Relationships

The discussion of equity theory helps explain the balance of power in long-term relationships. However, it provides very little information about how people actually use power, especially in beginning new relationships. Focussing first on flirtation and then on the process during which one person asks another for a date, we will discuss *how* men and women actually use power with new dating partners.

Flirtation

A flirtation "is a sequence of behaviour, mostly nonverbal, which brings two people into increasing sociosexual intimacy" (Perper and Fox 1980a, 23). To date, the best research on what actually happens during flirtation (as opposed to what people think happens) is by Timothy Perper and Susan Fox.

Clocking over 300 hours of observations of working-class and middle-class single people of varying ages in New Jersey and New York City bars, Perper and Fox have overturned two of our most beloved cultural myths. The first overturned cultural myth is that the man is always the sexual aggressor, eagerly pressing himself on the coy but reluctant woman. At least in the beginning of the flirtation process, men do not "swarm around a woman like bees about a lump of sugar." Instead, the woman often makes the first move. Because her move is subtle — usually nothing more than standing close to her target — it is understandable that the man might erroneously come to believe that *he* started the interaction.

According to the second overturned myth, men know more about flirtations and sex than do women. In glaring contrast with this expectation, women are the experts:

Figure I
Flirtation in Bars (note that either gender may initiate a flirtation — power is shared, neither partner dominates the outcome)

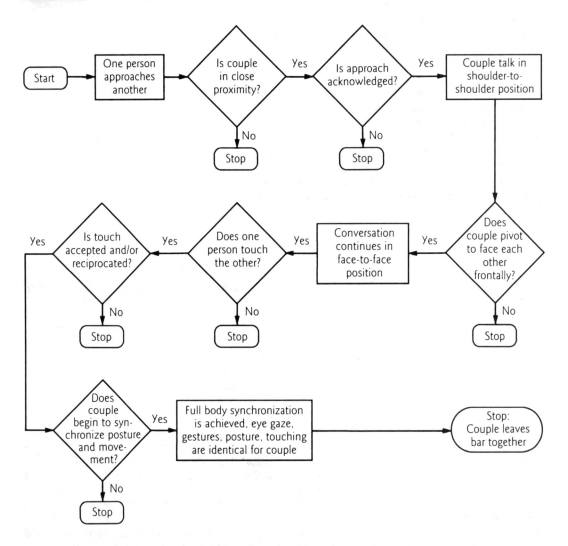

Source: Elizabeth Rice Allgeier and Naomi B. McCormick, *Changing Boundaries: Gender Roles and Sexual Behavior*, figure 3-1, p. 77. © 1983, Palo Alto, Mayfield Publishing Company. Reprinted by permission.

Typically, women are exquisitely familiar with what occurs during flirtations while men are generally quite ignorant. Women can describe in great detail how they and other women flirt and pick up men, and what men do (and just as frequently, what men *do not* do). In contrast, . . . [most] men were unfamiliar with all or most of the events of flirtations. Even quite successful men had no idea how they attracted women and what happened during a flirtation. Often men create vast and complex theories . . . but they seem to possess little or no information. (Perper and Fox 1980b, 4)

Now that we have established that women know more about flirting, at least in bars, it is still appropriate to ask, "Which gender has the most power?" Egalitarians should be delighted to know that flirtations are not under the control of one person. Instead, both genders have equal power.

A successful flirtation is one that will probably result in a new dating or sexual relationship. Such a flirtation depends on the influence or target signalling that the flirt's influence attempts are welcome at *each* stage of the flirtation. To clarify this, we have described the stages of a flirtation in Figure 1.

As you can see, neither gender dominates a successful flirtation. Indeed, it is hard to separate the influencing agent from the influencee. Each person takes a turn at influencing the partner and at signalling that the other's influence attempts are welcome. As the couple's relationship becomes more secure, flirtation strategies become more obvious:

[A woman] commonly touches the man before he touches her. Her touch is made, typically with the palm of the hand flat, and not with the fingertips, in a light, fleeting and pressing gesture. . . . She might brush against him with her hip or back, she may lean on him briefly, or she might brush against him while she turns to look at something. An alternative is for the woman to remove an otherwise nonexistent piece of lint from the man's jacket (men's jackets in bars collect such lint very readily). (Perper and Fox 1980a, 18)

An important aspect of touching is that it is safe, in that it can be interpreted as accidental. This saves face for the influencing agent should the flirtation prove unsuccessful. Touching during flirtation is similar to body language, a popular strategy for both men and women when they approach a date to have sexual intercourse (McCormick 1979). This strategy relates to a point made earlier: less obvious kinds of sexual power may be preferred because they are subtle enough to convince a partner that he or she wanted what happened just as much as the influencing agent did.

Asking for a Date

As you recall, Herbert Dumple asked Mildred Smedly out. North American gender-role norms are rather strict about who initiates a date. The traditional woman can, at most, make herself attractive. She is not allowed to call the man or to start a new relationship. In contrast, the traditional man (shy or not) is responsible for initiating any and all relationships with women. Does the man still have all the power when it comes to initiating a new dating relationship? Perhaps not. Current research sheds light on this issue.

Research fails to clarify whether women take more assertive roles in dating than in the past. Nevertheless, there are strong indications that traditional gender-role norms prevail. Men are more likely to say that they would initiate new heterosexual relationships than women are (Green and Sandos 1980). Moreover, both gender-typed and androgynous college students report that men typically initiate dates and pay for expenses incurred on dates (Allgeier 1981).

Men still have most of the power when it comes to initiating new dating relationships. However, not everyone is happy with this situation. Already, some college students are pushing for change (see Allgeier 1981). Liberals are experimenting with innovative dating patterns. Androgynous people, especially men, tend to have more experiences with female-initiated dates than do gender-typed individuals. Also, some men express dissatisfaction with the traditional date. Men are more positive about women initiating and paying for dates than women are.

In any event, the times may be ripe for change. A recent study at a southern university suggests that college men welcome female sexual initiation. In this study, women students approached strangers with this line: "I have been noticing you around campus. I find you very attractive." After saying this, most of the women are extremely successful in gaining men's verbal compliance with requests to go out on dates, to go to the women's apartments, and especially to go to bed with the women (Clark and Hatfield 1981). Apparently, more than a few college men enjoy being propositioned. However, as we shall see, wishes are not always realities.

Women are well advised to be cautious when contemplating whether to ask men out. The gender-role norms for male initiative in courtship are far from dead. When college students are asked how they feel about someone who either starts a friendly conversation or invites a coworker to dinner at a restaurant, responses are stereotyped (Green and Sandos 1980). Both men and women feel that it is more appropriate for the man than for the woman to take the initiative in either situation. Perhaps this helps explain why women are so conservative. Not surprisingly, women are more positive about men initiating dates than men are (Allgeier 1981).

There is more to power in courtship than asking someone out. People also have the power to refuse. Women are more pragmatic than are men about courtship. They want to size men up before committing themselves to relationships. Moreover, the double standard may still be operating. Women may be especially reluctant to go along with a man's sexual advances when he comes on "too strong." Clark and Hatfield's study (1981) supports this idea. When men ask strangers on a college campus for dates, they are successful. However, when they ask new acquaintances to go to their apartments or go to bed with them, they are not greeted with the warm enthusiasm that men give women for these same requests. Instead, most are flatly refused, with such responses as "You've got to be kidding" or "What is wrong with you? Leave me alone" (p. 17).

Changing Boundaries of Dating

We may conclude at this point that North American courtship is not as rigidly bound to the double standard as many of us suspected. Traditional gender-role norms are being challenged in three ways. First, with the exception of young adolescents, sexually active women are not exploited by men. Instead, the coitally experienced woman is likely to be independent and pro-feminist. Also, she is unlikely to have sex outside an equitable or balanced relationship. Second, men are not the experts when it comes to picking up dates. If knowledge is power, then women are more powerful than men when it comes to signalling men with whom they would like to become better acquainted. Finally, although it is not known if women are asking men out more than in the past, the times are ripe for change. Some men are highly receptive to women's invitations for dates and sex (Hite 1981). Probably the main thing that holds women back is the continued stereotype that such behaviour is unfeminine or inappropriate.

Courtship has changed, at least in its preliminary stages. However, what happens once a couple does have sex? In the remainder of this paper, we focus more specifically on the relationship between men and women during sexual intercourse. We also further identify and document the sexual value system — society's evolving rules for playing the courtship game.

Roles and Power During Sexual Intimacy

In general, dominant and extroverted people report engaging in more varied sexual behaviour and with more frequency than submissive, introverted people (DeMartino 1963; Eysenck 1971, 1972; Maslow 1963). Extroverts of both genders are more likely than passive individuals to be sexual nonconformists, willing to deviate from expected gender roles in their sexual encounters. For example, unlike her passive counterpart, the dominant and extroverted woman may be more likely to take the active sexual role. She is also more willing to experiment with nontraditional coital positions, such as being on top of her partner during sex.

Traditionally, women have been expected to play a relatively passive role in sexual encounters in our own and in some other societies (Ford and Beach 1951; Rainwater 1971; Rubin 1976, 134–54). It is no accident that the stereotype of the sexually passive woman is consistent with both the sexual double standard we have alluded to previously and our culture's idealization of the "passive-receptive" woman (Broverman et al. 1972, McKee and Sherriffs 1957; Rosenkrantz et al. 1968).

Consistent with the double standard and idealization of the passive-receptive woman, most dating and married couples report that a woman seldom actively initiates a couple's first intercourse (Peplau, Rubin, and Hill 1977). Generally, the woman is less likely to initiate sex than the man (Bell 1976; Carlson 1976; Crain and Roth 1977). These findings still leave many questions unanswered, however. For example, the need to look feminine might lead a woman to overlook or forget some subtle strategies she uses to give her partner the idea that *he* wants sex. What are the politics of deciding whether and how to have sexual intercourse?

Seduction and Rejection

Historically, the whole scenario of the sexual encounter, from initiation and timing to positioning of the bodies, was expected to be initiated by men (Long-Laws 1979). In contrast, the woman has been expected either to go passively along with men's sexual advances or to refuse to have sex (Ehrmann 1959; Gag-

non and Simon 1973; Komarovsky 1976; Peplau, Rubin, and Hill 1976, 1977).

Young people's sexual vocabularies characterize men as sexual actors and women as sexual objects. According to Sanders and Robinson (1979, 28), women describe the penis with "cute little euphemisms" such as "Oscar," "penie," "ding-a-ling," and "baby-maker." In contrast, young men are more likely to use power slang such as "womp," "rod," "pistol," and "stick." Similarly, men use slang for sexual intercourse, such as "poking," "stroking a hole," and "hosing," suggesting that men perceive sex as demonstrations of power. Their language contrasts strongly with women's vague, passive, and romantic images of sex: "doing it," "being inside," "going all the way," and "loving."

Women's typical words for describing sexuality (that is "penis," "vagina," and "make love") reveal attitudinal constraints that contrast strongly with men's verbal flexibility. Unlike women, men are able to communicate about sex with a variety of audiences (Sanders and Robinson 1979). Less free to talk about sex, women may also feel less free to be sexual actors than do men.

On the other hand, women may feel more comfortable about being sexual actors than they did in the past. A large proportion of both men and women in ongoing relationships report persuading their partners to have sex using such straightforward approaches as touching, snuggling, kissing, allowing their hands to wander, and asking directly (Jesser 1978). When asked how men responded to their sexual advances, women who ask directly to have sex are *not* more likely to report being rebuffed than those who fail to report asking directly. Predictably, women who are opposed to female sexual modesty and the need for women to pursue their interests inconspicuously are especially likely to consider directly asking their dates to have sex. Equally predictable, men whose partners had directly asked them to have sexual relations are also those who disagreed with the view that women must regard their bodies more modestly than men. These same men are especially likely to disagree with the position that men's dominant interest in women is sexual (Jesser 1978).

Could sexual role playing be on the wane among today's courting couples? Another study finds strong similarities between men's and women's use of influence in sexual encounters. When asked how they would influence a date to have sex in a hypothetical sexual encounter, both male and female college students prefer indirect strategies. For instance, one student said, "I would test my limits by holding hands, sitting closer to this person, etc." (McCormick 1979, 199). As you recall, using touch as an approach is also popular in flirtations.

Indirect strategies are preferred for good reasons. In their very subtlety, these strategies provide the influencing agent with a haven from possible rejection. For example, imagine that Mildred Smedly uses another indirect approach — environmental manipulation — to influence Herbert Dumple to have sex. After doing her best to set the stage for sex by dimming the lights, providing some liquor, and playing sensual music on the stereo, she is shocked when Herbert makes fun of her. Fortunately, her strategy permits her to avoid the hot seat when Herbert ridicules her.

> HERBERT (in challenging voice): Mildred, are you coming on to me?
> MILDRED (firmly): No, Herbert. I just like that record a lot. Also, candlelight is good for my eyes after a long day of typing my term paper.

Clearly, indirect strategies are useful for having sex. However, seduction, a highly direct and arousal-oriented strategy, is also popular with both men and women for influencing a hypothetical partner to have sex. Here are two quotes from students' essays describing how they would seduce their dates (McCormick 1976b):

> [Female college student:] I would start caressing his body and start kissing his chest, maybe

stomach. I would try to be very sexy; doing this especially with lots of eye contact. Probably a few sighs here and there to let him know I feel sexually stimulated. This would probably be all I would do aside from wearing something slinky and bare. I could not get myself to perhaps start unbuckling his pants.

> [Male college student:] I would proceed to use my charm and bodily contact to get what I want. (1) If she shys away in a huff, I would stop and try to talk it out. If we got nowhere from there, I would take my ass home. (2) If she gives me the come on, then I would proceed very vigorously. (3) If she pushed away gently, I would tell her what a good time we had, that we are not children, and since we relate so well, we should "Get it on."

Consistent with the stereotype that men are sexual actors and women are sex objects, men say they would use seduction significantly more than women say they would. However, both genders prefer seduction over all other strategies for influencing a partner to have sex. Women are clearly capable of experiencing men as sex objects.

Gender differences also disappear when college students are asked how they would avoid sexual intercourse with a turned-on partner. Both men and women prefer direct, obvious strategies. Moralizing — using religious convictions or moral opposition to argue against having sex — is one such strategy. As one volunteer put it, "I would state directly that that type of relationship is reserved for marriage" (McCormick 1979, 199).

Clearly, some of today's young singles are breaking out of sexual role playing. At any rate, the previously discussed findings suggest that male and female college students have the *potential* to enjoy courtship interactions that are free of gender-role stereotypes. Nevertheless, egalitarian readers should be advised to hold their applause. It is important to note that regardless of their gender-role attitudes, the overwhelming majority of college students stereotype men as using all possible strategies to have sex and women as using every strategy in the book to avoid having sex (LaPlante, McCormick, and Brannigan 1980; McCormick 1976a, 1979). If such stereotyping persists, it is likely that students believe that others want them to engage in sexual role playing and that such behaviour will be common with future dating partners.

In contrast with their lack of sexual role playing when asked what they would do within hypothetical sexual encounters with imaginary or future partners, students report strict adherence to gender-role stereotypes during their *actual* courtship experiences. When describing their personal use of power via various strategies, men use strategies significantly more than women do to influence dates to have sex, and women use strategies significantly more than men do when the goal is avoiding sexual intercourse. Complementing this finding, when asked to describe their experiences as influences within sexual encounters, men are more likely than women to report being influenced by all strategies for avoiding sex. Also, women report being more likely than men to be influenced by the majority of strategies for having sex (LaPlante, McCormick, and Brannigan 1980; McCormick 1977).

The continued importance of gender roles in sexual encounters is supported by the fact that a higher proportion of women than men say that they use extraordinarily subtle or indirect signals to indicate their sexual interest. For instance, they report using eye contact, changes of appearance or clothing, and changes in tone of voice. Could it be that these women are fearful of "turning off" their partners if they are more sexually assertive? Consistent with such an opinion, many women are hesitant about being assertive with dates with whom they want to have sex, perceiving this as unacceptable to men. Ironically, women may be holding themselves back sexually more than men would desire. Relatively unoffended by sexually assertive women (Jesser 1978), college men are more positive about women initiating sex than are women (Allgeier 1981). Just as they would

welcome greater female initiative in dating, men also desire more assertive sexual partners. For instance, many older men agree that "it's exciting when a woman takes the sexual initiative" (Tavris 1978, 113).

Overall, the research on strategies for having and avoiding sex has disappointing implications for those who prefer sexual behaviour that is liberated from gender roles. It may be that courtship is a bastion for the strict performance of stereotyped gender-role behaviour.

Are the Rules for Courtship Changing?

The courtship game has changed in three ways. First, thanks to the weakening of the double standard and encouragement from feminists, women are freer to make the first move in a flirtation and to have premarital sex than in the past. Second, men seem to be encouraging women to be more assertive in initiating sexual relationships. Third, given the opportunity, men would reject sex and women would try to have sex with the same strategies that are characteristically used by the other gender.

Despite these changes, the courtship game continues to follow gender-role stereotypes. Men ask women out more than vice versa. Men are more likely to influence a date to have sex; women are morely likely to refuse sex. The persistence of gender-role playing is associated with a number of factors, such as women's more conservative attitudes toward sexuality. Another factor that contributes to the courtship game is that North American society views people who behave "out of role" (that is, passive men and assertive women) as less well adjusted and popular (Costrich et al. 1975).

As the women's liberation movement gains increasing acceptance, the courtship game will probably become less rigid. For instance, although women prefer masculine over feminine men, male college students are *not* more attracted to feminine women than they are to masculine women (Seyfried and Hendrick 1973). Even more indicative of social change, recent research contradicts earlier reports (Goldberg, Gottesdiener, and Abramson 1975; Johnson et al. 1978) that men are turned off by pro-feminist women. Johnson, Holborn, and Turcotte (1979) found that men were more attracted to women who support the feminist movement than they were to those who are described as nonsupporters. As attitudes toward feminist women become more liberal, people may try out more egalitarian ways of dealing with courtship. However, such experimentation is likely to be minimal at first because out-of-role behaviour is especially risky within sexual encounters where people already feel emotionally vulnerable.

Some insight into future directions for male-female courtship is provided by a vocal and liberal group of physicians and sex therapists. In the past decade, a number of therapists have contributed their ideas in opinion articles with titles such as "Do Men Like Women to Be Sexually Assertive?" "Who Should Initiate Sexual Relations, Husband or Wife?" and "Who Should Take the Sexuual Lead — the Man or the Woman?" In many of these articles, medical personnel and sex therapists indicate that they favour sexual equality in the bedroom for all but those few patients who would experience emotional turmoil as a result of such equality.

If the public continues to be exposed to these liberal ideas, values of future generations will slowly but surely change. It may not be overly optimistic to predict that college students in the year 2000 will be less likely to stereotype strategies for having sex as something only men would do and strategies for avoiding sex as something only women use. Before we get carried away with optimism, however, it is important to note that not all opinion leaders reject the sexist courtship game. Indeed, a powerful backlash by psychiatrists and other sex therapists has indicated that they are highly alarmed by the supposedly explosive impact of the women's liberation movement on power in the sexual

encounter. According to this backlash, women who are assertive about sex endanger the security of otherwise solid relationships and make men neurotic, anxious, or insecure. Ruminating about the new impotence allegedly caused by sexually aggressive women, these conservative sex experts advise women to remain sexually passive in the bedroom or, at the very least, to be cautious when taking the sexual initiative with men (Ginsberg, Frosch, and Shapiro 1972; also see F. Lemere's and G. Ginsberg's commentary in Kroop 1978). Clearly, if the stereotyped courtship game does die, it will have an agonizing and elongated death rattle.

Works Cited

Allgeier, E.R. 1981. "The Influence of Androgynous Identification on Heterosexual Relations." *Sex Roles*, 7: 321–30.

Bell, R.R. 1976. "Changing Aspects of Marital Sexuality. *Sexuality Today and Tomorrow*. Eds. S. Gordon and R.W. Libby. Belmont, CA.: Wadsworth.

———. 1979. *Marriage and the Family Interaction*. Chicago, IL.: Dorsey.

Bem, D.J. 1972. "Self-Perception Theory." *Advances in Experimental Social Psychology*. Vol. 6. Ed. L. Berkowitz. New York: Academic.

Berkove, G.F. 1979."Perceptions of Husband Support by Returning Women Students." *The Family Coordinator* 28: 451–58.

Broderick, C.B. 1979. *Marriage and the Family*. Englewood Cliffs, NJ: Prentice-Hall.

Broverman, I., et al. 1972. "Sex Role Stereotypes: A Current Appraisal." *Journal of Social Issues* 28: 59–78.

Carlson, J. 1976. "The Sexual Role." *Role Structure and Analysis of the Family*. Ed. F.I. Nye. Beverly Hills, CA: Sage. 101–110.

Clark R.D., III, and E. Hatfield. 1981. "Gender Differences in Reciptivity to Sexual Offers." Unpublished manuscript. (Available from Dr. Elaine Hatfield, Psychology Department, 2430 Campus Road, Honolulu, HI 96822)

Coleman, J.S. 1966. "Female Status and Premarital Sexual Codes." *American Journal of Sociology* 72: 217.

Collins, B.E., and B.H. Raven. 1968. "Group

Structure: Attraction, Coalition, Communication, and Power." *The Handbook of Social Psychology*. 2d ed. Vol. 4. Eds. G. Lindzey and E. Aronson. Reading, MA: Addison-Wesley. 102–204.

Costrich, N., et al. 1975. "When Stereotypes Hurt: Three Studies of Penalties for Sex-Role Reversals." *Journal of Experimental Social Psychology* 11: 520–30.

Crain, S., and S. Roth. 1977. "International and Interpretive Processes in Sexual Initiation in Married Couples." Paper presented at the meeting of the American Psychological Association, San Francisco. August.

Critchfield, R. 1980. "Sex in the Third World." *Readings in Human Sexuality: Contemporary Perspectives*. 2d ed. Eds. C. Gordon and G. Johnson. New York: Harper and Row.

Cvetkovich, G., et al. 1978. "Sex Role Development and Teenage Fertility-Related Behaviour." *Adolescence* 13: 231–36.

Davidson, L., and L. Kramer-Gordon. 1979. *The Sociology of Gender*. Chicago: Rand McNally.

Deckard, B.S. 1975. *The Women's Movement*. New York: Harper and Row.

Degler, C. 1980. *At Odds: Women and Family in America from the Revolution to the Present*. New York: Oxford University Press.

DeMartino, M.F. 1963. "Dominance-Feeling, Security-Insecurity, and Sexuality in Women." *Sexual Behaviour and Personality Characteristics*. Ed. M.F. DeMartino. New York: Grove. 113–43.

Ehrmann, W. 1959. *Premarital Dating Behavior*. New York: Holt, Rinehart and Winston.

Eysenck, H.L. 1971. "Introverts, Extroverts, and Sex." *Psychology Today* 4: 48–51, 82.

———. 1972. "Personality and Sexual Behavior." *Journal of Psychosomatic Research*, 16: 141–52.

Ford, C.S., and F.A. Beach. 1951. *Patterns of Sexual Behaviour*. New York: Harper and Row.

French, J.R., Jr., and B.H. Raven. 1959. "The Bases of Social Power." *Studies in Social Power*. Ed. D. Cartwright. Ann Arbor: University of Michigan Press. 150–67.

Gagnon, J.H., and W.Simon. 1973. *Sexual Conduct: The Social Sources of Human Sexuality*. Chicago: Aldine.

Gillespie, D.L. 1971. "Who Has the Power? The Marital Struggle." *Journal of Marriage and the Family* 33: 445–58.

Ginsberg, G.L., W.A. Frosch, and T. Shapiro. 1972. "The New Impotence." *Archives of General Psychiatry* 26: 218–20.

Goldberg, P.A., M. Gottesdiener, and P.R. Abramson. 1975. "Another Put-down of Women? Perceived Attractiveness as a Function of Support for the Feminist Movement." *Journal of Personality and Social Psychology* 32, 113–15.

Gordon, M. 1980. "The Ideal Husband as Depicted in the Nineteenth-Century Marriage Manual. *The American Man*. Eds. E.H. Pleck and J.H. Pleck. Englewood Cliffs, NJ: Prentice-Hall.

Green, S.K., and P. Sandos. 1980. "Perceptions of Male and Female Initiators of Relationships." Paper presented at the meeting of the American Psychological Association, Montreal, September.

Hacker, H.M. 1975. "Gender Roles from a Cross-Cultural Perspective." *Gender and Sex in Society*. Ed. L. Duberman. New York: Praeger, 1975.

Hatfield, E., and J. Traupmann. 1980. "Intimate Relationships. A Perspective from Equity Theory." *Personal Relationships*. Eds. S. Duck and R. Gilmour. London: Academic. 165–78.

Heiss, J., ed. 1968. *Family Roles and Interaction*. Chicago: Rand McNally.

Hersch, B.G. 1980. "A Partnership of Equals: Feminist Marriages in 19th-Century America." *The American Man*. Eds. E.H. Pleck and J.H. Pleck. Englewood Cliffs, NJ: Prentice-Hall.

Hill, C.T., Z. Rubin, and L.A. Peplau. 1976. "Breakups Before Marriage: The End of 103 Affairs." *Journal of Social Issues* 32: 147–68.

Hite, S. 1981. *The Hite Report on Male Sexuality*. New York: Knopf.

Hooper, J.O. 1979. "My Wife, the Student." *Family Coordinator* 28: 459–64.

Hopkins, J.R. 1977. "Sexual Behavior in Adolescence." *Journal of Social Issues* 33: 67–85.

Hunt, M. 1974. *Sexual Behavior in the 1970s*. Chicago: Playboy.

Jesser, C.J. 1972. "Women in Society: Some Academic Perspectives and the Issues Therein." *International Journal of Sociology of the Family* 2: 246–59.

———. 1978. "Male Responses to Direct Verbal Sexual Initiatives of Females." *Journal of Sex Research* 14: 118–28.

Johnson, R.W., et al. 1978. "Perceived Attractiveness as a Function of Support for the Feminist Movement: Not Necessarily a Put-down of Women." *Canadian Journal of Behavioral Science* 10: 214–21.

Johnson, R.W., S.W. Holborn, and S. Turcotte. 1979. "Perceived Attractiveness as a Function of Active vs. Passive Support for the Feminist Movement." *Personality and Social Psychology Bulletin* 5: 227–30.

Kinsey, A.C., et al. 1953 *Sexual Behavior in the Human Female.* Philadelphia: Saunders.

Komarovsky, M. 1976. *Dilemmas of Masculinity: A Study of College Youth.* New York: Norton.

Kroop, M. 1978. "When Women Initiate Sexual Relations." *Medical Aspects of a Human Sexuality* 12, 16, 23, 28-29.

LaPlante, M., N. McCormick, and G. Brannigan. 1980. "Living the Sexual Script: College Students' View of Influence in Sexual Encounters." *Journal of Sex Research* 16: 338-55.

Larkin, R. 1979. *Suburban Youth in Cultural Conflict.* New York: Oxford University Press.

Leibowitz, L. 1978. *Females, Males, Families: A Biosocial Approach.* Belmont, CA: Wadsworth.

Long-Laws, J. 1979. *The Second X: Sex Role and Social Role.* New York: Elsevier, North Holland.

Mancini, J.A., and D.K. Orthner. 1978. "Recreational Sexuality Preferences Among Middle-Class Husbands and Wives." *Journal of Sex Research* 14: 96-106.

Maslow, A.H. 1963. "Self-Esteem (Dominance Feeling) and Sexuality in Women." *Sexual Behavior and Personality Characteristics.* Ed. M.F. DeMartino. New York: Grove. 71-112.

McCormick, N.B. 1976. "Impact of Sex and Sex Role on Subjects' Perceptions of Social Power in Hypothetical Sexual Interactions." Paper presented at the meeting of the Western Psychological Association, Los Angeles, April.

———. 1976b. Author's files. Unpublished data. (Information available from N. McCormick, Ph.D., Department of Psychology, State University of New York College at Plattsburgh, Plattsburgh, NY 12901)

———. 1977. "Gender Role and Expected Social Power Behavior in Sexual Decision-Making." Doctoral dissertation, University of California at Los Angeles. *Dissertation Abstracts International* 37: 422-B. (University Microfilms No. 77-1646, 151)

———. 1979. "Come-Ons and Put-Offs: Unmarried Students' Strategies for Having and Avoiding Sexual Intercourse." *Psychology of Women Quarterly,* 4: 194-211.

McKee, J., and A. Sherriffs. 1957. "The Differential Evaluation of Males and Females." *Journal of Personality,* 25: 356-71.

Mercer, G.W., and P.M. Kohn. 1979. "Gender Difference in the Interpretation of Conservatism, Sex Urges, and Sexual Behavior Among College Students." *Journal of Sex Research* 15: 129-42.

Murstein, B.I. 1980. "Mate Selection in the 1970s." *Journal of Marriage and the Family* 42: 777-92.

Peplau, L., Z. Rubin, and C. Hill. 1976. "The Sexual Balance of Power." *Psychology Today* 10: 142-47, 151.

———. 1977. "Sexual Intimacy in Dating Couples." *Journal of Social Issues* 33: 86-109.

Perper, T., and V.S. Fox. 1980a. "Special Focus: Flirtation Behavior in Public Settings." Paper presented at the meeting of the Eastern Region of the Society for the Scientific Study of Sex, Philadelphia, April.

———. 1980b. "Flirtation and Pickup Patterns in Bars." Paper presented at the meeting of the Eastern Conference on Reproductive Behavior, New York, June.

Pleck, J.H. 1979. "Men's Family Work: Three Perspectives and Some New Data." *Family Coordinator* 28: 481-88.

Rainwater, L. 1971. "Marital Sexuality in Four Cultures of Poverty." *Human Sexual Behavior: Variations in the Ethnographic Spectrum.* Eds. D.S. Marshall and R.C. Suggs. New York: Basic.

Raven, B.H. 1965. "Social Influence and Power." *Current Studies in Social Psychology.* Eds. I.D. Steiner and M. Fishbein. New York: Holt, Rinehart and Winston.

———. 1971. "The Comparative Analysis of Power and Power Preference." Paper presented at the meeting of the Albany Symposium on Power and Influence, Albany, New York. October 11-13.

Robinson, W.J. 1929. *Woman: Her Sex and Love Life.* 17th ed. New York: Eugenics.

Rosenkrantz, P., S. Vogel, H. Bee, I. Broverman, and D. Broverman. 1968. "Sex Role Stereotypes and Self-Concepts in College Students." *Journal of Consulting and Clinical Psychology* 32: 287-95.

Rubin, L.B. 1976. *Worlds of Pain: Life in the Working Class Family.* New York: Basic.

Safilios-Rothschild, C. 1977. *Love, Sex, and Sex Roles.* Englewood Cliffs, NJ: Prentice-Hall, Spectrum Books.

Sanders, J.S., and W.L. Robinson. 1979. "Talking and Not Talking About Sex: Male and Female Vocabularies." *Journal of Communication* 29: 22-30.

Scanzoni, J.H. 1970. *Opportunity and the Family.* New York: Free Press.

Scanzoni, J.H., and G.L. Fox. 1980. "Sex Roles, Family and Society: The 70s and Beyond." *Journal of Marriage and the Family* 42: 743-56.

Scanzoni, L., and J.H. Scanzoni. 1976. *Men,*

Women, and Change. New York: McGraw-Hill.

Seyfried, B.A. and C.Hendrick. 1973. "When Do Opposites Attract? When They Are Opposite in Sex and Sex-Role Attitudes." *Journal of Personality and Social Psychology* 25: 15–20.

Stephens, W.N. 1963. *The Family in Cross-Cultural Perspective.* New York: Holt, Rinehart and Winston.

Tavris, C. 1978. "40,000 Men Tell About Their Sexual Behavior, Their Fantasies, the Ideal Woman, and Their Wives." *Redbook Magazine* February: 111–13.

Walster, E., G.W. Walster, and E. Berscheid. 1978. *Equity Theory and Research.* Boston: Allyn and Bacon.

Walster, E., G.W. Walster, & J. Traupmann. 1978. "Equity and Premarital Sex." *Journal of Personality and Social Psychology* 36: 82–92.

Weber, M. 1964. *The Theory of Social and Economic Organization.* Trans. and eds. A.M. Henderson and T. Parsons. New York: Free Press.

Zelnick, M., and J.F. Kantner. 1977. "Sexual and Contraceptive Experience of Young Unmarried Women in the United States, 1976 and 1971." *Family Planning Perspectives* 9: 55–71.

———. 1979. "Reasons for Nonuse of Contraceptives by Sexually Active Women Aged 15–19." *Family Planning Perspectives* 11: 289–96.

———. 1980. "Sexual Activity, Contraceptive Use and Pregnancy Among Metropolitan-Area Teenagers: 1971–1979." *Family Planning Perspectives* 12: 230–37.

" MARRIAGE SQUEEZE: MATE
, MORTALITY, AND THE
RADIENT*

Among persons in midlife, about one in five is unmarried. The sex ratio in this group is about 80, which is markedly unbalanced. Although changes in fertility and mortality are contributing factors, the real squeeze is largely attributable to the ubiquitous norm that husbands should be older than their wives. This mating gradient is the most significant determinant of the competition for mates as it is experienced by older unmarried women compared with older unmarried men. The nature and magnitude of this marriage squeeze are demonstrated using Canadian vital statistics and census data. Age differentials of brides and grooms in all marriages registered in 1981 are used to create "availability indices" that estimate the number of unmarried persons of the opposite sex that are potentially available for every 100 unmarried persons. For men, availability indices are low in the 20s, and they increase with advancing age, to about one-to-one in the 50s. For women, access to potential grooms is highest in the 20s and decreases with advancing age until, in the 50s, there are only 50 potential grooms per 100 unmarried women. The implications of unbalanced sex ratios are discussed with reference to changes in marriage and the family. Markedly skewed sex ratios may shift the bal-

ance of power between the sexes and produce a demographic reaffirmation of the double standard.

Most people are socialized to expect that they will marry, and that, once married, they will spend most of their lives in the company of a husband or wife. In Canada, about 90 percent of all men and 92 percent of all women will marry at least once before the age of 80 (Adams and Nagnur 1981, 56). The observation that most people marry often leads to the perception that most adults are married, with the unmarried being viewed as a small residual category who are statistically and socially deviant.[1] When considering family life in contemporary North America, however, it is important to distinguish between persons who *have never been* married, the statistic that is usually given, and persons who are *currently* married. In actuality, the married state is not universal or even nearly universal. In Canada in 1981, the most recent census year, among persons 16 years of age and older, about one-third were not married (see Table 1). One adult out of three still constitutes a minority, but it is a substantial one.

Being unmarried is not necessarily problematic for young persons who have not married yet. At the other end of the life span, the approach of senescence may diminish the centrality of the married state. In midlife, however, marriage continues to be the status preferred by most men and women. Although some persons elect to remain single, being unmarried is most often viewed as being emo-

Source: *Sociological Perspectives* 31 (1988): 142–67. Reprinted with permission.

*A preliminary version of this article was presented to the Pacific Sociological Association at their annual meeting in Portland, Oregon, in April 1987. This research was made possible, in part, by a University of Victoria Faculty Research Grant. I am indebted to Mr. Dhruva Nagnur, now of the Social and Economic Studies Division of Statistics Canada, for providing unpublished data on marriages by sex and age in Canada in 1981. The research assistance of Ms. Linda Kriwtschenko and of Ms. Sandra Jenko is gratefully acknowledged.

Table 1
Proportion of Population Unmarried, by Age and
Sex: Canada, 1981

Age	Males	Females
16–19	92.95	88.31
20–24	79.02	58.25
25–29	39.57	27.42
30–34	21.15	18.20
35–39	16.59	17.47
40–44	14.19	16.71
45–49	12.79	16.23
50–54	13.71	18.88
55–59	14.55	23.52
60–64	15.97	33.29
65–69	16.95	42.74
70–74	22.19	58.48
75–79	28.86	73.86
80+	46.81	91.44
16–29	69.91	56.40
30–64	16.05	19.99
65+	25.22	63.19
All ages 16+	36.28	38.54

Source: Census of Canada (1981).
Note: Total population of Canada (N=24, 341, 700) rounded
to the nearest hundred. Unmarried persons includes all
persons who are never-married, divorced, or widowed.

tionally, socially, and economically problematic (Adams 1976; Stein 1981). Nevertheless,
among persons aged 30–64, about 16 percent
of men and about 20 percent of women are
unmarried.

The study of patterns of nuptiality has
tended to focus almost entirely upon young
persons contemplating primary marriages.
However, given that more than one in three
marriages now involve remarriages, the systematic study of mate selection needs to be
broadened to include the increasing number
of persons who might marry in midlife or
later. The purpose of the present article is to
document some of the demographic and social constraints that affect the mate-selection
opportunities for the one in three adults who
is currently unmarried, with special emphasis
on the situation of midlife adults aged 30–64.

At least three factors affect the marriage
market in midlife. First, fluctuations in fertility may cause a "marriage squeeze" as a result of a lack of cross-sex persons of a suitable
age. Second, increasing sex differentials in
mortality produce marked decreases in sex ratios in the later years. A third factor, which
to my mind is the most important, is the operation of age-based mate-selection norms
that produce large discrepancies in the *de facto*
pool of eligibles for men and for women. The
combined effects of these interacting factors
will be illustrated by the construction of
"availability indices," which estimate the
number of unmarried persons of the opposite
sex potentially available for every 100 persons
in various age–sex groupings. These "availability indices" are widely disparate for men
and women at different ages, a phenomenon
that has major implications for male–female
interaction in both familial and nonfamilial
settings.[2]

Sex Ratios in the Unmarried Population

In describing mate-selection patterns, the first
step is to define the pool of eligibles who are
considered to be at least minimally suitable
as potential partners. In our culture, this ordinarily means persons of the opposite sex
who are unmarried.[3] Given the increasing tolerance for remarriage, for most persons eligibles include both the never married and the
divorced or widowed.[4]

The most basic parameter that defines the
field of eligibles is simply the relative proportions in population of males and females of
approximately the same ages. Such data are
available for Canada for the 1981 census year
(see Table 2). In adolescence and young adulthood, the sex ratio approximates 100 and remains near unity until the late 50s. If marriage
patterns simply involved stable marriages between young persons of the same age, virtually everyone would have the opportunity to
marry, and the unmarried population would
consist primarily of widows past retirement
age. In fact, however, people do not marry

Table 2
Sex Distributions by Age, Marital Status, and Method of Comparison: Canada, 1981

Age	Sex Ratios[a] of All Persons	Sex Ratios of All Unmarried[b] Persons	Proportionate Distribution Among Unmarried Persons % male – % female[c]
16–19	104.13	109.91	52–48
20–24	100.41	136.22	58–42
25–29	99.19	143.18	59–41
30–34	100.43	116.69	54–46
35–39	101.77	96.67	49–51
40–44	101.72	86.37	46–54
45–49	102.27	80.64	45–55
50–54	99.97	72.57	42–58
55–59	92.95	57.51	37–63
60–64	89.46	42.88	30–70
65–69	86.07	34.14	25–75
70–74	79.86	30.31	26–74
75–79	71.59	27.98	22–78
80+	54.30	27.80	22–78
16–29	101.07	125.28	56–44
30–64	102.60	79.40	44–56
65+	74.87	29.89	23–77
All ages 16+	96.18	88.49	47–53

Source: Census of Canada (1981).
[a] The sex ratio is the number of men divided by the number of women times 100.
[b] Unmarried persons includes all persons who are never-married, divorced, or widowed.
[c] Proportions are rounded to the nearest whole percentage point.

others of the same age. A combination of fertility, mortality, and marriage patterns together produce markedly unbalanced sex ratios in the unmarried population. Among persons under 35, such ratios are unusually high; after 35, they decline systematically until, in old age, unmarried women outnumber unmarried men more than four to one. Among the younger populations, the factor of fertility contributes to these outcomes; at the later ages, mortality differentials are more important.

The Fertility Factor

During a time of rapid increase in fertility, some young women are "squeezed" out of the marriage market because there are not enough potential husbands of a suitable age, namely, two to three years older than themselves. The resulting phenomenon is known as the *marriage squeeze*, and has been of concern to demographers for more than 20 years (Glick, Heer, and Beresford 1963, 38).[5] However, this factor does not contribute substantially to the sex ratios of the unmarried at midlife. The only women who are affected by it are those born during the few years of rapid increase in fertility; once high fertility rates have been established, the sex ratios of eligible persons are again stabilized. At the other end of a baby boom, young men who are born during the time of rapid decrease in fertility will also experience a marriage squeeze, in that they will find insufficient numbers of women two to three years younger than themselves. The marriage squeeze seems to account for only a small proportion of persons who never marry, and to have had a substantial impact only on those few select cohorts born during extreme fluctuations in the fertility rate (Veevers 1988c).

The Mortality Factor

In the industrialized Western world, male death rates are consistently and substantially higher than female death rates, a discrepancy that has been increasing (Gee and Veevers 1983; Veevers and Gee 1985). Women can now expect to live about seven years longer than men. Although all sex ratios decline with advancing age, it is noteworthy that, in the general population, the decline does not begin until after age 50, and it is not really pronounced until after age 70. Among unmarrieds, however, the decline begins at age 35 and is much more pronounced. One factor that contributes to this situation is that married persons, especially husbands, have lower mortality rates than the unmarried (Fox, Bulusu, and Kinlen 1979; Boyd 1983). Another is the fact that the combination of female longevity plus a preference for marrying older men ensures that the incidence of wives who are widowed will vastly exceed that of husbands who become widowers.[6] At the time of a divorce, the sex ratio of persons involved is obviously balanced. However, once persons become unmarried as a result of death or divorce, the rates of remarriage are higher for men than for women, and the men's time spent before remarriage is shorter (Adams and Nagnur 1981, 56; Treas and Van Hilst 1976).

The effects of differential mortality, differential widowing, and differential remarriage rates combine to produce markedly different sex ratios among the unmarried population compared with the population as a whole, as shown in Table 2. Among persons aged 30–64 in the general population, the sex ratio is 102, which is about equal but slightly in the direction of an excess of males. Among unmarried persons aged 30–64, the sex ratio is only 79.

Before considering other factors that contribute to male–female imbalances, let us examine what sex ratios actually mean. By demographic convention, sex ratios are a convenient means of making between-group comparisons, or of assessing changes within a group over time. In terms of their consequences for a particular population, however, their meaning is less obvious. Another way of expressing the imbalances described by a sex ratio of 79 would be to note that it describes a group composed of about 44 percent men and about 56 percent women. Column 4 in Table 2 shows this alternate way of describing sex imbalances. Some imbalances may not seem dramatic for many purposes. However, if the population is to be grouped into cross-sex pairs, as it is in marriage, small distortions may produce significant results.

Let us consider a hypothetical population of 100 persons: 44 men and 56 women. If *all* of the available males were involved in a cross-sex pair, then 44 women could marry 44 men, and 88 percent of the population could be married. Of necessity, 12 women out of 56, or *21 percent of all women* could *not* be married. When talking about marriage markets, this way of looking at sex imbalances may be more relevant than conventional sex ratios.

The Hypergamy Factor: Age-Based Marriage Norms

The demographic facts that describe the distribution of the sexes in a population must be considered in the light of the social attitudes concerning them. Studies of mate selection provide extensive evidence supporting the generalization that *hypergamy*, the situation where the woman marries up in terms of status, is almost universally more acceptable and more common than the converse, *hypogamy*, in which the woman marries down. These norms structure the patterns of relative ages within marriage. Other things being equal, it is appropriate for a man to marry someone of his own age *or younger*; it is appropriate for a woman to marry someone of her own age *or older*. When women are seeking husbands, they tend to seek men who are considerably older than themselves. In contrast, men seeking wives tend to want relatively young wives. Technically, the word "nubile" means marriageable, but in common parlance it is synonymous with young.

Casual inspection of marriage patterns suggests that the "typical" marriage in Canada involves a bride between the ages of 21 and 24 marrying a groom between the ages of 23 and 26 who is two or three years her senior. Such an observation would hardly be thought controversial, and yet such a union involves only about one-quarter of all marriages. During the formation of primary marriages, in late adolescence or early adulthood, hypergamy norms are not usually problematic, in that approximately equal numbers of eligible men and women exist, and the age differences of spouses are usually not large. At the later ages, however, the age range of potential mates widens considerably (Bytheway 1982). In the 20s, most mates are selected from persons within a range of about five years. In later life, potential mates may be 10, 15, or even 20 years younger or older than oneself.

Nearly universal hypergamy norms mean that competition in the marriage market is quite different for men and for women. With advancing age, there are proportionately fewer and fewer unmarried men; those who are available can choose from a large pool of younger women and face few competitors. Conversely, with advancing age, there are proportionately more and more unmarried women; those who are available can choose from only a small pool of older men and face many competitors, including some women who are much younger.

The asymmetrical nature of marriage opportunities for unmarried men and women in midlife has been discussed from a number of perspectives (Novak 1983; Guttentag and Secord 1983; Espenshade 1985, 231–33). While various authors agree that it exists, and

that the disparities involved are "large," there have been few attempts to assess exactly how large the imbalances are, or how they are affected when a multiplicity of factors are taken into account simultaneously. In addressing this problem, we have developed a method of calculating *availability indexes* to quantify the sex-ratio imbalances in the unmarried population.

Calculating Availability Indexes

An availability index is defined as the number of eligible persons of the opposite sex available for every 100 unmarried persons. Availability indexes are created by relating two kinds of data: nuptiality data, which allow for a description of probable marriage patterns, and demographic data, which relate those patterns to particular age-sex distributions of unmarried persons. The present illustration will be limited to data on 190 082 registered marriages, with the exact age of brides cross-tabulated by the exact age of grooms. Statistics Canada provided population estimates; men and women classified as never-married, divorced, or widowed were grouped to produce a distribution of unmarried persons by age and sex.

The technique involved in the calculation of availability ratios will be illustrated by examining in detail the steps used to estimate the number of potential brides available for every 100 eligible men who were 40 years of age in Canada in 1981.

Step One: Age Range of Potential Eligibles

Theoretically, it is possible for any single person who is of legal age to marry any cross-sex single person who is also of legal age, and who is outside incest prohibitions. In fact, however, only persons of a "suitable" age are really viable as potential mates. For some individuals, an age difference of 20, 30, or even 40 years is acceptable. In most instances, however, persons marry within a few years of their own age.[7] By examining the age distributions of actual brides and grooms in 1981, one can avoid speculation about the choices that individuals might prefer in marriage, or might at least find acceptable, and rely only on what they actually do.

The age range within which persons generally find each other to be acceptable marriage partners was arbitrarily defined as the age range within which 80 percent of all marriages for persons of a given age occur. The range of ages that are acceptable is relatively restricted among the young, and it increases in midlife. For example, in Canada in 1981, of all brides aged 20, 80 percent chose grooms between 20 and 25, a six-year span; however, of all brides aged 40, 80 percent chose grooms between 32 to 52, a 21-year span.

To begin with our specific example: among grooms aged 40, 80 percent chose brides in the age range 26 to 42. As shown in Table 3, Column 4, in 1981 there were 520 200 unmarried women of these ages.

Table 3
The Calculation of an Availability Index: An Example Using Unmarried Men of 40: Canada, 1981

Age of "Suitable" Unmarried Women[a]	Number of Brides of This Age: Canada 1981[b]	Proportion of Brides Selecting Men of 40[c]	Number of Unmarried Women[d]	"Fair Share" of Potential Brides[e]
26	8 712	.459	57 100	262
27	7 230	.913	49 300	450
28	5 736	1.116	43 300	483
29	4 822	1.224	38 800	475
30	3 994	1.652	35 800	591
31	3 392	2.241	33 200	744
32	2 847	3.410	31 400	1 071
33	2 645	3.251	30 000	975
34	2 340	3.376	29 400	993
35	1 856	4.149	25 200	1 047
36	1 464	4.167	23 200	967
37	1 371	5.616	22 600	1 269
38	1 285	5.370	22 300	1 198
39	1 032	5.717	20 600	1 178
40	983	5.086	19 900	1 012
41	857	3.967	19 200	762
42	819	4.274	18 900	808
Totals:	51 385	2.133	520 200	14 284

[a] Of all men of age 40 who got married in Canada in 1981, at least 80 percent chose brides between the ages of 26 and 42.
[b] Of all brides who got married in Canada in 1981, there were 51 385 between the ages of 26 and 42.
[c] Of all brides aged 26–42, a total of 2.1 percent married men aged 40. Of brides aged 37, 5.6 percent married men aged 40.
[d] In Canada in 1981, there were a total of 520 200 unmarried women aged 26–42.
[e] The "fair share" for men of 40 is the percentage of unmarried women of a given age who select men of 40 as grooms. There are many young unmarried women aged 26, but only a few (0.5 percent) select men of 40, so their "fair share" is estimated to be 0.5 percent of 57 100 or 262. Conversely, there are fewer unmarried women at age 40, but more (5.1 percent) selected men of 40, so their "fair share" is estimated to be 5.1 percent of 19 900 or 1012.

Step Two: The "Fair Share" Ratio

One way to think about eligible mates would be simply to compare the number of single persons of a given age with the total number of persons in the population who are of the opposite sex, unmarried, and of a suitable age. Thus, in Canada in 1981, there were 18 000 unmarried men aged 40 who, theoretically, could choose as brides any unmarried woman aged 26–42, of which there were 520 200. Although this superficially seems to constitute very good odds, in reality it overlooks the very important factor of competition.

Although all women aged 26–42 may be suitable as brides for men of 40, they are not all really available, in that 40-year-old men must compete with other unmarried men of all ages. Some of these eligible women will want to marry men who are younger than 40; others will prefer men who are older. Realistically, the best that 40-year-old men can expect is their "fair share" of all women aged 26–42. How can the competition with men of other ages be taken into account to determine their "fair share" of the marriage market available to 40-year-olds?

To estimate the answer to this question, we need only consider how likely women aged 26–42 are to marry men aged 40 exactly (Table 3). In 1981, of all brides aged 26 (N = 8712), only 0.459 percent married men aged 40. Of all unmarried women aged 26 in Canada in 1981 (N = 57 100), we can then assume that 0.459 percent, or 262, are likely to select an unmarried man aged 40 rather than someone of any other age. Similarly of all brides aged 35 (N = 1856), 4.149 percent married men aged 40. Of all unmarried women aged 35 (N = 25 200), we can assume that 4.149 percent, or 1047, are likely to select an unmarried man aged 40 rather than any other age. This procedure is then repeated for all ages from 26 to 42. The result is that of all unmarried men aged 40 in 1981 (N = 18 000), a total of 14 284 unmarried women are theoretically available to them as potential brides. The availability index for men aged 40 is therefore 14 284 per 18 000, or 79 per 100.

Once we know the age range of potential mates, and the "fair share" that a given group has of that pool, it is easy to calculate the ratio between the number of potential brides or grooms and the number of eligible mates available to them. These steps were repeated to compute the availability indices of potential brides for selected ages for men aged 20 to 70, as shown in Table 4. The same procedures were applied to compute availability in-

---

Table 4

Availability Indexes of Potential Brides for Unmarried Men, by Age of Men: Canada, 1981

Age of Unmarried Men	Number of Unmarried Men	Age Range of "Suitable" Potential Brides[a]	"Fair Share" of Potential Brides[b]	Availability Indexes[c]
20	217 400	18–21	101 400	46
30	45 100	22–32	33 812	75
40	18 000	26–42	14 284	79
50	16 380	31–52	16 606	101
60	13 440	40–62	19 779	147
70	11 860	54–71	31 003	261

[a] Of all men of a given age getting married in Canada in 1981, at least 80 percent chose brides within this age range.

[b] "Fair share" is calculated as shown in Table 3.

[c] An availability index is the number of brides potentially available for 100 unmarried men.

Table 5
Availability Indexes of Potential Grooms for Unmarried Women, by Age of Women: Canada, 1981

Age of Unmarried Women	Number of Unmarried Women	Age Range of "Suitable" Potential Grooms[a]	"Fair Share" of Potential Grooms[b]	Availability Indexes[c]
20	170 600	20–25	176 977	104
30	35 800	26–39	26 176	73
40	19 900	32–52	11 929	60
50	22 820	43–62	11 447	50
60	32 360	53–71	10 652	33
70	38 960	64–75+	7 484	20

[a] Of all Canadian women of a given age getting married in Canada in 1981, at least 80 percent chose grooms within this age range.

[b] "Fair share" is calculated as shown in Table 3.

[c] An availability index is the number of grooms potentially available for 100 unmarried women.

dexes of potential grooms for selected ages of women aged 20 to 70, as shown in Table 5.

Step Three: Age-Sex Differences in Availability Indexes

A comparison of Table 4 and Table 5 shows the differences in circumstances for men and women at different ages in the life cycle. For men, advancing age means a progressive improvement in the availability ratios of unmarried men to potential brides. At age 20, the marriage market is very restricted: their availability ratio is only 46 potential brides for every 100 unmarried men. This ratio improves during the next two decades, until it is approximately one to one by age 50. After that time, it increases markedly, until it is better than two to one in old age. Thus, men begin with a situation of high competition for a limited number of women, and they end up with a situation of little competition for many women.

Conversely, the availability ratios of women to eligible men begin very high for young girls, who are eligible for many men, and then decline with advancing age, as more and more unmarried women compete for fewer and fewer unmarried men. The availability ratio

at age 20 is about one to one; it declines steadily, until, at midlife, there are only about 50 potential grooms for every 100 unmarried women. The ratio declines sharply from that point on, until in old age there are only about 20 potential grooms for every 100 unmarried women.

An Additional Complication: Cohabitation

Although the availability indices, as we have presented them, provide an estimate of the proportions of men and women available for marriage, they systematically exaggerate the opportunities as they exist in reality. Persons who are not legally married may still be outside the pool of eligibles if they are living in a common law marriage, an alternative that seems to be increasing (Glick and Spanier 1980). Strictly speaking, the availability ratios should be based only on unmarried persons who are not cohabiting.

An Additional Complication: Homosexuality

For most persons, an important criterion of eligibility for marriage is not only a person of the opposite sex, but one who is exclusively (or at least predominantly) heterosexual. The incidence of homosexuality in the population has been the subject of considerable speculation. Advocates of the Gay Liberation movement have a tendency to perceive the gay community — both in and out of the closet — as considerably larger than the straight community is likely to believe. The *minimum* estimate of the incidence of persons who are exclusively or predominantly homosexual is 6 percent of men and 1 percent of women (Gagnon and Simon 1973, 131). A *conservative* estimate is at least 15 percent of men and 6 percent of women (Hyde 1982, 378). Presumably, the rates of homosexuality are generally lower than average among husbands and wives, and substantially higher than average among unmarried persons, especially midlife bachelors and spinsters who have never married. Unfortunately, no data could be found to provide accurate estimates of the prevalence of homosexuality by sex, age, and marital status. Strictly speaking, the availability indexes should be modified by excluding from the pool of eligibles a certain percentage of men and women who are homosexual. Since all available studies confirm that homosexuality is much more common among men than among women, the fact of male homosexuality further reduces the sex ratio of the pool of eligibles.

An Additional Complication: Perennial Bachelors

Many analyses of family life in North America reflect an implicit pro-nuptialism, in that they assume that almost all unmarried persons would, under beneficent circumstances, want to get married. The present analysis cannot take into account the presence of unmarried persons who are, in fact, outside the pool of eligibles in that they have no interest in, or intention of getting married, regardless of their opportunities to do so. This population includes nuns and priests as well as voluntary celibates and other misogamists. Popular wis-

dom suggests that men are more likely than women to pronounce themselves "not the marrying kind," but without additional research this remains speculative.

A Singles Party

The "availability index" for unmarried women aged 40 is estimated to be 60 men per 100 women (see Table 5). A more meaningful conceptualization of these data is possible if we imagine what this distribution of the sexes means in a social setting. Suppose all the unmarried women aged 40 gave a party to which they invited all the unmarried men aged 32 to 52. If their "fair share" of this group came to a typical party of 100 persons, there would be approximately 38 men and 62 women. Some unknown proportion of those men are not truly eligible, because they are gay, or because they are already living with someone, or because they are uninterested. Nevertheless, if all the men wanted to dance — or all decided to get married — there would be only 38 men to couple with 38 women, leaving 24 women, or 24 percent of the entire group, without partners. Of the 62 women who came to the party, *more than one-third* would have no one to dance with.

If a similar singles dance were held by unmarried women of 50, where the "availability index" is 50, there would be 33 men and 66 women. Half of the women would be without partners. It is this situation that we are referring to as the *real* marriage squeeze.

Implications: The Demographic Double Standard

The double standard of ageing is not news. Like other manifestations of the double standard, it has its roots in misogynous attitudes that are a fundamental part of our cultural heritage, and that are accepted, in varying degrees, by both men and women. Like other manifestations, it changes slowly, if at all. Contemporary marriage norms do not go to the extreme of the Indian custom of suttee, which dictates that a widow should immolate herself on her husband's funeral pyre. However, contemporary norms do continue to devalue older widows or divorcees and to handicap them in the marriage market.

What is news is the *degree* to which the double standard of ageing has become manifest in recent years. Concomitant changes in fertility and mortality have combined to exaggerate greatly the imbalance between the sexes. Moreover, the imbalances, which in the past were a part of life in old age, have now become prevalent in midlife as well.

Dilemmas of Mate Selection

To this point, we have considered only the minimal criteria for defining someone as eligible for marriage — namely, being a cross-sex unmarried heterosexual person within a certain age range. In considering populations in national terms, we overlook regional differences in the distribution of population. Propinquity provides a major constraint, especially for persons outside major metropolitan areas. Moreover, in addition to important norms of racial and religious homogamy, the mating gradient that dictates that women should marry up and men should marry down applies not only to age, but also to height, weight, socioeconomic status, education, and perhaps intelligence (Doudna and McBride 1980).

When all of the factors constraining mate selection are taken into account, what is amazing is not that some people are unmarried, but that most people do have mates. Saxton (1983, 4) makes this point quite graphically. If one were to assume that a person had six criteria for selecting a mate, and that the chances of each of these standards being met in another person were, on the average, one in five, then the cumulative odds against finding one persons meeting all six of the criteria at once would be five to the sixth power, or 15 625. Many individuals will have more than six minimum standards in mind, and, for those with idiosyncratic preferences, the odds

of finding them in an eligible person may be much more than one in five. A distorted sex ratio such as we have described greatly complicates what was already a very complex problem.

Consequences of Male–Female Imbalances

A full discussion of the implications of the markedly unbalanced sex ratios is beyond the scope of the present article.[8] It is clear, however, that such imbalances will have repercussions, not only for marital relationships, but also for various aspects of all other relationships between the sexes (Heer and Grossbard-Schechtmen 1981). Very low sex ratios will be associated with a cluster of social, sexual, and cultural consequences. Some of these outcomes are suggested by the examination of groups, such as American blacks, who have already experienced very low sex ratios (Guttentag and Secord 1983, 199–230).

When considering what amounts to demographic determinism, it is important to note that this is one of many factors that may be leading the family in North America toward the same place. The degree of determination by any one factor is difficult to determine, but the sex-ratio factor is clearly one of importance.

In sorting out cause and effect, it is important not to think of the patterns of mate selection as being something "caused" by the male preference for younger women. It is also "caused" by the female preference for older men, who are, by and large, better providers and more established. One response to the dilemma of mate selection might be to accept as husband material persons of one's own age or even younger. However, this does not seem to be happening (Veevers 1984; Veevers and Gee 1985).

Among the many sequela that might result from too many women and too few men, we suggest the following hypotheses for further examination. With declines in sex ratios, one would expect to find:

- *Single subcultures*: an increase in the proportions of persons who delay marriage or remarriage, or who never marry or remarry.
- *Antinuptialism*: an increase in supportive ideologies that value a life of *Single Blessedness* (Adams 1976).
- *Innovations in mate selection*: a trend to marriage bureaus, classified advertisements, and other unorthodox strategies to increase access to potential mates (Jedlicka 1978).
- *Heterogamy*: a broadening in the field of eligibles to include a wider age range of persons, as well as those with dissimilar racial, religious, or marital characteristics (Glick and Spanier 1980).
- *Illegitimacy*: an increase in numbers and proportions of out-of-wedlock births (Guttentag and Secord 1983, 216–20).
- *Divorce*: an increase in separation and divorce, as a result of lower marital commitment among husbands and higher marital dissatisfaction among wives (Guttentag and Secord 1983, 215).
- *Female independence*: an increase attributable to a reluctance to depend upon marriage for social and economic status (Guttentag and Secord 1983, 215).
- *Female-headed households*: an increase as a result of illegitimacy and low marriage/remarriage rates.
- *Man-sharing*: an increase in tolerance for polygamous relationships, both premarital and extramarital (Richardson 1985).

The Principle of Least Interest

The traditional family system is based on the ideals of universal and life-long monogamous marriage, which, in turn, are based on balanced sex ratios. Assuming that, for most people, getting and staying married are important life goals, the bottom line in marital disputes is the threat of divorce. If a situation is defined as intolerable, walking away from it is an increasingly acceptable solution, as is subsequently entering a new and (one hopes) more satisfactory union. For young wives, especially attractive young wives, there is a large pool of men potentially available as mates; this means that the husband who does not create a satisfactory marital environment is in danger of losing his wife. However, by midlife, the wife's pool of eligibles has shrunk, while the husband's has expanded considerably. For the wife, the realistic choice may well be between staying married to her current husband or not being married at all.

In marriage, as in other relationships, there is a well-known *principle of least interest*: "that person is able to dictate the conditions of association whose interest in the continuation of the affair is the least" (Waller 1938, 275). The demographic reality is that, in a marriage at midlife, the onus for maintaining the union is more on the wife than on the husband; this situation, other things being equal, must tip the balance of power in his favour.

If we assume that most adults are heterosexual, and that their first preference is to live out their lives with a husband or wife in the context of a stable and monogamous marriage, then the imbalance of sex ratios results in a substantial, non-negotiable, and pervasive reinforcement of the power advantage that has traditionally been associated with the male role. In essence, what is involved in the "real" marriage squeeze is a *reaffirmation of the double standard*. The traditional double standard was based on a philosophy of patriarchy and on vestiges of Victorian morality. These underpinnings have recently been discredited in light of egalitarian norms and increasing permissiveness. In their place, however, there may well emerge a new basis for a double standard. Men and women may continue to be subjected to quite different expectations concerning their sexual and/or conjugal behaviour. The emergent rationale may be based, not upon androcentric ideologies, but upon the demographic reality of a social world in which there is a relative scarcity of men and a relative surplus of women.

Notes

1. For example, in a recent textbook, Kelley (1979, 271) writes that "despite our high degree

of interest in alternative lifestyles, it remains true that 95% of American women are married by age 54, and 94% of the men by age 64."

2. A comparable situation exists in the white population of the United States (Stein 1981, 29). In the black population, mortality rates for young males are so high that balanced sex ratios are not found, even at the young ages. In 1970, among black women over 20, 30 or more out of 100 did not have a potential partner in the marriage pool (Guttentag and Secord 1983, 201). The greatly exaggerated marriage squeeze among black populations is discussed separately (Veevers 1988b).

3. Farber (1964) has suggested that the family system in North America is moving toward a condition of permanent availability, in which every adult in the society will be considered as potentially eligible as a mate for every other cross-sex adult outside the incest taboo, regardless of their current marital status. While there is evidence of trends toward such a situation, in which divorce and remarriage will be possible and acceptable in a wide variety of circumstances, such expectations are not yet widely shared, and, in most circumstances, persons who are married and who are living with their spouse are not considered marriageable (Veevers 1982).

4. This has not always automatically been assumed to be true. For example, writing in 1961, Peterson notes that "the sex ratio of that portion able to wed . . . is delimited, first of all, by age (it is usual to include that sector of the population aged 14 and over), and secondly by marital status. . . . Whether to include widowed and divorced persons is a moot point. Legally they are marriageable, but actually in the United States a large proportion of the persons so designated in any census will never marry" (Peterson 1961, 72). He goes on to discuss sex ratios in terms of marriageable persons, defined as aged 14 years or over and never married. He reports that, in 1950, among single persons, there were more than five males to every four females.

5. Alternative strategies for describing and assessing the marriage squeeze are discussed separately (Veevers 1988c).

6. In the United States, Nye and Berardo (1973, 600) estimate that, if a husband and wife are the same age, there is about a 60 percent chance that the woman will be widowed. If she is five years his junior, the probability increases to 70 percent, and if she is ten years younger, it is about 80 percent. In 1969, widows in the United States outnumbered widowers by more than three to one;

in 1970, the ratio was about four to one; in 1980, it was more than five to one (U.S. Bureau of the Census 1981).

7. In defining the field of eligibles that determine mate selection, it is important to remember that what is involved is not a description of all couples who may go together as dating and/or sexual partners, but rather only that small proportion of all relationships *that lead to marriage.* For example, of the many romantic and/or erotic liaisons between blacks and whites, only a very small proportion lead to marriage. Racially mixed couples are more likely than others to live together without marriage (Glick and Spanier 1980). In the same way, although there may be many romantic involvements between older men and much younger women, and even some involvements between older women and much younger men, these relationships are unlikely to be formalized by marriage.

8. The implications of low sex ratios have been discussed in some detail in *Too Many Women? The Sex Ratio Question* (Guttentag and Secord 1983). A lay person's view of some implications is presented by Novak (1983) in *The Great American Man Shortage and Other Roadblocks to Romance.* The available evidence concerning these nine hypotheses and other possibilities is discussed separately (Veevers 1988a).

Works Cited

Adams, Margaret, 1976. *Single Blessedness.* New York: Basic.

Adams, O.B., and D.N. Nagnur. 1981. *Marriage, Divorce and Mortality: A Life-Table Analysis for Canada.* Catalogue 84–536. Ottawa: Statistics Canada.

Boyd, M. 1983. "Marriage and Death." *Marriage and Divorce in Canada.* Ed. K. Ishwaran. Toronto: Met' ⁸⁰ ¹⁰⁶

Bytheway, W
Age of Ag
Marriage a

Doudna, Cl
"Where *A*
Top?" *Sav*

Espenshade,
America:
ing Cause
11: 193–2

Farber, Berr
teraction.

Sax
Fam
Stein, Pe
in a Socia
Treas, J., an
Remarriage R
Gerontologist 16:

Fox, J.A., L. Bulusu, and L. Kinlen. 1979. "Mortality and Age Differences in Marriage." *Journal of Biosocial Science* 11: 117–31.

Gagnon, William, and John Simon. 1973. *Sexual Conduct: The Social Origins of Human Sexuality.* Chicago: Aldine.

Gee, Ellen M., and Jean E. Veevers. 1983. "Accelerating Sex Mortality Differentials: An Analysis of Contributing Factors." *Social Biology* 30: 75–85.

Glick, P.C., D. Heer, and J.C. Beresford. 1963. "Family Formation and Family Composition: Trends and Prospects." *Sourcebook of Marriage and the Family.* Ed. M.B. Sussman. New York: Houghton Mifflin. 30–40.

Glick, Paul C., and Spanier, Graham B. 1980. "Married and Unmarried Cohabitation in the United States." *Journal of Marriage and the Family* 42: 19–30.

Gove, W.R. 1973. "Sex, Marital Status and Mortality." *American Journal of Sociology* 79: 45–67.

Guttentag, M., and P.F. Secord. 1983. *Too Many Women? The Sex Ratio Question.* Beverly Hills, CA: Sage.

Heer, D.M., and A. Grossbard-Schechtmen. 1981. "The Impact of the Female Marriage Squeeze and the Contraceptive Revolution on Sex Roles and the Women's Liberation Movement in the United States 1960–1975." *Journal of Marriage and the Family* 43: 49–65.

Hyde, Janet Shibley. 1982. *Understanding Human Sexuality.* New York: McGraw-Hill.

Jedlicka, D. 1978. "Sexual Inequality, Aging, and Innovation in Preferential Mate Selection." *Family Coordinator* 27: 137–40.

Kelley, R.K. 1979. *Courtship, Marriage and the Family.* New York: Harcourt Brace Jovanovich.

Novak, William. 1983. *The Great American Man Shortage and Other Roadblocks to Romance.* New York: Rawson.

Nye, F., and F. Berardo. 1973. *The Family: Its Structure and Function.* New York: Macmillan.

Peterson, W. 1961. *Population.* New York: Macmillan.

Richardson, Laurel. 1985. *The New Other Woman: Contemporary Single Women in Affairs with Married Men.* New York: Free Press.

ton, L. 1983. *The Individual, Marriage, and the ily.* Belmont, CA: Wadsworth.

er, ed. 1981. *Single Life: Unmarried Adults Context.* New York: St. Martin's.

A. Van Hilst. 1976. "Marriage and tes Among Older Americans."
32–36.

U.S. Bureau of the Census. 1981. *Marital Status and Living Arrangements: March 1980.* Current Population Report. Washington, DC: Government Printing Office.

Veevers, Jean E. 1982. "Permanent Availability for Marriage: Considerations of the Canadian Case." Paper presented to the International Sociological Association, Mexico City.

———. 1984. "Age-Discrepant Marriages: Cross-National Comparisons of Canadian-American Trends." *Social Biology* 30: 75–85.

———. 1988a. "Supply and Demand: Family Implications of Skewed Sex Ratios." Unpublished.

———. 1988b. "The Marriage Squeeze for Black Americans: Causes, Trends and Consequences." Unpublished.

———. 1988c. "Baby Boom, Baby Bust and the Marriage Squeeze: A Simplified Measure." Unpublished.

Veevers, Jean E., and Ellen M. Gee. 1985. "Accelerating Sex Mortality Differentials Among Black Americans." *Phylon: A Review of Race and Culture* 46: 162–75.

Waller, Willard. 1938. *The Family: A Dynamic Interpretation.* New York: Dryden.

ETHNIC INTERMARRIAGE AND ET
IDENTITY*

Jay Goldstein
Alexander Segall

Ethnic intermarriage is usually viewed as posing a problem for the maintenance of ethnic
identity. The hypothesis that intermarriage
weakens both internal and external ethnic
identity of offspring is tested on a representative sample of Winnipeg adults. Results show
that the presence of ethnically mixed parentage is inversely related to both of the indicators of internal identity and all three indicators of external identity. Multiple regression
analysis reveals that relative to socioeconomic
status (SES), age, sex, and ethnic generation,
mixed parentage is the best or is among the
best predictors of four of the five indicators
of identity. The implications of these findings
for subsequent research on the retention/loss
of ethnic identity are discussed.

Introduction

The attitudes of Canadians toward ethnic intermarriage have become increasingly favourable over the past 15 years.[1] Evidence also
points to an increase in the actual rate of intermarriage (see, for example, Kalbach 1974;
Lasry and Bloomfield-Schacter 1975). The
1981 Census of Canada, for the first time,
acknowledged the growing number of ethnic
intermarriages by allowing individuals to
specify more than one ethnic origin, and

nearly one Canadian in ten indicated multiple
origins (Statistics Canada 1983).

Sociologists have tended to view ethnic intermarriage as posing problems for the maintenance of ethnic identity. Given the important role of the family in the socialization
process, it is not surprising that intermarriage
should be seen as problematic for the intergenerational transmission of an ethnic group's
culture. Furthermore, the presence in the family of parents with different ethnic origins may
present difficulties for a child when it comes
to selecting a role model for his/her ethnicity
(A.I. Gordon 1964, 317ff).

It is primarily with regard to the extent of
the erosive influence of intermarriage that sociologists differ. One point of view is that
marriage across ethnic boundaries inevitably
leads to a loss of identity among minority
groups (M.M. Gordon 1964). In this vein,
Steinberg (1981) has asserted that intermarriage signifies that a group is disintegrating,
both socially and culturally. Steinberg claims
that even if the parents in a mixed marriage
are able to agree on a single identity for their
offspring, it is quite doubtful that their children will be able to develop or sustain a stable
ethnic identity.

In contrast to the preceding view is the belief that, in some cases, intermarriage can be
a means of recruiting members to an ethnic
group. Dinnerstein and Reimers (1975) see
this outcome as possible in the case of religiously based ethnic groups who can acquire
converts through intermarriage. Along similar
lines, Reitz (1980) contends that, while intermarriage may be an indication that the

Source: Canadian Ethnic Studies 17 (1985): 60–71. Reprinted with
permission.

*The research reported in this paper was part of the 1983 Winnipeg
Area Study. It was supported by grants from the Social Sciences and
Humanities Research Council of Canada and the University of Man-
itoba Institute for Social and Economic Research.

ohesion of an ethnic group has diminished, it may not indicate that, *if* the children of such marriages become members of the ethnic group of one (or both) parent(s).

Empirical research on the consequences of intermarriage in Canada is sparse. A review of the literature reveals that studies on this topic have had two principal foci. One of these is the impact of intermarriage on language retention among French Canadians, while the other is the effect of intermarriage on ethnic identity among Jews.

Studies by Castonguay (1982) and Li and Denis (1983) have demonstrated an association between an exogamous marriage and a shift from the use of French to the use of English among adult francophones. Mougeon (1977) reported that, in a predominantly English-speaking community, linguistically mixed marriages played an important role in the displacement of French by English.

The consequence of intermarriage for the Jewish ethnic group seems to vary, depending on whether one considers the partners in such marriages or their offspring. Recent studies of married couples in both Canada (Weinfeld 1981a) and the United States (Mayer 1980; Lazerwitz 1981) suggest that, if the non-Jewish partner converts to Judaism, then there is a high degree of Jewish religious expression in the family. However, when the non-Jewish spouse does not convert to Judaism (or the Jewish partner converts to his/her spouse's faith), there is a low level of Jewish religious expression. Less is known about the effect of Jewish–Gentile intermarriage on offspring. The available evidence points to a reduction of Jewish ethnic identification among children with one Jewish and one non-Jewish parent (Frideres, Goldstein, and Gilbert 1971). Lazerwitz (1981) reported that, among adults who maintained a Jewish identity, those with mixed parentage were much less involved in Jewish ritual and were much less likely to belong to Jewish organizations than Jewish adults whose parents were both Jewish. Mayer (1980) observed that parents in Jewish–Gentile marriages were more likely than Jewish couples to expect their children to

make their own choice of religious identification upon reaching adulthood. It appears from Lazerwitz's data that, when the offspring of Jewish–Gentile intermarriages attain adulthood, if they do maintain a Jewish identity, it is a relatively low degree of identity.

On balance, previous research supports the position that intermarriage is conducive to a loss of ethnic identity. However, since these studies have concentrated upon French Canadians and Jews, the extent to which their conclusions may be applied to other groups in Canada is not known.

Research Problem

The study reported here was undertaken to assess the impact of ethnic intermarriage on the ethnic identity of the *offspring* of such marriages. Specifically, it was hypothesized that the adult offspring of ethnically mixed marriages will have a lower degree of ethnic identity that the offspring of ethnically non-mixed marriages. Focussing on the children of, rather than the partners in, mixed and nonmixed marriages has an advantage in terms of clarifying the direction of the linkage between intermarriage and ethnic identity.

If intermarried individuals are found to differ in ethnic identity from their counterparts in nonmixed marriages, it is difficult to determine whether this difference is an *effect* of involvement in an ethnically mixed marriage, or whether variations in ethnic identity preceded (and perhaps affected the likelihood of) intermarriage.[2] In contrast, a comparison of the adult offspring of mixed and nonmixed marriages eliminates the problem of establishing a temporal sequence. In this kind of comparison, an ethnic intramarriage or intermarriage preceded the individual's ethnic identity and provided a context within which such an identity developed. If it is found that adults from mixed and nonmixed families of orientation differ in their ethnic identity, then this difference can be viewed (after controlling for other relevant variables) as a consequence of intermarriage.

Data Collection

The data used to test the hypothesized relationship between intermarriage and ethnic identity were collected as part of the 1983 Winnipeg Area Study, a survey of residents of Winnipeg, Manitoba. The survey was conducted during February and March of 1983. A simple random sample of 701 addresses was selected from all dwelling units listed in the 1982 property-tax assessment file of the city of Winnipeg. The household was the primary sampling unit, and one adult per household was selected for an interview lasting about one hour.[3] Interviewers were instructed to try to obtain an equal number of male and female respondents. A total of 524 interviews were completed, yielding a response rate of 75 percent.

A comparison of the sample and 1981 census data for Winnipeg revealed that the sample was quite similar to the Winnipeg population in regard to sex, age, and household size. However, the proportion of married persons in the sample was notably greater than in the Winnipeg population. This difference was attributable, in large part, to the fact that the sampling procedure used in the survey excluded persons under 18 years of age. In contrast, the 1981 census data included 15- to 17-year-olds, a segment of the population that was predominantly unmarried.

Measurement

The independent variable in the study was the respondent's parentage. Each respondent was asked to specify the ethnic group to which his/her father's side of the family belonged, and the ethnic group on his/her mother's side of the family. Respondents who reported exactly the same ethnic origin on both sides of their families of orientation (59 percent of the sample) were categorized as having nonmixed parentage. The remaining 41 percent of respondents reported different ethnic origins for their parents. These respondents were categorized as having mixed parentage.

The dependent variable, ethnic identity, was conceptualized as comprising two distinct components: an internal component and an external component (Isajiw 1981). The internal (or subjective) component of identity consists of an individual's beliefs, feelings, and attitudes about his/her ethnicity. The external (or objective) component involves readily observable behaviour patterns that derive from membership in an ethnic group. These behaviour patterns include such things as adherence to the cultural traditions of one's ethnic group, participation in primary relationships with persons from one's ethnic group, membership in ethnic secondary groups (such as clubs, service organizations, and churches), and making financial contributions to ethnic-group causes or activities. In this study, indicators of both internal and external components of ethnic identity were employed.

Two facets of internal identity were measured. One of these was the individual's ethnic self-identification, that is, the individual's perception of the ethnic group (if any) to which he or she belonged. Respondents were asked "How would you describe your ethnic identity?" Answers to this open-ended question were collapsed into four categories: "Simply ethnic" (e.g., Polish, Filipino, Irish); "ethnic Canadian" (e.g., French Canadian, Chinese Canadian, Jewish Canadian); "simply Canadian"; and "other" (e.g., WASP, Protestant). The second facet of internal identity was the salience of ethnicity to the individual. This was measured by asking respondents to specify the extent to which they agreed or disagreed with the statement "My ethnic identity is important to me."

Three aspects of external ethnic identity were tapped. First, the extent to which respondents (excluding those with a Canadian ethnic self-identification) adhered to the culture of their ethnic group was assessed by asking "To what extent do you follow the customs and traditions of your ethnic group?". Second, involvement in secondary relationships with fellow members of one's ethnic group was measured (for all respondents except those with a Canadian self-identification) by the question "Do you belong to any clubs, groups, or organized activities of your ethnic group?" Finally, involvement in primary relationships with members of one's ethnic group was assessed by asking those respondents who had ever been married whether their spouse's ethnic background was the same as, or different from, their own.

The hypothesis that intermarriage reduces ethnic identity leads to the following specific predictions concerning the relationship between parentage and the indicators of internal and external identity. Parentage and ethnic self-identification should be inversely related (i.e., respondents with mixed parentage should be more likely to identify themselves as Canadian or other, and less likely to identify themselves as simply ethnic, than respondents with nonmixed parentage). Parentage and the salience of ethnic identity should be inversely related. Respondents with mixed parentage should tend to express disagreement with the assertion that their ethnic identity is important to them, while the opposite should hold true for respondents from ethnically homogeneous families. Parentage and observance of ethnic-group customs should be inversely related. Respondents with mixed parentage should report that they follow the customs of their ethnic group to a lesser extent than should respondents with nonmixed parentage. An inverse relationship between participation in ethnic organizations and parentage is predicted; respondents with mixed parentage should report fewer organization memberships than should those with nonmixed parentage. Finally, parentage and ingroup marriage should be inversely related. Respondents whose parents had different ethnic origins should be less likely to marry within their own ethnic group than should respondents with nonmixed parentage.

For the purposes of testing these hypotheses, the independent variable (parentage) was treated as a dummy variable: the presence of mixed parentage was assigned a score of 2 while its absence was assigned a score of 1. The responses to the item measuring ethnic self-identification were scored as follows: simply ethnic was assigned a score of 2, ethnic Canadian was scored as 1, and Canadian and other were scored as 0. Scores on the salience scale could range from 1 (low salience) to 7 (high salience). On the scale measuring observance of ethnic customs, scores could range from 1 ("never") to 5 ("always"). Organization-membership scores could range from 0 (no memberships) to 3 (three or more memberships). The respondent's own marriage was treated as a dummy variable. The presence of an in-group (i.e., ethnically homogamous) marriage was scored as 2 and the absence of an in-group marriage was scored as 1.

Findings: Bivariate Analysis

Table 1 shows the frequency distributions of the five indicators of ethnic identity. Less than 1 percent of the sample failed to respond to the question on ethnic self-identification, revealing that awareness of having an ethnic affiliation of some kind was nearly universal among Winnipeggers. Nearly one-half of the respondents described their ethnic origin simply in terms of an ethnic-group label, while roughly one-third said that they were Canadian. Regarding the salience of ethnic identity, nearly one-half of the sample expressed strong agreement with the assertion that their ethnic identity was important to them. The mean score on the salience scale was 5.05, indicating the importance of ethnic identity to these respondents.

Regarding the three indicators of external identity, Table 1 shows that nearly one-half of the respondents said that they rarely or never followed the cultural traditions of their ethnic group, while about one-fifth often or always did so. Membership in ethnic secondary groups was uncommon, with 82 percent of the respondents reporting no memberships at all. Finally, of the respondents who had ever been married, 49 percent had a spouse whose ethnic origin was the same as their own, while 51 percent had an ethnically heterogamous marriage.

Table 1
Frequency Distributions for Indicators of Ethnic Identity and Correlations with Parentage

Self-Identification	(Value)	N^a	Percent
Simply Ethnic	(2)	248	47.7
Ethnic Canadian	(1)	67	12.9
Simply Canadian	(0)	186	35.8
Other	(0)	19	3.7
		520	100.1

Correlation with parentage = −.113 (N = 508, p ≤ .01)

Is Ethnic Identity Important?

(Strongly Disagree)	(1)	31	6.0
	(2)	34	6.6
	(3)	32	6.2
(Neutral)	(4)	73	14.2
	(5)	93	18.1
	(6)	113	22.0
(Strongly Agree)	(7)	137	26.7
		513	99.8

Correlation with parentage = −.116 (N = 501, p ≤ .01)

Adherence to Cultural Traditions[b]

Never	(1)	82	26.2
Rarely	(2)	61	19.5
Sometimes	(3)	101	32.3
Often	(4)	33	10.5
Always	(5)	36	11.5
		313	100.0

Correlation with parentage = −.236 (N = 301, p ≤ .001)

Organization Memberships[b]

None	(0)	261	81.6
One	(1)	41	12.8
Two	(2)	10	3.1
Three or more	(3)	8	2.5
		320	100.0

Correlation with parentage = −.132 (N = 308, p ≤ .05)

Respondent's Own Marriage[c]

Ethnically Homogamous	(2)	187	49.2
Ethnically Heterogamous	(1)	193	50.8
		380	100.0

Correlation with parentage = −.204 (N = 369, p ≤ .001)

---

[a] Ns vary because of missing data.
[b] Excludes respondents with Canadian self-identification.
[c] Excludes never-married respondents

In his discussion of ethnic identity, Isajiw (1981) remarked that the internal and external components of identity can vary independently. If the responses to the items on self-identification and the salience of identity are compared with the responses to the three items tapping external identity, it is apparent that the internal (i.e., attitudinal and belief) component was stronger than the external (i.e., behavioural) component in this sample of Winnipeggers.[4]

The results of the tests of the hypotheses concerning parentage and ethnic identity are also presented in Table 1. The two indicators of internal identity and the three indicators of external identity were expected to vary inversely with the respondent's parentage. All of the correlations were in the anticipated direction, and all correlations were statistically significant. These findings furnish support for the proposition that intermarriage tends to reduce the ethnic identity of the offspring of such marriages.

Since previous Canadian research on intermarriage has focussed on specific ethnic groups, it was decided to investigate whether the relationship between intermarriage and identity found in this sample held up across different ethnic categories. This relationship was examined for respondents belonging to

Table 2
Correlation Between Parentage (Mixed vs. Nonmixed) and Ethnic Identity, Controlling for Ethnic Heritage

A. Ethnic Heritage (Based on Father's Side of Respondent's Family).

Correlation Between Parentage and:	British Isles		North and West European		Central and East European	
	r	(N)	r	(N)	r	(N)
Self-Identification	−.040	(143)	−.192[a]	(124)	−.157	(94)
Salience of Ethnic Identity	.054	(141)	−.145	(123)	−.153	(92)
Adherence to Customs	−.167	(74)	−.282[a]	(79)	.048	(65)
Organization Memberships	−.018	(79)	−.099	(79)	.109	(65)
In-Group Marriage	−.147	(112)	−.079	(82)	−.228[a]	(75)

B. Ethnic Heritage (Based on Mother's Side of Respondent's Family).

Correlation Between Parentage and:	British Isles		North and West European		Central and East European	
	r	(N)	r	(N)	r	(N)
Self-Identification	−.125	(139)	.040	(90)	−.291[b]	(86)
Salience of Ethnic Identity	.041	(138)	−.360[c]	(89)	−.239[a]	(84)
Adherence to Customs	−.189	(65)	−.345[b]	(57)	.157	(62)
Organization Memberships	−.042	(70)	−.305[a]	(59)	.179	(60)
In-Group Marriage	.162	(106)	.136	(68)	.017	(68)

[a] $p \leq .05$
[b] $p \leq .01$
[c] $p \leq .001$

three broad ethnic categories: British Isles, North and West European, and Central and East European.[5] Separate analysis was carried out, using ethnic origin on both the father's side and the mother's side of the respondent's family. For the three categories, the correlation between parentage and each of the five indicators of ethnic identity was computed. The results in Table 2 show that mixed marriage tended to be associated with a lower level of ethnic identity: parentage and ethnic identity were inversely related in 12 of the 15 tests when the father's ethnicity was used (see Table 2A), and in 8 of the 15 tests when the mother's ethnicity was used (see Table 2B).

The results of the hypothesis tests for the three ethnic categories generally were consistent with the argument that intermarriage reduces rather than enhances ethnic identity among the offspring of such marriages. It must be noted that the cross-sectional nature of the sample meant that a variety of ethnic origins had to be subsumed under three broad categories in order to be able to carry out the correlational analysis. It is therefore possible that important differences between ethnic groups in terms of the effect of intermarriage may have gone undetected.

Findings: Multiple Regression

To gain further insight into the impact of intermarriage on identity, a stepwise multiple regression analysis was undertaken. In this analysis, three measures of SES, along with age, sex, and ethnic generation, were allowed to compete with the parentage variable to explain variation in each component of ethnic identity.[6] This procedure shows whether parentage appears in the particular combination of independent variables that explain the largest portion of variation in each component of ethnic identity. The standardized regression coefficients (betas) for the independent variables explaining the greatest variation in a dependent variable reveal the explanatory value

of each variable while holding the effects of all other independent variables constant.

The indicators of SES were occupational status, education, and family income. The Blishen revised socioeconomic index (Blishen and McRoberts 1976) was used to assign a status score to the respondent's occupation. This score reflected the income and educational levels of incumbents of an occupation as well as the prestige of the occupation.[7] The educational attainment of the respondent was indicated by the actual number of years of education he or she reported. Family income was measured by having respondents specify into which of 26 categories (ranging from "less than $6000" to "75 000 and over") the total income (before taxes) of his or her household fell in the previous 12 months. The respondent's age in years was recorded. Sex was treated as a dummy variable (with male = 1 and female = 2). Ethnic generation was scored as follows: first = 1, second = 2, and third = 3.

The results of the multiple regression analysis are shown in Table 3. It is readily apparent that only a small proportion of the variation in any of the five components of ethnic identity could be explained by the independent variables included in the analysis. Since the objective here was to assess the relative explanatory value of mixed parentage (rather than to find the combination of independent variables that would maximize the explained variation in each dependent variable), we will focus on the standardized regression coefficients rather than on the squared multiple regression coefficients (multiple r^2).

The multiple regression analysis demonstrated that parentage was the best predictor of both the respondent's adherence to ethnic customs and the respondent's own marriage type and was among the best predictors of self-identification and the salience of ethnic identity. Only in the case of organization membership did parentage not meet the criteria for inclusion in the regression model. The fact that parentage was inversely related to identity when the effects of SES, age, sex, and ethnic generation were taken into account

Table 3

Stepwise Multiple Regression Analysis of the Relationship Between Parentage, SES, Generation, Age, Sex, and Components of Ethnic Identity

Component of Ethnic Identity	Independent Variables in Model	b
1. Self-identification	Generation	−.173
	Family Income	.098
	Education	−.095
	Parentage	−.071
	Age	−.057
	Multiple r^2 = .065 (F = 6.14, p≤.0001)	
2. Salience of ethnic identity	Occupation	−.137
	Parentage	−.091
	Age	.057
	Sex	.047
	Multiple r^2 = .037 (F = 4.26, p≤.01)	
3. Adherence to ethnic customs	Parentage	−.186
	Education	.160
	Sex	.119
	Family Income	.096
	Generation	−.085
	Multiple r^2 = .099 (F = 5.53, p≤.0001)	
4. Organization memberships	Generation	−.247
	Age	.095
	Occupation	.093
	Education	.073
	Multiple r^2 = .083 (F = 5.90, p≤.0001)	
5. In-group marriage	Parentage	−.165
	Age	.125
	Sex	.051
	Generation	.040
	Multiple r^2 = .068 (F = 5.93, p≤.0001)	

provided further evidence that marriage across ethnic boundaries tends to diminish ethnic identity in the offspring of such marriages.

Conclusion

This study of the impact of intermarriage on the ethnic identity of the adult offspring of such marriages has furnished evidence consistent with the proposition that mixed parentage tends to be associated with lower levels of both internal and external dimensions of ethnic identity. While the magnitude of this association was not especially great in absolute terms, relative to other variables (such as generation and age) included in the study, parentage proved to be an important predictor of ethnic identity.

If the rate of ethnic intermarriage continues to rise (and it is quite probable that it will do so), then persons with ethnically mixed family backgrounds will comprise an increasingly large portion of the Canadian population. In view of this trend and the findings reported here, researchers would be well advised to incorporate an indicator of parentage in future studies of ethnic identity retention/loss. If this is done, more evidence on the linkage between intermarriage and identity will become available. Such evidence will shown whether the inverse relationship between parentage and identity found here applies to all ethnic groups, or whether some groups indeed can "gain" more than they "lose" from intermarriage.

Notes

1. A 1983 Canadian Gallup Poll (Canadian Institute of Public Opinion 1983) reported that tolerance of interracial and interfaith marriage had increased considerably between 1968 and 1983. Acceptance of Catholic–Protestant intermarriage increased from 61 percent to 84 percent; acceptance of marriages between Jews and non-Jews rose from 52 percent to 77 percent; and acceptance of marriages between blacks and whites grew from 36 percent to 70 percent. Age was related to attitudes toward intermarriage, with persons between 18 and 49 being more tolerant than those aged 50 and above. In the United States, the Gallup poll (1983) revealed a similar trend to greater tolerance of intermarriage. A comparison of the two surveys shows that, in 1983, Canadians were much more tolerant than Americans of interracial marriage (70 percent vs. 43 percent) and slightly more tolerant of Protestant–Catholic marriages (84 percent vs. 79 percent). Acceptance of marriages between Jews and non-Jews was equal in the two societies.
2. Castonguay (1982) argued that the direct relationship between the rate of exogamy and the shift to the usage of English among francophones could have arisen because anglicization increased the likelihood of francophones marrying outside their group. In other words, it is possible that knowledge of English facilitated intermarriage rather than having been a consequence of intermarriage. His own position is that *both* exogamy and language shift among French Canadians have resulted from changes in Canadian society that have led to greater contact between ethnic groups.
3. The eligibility criteria were (1) that the dwelling was the individual's usual place of residence,

and (2) that the person was betw[...] years of age.
4. Precise comparisons of the level of et[...] tity in Winnipeg and other communities i[...] problematic by variations in such factors as sa[...] design, the components of identity that were mea[...] ured, and the operationalization of these components in previous research. It is possible, however, to make some broad comparisons. In terms of self-identification and the extent of in-group marriage, the Winnipeg data closely resemble Reitz's (1980) findings based on a national sample of urban ethnic groups and Isajiw's (1981) sample of ethnic groups in Toronto. Isajiw measured adherence to ethnic cultural traditions and membership in ethnic organizations in Toronto, and here, too, the present findings were quite similar. It appears that, for those aspects of ethnic identity that were measured, Winnipeggers were not markedly different from other populations that have been studied in Canada.
5. The British Isles category included respondents of English, Irish, Welsh, and Scottish ancestry. The North and West European category included the following specific ethnic origins: French (and French Canadian), German (and German Canadian), Scandinavian, Dutch, and Belgian. The Central and East European category included respondents of Ukrainian (and Ukrainian Canadian), Hungarian, Polish, Czech, Russian, and Yugoslavian ancestry. These categories (which included roughly two-thirds of the sample) were used to maximize the number of cases included in the correlational analysis.
6. Previous studies (e.g., O'Bryan, Reitz, and Kuplowska 1975; Reitz 1980; Weinfeld 1981b) have shown that measures of ethnic identity tend to vary inversely with the individual's ethnic generation and SES (measured in terms of education, job status, income, etc.). In this study, the first generation consisted of persons who had migrated to Canada either as children or as adults; the second generation was persons born in Canada with both parents foreign-born; the third generation was persons born in Canada with one or both parents Canadian-born.
7. The four-digit Standard Occupational Classification code (Statistics Canada 1980) for the respondent's job title was ascertained. The Blishen score for that occupational classification was recorded. Those occupations for which no socioeconomic index was available (including the occupation of housewife) were treated as missing data. On the revised Blishen scale, index scores could

4 to a maximum of
he sample was 20.6
eing 46.5.

)berts. 1976. "A Re-
for Occupations in
of Sociology and An-
thropology 13(1): 71-79.

Canadian Institute of Public Opinion. 1983. "Canadians Today Are More Tolerant to Intermarriage." The Gallup Report, June 2.

Castonguay, C. 1982. "Intermarriage and Language Shift in Canada, 1971 and 1976."
Canadian Journal of Sociology 7(3): 263-77.

Dinnerstein, L., and D.M. Reimers. 1975. Ethnic
Americans. New York: Dodd, Mead.

Frideres, J.S., J. Goldstein, and R. Gilbert. 1971.
"The Impact of Jewish-Gentile Intermarriages in
Canada: An Alternative View." Journal of Com-
parative Family Studies 11(2): 268-75.

Gallup Poll. 1983. "Survey Finds Greater Acceptance of Interracial/Interfaith Marriages." Report
No. 213 (June): 7-10.

Gordon, A.I. 1964. Intermarriage. Boston: Beacon
Press.

Gordon, M.M. 1964. Assimilation in American Life.
New York: Oxford University Press.

Isajiw, W.W. 1981. "Ethnic Identity Retention."
Research Paper No. 125. Centre for Urban and
Community Studies, University of Toronto.

Kalbach, W.E. 1974. "Propensities for Intermarriage in Canada as Reflected in the Ethnic Origins of Native-born Husbands and Their
Wives." Paper presented at the Canadian Sociology and Anthropology Association annual
meeting, Toronto, Ontario, August 24.

Lasry, J.-C., and E. Bloomfield-Schachter. 1975.
"Jewish Intermarriage in Montreal." Jewish Social
Studies 37 (3-4): 267-78.

Lazerwitz, B. 1981. "Jewish-Christian Marriages
and Conversions." Jewish Social Studies 43(1):
31-46.

Li, P.S., and W.B. Denis. 1983. "Minority Enclave
and Majority Language: The Case of a French
Town in Western Canada." Canadian Ethnic
Studies 15(1): 18-32.

Mayer, E. 1980. "Processes and Outcomes in Marriages Between Jews and Non-Jews." American
Behavioural Scientist 23(4): 487-518.

Mougeon, R. 1977. "French Language Replace-
ment and Mixed Marriages: The Case of the
Francophone Minority of Welland, Ontario."
Anthropological Linguistics 19(8): 368-77.

O'Bryan, K.G., J.G. Reitz, and O. Kuplowska.
1975. Non-Official Languages: A Study in Canadian Multiculturalism. Ottawa: Supply and Services Canada.

Reitz, J.G. 1980. The Survival of Ethnic Groups. Toronto: McGraw-Hill Ryerson.

Statistics Canada. 1980. Standard Occupational
Classification. Ottawa: Supply and Services
Canada.

———. 1983. Update from the 1981 Census: Highlight Information on Ethnicity, Language, Etc. Ottawa: Supply and Services Canada.

Steinberg, S. 1981. The Ethnic Myth. Boston: Beacon Press.

Weinfeld, M. 1981a. "Intermarriage: Agony and
Adaptation." The Canadian Jewish Mosaic. Eds.
M. Weinfeld, W. Shaffir, and I. Cottler. To-
ronto: Wiley. 365-382

———. 1981b. "Myth and Reality in the Canadian
Mosaic: 'Affective Ethnicity'." Canadian Ethnic
Studies 13(3): 80-100.

Part Four

THE PRIVATE LIVES OF HUSBANDS AND WIVES

• • •

You never know the truth about anyone else's marriage: you only know the truth about your own, and you know exactly half of that.
Richard Needham, *Wit and Wisdom*, (1982)

The social meaning of the distinction between married and unmarried persons is becoming increasingly blurred. On the one hand, persons who are bonded together into couples and who are recognized as forming a social unit may or may not be legally married. As cohabitation becomes increasingly commonplace, the distinction between a legal marriage, based on a government-sanctioned agreement, and a common law marriage, based only on a shared understanding, is becoming less and less critical for many persons. In terms of social and psychological dynamics, it may be more useful to refer to *formal marriage*, which is one with a licence, and *informal marriage*, which is one without. In most of the articles, one could use the term "marriage" or "marriage-like union" interchangeably. Similarly, in many instances two people who are technically married may have physically and socially separated from each other, and have begun to act like single persons. Their separation is, in effect, an *informal divorce*, which may occur considerably earlier than its recognition in the courts with a *formal divorce* decree.

The roles of husband and wife have evolved over time until they now include a wide range of expectations. The Victorian model of an authoritarian husband with a wife who was basically his chattel or property can still be found in some couples, but it has generally been supplanted by companionate marriages or by more egalitarian models. The focus on the changing role of wives has often obscured the fact that changes in the woman's role necessitate comparable changes in the man's role, and that the status of the husband has therefore also been modified over the years. Our study of husband–wife roles is further complicated by the fact that couples' behaviour in the presence of others is often very different from their private conduct. Depending on the normative expectations of a given community, they may well seem to be more autocratic or more democratic than they actually are.

From many perspectives, the issues involved in moving away from a patriarchal system and toward an egalitarian one seem to offer clear-cut polarizations. We anticipate that women will be advocates of change, which they will define as progress toward justice, and that men will be resistant to such change, and loath to give up the privileges usually associated with the assumptions supporting male supremacy. In practice, the issues are not so clear-cut. The role of a male breadwinner in the instrumental role, bonded to a female homemaker in the expressive role, had a balance of privileges and obligations on both sides. While men are often reluctant to relinquish the privileges of male dominance, they are not unaware of its attendant costs. On the other side, there are women who perceive the movement advocating women's "rights" as an aspect of social change that sacrifices the traditional "rights" of women to be dependent and to raise as many children as they want while giving them their undivided attention.

A marriage is a single social unit, but it is composed of two people, and, of necessity, they view their shared venture differently. Jessie Bernard has pointed out that, rather than talking about *the* marriage that a couple experiences, we should talk about *her* marriage and *his* marriage. If both people were to tell us the whole truth, to the best of their knowledge and ability, these two halves of a single whole might appear to be quite different.

About the Articles

It is easy to pinpoint the date in a person's *public biography* when he or she moves in with someone or is officially married: it is much more difficult to recognize the point in a person's *private biography* when he or she begins to feel like a married person. Marriage is, among other things, an interminable conversation. Berger and Kellner show, in convincing detail, the process by which some marriage partners are able to mold each other's view of the world until they have created a new shared social reality. This process can happen in informal arrangements as well as in formal marriages. Conversely, for some couples, it never happens at all.

A preoccupation with marital problems has caused researchers to overlook those unusual couples whose vital marriages approximate the romantic ideal. Ammons and Stinnet suggest a number of factors that contribute to the ability of couples to form and sustain vital marriages.

An often-overlooked psychological truism is that, in any given behaviour pattern, a plurality of motives may exist: the reasons for beginning the behaviour may be quite differ-

ent from the reasons for continuing it. Trost implicitly takes this factor into account when he examines what holds marriages together. As he explains, the marriage process supplements the emotional bonds of the courtship period with other bonds, such as childrearing obligations, financial advantages, and social networks.

The dynamics of the private lives of husbands and wives are often positive, but there is also a dark side to many marriages. Spouse abuse has only recently been recognized as a widespread and endemic problem. Dutton reviews a number of responses to the social problem of wife abuse, and suggests strategies for intervention and prevention.

Further Readings

Blumstein, Philip, and Pepper Schwartz. 1983. *American Couples: Money, Work, Sex.* New York: William Morrow.

Brinkerhoff, Merlin B., and Eugen Lupri. 1988. "Interspousal Violence." *Canadian Journal of Sociology* 13: 407–34.

D'Arcy, Carl, and C.M. Siddique. 1985. "Marital Status and Psychological Well-Being: A Cross-National Comparative Analysis." *International Journal of Comparative Sociology* 26: 149–66.

Hobart, Charles, and David Brown. 1988. "Effects of Prior Marriage Children on Adjustment in Remarriage: A Canadian Study." *Journal of Comparative Family Studies* 19: 381–96.

Lupri, Eugen, and James S. Frideres. 1981. "The Quality of Marriage and the Passage of Time: Marital Satisfaction and the Family Life Cycle." *Canadian Journal of Sociology* 6: 283–305.

Mackie, Marlene. 1987. *Constructing Men and Women: Gender Socialization.* Toronto: Holt, Rinehart and Winston.

MARRIAGE AND THE CONSTRUCTION OF REALITY: AN EXERCISE IN THE MICROSOCIOLOGY OF KNOWLEDGE

Peter Berger
Hansfried Kellner

Ever since Durkheim, it has been a commonplace of family sociology that marriage serves as a protection against anomie for the individual. Interesting and pragmatically useful though this insight is, it is but the negative side of a phenomenon of much broader significance. If one speaks of *anomic* states, then one ought properly to investigate also the *nomic* processes that, by their absence, lead to the aforementioned states. If, consequently, one finds a negative correlation between marriage and anomie, then one should be led to inquire into the character of marriage as a *nomos*-building instrumentality; that is, of marriage as a social arrangement that creates for the individual the sort of order in which he can experience his life as making sense. It is our intention here to discuss marriage in these terms. While this could evidently be done in a macrosociological perspective, dealing with marriage as a major social institution related to other broad structures of society, our focus will be microsociological, dealing primarily with the social processes affecting the individuals in any specific marriage; although, of course, the larger framework of these processes will have to be understood. In what sense this discussion can be described as microsociology of knowledge will hopefully become clearer in the course of it.[1]

Marriage is obviously only *one* social relationship in which this process of *nomos*-building takes place. It is, therefore, necessary to first look in more general terms at the character of this process. In doing so, we are influenced by three theoretical perspectives — the Weberian perspective on society as a network of meanings (Weber 1956, 1961), the Meadian perspective on identity as a social phenomenon (Mead 1934), and the phenomenological analysis of the social structuring of reality, especially as given in the work of Schutz (1960, 1962) and Merleau-Ponty (1945, 1953). Not being convinced, however, that theoretical lucidity is necessarily enhanced by terminological ponderosity, we shall avoid as much as possible the use of the sort of jargon for which both sociologists and phenomenologists have acquired dubious notoriety.

The process that interests us here is the one that constructs, maintains, and modifies a consistent reality that can be meaningfully experienced by individuals. In its essential forms this process is determined by the society in which it occurs. Every society has its specific way of defining and perceiving reality — its world, its universe, its overarching organization of symbols. This is already given in the language that forms the symbolic base of society. Erected over this base, and by means of it, is a system of ready-made typifications, through which the innumerable experiences of reality come to be ordered (Schutz 1960, 202–20; 1962, 3–27, 283–86). These typifications and their order are held in common by the members of society, thus acquiring not only the character of objectivity, but being

Source: *Diogenes* 46(1964): 1–25. Reprinted with permission.

taken for granted as *the* world *tout court,* the only world that normal men can conceive of (Schultz 1962, 207–28). The seemingly objective and taken-for-granted character of the social definitions of reality can be seen most clearly in the case of language itself, but it is important to keep in mind that the latter forms the base and instrumentality of a much larger world-erecting process.

The socially constructed world must be continually mediated to and actualized by the individual, so that it can become and indeed remain *his* world as well. The individual is given by his society certain decisive cornerstones for his everyday experience and conduct. Most importantly, the individual is supplied with specific sets of typifications and criteria of relevance, predefined for him by society and made available to him for the ordering of his everyday life. This ordering or (in line with our opening considerations) nomic apparatus is biographically cumulative. It begins to be formed in the individual from the earliest stages of socialization on, then keeps on being enlarged and modified by himself throughout his biography (cf. Piaget 1954). While there are individual biographical differences making for differences in the constitution of this apparatus in specific individuals, there exists in the society an overall consensus on the range of differences deemed to be tolerable. Without such consensus, indeed, society would be impossible as a going concern, since it would then lack the ordering principles by which experience alone can be shared and conduct can be mutually intelligible. This order, by which the individual comes to perceive and define his world, is thus not chosen by him, except perhaps for very small modifications. Rather, it is discovered by him as an external datum, a ready-made world that simply is *there* for him to go ahead and live in, though he modifies it continually in the process of living in it. Nevertheless, this world is in need of validation, perhaps precisely because of an ever-present glimmer of suspicion as to its social manufacture and relativity. This validation, while it must be undertaken by the individual himself, requires ongoing interaction with others who coinhabit this same socially constructed world. In a broad sense, *all* of the other coinhabitants of this world serve a validating function. Every morning the newspaper boy validates the widest coordinates of my world and the mailman bears tangible validation of my own location within these coordinates. However, some validations are more significant than others. Every individual requires the ongoing validation of his world, including crucially the validation of his identity and place in this world, by those few who are his truly significant others (Mead 1934, 135–226). Just as the individual's deprivation of relationship with his significant others will plunge him into anomie, so their continued presence will sustain for him that *nomos* by which he can feel at home in the world at least most of the time. Again in a broad sense, all the actions of the significant others and even their simple presence serve this sustaining function. In everyday life, however, the principal method employed is speech. In this sense, it is proper to view the individual's relationship with his significant others as an ongoing conversation. As the latter occurs, it validates over and over again the fundamental definitions of reality once entered into, not, of course, so much by explicit articulation, but precisely by taking the definitions silently for granted and conversing about all conceivable matters on this taken-for-granted basis. Through the same conversation, the individual is also made capable of adjusting to and changing new social contexts in his biography. In a very fundamental sense it can be said that one converses one's way through life.

If one concedes these points, one can now state a general sociological proposition: the plausibility and stability of the world, as socially defined, is dependent upon the strength and continuity of significant relationships in which conversation about this world can be continually carried on. Or, to put it a little differently, the reality of the world is sustained through conversation with significant others. This reality, of course, includes not only the imagery by which fellowmen are viewed, but also includes the way in which one views oneself. The reality-bestowing force of social relationships depends on the degree of their nearness (Schutz 1960, 181–95); that is, on the degree to which social relationships occur in face-to-face situations and to which they are credited with primary significance by the individual. In any empirical situation there now emerge obvious sociological questions out of these considerations; namely, questions about the patterns of the world-building relationships, the social forms taken by the conversation with significant others. Sociologically, one must ask how these relationships are *objectively* structured and distributed, and one will also want to understand how they are *subjectively* perceived and experienced.

With these preliminary assumptions stated, we can now arrive at our main thesis here. Namely, we would contend that marriage occupies a privileged status among the significant validating relationships for adults in our society. Put slightly differently, marriage is a crucial nomic instrumentality in our society. We would further argue that the essential social functionality of this institution cannot be fully understood if this fact is not perceived.

We can now proceed with an ideal–typical analysis of marriage; that is, seek to abstract the essential features involved. Marriage in our society is a *dramatic* act in which two strangers come together and redefine themselves. The drama of the act is internally anticipated and socially legitimated long before it takes place in the individual's biography, and is amplified by means of a pervasive ideology, the dominant themes of which (romantic love, sexual fulfilment, self-discovery, and self-realization through love and sexuality, the nuclear family as the social site for these processes) can be found distributed through all strata of the society. The actualization of these ideologically predefined expectations in the life of the individual occurs to the accompaniment of one of the few traditional rites of passage that are still meaningful to almost all members of the society. It should be added that, in using the term "strangers," we do not mean, of course, that the candidates for the marriage come from widely discrepant social backgrounds — indeed, the data indicate that the contrary is the case. The strangeness, rather, lies in the fact that, unlike marriage candidates in many previous societies, those in ours typically come from different face-to-face contexts — in the terms used above, they come from different areas of conversation. They do not have a shared past, although their pasts have a similar structure. In other words, quite apart from prevailing patterns of ethnic, religious, and class endogamy, our society is typically exogamous in terms of nomic relationships. Put concretely, in our mobile society the significant conversation of the two partners previous to the marriage took place in social circles that did not overlap. With the dramatic redefinition of the situation brought about by the marriage, however, all significant conversation for the two new partners is now centred in their relationship with each other — and, in fact, it was precisely with this intention that they entered upon their relationship.

It goes without saying that this character of marriage has its roots in much broader structural configurations of our society. The most important of these, for our purposes, is the crystallization of a so-called private sphere of existence, more and more segregated from the immediate controls of the public institutions (especially the economic and political ones), and yet defined and utilized as the main social area for the individual's self-realization (Gehlen 1957, 57–69; 1961, 69–77, 127–40; Schelsky 1955a, 102–33; Luckmann 1963). It cannot be our purpose here to inquire into the historical forces that brought forth these phenomena, beyond making the observation that these are closely connected with the industrial revolution and its institutional consequences. The public institutions now confront the individual as an immensely powerful and alien world, incomprehensible in its inner workings, anonymous in its human character. If only through his work in some nook of the economic machinery, the individual must find a way of living in this alien world, come to terms with its power over him, be satisfied with a few conceptual rules of thumb to guide him through a vast reality that otherwise remains opaque to his understanding, and modify its anonymity by whatever *human relations* he can work out in his involvement with it. It ought to be emphasized, against some critics of "mass society," that this does not inevitably leave the individual with a sense of profound unhappiness and lostness. It would rather seem that large numbers of people in our society are quite content with a situation in which their public involvements have little subjective importance, regarding work as a not too bad necessity and politics as at best a spectator sport. It is usually only intellectuals with ethical and political commitments who assume that such people must be terribly desperate. The point, however, is that the individual in this situation, no matter whether he is happy or not, will turn elsewhere for the experiences of self-realization that do have importance for him. The private sphere, this interstitial area created (we would think) more or less haphazardly as a by-product of the social metamorphosis of industrialism, is mainly where he will turn. It is here that the individual will seek power, intelligibility and, quite literally, a name — the apparent power to fashion a world, however Lilliputian, that will reflect his own being: a world that, seemingly having been shaped by himself and thus unlike those other worlds that insist on shaping him, is translucently intelligible to him (or so he thinks); a world in which, consequently, his is *somebody* — perhaps even within its charmed circle, a lord and master. What is more, to a considerable extent these expectations are not unrealistic. The public institutions have no need to control the individual's adventures in the private sphere, as long as they really stay within the latter's circumscribed limits. The private sphere is perceived, not without justification, as an area of individual choice and even autonomy. This fact has important consequences for the shaping of identity in modern society that cannot be pursued here. All that ought to be clear here is the peculiar location of the private sphere

within and between the other social structures. In sum, it is above all and, as a rule, only in the private sphere that the individual can take a slice of reality and fashion it into his world. If one is aware of the decisive significance of this capacity and even necessity of men to externalize themselves in reality and to produce for themselves a world in which they can feel at home, then one will hardly be surprised at the great importance that the private sphere has come to have in modern society.[2]

The private sphere includes a variety of social relationships. Among these, however, the relationships of the family occupy a central position and, in fact, serve as a focus for most of the other relationships (such as those with friends, neighbours, and fellow members of religious and other voluntary associations). Since, as the ethnologists keep reminding us, the family in our society is of the conjugal type, the central relationship in this whole area is the marital one. It is on the basis of marriage that, for most adults in our society, existence in the private sphere is built up. It will be clear that this is not at all a universal or even cross-culturally wide function of marriage. Rather marriage in our society has taken on a very peculiar character and functionality. It has been pointed out that marriage in contemporary society has lost some of its older functions and taken on new ones instead (Parsons and Bales 1955, 3–34, 353–96). This is certainly correct, but we would prefer to state the matter a little differently. Marriage and the family used to be firmly embedded in a matrix of wider community relationships, serving as extensions and particularizations of the latter's social controls. There were few separating barriers between the world of the individual family and the wider community, a fact even to be seen in the physical conditions under which the family lived before the industrial revolution (Ariés 1962, 339–410). The same social life pulsated through the house, the street, and the community. In our terms, the family and, within it, the marital relationship were part and parcel of a considerably larger area of conversation. In our contemporary society, by contrast, each family constitutes its own segregated subworld, with its own controls and its own closed conversation.

This fact requires a much greater effort on the part of the marriage partners. Unlike an earlier situation in which the establishment of the new marriage simply added to the differentiation and complexity of an already existing social world, the marriage partners are now embarked on the often difficult task of constructing for themselves the little world in which they will live. To be sure, the larger society provides them with certain standard instructions as to how they should go about this task, but this does not change the fact that considerable effort of their own is required for its realization. The monogamous character of marriage enforces both the dramatic and the precarious nature of this undertaking. Success or failure hinges on the present idiosyncrasies and the fairly unpredictable future development of these idiosyncrasies of only two individuals (who, moreover, do not have a shared past) — as Simmel has shown (Wolff 1950, 118–44), the most unstable of all possible social relationships. Not surprisingly, the decision to embark on this undertaking has a critical, even cataclysmic connotation in the popular imagination, which is underlined as well as psychologically assuaged by the ceremonialism that surrounds the event.

Every social relationship requires objectivation; that is, requires a process by which subjectively experienced meanings become objective to the individual and in interaction with others become common property and thereby massively objective (Schutz 1960, 29–36, 149–53). The degree of objectivation will depend on the number and the intensity of the social relationships that are its carriers. A relationship that consists of only two individuals called upon to sustain by their own efforts an ongoing social world will have to make up in intensity for the numerical poverty of the arrangement. This, in turn, accentuates the drama and the precariousness. The later addition of children will add to the, as

it were, density of objectivation taking place within the nuclear family, thus rendering the latter a good deal less precarious. It remains true that the establishment and maintenance of such a social world makes extremely high demands on the principal participants.

The attempt can now be made to outline the ideal–typical process that takes place as marriage functions as an instrumentality for the social construction of reality. The chief protagonists of the drama are two individuals, each with a biographically accumulated and available stock of experience (Schutz 1960, 186–92, 202–10). As members of a highly mobile society, these individuals have already internalized a degree of readiness to redefine themselves and to modify their stock of experience, thus bringing with them considerable psychological capacity for entering new relationships with others.[3] Also, coming from broadly similar sectors of the larger society (in terms of region, class, ethnic, and religious affiliations), the two individuals will have organized their stock of experience in similar fashion. In other words, the two individuals have internalized the same overall world, including the general definitions and expectations of the marriage relationship itself. Their society has provided them with a taken-for-granted image of marriage and has socialized them into an anticipation of stepping into the taken-for-granted roles of marriage. All the same, these relatively empty projections now have to be actualized, lived through, and filled with experiential content by the protagonists. This will require a dramatic change in their definitions of reality and of themselves.

As of the marriage, most of each partner's actions must now be projected in conjunction with those of the other. Each partner's definitions of reality must continually be correlated with the definitions of the other. The other is present in nearly all horizons of everyday conduct. Furthermore, the identity of each now takes on a new character, having to be constantly matched with that of the other, indeed being typically perceived by people at large as being symbiotically conjoined with the identity of the other. In each partner's psychological economy of significant others, the marriage partner becomes the other *par excellence*, the nearest and most decisive coinhabitant of the world. Indeed, all other significant relationships have to be almost automatically reperceived and regrouped in accordance with this drastic shift.

In other words, from the beginning of the marriage each partner has new modes in his meaningful experience of the world in general, of other people and of himself. By definition, then, marriage constitutes a nomic rupture. In terms of each partner's biography, the event of marriage initiates a new nomic process. Now, the full implications of this fact are rarely apprehended by the protagonists with any degree of clarity. There, rather, is to be found the notion that one's world, one's other-relationships and, above all, oneself have remained what they were before — only, of course, that world, others, and self will now be shared with the marriage partner. It should be clear by now that this notion is a grave misapprehension. Just because of this fact, marriage now propels the individual into an unintended and unarticulated development, in the course of which the nomic transformation takes place. What typically *is* apprehended are certain objective and concrete problems arising out of the marriage — such as tensions with in-laws or with former friends, or religious differences between the partners, as well as immediate tensions between them. These are apprehended as external, situational, and practical difficulties. What is *not* apprehended is the subjective side of these difficulties — namely, the transformation of *nomos* and identity that has occurred and that continues to go on, so that all problems and relationships are experienced in a quite new way — that is, experienced within a new and ever-changing reality.

Take a simple and frequent illustration — the male partner's relationships with male friends before and after the marriage. It is a common observation that such relationships, especially if the extramarital partners are single, rarely survive the marriage, or, if they do, are drastically redefined after it. This is typ-ically the result of neither a deliberate decision by the husband nor deliberate sabotage by the wife. What rather happens, very simply, is a slow process in which the husband's image of his friend is transformed as he keeps talking about this friend with his wife. Even if no actual talking goes on, the mere presence of the wife forces him to see his friend differently. This need not mean that he adopts a negative image held by the wife. Regardless of what image she holds or is believed by him to hold, it will be different from that held by the husband. This difference will enter into the joint image that now needs to be fabricated in the course of the ongoing conversation between the marriage partners, and, in due course, must act powerfully on the image previously held by the husband. Again, typically, this process is rarely apprehended with any degree of lucidity. The old friend is more likely to fade out of the picture by slow degrees, as new kinds of friends take his place. The process, if commented upon at all within the marital conversation, can always be explained by socially available formulas about "people changing," "friends disappearing," or oneself "having become more mature." This process of conversational liquidation is especially powerful because it is one-sided — the husband typically talks with his wife about his friend, but *not* with his friend about his wife. Thus the friend is deprived of the defence of, as it were, counterdefining the relationship. This dominance of the marital conversation over all others is one of its most important characteristics. It may be mitigated by a certain amount of protective segregation of some nonmarital relationships (say, "Tuesday night out with the boys," or "Saturday lunch with mother"), but even then there are powerful emotional barriers against the sort of conversation (conversation *about* the marital relationship, that is) that would serve by way of counterdefinition.

Marriage thus posits a new reality. The individual's relationship with this new reality, however, is a dialectical one — he acts upon it, in collusion with the marriage partner, and it acts back upon both him and the partner, welding together their reality. Since, as we have argued before, the objectivation that constitutes this reality is precarious, the groups with which the couple associates are called upon to assist in codefining the new reality. The couple is pushed toward groups that strengthen their new definition of themselves and the world, avoids those that weaken this definition. This, in turn, releases the commonly known pressures of group association, again acting upon the marriage partners to change their definitions of the world and of themselves. Thus the new reality is not posited once and for all, but goes on being redefined not only in the marital interaction itself but in the various maritally based group relationships into which the couple enters.

The individual's biography marriage, then, brings about a decisive phase of socialization that can be compared with the phases of childhood and adolescence. This phase has a rather different structure from the earlier ones. There the individual was in the main socialized into already existing patterns. Here he actively collaborates rather than passively accommodates himself. Also in the previous phases of socialization, there was an apprehension of entering into a new world and being changed in the course of this. In marriage there is little apprehension of such a process, but rather the notion that the world has remained the same, with only its emotional and pragmatic connotations having changed. This notion, as we have tried to show, is illusionary.

The reconstruction of the world in marriage occurs principally in the course of conversation, as we have suggested. The implicit problem in this conversation is how to match two individual definitions of reality. By the very logic of the relationship, a common overall definition must be arrived at — otherwise the conversation will become impossible and, ipso facto, the relationship will be endangered. Now, this conversation may be understood as the working away of an ordering and typifying apparatus — if one prefers, an objectivating apparatus. Each partner ongoingly

contributes his conceptions of reality, which are then *talked through*, usually not once but many times, and in the process become objectivated by the conversational apparatus. The longer this conversation goes on, the more massively real do the objectivations become to the partners. In the marital conversation, a world is not only built but is also kept in a state of repair and ongoingly refurnished. The subjective reality of this world for the two partners is sustained by the same conversation. The nomic instrumentality of marriage is concretized over and over again, from bed to breakfast table, as the partners carry on the endless conversation that feeds on nearly all they individually or jointly experience. Indeed, it may happen eventually that no experience is fully real unless and until it has been thus "talked through."

This process has a very important result — namely, a hardening or stabilization of the common objectivated reality. It should be easy to see now how this comes about. The objectivations ongoingly performed and internalized by the marriage partners become ever more massively real, as they are confirmed and reconfirmed in the marital conversation. The world that is made up of these objectivations at the same time gains in stability. For example, the images of other people that before or in the earlier stages of the marital conversation may have been rather ambiguous and shifting in the minds of the two partners, now become hardened into definite and stable characterizations. A casual acquaintance, say, may sometimes have appeared as lots of fun and sometimes as quite a bore to the wife before her marriage. Under the influence of the marital conversation, in which this other person is frequently "discussed," she will now come down more firmly on one *or* the other of the two characterizations, or on a reasonable compromise between the two. In any of these three options, though, she will have concocted with her husband a much more stable image of the person in question than she is likely to have had before her marriage, when there may have been no conversational pressure to make a definite option at all. The same process of stabilization may be observed with regard to self-definitions as well. In this way, the wife in our example will not only be pressured to assign stable characterizations to others but also to herself. Previously uninterested politically, she now identifies herself as a liberal. Previously alternating between dimly articulated religious positions, she now declares herself an agnostic. Previously confused and uncertain about her sexual emotions, she now understands herself as an unabashed hedonist in this area. And so on and so forth, with the same reality — and identity — stabilizing process at work on the husband. Both world and self thus take on a firmer, more reliable character for both partners.

Furthermore, it is not only the ongoing experience of the two partners that is constantly shared and passed through the conversational apparatus. The same sharing extends into the past. The two distinct biographies, as subjectively apprehended by the two individuals who have lived through them, are overruled and reinterpreted in the course of their conversation. Sooner or later, they will "tell all" — or, more correctly, they will tell it in such a way that it fits into the self-definitions objectivated in the marital relationship. The couple thus constructs not only present reality but reconstructs past reality as well, fabricating a common memory that integrates the recollections of the two individual pasts (Halbwachs 1952, 146–77; Berger 1963, 54–65). The comic fulfilment of this process may be seen in those cases when one partner "remembers" more clearly what happened in the other's past than the other does — and corrects him accordingly. Similarly, there occurs a sharing of future horizons that leads not only to stabilization but inevitably to a narrowing of the future projections of each partner. Before marriage, the individual typically plays with quite discrepant daydreams in which his future self is projected (Schutz 1962, 72–73, 79–82). Having now considerably stabilized his self-image, the married individual will have to project the future in accordance with this maritally defined identity. This narrowing of future horizons begins with the obvious

external limitations that marriage entails — for example, with regard to vocational and career plans. However, it extends also to the more general possibilities of the individual's biography. To return to a previous illustration, the wife, having "found herself" as a liberal, an agnostic, and a "sexually healthy" person, ipso facto liquidates the possibilities of becoming an anarchist, a Catholic, or a lesbian. At least until further notice she has decided upon who she is — and, by the same token, on who she will be. The stabilization brought about by marriage thus affects the total reality in which the partners exist. In the most far-reaching sense of the word, the married individual "settles down" — and *must* do so, if the marriage is to be viable, in accordance with its contemporary institutional definition.

It cannot be sufficiently strongly emphasized that this process is typically unapprehended, almost automatic in character. The protagonists of the marriage drama do *not* set out deliberately to re-create their world. Each continues to live in a world that is taken for granted, and keeps its taken-for-granted character even as it is metamorphosed. The new world that the married partners, Prometheus-like, have called into being is perceived by them as the normal world in which they have lived before. Reconstructed present and reinterpreted past are perceived as a continuum, extending forwards into a commonly projected future. The dramatic change that has occurred remains, in bulk, unapprehended and unarticulated. And, where it forces itself upon the individual's attention, it is retrojected into the past, explained as having always been there, though perhaps in a hidden way. Typically, the reality that has been "invented" within the marital conversation is subjectively perceived as a "discovery." Thus the partners "discover" themselves and the world, "who they really are," "what they really believe," "how they really feel, and always have felt, about so-and-so." This retrojection of the world being produced all the time by themselves serves to enhance the stability of this world and at the same time to assuage the "existential anxiety" that, probably inevitably, accompanies the perception that nothing but one's narrow shoulders support the universe in which one has chosen to live. If one may put it like this, it is psychologically more tolerable to be Columbus than to be Prometheus.

The use of the term "stabilization" should not detract from the insight into the difficulty and precariousness of this world-building enterprise. Often enough, the new universe collapses *in statu nascendi*. Many more times it continues over a period, swaying perilously back and forth as the two partners try to hold it up, finally to be abandoned as an impossible undertaking. If one conceives of the marital conversation as the principal drama and the two partners as the principal protagonists of the drama, then one can look upon the other individuals involved as the supporting chorus for the central dramatic action. Children, friends, relatives, and casual acquaintances all have their part in reinforcing the tenuous structure of the new reality. It goes without saying that the children form the most important part of this supporting chorus. Their very existence is predicated on the maritally established world. The marital partners themselves are in charge of their socialization *into* this world, which to them has a pre-existent and self-evident character. They are taught from the beginning to speak precisely those lines that lend themselves to a supporting chorus, from their first invocations of "Daddy" and "Mummy" to their adoption of the parents' ordering and typifying apparatus that now defines *their* world as well. The marital conversation is now in the process of becoming a family symposium, with the necessary consequences that its objectivations rapidly gain in density, plausibility, and durability.

In sum: The process that we have been inquiring into is, ideal-typically, one in which reality is crystallized, narrowed, and stabilized. Ambivalences are converted into certainties. Typifications of self and of others become settled. Most generally, possibilities become facticities. What is more, this process

of transformation remains, most of the time, unapprehended by those who are both its authors and its objects.[4]

We have analyzed in some detail the process that, we contend, entitles us to describe marriage as a nomic instrumentality. It may now be well to turn back once more to the macrosocial context in which this process takes place — a process that, to repeat, is peculiar to our society as far as the institution of marriage is concerned, although it obviously expresses much more general human facts. The narrowing and stabilization of identity is functional in a society that, in its major public institutions, must insist on rigid controls over the individual's conduct. At the same time, the narrow enclave of the nuclear family serves as a macrosocially innocuous "play area," in which the individual can safely exercise his world-building proclivities without upsetting any of the important social, economic, and political apple carts. Barred from expanding himself into the area occupied by those major institutions, he is given plenty of leeway to "discover himself" in his marriage and his family, and, in view of the difficulty of this undertaking, is provided with a number of auxiliary agencies that stand ready to assist him (such as counselling, psychotherapeutic, and religious agencies). The marital adventure can be relied upon to absorb a large amount of energy that might otherwise be expended more dangerously. The ideological themes of familism, romantic love, sexual expression, maturity, and social adjustment, with the pervasive psychologistic anthropology that underlies them all, function to legitimate this enterprise. Also the narrowing and stabilization of the individual's principal area of conversation within the nuclear family is functional in a society that requires high degrees of both geographical and social mobility. The segregated little world of the family can be easily detached from one milieu and transposed into another without appreciably interfering with the central processes going on in it. Needless to say, we are not suggesting that these functions are deliberately planned or even apprehended by some mythical ruling directorate of the society. Like most social phenomena, whether they be macro- or microscopic, these functions are typically unintended and unarticulated. What is more, the functionality would be impaired if it were too widely apprehended.

We believe that the above theoretical considerations serve to give a new perspective on various empirical facts studied by family sociologists. As we have emphasized a number of times, our considerations are ideal–typical in intention. We have been interested in marriage at a normal age in urban, middle-class, Western societies. We cannot discuss here such special problems as marriages or remarriages at a more advanced age, marriage in the remaining rural subcultures, or in ethnic or lower-class minority groups. We feel quite justified in this limitation of scope, however, by the empirical findings that tend toward the view that a global marriage type is emerging in the central strata of modern industrial societies (Mayntz 1955; Schelsky 1955b; Sorre 1955; Anshen 1959; Bell and Vogel 1960). This type, commonly referred to as the nuclear family, has been analyzed in terms of a shift from the so-called family of orientation to the so-called family of procreation as the most important reference for the individual (Parsons 1949, 233–50). In addition to the well-known socioeconomic reasons for this shift, most of them rooted in the development of industrialism, we would argue that important macrosocial functions pertain to the nomic process within the nuclear family, as we have analyzed it. This functionality of the nuclear family must, furthermore, be seen in conjunction with the familistic ideology that both reflects and reinforces it. A few specific empirical points may suffice to indicate the applicability of our theoretical perspective. To make these we shall use selected American data.

The trend toward marriage at an earlier age has been noted.[5] This has been correctly related to such factors as urban freedom, sexual emancipation, and egalitarian values. We would add the important fact that a child raised in the circumscribed world of the nuclear family is stamped by it in terms of his psychological needs and social expectations. Having to live in the larger society from which the nuclear family is segregated, the adolescent soon feels the need for a "little world" of his own, having been socialized in such as way that only by having such a world to withdraw into can he successfully cope with the anonymous "big world" that confronts him as soon as he steps outside his parental home. In other words, to be "at home" in society entails, *per definitionem*, the construction of a maritally based subworld. The parental home itself facilitates such an early jump into marriage precisely because its controls are very narrow in scope and leave the adolescent to his own nomic devices at an early age. As has been studied in considerable detail, the adolescent peer group functions as a transitional *nomos* between the two family worlds in the individual's biography (Riesman 1953, 29–40; Elkin 1960).

The equalization in the age of the marriage partners has also been noted.[6] This is certainly also to be related to egalitarian values and, concomitantly, to the decline in the "double standard" of sexual morality. Also, however, this fact is very conducive to the common reality-constructing enterprise that we have analyzed. One of the features of the latter, as we have pointed out, is the reconstruction of the two biographies in terms of a cohesive and mutually correlated common memory. This task is evidently facilitated if the two partners are of roughly equal age. Another empirical finding to which our considerations are relevant is the choice of marriage partners within similar socioeconomic backgrounds (Warner and Lunt 1941, 436–40; Hollingshead 1950; Burgess and Wallin 1943). Apart from the obvious practical pressures toward such limitations of choice, the latter also insure sufficient similarity in the biographically accumulated stocks of experience to facilitate the described reality-constructing process. This would also offer additional explanation to the observed tendency to narrow the limitations of marital choice even further, for example in terms of religious background (Lenski 1961, 48–50).

There now exists a considerable body of data on the adoption and mutual adjustment of marital roles (Cottrell 1933; Waller and Hill 1951, 253–71; Zelditch 1955).[7] Nothing in our considerations detracts from the analyses made of these data by sociologists interested primarily in the processes of group interaction. We would argue only that something more fundamental is involved in this role-taking — namely, the individual's relationship to reality as such. Each role in the marital situation carries with it a universe of discourse, broadly given by cultural definition, but continually re-actualized in the ongoing conversation between the marriage partners. Put simply: Marriage involves not only stepping into new roles, but, beyond this, stepping into a new world. The *mutuality* of adjustment may again be related to the rise of marital egalitarianism, in which comparable effort is demanded of both partners.

Most directly related to our considerations are data that pertain to the greater stability of married as against unmarried individuals (Waller and Hill 1951, 253–71). Though frequently presented in misleading psychological terms (such as "greater emotional stability," "greater maturity," and so on), these data are sufficiently validated to be used not only by marriage counsellors but in the risk calculations of insurance companies. We would contend that our theoretical perspective places these data into a much more intelligible sociological frame of reference, which also happens to be free of the particular value bias with which the psychological terms are loaded. It is, of course, quite true that married people are more stable emotionally (that is, operating within a more controlled scope of emotional expression), more mature in their views (that is, inhabiting a firmer and narrower world in conformity with the expectations of society), and more sure of themselves (that is, having objectivated a more stable and fixated self-definition). *Therefore*

they are more liable to be psychologically balanced (that is, having sealed off much of their "anxiety," and reduced ambivalence as well as openness toward new possibilities of self-definition) and socially predictable (that is, keeping their conduct well within the socially established safety rules). All of these phenomena are concomitants of the overall fact of having "settled down" — cognitively, emotionally, in terms of self-identification. To speak of these phenomena as indicators of "mental health," let alone of "adjustment to reality," overlooks the decisive fact that reality is socially constructed and that psychological conditions of all sorts are grounded in a social matrix.

We would say, very simply, that the married individual comes to live in a more stable world, from which fact certain psychological consequences can be readily deduced. To bestow some sort of higher ontological status upon these psychological consequences is ipso facto a symptom of the mis- or non-apprehension of the social process that has produced them. Furthermore, the compulsion to legitimate the stabilized marital world, be it in psychologistic or in traditional religious terms, is another expression of the precariousness of its construction (Nash and Berger 1962). This is not the place to pursue any further ideological processes involved in this. Suffice it to say that contemporary psychology functions to sustain this precarious world by assigning to it the status of "normalcy," a legitimating operation that increasingly links up with the older religious assignment of the status of "sacredness." Both legitimating agencies have established their own rites of passage, validating myths and rituals, and individualized repair services for crisis situations. Whether one legitimates one's maritally constructed reality in terms of "mental health" or of the "sacrament of marriage" is today largely left to free consumer preference, but it is indicative of the crystallization of a new overall universe of discourse that it is increasingly possible to do both at the same time.

Finally, we would point here to the empirical data on divorce (Bureau of the Census 1956, 1958). The prevalence and, indeed, increasing prevalence of divorce might at first appear as a counterargument to our theoretical considerations. We would contend that the very opposite is the case, as the data themselves bear out. Typically, individuals in our society do not divorce because marriage has become unimportant to them, but because it has become so important that they have no tolerance for the less than completely successful marital arrangement they have contracted with the particular individual in question. This is more fully understood when one has grasped the crucial need for the sort of world that only marriage can produce in our society, a world without which the individual is powerfully threatened with anomie in the fullest sense of the word. Also, the frequency of divorce simply reflects the difficulty and demanding character of the whole undertaking. The empirical fact that the great majority of divorced individuals plan to remarry and a good majority of them actually do, at least in America, fully bears out this contention (Parsons 1942; Glick 1949; Goode 1956, 259–85).

The purpose of this article is not polemic, nor do we wish to advocate any particular values concerning marriage. We have sought to debunk the familistic ideology only insofar as it serves to obfuscate a sociological understanding of the phenomenon. Our purpose has rather been twofold. First, we wanted to show that it is possible to develop a sociological theory of marriage that is based on clearly sociological presuppositions, without operating with psychological or psychiatric categories that have dubious value within a sociological frame of reference. We believe that such a sociological theory of marriage is generally useful for a fully conscious awareness of existence in contemporary society and not only for the sociologist. Second, we have used the case of marriage for an exercise in the sociology of knowledge, a discipline that we regard as most promising. Hitherto this discipline has been almost exclusively concerned with macrosociological questions, such as those dealing with the relationship of intellectual history to social processes. We believe that the microsociological focus is equally important for this discipline. The sociology of knowledge must not only be concerned with the great universes of meaning that history offers up for our inspection, but with the many little workshops in which living individuals keep hammering away at the construction and maintenance of these universes. In this way, the sociologist can make an important contribution to the illumination of that everyday world in which we all live and which we help fashion in the course of our biography.

Notes

1. The present article has come out of a larger project on which the authors have been engaged in collaboration with three colleagues in sociology and philosophy. The project is to produce a systematic treatise that will integrate a number of now separate theoretical standards in the sociology of knowledge.

2. In these considerations we have been influenced by certain presuppositions of Marxian anthropology, as well as by the anthropological work of Max Scheler, Helmuth Plessner, and Arnold Gehlen. We are indebted to Thomas Luckmann for the clarification of the social-psychological significance of the private sphere.

3. David Riesman's well-known concept of "other-direction" would also be applicable here.

4. The phenomena here discussed could also be formulated effectively in terms of Marxian categories of reification and false consciousness. Jean-Paul Sartre's recent work, especially *Critique de la raison dialectique*, seeks to integrate these categories within a phenomenological analysis of human conduct (cf. Lefebvre 1958-61).

5. and 6. In these as well as the following references to empirical studies we naturally make no attempt at comprehensiveness. References are given as representative of much larger body of materials (see, for example, Glick 1957, 54; 1947; Bureau of the Census 1956, 1958; Current Population Reports, 1959).

7. For a general discussion of role interaction in small groups, cf. Homans 1950.

Works Cited

Anshen, Ruth, ed. 1959. *The Family — Its Function and Destiny.* New York: Harper and Row.

Ariés, Philippe. 1962. *Centuries of Childhood.* New York: Knopf.

Bell, Norman, and Ezra Vogel. 1960. *A Modern Introduction to the Family.* Glencoe, IL: Free Press.

Berger, Peter. 1963. *Invitation to Sociology — A Humanistic Perspective.* Garden City, NY: Doubleday/Anchor.

Bureau of the Census. *Statistical Abstracts of the United States,* 1956 and 1958.

Burgess, Ernest, and Paul Wallin. 1943. "Homogamy in Social Characteristics." *American Journal of Sociology* (September): 109–24.

Cottrell, Leonard. 1933. "Roles in Marital Adjustment." *Publications of the American Sociological Society.* 27: 107–15.

Current Population Reports. 1959. Series P-20, No. 96 (November).

Elkin, Frederick. 1960. *The Child and Society.* New York: Random House.

Gehlen, Arnold. 1957. *Die Seels im technischen Zeitalter.* Hamburg: Rowohlt.

———. 1961. *Anthropologische Forschung.* Hamburg: Rowohlt.

Glick, Paul. 1947. "The Family Cycle." *American Sociological Review* (April): 164–74.

———. 1949. "First Marriages and Remarriages." *American Sociological Review* (December): 726–34.

———. 1957. *American Families.* New York: Wiley.

Goode, William. 1956. *After Divorce.* Glencoe, IL: Free Press.

Halbwachs, Maurice. 1952. *Les cadres sociaux de la mémorie.* Paris: Presses Universitaires de France.

Hollingshead, August. 1950. "Cultural Factors in the Selection of Marriage Mates." *American Sociological Review* (October): 619–27.

Homans, George. 1950. *The Human Group.* New York: Harcourt Brace.

Lefebvre, Henri. 1958–61. *Critique de la vie quotidienne.* Paris: L'Arche.

Lenski, Gerhard. 1961. *The Religious Factor.* Garden City, NY: Doubleday.

Luckmann, Thomas. 1963. "On Religion in Modern Society." *Journal for the Scientific Study of Religion* (Spring): 147–62.

Mayntz, Renate. 1955. *Die moderne Familie.* Stuttgart: Enke.

Mead, George H. 1934. *Mind, Self, and Society.* Chicago: University of Chicago Press.

Merleau-Ponty, Maurice. 1945. *Phénoménologie de la perception.* Paris: Gallimard.

———. 1953. *La structure du comportement.* Paris: Presses Universitaires de France.

Nash, Dennison, and Peter Berger. 1962. "The Family, the Child and the Religious Revival in Suburbia." *Journal for the Scientific Study of Religion* (Fall): 85–93.

Parsons, Talcott. 1942. "Age and Sex in the Social Structure of the United States." *American Sociological Review* (December): 604–16.

———. 1949. *Essays in Sociological Theory.* Glencoe, IL: Free Press.

Parsons, Talcott, and Robert Bales. 1955. *Family, Socialization, and Interaction Process.* Glencoe, IL: Free Press.

Piaget, Jean. 1954. *The Construction of Reality in the Child.* New York: Basic.

Riesman, David. 1953. *The Lonely Crowd.* New Haven: Yale University Press.

Schelsky, Helmut. 1955a. *Soziologie der Sexualitaet.* Hamburg: Rowohlt.

———. 1955b. *Wandlungen der deutschen Familie in der Genenwart.* Stuttgart: Enke.

Schutz, Alfred. 1960. *Der sinnhafte Aufbau der sozialen Welt.* Vienna: Springer.

———. 1962. *Collected Papers,* I. The Hague: Nijhoff.

Sorre, Maximilien, ed. 1955. *Sociologie comparée de la famille contemporaine.* Paris: Centre National de la Recherche Scientifique.

Waller, Willard, and Reuben Hill. 1951. *The Family — A Dynamic Interpretation.* New York: Dryden.

Warner, W. Lloyd, and Paul Lunt. 1941. *The Social Life of a Modern Community.* New Haven: Yale University Press.

Weber, Max. 1956. *Wirtschaft und Gesellschaft.* Tübingen: Mohr, 1956.

———. 1951. *Gesammelte Aufsaetze zur Wissenschaftslehre.* Tübingen: Mohr.

Wolff, Kurt, ed. 1950. *The Sociology of Georg Simmel.* Glencoe, IL: Free Press.

Zelditch, Morris. 1955. "Role Differentiation in the Nuclear Family." Parsons and Bales 307–52.

THE VITAL MARRIAGE: A CLOSER LOOK*

Paul Ammons
Nick Stinnett

Although most couples enter marriage expecting that theirs will be a vital relationship replete with intrinsic rewards, few achieve this lofty ideal. This paper identifies and describes those personality characteristics that enable couples to develop and sustain a vital relationship. The findings, taken from data gathered by a questionnaire, indicate that vital marital partners are in possession of personality needs that promote sexual expressiveness, "otherness" rather than selfness, determination, and high ego strength. These findings are discussed in terms of an individuation-mutuality paradigm.

A recurrent theme in the literature describing American marriages during the past 30 years has been the emergence of the companionate marriage (Mace and Mace 1975). An emphasis on clearly defined instrumental or task-oriented roles is seen as giving way to fluid relationships based on interpersonal competence (Foote and Cottrell 1955). The vital marital dyad, a companionate marriage *par excellence* (Cuber and Haroff 1965), was selected as an area for study because most couples enter marriage expecting theirs to be this type of relationship. Although newlyweds generally expect their spouse to become their best friend, lover, and source of primary emotional gratification, often husbands and wives soon discover they are at a loss to know how to realize these aspirations.

While much of the marriage enrichment literature has sought to teach the requisite knowledge and skills for developing an in-depth relationship (Mace and Mace 1975), surprisingly little research has been done to determine the personality characteristics of vital marital partners. This type of information is needed because the interpersonal competence necessary for the successful relationships that contribute to vital marriages is influenced in large part by the personalities of husbands and wives. And, in turn, successful marriages contribute to the development of strong families. Satir (1972) graphically illustrates this point when she refers to the marital dyad as the "axis" on which the family turns.

Method

Procedure

In an attempt to find out more about vital marriages and healthy families, extension home economists in all counties in Oklahoma were asked to recommend several strong families for study. To assist in their selection, the home economists were furnished with a set of guidelines that operationally defined strong marriages and families. A questionnaire was developed and mailed to recommended families. Only those respondents scoring 25 out of 35 possible points ($N = 48$) on the Vital-Total Marriage Relationship Scale were used in the final analysis of data.

*The authors wish to express their appreciation to Lynda Henley Walters, James Walters, and James Pippin of the University of Georgia for their helpful critiques of earlier drafts of this paper.

Source: Family Relations 29 (1980): 37–42. Reprinted with permission.

Instruments

Vital-Total Marriage Relationship Scale (VTMRS)

The VTMRS consisted of seven statements designed to measure the degree to which respondents expressed marital vitality according to Cuber and Haroff's (1965) conceptualization. The VTMRS is designed to measure the degree of satisfaction a person derives from his marriage relationship, the degree of emotional involvement the couple has with each other, the degree to which the couple does things together, and the degree to which they enjoy living their lives together.

A five-point Likert-type scale was utilized on which respondents were asked whether they strongly agree, agree, are undecided, disagree, or strongly disagree with statements such as, "I receive more satisfaction from my marriage relationship than from most other areas of my life." The responses were scored in such a way that the highest score represented the highest degree of vital-total relationship.

The validity of VTMRS is reflected in that an item analysis using the chi-square test showed each of the items to be significantly discriminating beyond the .0001 level between upper and lower quartiles of the sample (see Table 1). A split-half reliability coefficient of .83 was obtained in determining an index of reliability of the items in the scale.

Edwards Personal Preference Schedule (EPPS)

A modified version of the EPPS (Edwards 1959) as reported by Constantine and Constantine (1971) was used to determine the degree to which respondents possessed each of 15 personality needs.

Sample

Primarily, the sample (N = 72) was composed of rural, middle-aged, middle-class individuals. The majority of the respondents were either from the upper-middle (50 percent) or lower-middle (29 percent) socioeconomic class as measured by the McGuire-White Index of Social Status (1955). Most were between the ages of 31–45 (79 percent). Although the majority (66.2 percent) of the sample had been married between 15 and 25 years, the range was from 5 to over 35 years of marriage. The number of children ranged from 2 to 12.

Findings and Discussion

Sex

Sex appears to play a central and profoundly important role in the vital marriage. Its importance is highlighted by the findings of this

Table 1
Item Analysis[a] of Vital-Total Marriage Relationship Scale Scores

Item	X^2	f
My spouse and I enjoy doing many things together	27.51	.0001
I enjoy most of the activities I participate in more if my spouse is also involved	26.47	.0001
I receive more satisfaction from my marriage relationship than most other areas of life	24.44	.0001
My spouse and I have a positive, strong emotional involvement with each other	34.00	.0001
The companionship of my spouse is more enjoyable to me than most anything else in life	27.24	.0001
I would not hesitate to sacrifice an important goal in life if achievement of that goal would cause my marriage relationship to suffer	26.66	.0001
My spouse and I take an active interest in each other's work and hobbies	26.69	.0001

[a] Based on comparison of upper and lower quartiles of scores.

study in several ways. First, a majority (85.51 percent) of the respondents reported moderately high to very high needs for sexual activity as measured by the EPPS sex subscale. The relationship between sexual dysfunction and marital problems has been well documented (e.g., Neuhaus and Neuhaus 1974). But others (Lederer and Jackson 1968) have maintained that sex is an overrated commodity in the determination of marital success.

The apparent contradiction between the observations of Lederer and Jackson and the findings of this study may be explained by examining the nature of the vital relationship more closely. Cuber and Haroff (1965) noted that vital couples were markedly different from what they termed utilitarian couples. Utilitarian couples gratify many of their needs outside the marital relationship. They tend to view their marriage as a mutually advantageous, but hardly thrilling merger, whereas vital couples strive to become soul mates, filling their relationship with an "exciting mutuality of feelings and participation together . . . becoming . . . intensely bound together psychologically in important life matters" (pp. 55, 56).

Among vital marital couples, the need for sex on the part of one spouse was found to be associated with the need for strong attachments on the part of his or her mate as measured by the EPPS affiliation subscale ($r_s = .60$, $p < .0001$ for wives; $r_s = .43$, $p < .02$ for husbands). This finding suggests that these couples viewed sex as an important component of their overall interpersonal relationship and as one of the means of sustaining the dynamic intimacy they desire. It is logical, then, to assume that sex would be more important for the vital marital couple than for the utilitarian couple. This assumption was borne out by the findings of this study in that vital marital partners expressed significantly ($H = 11.38$, $p < .01$) higher needs for sex than did those with lower VTMRS scores.

Sex appears to be a mutual adventure for the vital marital couple in that the needs of both partners among pairs who had this type of relationship were found to be similar (r_s = .46, $p < .01$). This finding suggests that compatibility is enhanced when the needs of each partner are similar or when both partners make adjustments for compatibility. In addition, their similar, high need for sex also indicates that these vital marital partners invest a great deal in their relationship, thus increasing the likelihood of a mutually satisfying sex life (cf. Nye 1976).

Reciprocity

A majority of the vital marital partners expressed high levels of need to be understanding and supportive as measured by the EPPS intraception (75 percent) and nurturance (97.49 percent) subscales. Expression of these needs increases the likelihood of husband and wife mutually reinforcing each other's positive self-concept and giving each other psychological strokes. Others (e.g., Otto 1975) have noted that strong family members provide support for one another. Rarely, however, has it been demonstrated that marital partners gratify their own needs in the process of gratifying their mate's need to be understood and supported.

The emphasis in our era on individual rights, personal growth, and self-awareness seems to map out the road to happiness via the route of narcissistic "selfism" (Neubeck 1979). Selfism as a marital frame of reference lessens each partner's sense of responsibility for the success of the relationship and promotes moving in and out of marriage. Specifically, from a social-exchange perspective, selfism increases the anticipated rewards from the relationship while reducing each partner's willingness to make necessary investments. Decreased investments on the part of one spouse decrease the likelihood of the other spouse receiving the rewards he or she deems desirable, resulting in marital instability because "associations are continued only if each participant feels he is receiving what he deserves based upon what he expects" (Bagarozzi and Wodarski 1977, 53; Thibaut and Kelly 1959).

There are some indications that seeking self-gratification has not enabled individuals to live happier, more fulfilling lives (Nye 1978). The findings of this study strongly indicate that "otherness" rather than "selfness" contributes to each partner's emotional well-being and personal growth.

Expression of the need to be understanding and supportive encourages reciprocity (Lederer and Jackson 1968). Hence, when the husband demonstrates that he understands his wife, he meets both her need to be understood and his own need to be understanding. His empathy encourages her to express her need to be understanding of him, and, as she does so, both their needs are met once again.

Too often, there is the assumption that if giving in a marriage is necessary for its success, then, in order to focus on the needs of the mate, it is necessary to sacrifice one's individuality and the right to personal need gratification. The findings of this study clearly indicate a mutually gratifying relationship is one in which affective rewards are multiplied in response to the co-operative efforts of both partners. Such mutually gratifying exchanges between vital marital partners not only meet the needs of each individual partner but also solidify the cohesiveness of the relationship (Nye 1976).

Determination and Commitment

These couples viewed developing and sustaining a vital relationship as one of their most important life goals, as indicated by their VTMRS scores. They expressed high levels of personality need that reflected a strong desire to accomplish this goal and the determination to see it through, as indicated by a vast majority of the respondents reporting moderately high to very high needs for achievement (87.47 percent) and endurance (85.47 percent) on the EPPS.

Commitment to developing a vital marital relationship and the determination and perseverance to honour that commitment are often ignored in the literature, although they

may well be among the more important enabling factors in marital success. Commitment and determination may help explain several findings of this study that differ from the results of previous studies. For example, determination may explain why these couples, unlike those studied by Blood and Wolfe (1960) or Rollins and Cannon (1974), demonstrated a concomitant increase in marital vitality with the number of years of marriage (r_s = .27; $p<.01$). Determination may also explain why the inverse relationship between marriage satisfaction and number of children reported by others (Hicks and Platt 1970) was not experienced by these couples (r_s = .19). Finally, Christenson and Johnson (1971) have observed that, if there is a strong desire for marriage success, couples may develop patterns of complementary need meeting after marriage; this hypothesis offers a plausible explanation for the presence of such a pattern among these couples (Ammons and Stinnett 1977) when scant research support for complementary need meeting has been found previously (Hicks and Platt 1970).

In short, these couples seem to have learned to pull together to resolve inevitable life crises successfully and achieve satisfying marriage and family relationships. They are able to do so because they have a clear vision of what they want and they express personality needs that enable them to realize their aspirations.

Ego Strengths

Vital marital partners appear to have well-developed ego strengths; that is, they have characteristics that enable them to function autonomously and to separate themselves from their mate. Healthy ego strength is indicated in that a majority (75 percent) of the respondents expressed a moderate need to make independent judgments and take independent actions as measured by the EPPS autonomy subscale. Further, only 2 percent expressed high dependency needs as measured by the EPPS deference subscale. Moreover, not one of the respondents reported high needs to accept undue blame or admit inferiority as measured by the EPPS abasement subscale.

The importance of healthy ego strength to the vital relationship is underscored by previous research, which has found ego strength to be related to: (a) the ability to form rewarding personal relationships (Frank 1975); (b) the ability to handle stress well (p. 121); and (c) sexual gratification (Barton, Kawash, and Cattell 1972).

Stress and conflict are inevitable in an intimate relationship. Stressful times are debilitating for the husband or wife with low ego strength. Their underlying insecurity and fear of losing the relationship may cause them to adopt a posture of overaccommodation as they cling to their mate in neurotic desperation. High ego strength enables couples to weather stressful times and frees them to work toward their resolution while leaving each partner's basic integrity as an individual intact.

Concluding Comment

Although these couples have effected a vital marriage relationship, the evidence of mutuality in their relationships may be misleading. Without the strength of individuality, it might not have been possible for them to think so positively about their togetherness. The need for individuality within a committed relationship is not a new concept.

Healthy family functioning has been discussed in terms of an individuation-mutuality paradigm (Barnhill 1979). Individuation has been defined as "independence of thought, feeling, and judgment of individual family members. It includes a firm sense of autonomy, personal responsibility, identity, and boundaries of self." Mutuality refers to "a sense of emotional closeness, joining or intimacy" (p. 95).

The twin notions of individuation and mutuality are separate concepts, yet they are inextricably wed. Paradoxically, healthy mutuality occurs only when there is individuation. A normative but critical task for contemporary couples is to figure out how to balance the individuation-mutuality see-saw (Sheehy 1976).

Lederer and Jackson (1968) used overlapping circles to discuss the blending of the two concepts. In their conceptualization, each person's circle overlaps the circle representing the relationship, but does not overlap with the circle representing the partner. Mutuality is the individual's identification with, involvement in, and commitment to the relationship (represented by the individuals' circles overlapping the relationship circle). The relationship consumes most, but not all, of each individual's circle.

A homeostatic balance between individuation and mutuality eludes many couples. The two concepts exist in a state of dynamic tension within the marital arena. This tension creates the ever-present danger either that mutuality will be lost as individuation is increased or that the autonomy of individual partners will be swallowed up by the corporate mutuality of the relationship. Either extreme is emotionally unhealthy. To have individuation without mutuality promulgates isolation, despair, alienation, and insecurity. Mutuality, without the firm boundaries of an individuated self, promulgates a neurotic dependency (Barnhill 1979).

Perhaps the gravest danger to the vital marital relationship, with its emphasis on becoming "bound together in important life matters," is that the see-saw will be tipped too far in the direction of mutuality. It is well worth noting that these couples appeared to have mastered the art of losing themselves in their relationship without losing their sense of self in the process. Husbands and wives in vital marriages both give and receive a great deal from each other. However, like the ancient god Janus, they face two directions — inward toward their conjoint relationship and outward toward their functional autonomy. Mutuality is furthered by their commitment to the relationship and through reciprocal need meeting. Individuation, on the other hand, is furthered by the presence of sufficient ego strength to avoid losing their independence.

Vital marital partners further enhance mutuality as they express their needs for individuation. An autonomous person "appreciating his own worth . . . is ready to see and respect the worth of others" (Satir, 1972). Conversely, expressions of mutuality generate energy and security from within the relationship, providing a stable springboard for autonomous functioning. Thus, individuality and mutuality coexist harmoniously, forming the warp and woof of an interdependent relationship pattern that encourages both the individual and the relationship to flourish.

Works Cited

Ammons, P., and N. Stinnett. 1977. "Personality Patterns Among Strong Families." Paper presented at the meeting of the National Council on Family Relations, October.

Bagarozzi, D.A., and J.S. Wodarski. 1977. "A Social Exchange Typology of Conjugal Relationships and Conflict Development." *Journal of Marriage and Family Counseling* 5: 53–60.

Barnhill, L.R. 1979. "Healthy Family Systems." *The Family Coordinator* 28: 94–100.

Barton, K., G. Kawash, and R.B. Cattell. 1972. "Personality Motivation and Marital Role Factors as Predictors of Life Data in Married Couples." *Journal of Marriage and the Family* 34: 474–80.

Blood, R.V., and D.M. Wolfe. 1960. *Husbands and Wives: The Dynamics of Married Living.* Glencoe, IL: Free Press.

Christenson, H.J., and K. Johnson. 1971. *Marriage and the Family.* 3rd ed. New York: Roland.

Constantine, L.M., and J.M. Constantine. 1971. "Sexual Aspects of Multilateral Relationships." *Journal of Sex Research* 7: 204–25.

Cuber, J.F., and P.B. Haroff. 1965. *Sex and the Significant Americans.* New York: Penguin.

Edwards, A.I. 1959. *Edwards Personal Preference Schedule.* Manual. New York: Psychological Corporation.

Foote, N.R., and L.S. Cottrell. 1955. *Identity and Interpersonal Competence.* Chicago: University of Chicago Press.

Frank, J.D. 1975. "General Psychotherapy: The Restoration of Morale." *American Handbook of Psychiatry,* Vol 5. 2d ed. Eds. D.X. Freedman and J.E. Dyrud. New York: Basic.

Hicks, M.W., and M. Platt. 1970. "Marital Happiness and Stability: A Review of the Research in the Sixties." *Journal of Marriage and the Family* 33: 553–57.

Lederer, W.J., and D.D. Jackson. 1968. *The Mirages of Marriage.* New York: Norton.

Mace, D., and V. Mace. 1975. "Marriage Enrichment: Wave of the Future." *The Family Coordinator* 24: 132–36.

McGuire, C., and G.D. White. 1955. "The Measurement of Social Status." Research paper in Human Development. No. 3. (Available from C. McGuire, University of Texas, Austin, TX)

Neubeck. G. 1979. "In Praise of Marriage." *The Family Coordinator* 28: 115–17.

Neuhaus, R., and R. Neuhaus. 1974. *Family Crises.* Columbus, OH: Merrill.

Nye, F.I. 1976. "Ambivalence in the Family: Rewards and Costs in Group Membership." *The Family Coordinator* 25: 21–31.

———. 1978. "Socialization in the 1970's: Over Emphasis on Individualism?" *Family Perspective* 17: 105–16.

Otto, H.A. 1975. *The Use of Family Strength Concepts and Methods in Family Life Education: A Handbook.* Beverly Hills, CA: Holistic.

Rollins, B.C., and K.L. Cannon. 1974. "Marital Satisfaction Over the Family Life Cycle: A Reevaluation." *Journal of Marriage and the Family* 36: 271.

Satir, V. 1972. *Peoplemaking.* Palo Alto: Science Behavior.

Sheehy, G. 1976. *Passages.* New York: Dutton.

Thibaut, J.W., and H.H. Kelly. 1959. *The Social Psychology of Groups.* New York: Wiley.

WHAT HOLDS MARRIAGES TOGETHER?

Jan E. Trost

The question of why some divorce is turned around to the question of why some do not divorce. When a number of marital bonds keeping marriages together are weakened, the likelihood of divorce increases. Initially, only an emotional bond exists. Gradually, more bonds form. If the emotional bond disappears, the other bonds might keep the marriage intact. The increase in the divorce rate is explained in the various marital bonds.

The question "Why do people divorce?" could be dealt with by turning it around: "Why do not all divorce?" Of course, we can never reach a divorce rate of 100 percent simply because some marriages are dissolved by the death of one of the spouses before the partners manage to get a divorce. This article aims to undertake a theoretical discussion of marital stability/instability.

In social science, we normally look upon groups as having a goal or an aim to fulfil; and when the goal is reached, the group can dissolve. However, we are inclined to look upon some groups somewhat differently, because the goal can be so diffuse or unspecified that we do not know when it is reached. Examples are friendship groups and marital groups. Traditionally speaking, the marital group or dyad should last forever, which means until death.

When a marriage is dissolved by divorce, we often assume that it was a failure, or that it had broken down or was disrupted. Why do we as scientists, practitioners, or laymen make such an assumption? There are two reasons. If we look at marriage as a social system,

it is reasonable to say that divorce is a breakdown of the system. However, then we would also have to classify the ending of the marriage by the death of one of the spouses as a breakdown. Is it also reasonable to classify the system as a failure whether marriages end by divorce or death? Yes, if by failure we mean not being able to meet the expectations of the system. Most of us presume that, if a marriage fails, that is, is ended by divorce, then failure means that the marriage as such was a mistake or was bad.

One could, instead, say that marital failure occurred only at the final stage of the marriage — that is, immediately prior to the divorce. Many marriages are successful for some time (from the perspective of one or both partners), less successful during other periods, and then successful again for some periods of time. When we use the term "failure," however, we are probably classifying *all* the marriage as a "failure," and for both spouses. Yet, most marriages that have ended in divorce were certainly not always failing. As laymen and practitioners, we have heard many divorcees remark: "It was a mistake to marry." For most people, it was no mistake at all to marry and to stay married for a while; it might have been a mistake not to have divorced somewhat earlier. For others, the mistake might have been the problems that occurred during the divorce process.

From our perspective, it is fully relevant to use professional jargon such as "breakdown" or "failure" when referring to a system's approach. However, in other instances or when addressing noncolleagues, we make the mistake of imposing (mostly unconsciously) a negative evaluation on divorce and the

Source: *Acta Sociologica* 4 (1986): 303–10. Reprinted with permission.

divorced. We have to try to avoid making such value judgments (cf. Sprey 1985).

Traditionally, however, in our Western societies, the idea of everlasting marriage has existed and still exists. The idea of everlasting marriage is based on religious stands and on tradition. It is our task to study traditions, but it is not our task to use value-laden terminology. Most people who start a relationship such as marriage or cohabitation look upon it as something that will last. Although we know that one of us will die sometime in the future, we normally do not take this into consideration. Also, although we know of the high statistical probability of divorce, we do not consider it as applying to us. It is more or less like driving a car; we know that there are many accidents, but presume we won't be involved in one, at least not today. It is not so much a matter of taking risks as of being optimistic (or one might say unrealistic).

Bonds

These reflections lead us to the question of what keeps a marital dyad together. Our approach here is based on the idea of bonding, that is, the reason not all marriages end in divorce is that there are a number of bonds keeping the two spouses in the marriage. It might be more correct to state that the bonds keep the marital dyad from splitting up.

Turner (1970, 41), states that a "bond, or tie, exists when some *value* of the individual's — shared or unique — is felt to be fostered by association and interaction with some other person or group." It is more important to note that the bonds are thus the individual's and not the dyad's; bonds have effects upon the dyad, but they are still individual. Also it is important to note that we stress the perception of the individual, and not objective criteria; the perception can, of course, be on an unconscious or a conscious level, but is usually unconscious.

This approach is close to Lewin's old idea (1951) and his field theory stressing barriers of restraining forces. It seems somewhat odd

to us, however, to label positive emotions as restraining forces; bond is a more fitting label.

At the start of a marriage (or cohabitation), the only bond typically present is an emotional one, with high attraction, love, or whatever we might want to call it. We start the relationship because we love the other person, and we want to be together as much as possible (to live together). We marry because we are socialized to equalize living together and marriage, except in cultures where cohabitation without marriage is a social institution alongside marriage (cf. Trost 1979). The emotional bond is the basis for our marriage or cohabitation.

There are, however, some exceptions, even in cultures where the partners themselves decide if and when to marry. We are thinking of what are often called "forced marriages," where the bride is pregnant at the time of marriage. Some of these are truly forced marriages, in the sense that they would not have occurred had the bride not become pregnant. Such marriages are probably rare in modern societies because of efficient and easily available contraception and relatively easily available abortions. There are, however, two types of marriages that are erroneously called "forced." In one type, a couple decides to marry some time in the future, but the unplanned pregnancy has resulted in their decision to marry sooner. In the other type, the couple has decided to marry soon; in this case, they are less careful about contraceptives since they want a child soon anyway.

In the truly forced marriage, there is no emotional bond at the beginning; only a kind of social bond. In the other two types of "forced" marriages, erroneously so labelled, the emotional bond is the primary one.

In many cases, at the time of marriage or soon after, economic/technical bonds appear; spouses take out loans and buy furniture and other household goods. As time passes, these bonds become stronger and stronger; the couple may buy a boat, a summer cabin, or a house. Often, the longer the couple is married, the stronger the economic bonds become. In some cases, however, when both spouses are earning a high income and doing quite well financially, these economic bonds can become considerably less important.

If and when offspring enter the marriage, two types of bonds related to the offspring occur. One is the emotional bond to the children; strictly speaking this is not a marital bond, but rather a parent–child bond. In reality, most of us would perceive these bonds as so closely connected with the marriage that they ought, in fact, to be classified as marital bonds. The other type of bond related to the offspring is of a more social nature, each parent taking care of the offspring in the family/marital setting. The parents perceive social expectations or social norms that children need the family, based upon an existing marriage. These social bonds are stronger when the children are minors; when the children are older, and especially when they have been launched, this bond will begin to disappear (Luckey and Bain 1970).

Another type of social bond is the one based on perceived expectations from the individual's social network (relatives, friends, workmates, and acquaintances). These perceived expectations or bonds exist at the start of the marriage and remain; their strength, however, is based on religious and other traditions; "it is proper behaviour not to divorce," "to be responsible," or a Nordic expression "if you have taken the devil onto the boat, you have to row him ashore" (cf. Goode 1964–65).

A third type of social bond does not relate to social pressure, but concerns the risk of losing an important part of one's social network. The bridge parties and other social activities we enjoy and highly value are performed in established pair-relationships. The old saying "you should not be your friend's enemy's friend" is a social reality in our societies; to be your friend's enemy's friend could easily be interpreted as a lack of loyalty or as dishonesty.

A fourth type of social bond is the law. If the law totally forbids divorce, as in Ireland, and in Spain until recently, the legal bond is complete — if we disregard annulments and legal separations, *a mensa et toro* (from board and bed). On the other hand, in some countries there is no legal bond, since the law states the right to divorce, and the courts are not allowed to ask for any ground, reason, or cause. Even in those cultures, however, there might be a possibility for a semilegal bond; one might feel that one has to consult a legal adviser, and the legal adviser might be a hindrance or act as a bond, by behaviour and advice or by his or her mere existence. It takes some initiative to contact the legal adviser, or to write to the court demanding a divorce. So, even when the law is very permissive, the legal system is a sort of bond.

Human beings are not just human and social, they are also sexual, and typically in our society there is a strong connection between sexuality and marriage. This is true even if there are no strong social norms against premarital sex or against extramarital sex. Therefore, we can claim that there are also sexual bonds in almost all marriages. These sexual bonds are also reinforced in many societies by norms against extramarital sex.

In a dyadic relationship, one's perceptions of the other partner's bonds are of importance for one's own bonds — these can be labelled "counterbonds." If, for example, a spouse in a marriage perceives the other to have very strong emotional bonds, this perception would likely influence the strength of the counterbonds. These bonds relate to the perceived or anticipated effects of a separation or divorce: "if we divorced he/she would never manage" (financially, socially, or emotionally).

Not all the marital bonds have been enumerated here, but the more salient ones have been addressed.

Expectations, Perceived Reality, and Bonds

We assume that an individual's expectations as to what a marital relationship should be are related to the strength of the bonds. If a person has high expectations of his or her marital relationship and if the perceived reality does not meet the standards set by the expectations, then that person has lower satisfaction with the relationship. In such cases, the bonds are weaker than they would be had the expectations been met. This also means that, if a person has low expectations, it is more likely that expectations will be met, and thus the bonds are that much stronger. This seems to be true for the internal bonds, such as those based upon emotions and sexuality. Thus, we assume that the higher the expectations, the lower the satisfaction, and the lower the satisfaction, the weaker the bonds.

With time, changes take place in the expectations of the individual in a marriage. Sometimes they grow greater, perhaps because of external influences. We might be told by friends or read somewhere that our sex lives could be much more pleasurable, we might change our libido, or we might have experienced extramarital sexual intercourse. These external influences can make our expectations higher or lower. An unpleasant extramarital sexual experience might cause us to believe our earlier expectations on intramarital sex were too high, such that we change our expectations. Our extramarital sexual experiences might have been much more enjoyable than we could believe, so we change our expectations as regards intramarital sexuality.

Sanctions and Bonds

Some bonds are based on fear of sanctions if the bonds are broken. Normally, the stronger these sanction-based bonds are, the more severe the predicted sanctions will be, and of course, *vice versa*.

The predicted or anticipated sanctions as a person perceives them are related to the perceived strength of the bonds. The stronger the bonds, the more severe the sanctions. The closer we are to breaking the bonds, and thus the more prone we are to a divorce initiated by ourselves, the weaker we perceive the sanctions to be. Note that we do not take into consideration here the real outcome of a divorce. This real outcome of a divorce is its aftermath, but here we are looking at the situation while the spouses are still married and living together. A person might fear strong sanctions or negative effects of the divorce; if the spouses divorce the outcome can be much less dramatic, and *vice versa*.

Some couples do not have many friends; others do (cf. Bell 1981). For those with many common friends, the perceived outcome is more traumatic than for those who have only a few or no common friends. It is, however, more complicated; some persons are more optimistic about the outcome than others. For the optimists, the presumed or anticipated outcome is less severe than it is for the pessimists. Generally speaking, the optimists presume less severe and fewer sanctions from a divorce than the pessimists. On the other hand, some are optimistic about the future of the marriage, and for them the bonds are stronger. They may very well also be inclined to decrease their expectations of the marital relationship.

It seems reasonable to assume that those who are dissatisfied with the marital relationship are more likely to define away some of the sanctions; for example, a Catholic, for whom divorce is not available according to the Church, may presume that the Church will give an annulment; another Catholic in this situation may leave the Church and in that way remove the religious sanctions.

There is also the question of alternatives. The dissatisfied spouse who has someone else he or she wishes to live with will define the bonds as less binding and the sanctions as less severe, and will be compensated by the new relationship and its presumed rewards.

Some spouses define their marital situation as so bad that they see the future as better even though they might foresee loneliness and a very precarious financial situation. They may well feel that the problems in the marriage are so intolerable that anything else is better than staying married. (Cf. the theory of Thibaut and Kelley 1959, about alternatives and comparison levels).

More and More Divorces

Divorce rates have increased in most countries in the western world. This is true for the United States, the Nordic countries, and most of continental Europe (Le divorce . . . 1975). If one looks at the crude rates (relative to population size) or the rates relative to the number of existing marriages, one might find that the statement is not true. However, if one looks at cohort data — that is, if one follows those who married at specific times — one will find that the statement is true. This effect is partly the result of varying birth rates during earlier decades and partly of decreases in the marriage rates (which also should be studied by cohorts, or by age-specific rates).

Why have divorce rates increased and why do they continue to do so? With our perspective, the answer can be arrived at by looking at the bonds and their changes as discussed in this article.

As stated above, new marriages are based normally on only the emotional bonds. If the emotional bonds weaken or disappear after some time, other bonds are then added to the marital relationship. If a couple do not divorce when the emotional bonds have disappeared, or when the emotions between the spouses have become negative, other emotional bonds will replace them. It is not difficult to find elderly couples today who had bad times together some decades ago, and who now, in old age, feel much affection for each other. In some cases these persons have changed their expectations so that the perceived reality fits, and they are now satisfied. In other cases, what is often labelled as old-age love and concern are not emotions per se, but, for example, a physical dependency because of mutual weakness and lack of alternatives.

It is a moral and political dilemma as to whether society should help or force a dissatisfied spouse to stay in a marriage or to divorce. In a marriage that does not end in divorce, for example, the early marital period may be satisfactory, followed by some periods characterized by dissatisfaction, further intermingled with satisfactory periods, and be followed by a satisfactory ending. Would it have been better for the individual, for third persons (mainly the children), or for society if there had been a divorce? Is a long period of dissatisfaction compensated by old-age satisfaction in the same marriage? No one knows.

We know that offspring of divorced parents have higher crime rates and other societal and personal problems. However, as Manniche (1985) has shown, the frequency of negative outcomes among children of divorced parents is the same as for children of parents who are highly dissatisfied in their marriages!

Over the last decade, there has been a tendency in the western world, among politicians, to take the position that those who really want to divorce should also have the right to do so (SOU 1972). The introduction of no-fault divorce laws reflects this view. Thus, the legal bonds have changed; today society, more than in the past, accepts divorce via the matrimonial laws. This means that the legal marriage bonds are less strong than some decades ago. The legal procedure has also changed in the same direction with the same effect.

In many societies, the possibility of one of the ex-spouses getting lifelong alimony has decreased considerably. This legal change also weakens the legal bonds in the marriages, particularly if the better-off spouse is aware of the change. This is an example not only of changes in legal bonds but, even more, of changes in economic bonds.

The number of women in the work force has increased over recent decades (Lupri 1983). This is true for all categories of women, including wives and married mothers. Because many of these women are gainfully employed, they can look forward to a decent living standard, even after a divorce. This holds true especially for wives with no minor children. In some countries, the state guarantees decent child support. In these situations, if the custodian (often still the mother) does not receive child support from the noncustodian, the state will make a payment on behalf of the delinquent parent. In some countries, the amount paid by the state is a minimum that is higher than that many of the noncustodians are expected to pay according to the court's decision. Again, these changes weaken the economic bonds.

We are not ready to claim that emotional bonds between the parent and the offspring per se have changed. However, since there are fewer children in today's family in the Western world, the time during which there are minor children tied to the marital unit is shorter. This change in family size weakens this type of emotional bond from a time perspective.

The bonds related to the socially required responsibility for minor children have also weakened in some countries. The possibility of joint custody after divorce (which is possible in, for example, many of the states of the United States, Denmark, Norway, Sweden, and Australia) makes it likely that some spouses who have minor children will presume they will continue to take care of them, even after divorce. Thus, this type of bond, too, has weakened in some countries.

We have mentioned bonds based on pressure from the individual's social network. Partly because divorces have become more common, divorce and divorcees have become better accepted as social phenomena (cf. Bernard 1979). Thus, the perception of sanctions from the social network has changed and has weakened this type of bond.

Another bond mentioned here has been the perceived risk of network losses. Again, parents, relatives, and friends do not withdraw their support as much now as in earlier times, because divorce is so common and is no longer shameful. With the increase in the number of women in the labour force, more of the wife's friends are her own and relatively fewer friends are based on the marital dyad. Therefore, because the risk of losses of friendships because of a divorce appears to be less, there are fewer binding network bonds.

It is unclear whether extramarital intercourse has become more or less common, or if there has been no change. What is clear, however, is that, in the Western world, especially since the publications by Masters and Johnson in the 1960s, there has been an increasing concern for sexual satisfaction, with higher expectations by both sexes, but particularly by women. As we have argued earlier, if the expectations increase, the satisfaction decreases, and if the satisfaction decreases, the bonds become weaker. Consequently the sexual bonds may be weaker now that they were some decades ago.

Finally, what is happening to what we call "counterbonds"; that is, the anticipated effects upon the other spouse? It is reasonable to assume that these have changed as well. The situation for the other spouse is probably anticipated to be not as bad as it once was. With a perception of easier survival for the other spouse — financially, socially, etc. — follows a weakening of the counterbonds, or a lessening of concern for the future effects upon the other spouse.

Summary and Conclusions

Our perspective on the marital dyad; has been on what holds the pair together — that is, the various marital bonds that have been briefly discussed in this article. These may be summarized as follows:

- Emotional bonds vis-à-vis the spouse
- Emotional bonds between the parent and the offspring
- Economic bonds
- Social bonds, responsibility for the offspring, social pressure, importance of the contribution of the social network
- Counterbonds
- Legal bonds
- Sexual bonds.

As indicated, the strength of these bonds seems to have changed, making them weaker and lessening the presumed sanctions when breaking the bonds. The increases in the divorce rates can thus be explained by these changes in the bonds.

We want to stress the importance of looking at the individual spouse and not at the couple when trying to understand why some divorce and others do not. To be sure, divorce affects the dyad (it dissolves) as well as the individual. Nevertheless, the effects are different from the forces leading to divorce. If neither spouse takes the initiative to divorce, there will be no divorce, so initiative from at least one of the spouses is a necessity for divorce to occur. Our answer to the question of who divorces and why would, thus, be stated as follows:

- The one who divorces is characterized by some initiative.
- The one who divorces does so because he or she perceives fewer and less demanding bonds
- The one who is divorced (that is, affected by the one who divorces) is characterized as having had a spouse who divorced.

Works Cited

Bell, Robert R. 1981. *Worlds of Friendship*. Beverly Hills, CA: Sage.

Bernard, Jessie. 1979. Foreword. *Divorce and Separation*. Eds. George Levinger and Oliver C. Moles. New York: Basic.

Goode, William J. 1964–65. *The Family*. Englewood Cliffs, NJ: Prentice-Hall.

Le Divorce . . . 1975. *Le divorce en Europe occidental*. La Documentation Français. Paris.

Lewin, Kurt. 1951. *Field Theory in Social Science*. New York: Harper & Row.

Luckey, E.B., and J.K. Bain. 1970. "Children: A Factor in Marital Satisfaction." *Journal of Marriage and the Family* 32: 43–44.

Lupri, Eugen, ed.. 1983. *The Changing Position of Women in Family and Society*. Leiden: Brill.

Manniche, Erik. 1985. *The Family in Denmark*. Helsingör: IPC.

Masters, William, and Virginia Johnson. 1966. *Human Sexual Response*. Boston: Little, Brown.

SOU 1972:41 1972. *Familj och äktenskap*. Stockholm: Liber.

Sprey, Jetse. 1985. Editorial Comments. *Journal of Marriage and the Family* 47: 807–808.

Thibaut, J.W., and H.H. Kelley. 1959. *The Social Psychology of Groups*. New York: Wiley.

Trost, Jan. 1979. *Unmarried Cohabitation*. Västerås: International Library.

Turner, Ralph H. 1970. *Family Interaction*. New York: Wiley.

INTERVENTIONS INTO THE PROI OF WIFE ASSAULT: THERAPEUTI POLICY, AND RESEARCH IMPLIC

Donald G. Dutton

Psychological contributions to the social problem of wife assault are reviewed in the following areas: assessing police response to family-crisis calls, training police for family-crisis intervention, evaluation of training and policy change, treatment of wife assaulters, research on the causes of wife assault and its effects on the victim.

This research constitutes a "problem-focussed" approach that incorporates the study of basic processes such as the cognitive interpretation of affective states, applied issues such as treatment strategies for assaultive males, and policy issues such as the ideal model for delivery of services to diminish wife assault. The author argues that each of the three areas stimulates new insights in the other two.

Although wife assault seems to have occurred in both Western and Eastern cultures since earliest recorded history (Davidson 1977; de Reincourt 1974; Taylor 1954), and appears to be prevalent in contemporary North America (Schulman 1979; Straus, Gelles, and Steinmetz 1980), scant attention was paid to it in the psychological literature before 1970. Since that time, however, psychologists' contributions have been threefold:

1. development of crisis-intervention programs for police and other professionals who intervene in family disturbances that frequently involve wife assaults (Bard 1972; Dutton 1981a; Liebman and Schwartz 1972);

2. a development of a substantive literature on the causes of wife assault in males (Dutton and Browning 1983, 1984; Straus and Hotaling 1980) and the cognitive and affective consequences in female victims (Dutton and Painter 1981; Porter 1981); and

3. development of treatment groups for assaultive males based largely on social learning theory (Bandura 1979; Ganley 1981; Novaco 1975).

The studies reported below include such apparently diverse aspects as training and evaluation of police performance, basic research on the causes of wife assault and effects on the victim, and treatment program development for wife assaulters. A guiding principle of this work has been that mutual benefit accrues to basic research and its application to current social issues: basic research has much to offer toward policy development, and research is stimulated by the challenge of application.

Wife assault presents special problems for the researcher, clinician, and policy maker because of its inherently private nature. Only about 8.6 percent[1] of wife assaults are reported to police (Schulman 1979) compared to 34 percent of all assaults (Canadian Urban Victimization Survey 1983). Hence, detection of wife assault by the state is difficult and subsequent criminal-justice-system programs that depend on improved detection as a necessary step toward specific deterrence (Wilson 1983) must counter resistance from both

*The research reported in this paper has been funded by Health and Welfare Canada; the Research Division, Ministry of the Solicitor General of Canada; and by the Social Sciences and Humanities Research Council of Canada.

Source: Canadian Journal of Behavioural Science 16 (1984): 281–97.

blic and professionals about involving state in "family business" (Steiner 1981). Researchers have to solve the problems of access to populations of assaultive males and sample representatives (Dutton and Browning 1983). Clinicians have difficulty in gaining access to corroborative information about frequency and severity of abuse that they can use to confront the denial or minimizing of violence that occurs in treatment groups for batterers (Browning and Dutton 1984). As a widely recognized social problem, wife assault has taken one step out of the closet, but misinformation and dubious generalizations still abound. In particular, incidence estimates of wife assault vary widely, in part because of definitional problems about what constitutes an assault. Two large-sample victim surveys have indicated that "serious assault" (hitting, biting, kicking, or worse) occurs for 10.7 percent of women over the course of their marriage (Schulman 1979; Straus, Gelles and Steinmetz 1980). Wife assaulters are widely believed to have learned to be assaultive in their family of origin, although evidence for this assertion is mixed and proper baseline measures of exposure to violence in non-assaultive populations are just now becoming available (Dutton and Browning 1983). The public is viewed as condoning wife assault (Straus 1976), although survey evidence (Stark and McEvoy 1970) suggests otherwise, and battered women are believed by some professionals to be "masochistic" (Snell, Rosenwald, and Robey 1964), although evidence again suggests otherwise (Caplan 1984; Dutton 1983c, Dutton and Painter 1981; Rounsaville 1978). Below, I will review my work on training police to intervene in family disputes, discuss criminal-justice policy on wife assault, and review my current working assumptions for understanding the wife assaulter and the effects of assault on the victim.

Wife Assault and the Police

In attempting to improve police training for "family crisis calls," current training proce-

dures and police job requirements were assessed in a previous paper (Dutton 1981b). It was found that, while training was heavily "law enforcement" oriented, 80 percent of police time was spent on "order maintenance" activities where clear evidence of lawbreaking was lacking (Wilson 1969). Order-maintenance activities emphasize conflict management and problem-solving skills rather than use of legal authority and pertain to a wide variety of situations such as landlord–tenant and neighbour disputes and family conflicts. In the latter area, police are involved in situations where wife assault is frequent. For example, Bard and Zacker (1975) found that evidence of wife assault existed in over one-third of 1000 "family conflicts" they attended with the New York City Police.

In 1974, when revision of the police training curriculum was begun, little formal training was provided by any Canadian police force to enable recruits to intervene successfully in family disputes, despite pubic demand. This disjunction between formal training and job requirements led to the development of a training module for conflict resolution (Dutton 1981b) that was designed to train police with a set of procedures to improve their ability to detect chargeable assaults during family-crisis intervention, improve their ability to decide a course of action (such as arrest, referral, mediation, or removing one party), improve their ability to implement a successful course of action, and diminish the physical risk to police and citizens.

Training Police for Family-Dispute Intervention

A comprehensive description of the implementation, content, and evaluation of a police training program is contained in Dutton (1981b). The program used attitude change (Zimbardo and Ebbesen 1969) and group process techniques (Yalom 1975) and involved a five-step procedure for crisis intervention (safety, defusing of violence, problem resolution, mediation techniques, referral techniques) taught in modular fashion so that each step both augmented and reviewed prior steps. Drawing on the social-psychological literature in such areas as proxemics (Baxter and Rozelle 1975), stereotypes (Bayley and Mendelsohn 1968), and self-fulfilling prophecies, the training succeeded in diminishing violence directed toward police by disputing families (Dutton and Levens 1977) largely through decreasing what Bard (1971) had termed *iatrogenic violence.* Furthermore, trained police were more likely to initiate long-term solutions to conflict resolution (such as referral to a social agency) and were less likely to restrict themselves to short-term solutions (such as merely removing one person for the night). Wilt and Breedlove (1977) have pointed out the danger of short-term solutions. In Kansas City, where the police forced used only short-term solutions, 90 percent of homicide victims or suspects and 85 percent of aggravated-assault victims or suspects had had one prior "disturbance" call at their residence. Fifty percent had had five or more disturbance calls. A disturbance call to police may be viewed as an opportunity for preventive policing, in that many couples appear to have repeated, escalating conflicts that short-term intervention does not stop. To this date, debate exists over the optimal solution for "disturbance" calls where assaults are suspected and future violence seems possible. At the time we began training, police were unwilling to increase their low (3–7 percent) arrest rate on disturbance calls, despite evidence that a higher arrest rate was warranted. Jaffe and Burris (1982) found that, of 222 disturbance calls they monitored in London, Ontario, police arrested in only 3 percent of the cases, although 17 percent of the woman victims required medical attention as a result of the altercation. Since increased arrest rates were unlikely at that time, we attempted to get police to increase referral rates to outside agencies (that is, to divert cases). Subsequent evaluation showed that referral rates increased to 18 percent of cases for trained police, compared to 8 percent for untrained

(Levens and Dutton 1980). Correspondingly, a constellation of attitudinal items consonant with attempting long-term solutions to family disturbance, and recognizing the severity of family violence, showed change in the desired direction up to seven months after training. All results were significant at the .05 level or better (Levens and Dutton 1980).

Policy and Practice of Police Response to "Family Disturbance"

Before this training was implemented, a unique opportunity to measure the police organizational change in policy and practice of handling "family dispute" calls presented itself. The Vancouver Police Department agreed to co-operate in having its system of dispute handling monitored from the time when public requests for service came to the police via telephone through the actual police handling of calls to which they were dispatched. At the same time, the chief constable of the Vancouver Police and the chairman of the Provincial Police Commission publicly stated, in response to public demand, that police would begin a more aggressive policy of handling family dispute calls. Hence, we were provided with a situation that allowed us, first, to develop sound family intervention training for police recruits as described above, and assess the effects of training on performance; second, to provide in-service intervention training to police veterans; and third, to assess the combined effects of training and policy change on actual changes in police intervention into family disputes.

This assessment was made by, first, having researchers listen to 174 hours of taped calls from citizens to police; second, examining police time and contact records for all relevant police activity; third, having police officers fill out research reports on each family dispute they attended; and, finally, making field observation of dispute intervention. Baseline data were collected for a six-month period in January–June 1975 before trained recruits began duty and before official statements of policy change had been made. Follow-up data were collected for four weeks in July–August 1976, nine months after trained recruits had begun police service, when in-service training was in operation and policy directions had been issued. The main findings were that family-dispute calls constituted 17.5 percent of all calls to the Vancouver police (based on six-month baseline data) and typically increased from the beginning to the end of the week, with husband–wife disputes[2] constituting 77 percent of all family-dispute calls (Levens and Dutton 1980).

Analysis of police dispatch records yielded a subsample of 96 husband–wife disturbances for which police presence was requested. Police attended on 43/80 of these calls when their presence was requested (53.8 percent of the time). This dispatch rate was surprisingly low given the high violence potential of these calls. When police did not attend, the caller was told that the call was not a police matter or was given legal advice. To assess changes in dispatch probabilities as a result of training and policy changes, we traced 117 requests for police service in July–August 1976 through police records. The dispatch rate for these calls was 78.6 percent during peak periods, a significant ($p<.01$) increase over the 58.8 percent rate for the baseline period.

Initially, we regarded an increase in use of social agencies as a positive step, on the assumption that the agency could help the couple initiate long-term solutions to their marital problems. However, as it turned out, many agencies had little understanding of the dynamics and issues surrounding wife assault and some assaulted women were, as a consequence, put in a position of receiving counselling for having been assaulted by their husbands. The husband would refuse to seek counselling, so the problem of his violence toward his wife was not being dealt with. One way to do this, of course, would be for police to arrest the husband, thereby demonstrating that the state considered wife assault a serious crime.

Much has been written about the unwillingness of police both to attend family disputes and to take legal action on behalf of battered women. Women's groups have petitioned criminal-justice agencies to arrest wherever reasonable and probable grounds exist to suspect an assault has occurred (see, for example, U.S. Commission on Civil Rights 1978; Standing Committee of Health, Welfare and Social Affairs 1982). Studies by Bard (1972), Jaffe and Burris (1982), Levens and Dutton (1980), Loving and Farmer (1981), Dutton (1981b), and Sherman and Berk (1983) suggest that an increased arrest rate in conjunction with increased prosecution and effective treatment might improve protection for victims and decrease recidivism rates.

No pre–post differences in arrest rates were found in the Levens and Dutton (1980) study, however. Arrest rates remained extremely low (6 percent), reflecting either a refusal by the police to view wife assault as a serious crime, or a realistic appraisal that the case will not lead to a conviction because the Crown will not prosecute, the judge will not convict, or the victim herself will drop the charges. Some evidence exists that all three occur frequently (Dutton 1981a; Lehrman 1981). There is some evidence that arrest is the best strategy for preventing immediate recidivism. Sherman and Berk (1983) had Minneapolis police arrest, mediate, or remove one party at random for less serious wife assaults. During the next six months, only 10 percent of those arrested generated a new official report of domestic violence, compared to 16 percent of those whose cases were mediated by police and 22 percent of those ordered out of the house. However, since proceedings against the accused were in progress during this six-month period, the study does not tell us what long-term effects of arrest might be. Arrested men in the Sherman study may only have been on "good behaviour" prior to their court hearings.

For some time I have argued that coupling arrest with mandatory treatment groups for convicted assaulters is a program worth exploring (Dutton 1981a). One advantage is the potentially effective sentencing option provided to judges. Judges have been reluctant to convict in wife-assault cases where the couple wishes to remain together, not wanting to incarcerate a wage earner. One consequence of this reluctance is a very weak correlation (gamma = .28) between severity of wife assault and severity of sentence (Dutton and Muller 1984). Effective treatment has the potential of providing a means for batterers to learn more acceptable reactions to stress and conflict (Ganley and Harris 1978). Anger-management training with other groups has proven effective (Novaco 1975). It seems clear that police operate within parameters set by other parts of the criminal-justice system. If the Crown and judges do not treat wife-assault cases seriously and convict (cf. Hogarth 1980), police will not arrest. Hence, if a stronger arrest policy is desired, providing a sentencing option to judges and convincing Crown counsel of the seriousness of wife-assault cases are necessary precursors to policy change (Dutton 1981a).

Treatment Groups for Wife Assaulters

Although behaviour modification and "cognitive" behaviour modification for anger has been used in other contexts (Meichenbaum and Novaco 1978; Novaco 1975), its application to anger stemming from spousal conflicts is relatively recent (Ganley and Harris 1978). In 1979, along with Dale Trimble, I began to use a combination of group experiential (Yalom 1975) and cognitive behaviour-modification techniques to modify anger and violence in wife assaulters. Based on the social-learning assumption that wife assault is a learned response to stress (Ganley 1981) and to perceived threat within the spousal dyad (Dutton 1984), we began to examine and attempt to modify the beliefs, perceptions, attitudes, and behaviours of wife assaulters in weekly group sessions. Assaulters were required, among other things, to keep an "anger diary" (cf. Ganley 1981) in which they listed events that caused them to feel

angry, their "internal monologue or self-talk" in response to the event, how angry they felt, and how they knew they were angry (by bodily reactions, etc.). This not only helped batterers become more sensitive to monitoring the buildup of anger cues prior to violence, and the extent to which their interpretation of an event led to their anger, but also helped serve as a didactic device to instruct batterers how much control and responsibility they had for their own violence. In addition, it served as an assessment device, allowing us to separate cases where profound distortion of events occurred (including "conjugal paranoia" (American Psychiatric Association 1980) or what Bandura (1979) calls "delusional instigators") from cases where provocation was real and contained in combative interchange (Benjamin 1974, 1979; Kiesler 1983). To say that provocation exists is not to condone or excuse assaultive behaviour but rather to suggest that couple therapy might follow the male's individual treatment.

At present, considerable enthusiasm exists among practitioners for the use of treatment groups for wife assaulters. In part, this enthusiasm is based on the success of anger management in other contexts (Novaco 1975), in part on subjective assessments of therapeutic success (Ganley and Harris 1978) and in part because there is no obvious alternative (Dutton 1981a). Without an effective sentencing option to incarceration, a more effective criminal-justice policy to wife assault is unlikely. At the time of writing, 27 such treatment groups exist as a "best hope" in a variety of Canadian cities. To date, no thorough and well-designed evaluation of outcome (such as diminished violence as reported by both men and wives on the Straus Conflict Tactics Scale [1979]) has been carried out. The need for such an evaluation is great.

Essentially, such an evaluation would monitor males convicted or self-referred for wife assault. Control groups, matched with treatment groups on relevant demographics and history of violence, could be obtained either from standby waiting lists or from family courts not involved in referrals to treatment programs. Long-term outcome as determined from Straus (1979) Conflict Tactics Scale measures of violence that are obtained from both husbands and wives and corroborated where necessary through police reports and hospital records would provide an essential first step toward effective evaluation.

A Theory of Wife Assault

Our research orientation has been designed to implement and augment our treatment approach. To that end, our research hypotheses are derived from clinical observation and are useful not only insofar as they add to our understanding of the dynamics of wife assault but also in their applicability for therapists and practitioners. Since many cases of wife assault that we treated involved violence in an interpersonal context as a means of restoring a perceived loss of control, we have cast our research in social-psychological terms (see also Hendrick 1983), drawing on the literatures of power motivation (McClelland 1975; Winter 1973), social learning (Bandura 1974, 1977, 1979), intimacy (Derlega and Chaikin 1975; Dutton, Fehr, and McEwen 1982; Patterson 1976) and deindividuation (Dutton, Fehr, and McEwen 1982; Zimbardo 1969).

At the time our research began, most theoretical views of the etiology of wife assault were either clinical or sociological. Clinical theorists treated wife assault as abnormal and ascribed assault to a clinical syndrome in the assaulter such as a sadistic personality (Pizzey 1974), pathological dependency (Snell, Rosenwald, and Robey 1964) or temporal lobe epilepsy (Elliot 1977). Most clinical explanations were based on studies that suffered from a wide variety of methodological problems such as a tendency to generalize from psychiatric case studies (Symonds 1978) or from prison populations (Faulk 1974), a failure to assess systematically a large sample of wife assaulters and to use proper control groups,

and a tendency to rely on descriptive data supplied by the victim (Rosenbaum and O'Leary 1981). These methodologies may have inflated the incidence of wife assaulters who belonged to subpopulations with diagnosable psychopathologies (Dutton and Browning 1983).

In contrast to this clinical approach, sociologically influenced explanations have been focussed on the "normality" of wife assault, viewing it as a product of norms and values in Western society. These norms supported the notion that power advantages should accrue to males within family structures (de Reincourt 1974; Safilios-Rothschild 1970) and that males had a right to use force to maintain their power advantage (see, for example, Dutton 1983b). Male dominance and the romanticizing of male violence were viewed as contributing to a cultural milieu in which physical dominance of women was accepted (Martin 1977; Roy 1977; Straus 1976; Whitehurst 1974).

Victim surveys (for example, Schulman, 1979; Straus, Gelles, and Steinmetz, 1980) have not generally supported the contention that a norm exists for acceptance of wife assault. Especially as the assault becomes more severe, fewer people condone the action or practise it. Stark and McEvoy (1970), for example, found that only 20 percent of North Americans approved a man's slapping his wife "on appropriate occasions." Given the leading phrasing of this item, the agreement rate is too small to support the notion of a culture norm. Also, the victim surveys by Schulman and Straus showed that serious wife assault occurred in 10.7 percent of marriages. While this clearly constitutes a serious social problem, it does not suggest a norm for wife assault.

Nested ecological perspectives (Belsky 1980; Dutton 1981c, 1984) avoid the limitations of both clinical and sociological perspectives by treating violence as multiply determined by forces in the broader culture (macro system); community systems of connection to the broader culture (exosystem), such as occupational or friendship groups;

family dynamic (microsystem); and the individual (ontogentic). Nested ecological theories posit that narrow-focus factors operate within parameters set by broader factors. The interactive nature of the theory can be demonstrated by the following hypothetical "profile" of a male at risk for wife assault: if a male with a strong need for dominance or control of others but poor verbal skills through which to realize such control has witnessed violence as a means of conflict resolution in his family of origin and is currently engaged in conflict in his marital relationship, the likelihood of wife assault increases. If the content of the conflict involves intimacy or other issues that are essential to the form of the relationship, attempts by the male to gain control through increased pressure on the female to submit to his demands will increase. If these appear to fail, the likelihood of violence increases.

If job stress or unemployment exist and if this male has no intimate support group or lacks the capacity to be intimate with friends who could serve to mitigate his stress, the likelihood of marital violence increases further. Finally, if this male lives in a culture that devalues women, provides conflicting notions of appropriate husband–wife roles, condones the use of violence for instrumental purposes, and believes strongly in noninterference in family interaction, the likelihood of wife assault will increase further.

This theoretical framework is conceptually elaborate, heuristically rich, avoids the limitations of clinical viewpoints, which focus too exclusively on the ontogenetic level, and sociological viewpoints, which focus too exclusively on the macrosystem level. The framework will eventually require data-analysis techniques such as causal modelling (Joreskog 1979) that allow the theoretical preconception of pathways of influence to determine the causal model.

While we have set our research within this nested ecological framework, our current focus is on the interaction of ontogenetically learned predispositions in males with microsystem processes to produce violence. Our exploratory studies have examined the power motive (McClelland 1975) in assaultive males and how sociocultural definitions of the male role might shape this motive into a need for control within the primary relationship (Dutton and Browning 1983). On the basis of our clinical experience, we felt that a useful organizing concept for content issues presented by men in conflicted relationships was that of interpersonal intimacy. Some evidence existed to suggest that a frequent instigating mechanism of wife assaults was sudden perceived increases (Gelles 1975) or decreases (Martin 1977) in the socioemotional distance between man and woman. Dutton, Fehr, and McEwen (1982) posited a homeostatic process in which males attempted to maintain interpersonal intimacy in an "optimal zone" similar to Patterson's (1976) model for interpersonal spacing. Departures from this optimal zone are hypothesized to produce arousal that males experience as anger. Our clinical experience also suggested that considerable anxiety accompanied departures from the optimal zone, but sex-role socialization maximizes the likelihood that males will interpret such arousal as anger. Novaco (1975) has listed a variety of sources of reinforcement that may shape the interpretation of arousal states of anger. These include the greater energizing function of anger as opposed to anxiety, feelings of agency or effectance that accompany anger, and an increase in anger when the male is in (or feels he should be in) a position of coercive power in a hierarchy. Such a perspective is more consistent with a "labelling" or two-factor theory of emotion (Schachter 1964), which suggests that social factors shape the interpretation of physiological states. At present, a continuing debate exists in the basic research literature between two-factor theorists and expressive-motor theorists (Leventhal 1980) who view social factors as having a diminished role in shaping emotions. Consistent with the notion that sex-role expectations may shape interpretations of emotion is a recent study by Dutton and Aron (1984) which showed that for males a significant positive correlation exists between self-reports of arousal and anger in response to witnessing interpersonal conflict. For females, significant correlations existed between self-reports of arousal and anxiety in response to the same stimulus array.

In our research on assaultive males we hypothesized that, to the extent that violence had been vicariously learned as a response to anger, the likelihood of violence should increase in relationship situations where perceived uncontrollable changes in socioemotional distance occur. This may happen, for example, when a woman shows signs of increased independence from the relationship (such as a new job, increase in outside social contacts, or threatening to leave or leaving the relationship). We describe these situations as "abandonment" situations from the male perspective. Conversely "engulfment" situations are defined as those in which the female demonstrates increased dependence on the male (pregnancy, increase in demands for affection, time spent together, etc.). While issues of socioemotional distance occur for most couples, wife assaulters may be particularly inept at communicating their own needs in response to intimacy changes or may have exaggerated needs to control intimacy and maintain an "optimal zone." Consequently, they may experience arousal that they interpret as anger. If their verbal skills are poor, their prepotent response to anger may be violence.

To assess these hypotheses, we compared physiological and self-report responses of wife assaulters and control males to videotaped scenarios of husband–wife arguments. Three levels of socioemotional distance (abandonment, neutral, and engulfment) were represented in which either the husband (male dominant) or wife (female dominant) verbally dominated the argument (spoke more, interrupted more, generated eventual concessions from his or her partner). Each scenario was five to seven minutes long, was acted by professional actors, and depicted a moderate level of husband–wife conflict in a home setting.

Preliminary examination of these data (Dutton and Browning 1983) revealed that physically assaultive males demonstrated ex-aggerated anger self-reports in circumstances in which the female was presented as dominant and leaving the relationship. Furthermore, they were more likely than control subjects to report the abandonment issue as relevant for their own relationship (X^2 [4,N = 54] = 36.13, p = .0001). Interestingly, self-reports of humiliation frequently occurred while watching the conflict scenarios, and correlated +.4 (p = .001) with the male's report of being verbally abused by his mother in the family of origin.

Our initial studies have also indicated greater within-group variance than we initially anticipated. While we are currently planning to expand and improve our initial studies of power and intimacy issues, we are also becoming more aware that a variety of subpopulations may constitute the group currently called physically assaultive. Future studies may determine whether differences in affective reaction patterns exist for the "overcontrolled" vs the "undercontrolled" wife assaulter (Subotnik 1983) or for the assaulter whose use of assault is specific to his wife, as opposed to a general pattern of aggression.

Finally, the results of this study and others (e.g., Dutton and Painter 1981; Rosenbaum and O'Leary 1981) have highlighted the need for proper comparison groups in examining the correlates of physically abusive behaviour in husbands. The Rosenbaum and O'Leary study (1981) and our study showed some similarities in the responses of wife assaulters and maritally distressed controls, indicating the importance of such controls for interpretation of the results.

Research on the Victims of Wife Assault

Studies on the impact of assault on the victims have paralleled research on the causes of wife assault. An extensive literature has developed over the past decade on the psychological consequences of victimization (e.g., Dutton and Painter 1981; Fattah 1981; Flynn

1983). Some of this work has concentrated on affective reactions such as depression (Seligman 1975), lowered self-esteem, and lowered feelings of self-worth (Frieze 1979), while other work has focussed on cognitive reactions (Bulman and Wortman 1977; Porter 1983) or behavioural consequences (Seligman 1975; Walker 1979). My own work has attempted to explain the paradoxical phenomenon of battered women strongly bonding to their assaulter (Dutton and Painter 1981) with consequent reluctance to initiate criminal justice system proceedings (Dutton 1981a), to contrast legal and psychological perspectives and expectations for battered women (Dutton 1983c), and to contrast social psychological and predispositional explanations for the victimhood of battered women (Dutton and Painter 1981; Dutton 1983a).

In attempting to account for the "bonding" of battered women to their aggressor, Susan Painter and I interviewed 24 battered women in Vancouver transition houses. Further data came from the dissertation of one of my doctoral students (Porter 1983) who interviewed 50 battered women in a San Jose, California transition house. As a result of these studies, I have come to view the victimhood of battered women as an example of a "social trap" (see Platt 1973) in which immediate payoffs obscure long-term consequences. Battered women start out in marital relationships with expectations and a sense of role responsibilities similar to those of other women (Williams 1977). Specifically, they have a socialized sense of personal responsibility for relationship outcome (Williams 1977) and for the affective state of their partner (Williams 1977). They may be somewhat more likely to tolerate physical aggression because they are more likely to have witnessed it in their family of origin (Rounsaville 1978), but there is no evidence that they have masochistic predispositions that lead them to seek out violent situations (Caplan 1984; Dutton 1983a; Rounsaville 1978). Violent episodes typically begin in the first year following marriage (Dutton and Painter 1980; Rosenbaum

and O'Leary 1981) and are initially less severe than later on (Wilt and Breedlove 1977). At this point, since they are infrequent and are typically followed by considerable contrition by the male (Walker 1977) wives may view them as an anomaly that is not likely to recur. Repeated assaults of increasing severity change this perception, but as the cognitive component begins to shift toward the realization that the violence is permanent and dangerous, affective reactions to battering have already developed strong bonds to the batterer. Following his study of battered women, Rounsaville concluded: "The most striking phenomenon that arose in the interview and in treatment with battered women was the tenacity of both partners to the relationship in the face of severe abuse sustained by many of the women" (1978, 20). Part of this "traumatic bonding" process occurs because of the intermittent nature of the abuse, interspersed with strong positive reinforcement (Walker 1979).

Dutton and Painter (1981) reviewed the bonding effects of intermittent positive-negative treatment in both the human (Kempe and Kempe 1980) and animal (Rajecki, Lamb, and Obsmacher 1978) literatures. Consistent evidence for association of this particular reinforcement pattern with powerful social bonds was found in both humans and animals. We viewed the positive–negative treatment pattern as creating a double intermittent reinforcement effect through intermittent positive reinforcement (Rounsaville 1978; Walker 1979) and intermittent negative reinforcement through the removal of aversive arousal (Kendrick and Cialdini 1977; Zuckerman 1979) by the husband following a battering incident. Since this mechanism provides an explanation for staying in an abusive relationship that is an alternative to the predispositional explanation of female masochism, it deserves, in our opinion, further exploration.

A second major contribution to traumatic bonding is the exaggerated power differential that results from the violence. As the male gains more power in the marital dyad through threats of future violence, the woman is increasingly put into a position of exaggerated powerlessness and consequent depression (Rounsaville 1978), low self-appraisal (Walker 1979), dependency on the aggressor (cf. Bettleheim 1943) and self-blame (Porter 1981) that incrementally bond her to a relationship that is becoming increasingly dangerous. When these psychological effects are coupled with economic dependency, criminal-justice-system apathy (Dutton 1981a) and the belief that she cannot escape her assaulter, the net effect is to produce a victim who is psychologically ill-equipped for either self-defence or escape. When battered women finally do break away from battering relationships, it appears to be because of fear for their own lives and the safety of their children (Rounsaville 1978). Jaffe and Burris (1982) found that women in London, Ontario, who charged their husbands with assault had been previously assaulted an average of 35 times. It is our contention that this "battered woman syndrome" of low self-esteem, poor coping skills, loyalty to the aggressor, etc., develops incrementally as a joint function of female socialization and aversive events (batterings). To ascribe the syndrome to a personality trait such as masochism seems to be an example of the fundamental attribution error (Dutton 1983a) of paying insufficient attention to the circumstances of determining the action (Nisbett and Ross 1980). Battered women appear to remain in abusive relationships despite the abuse, and depicting them as masochistic has as little basis as depicting all wife assaulters as sadistic or paranoid. Clearly, the plight of battered women presents a difficult problem for policy makers: if the state maintains an apathetic response to "family dysfunction" (Steiner 1981), then battered women are not afforded protection and are unrealistically expected to initiate legal proceedings despite "cooling off periods" and other bureaucratic entanglements (Dutton 1981a). If the state takes too aggressive a policy in intruding into family issues, some people will view it as an infringement on their right to privacy. Perhaps the best that

can be done is to increase arrest rates for wife assault, encourage battered women not to drop charges, prosecute and convict batterers, and develop effective treatment means to end the violence.

As with most research projects, this one has opened up a surplus of new questions. Several types of batterers may exist, who differ in their patterns of violence, cognitive distortions, and affective reactions. Battered women are frequently deprived of help by a criminal-justice system that is largely uninformed about the dynamics of family violence. Criminal-justice models of cause and effect and of personal responsibility (Hart and Honoré 1959) are not well suited to considerations of the post-trauma immobility of battered women. Yet, some improvement, in the sense of a more rational criminal-justice policy, seems imminent (Standing Committee on Health, Welfare and Social Affairs, 1982). Some major gains have been made in the past fifteen years, not only in recognizing and documenting the seriousness of wife assault, but in analyzing forces that contribute to the actions of the assaulter and the apparent apathy of his victim. This analysis serves a useful function; it precludes labels that are reductionistic or victim-blaming and points the way for effective and informed policy.

Notes

1. This figure assumes no underreporting to telephone interviewers in victim surveys.
2. This category includes all calls involving husband–wife, common law partners, boyfriend–girlfriend, and man–woman fights where the relationship was unknown.

Works Cited

American Psychiatric Association. 1980. *Diagnostic and Statistical Manual of Mental Disorders*, 3rd ed. Washington, DC: American Psychiatric Association.

Bandura, A. 1974. *Aggression: A Social Learning Analysis*. Englewood Cliffs, NJ: Prentice-Hall.

——. 1977. "Self-efficacy: Toward a Unified Theory of Behavioral Change." *Psychological Review* 84: 191–215.

——. 1979. "The Social Learning Perspective: Mechanisms of Aggression. *Psychology of Crime and Criminal Justice*. Ed. H. Toch. New York: Holt, Rinehart and Winston.

Bard, M. 1970. "Training Police as Specialists in Family Crisis Intervention." Washington, DC: Law Enforcement Assistance Administration, U.S. Government Printing Office.

——. 1971. "Iatrogenic Violence." *The Police Chief*.

——. 1972. "The Role of Law Enforcement in the Helping System." *The Urban Policeman in Transition*. Eds. J. Snibbe and H. Snibbe. Springfield, IL: Charles Thomas.

Bard, M, and J. Zacker. 1975. *Police — Interpersonal Conflict: Third Party Intervention Approaches*. Washington, DC: Police Foundation.

Baxter, J.C., and R.M. Rozelle. 1975. "Nonverbal Expression as a Function of Crowding During a Simulated Police-Citizen Encounter." *Journal of Personality and Social Psychology* 32: 40–54.

Bayley, D.H., and H. Mendelsohn. 1968. *Minorities and the Police*. New York: Free Press.

Belsky, J. 1980. "Child Maltreatment: An Ecological Integration." *American Psychologist* 35(4): 320–35.

Benjamin, L.S. 1974. "Structural Analysis of Social Behavior." *Psychological Review* 81: 392–425.

——. 1979. "Use of Structural Analysis of Social Behavior and Markov Chains to Study Dyadic Interactions." *Journal of Abnormal Psychology* 88: 303–19.

Bettleheim, B. 1943. "Individual and Mass Behavior in Extreme Situations." *Journal of Abnormal and Social Psychology* 38: 417–52.

Browning, J.J., and D.G. Dutton. 1984. "Using Couple Data to Quantify the 'Pirandello Effect'". Paper presented at the meeting of the Canadian Psychological Association, Ottawa.

Bulman, R.J., and C.B. Wortman. 1977. "Attributions of Blame and Coping in the 'Real World'. Severe Accident Victims React to Their Lot." *Journal of Personality and Social Psychology* 35: 351–63.

Canadian Urban Victimization Survey. 1983. Ottawa: Solicitor General of Canada.

Caplan, P. 1984. "The Myth of Women's Masochism." *American Psychologist* 39: 130–39.

Davidson, T. 1977. "Wifebeating: A Recurring Phenomenon Throughout History." *Battered

women: A Psy... tic Violence. / trand Reinh... de Reincourt / New York / Derlega, V./ timacy: ... glewoo... Dutton, ... to Wife Ass... licitor General o...

——. 1981b. "Training... vene in Domestic Violence. *Social Learning Approaches to Predic... ment and Treatment*. Ed. R. Stuart. New Brunner/Mazel.

——. 1981c. "An Ecologically Nested Theory of Male Violence Towards Intimates." Papers presented at the meeting of the Canadian Psychological Association, Toronto.

——. 1983a. *Masochism as an "Explanation for Traumatic Bonding": An Example of the "Fundamental Attribution Error."* Boston: American Orthopsychiatric Association.

——. 1983b. "A Systems Approach for the Prediction of Wife Assault: Relevance for Criminal Justice System Policy." *Probability and Prediction: Psychiatry and Public Policy*. Eds. C. Webster and S. Hucker. Cambridge: Cambridge University Press.

——. 1983c. "The Victimhood of Battered Women: Psychological Versus Criminal Justice System Perspectives." *International Society of Criminology*, Vancouver.

——. 1984. "A Nested Ecological Theory of Male Violence Towards Intimates." *Feminist Psychology in transition*. Ed. P. Caplan. Montreal: Eden.

Dutton, D., and A. Aron. 1984. "Romantic Attraction and Generalized Liking for Others Who Are Sources of Conflict-Based Arousal" Unpublished manuscript.

Dutton, D., and J.J. Browning. 1983. "Violence in intimate relationships." *International Society for Research on Aggression*, Victoria, BC.

——. 1984. "Power Struggles and Intimacy Anxieties as Causative Factors of Violence in Intimate Relationships." *Violence in Intimate Relationships*. Ed. G. Russell. New York: Spectrum.

Dutton, D., B. Fehr, and H. McEwen. 1982. "Severe Wife Battering as Deindividuated Violence." *Victimology: An International Journal* 7: 13–23.

Dutton, D., and B. Levens. 1977. "An Attitude

ned and Untrained Police Offi-
dian Police College Journal 1(2):

, and L. Muller. 1984. "Deterrence of
ssault: What Can the Criminal Justice
Accomplish?" University of British Co-
ia. Unpublished manuscript.
on, D., and S.L. Painter. 1980. Male Domestic
Violence and Its Effects on the Victim. Ottawa:
Health and Welfare Canada.
———. 1981. "Traumatic Bonding: The Develop-
ment of Emotional Attachments in Battered
Women and Other Relationships of Intermittent
Abuse." Victimology: An International Journal 6:
139–55.
Elliot, F. 1977. "The Neurology of Explosive Rage:
The Episodic Dyscontrol Syndrome." Battered
Women: A Psychosociological Study of Domestic Vi-
olence. Ed. M. Roy. New York: Van Nostrand
Reinhold. 98–109.
Fattah, E.A. 1981. "The Victimization Experience
and Its Aftermath." Victimology: An International
Journal 6: 29–47.
Faulk, M. 1974. "Men Who Assault Their
Wives." Medicine, Science and the Law, 180–83.
Flynn, E. 1983. "Victims of Terrorism." Paper pre-
sented at the meeting of the International Society
for Criminology, Vancouver, BC.
Frieze, I.H. 1979. "Perceptions of Battered Wives."
New Approaches to Social Problems. Eds. I.H.
Frieze, D. Bar-Tal, and J.S. Carroll. San Fran-
cisco: Jossey-Bass.
Ganley, A. 1981. Court Mandated Therapy for Wife
Assaulters. Washington, DC: Center for Women
Policy Studies.
Ganley, A., and L. Harris. 1978. Domestic Violence:
Issues in Designing and Implementing Programmes
for Male Batterers. Toronto: American Psycho-
logical Association.
Gelles, R. 1975. "Violence and Pregnancy: A Note
on the Extent of the Problem and Needed Serv-
ices." Family Coordinator 24: 81–86.
Hart, H., and A. Honoré. 1959. Causation in the
Law. London: Oxford University Press.
Hendrick, C. 1983. "Clinical Social Psychology:
A Birthright Reclaimed." Journal of Social and
Clinical Psychology 1: 66–87.
Hogarth, J. 1980. "Battered Wives and the Justice
System." University of British Columbia. Un-
published manuscript. Faculty of Law.
Jaffe, P., and C.A. Burris. 1982. An Integrated Re-
sponse to Wife Assault: A Community Model. Ot-
tawa: Solicitor General of Canada.

Joreskog, K. 1979. "Statistical Estimation of Structural Models in Longitudinal Development Investigations." Longitudinal Research in the Study
of Behavior and Development. Eds. J. Nesselroade
and P. Baltes. New York: Academic. 303–51.
Kempe, R.S., and C.H. Kempe. 1978. Child Abuse.
Cambridge, MA: Harvard University Press.
Kendrick, D.T., and R.B. Cialdini. 1977. "Romantic Attraction: Misattribution Versus Reinforcement Explanations." Journal of Personality and Social Psychology 35: 381–91.
Kiesler, D.J. 1983. "The 1982 Interpersonal Circle:
A Taxonomy for Complementarity in Human
Transactions." Psychological Review 90: 184–214.
Lehrman, L. 1981. Prosecution of Spouse Abuse: In-
novations in Criminal Justice Response. Washing-
ton, DC: Center for Women Policy Studies.
Levens, B.R., and D.G. Dutton. 1980. The Social
Service Role of the Police: Domestic Crisis Inter-
vention. Ottawa: Solicitor General of Canada.
Leventhal, H. 1980. "Toward a Comprehensive
Theory of Emotion." Advances in Experimental
Social Psychology 13: 140–208.
Liebman, D.A., and J.A. Schwartz. 1972. "Police
Programs in Domestic Crisis Intervention: A Re-
view." The Urban Policeman in Transition. Eds.
J. Snibbe and H. Snibbe. Springfield, IL: Charles
Thomas. 421–72.
Loving, N., and M. Farmer. 1981. Police Handling
of Spouse Abuse and Wife Beating Calls: A Guide
for Police Managers. Washington, DC: Police Ex-
ecutive Research Forum.
Martin, D. 1977. Battered Wives. New York:
Kangaroo.
McClelland, D. 1975. Power: The Inner Experience.
New York: Halstead.
Meichenbaum, D., and R.W. Novaco. 1978.
"Stress Inoculation: A Preventative Approach."
Stress and Anxiety, Vol. 5. Eds. C. Spielberger
and I. Sarason. New York: Halstead. 317–30.
Nisbett, R., and L. Ross. 1980. Human Inference:
Strategies and Shortcomings of Social Judgment. En-
glewood Cliffs, NJ: Prentice-Hall.
Novaco, R. 1975. Anger Control : The Development
and Evaluation of an Experimental Program. Lex-
ington, MA: Lexington.
Patterson, M.L. 1976. "An Arousal Model of In-
terpersonal Intimacy." Psychological Review 83:
325–45.
Pizzey, E. 1974. Scream Quietly or the Neighbours
Will Hear. Harmondsworth: Penguin.
Platt, J. 1973. "Social Traps." American Psychologist
28: 641–51.

Porter, C.A. 1981. "The Interrelation of Attributions, Coping and Affect in Battered Women." Paper delivered at the meeting of the Canadian Psychological Association, Toronto.

———. 1983. *Blame, Depression and Coping in Battered Women.* Vancouver: U.B.C. Department of Psychology.

Rajecki, P., M. Lamb, and P. Obsmacher. 1978. "Toward a General Theory of Infantile Attachment: A Comparative Review of Aspects of the Social Bond." *Behavioral and Brain Sciences* 3: 417–64.

Rosenbaum, A., and K.D. O'Leary. 1981. "Marital Violence: Characteristics of Abusive Couples." *Journal of Consulting and Clinical Psychology* 41: 63.

Rounsaville, B. 1978. "Theories of Marital Violence: Evidence from a Study of Battered Women." *Victimology* 3: 11–31.

Roy, M. 1977. *Battered Women: A Psychosocial Study of Domestic Violence.* New York: Van Nostrand Reinhold.

Safilios-Rothschild, C. 1970. "The Study of Family Power Structure: A Review 1960–1969." *Journal of Marriage and the Family* 32: 539–53.

Schachter, S. 1964. "The Interaction of Cognitive and Physiological Determinants of Emotional State." *Advances in Experimental Social Psychology.* Ed. L. Berkowitz. New York: Academic. 49–80.

Schulman, M. 1979. *A Survey of Spousal Violence Against Women in Kentucky.* Washington, DC: U.S. Dept. of Justice: Law Enforcement Assistance Administration.

Seligman, M.E. 1975. *On Depression, Development and Death.* San Francisco: Freeman.

Sherman, L.W., and R.A. Berk. 1983. "The Specific Deterrent Effects of Arrest for Domestic Assault: Preliminary Findings." Unpublished paper, Police Foundation, Washington, DC.

Snell, J.E., P.J. Rosenwald, and A. Robey. 1964. "The Wifebeater's Wife." *Archives of General Psychiatry* 11: 107–13.

Standing Committee on Health, Welfare and Social Affairs. 1982. *Proceedings and Evidence from the Inquiry into Violence in the Family.* No. 25. Ottawa: House of Commons. 3–33.

Stark, R., and J. McEvoy. 1970. "Middle-Class Violence." *Psychology Today* 4(6): 107–12.

Steiner, G. 1981. *The Futility of Family Policy.* Washington, DC: Brookings Institute.

Straus, M. 1976. "Sexual Inequality, Cultural Norms and Wife Beating." *Victimology* 1: 54–76.

———. 1979. "Measuring Intrafamily Conflict and Violence: The Conflict Tactics Scale." *Journal of Marriage and the Family* 41: 75–88.

Straus, M., R.J. Gelles, and S. Steinmetz. 1980. *Behind Closed Doors: Violence in the American Family.* New York: Anchor Press/Doubleday.

Straus, M., and G. Hotaling. 1980. *The Social Causes of Husband Wife Violence.* Minneapolis: University of Minnesota Press.

Subotnik, L.S. 1983. "Overcontrolled and Undercontrolled Types of Men Who Batter Women." Paper presented at International Society for Research in Aggression, Victoria, BC.

Symonds, M. 1978. "The Psychodynamics of Violence-Prone Marriages." *American Journal of Psychoanalysis* 38: 213.

Taylor, G. Rattray. 1954. *Sex in History.* New York: Vanguard.

U.S. Commission on Civil Rights. 1978. *Battered Women: Issues of Pubic Policy.* Washington, DC: Government Printing Office.

Walker, L. 1977. "Battered Women and Learned Helplessness." *Victimology: An International Journal* 2: 525–34.

———. 1979. *The Battered Woman.* New York: Harper & Row.

Whitehurst, R.N. 1974. "Violence in Husband-Wife Interaction." *Violence in the Family.* Eds. S.K. Steinmetz and M.A. Straus. New York: Harper & Row. 75–81.

Williams, J.H. 1977. *Psychology of Women: Behavior in a Biosocial Context.* New York: Norton.

Wilson, J.Q. 1969. "What Makes a Better Policeman?" *Atlantic Monthly,* March.

———. 1983. *Thinking About Crime.* New York: Basic.

Wilt, G.M., & R.K. Breedlove. 1977. *Domestic Violence and the Police: Studies in Detroit and Kansas City.* Washington, DC: Police Foundation.

Winter, D.G. 1973. *The Power Motive.* New York: Free Press.

Yalom, I. 1975. *The Theory and Practice of Group Therapy.* New York: Basic.

Zimbardo, P. 1969. "The Human Choice: Individuation, Reason and Order vs. Deindividuation, Impulse and Chaos." *Nebraska Symposium on Motivation.* Lincoln: University of Nebraska Press.

Zimbardo, P., and E. Ebbesen. 1969. *Influencing Attitudes and Changing Behavior.* Menlo Park, CA: Addison-Wesley.

Zuckerman, M. 1979. *Sensation Seeking: Beyond the Optimal Level of Arousal.* Hillside, NJ: Erlbaum & Associates.

Part Five

THE DIVISION OF LABOUR: MEN'S WORK, WOMEN'S WORK

• • •

However co-operative the relation between husband and wife, there is usually the tacit assumption that the household is basically the wife's responsibility. If she can cope with that and another job, fine, but the domestic burden is primarily hers.
Edna G. Rostow, *The Woman in America*
(1965)

If women are working "like men," then to some extent men will be expected to work "like women" and be involved in housework and child care. Given recent history, the prospects of husbands taking on more housework are not good. How are we to account for the ubiquity and persistence of these perceived inequities? One factor may simply be the ingrained nature of sex roles. Nevertheless, adaptations have been made by some couples and theoretically would be possible for many more. Why have they not occurred?

The idea of a symmetrical family, in which both husband and wife work full-time, and in which they both assume equal responsibility for housework, personal maintenance, and child care, assumes that the work of one person is more or less equivalent to the work of the other. While work may often be equivalent in terms of the number of hours involved, or in terms of the subjective degree of sacrifice and difficulty experienced, it is seldom equal in terms of value, or at least as value is objectified and made explicit by translation into dollars. Even if both husband and wife are employed full-time, their contributions to family life are not necessarily valued

as equal unless their earned incomes are approximately on the same level.

Even among dual-income couples in which both persons work full-time, husbands usually earn substantially more than do their wives. For example, in British Columbia in 1980, in all dual-income couples in which both persons worked full-time, only 10 percent of couples involved persons with approximately equal incomes, and more than half of the husbands earned *twice* as much as their wives (Veevers 1986). When the contributions of two working adults are this markedly and visibly asymmetrical, it seems likely that the traditional pattern of male dominance and superiority on the basis of superior assets will remain unchallenged. The man's sense of distributive justice, and to a lesser extent the woman's sense as well, incorporates the trade-off that those persons who *pay more* are therefore entitled to *do less*. This does not violate the norm of reciprocity, but merely changes its basis, even as this occurs in other unequal partnerships or friendships. It is commonplace to observe that "time is money." It is less usual to note the truism that the obverse is also true: "money is time." In terms of the micropolitics of everyday life, the advantages of power and dominance continue to lie with the person who makes, and subsequently takes, the lion's share.

About the Articles

An opportunity is not really an opportunity unless one is psychologically prepared to take advantage of it. Although sex roles are changing in the larger society, the process is gradual. Opportunities for change do exist, but many children are socialized so that they learn to want, or at least to expect, family lives much like the lives of their parents. Gaskell describes in some detail the process of the reproduction of family life as experienced by teenagers in Vancouver.

Most wives and mothers who are employed outside the home experience a "double shift" of responsibilities: they work full-time at a paying job and then come home to work almost as many hours doing housework and child care. De Koninck points out the various ways in which this situation increases psychosocial and health problems for women, and calls on professionals to address the issues raised by double work as a risk factor.

In many families, the husband's main role has been that of breadwinner. The financial well-being of the family has been defined as basically "his" responsibility, even though the wife is increasingly likely to help him with his obligations. In the same way, the wife's main role has been that of mother. The physical, psychological, and emotional care of children have been defined as basically "her" responsibility. Occasionally, the husband–father might help with "her" children or "her" housework, but she has remained the primary child-care person just as he has remained the primary wage-earner. Lupri discusses the extent to which the role of fatherhood is being redefined and expanded, at least among dual-earner families.

The redefinition of family roles occurs hand-in-hand with the redefinition of gender roles. Livingstone and Luxton point out the interface between the changes occurring in the work world of steelworkers and the expansion of gender consciousness to husband–wife interaction.

Further Readings

Canadian Advisory Council on the Status of Women. 1987. *Growing Strong: Women in Agriculture*. Ottawa: Canadian Advisory Council on the Status of Women.

Cebotarev, N., W.M. Blacklock, and L. McIsaac. 1986. "Farm Women's Work Patterns." *Atlantis* 11: 1–22.

Kohl, Seena B. 1978. "Women's Participation in the North American Family Farm." *Women's Studies International Forum* 1: 47–54.

Luxton, Meg, and Harriet Rosenberg. 1986. *Through the Kitchen Window: The Politics of Home and Family*. Toronto: Garamond.

Marsden, Lorna. 1988. "What Is the 'Labour Force?'" *Readings in Sociology: An Introduction*. Eds. Lorne Tepperman and James Curtis. Toronto: McGraw-Hill Ryerson. 595–600.

Meissner, Martin, et al. 1975. "No Exit for Wives: Sexual Division of Labour and the Culmination of Household Demands." *The Canadian Review of Sociology and Anthropology* 12: 424–39.

Veevers, Jean E. 1986. "The Lion's Share: Relative Contributions of Husbands and Wives in Two-Income Families." Paper presented to the Canadian Sociology and Anthropology Association, Winnipeg.

Wilson, S.L. 1986. *Women, the Family and the Economy*. 2d ed. Toronto: McGraw-Hill Ryerson.

THE REPRODUCTION OF FAMILY LIFE: PERSPECTIVES OF MALE AND FEMALE ADOLESCENTS*

Jane Gaskell

The literature on the transition from school to work emphasizes the experience of males rather than females, as does a good deal of work in the sociology of education (Acker 1981). Osterman (1980), Bazalgetti (1978), Willis (1977), Ryrie and Wier (1978), Ornstein (1976), Thomas and Wetherall (1974), and Bullock (1973) constitute just some examples of work that has been carried out only on males. This neglect of women's experiences has meant not only that findings on males are misleadingly generalized to "youth," but also that the analysis remains incomplete, failing to make visible assumptions based on the experience of males; these assumptions become visible only when the experience of females is addressed.

One important assumption is the role of domestic labour. When the focus shifts to young women, it is clear that family issues must be addressed alongside issues of paid employment in order to understand the ways young people approach working life. But it is not just the young women who make assumptions about how their family lives will affect their work outside the home. The choices all young people make are embedded in assumptions about family life. For the males, however, family issues have appeared neither important nor problematic. It is assumed that they will get older, marry, and

"settle down" to an uninterrupted work life, provided that a job is available.

When researchers have turned their attention to women's place in the labour force, one of the first variables that is added to the analysis is family plans (Sokoloff 1980). A husband's "support" and the necessity of interrupting their work lives for childbearing and rearing differentiate the labour-force behaviour of some women from others (Almquist and Angrist 1975; Bielby 1978).

This leads in the same direction as the argument, made theoretically by Barrett (1980), Kuhn (1978), and others, that the continuing location of women in the family is central to understanding women's subordination in both capitalist and socialist societies. Women continue to be primarily responsible for domestic labour, even as their participation in the labour force increases (Meissner 1975, 1981; Vanek 1974, 1980). Employers and state agencies assume women are primarily located in the family (Coser and Rokoff 1971; Wolpe 1974; Thurow 1975; David 1980) and by basing policy on this assumption, serve to ensure its continuation. But it is not just women who are located in families. Fully theorizing the organization of families and the role they play in locating people is critical to an adequate notion of how paid work is treated by everyone, not simply to understanding the oppression of women.

This paper will take data gathered in a study of 17- and 18-year-olds who are just leaving school and entering work and will focus on the way they construct their family lives in

*The author wishes to thank Jean Anyon and Nancy Jackson for their help with this paper.

Source: British Journal of Sociology of Education 4 (1983): 19–38. Reprinted with permission.

219

relation to their work. It will try to fill in a gap in the literature on the transition to adulthood by addressing the reproduction of family life alongside the reproduction of wage labour. What I will try to explore is how these young people come to expect and plan family lives of their own where the woman will take primary responsibility for domestic work and where the man will "help out." Of course, expectations and decisions at this age are not binding. Young people's anticipation and planning for domestic life will not take into account all the contingencies they will face or accurately predict their own responses. However, they way they anticipate the future affects what the future will bring them. It is only a first step in determining how the allocation of domestic duties occurs, but it is an important step in reproducing families in which domestic work depends largely on women.

In addressing the question of reproduction, this study follows a great deal of other work in the sociology of education. Although there has been less emphasis on the reproduction of gender categories than on the reproduction of class, increasing attention is being given to the ways the reproduction of gender occurs (Arnot 1981; David 1980; Deem 1978; Wolpe 1978). As Willis (1981) notes, the term has come to subsume many different approaches. To locate my own work, I will begin by briefly describing two approaches to reproduction that I find incomplete.

The first is structural theory, which accounts for the reproduction of family life through its functional necessity for capital accumulation or, in a feminist version, for patriarchy. Arguing that women's subordination in the family is "necessary" looks at the consequences of particular family forms, but does not show how they are produced, or how capitalists or men manage to bring about conditions that ensure people will do what is not in their interest. Functional approaches overemphasize the power and clarity of purpose of the dominant group. Capitalism and male domination have managed to survive many

different forms of marital and childrearing relationships. The forms these relationships take are created not simply by what the powerful want, important as this may be, but also by the ways ordinary people have collectively and individually won space for their own ways of doing things. While structures of domination define some of the conditions that a new generation confronts, the solutions people work out for themselves are not predetermined. To understand them, we must move from the level of abstraction of structural theory to the level where individuals can be seen making decisions.

Second, socialization theories have attempted to explain the continuation of family forms where women take responsibility for child care and housekeeping, through the internalization of the dominant ideology by young men and women. Educational research on gender has emphasized the way the dominant ideology of women's domesticity is transmitted to the young in teachers' and parents' attitudes, and in school practices and textbooks. This research has exposed an important set of sexist practices that had been hidden. But as Anyon (1981) has pointed out, the assumption is that this socialization is, unfortunately, successful and that little girls emerge content to re-create traditional forms of behaviour. But recent research has begun to take seriously the resistance of young people and the ways the dominant ideology is mediated through a prism of class- and gender-specific life conditions and experiences and only selectively incorporated. The result is a blend of oppositional tendencies and acquiescence, self-interest and acceptance of domination (McRobbie 1978; Hall and Jefferson 1977). This approach allows a more dialectic approach to ideology and structure and makes change possible, open to human agency.

In this paper, I will point to the ways in which structures of capitalism and patriarchy, and dominant ideologies of gender impinge on the experience of working-class youth, and on the ways they think about organizing domestic work in their own lives. I will present the youth not as passive recipients of cultural and economic imperatives, but as creative, active participants in making "sense" and making choices for themselves. They do choose, or at least plan for, patterns of domestic labour that continue women's subordination in the family and in the workplace. But neither the women nor the men are powerless in this process — they resist some aspects of it, they see through some of the inequity, and they find advantages for themselves in traditional patterns. Looking at how they decide to organize domestic labour and why, exposes the structural and ideological factors that become critical in reproducing old patterns, and the factors that might change and lead to different kinds of decisions, with different consequences for themselves and others. It exposes the struggle, the weighing of forces, and the problems confronting them, rather than granting total power to the system.

Methodology

Eighty-three students were interviewed for this study from three schools in different working-class neighbourhoods of Vancouver, British Columbia. They all graduated from Grade 12 in 1977 and planned to go directly into the labour market. Thirty-six of the students were male; 47 were female. The students volunteered to participate in the study during a spare period in school hours and as a result cannot be said to be "representative" of all the students in the school who were planning to go to work. But the schools were not randomly picked to be representative of Vancouver schools: they also volunteered to participate. And Vancouver is not representative of British Columbia or Canada. The study should then be seen as an exploration of the ways in which a specific group of young people approaches growing up and the ways ideology and structure affect this process. How much the findings can be generalized can be determined only through other similar work.

The first interview took place in May of the students' final high-school year. The interview covered educational plans, job plans, course selection, and attitudes toward the division of labour between men and women in the home, at school, and at work. A second interview took place between February and April, 1978, when 80 of the original students were recontacted. They were asked about their work, about their transition from school to work, and about the ways they were organizing and planning to organize their domestic lives.

The process of coding and using the interview comments was complex. The interviews were transcribed and read over several times. They were then analyzed by recording comments in categories such as division of labour in the home, bringing up children, the importance of work for women, etc. Profiles of individual students were also developed in order to understand the interrelationships among attitudes. The original transcripts were often reread in the process of developing interpretations of the interviews, to check for accuracy and relevant additional information.

Two interviews cannot provide the same depth of information as participant observation over a longer period of time. However, interview comments do reveal ways of thinking that cannot be measured by more standardized procedures. The young people describe the way their world works, what they like about it, and what they do not. They can be pushed to explain what they take for granted and to consider why alternative plans are not feasible. Their explanations and common sense do become clear.

The Girls

All of these girls plan to work outside the home. However, they feel that their right to work outside the home needs to be justified, rather than taken for granted. It is striking how many of them say women "should be able" to work "too"; "It's okay for women to earn money. She [sic] is helping out"; "I think if she wants to work, she can."

This is because they all assume they will have primary responsibility for domestic work — for child care and for housekeeping. They assume that paid work outside the house will be possible only when domestic duties have been taken care of. If they want to make space for other activities, they feel they are responsible for making alternative domestic arrangements — by working harder themselves, "bullying" their husbands, finding someone else to care for the children, or buying other necessary services.

This belief that work outside the home will be secondary to work inside the home is critical in understanding how these girls plan their lives and "voluntarily" choose paths that will tend to reproduce their secondary status at work and, paradoxically, in the home. It limits their aspirations, or at least reconciles them to less attractive jobs (Gaskell 1977). As the girls in this study put it:

If I had a job that was really important, I probably wouldn't be able to raise my own children the way I want to.

I considered engineering pretty seriously [but] . . . if I'm going to get married that's the most important thing I'm looking forward to.

It also means that whatever job a woman aspires to is treated as less important than her husband's, allowing him to devote time and family resources to performing his job well, while she takes them from hers. Her lack of resources, especially monetary, limits her power in the home, even though she devotes her energy there.

These girls, then, are not part of a new generation of "liberated" women who reject old roles explicitly. (Some young women today undoubtedly do, and the processes involved in this need to be understood.) In their assumption of domestic responsibilities, these girls fit the abstracted models of "reproducing patriarchal structures" and being "success-fully" socialized. However, the girls arrive at what they expect to do not through a straightforward response to structural imperatives or through a complete internalization of a domestic ideology. To understand the processes involved, it is necessary to explore both ideological and structural factors, showing how individual beliefs and choices are dialectically related to social forces that are beyond their choice or control.

The Domestic Ideology and the Role of Experience

The dominant ideology tells these girls that putting family responsibilities first is the preferred pattern for women. Domestic work will be as satisfying, fulfilling, and challenging as putting a career first. It reflects a woman's special interests and abilities, making her different from, but not unequal to, a man. The ideology obscures power differences and uses gender, rather than choice or achievement, as the criterion for determining who does what.

To the extent that these girls have been successfully socialized into femininity, they should accept this pattern, prefer to do the domestic work, and see themselves as more suited to it than any man. About a quarter of the girls did this, turning domestic work into a romantic idyll ("Her main job is doing things that you know, he likes. And making the house their own. Making it a nice and comfortable place to come home to. Supporting him and his problems, sort of thing"). They regarded housework as a good alternative to the stresses of a paid job ("I'd rather be at home. I don't want to work the rest of my life. I'd rather do the housework"); a rewarding way to spend time ("The advantage of being a girl is that you have kids and bring up a family"); or just the way it is ("I feel that the woman's place is in the home, and I feel that she should work at making their marriage work"). For these girls, their experiences have reinforced the notion that they belong in the home. They have become interested in domestic work, they value it, and they like it. As a result, they prefer traditional patterns and use the domestic ideology to defend their choice.

Although we can see them as "well socialized," this is an active process for them. They find advantages in traditional patterns. They discount experiences that might bring their beliefs into question. A job is nice, they admit, but only for a while. Housework can be a chore, but a tidy house is satisfying.

The other three-quarters of the girls do not describe their experiences as so nicely congruent with the domestic ideology. For them, making sense of their everyday experience produces beliefs that run counter to the stereotype of the happy housewife, beliefs that they feel impelled to take seriously.

They have seen that paid work provides status, money, and independence. They are enthusiastic about moving into jobs after high school, despite the low wages and the low-level and boring jobs most had. They find that work provides a period of relative independence in their lives, when parental control is eased, and the school in loco parentis disappears. They are treated as responsible adults and paid a wage, signalling that they are competent to perform a task that is of real value to someone else. Furthermore, work provides more free time and the money to enjoy it (Gaskell and Lazerson 1981).

These positive feelings about paid work are projected into the future, and buttressed by their observations of their mothers' lives. Sixty percent of their mothers work, but the daughters of both working and nonworking mothers share the view that life at home is isolating, boring, and cuts you off from the "real world."

> You get bored staying at home. Women should get into things more. My mum is at home. She doesn't know what is going on in the world.

> I think women should be able to work. My mum did. She didn't do it because we were starving or anything. She did it because she was really bored. She needed to come out of her shell.

Rubin (1976) finds the same attitudes among married working-class women. Despite the fact that they are often forced to work by financial pressures, "most find the world of work a satisfying place — at least when compared to the world of the housewife" (p. 169). Work provides independence, and more ability to control one's own life, even when the jobs appear routine, low paying, and dead-end. The socialization into femininity that these girls have received has not been enough to convince them that paid work does not matter for a woman and that they should define their achievement simply in terms of a domestic role.

Most of the girls are well acquainted with housework. Eighty-five percent of them were regularly expected to do household chores and half of them took a major responsibility for housework for the whole family. In their descriptions of how housework gets done in the family, it is clear that mothers take primary responsibility, whether they are working outside the home or not. Female children are the primary helpers and males rarely do much.

> When I was younger my parents were working and me and my sister were young but we swept the floor and vacuumed and washed the dishes and then when Mom came home she'd do the heavy stuff, like washing clothes, and that.

> I don't have to do chores around the house. Like I help my mum with the dishes. Sometimes I'll wash and dry for a week if I feel like it. Sometimes I won't even touch them. But usually, I must admit, I either wash or dry for her, you know. . . . On Saturdays and Sundays, like, I clean the basement, mop it up and that. Saturday my mom does the upstairs. But I like to cook too, like a lot of times I'll come home and cook dinner.

Even girls who by their own assessment, "didn't do much" were able to list household tasks that they performed fairly regularly. Females' responsibility for this work is so deeply ingrained that it is barely noticed.

Housework is seen as unglamorous and boring work, by and large, not something that provides great rewards. At their most positive, the girls might say, "Housework is tolerable. I will do it if it has to be done." This view of housework feeds the desire for work outside the home, which is less boring, more socially rewarding, and more challenging.

Child care is the most critical and demanding part of domestic work and, although these girls were committed to having families, they were very ambivalent about the joys of mothering. They have experiences in babysitting and they have watched their own mothers. Some of the strongest expressions of the negative impression this left were:

I don't ever want to have kids. I can't stand being around little kids. They drive me totally out of my mind.

I think 95 percent of mothers don't want their kids. You always have to do things you don't want to do. You don't have any respect for yourself. The kids are dirty and crabby and you get treated like dirt by your husband.

In milder language, many described women at home with small children as "depressed and hypochondriac," "tired out," and "really bored." This ambivalence about motherhood — I want children, but staying home for long periods with children is a nuisance — is also described by Prendergast and Prent (1980). Using a somewhat different methodology, they also discovered that the accounts most teenage girls give of motherhood are dominated by fears of isolation, boredom, and depression rather than the stereotypical joy in children.

Three-quarters of the girls, then, valued paid work over domestic work. In this, they reflect and find support from the dominant achievement values of the society, if not from feminine values. But they overwhelmingly agree that they would be the ones who would take primary responsibility for domestic work. How did they agree to this, agree to collude in their own subordination, to take

on the less desirable tasks, if their socialization had not succeeded in making it a preferred choice for most of them?

Ideology and Structure: The Dialectic of Reproduction

Even though these girls did not accept the whole ideology of domesticity, elements of this ideology continued to exert considerable influence on how they interpreted what they saw around them, and what they took for granted. These elements existed alongside an understanding of the way existing social structures prevented change. The particular mixture of critical awareness, social analysis, and dominant ideology that they produce illustrates both the active part the girls themselves play in reproduction and the role of ideological hegemony and social structure.

Masculinity
For many, the barriers to change lie in the nature of men. Men, these girls said over and over again, cannot or will not share domestic work. They are not like that. So if you want a tidy house and you want to live in relative harmony with men, you have to do it yourself.

Sharing the housework would be wonderful. But it is not going to happen. He'd [her boyfriend] never help with the floors or with the dishes. I know him too well. I don't expect him to do it because I know he wouldn't.

I just couldn't picture my husband doing it — cleaning, making beds, making supper. I guess it's picturing my brother and dad.

Men don't know the first thing about a laundry machine.

Similarly, men are seen as incapable of, or at least not very competent at, bringing up children.

I can't give a distinct reason why a mother [rather than a father] should bring up her children, but I think it should be the wife that brings them up. It's because kids really relate better to mothers.

The woman has more affection for a baby when it is small. Men aren't used to it, and don't want to do it.

Men are rough, their tone of voice. Babies like softness.

I don't think men are very good at raising children. From what I have seen of fathers, I don't think they could hack it. I guess that is just the way they were brought up when they were young. Women have a better knack for it than men do.

In all these ways, men are seen as incapable and/or unwilling to be full-time fathers. Their masculinity is threatened by involvement with small children. As one girl put it, "I always look at them as fags. I really do. I can't help it."

This view of men, masculinity, and the limits of acceptable or "natural" male behaviour has been noted before (Oakley 1974, 153–60; Gaskell 1977; Tolson 1977). These beliefs show few signs of change, despite the women's movement and more media attention to the issue. The girls express an enormous amount of incredulity when presented with the notion that men might be domestic.

Their construction of masculinity is rooted in an ideology that suggests that what men are like is what men must be like. Biological explanations of the differences between men and women and the domestic ideology's construction of the special nature of men and women shape their perceptions. A culture based on gender differences makes it easy to incorporate this element into the way they construct their lives.

Their views are also validated by their experience of patriarchal family structures. They have not seen men in domestic roles. Their fathers, brothers, and boyfriends do housework only as a special favour for a woman. The knowledge that some men do housework — that it is not inherent in the nature of man not to do housework — seems hard to come

by, but can be powerful when it does. One of the two girls who said they would fight for equal sharing of the housework said:

He [her boyfriend] is neat and I'm not. The regular way is the way it's mostly done. You don't see people going against it. Why not? I want to be equal. Men and women should share the housework. I know guys who vacuum and sew and do the laundry.

When they were presented with the possibility of having a man stay at home while the woman worked, the girls also alluded to the role their experience played: "It could be okay, I guess. It's strange because I'm not used to it. I still feel that a child needs his mother." This view of men is important in shaping the dilemma the girls confront. It limits the way they see their options, to having no children and a messy house, or making the adjustments themselves. Men remain outside the whole process of negotiation.

The Labour Market

A further constraint that these girls saw impinging directly on their ability to plan their future was a realistic assessment of the probable earnings of themselves and the men they would live with. Men earn more money than women. Women can expect, on the average, to earn about 60 percent of what men earn in Canada. These girls were in and were expecting to continue in jobs that were firmly located within the female part of a sexually segregated labour market. Fifty-four percent were in clerical jobs, 18 percent were in sales jobs, and 16 percent were working as waitresses (Gaskell 1981).

With occupational prospects like these, the girls realized that if they worked and their husbands stayed home to look after the children, the family would not be well off financially. Assuming a parent must stay at home with young children, it makes more financial sense for the woman to be the one who gives up her job, if only for a while. This economic reason for the belief that it should be women who stay home was often used by girls who wanted to keep working: "It would be quite all right for him to stay home if the wife went to work. As long as she made enough money to support them.''

Girls with more traditional views were also able to point to economic constraints to bolster their views.

> One parent should be able to stay home until the kids are old enough for school. The most practical approach is that the one with most money would work. But really I'd probably stay home anyway. I'd have more patience.

Financial pressure also has the effect of pushing women into the labour market. These girls are aware of how tenuous the financial position of single-income households has become.

> I think that now most women are going to have to work. In our age it is impossible to buy a house or anything, and I think we are going to have to work and support him and work equally.

> I think if only one works, they don't have hardly any money. They don't eat good.

This push, however, is adding the responsibility of earning money on to women's existing domestic responsibilities, not making the responsibility for domestic labour equal. Women will not earn an equal share of the family income and Lein et al. (1977) have pointed out that this tends to make women feel they have to work even harder around the house to "make up for" their lack of earning power.

The fact that women can expect to earn lower wages than men becomes a critical structural element in reproducing a traditional division of labour in the home. It becomes a financially rational decision. Involved in this decision is the incorporation of an element of dominant ideology, the view that how much you earn determines the importance of your work. Financial criteria become the primary mode of valuing work. Work that brings in a lot of money deserves more respect than

work that does not. This, in turn, serves to devalue domestic labour even further, as well as devaluing the work women do outside the home. Again, ideology, along with the structural reality of a sexually segregated labour market, become the elements that combine to lead to "reproduction."

Child Care

Finally, the availability of acceptable child care outside the family limits these girls' notions of how they will handle domestic labour and a paid job. This constraint need not differentially affect men and women. If domestic responsibilities were shared, the problems of finding substitute child care would be also. But because, as we have seen above, the girls assume responsibility, child care constrains their job planning and not the boys'.

Their view that child care is a "drag" and that paid work is rewarding coexists with the belief that young children need to be cared for by their mothers, if they are to grow up healthy, happy, and well adjusted. This belief is widespread. Public polls reveal that Canadians overwhelmingly endorse equal opportunities for women, but just as strongly believe that "when children are young a mother's place is in the home" (Gibbins, Ponting, and Symons 1978; see also Yankelovitch 1974). It is this conflict that the girls must come to terms with.

> Women shouldn't work with small children. It's hard on the kids.

> One thing I learned in Child Care and feel strongly about, if a woman is working she doesn't get to know the kids. Mothers shouldn't stick the kids with a babysitter until Grade 1.

> One thing I'm really against is leaving kids when they are really small. Kids come first. Wait till they're a few years into school.

This ideology exerts a powerful influence on these young women. It may be learned in a child-care course, as one of the girls above indicated, or picked up from family, friends, TV, newspapers, magazines, and child-care manuals. The view that one must stay at home with young children is also fed by the inadequacy of any perceived alternatives to child care by full-time mothers until the school takes over at the age of five or six. Although school is an approved alternative to mother, other publicly available alternatives, such as babysitting and day care at an earlier age, are seen as "dumping grounds," lacking in "love," and alienating parents from children (see also Lein et al. 1977).

> You'll be a better mother if you were with the kids, and not throw them out with the babysitter . . . because they learn bad habits.

> I don't believe in leaving little kids at home with the babysitter and their mother not knowing them very well. I'd wait to go back to work until they were in about Grade 1 or 2.

> Like when you have kids, you'd have to shove them off into a day care (if you went back to work). But if you don't see them, it isn't so good.

> There's a day care across the street and I feel those children won't grow up as part of those parents. Day care workers have more influence. If both parents want to work, they should realize they can't give a child what he deserves. They shouldn't have children.

These views reflect the real fact that the availability, quality, and funding of day care is less than desirable because of the very low priority given to it within the social-service area and the very low salaries that are paid to anybody embarking on a career in day care. Decent child care is hard to find, but then, one could argue, so is a decent first-grade classroom. The notion that the age of five or six is the desirable age to have children in "school" is clearly a reflection of the way child care has been publicly organized — at five the state pays and indeed demands attendance. Before

that the parent pays and the state provides subsidies only to parents with low incomes, making day care a suspect institution, appropriate only for "inadequate" parents. In this area the ideology of mothering, instead of being contradicted by experience, is supported by it. The organization of society — the structure — produces the experience that validates the ideology and produces constraints that any parent must contend with in order to change traditional patterns of behaviour. Ideology and structure come together to reproduce mother-centred patterns of child-rearing for another generation.

The Potential for Change

Although incorporation of elements of the dominant ideology, the constraints of child care and the labour market, and their experience of men combined to produce in all of these girls the view that domestic work is primarily their responsibility, there are differences in the ways they plan to deal with the domestic responsibilities they assume. Some are more likely to challenge the usual behaviour patterns than others.

A couple of girls, seeing the dilemmas, concluded that marriage and a family were not for them. The only way to stay independent was not to get married, not to have children. Although only two contemplated this as a long-term solution, many commented that they would put off marriage and certainly having children, for a while (at least until age 25, which seemed like a long time to them) to enjoy their independence while it was possible.

It was the potential availability of acceptable alternatives for child care that was critical in setting apart that quarter of the girls who planned to return to work while their children were preschoolers.

> I would work if my mum would take care of the kids.

> I guess I'd have to stay at home for awhile, at least until they're one and a half or two years old. Unless my husband worked graveyard.

> I'd go back to work when they were old enough for day care — one and a half or two.

The most acceptable alternative forms of child care are family arrangements, with the husband or with the grandmother. But if day care is seen as acceptable, it makes it possible to return to work when the child is 18 months or perhaps three years, instead of when she is five.

There were also a few girls who, while accepting that they "should" stay home for the sake of the children, were prepared to put their own needs above their responsibilities.

> It would be better to stay at home, but personally, I don't think I could.

> I hate staying at home. I'd really be going crazy without a job. But with children, part-time is best.

Similarly, a couple of girls were committed enough to sharing housework to be willing to do battle over it.

> You should share everything when you're married. Even now my boyfriend does the dishes. He complains and bitches sometimes. Sometimes I do it. He is trying hard to change his habits. It creates tension between us.

This girl's expressed willingness to create tension and take on her boyfriend distinguishes her from the great majority of other girls who, if they do it, do it more quietly, less on principle.

The girls anticipate that experience in the labour market will also make a difference to how much paid work they do, and perhaps to the division of domestic work.

> If I really love my job, and the boss needs me, maybe. . . .

> It should be the husband [who works], unless he's unemployed and I could get outside work.

This suggests that change can occur when a girl takes her own needs seriously and when the social structure provides her with alternatives. Structural factors — the availability of child care, male unemployment, women getting higher pay — may produce shifts in who does what, if not immediately in whose responsibility it is seen to be. The girls are certainly not so committed to traditional patterns that new opportunity structures would make no difference. These changes in behaviour would then become part of their, and other girls', experience and provide potential challenges to received ideology. Understanding this dialectical relation between ideology and structure allows us to see how reproduction occurs systematically, but is not a necessary and inevitable outcome of the situation in which these girls find themselves.

The Boys

The boys also make decisions about how they plan to manage domestic work. Although paid work is their primary focus in planning the future, they also want to get married and have children, just as the girls do. They, however, do not plan to take a lot of responsibility for these tasks, which allows them to treat paid work as their main focus of concern.

It is perhaps easier to understand the boys' decision — who wouldn't want to have the more powerful and independent position and to let someone else take responsibility for getting the domestic work done? Who wouldn't like a "wife"? Because the dominant ideology supports their immediate self-interest, reconstituting this ideology to make it congruent with their experience and desires is not as pressing for them. In this section, I will outline the boys' notion of the division of labour in the home and examine how accurate the girls' constructions of the boys' views are.

The Ideology of Domesticity and Self-Interest

Most of the boys accept the traditional view of the division of labour in the home. They are significantly more conservative than the girls, significantly more likely to swallow the "domestic ideology" whole.

> I wouldn't let her work if I could support the family.

> If I work and get a lot of money, I wouldn't want her to work. She could look after the kitchen or something. There's a lot to do.

> I'm traditional. Women's Lib can never make a husband pregnant. Mother's place is at home until the kids can take care of themselves.

> I don't think it should be equal. I think the wife should stay home and clean the house and cook, while the male goes out and works.

They accept some variations — the woman can "help" the man by getting a paid job and the man can "help" the woman around the house. But a differentiation of roles is assumed.

> A wife helps out. It's not as important [for her to work] as long as you can get along on his wages. It's not right if she has a kid.

> When the kids get to be about 16 and they're in school all day and she's got five hours to kill she should go out and get a job not far from home so she can get home and make supper.

> Well, if the husband happens to be at home and his wife is working (like if he's sick or something) there's no reason why he can't do the cooking.

And a reversal of roles is outrageous.

> I'd never let her do that. It's just a person's morals. It's how you're brought up. . . . The man is supposed to go and collect the bread and the woman stays home. . . .

> No, if you have a lot of kids, she's got to stay home all the time and he brings in the money. It's the husband's duty to keep the household going. I don't know why. That's the way it's always been.

It became apparent in the interviews that they had not spent a lot of time worrying about it — it's "just the way it is," they said. Their own households ran along these lines, and they took these patterns for granted.

> The males and females don't share the work in our house. The females got nothing else to do. When mother was working, she did all the housework too, but that's because my sister wouldn't do it.

> I sleep and eat. Sometimes wash the dishes. Pick up the mail and paper if I step on it. I don't really care if the housework is done. Mother does it. She works part-time.

> The odd time I cut the grass, or work in the garage. Help Dad fix things around the house. No housework, not even making my own bed. Mother does it. She doesn't work. My sister should help.

And they were quite aware of their own self-interest. They did not like domestic work. They did not want to change what was obviously an advantageous status quo. Although they said the same things as the girls — housework is a drag and child care drives me nuts — they were much more willing to take their own self-interest seriously than the girls were.

> I just couldn't stand staying in the house, really. It would drive me bananas.

> I can't picture myself staying at home and looking after kids for five years, while she works. I'd just feel sheer lazy.

> For one thing, I don't like kids and housework, kids and housework. . . . I wouldn't want to do it all the time.

When they were prodded, they recognized that their assumptions were not quite fair — that they "should" share. This was clearest in the area of housework.

> I don't do a hell of a lot. I'm too lazy . . . I'm bagged after work. I want the weekends for myself. Biking, skiing, my girlfriend. I should help more — there should be two of me — one to stay around. My mum and sister do the work.

> If I marry, I should share; but I wouldn't want to.

> If I marry my girlfriend, I'd help her out. I don't like doing it. If someone doesn't ask me, I won't do it.

> If she's going to be a stickler about it, well, I guess I could volunteer sometimes. It depends upon the person.

In the area of child care, it was not so much fairness as a desire to retain their primacy in family affairs that motivated them to take part in domestic work. They set out how important their role in child care was, retaining their father's prerogatives and his ultimate authority, while leaving women to do the primary caregiving.

> There's a difference between raising kids and looking after them. The woman might spend more time with the kids, but the father has the authority.

> From age one to seven you are mom's boy; and then from seven to fourteen, you are daddy's boy. The kids need the female, but they need the male image too. They act differently to males and females. They can get away with more with the female, like with their mothers. But the father comes home and he's ready to hit the kid over the head.

In the interview, then, the boys overwhelmingly presented very conservative views.

When asked, what came most easily to mind was what their parents did, what the dominant ideology told them, a justification for their own present behaviour. This makes the girls' description of men fairly accurate. They are, as the girls described, unused to and unwilling to do much about domestic duties. They incorporate the dominant ideology gladly, actively to serve their own interests.

Equality and Structural Barriers

The boys were not universally as reactionary as the above views suggest. Some boys did take seriously the notion of women's equal rights, especially to a job.

> Sure I think [career women] are a really good idea. But I think it's going to be a long time before women are really into top positions . . . because so many men still feel that women should be at home and doing the routine jobs.

> Women should be able to work outside the home. We shouldn't expect them to get married, have babies, and stay home. They do have their own freedom, their own life. They can enjoy it.

> She should believe in something, you know, and she should go for it. Like what usually happens is that she just goes for the husband to compliment him. Because I think that women think that like if they can please the husband that's what they're looking for.

The general values of achievement and fairness present a challenge to the traditional views of these boys. They admire women with more independence; they feel everyone should be treated equally. Achieving these goals, however, will involve some concessions by men in the area of domestic labour. Are they willing to follow through? To a certain extent, although it often becomes "helping" rather than sharing equally. On housework:

> Yeh, they [men] should do that, you know; they shouldn't just say "Oh I worked eight

hours and I'm tired and I'm gonna go to sleep or something." They both occupy the same house, and . . . we have to look [after] our own things, and if we can't split the duties. . . .

They should share. It's something that has to be done. I help my fiancée with her housework. She has a two-year-old son.

On child care:

I think it's sort of an equal responsibility, too. If a man's home, why not be involved? He sort of groans changing those diapers. I'd probably end up doing it. Changing the kid at 2 o'clock in the morning . . . yuk. It's important, like . . . they have to do it.

The way it is in most families is what I *don't* want. I want to have some part in what the kids are doing. I want to be at home; I still want to have something that I would do as a career. . . . But I really think that it should be equally done.

As with the girls, structural barriers become important in their thinking. For the boys, these come down on the side of not taking equal responsibility at home, which is what they prefer anyway. The labour market makes it more reasonable for women to stay home because they earn less.

I wouldn't mind doing child care if she had a large income; I would stay at home. But I would prefer to be working and have my wife at home.

I could stay home with the kids if her job was more [money] than mine. . . . Times change. I haven't heard of any men staying home, but it could be all right.

Staying home is a little weird; the guys have to be a little strange, or, unless the guy's a cripple and can't help it. . . . If she'd earn more money than him it would probably work out that she'd go to work and he'd stay home.

And the person who stays home should do the housework; so they can assume women will do it for them.

I figure if I'm gone all day and my wife is home she can clean up.

Whoever has the job shouldn't have to do the housework. It could be either person. But, I'd have the job.

I think the person who spends the most time at home should do the majority of the work.

If [my] wife wasn't working, I'd expect her to keep the house clean. Whoever has time should do it.

A woman might handle child care in some other way besides staying home, but day care is unacceptable and alternate child care is hard to come by.

If there was somebody to take care of the kids I wouldn't mind if she worked or when she is very well trained for or involved in her work.

She could have a small part-time job if she wants to. But not with the kids in day care.

So it becomes "reasonable" to assume the woman will stay home, even for those more liberal boys who do not assume it is their prerogative to tell their wives what to do, and who do not find the notion of equality absurd before it is even addressed by factors in the real world. The application of universal principles — whoever earns most money, whoever is at home — becomes the reason for women to do the work.

For the more liberal boys, resolving the issue of domestic labour becomes a struggle to integrate principles of fairness and achievement with relegating women to the home. For the more conservative boys, this is a less difficult issue because they incorporate an ideology of domesticity for women more completely, and they are less concerned about putting their self-interest above fairness. For neither group of boys does their concrete experience play a large role in refracting and forcing them to reinterpret the ideologies they hear. It is a much more abstract issue. It does not have the immediate meaning it has for the girls.

Conclusions

I have argued that the reproduction of family life has been ignored in the mostly male literature on the transition to adulthood. The issue of family organization is important in itself, and it makes visible a set of assumptions in which the vocational planning of boys and girls is embedded. Despite the initial similarity in their enthusiasm for leaving school and finding work, males and females make different long-term assumptions about what a paid job will mean, because of its relation to domestic labour.

In exploring the reasons for this, I have stressed the incorporation of elements of the dominant ideology and their interaction with social institutions, notably the labour market and the provision of child care, and with their immediate experiences of family and friends. Income differences between men and women, the inadequate provision of public child care facilities, and the predominance of families with a traditional division of labour are all part of the world these young people know, and they interpret it through incorporation of selected elements of the dominant ideology. Their experience then takes on meanings that lead to an expectation that traditional patterns will be continued. Whether these expectations will come to pass cannot be determined here, but I have suggested that changes in opportunities — a good job for a woman, an excellent child-care facility, a liberal husband — could make a difference. The trouble is that these changes are unlikely to occur on a wide scale.

Both the young men and the young women in this study expect that the young women will add work outside the home to their domestic work. Paid labour for women gets incorporated into the old directives that women be primarily mothers and housekeepers, helpmates to their husbands rather than equal participants in the labour force or the home. It means that while these young women are pleased by their transition from school to work and find their jobs important and rewarding, they still assume they will give them up in a few years and, for the most part, will not allow the demands of their paid work to interfere with their family life.

There is perhaps nothing surprising about this. Much of the literature tells us that, although paid labour can increase women's power in the household, it does not equalize their power. Women's jobs provide them with less income than men's and are seen as less important. Even working women continue to do most of the domestic labour, both reflecting and producing their "secondary" status as workers.

These interviews give some insight into the way this pattern begins in the expectations of young people about to embark on adult life and into the factors that begin to produce change in their expectations. A few girls accept happily, indeed glorify, the traditional role of women. They want to be primarily lovers of their husbands, mothers to their children. They see advantages in the traditional pattern; they appropriate the traditional ideology. They recognize often that their attitudes reflect the way they have been brought up, the way they have learned to deal with the world, the skills and abilities that they have developed over time. But they accept these prescriptions.

But most girls do not embrace these traditional tasks so cheerfully. The majority do not particularly like housework, and they see being at home with children as confining. Work brings them independence, responsibility, and money, all of which they are enjoying. Marriage and children bring a return to dependence on a male wage, personalized control and authority in the family, and little time that is not available to the demands of others. However, incorporating domestic duties into their lives seems necessary, given the way they see the men around them behaving, the state of child care, and the incomes they can expect. Elements of the domestic ideology still shape the way they see acceptable options. The social organization of child care, the nature of men, and the fact of segregated labour markets make change unlikely. They therefore determine to cope with their lack of alternatives with good grace, not asking the impossible, not complaining about the inevitable.

> I don't know if I'm looking forward to that, but I accept it.

> I feel strongly that people should be equal, but how can you, unless you start from scratch?

Facing up, as they feel, realistically, to the constraints of their lives, they accept them and constrain themselves accordingly. Some feel they will be more able to work out individual solutions, through struggling with the men in their lives or finding a neighbour to babysit, than others.

In the young people in this study, we can see both the passivity that reproduces traditional roles and the beginning of discontent that provides the possibility of change. There are many youth, most notably a large number of the girls, who would challenge the idea that the traditional division of labour by sex is equally fulfilling for males and females and is the only proper way to organize families and work. But it is clear that this discontent is not enough to bring about equality for men and women. The waning of domestic ideology among the girls is not enough to stop them planning their lives around it. Life choices come not merely from some abstract principles of what should happen, but from an assessment of the way the world works, what opportunities are open, what paths are possible. In this construction of how the world works, ideological elements incorporated from outside are critical. Young people with more liberal attitudes thought little change seemed realistically possible. Instead of expressing much anger about this, or trying to combat it, which might begin a process of change, they resign themselves to it and re-

solve to get on with life as it presents itself. Richard Hoggart writes:

> When people feel they cannot do much about the main elements of their situation, feel it not necessarily with despair or disappointment or resentment but simply as a fact of life, they adopt attitudes towards that situation which allow them to have a liveable life under its shadow, a life without a constant and pressing sense of the larger situation. The attitudes remove the main elements in the situation to the realm of natural laws, the given and the raw, the almost implacable material from which a living has to be carved. (1960, 322)

This analysis implies that any attempt to give young people a sense of their own agency in the world, to show them that the world is constructed through a series of political and personal actions that might be changed, involves not just talking to them but also showing them that conditions can indeed be altered. In other words, it involves not just ideological work but also political movements for institutional change that demonstrate the possibility of change. This might occur in many ways — for example, in a movement for satisfactory child care that demonstrates its potential value, or in a struggle for equal pay that shows women's jobs are valuable and can be rewarded. The limits of reform will be set not just by how well an alternative account of the world can be conveyed but also by how much the lived world of such young people can actually be demonstrated to be changeable.

Works Cited

Acker, S. 1981. "No Woman's Land: British Sociology of Education 1960–1979." *Sociological Review* 29(1): 77–104.

Almquist, E.M., and S.S. Angrist. 1975. *Careers and Contingencies.* Port Washington, NY: Dunnellen.

Anyon, J. 1981. "Accommodation, Resistance and Female Gender." Paper presented at the International Sociology of Education Conference,

Birmingham, England.

Arnot, M. 1981. *Class, Gender and Education*. Milton Keynes: Open University Educational Enterprises.

Barrett, M. 1980. *Women's Oppression Today: Problems in Marxist Feminist Analysis*. London: Verso Educations.

Bazalgetti, J. 1978. *School Life and Work Life: A Study of Transition in the Inner City*. London: Hutchinson.

Bielby, D. 1978. "Career Sex: Atypicality and Career Involvement of College Education Women." *Sociology of Education* 51(1): 7–28.

Bullock, P. 1973. *Aspirations vs. Opportunity: Careers in the Inner City*. Ann Arbor: Institute of Labor and Industrial Relations, University of Michigan.

Coser, R.L., and G. Rokoff. 1971. "Women in the Occupational World: Social Disruption and Conflict." *Social Problems* 18(4): 535–54.

David, M. 1980. *The State, the Family and Education*. London: Routledge and Kegan Paul.

Deem, R. 1978. *Women and Schooling*. London: Routledge and Kegan Paul.

Gaskell, J. 1977. "Sex Role Ideology and the Aspirations of High School Girls." *Interchange* 8(3): 43–53.

———. 1981. "Sex Inequalities in Education for Work: The Case of Business Education." *Canadian Journal of Education* 6(2): 54–72.

Gaskell, J., and M. Lazerson. 1981. "Between School and Work: Perspectives of Working-Class Youth." *Interchange* 11(3): 80–96.

Gibbins, R., J.R. Ponting, and G. Symons. 1978. "Attitudes and Ideology: Correlates of Liberal Attitudes Towards the Role of Women." *Journal of Comparative Family Studies* 9(1): 19–40.

Hall, S., and T. Jefferson. 1977. *Resistance Through Rituals: Youth Subcultures in Post-War Britain*. London: Hutchinson.

Hoggart, R. 1960. *The Uses of Literacy*. Harmondsworth: Penguin.

Kuhn, A. 1978. "Structures of Patriarchy and Capital in the Family." *Feminism and Materialism*. Eds. A. Kuhn and A.M. Wolpe. Boston: Routledge.

Lein, L., et al. 1977. *Working Family Project Final Report: Work and Family Life*. Wellesley, MA: Wellesley College Research Center for Research on Women.

McRobbie, A. 1978. "Working Class Girls and the Culture of Femininity." Women's Study Group, Centre for Contemporary Cultural Studies. *Women Take Issue*. Birmingham: Centre for Contemporary Cultural Studies, University of Birmingham, Women's Studies Group.

Meissner, M. 1975. "No Exit for Wives: Sexual Division of Labour and the Cumulation of Household Demands." *Canadian Review of Sociology and Anthropology* 12: 424–39.

———. 1981. "The Domestic Economy: Now You See It, Now You Don't." Paper prepared for SSHRC conference on Women in the Labour Force, Vancouver.

Oakley, A. 1974. *The Sociology of Housework*. New York: Pantheon.

Ornstein, M.D. 1976. *Entry Into the American Labour Force*. New York: Academic.

Osterman, P. 1980. *Getting Started: The Youth Labour Market*. Cambridge, MA: MIT Press.

Prendergast, S., and A. Prent. 1980. "What Will I Do? Teenage Girls and the Construction of Motherhood." *Sociological Review* 28(3): 517–32.

Rubin, L. 1976. *Worlds of Pain: Life in the Working Class Family*. New York: Basic.

Ryrie, A.C., and A.D. Wier. 1978. *Getting a Trade*. Hodder and Stoughton.

Sokoloff, N. 1980. *Between Money and Love*. New York: Praeger.

Thomas, R., and D. Wetherall. 1974. *Looking Forward to Work*. London: H.M.S.O.

Thurow, L. 1975. *Generating Inequality*. New York: Basic.

Tolson, A. 1977. *The Limits of Masculinity*. London: Tavistock.

Vanek, J. 1974. "Time Spent in Housework," *Scientific American* 231: 116–20.

———. 1980. "Household Work, Wage Work and Sexual Equality. *Women and Household Labour*. Ed. S.F. Berk. Beverly Hills: Sage Publications.

Willis, P. 1977. *Learning to Labour*. Farnborough: Saxon.

———. 1981. "Cultural Production Is Different from Cultural Reproduction Is Different from Social Reproduction Is Different from Reproduction." *Interchange* 12(2–3): 48–67.

Wolpe, A.M. 1974. "The Official Ideology of Education for Girls." *Educability, Schools and Ideology*. Eds. J. Ahier and M. Flude. London: Croom Helm.

———. 1978. "Education and the Sexual Division of Labour." *Feminism and Materialism*. Eds. A. Kuhn and A.M. Wolpe. London: Routledge and Kegan Paul. 138–59.

Yankelovitch, D. 1974. *The New Morality: A Profile of American Youth in the 1970's*. New York: McGraw-Hill.

DOUBLE WORK AND WOMEN'S HEALTH*

Maria de Koninck

In Canada, although a high percentage of wives and mothers have full-time or part-time paid employment outside the home, the expectation that they will assume primary responsibility for domestic work persists. As a result, women who work outside the home experience cumulative stress: too many physical and emotional demands to meet, too many hours of work, and a continuous struggle to reconcile the demands of the two work settings. The author considers double work from a socioeconomic, structural viewpoint, and from the perspective of increased psychosocial and health risks. She calls on professionals to address the complex and controversial issues raised by the identification of double work as a risk factor.

Addressing the issue of women's work and women's health requires, for many people, some preliminary reflection. Indeed, to some minds the words "work" and "women" are largely incompatible. When discussing women's activities, is it not common to label a large number of women as "not working"? It can be argued that this is merely a matter of semantics and that the reference is solely to paid labour. But what about work done without pay? Feminist claims have brought about some refinement in terminology, and one now speaks with increasing care of "work outside the home" as opposed to work in the home, without quite knowing how to define the activities performed in the home in terms of the conventional concept of work. Furthermore, the differentiation between work performed inside and outside the home is more than a distinction between workplaces, referring as it does to a particular style of economic organization.

Labour activity in our society is divided into two main categories, namely "productive" work, which is assigned a market value, and "nonproductive" work, which has no market value and is not counted as a factor when evaluating production. The first category involves the production of goods and services; the second entails "reproduction" and the maintenance of the labour force.[1] Productive activities take place in the labour market, whereas reproductive activities take place in the domestic sphere, the basic unit of which is still the family (Vandelac 1981).

The activities classed under the heading of "reproduction," in the broad meaning of the term, fall mainly to women. They encompass not only biological reproduction but also child-rearing (training, affective care, and socialization) and those activities involved in maintenance of the domestic unit. For some women, reproductive tasks represent a full-time occupation; for others, they are coupled with paid employment on a full-time or a part-time basis, as dictated by the needs of the labour market.

An economic approach to the issue of double work and women's health has been emphasized here; it is important to broach the problem in these terms since the "invisible" part of women's work conditions the overall approach to the issue. To deny the exigencies of this work would be to deny the potential constraints that it imposes on health. Domestic work is the main occupation of large numbers of women; for others, it is an occupation over and above paid employment.

*Translated from the original French article, "Double travail et santé des femmes."

Source: *Canada's Mental Health* 32 (1984): 28–31. Reproduced with permission of the Minister of Supply and Services Canada.

235

Such work entails, in our view, health hazards that, because they are not recognized as stemming from occupational activities, tend to be given individualist or even psychological interpretations.[2] The mere fact that work in the home does not enjoy the social recognition bestowed by the assignment of monetary value can in itself be cited as a potential source of stress since this situation generates dissatisfaction (Stellman 1978).

The Labour Market

Women workers occupy a particular position in the labour market. They are concentrated in the tertiary sector where, by and large, they are relegated to service jobs. In the secondary sector, they are concentrated in certain types of industries that are characterized by relatively low productivity (Armstrong and Armstrong 1978). They generally receive lower pay and are less likely to be unionized than are their male colleagues, and they are more likely to be working on a part-time basis (Lepage and Gauthier 1981).

We establish a link between women's reproductive responsibilities and their labour-market position because the tremendous load of unpaid, uncounted, and unrecognized work that women carry is tied to their second-class market status. Without such work, commerce could not function as it does now; on the other hand, if women enjoyed the same access to the market as do men, domestic work would not be performed in the same way (Conseil du statut de la femme 1983).[3]

Increasing numbers of women are entering the paid labour market. This trend represents a profound change in the female work profile triggered by the demands of economic development (Oakley 1981; Clio 1982). Women's share in the market is also increasingly stable, a phenomenon observed in most industrialized countries (Silbermane 1982). In 1982, the Canadian labour market included 4.5 million women workers, for a female "economic activity rate" of 51.6 percent. Of that total, 3.3 million (75 percent) held full-time jobs

and typically worked an average of 38.9 hours a week, whereas 1.1 million women were employed part-time, averaging a working week of 15.3 hours (Statistics Canada 1983).[4] Available data for Quebec indicate that, in 1981, 64.4 percent of the women in the labour market were mothers, 79.3 percent of whom held full-time jobs (Messier 1983). To this number must be added the number of female employees who were married with no children. The cumulation of domestic labour and paid labour would thus appear to be the daily way of life for many women.

Today, more than ever, women are combining labour-market participation with domestic responsibilities; they are thus active in two different workplaces governed by different standards. More and more women are engaging in what is commonly referred to as a double job or double workday — or, in more economic terms, double labour.

However, it should not be assumed that increased female participation in the labour market opens the door to a professional life that women can plan in the same manner as can their male colleagues. Charged with the responsibility for family life, women organize their occupational activities with reference to the domestic unit. Despite the practice of contraception, which allows for better family planning (Recherches et familles 1983), women's movements in and out of the market still revolve around periods of childbearing. These movements shape the organization of female labour-market participation; women's participation is defined and governed by the needs arising from their domestic responsibilities. The results may include such arrangements as part-time work, casual work, or paid work done at home. The relationship between women's professional life and their family life can be described as a series of compromises and successive, mutually competitive movements between two workplaces (Recherches et familles 1983). The fact that half of the female population is now in the labour market has not altered the market's structure fundamentally, and women are still expected to adapt to its demands.

Domestic Labour

A number of time-budget studies have been conducted to measure the number of hours housewives spend performing their different domestic activities. They estimate that a full-time housewife works about 50 hours a week, with lower and upper limits of 36 and 73 hours, depending on the number of children in the family (Proulx 1978; Michel 1978; Chadeau and Fouquet 1981). However, time-budget analyses run into problems, especially since a number of duties are performed simultaneously (Conseil du statut de la femme 1983). Furthermore, it is always difficult to evaluate the time housewives spend organizing the domestic unit and planning the various activities that take place within that environment; and how can the emotional involvement and personal availability inherent in domestic labour be quantified?

Domestic labour is divided into two main classes of activities, the first centred on care, e.g., childrearing, and the second on domestic maintenance, involving such duties as cleaning, cooking, budgeting, and shopping. Contrary to widespread belief, there has been no real reduction in the number of hours spent on work in the home, because the advantages of domestic technology are offset by more stringent standards of hygiene, childrearing, and so on. It is frequently forgotten that these domestic duties also fall to women who do paid work outside the home. A 1977 survey by Kim Chi Tran Van among Quebec working mothers revealed that the subjects spent an average of 36.2 hours a week on housework (Tran Van 1980), boosting the cumulative total of domestic labour and paid labour to more than 70 hours a week. Overall, this evaluation falls in line with surveys conducted in the United States and France (Michel 1978; Chadeau and Fouquet 1981).

The Domestic Labour/Paid Labour Combination

Considered globally, the general working conditions of salaried women workers are not all that different from those of housewives (Stellman 1977). For instance, both types of work involve dull, repetitive tasks, little opportunity for advancement, and little opportunity for workers to act collectively to defend their interests. Both types of work also involve a sum of affective care and availability that is taken for granted as "inherent in feminine nature." Being concentrated in certain jobs, women workers on the whole occupy a precarious market position, making them more vulnerable to unemployment. They are also exposed to abusive conditions such as sexual harassment; many women must deal with such abuses from a position of weakness, knowing that their jobs are at stake.

Women's work in the market is geared mainly to ensuring the well-being of others (Oakley 1981; Sokoloff 1980), with job ghettos generally centred on service occupations ("reproduction" in the broad sense). Domestic work, waitressing, secretarial work, nursing . . . these "typically female" jobs are different expressions of the mothering function that women exercise in our society. The expected prerequisites for these jobs, like those for mothering, are regarded not as skills but rather as attributes of feminine socialization (Recherches et familles 1983). This does not, however, prevent the demands of such jobs from producing stress (Stellman 1978). Society's total lack of recognition of full-time housework holds also for the housekeeping activities of women wage-earners. This lack of recognition applies both to the actual domestic component of their work and to its interference with their professional activity.

Double Work from the Health Standpoint

Paid employment should certainly not be regarded as negative in itself. On the contrary: for some women, paid work is a means of liberation, providing newfound financial independence and breaking the isolation experienced by many housewives. Having reviewed U.S. national statistics spanning several years,

C + R

Ingrid Waldron (1980) concludes that paid employment apparently has both positive and negative effects on women's health but that no clear, definitive conclusions can be drawn. However, these considerations must not obscure the fact that the contribution of women wage-earners in the form of housework is still not acknowledged, and that their position in the labour market most often entails second-class, unrewarding, and low-status working conditions. This is the backdrop for our preferred approach to the issue; we develop this approach around two axes, namely cumulation and reconciliation.

The Inherent Cumulation of Double Work

We have underscored the total workload with which women workers have to contend. This workload, which entails an excessive number of working hours, can itself be a source of tension, fatigue, stress, and emotional vulnerability (Stellman 1978; Walsh, Chapman, and Richard 1980). Women who have 70-hour work weeks without sick leave or vacations — family vacations are rarely times of rest and relaxation for housewives (Vie Ouvrière 1982) — and who get up at night to tend sick children live under conditions that promote the development of health problems.

Cumulation can also be viewed from the standpoint of multiplied risks. Women's jobs, which often demand considerable affective involvement, add to the demands encountered in the domestic unit. Female teachers and nurses provide key examples of the amount of affective input that may be required of women. Responding to children at school or tending patients in a hospital and then mothering in the family requires tremendous affective availability. We should not lose sight of the fact that the family has become the main source for the fulfilment of an individual's affective needs (Johnson and Johnson 1977). Furthermore, job burnout is associated with work involving functions of an essentially maternal nature in the broad sense

— care of children and chronically ill patients, nursing and social work (Bibliography Series 1981). The growing concern over burnout is particularly interesting in that it focusses on the qualitative aspect of job content. New emphasis is thus placed on a dimension of the demands of certain occupations — including indirectly the occupation of motherhood — that has been too long ignored.

For unskilled female workers, the extent of the workload may be particularly evident with respect to the physical demands of the job (Stellman 1977; Oakley 1981), with the cumulation in many cases exceeding the limits considered to be tolerable up to that point.

The Farmingham heart study, which singles out domestic responsibilities as one of the factors in the coronary problems of female office workers, paves the way for many hypotheses (Haynes and Feinleib 1980). The approach used in this study proves far broader than the conventional risk analysis centred on a given situation without regard for the associated context.

The cumulation observed in double work takes on more complex forms than the sum total of activities, demands, and availability. It also shows itself in the overlapping of activities stemming from each form of work, and in the functional continuity between the work settings themselves. In effect, the workday of women with domestic responsibilities consists of a constant shifting between two functions, two sets of tasks. Even the travel time to and from the outside workplace is often used for shopping and chauffeuring children. Lunchtime is sometimes spent shopping for the family.

Nor can the home be regarded by women as a place in which they can renew their resources; it is, instead, the site for their second workday, with "holidays" designated as times for catching up on tasks set aside during paid working hours. While the home is generally perceived as a place of repose, in contrast with the workplace, this perception does not apply in the case of women wage-earners. The home, which is the workplace of housewives, is a workplace for salaried women as well.

Reconciliation

"Reconciliation" as an aspect of double work has not yet attracted a great deal of attention, except among women themselves. Like cumulation, reconciliation is inherent in double work. Used in this context, the term denotes the need for female workers not only to perform double work but to perform each job well, without interference from the other job. In practical terms, this means that, notwithstanding her paid employment, a woman must be a good housewife, and *vice versa*. In our opinion, this is the aspect of double work that has the most important impact on mental health. It translates into stress over day care for children, problems of concentration, and a constant affective load. Women workers are faced with a number of difficult decisions that generate dissatisfaction regardless of the choice made, for example, when they are assigned overtime, or when a child is sick. This situation is conducive to stress. A number of studies have examined the problem of reconciling tasks from the perspective of role conflicts. Ingrid Waldron (1980) clearly points up the complexity of this issue when she states that the demands linked to double work may produce stress but that, on the other hand, many housewives live under stress because they regard housework as monotonous and not highly valued.

The issue of reconciliation emerges most frequently when women discuss their situation; a situation that is all the more problematical because, in our view, it is quite impossible for the vast majority of women to handle double work in a satisfactory manner. The quantity and quality of work demanded are simply beyond their capacities. The problems are compounded by the self-regulating mechanism of guilt found in most women; research has shown that mothers who work outside the home experience guilt (Johnson and Johnson 1977). Greater attention should thus be paid to the pressure for reconciliation as a risk factor for health problems.

Although the "role conflict" approach highlights problems, it sets them in a psychological perspective, whereas they should, we feel, be viewed from the standpoint of labour organization.

Double Work and Health

The analysis of relationships between double work and physical and mental health (with the possible exception of role-conflict analysis) is in its infancy; not even the questions have been clearly formulated. This may be explained first by the magnitude of the challenge inherent in these questions. Acknowledging the existence of double work for women entails implicit acknowlegment of the sexual division of labour. Such an analysis places health-care researchers, male as well as female, in a political and social arena in which they are often ill at ease. Addressing the sexual division of labour as a physical and mental health hazard challenges the narrow definition of health that still prevails in most institutional contexts. Yet, these are the terms in which women describe their situation. Most of those whom the author has encountered cite double work as the major problem confronting them. They realize that the concepts of both "work" and "health" must be broadened to encompass this problem.

But this is not all. Reflection on the health implications of double work is starting to overflow the bounds that some people tried to establish so as not to impede the long and painful collective struggle for the recognition of women's right to paid employment. It should be added that many are beginning to see through the illusion of task-sharing (Meissner 1975; Conseil du statut de la femme 1983; Haas 1982); this prompts new questions and, above all, a search for more fundamental solutions. In short, the issue of double work is characterized by a great deal of ambivalence, which complicates the pursuit of practical solutions (Conseil du statut de la femme 1983).

Records continue to show that women frequently have recourse to medical services and drugs (Guyon, Simard, and Nadeau 1981).

This could be attributed to their collective status, of which work is a determinant aspect. Housework, in the broad sense, is the main or secondary occupation of the vast majority of women. Such work — as well as the conditions under which it is performed — is increasingly perceived as one of the factors to be explored by researchers studying the question of women's health. Given this overall perspective, the approach of Quebec's Council of Social and Family Affairs (CASF) has led to some interesting new contributions. Introducing a qualitative dimension to the analysis of health statistics, the council observes that a crude accounting of the longer life expectancy of women as opposed to men is inadequate, since most of those additional years are not years of good health (Dillard 1983). This type of reflection can only prove beneficial to women, for it calls into question approaches that have often tended to minimize their problems.

In the summer of 1982, we heard eloquent testimony from a group of women.[5] According to them, the problem of day care for children was of such concern to some women workers and created such mental strain that they saw it as more harmful to their health than the unhealthy conditions they had identified in their working environment. (The subjects were seamstresses in the garment industry.) Without diminishing the importance of current occupational health-research efforts or disregarding research into the dramatic hazards to which more men than women are exposed in their workplaces, new questions must be raised to achieve a better understanding of the situation of women and work. One of these questions is that of double work. The avenues to explore are many — for example, use of health services, use of drugs, fatigue, and premature ageing. Feminists contend that these manifestations, which are often analyzed as individual situations, originate in the collective situation. Thus, double work is experienced by women as individuals; but it is as a group that they assume responsibility for domestic work in our society. It is this situation that must be questioned in interventions with women. The approach used in stress research and in studies on the psychosocial risks involved in work provides interesting avenues for exploring these issues.

Conclusion

If we have deemed it important to raise the issue of double work at this time, although it has not yet been clearly formulated, it is because this issue requires urgent consideration. Mental-health workers — and, indeed, workers in health services as a whole — should take account of this problem; many women are carrying the double burden of domestic work and paid work, and they often describe this cumulation as a far-reaching but little-known problem. We realize that, as with any analysis of the relationships between different socioeconomic conditions and health, identifying double work as a health hazard carries us into an area where there are many uncertainties. But this is also partly our intention. The questions raised by the recognition of double work pertain to the collective situation of women. The complexity of this situation must not serve as a pretext for shrouding its effects in silence.

Notes

1. The portion of the economy that can be characterized as "underground" or "informal" goes beyond "reproductive" activities. These aspects are not dealt with in this paper.
2. We need only refer to the different interpretation of health problems related to "working" life as opposed to the interpretations of the health problems of housewives and mothers.
3. Quebec's Conseil du statut de la femme (Council on the Status of Women) conducted a wide-ranging study on domestic production. The research effort, co-ordinated by Louise Vandelac, was written up in seven volumes — one a synthesis — available on request. The address is 8 rue Cook, Bureau 300, Québec (Québec) G1R 5J7.
4. In 1982, 1 001 000 Quebec women were employed, 787 000 of them full-time (78.6 percent) and 214 000 part-time (Statistics Canada 1983).

5. This testimony was gathered during a meeting with representatives of Montreal's cultural communities on the matter of occupational-health priorities for women workers.

Works Cited

Armstrong, Pat, and Hugh Armstrong. 1978. *The Double Ghetto: Canadian Women and Their Segregated Work*. Toronto: McClelland and Stewart.

Bibliography Series 1981. *Job Burnout in the Human Services* (February).

Chadeau, Ann, and Annie Fouquet. 1981. "Peut-on mesurer le travail domestique." *Économie et Statistiques*. No. 136. Paris: INSEE. 29-42.

Clio. 1982. *L'histoire des femmes du Québec depuis quatre siècles*. Montréal: Quinze.

Conseil du statut de la femme (CSF). 1983. *Rapports de recherche sur la protection domestique*.

Dillard, Sylvie. 1983. *Durée ou qualité de la vie?* Quebec: Conseil des affaires sociales et de la famille.

Guyon, Louise, Roxanne Simard, and Louise Nadeau. 1981. *Va te faire soigner, t'es malade*. Montréal: Stanké.

Hass, Linda. 1982. "Parental Sharing of Child Care Tasks in Sweden." *Journal of Family Issues* 3(3): 289-412.

Haynes, Suzanne G., and Manning Feinleib. 1980. "Women, Work and Coronary Heart Diseases: Prospective Findings from the Farmingham Heart Study." *American Journal of Public Health*. 70(2): 133-41.

Johnson, Colleen Leahy, and Frank Arvid Johnson. 1977. "Attitudes Toward Parenting in Dual-Career Families." *American Journal of Psychiatry* 134(4): 391-95.

Lepage, Francine, and Anne Gauthier. 1981. *La syndicalisation: Droit à acquérir, outil à conquérir*. Québec: CSF.

"La maladie des femmes elle s'appelle oppression." 1982. *Vie Ouvrière*. Vol XXLL, No 160.

Meissner, Martin. 1975. "Sur la division du travail et l'inégalité entre les sexes." *Sociologie du travail*. 4-75: 329-50.

Messier, Suzanne. 1983. "Chiffres en mains." Unpublished revision. Quebec: CSF.

Michel, Andrée. 1978. *Les femmes dans la société marchande*. Paris: PUF.

Oakley, Anne. 1981. *Subject Women*. Oxford: Martin Robertson.

Proulx, Monique. 1978. *Five Million Women*. Ottawa: Advisory Council on the Status of Women.

Recherches et familles. 1983. Rapport des groupes préparatoires au colloque national, Ministère de la Recherche et de l'Industrie, Secrétariat chargé de la famille auprès des ministères des affaires sociales et de la Solidarité nationale: 18-23, 77-116.

Silbermane, Roxanne. 1982. "L'emploi féminin: le grand embouteillage." *Terre des femmes*. Paris/Montréal: La découverte/Maspéro, Boréal Express. 27-30.

Sokoloff, Natalie J. 1980. *Between Money and Love*. New York: Praeger.

Statistics Canada. 1983. *The Labour Force*. Monthly Catalogue 71-001 (December).

Stellman, Jeanne Mager. 1977. *Women's Work, Women's Health: Myths and Realities*. New York: Pantheon.

———. 1978. "Occupational Health Hazards of Women: An Overview." *Preventive Medicine*. 7: 281-93.

Tran Van, Kim Chi. 1980. *Étude sur les caractéristiques des travailleuses québécoises*. Québec: MTMO.

Vandelac, Louise. 1981. "Et si le travail tombait enceinte?" *Sociologie et Sociétés* (October): 67-81.

Waldron, Ingrid. 1980. "Employment and Women's Health: An Analysis of Causal Relationship," *International Journal of Health Services*. 10(3): 435-55.

Walsh, Diana, Egdahl Chapman, and H. Richard., eds. 1980. *Women, Work and Health: Challenge to Corporate Policy*. Industry and Health Care Series, No. 8. New York: Springer-Verlag.

FATHERS IN TRANSITION: THE CASE OF DUAL-EARNER FAMILIES IN CANADA*

Eugen Lupri

This chapter examines one aspect of a larger research program focussing on the relationship between family and work in the lives of Canadian couples. Two major goals of this study are to analyze how fathers in dual-earner families combine work and family tasks and to show how these role enactments vary by stage in the family life cycle.[1]

Objectives

A focus on fathers is timely because both experts and lay persons often claim that many men, especially younger men, want to see fatherhood expanded and redefined. Increasingly, fathers are participating with mothers in prenatal classes and in childbirth itself. Fathers and mothers alike are found to be eager for information on infant behaviour, health, growth, and developmental landmarks (Kliman and Vukelich 1985). Researchers in various disciplines have been discovering the crucial part played by fathers in various aspects of children's developments, affectional bonds, and nurturance behaviour (Lamb 1976; Lamb, Pleck, and Levine 1986; Lewis and O'Brien 1987a; McAdoo 1986; Russel 1983). Clearly, the traditional *image* of fatherhood is in transition. In fact, the most significant changes in contemporary family life are occurring in fathers' roles because an increasing number of young fathers are assuming the role of caregivers (Russel 1986).

These optimistic predictions, which seem to be congruent with normative expectations, have, on their face, a certain amount of validity and are therefore exceedingly appealing both to the general public and to social scientists. Indeed, the shift by both women and men toward egalitarian gender-role attitudes during the past decade has been documented widely by annual surveys and polls of the Canadian adult population (*Maclean's* 1988). We cannot assume, however, that these attitudinal changes will translate automatically into behavioural changes, because attitudes and behaviour do not always coincide. The degree to which contemporary fathers actually assume caregivers' roles remains highly problematic and needs careful empirical scrutiny.

What changes, if any, have occurred in this important area of men's lives? To answer this question, it is important to recognize that men's family and work roles exist in relation to women's family and work roles, and that gender comparisons must be made to show whether comparable changes have occurred in the roles of both fathers and mothers. For this reason, I examine fathers and mothers in dual-earner families in which both partners work for pay; in Canada, the two-earner family is no longer a variant family form but a viable option for an increasing number of couples, young and old. This paper emphasizes the unitary character of family and work and assumes that the dual-earner families of today are harbingers of tomorrow.

Source: *Zeitschrift für Sozialisationforschung und Erziehungssoziologie* (ZSE) 8. Jahrgang / Heft 4 / 1988. S.281-97. Reprinted with permission.

*This research was supported by the Social Sciences and Humanities Research Council of Canada and the University of Calgary Research Grants Committee. Some of the data used in this paper have been reported in Lupri and Mills (1987) and in Horna and Lupri (1987).

The "life cycle" approach used here is an analytical strategy that allows us to make tentative generalizations about changes in family behaviour over time. In the absence of longitudinal studies, the family life cycle is meaningful theoretically because it represents variation in role enactments of both fathers and mothers during couples' lives; family scholars often have ignored this variability (Mattesich and Hill 1987).[2]

Background

The Increase in Mothers' Paid Employment

More than 30 years ago, Alva Myrdal and Viola Klein introduced the notion of "women's two roles." In their pioneering work, *Women's Two Roles: Home and Work* (1956), they pointed out that it is wives who added a second role, that of paid employment. A decade later, Myrdal (1967) contended that women could not compete successfully with men in the marketplace unless men also were willing to have two roles, adding household tasks and child care to their occupational role. Those observations prompted Rapoport and Rapoport (1976) to conceptualize the slower rate of change in men's family roles, compared with the rapid change in women's roles outside the home, as a "psychological lag." To the American sociologist Pleck (1978, 1983), the uneven evolution of family and work roles for both women and men represents a "transitional problem of adjustment" of the 1960s and 1970s, suggesting that gender equity in the home can be achieved in the near future. Yet, despite its historical underpinnings, the Rapoports' and Pleck's evolutionary perspective underestimates the structural grounding of much of today's sexual inequality in family and work relations, as documented by time-budget studies in capitalist and socialist countries (Lupri 1983; Szalai et al. 1972; Lupri and Vianello 1990).

While researchers in the early 1980s were busy coming to grips with new family trends

and predicting the emergence of the "symmetrical family" (Bane 1984; Lupri and Symons 1982; Young and Willmott 1975), in which both partners share family and workloads equally, women everywhere continued to enter the marketplace in droves. By 1985, Canadian married women's share in paid work had grown so dramatically that now we have come almost full circle since the preindustrial era, when women played an integral productive role in the family economy. From 1931 to 1985, labour-force participation rates for all women increased from 20 percent in 1931 to an all-time high of 56 percent, or two and one-half times. In the same period, the rate for married women increased 13 times from a low of 4 percent in 1931 and 1941 to another all-time high of 55 percent in 1985. Even more dramatic is the increase in labour-force activity among young mothers, the group generally viewed in the past as least likely to work for pay outside the home. As trend data from 1971 and 1985 show, mothers with at least one child under six in the home registered the largest increase in participation (51.0 percent), followed by mothers with children 6 to 15 years old (30.6 percent). In short, increasing numbers of Canadian mothers share the economic burdens of households by seeking paid employment.

These two patterns — the increases in employment among married women and among young mothers — represent important changes in women's roles. First, they reflect the ever-increasing intersection of women's roles in family and in paid work. Second, they indicate that, to an increasing degree, Canadian wives, young and old, combine family and work roles by seeking employment outside the home. Third, they show the likelihood of growth in the number of families with small children in which both parents work for pay. Fourth, they seem to signify that paid work is becoming crucial to both Canadian men's and women's sense of identity. Finally, these patterns show that the dual-earner family is rapidly becoming dominant in Canadian society.

Pressure for Change in Men's and Fathers' Roles

The tremendous growth in women's labour-force activity, especially in the recent decade, fulfils one basic goal of the new women's movement that began in the late 1960s: to break the restrictive molds of the household and to provide equal opportunity for women in the marketplace (Wilson 1986). This goal was inspired by the recognition that power and prestige derive not from unpaid housework but from participating fully in the economy and the polity. Equal opportunity, however, has not translated into equal treatment, as we have shown elsewhere (Lupri and Mills 1983). Canadian women, like women around the world, remain clustered in a few occupations with low prestige, low pay, and limited opportunities for promotion and advancement. Feminists argue that women's limited access to the more interesting, demanding, and rewarding jobs and to political involvement and other opportunities outside the home are related largely, if not entirely, to the heavy burden they carry in the home. Thus, another goal of the women's movement is to seek an increase in men's participation in the household.

As more and more wives and mothers take on work for pay outside the home, husbands and fathers are increasingly subject to pressure, practical as well as moral, to share household tasks and child care equally with their partners. This pressure comes especially from young women and mothers, who want "fatherhood expanded," as Jessie Bernard wrote (1974, 175) more than a decade ago. The sharing of the provider role by the mother is believed to call forth a sharing of the parental role in the child care and socializing function. Role sharing means that both parents assume equal responsibility for the children and take this responsibility into account as they integrate occupational and family roles.

The optimal setting for testing this type of role sharing is the dual-earner family, in which both parents pursue work outside the home. Such a testing ground allows us to examine the extent to which Canadian fathers expand their traditional roles as providers and assume roles as caregivers.

Study Design[3]

Research Locale

A cross-section of couples was chosen from Calgary, Alberta, Canada's sixth largest census metropolitan area, with more than 670 000 inhabitants in 1981. During the late 1970s, when the oil and gas industry was booming, Calgary grew faster than any other metropolitan area in Canada. It has a relatively high concentration of young adults because of the heavy influx of migrant workers and families with small children.

The population of Calgary is relatively well educated: in 1981, 14 percent of the population 15 years old and over were university graduates, compared with 8 percent for Canada as a whole. The labour-force participation rates were high (64 percent for women vs. 52 percent for Canada; for men, 87 percent vs. 78 percent). Nearly 23 percent of the labour force were engaged in managerial, scientific, and related occupations, compared with 15 percent for Canada. Incomes in Calgary are well above those for Canada as a whole: in 1981, the median income had risen to $17 000, almost 24 percent above the national figure.

This highly dynamic social setting provides a challenging opportunity to observe elements of family interaction and emerging styles of fatherhood among dual-earner couples.

Sample

A systematic random sample of 562 matched couples was drawn from a current special directory by taking every nth residence, excluding businesses, after a random start. Because the research design required collecting information from both members of a couple, the refusal rate was about 28 percent. Whenever the simultaneous participation of two persons is required, it is always more difficult to obtain a high response rate than when only one person's participation is required. Even so, the sample of 562 couples is fairly representative of the 133 135 Calgary husband–wife families (including common law unions) because the sample characteristics reflect the proportions reported for the total population of Calgary regarding family life-cycle profiles, age, employment characteristics, socioeconomic status, and educational level.

Data Collection and Measures

The data were collected in 1981 by means of an interview schedule, a self-administered questionnaire, and a drop-off questionnaire. After rapport was established with the couple and instructions were explained clearly, the interviewer selected one partner to be interviewed and asked the other to complete a self-administered questionnaire in another part of the dwelling. This dual approach was employed because the self-administered questionnaire could deal more validly with potentially sensitive data such as marital power, family conflict, and violence, whereas the personal interview could maintain rapport while gathering background information such as age, employment status, time budgets, and pertinent family characteristics. This procedure of simultaneous but physically separated data acquisition by two different methods minimized contaminating responses by either partner.

The third instrument used in our study was a self-administered drop-off questionnaire that interviewers left behind after the interview, together with a self-addressed stamped envelope, to be completed and returned by both partners. This procedure yielded completed questionnaires from 367 female and 359 male respondents, including 346 matched couples. The self-administered questionnaire included additional questions on estimated typical time expenditures (separately on a

workday, a Saturday, and a Sunday) for all daily activities including work, nonwork, and leisure pursuits. The time-budget portion was followed by questions on annual frequencies of involvement in all earlier listed activities, other participants in those activities, reasons for performing them, and several other topics.

The responses reported in this paper are drawn selectively from all three instruments. They come largely from a subsample of fathers and mothers in dual-earner families, in which both parents work for pay full time (30 hours or more per week). For comparative purposes, we also examine data from childless dual-earner couples and from single-earner families, in which only the fathers work for pay and the mothers are not employed gainfully. Other comparison groups will be identified later in the appropriate context.

Results

The concept of role entails two components: "expectations," including beliefs and cognitions, and "enactments" or conduct. The analytical distinction between these two components is useful because expectations and norms do not always coincide with conduct or behaviour.

Following an earlier research strategy (Horna and Lupri 1987; Lupri and Mills 1987), we conceptualize the parental role as being enacted through a series of tasks that are carried out by either parent or by both. In doing so, we recognize the unitary character of family and work relations, and conceptualize the family as a unit with a set of developmental task requirements inside and outside the household. In dual-earner families, these tasks involve the couples' sharing in the economic-provider role as well as the "expected" joint parental involvement in at least two additional family roles: that of the homemaker and that of the caregiver. In the following pages, we present estimates of time budgets on the extent to which fathers and mothers enact these three roles over the course of the family life cycle. These estimates will be supplemented by proportional measures of estimated role enactments.

Fathers as Economic Providers

Although women and men in dual-earner couples (with or without children) are free to allocate essentially identical amounts of time to their regular jobs and careers, they do not do so. As Table 1 shows, childless men and fathers across all five life-cycle stages spend between three and ten hours more each week in paid work than do their partners. Fathers also are more likely than mothers to work overtime and on weekends. Certainly these differences reflect divergent occupational pursuits due to gender segregation in the workplace. Thus women of all ages have been drawn into the labour force to take sex-segregated jobs that typically are unstable, are low in rank and prestige, and offer few opportunities for advancement. No wonder, then, that work performed by women does not command remuneration equal to that performed by men. Such structurally grounded gender inequities make a man's occupational

Table 1

Mean Hours in Tasks of Dual-Earner Parents' Work Week, by Stage in the Family Life Cycle

| | Absolute and Relative Time Per Week in . . . | | | | | | | |
| | Paid Work | | Housework[b] | | Child Care | | Weekly Total | |
Family Life-Cycle Stage[a]	Absolute	Relative	Absolute	Relative	Absolute	Relative	Absolute	Relative
Young Childless Couples (I)								
(N = 80)								
Husbands	41.5	.525	10.00	.392	—	—	51.5	.493
Wives	37.5	.475	15.5	.608	—	—	53.0	.507
All Children Under 6 (II)								
(N = 60)								
Fathers	43.0	.566	9.0	.261	8.5	.254	61.5[c]	.424
Mothers	33.0	.434	25.5	.739	25.0	.746	83.5	.576
Children 7–14 Years Old (III)								
(N = 58)								
Fathers	42.5	.547	9.8	.295	4.5	.243	57.8[c]	.441
Mothers	36.0	.453	23.4	.705	14.0	.757	73.4	.559
Children 15 Years and Older (IV)								
(N = 46)								
Fathers	42.0	.542	9.8	.311	3.5	.219	55.3[c]	.442
Mothers	35.5	.458	21.8	.689	12.5	.781	69.8	.558
Empty Nest (V)								
(N = 58)								
Fathers	40.5	.519	9.3	.369	—	—	49.8	.483
Mothers	37.5	.481	15.9	.631	—	—	53.4	.517

[a] Stage I: married or common law couples with no children, in which the wife is age 44 or younger; Stage II: couples with children under the age of 6; Stage III: couples with children between the ages of 7 and 14; Stage IV: couples with children of age 15 and older living at home; Stage V: couples whose children have left home and in which fathers are under age 65 and not yet retired.

[b] Housework includes household chores, maintenance, repairs, yard work, cooking, and shopping.

[c] Parents' differences in mean hours are statistically significant.

world quite different from a woman's; this difference should be kept in mind when we examine styles of fatherhood in dual-earner families. These occupational differences diminish considerably in dual-*career* families ($N = 21$ in our subsample of dual earners with children at home), in which both spouses pursue professional work.

Although on the average fathers spend more time each week than mothers doing paid work (41.8 versus 35.7 hours, respectively), both women's and men's time in paid work varies considerably with the stage of family life. Not surprisingly, young fathers in dual-earner families with at least one child under the age of six (Stage II) devote more time to making money (an average of 43 hours per week) than do their counterparts in any of the other stages shown in Table 1. In addition, young fathers in Stage II spend ten more hours in paid work per week than do their sexual partners, who are forced to limit their outside work for pay and to assume a disproportionate share of unpaid domestic labour, including child care. Obviously the addition of a young child to the family adds financial burdens: young fathers may therefore need to make up the economic loss of their partners' reduced pay-cheque and to supplement their income to meet the increased demands of an expanding household — Oppenheimer's (1982) first "life-cycle squeeze." To cope with the emerging economic life-course constraints, young fathers work overtime, engage in job-related work on weekends, and take moonlighting jobs.

As Table 1 shows, the adaptive strategy in the later stages of the family life cycle involves the restructuring of provider and domestic roles: while fathers decrease somewhat the time they devote to paid work over the life course, mothers correspondingly increase their time. As fathers and mothers in dual-earner families reach the empty-nest stage at midlife, their *proportionate share* in paid work approaches an equitable division of provider roles as measured by time expended (51.9 percent versus 48.1 percent, respectively), a division similar to that of young couples without children (52.5 percent versus 47.5 percent, respectively).[4]

With the exception of our small sample of 21 dual-*career* couples, in which near-parity of wages prevails between the partners, mothers in dual-earner families are more likely than fathers, on average, to be secondary earners with lower remuneration. Thus, their contribution to family resources is likely to be relatively minor. The widest gap was found to exist between couples in Stage II, in which mothers contribute 30.9 percent of the reported annual family income of $27 850. Wage differentials for mothers and for fathers in later stages of the family life cycle are smaller, but the gap persists nonetheless. Occupation, as we have argued, has an important effect on wage disparities between women and men. Additional reasons for income differences include differences in educational attainment, career continuity, and number of hours worked.

In sum, even in dual-earner families, fathers appear to remain the major economic providers, especially in the earlier stages of the family life cycle. Only among the dual-career couples did we observe an equitable sharing in provider roles by fathers and mothers across the life course. This finding suggests that the relative status of the husband and the wife, especially in occupational terms, is important in understanding the family division of labour and the enactment of parental roles.

Fathers as Homemakers

According to traditional gender ideology, women's place is in the home and housework is women's work. How deeply these attitudes go — and how slowly they seem to be changing — have been the subjects of considerable research during the past decades. The household division of labour in dual-earner families is central to a fuller understanding of the changing roles of parents in contemporary society (Horna and Lupri 1987). Because household labour is unpaid, women's economic contribution to the family has been devalued and ignored by experts and lay persons alike until very recently. The very nature of work performed in the home, its variability and discontinuity, make domestic labour difficult to measure in economic terms or even to define. Our measure of housework includes time devoted to household chores, household maintenance and repairs, yard work, shopping, and meal preparation.

Estimates of absolute and relative (proportional) time spent in housework by childless couples and by parents are set out in the second column of Table 1. Although our main focus is on role enactments of fathers and mothers, childless couples (Stage I) and couples whose children have left the home (Stage V) offer interesting contrasts to the parents in the childrearing stages (II, III, and IV). Most noteworthy in this comparison are the uniform patterns of housework involvement by men across the life course, in view of the reduction in the time they devote to paid work over the life-cycle stages. By contrast, both childless wives and mothers allocate considerably more time to housework; further, their involvement in domestic labour is affected considerably more than men's involvement by the stage in the family life cycle. In fact, the number of hours that women devote to housework exhibits a *curvilinear* relationship with the family life cycle. Mothers in particular, whatever the age of the children, are forced to expend an average of four and one-half hours per *workday* at domestic tasks. In contrast, fathers in the childrearing stages get by with less than two hours *daily* during the work week. Fathers with very young children in the home (Stage II) make the smallest contribution to housework both in absolute time (nine hours per week) and in relative time (26.1 percent). In striking contrast, young mothers with children under six years of age in the home are forced to carry more than a double load: they contribute 25.5 hours per week to housework and have the largest proportionate share (73.9 percent) of any comparison group.

The fathers' low level of commitment to domestic labour can be demonstrated most clearly by comparing dual earners with single earners whose partners do not work for pay but are homemakers. Our findings indicate, for example, that whether or not their wives work for pay or whether or not they have children, the men's contribution to housework does not differ significantly (Lupri and Mills 1987). Further, as expected, the fathers' proportionate share is consistently less than the mothers' in both comparison groups. This pattern persists on weekends: although fathers increase their help with housework, mothers increase their share of housework even more (data not shown).

Clearly the fathers' contribution to domestic labour in dual-earner households is relatively low when compared with the time that mothers allocate to housework. Although mothers in our subsample of dual-career couples shared fully in the provider role, and although their husbands participated more in housekeeping and meal preparation than did their counterparts in dual-earner families, dual-career fathers' proportionate share in domestic labour was only slightly higher than that obtained for childless couples shown in Table 1: 40.7 percent versus 39.2 percent. Three of four dual-*career* couples, however, were able to hire household help, compared with only about 6 percent of dual-earner families.

Fathers as Caregivers

As suggested earlier, recent research shows that men are beginning to rethink their fatherhood role and to reflect on the options open to them. Some men want to expand their role as fathers and to become caregivers because they find intrinsic fulfilment in relating to their children in expressive and affective ways (Russel 1983). These "androgynous fathers" (Robinson and Barret 1986) differ from their traditional counterparts in that they are more nurturant, are more involved emotionally with their children, and engage more in child-care activities. Other men feel obligated to participate more in child care because their partners share equally in the breadwinner role; they want to reciprocate out of a sense of fairness (Bernard 1983; Bohen and Viveros-Long 1984). Still others increase their child-care tasks because they feel pressured by their partners, whether or not they are employed (Cohen 1987). Yet many men, including young men, remain entrenched in the traditional role, focus largely on their careers or jobs, and view caring for children as "women's work" (LaRossa and LaRossa 1981). These fathers feel that they make a better contribution to their children's lives by concentrating on their role as economic providers.

Because men's opportunities, choices, and personal preferences vary considerably, it is unlikely that a single "ideal" father model will emerge in the near future (Robinson and Barret 1986). Instead we expect current fatherhood roles to range between the traditional instrumental type and the emerging androgynous type. We expect fathers in dual-earner families to assume a significantly larger share in caregiving than their counterparts in single-earner families, in which the mother is a full-time homemaker. We also expect younger fathers of both comparison groups to be more responsive than older fathers to the demands of expanding households.

Estimates of absolute and relative time devoted to child care each work week by fathers and mothers are set out in the third column of Table 1. Table 2 provides estimates both for weekdays and for weekends because no domestic tasks are potentially more time-consuming, are more onerous, and demand greater and more constant attention than those related to childrearing. As expected, fathers typically allocate a significantly lower amount of time to child care than do mothers on both workdays and weekends in each of the three childrearing stages. Even so, a close inspection of the estimates presented in both tables reveals a few noteworthy and unexpected findings.

Fathers in dual-earner families appear to be "weekend fathers." The number of absolute hours they devote to child care on weekends exceeds the total hours they devote to these tasks on the five weekdays. This pattern

Table 2

Mean Total Hours Spent in Child Care on Weekdays and Weekends for Fathers and Mothers Who Are Employed Full-Time, by Stage in the Family Life Cycle

Stage in Family Life Cycle[a]	Absolute and Relative Time in Child Care					
	Weekdays (5)		Saturdays & Sundays		Weekly Total	
	Absolute	Relative[b]	Absolute	Relative[b]	Absolute	Relative[b]
Children Under 6 (II)						
Fathers	8.5	.254	11.0	.374	19.5[c]	.310
Mothers	25.0	.746	18.4	.626	43.4	.690
Children 7–14(III)						
Fathers	4.5	.243	4.9	.314	9.4[c]	.276
Mothers	14.0	.757	10.7	.686	24.7	.724
Children 15+ (IV)						
Fathers	3.5	.219	3.7	.366	7.2[c]	.276
Mothers	12.5	.781	6.4	.634	18.9	.724

[a] For definitions of life-cycle stage and number of matched parents, see Table 1.
[b] For definitions of relative measures of time, see note 4 at end of article.
[c] Parents' differences in mean hours are statistically significant at ≤.001.

emerges in each of the three childrearing stages, even though fathers, like mothers, decrease their overall time commitment to child care as the children grow older. As Table 2 shows, fathers' proportionate share in child care is consistently higher on weekends than on weekdays in each of the three stages.

Another striking feature of Table 2 is the mothers' total time investment in child care in comparison with that of fathers, and how the absolute hours vary by stage in the family life cycle. Most obviously, the time spent by mothers in child care increases sharply to 43.4 hours per week when there is at least one child under 6, decreases to 24.7 hours when there are children between 7 and 14 years of age, and declines further to 18.9 hours when there are children 15 years of age or older in the home. The fathers' total absolute hours are always less than half those of the mothers. In relative time, fathers carry 30 percent of the childcare load and mothers 70 percent in each of the three stages. Among the 21 dual-career families, fathers' proportionate share varied somewhat by life-cycle stage. Dual-career fathers' relative time was highest among those with children under six (Stage II, 44.3 percent), and lowest among fathers in Stage IV (31.9 percent); fathers in Stage III fell between the two extremes (36.8 percent).

The time budgets show that a growing number of dual-earner parents are confronted with the daily demands that young children make on their households. Time analysis, however, masks not only the quality of child care but also the different roles that parents play when they take care of their children. As numerous studies document, fathers frequently are nurturant toward their children: touching, vocalizing, smiling, and playing (Cohen 1987; Robinson and Barret 1986). Mothers, however, are the primary caretakers for young children: feeding them, keeping them clean, and watching out for their safety. Fathers' exposure to children is typically secondary: they develop interest and activities as the children grow older, and they appear to have the "fun" role of playing with their children (Booth and Edwards 1980; Lamb and

Lamb 1976). A recent study of families in which men do engage in some primary-care parenting found that when fathers take over these activities they define what they are doing as "helping their wives," not as "sharing the child care" (LaRossa and LaRossa 1981, 72). The fathers do not believe that they have an equal responsibility and hence do not invest an equal amount of time.

Our survey findings corroborate the results from qualitative studies on primary and secondary caretaking of children as reported elsewhere (Horna and Lupri 1987). Proportional measures indicate that when fathers with young children participate in child care, only 5 percent report caring for the child alone, while 62.5 percent perform this task with the wife and 15.8 percent with her and another child. Similarly, if fathers participate in any housework at all, the vast majority (66 percent) do so jointly with their partners. In meal preparation as well, fathers typically are "mother's helpers": only 15 percent are solely responsible for this task. When asked to define their daily activities as leisure, semi-leisure/work, or neither work nor leisure, significantly more fathers than mothers perceive domestic chores, child care, and games with children as leisure (Horna and Lupri 1987). Because fathers are more at liberty to participate (or not to participate) in child care and domestic tasks, they find them more relaxing and more like leisure than do the mothers. No wonder!

Discussion and Summary

As the vanguard of the future, dual-earner families challenge the traditional instrumental father role. Theoretically, the dual-earner family lifestyle embraces conjugal and parental-role symmetry rather than role complementarity inside and outside the household. The division of parental responsibilities becomes more egalitarian because instrumental and expressive roles are no longer gender-based, but are enacted by both father and mother. Parental-role symmetry implies role interchangeability, which allows fathers (and mothers) to share family and work roles and to experience a more rewarding, more humane, more meaningful life with their children. Recent studies into men's changing roles point the way to the future: men are rethinking their roles as fathers and more options are available to them today than ever before in history (Russel 1983).

The weight of the evidence from this research suggests that androgynous fathers are exceedingly rare, but that the fathers in dual-earner families are in a transitional state, moving from a traditional to a symmetrical fatherhood role. They participate in housework, meal preparation, and child care, but the vast majority still give primacy to their role as economic provider, both in perception and in enactment. Nonetheless, compared with their single-earner counterparts, dual-earner parents are setting the stage for an emerging transformation in parental responsibilities.

Despite this promising shift, the redistribution of domestic labour and child care is highly selective. The fathers tend to be secondary caregivers, taking on tasks that are defined more clearly or are sociable and pleasurable, while leaving the more ill-defined, unpleasant, or time-consuming tasks to mothers (Luxton 1987). Thus, mothers in dual-earner families remain primary caretakers and caregivers.

The inequitable division of parental responsibilities is most apparent when the total weekly time devoted by fathers and by mothers to paid work, household chores, and child care is summed and compared graphically across the stages of the family life cycle (Figure 1). The most striking observation in Figure 1 is that the mothers' work week is considerably longer than the fathers' in all three childrearing stages; the pattern persists on weekends. Most of the difference can be attributed to differences in the amount of time allocated to housework and child care, because mothers in dual-earner families spend only six to ten fewer hours than their partners in paid work in each of the childrearing stages. Thus, in dual-earner families, fathers do not increase their time in housework and child care comparably. These findings are supported by other studies, but our results show specifically that these differences vary significantly by stage in the family life cycle.

Parental gender inequity is most pervasive where the greatest need for equal sharing appears to exist: among dual-earner families with one child or more under six (Stage II). Although fathers in this stage of the family life cycle contribute 10 more hours to paid work than do their partners, the mothers' estimated work week is 23 hours longer. Although fathers are by no means unresponsive to their partners' accumulated demands in households with young children, and although they increase their proportionate share in domestic labour and child care on weekends, mothers' weekend workloads nevertheless exceed those of fathers by over six hours. That is, young mothers contribute almost 30 hours (!) more each week than fathers to meeting the demands of households with children under six. This situation is quite problematic in view of the rapid increase in labour-force participation among young mothers.

As Figure 1 shows, these pronounced gender differences in workloads diminish as the children grow older. Because the absence of children reduces considerably the total time required for domestic labour, a more equitable role sharing ensues, as can be observed among childless couples and among those in the empty nest.

All told, the road to androgynous fatherhood is arduous and long, beset with inherent contradictions. Our time-budget analysis revealed that in our subsample of 182 dual-earner fathers in the childrearing stages, only 26 fathers, or 14.2 percent, registered high enough proportionate shares (.45 or above) in both housework and child care to be regarded as full-fledged caretakers and caregivers, or androgynous fathers. In those families, at least one parent held a professional job or worked in a setting that allowed for the arrangement of flexible schedules.

Figure 1.
Mean Total Hours in Work Week and Weekend Work for Parents Who Are Employed Full-Time, by Stage in the Family Life Cycle

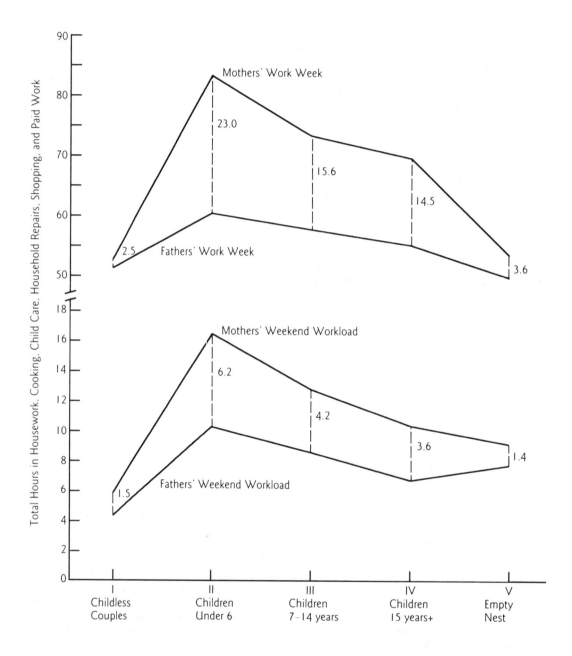

Family Life Cycle Stages

From our limited findings on dual-career families, we may infer that a great variety of class-related factors, both normative and structural, mediate between the emergence of new styles of fatherhood and the persistence of residual traditionalism. Despite recent corporate innovations to promote better integration of work and family life, in general the response of corporate Canada has not kept pace with the changing dynamics of family life. Very few Canadian employers offer any kind of child care to employees with young children. Paternity leaves have not been institutionalized and probably never will be accepted fully by employers and employees because career and family demands conflict, particularly in Stage II of the family life cycle. Institutional changes that would increase the flexibility of the occupational structure would also help in reducing those traditional barriers that still impede the development of new styles of fatherhood. Flexible scheduling exists, but it is limited primarily to fathers who pursue a professional career.

Historically, it has been expected that the family should adjust to the demands of the workplace. If the androgynous father role is to have a chance of becoming institutionalized, however, it may be necessary to alter work rather than the family.

Notes

1. For a detailed description of the research program's theoretical rationale, sampling design, and setting, see Horna, Lupri, and Mills (1984).
2. Lack of space does not permit me to detail the inherent pitfalls of inferring change from cross-sectional studies — i.e., the confounding influences of time (age, stage) and culture. On this point, see, for example, Lupri and Frideres (1981).
3. For a detailed description of the study design, see Lupri and Mills (1987) and Horna and Lupri (1987).
4. Relative measures of parents' time in paid work are obtained by dividing fathers' (or mothers') time in paid work by the total number of hours spent by both parents in paid work each week. The same calculation is used for arriving at proportionate shares in housework and child care.

Works Cited

Bane, Mary Jo. 1984. *Here to Stay*. New York: Basic.

Bernard, Jessie. 1974. *The Future of Motherhood*. New York: Dial.

———. 1983. "The Good Provider Role: Its Rise and Fall." *Family in Transition*. Eds. A. Skolnick and J. Skolnick. Boston: Little Brown. 155-75.

Bohen, M., and A. Viveros-Long. 1984. "Balancing Jobs and Family Life." *Work and Family: Changing Roles of Men and Women*. Ed. P. Voydanoff. Palo Alto, CA: Mayfield.

Booth, A., and J.N. Edwards. 1980. "Fathers: The Invisible Parent." *Sex Roles* 6 (3): 445-56.

Cohen, Theodore F. 1987. "Remaking Men." *Journal of Family Issues* 8 (March): 57-77.

Horna, Jarmila, and Eugen Lupri. 1987. "Fathers' Participation in Work, Family Life and Leisure: A Canadian Experience." *Reassessing Fatherhood: New Observations on Fathers and the Modern Family*. Eds. Charlie Lewis and Margaret O'Brien. London: Sage. 54-73.

Horna, Jarmila, E. Lupri, and D.L. Mills. 1984. "Dilemmas in Researching Family Work Roles." *International Journal of Comparative Sociology* 25 (3-4): 189-96.

Kliman, Deborah S., and Carol Vukelich. 1985. "Mothers and Fathers: Expectations for Infants." *Family Relations* 34 (July): 305-13.

Lamb, Michael E. 1976. *The Role of the Father in Childhood Development*. New York: Wiley.

Lamb, Michael E., and J.E. Lamb. 1976. "The Nature and Importance of the Father–Infant Relationship." *The Family Coordinator* (25)4: 370-85.

Lamb, Michael E., Joseph Pleck, and James A. Levine. 1986. "Effects of Paternal Involvement on Fathers and Mothers." *Men's Changing Roles in the Family*. Eds. R.A. Lewis and M.B. Sussman. New York: Haworth. 67-83.

LaRossa, Ralph, and Maureen M. LaRossa. 1981. *Transition to Parenthood*. Beverly Hills, CA: Sage.

Lewis, Charlie, and Margaret O'Brien, eds. 1987a. "Constraints on Fathers: Research, Theory and Clinical Practice." Lewis and O'Brien 1-19.

———. 1987b. *Reassessing Fatherhood: New Observations on Fathers and the Modern Family*. London: Sage.

Lupri, Eugen, ed. 1983. *The Changing Position of Women in Family and Society: A Cross-National Comparison*. Leiden: E.J. Brill.

Lupri, Eugen, and James Frideres. 1981. "The Quality of Marriage and the Passage of Time: Marital Satisfaction Over the Family Life

Cycle." *Canadian Journal of Sociology* 6(3): 283–305.

Lupri, Eugen, and Donald L. Mills. 1983. "The Changing Roles of Canadian Women in Family Work: An Overview." Lupri 43–77.

———. 1987. "The Household Division of Labour." *International Review of Sociology*. New Series (2): 33–54.

Lupri, Eugen, and Mino Vianello. 1990. "Gender Differences in the Family." *The Crystallized Barrier*. Ed. Mino Vianello. London: Sage.

Luxton, Meg. 1987. "Two Hands for the Clock: Changing Patterns in the Gendered Division of Labour in the Home." *Gender Roles: Doing What Comes Naturally*. Eds. E.D. Salamon and B.W. Robinson. Toronto: Methuen. 213–26.

Maclean's. 1988. "A Volatile National Mood." 5 (January): 26–74.

Mattesich, Paul, and Reuben Hill. 1987. "Life Cycle and Family Development." *Handbook of Marriage and the Family*. Eds. Marvin B. Sussman and Suzanne K. Steinmetz. New York: Plenum. 437–69.

McAdoo, John Lewis. 1986. "A Perspective on the Father's Role in Child Development." *Marriage and Family Review* (Winter): 117–33.

Myrdal, Alva, and Viola Klein. 1956. *Women's Two Roles: Home and Work*. London: Routledge and Kegan Paul.

Myrdal, Alva. 1967. Foreword. *The Changing Roles of Women and Men*. Ed. E. Dahlstrom. London: Duckworth. 9–15.

Oppenheimer, Valerie K. 1982. *Work and the Family. A Study in Social Demography*. New York: Academic.

Pleck, Joseph H. 1978. "The Work-Family Role System." *Social Problems* (24): 417–27.

———. 1983. "Husband's Paid Work and Family Roles: Current Research Issues." *Research in the Interweave of Social Roles: Families and Jobs*. Eds. H. Lopata, and J. Pleck. Greenwich, CT: JAI.

Rapoport, Rhona, and Robert Rapoport. 1971. *Dual-Career Families*. Baltimore: Penguin.

———. 1976. "The Working Woman and the Enabling Role of the Husband." Paper presented at the XII International Family Research Seminar. International Sociological Association, Moscow.

Robinson, Brian, and Robert L. Barret. 1986. *The Developing Father. Emerging Roles in Contemporary Society*. New York: Guildford.

Russel, Graeme. 1983. *The Changing Role of Fathers?* St. Lucia, Queensland: University of Queensland Press.

Szalai, Alexander, et al. 1972. *The Use of Time*. The Hague: Mouton.

Wilson, S.M. 1986. *Women, the Family and the Economy*. Toronto: McGraw-Hill Ryerson.

Young, Michael, and Peter Willmott. 1975. *The Symmetrical Family*. Harmondsworth: Penguin.

GENDER CONSCIOUSNESS AT W MODIFICATION OF THE MALE-BREADWINNER NORM AMONG STEELWORKERS AND THEIR SPOUSES[*]

D.W. Livingstone
Meg Luxton

This paper reviews the limited research to date on gender consciousness from liberal, radical, and socialist–feminist perspectives. It outlines an emergent approach that recognizes both gender identities and broader social forms of gender consciousness as continually constructed by men and women in class- and race-specific practices within paid workplace, household, and community spheres. This approach is applied to a study of Hamilton couples, especially steelworkers and their spouses. We focus on assessing expressions of one central aspect of gender identity — the male-breadwinner norm — through steelworkers' shop-floor culture and the attitudes of both spouses in steelworker households. We attempt to show how the male-breadwinner stereotype is currently being both reproduced and modified in response to women's growing participation in paid employment and particularly the recent presence of women steelworkers within a presumed bastion of traditional working-class masculinity.

↑ ♀'s participation in paid employment

Source: *Canadian Review of Sociology and Anthropology* 26 (1989): 240–75. Reprinted with permission of the *Canadian Review of Sociology and Anthropology*.

*The findings reported here are part of the Steelworker Families Research Project funded by the Social Science and Humanities Research Council (SSHRC) (Grant number: 410-83-0391). We are grateful to our co-investigators, Wally Secombe and June Corman, for their general assistance, as well as to Ellen Long for library research and Lucy Tantalo and Jill Given-King for typing services on this paper and Pat Armstrong for her research on York University C.V. instructions. We would also like to thank Mary O'Brien and Robert Brym and three anonymous reviewers for their comments on a previous draft.

Introduction

The contemporary women's movement has seriously challenged both the naturalization of gender differences and the assumed necessity of the subordination of women to men. The women's movement and the lesbian and gay liberation movements have also directly challenged traditional distinctions between the categories of man/women and masculine/feminine. As a result, the social construction of gender has become an increasingly visible and problematic process.[1] Critical analyses of female subordination, male domination, and sexual oppression are currently the most vibrant subject in the social sciences; they are extensive and extremely diverse in both paradigmatic and political terms.[2]

But one issue that scholars have only just begun to investigate is the nature and content of gender consciousness. Since the re-emergence of the women's movement, gender consciousness is increasingly revealed in commonsense, everyday expressions such as "she's a real women's libber . . ."; "that man is in the stone age as far as his attitudes to women are concerned"; "she doesn't laugh at the guy's jokes anymore — she says they're sexist." Such comments demonstrate that people rank gradations of attitudes, negotiate or confront differences in gender consciousness, and notice changes over time in the gender consciousness of individuals or groups.

sent, in the social sciences, this concept oorly articulated, and is used differently various scholarly traditions. For the most part, studies of gender consciousness have been limited to discussions of women, and this work tends, incorrectly, to equate gender and women (Porter 1983; Gurin 1985; Maroney and Luxton 1987a). Very few studies have been done of men's gender consciousness (Tolson 1977; Willis 1979; Cockburn 1983; Buchbinder 1987; Kaufman 1987) and even fewer on the interactions of the gender consciousness of women and men. For the most part, what exists at present is a working assumption that there is such a thing as gender consciousness and that it describes significant attitudes and behavioural dispositions on the part of (usually) women (Gurin 1985). This paper reviews earlier efforts to conceptualize and assess gender consciousness, argues for the importance of understanding different aspects of current gender consciousness in connection with social practices — particularly in paid workplace and household spheres — and draws on a general survey of Hamilton couples and a more intensive study of Stelco steelworkers and their spouses to examine the notion of the male breadwinner and the sex/gender division of labour — a central aspect of the gender consciousness of both women and men.

Conceptualizing Gender Consciousness

Many analysts have identified three main tendencies within the contemporary women's movement as liberal, radical, and socialist feminism (e.g., Jaggar 1983). While these perspectives often overlap, influence each other, and are constantly evolving, they represent distinct theoretical orientations with particular political implications. These theoretical perspectives have placed different emphases on issues of gender consciousness.

Liberal feminism has emphasized socialization, particularly the way sex stereotyping produces and transmits sex roles. This perspective has been primarily concerned with sex-role or, more recently, gender identity based on shared perceptions of normal female/male attributes.[3] Radical feminism has generally tended to take the biological sex dichotomy of women and men as a set of established categories, focussing on the power relations between them in terms of sexual politics and patriarchy. This approach has stressed the importance of consciousness raising and women's feminist consciousness, based on recognition of and opposition to the subordination of women. Socialist feminism, also recognizing the political power of consciousness raising and the importance of feminist consciousness for political action, has traced the continuing construction of both gender identity and feminist consciousness through the power relations of women and men in specific spheres of social practice and has paid particular attention to working-class women. Thus, at present in the literature related to gender consciousness, there are three main concepts — sex-role identity and attitudes, feminist consciousness, and gender consciousness per se.

Sex-Role Identity and Attitudes Research

Sex-role socialization theories have focussed on the processes through which female and male personalities are created. This approach may be traced back to the psychoanalytic revolution, but received its major impetus in social science through the functionalist paradigm that prevailed in academic social science in the immediate post–World War II period (Komarovsky 1946; Mead 1950; Parsons and Bales 1953). Its resurgence over the past 15 years has been preoccupied with documenting dominant perceptions of the social meaning of the categories of women and men. Some of the principal cumulative findings with regard to personal sex identities are as follows:

- popular notions of "women" and "men" are not simply bipolar but multidimensional, with some overlapping personal attributes (Spence and Helmreich 1978; Bem 1981);

• images of men remain centred around a quite sharply defined concept of heterosexual masculinity in terms of instrumental competence and power dominance, while images of women have become somewhat more diffuse and flexible, to include not only loosely related dimensions of nurturing, expressiveness, submissiveness, and emotional vulnerability, but also the more specific female subtypes (e.g., housewife, woman athlete, sexy woman, businesswoman) that are commonly perceived to have diverse combinations of personal attributes (Ruch 1984; Thompson et al. 1985; Deaux and Ullman, 1983); but

• in descriptive terms of the fundamental dimensions of instrumentality/expressivity and power/submissiveness, sex-role stereotypes have changed very little over the past generation (Werner and La Russa 1985; Gibbs 1985).

Sex-role researchers have also surveyed general social attitudes and their demographic correlates and have increasingly assessed popular attitudes about appropriate social roles for women and men. Notable among the empirical findings are the following:

• a growing recognition of the multidimensionality of sex roles and of the inconsistency of sex-role attitudes across public or societal, family, and general interpersonal spheres (Mason and Bumpass 1975; Giordano and Cernkovich 1979; Figueira-McDonough 1985);

• a definite trend toward more egalitarian conceptions of women's social roles (Boyd 1984; Anderson and Cook 1985; Gurin 1985; Mansbridge 1986); and

• consistent verification that women's engagement in paid employment, as well as youthfulness and higher educational attainment are associated with more egalitarian views of women's roles (Smith and Fisher 1982; Thornton, Alwin, and Cambwin 1983; Boyd 1984; Smith 1985).

Recently sex-role researchers have begun to assess empirically associations between personal gender identities and attitudes toward sexual equality (Figueira-McDonough 1985; Percival and Percival 1986), as well as to conceptualize dimensions or developmental stages of women's gender consciousness (Green 1979; Gurin 1985; Downing and Roush 1985).

Informative as this research may be in descriptive terms (and certainly our findings confirm its conclusions), it remains limited by the inherent weaknesses of functionalist role theory. As Gerson (1985, 32–37) has observed, sex-role socialization theories tend to oversimplify the relations between internalized norms and behaviour, to underestimate ambivalent socializing influences, and to overemphasize individual conformity, while ignoring the dynamics of individual and social change. Most fundamentally, as Connell (1985, 263) puts it:

> The problem is that role theory cannot grasp social change as history, that is, as transformation generated in the interplay of social practice and social structure. Change is always something that *happens to* sex roles, that impinges on them. It comes from outside, as in discussions of how technological and economic changes demand a shift to a "modern" male role for men. Or it comes from inside the person, from the "real self" that protests against the artificial restrictions of constraining roles. Sex role theory has no way of grasping change as a dialectic arising within gender relations themselves.

More specifically, changes in attitudes of and about women continue to be regarded, in sex-role research, either as necessary responses to externally imposed structural changes or as a clearer expression of women's internalized interests. Such assumptions fail to recognize either the connections with specific changes in the economic, domestic, and political power that men exercise over women, or the impact of the political mobilization of feminism (see Bashevkin 1984 for graphic examples).

Studies of Feminist Consciousness

Approaches that emphasize the power dynamics of sex and gender relations found one of their earliest sustained expressions in the writing of Simone de Beauvoir (1949), and have been given more systematic forms since by radical feminists, who have focussed on men's sexual domination and violence toward women and society as a whole (especially through militarism and the violation of the environment), and on the institutional dynamics of women's general subordination to men, especially in the family sphere and sexuality (Firestone 1971; Mitchell 1971; Delphy 1979; Daly 1978; O'Brien 1981). Although more recent radical-feminist scholarship appears to have placed greater emphasis on differences among women (recognizing, in particular, the importance of race), there has been a strong tendency to treat "women" and "men" as undifferentiated universal categories (Stimpson 1984).[4] This is clearly the case in most attempts to date to define feminist consciousness (Mitchell and Oakley 1986). The growth of the women's movement in the 1960s produced widespread use of the concept of feminist consciousness. Many women joined small consciousness-raising groups in which they discussed their own personal lives, and through that sharing came to understand the ways in which "the personal is political"; that is, the ways in which their individual experiences were shaped by social patterns common to most women. Those who recognized that women are oppressed were said to have a feminist consciousness. For example, Gerda Lerner (1986, 242) defines feminist consciousness as the recognition of collective wrongs suffered, leading to efforts to remedy these wrongs in political, economic, and social life. Appeals to the solidarity of sisterhood, often in terms comparable to earlier Marxist appeals to the solidarity of the working class, were commonly made during the consciousness-raising phase of the women's movement (Shulman 1980) and continue to be made (Morgan 1984). Even those who reject such conceptions as the imposition of

arbitrary stages (that is, movement from false consciousness through consciousness raising to true revolutionary consciousness) and argue instead for a multiplicity of contextually grounded feminist consciousness, tend to treat the oppression of women as a primitive universal term (Stanley and Wise 1983).

Some feminists have argued that there is a consciousness shared by women of all societies. Merle Thornton (1980) and Mary O'Brien (1981) argue that reproductive consciousness generated by the labour of birth is universal among women. Temma Caplan (1982, 546) similarly claims that, within all cultures, women share an essential consciousness: "the bedrock of women's consciousness is the need to preserve life." She argues that, as a result, women's domestic responsibilities in class societies reinforce a revolutionary potential of their consciousness, because when women's responsibilities are threatened (especially their responsibility to preserve life), women mobilize as a group through traditional female networks to protest and resist. While the shared material bases of women's condition should be recognized, other feminists have argued that women's experiences of biological reproduction vary greatly and are shaped by diverse historical and cultural conditions. As Rosalind Petchesky (1984, 364) observes with regard to reproductive consciousness: "no universal consciousness grows out of the conditions of reproduction, for abortion, pregnancy, and childbearing are different in different social circumstances and consciousness will reflect those differences."

The basic limitations of radical-feminist studies of women's consciousness to date have been: an overemphasis on, and often an ahistorical treatment of, the force of patriarchal structures to the exclusion of the active practices of actual women and men as motivated social agents; an undemonstrated assumption that all women and all men, respectively, share not only common experience but unified, internally consistent sets of interests; and a tacit denial that material and emotional needs for mutual support both diminish most men's motivation to dominate women and generate contradictions in most women's relations with most men (cf. Gerson 1985, 24–29).

Studies of Women's Gender Consciousness

While whole societies may be gender divided in such a way that some aspects of gender consciousness hold for all women or men of that society, in most large-scale societies there are significant differences within genders based on class, race, region, ethnicity, or generation.[5] Most pertinently, socialist feminist historical studies have recognized that, while a pervasive ethos of heterosexual masculinity and femininity has been intimately connected with the institutionalization of men's dominance over women in industrial capitalist societies, this ethos has had distinctive bases in ruling-class, middle-class, and working-class settings (Barrett and McIntosh 1982; Davidoff and Hall 1987). Much socialist feminist research pertaining to gender consciousness has focussed on the construction of women's gendered subjectivity as domestic labourers, family members, and sexual beings, especially in the context of family households as a central institutional site of women's oppression (Mitchell 1966; Rowbotham 1974; Rapp 1978). Over the past decade, the topic of female wage labour in capitalist society has gained greater attention, as have employment-based influences on women's gender identities and political orientations (Vogel 1986, 13–15).

The most detailed insights into the historical development of women's gender consciousness have come from studies of working-class women in Britain and America. Ellen Ross's (1983) study of women in East London shows how their shared experiences bred gender solidarity that empowered their contestation of male power and provided a basis for occasional challenges to the authorities. Sarah Eisenstein (1983), studying working women in the United States around the turn of the century, argues that women are

able to develop a group gender consciousness when they move out of their family household and are able to come together with other women in groups at work or in the community. Some historical studies demonstrate the existence among working-class women of a collective sense of themselves that certainly provided them with resources for struggle. For example, Susan Benson (1983) shows how women's work culture has provided department-store saleswomen with a framework for understanding and resources for coping with their jobs. Ardis Cameron (1985) describes how working-class women of Lawrence, Massachusetts, used existing women's networks to resist police and scabs during the strike of 1912. These women violated norms of women's behaviour mainly to protest against the ruling class "ladylike" attributes that were inappropriate for working-class women rather than as a challenge to femininity itself or to masculine dominance. However, there is no evidence in the existing studies that such women were critical of the dual categories, "feminine" and "masculine," or that their gender consciousness ever took on a sustained oppositional form. Furthermore, the idea of gender consciousness has been used by historians to describe phenomena rather than as a concept to be theorized.

Comparative studies of societies in which women and men are sharply differentiated and confined to same-sex groups have noted that common economic responsibilities, often shared residence, and social expectations of shared characteristics do result in gender-specific cultures (Pettigrew 1981; Chafetz 1984). So, within one society there may be a men's culture and a women's culture, each of which has its own understanding of itself, of the other culture, and of the social totality (Turnbull 1981). When, as is often the case, the society as a whole is male-dominated, women's material condition may be dictated by men and of benefit to men; nevertheless, the internal workings and meanings of women's culture may be only partially understood by the men. While these situations are often very oppressive for women, the existence of a distinct women's culture offers the potential for certain efforts on the part of women to at least provide themselves with support and solidarity — in a sense, a culture of consolation (Abu-Lughad 1985; Smith-Rosenberg, 1980). Discussing middle-class women in nineteenth-century American society, Nancy Cott (1977, 100) argues that "the canon of domesticity intensified women's gender group identification by assimilating diverse personalities to one work-role that was also a sex role signifying a shared and special destiny." In certain circumstances, where the women are able to wield relative power, their shared women's culture offers the potential for them to challenge their domination by the men's culture and to offer alternative definitions to the male interpretation of the social totality (Murphy and Murphy 1974). Insofar as women share some collective sense of their common experience, they may be said to share a gender consciousness.

Other, often socialist–feminist, researchers have begun to document carefully women's gender consciousness in contemporary capitalist societies. The main focus of this work has been on the ways in which awareness of gender and class interests are related. Ethnographies of working-class couples have illustrated how women's greater concern with home affairs influences both their attitudes toward social relations in employment and their connection with broader social issues (Hunt 1980; Porter 1983). More detailed case studies of women's recent paid work experience show that gender consciousness is often negotiated between the work culture and the world of home and family. For example, Heidi Gottfried and David Fasenfest (1984), Sallie Westwood (1984), and Louise Lamphere (1985) argue that working-class women use women's family-related interests and concerns (for example, the celebration of weddings, pregnancies, and births) to create a social space that male workers and bosses find difficult to penetrate. This allows women to provide themselves with some measure of control over the workplace. Women's collective experience of wage labour itself has been

shown to lead to their growing, if often ambivalent, awareness that the male family wage is a myth and the ideal of a male breadwinner is inappropriate, that they themselves are essential earners, and that their own shared work cultures provide a key resource in struggles for both job rights and fairer domestic division of labour (Pollert 1981; Costello 1985).

An Emergent Approach to Understanding Gender Consciousness

These cumulative findings, particularly from socialist–feminist research, have provoked a rethinking of the theoretical underpinnings of both gender consciousness and class consciousness (Bartky 1975; Tiano and Bracken 1984; Wilson and Sennott 1984). Conventional Marxist notions of class consciousness that ignore gender relations and focus narrowly on the relations between workers and bosses at the point of production, often explicitly denying the significance of other experiences, are seen as inadequate for proper understanding of class consciousness (Livingstone and Mangan, forthcoming), as are global assertions of feminist consciousness based on class-blind gender relations. Roberta Goldberg (1984, 84) concludes her study of the consciousness of women clerical workers:

How consciousness develops to enable people to challenge their roles is a question that cannot be answered using classical theories of class consciousness. A new theory of consciousness encompassing the two major areas of production, work and the family, must take into account the profound expectations of gender roles and the accompanying consciousness that arises when people are confronted by the contradictory expectations of the workplace and the family.

This understanding of social consciousness from a Marxist feminist perspective is explicitly based on an expanded conception of the capitalist mode of production that recognizes the family household and the paid workplace as two equally important points of production (Seccombe 1980; Goldberg 1984, 76). Our own general view is that class and gender relations in capitalist societies, as well as race and ethnic relations, are constituted through practices in three primary spheres of activity: paid workplaces, households, and communities. We conceive of a hierarchy of determination in which paid-workplace production relations tend to constrain the autonomy of household activities more than vice versa, while communities extending from both household and paid-workplace spheres take up residual and more discretionary parts of people's time and energies (Luxton, Livingstone, and Seccombe 1982; Corman 1988; Livingstone and Mangan, forthcoming). Certainly, research findings to date appear to support a general assumption that, in addition to family household-based relations, class-specific, gender-based changes in contemporary paid-workplace relations are critical to understanding both women's resistance and the gender consciousness of women and men in contemporary capitalist societies (Pollert 1983, 113–14; Game and Pringle 1983).

The well-developed Marxist conceptualizations of class consciousness offer a framework for thinking about gender consciousness. Marxists have commonly distinguished at least three aspects of class consciousness:

1. class identity, which is awareness of classes and identification with one's own class;
2. oppositional class consciousness, which is recognition of antagonistic interests with another class or classes; and
3. hegemonic class consciousness, which is readiness to act to achieve or maintain a form of society based on the assumption that specific class interests are universal.[6]

Simple comparable distinctions are not directly applicable to gender consciousness. Where class differences are entirely social, gender differences and gender identity have a basis in sex differences. Furthermore, at least in contemporary capitalist societies, an individual's sex (female or male) is explicitly stressed from the moment the birth is announced and is reiterated daily in almost all activities, including the most intimate ones; class membership is more rarely acknowledged and many people are able to live unaware of their class location. In addition, the elimination of ruling classes is possible in a way that the elimination of men is not (except in the daydreams of frustrated feminists). Thus, gender identity and some form of gender consciousness are fundamental to social relations in a way that class membership and consciousness are not.

Nevertheless, using the analogy of class consciousness as a starting point, we might think of gender consciousness in contemporary society in terms of the following:

• gender identities, as our understanding of the normal meanings of femininity and masculinity and our personal sentiments of affinity with these distinctions;
• oppositional gender consciousness, as a sense that gender identities of feminine and masculine have been arbitrary and constraining for both women and men and a recognition that gender relations have involved domination and oppression of women by men; and
• hegemonic gender consciousness, as the willingness to either maintain or create a form of society based on the assumption that one's own gender interests can be generalized for all.

At one extreme, we could distinguish those with hegemonic masculinist consciousness — that is, a strong heterosexual masculine personal identity and affinity, a consistent sense of resistance to men's sharing power with women in any sphere, and the continual assertion in practice of male dominance as the natural state of life. Conversely, a counter-hegemonic feminist consciousness might involve a strong sense of one's own personal identity as a woman and a clear sense of commonality with other women, a coherent belief in women's right to contest male dominance in any sphere, and a disposition to create a future society organized on principles consistent with women's complete liberation. Just as people of dominant class origins have sometimes developed profound sympathies with and taken the standpoint of subordinate classes, men can develop a pro-feminist consciousness — that is, sympathies with women's interests and a rejection of male power and masculinist discourse — without denying their own male identities. Similarly, just as some working-class people can ally themselves with the ruling class in apparent opposition to their own long-term class interests, so many women support systems of male domination.

We could further expect that most people would exhibit more mixed forms of gender consciousness in most circumstances. Partly as a consequence of inconsistencies between ruling-class ideology/discourse and the lived experiences of subordinate class cultures, working-class people have commonly exhibited forms of contradictory class consciousness (Gramsci 1971; Emmison 1985). Similarly, the dominant masculine ideology/discourse that many women have had imposed on them often contrasts sharply with their lived personal experiences and results in bifurcated forms of gender consciousness (Smith 1978; Kasper 1986).

While construing forms of gender consciousness in these terms may be useful, we need to be wary of a gender reductionism that, in effect, repeats common Marxist errors of class reductionism. The demonstrated empirical inadequacy and political irrelevance of simple unitary conceptions of material class interests and associated imputations of false consciousness in the attempts of many Marxist scholars to comprehend Western working-class thinking (Katznelson and Zolberg 1986) should be sufficient warning to proceed more circumspectly in studies of gender consciousness.

The current practice, by which studies of gender consciousness are conflated with studies of women's consciousness, must be avoided. Hence, studies of men's gender consciousness, both alone and in interaction with women's, are much needed (Brod 1987; Kaufman 1987). Such studies must recognize that experiences of gender relations are not only class-specific, but also grounded in race/ethnic and age relations as equally irreducible features of social reality (Davis 1981; Anthais and Yuval-Davis 1983; Dixon 1983; Brittan and Maynard 1985). Conceptualization and study of race/ethnic consciousness and age consciousness remain at an even more primitive level (Gurin, Miller, and Gurin 1980; Gurin 1985). But everyone's social consciousness presumably remains constrained and mediated by his/her own class, gender, age, and racial identities in complex ways (Simpson and Mutran 1981; Hraba and Yarborough 1983). At this stage of knowledge, the extension of more modest inquiries into the interplay of specific aspects of gender identities and oppositional gender consciousness among men and women in specific class and racial settings may be most fruitful. Finally, we need to recognize that both gender identities and any such broader notions of existing and desirable relations between the sexes are continually being socially constructed by diverse motivated agents under the constraints of institutionalized forms of organizational and ideological practices in workplace, household, and community (cf. Connell 1985). In short, we must recognize that women as well as men make the history of gender relations, even if not under conditions of their own choosing (Gerson 1985, 29).

Gender Consciousness at Work: A Study of Steelworkers and Their Spouses

Probably the predominant ideological notion connected with gendered social practices in advanced capitalist societies is that heterosexual marriage is the ideal for all women and men and that within such marriages the preferred division of labour is one in which the man is the breadwinner and the woman is the homemaker (Hunt 1980, 180). Whatever the actual extent of this practice (and where it actually has been practised most extensively is among white, urban populations), the ideology is profoundly pervasive, affecting most aspects of contemporary life from building codes, tax laws, and health-care plans to access to the labour market and wage levels (Luxton 1987).[7] As Archer and Lloyd (1984, 242) summarize:

> Perhaps the most pervasive [gender] stereotype is the belief that a man's main responsibility is to go out to work and a woman's is to look after her family. One consequence of this belief is that a working man is seen as the breadwinner and a woman as merely working for "pin money." This view may also be used as a reason for undervaluing the contribution of women workers, for justifying lower pay for women, and for regarding men's careers as being of greater importance than women's. Despite this belief, a large proportion of women workers . . . were the chief economic supporters of households in the 1970s.

The class, race, and gender composition of the employed work force in most advanced capitalist societies, including Canada's, has changed dramatically in the post–World War II period, with changing patterns of immigration and the increasing participation of married women, especially in working-class jobs (Armstrong 1984). The infusion of married women into paid employment has forced both men and women to rethink the mother–wife–homemaker role as the taken-for-granted female gender identity in society. Where women have found employment in so-called women's jobs, the dominant ideology has been modified; when women take on so-called men's jobs that ideology is seriously challenged.[8]

The remainder of this paper focusses on particular aspects of gender consciousness by investigating the reproduction and modification of the male-breadwinner norm in a factory in the steel industry. The latter is widely regarded as one of the strongest preserves of traditional white working-class masculine identity and opposition to women trying to do a "man's job." By examining the shop-floor cultural practices and expressed attitudes of married, white working-class men employed in the steel industry, the perceptions of their spouses, and the experiences of a small number of women who were hired in the steel plant, this paper documents the articulation of the male-breadwinner norm and assesses the various experiences that either lead to a modification of or actually challenge that norm.

Views on the gendered division of labour, as expressed most explicitly through acceptance or rejection of the male-breadwinner norm, are among the most basic ingredients of oppositional gender consciousness. Whether one is inclined to a feminist, male chauvinist, or more ambivalent sense of oppositional gender consciousness is likely to be intimately related to both dispositions on fundamental dimensions of gender identity and predispositions to act to maintain or create alternative forms of gender relations.

The Hilton Works of the Steel Company of Canada (Stelco), in Hamilton, Ontario, is one of the largest manufacturing plants in Canada. With a labour force of between 8000 and 14 000, it has been the major employer in the city of Hamilton since the early twentieth century. Unionized in the late 1940s by the United Steelworkers of America (Local 1005), the plant offers relatively high wages and benefits, which have made it one of the most desirable industrial workplaces in the city. The production labour force has been almost entirely white and male.[9]

Until recently, because of the relatively high wages and the relative job security, the vast majority of men at Stelco were economically able to support dependent wives and children, thus realizing the male-breadwinner ideal. Indeed, from 1945 to 1981, when there was a world decline in steel manufacturing, Hamilton consistently had among the lowest rates of women's employment in Canada. This was made possible by the wages from the heavy industry that dominates the city and was, of course, supported by the discriminatory hiring practices of those same industries (Webber 1986). During World War II, women were employed to replace male workers who had joined the army but, after the war, almost all those women were let go. Between 1946 and 1961, a few women were hired, but by 1961 they were all employed in one particular work site — the tin mill. Between 1961 and 1978, no women were hired, although approximately 30 000 women applied for jobs during those 19 years (Luxton, forthcoming). By 1978, there were 28 women working in the tin mill; the rest of the production workers were men. In 1979–80, a union-supported committee, The Women Back Into Stelco Committee, launched a highly public campaign, which included a discrimination complaint with the Ontario Human Rights Commission, to force Stelco to hire women for production jobs in the Hilton Works. As a result, Stelco hired approximately 200 women. The highly publicized campaign and the subsequent hiring of a number of women focussed attention on the question of gender and paid employment and for the women and men involved posed sharply the issue of gender identity (Eason, Field, and Santucci 1983).

We examined patterns of gender consciousness among married white male steelworkers and their spouses, and among white female steelworkers who entered Stelco as a result of their political campaign. Our study was conducted in 1983–84 in the wake of massive layoffs by Stelco, including most of the women hired in this campaign. We interviewed a random sample of 184 married steelworkers (182 were men), drawn from the Local 1005 membership list, who were living with their spouses and employed at Stelco. We also interviewed their spouses (76 of the women spouses were full-time housewives and 106 were in paid employment; the 2 male spouses were employed). In-depth followup interviews were also conducted selectively. For comparative purposes, a representative sample of individuals living with partners in

the Greater Hamilton Area was given a similar interview ($N = 795$). We also interviewed the leaders of the Women Back Into Stelco Campaign and 25 women who, though not part of the original campaign, were hired as a result of it. This paper investigates patterns of gender consciousness among men and women who, for the most part, are living in nuclear families where the man's income forms the greater part of the household income. It also looks at the impact on that consciousness of the women who got jobs at Stelco. We consider what factors foster support for a sharply differentiated sex/gender division of paid labour and, particularly, the ideal of the male breadwinner, and conversely what leads to a recognition that women and men can and ought to do the same paid work for the same remuneration. Most specifically, we attempt to investigate the links of masculine shop-floor culture with ideologies of work and the male-breadwinner norm in this core of the Hamilton working class.

Masculine Shop-Floor Culture

In occupational settings where the large majority of workers are male, there is often an equation of paid work with masculinity. It is assumed that workers in that field are, and should be, male. Such ideas are part of a larger ideology that accepts the existence of a decisive sex/gender division of labour, fundamental to which is the belief that women should be first and foremost wives and mothers and that men should primarily be breadwinners. In describing professional occupations, this assumption is articulated in phrases that call attention to the exception such as "a lady doctor," "a woman pilot," or "a female professor."[10] As Paul Willis (1979) and Cynthia Cockburn (1983) have demonstrated, the equation of paid work with masculinity is frequently characteristic of large-scale industrial settings where much of the work involves manual labour or where the work environment is particularly noisy, dirty, and noxious. Existing studies of masculine shop-floor culture also describe the meaning and pleasure that men extract in the midst of boring and alienating work situations. The assertion of masculinity is partially a defence, a way of insisting on the exclusion of women to protect specific jobs and more general job skills from increased competition (Cockburn 1985). It is also an integral part of the ideology of the male breadwinner. Such studies show why male camaraderie, based on masculinity, is important and why the men are often threatened if their culture is challenged (for example, by the presence of women).

In workplaces such as Stelco, where many parts of the plant have involved dangerous or heavy work, and where — with the exception of the cafeteria staff, the cleaning and office staff, and the tin-mill workers — all workers were men from 1945 until the challenge in 1979, manual labour, dangerous work, or even work with large machinery is often identified as men's work. This may militate against individuals recognizing the class nature of this work and therefore retard their sense of class identity. A male steelworker described the qualities needed to work at Stelco: "You got to be tough and you got to be willing to take risks. You got to be strong. It takes a real man to work here."

The shared experience of work, the camaraderie of co-workers, is shaped by their shared masculinity (Stewart 1981). As John Lippert (1977, 208) observed of his experience as an auto worker:

Each member of the group seems concerned mainly with exhibiting sexual experience and competency through the competition. . . . None of what happens between men in the plant is considered "sexuality." That remains as what we do with (or to) our women when we get home. . . . But even through this competition, it is easy to see that many, many men enjoy their physical interaction and that they receive a kind of physical satisfaction from it that they just don't get [from the work itself or] when they go home.

The unpleasantness and the brutality of the working situation is sometimes reinterpreted into a heroic exercise of manly confrontation with the task. In this way, a potential for developing oppositional class consciousness may be modified or even deflected by a gender consciousness that validates certain stereotypic notions of masculinity. Difficult, uncomfortable, or dangerous working conditions are not seen directly as employer-imposed hazards for the workers, but as challenges to masculine prowess. A male steelworker noted: "The coke oven, where I am, is really rough. The men who work there, they got to be really tough you know, just to keep at it, day after day."

Discontent with work in male-dominated factory environments is often not articulated as political discontent directed against the bosses but rather is mediated through forms of language and interplay among workers that express sexual competition and antagonism (Gray 1984; Meissner 1986). Sexually antagonistic language pervades the steel mill. Work itself — especially difficult work — is characterized as feminine and to be conquered: "it's a real bitch;" "give her hell." Similarly, malfunctioning machinery is called by derogatory terms for women — bitch, slut — that often have explicit sexual connotations. Disliked bosses are similarly described by terms that either cast aspersion on their masculinity and sexual ability — wimp, cream puff, dick — or identify them with negative female terms — bitch. Specific anger is expressed using terms for sexual intercourse, and workers' descriptions of their exploitation by management are usually articulated using rape terms — "we're getting fucked" or "we're getting screwed around."

Gender codes are central to the ways in which male workers approach other aspects of their work. One of the few ways workers can influence the design of the work sites is in their choice of pictures on the walls. Frequently lunch rooms are wallpapered with pinups of apparently sexually available women — imagery that both continues the theme of sexual symbolism and suggests a potential alternative activity that sharply contrasts with the workplace. This alternative for men involves both fantasized sexual activity, which is deemed to be physically and emotionally pleasurable in ways that the reality of work is not, and sexual domination, where the male (at least as viewer) is in a position of power over (at least the image of) the woman; this is a power that the worker never has at work.

Even when discontent at work is expressed as direct political opposition to management, it is filtered through a language of masculinity. Male workers describe standing up to management in masculine terms. One male Stelco worker described another approvingly: "He never takes any shit from the foreman and when they give him a hard time, he fights back hard — he's a real man." In plant-floor confrontations, and in contract negotiations, masculine characteristics and behaviours are commonly mobilized. As Paul Willis has noted (1979, 198), the spectacle, especially of the potential fist fight, and the bluff, or strong and combative language, register real expressions of anger and opposition. These may be very effective in the short run and certainly represent a strong force. But this "masculine style of confrontation demands an appropriate and honourable resolution: visible and immediate concessions" (Willis 1979, 198). As a consequence, contract negotiations often result in cash settlements, gains that are immediately visible but may "actually conceal longer-term defeats over the less visible issues of control and ownership" (Willis 1979, 198; Winter and Robert 1980). Most significantly, such masculinist worker consciousness is usually taken for granted as a normal part of how work is understood. Even men who do not like it tend rather to distance themselves from particular manifestations of it, objecting, for example, to swearing or to food throwing, than to develop a critique or opposition to the total culture. It is only when challenged explicitly that the dynamics of this gender consciousness can be seen at work. The Women Back Into Stelco campaign posed such a challenge.

The Challenge from Women and the Modification of the Male-Breadwinner Norm

When women attacked the policies that had excluded them from employment at the Hilton works, they were also, intentionally or not, attacking the legitimacy and attending beliefs both of the equation of steelmaking and masculinity and of the male-breadwinner ideal. In so doing, they were challenging existing ideologies of gender. The mere presence of female steelworkers, whatever their personal gender consciousness or motivation for seeking Stelco employment, acted as a "consciousness raising" for those involved.

There were about 14 000 men employed at Stelco when the first women walked through the doors after the campaign had succeeded. Their responses to women's employment at Stelco varied. One of the women noted:

> Some of them feel if you can do your job you got a right to be there. And others feel you got a right to be there if you are the only breadwinner. And then others . . . you shouldn't be there. And then there are others, that you should be there.

Male steelworkers, their spouses, and women steelworkers almost unanimously supported, in the abstract, the general principle of equal opportunities for women in the labour market. This is not surprising, given that, over the past 30 years, Canadian opinion surveys have found growing majority support among both women and men for the general principle of sex equality in paid workplaces. By 1970, over four-fifths of Canadian women and men supported equal pay for the same kind of work, and by the early 1980s support for the view that women could run most businesses as well as men had grown to about four-fifths of both women and men (Boyd 1984). Similarly, in our interview survey, male steelworkers and their spouses both expressed strong consensus (>70 percent) on the general statement: "If given the chance, women could and should do the same work as men now do, and men could and should do the same work as women now do (except for pregnancy)." They also demonstrated support for the principle of equal pay for equal work when they strongly disagreed (>85 percent) with the proposition: "women should not be paid the same as men."

The comments of the following male steelworkers in our in-depth followup interviews are representative:

> You can't turn the clock back. Every woman has the right to enter the market.

> I think it should be equal pay for sure. There is no argument there for me at all. You know, if a woman does the job of men, then, pay her accordingly.

> I figure the opportunity's there for everyone. It all depends on the individual. . . . I think if a woman can do the job, I feel that she should have it. The opportunity should be there.

Wives of steelworkers shared that general principle:

> It is okay for a woman to want to do different kinds of work.

> There are women who could handle jobs like men.

However, despite this general support in principle for women's right to paid employment and equal pay for equal work, attitudes toward more specific aspects of full sex/gender equality are much more mixed. Canada-wide opinion survey responses suggest that support for the male-breadwinner norm also generally appears to be diminishing; by the early 1980s, the majority of Canadian women and men expressed support for equal job opportunities for married women. However, in spite of growing support in recent years, small majorities are still opposed to married women with young children taking a job outside the home (Boyd 1984; Reid 1987). This pattern appears to be confirmed by our Hamilton surveys.

The most pertinent questions asked in both our Hamilton-wide and steelworker household surveys dealt with priority for jobs in hard times, and affirmative action in traditionally male jobs (Tables 1 and 2). Overall, the pattern of responses indicated that Hamilton couples also remained quite divided on these more specific issues of gender equality, that male Stelco workers were somewhat less supportive than Hamilton men in general, and that employed women were more supportive than homemakers.[11]

As Table 1 shows, small majorities of women and men in Hamilton couples rejected men's priority for jobs in hard times. A bare majority of Stelco wives did as well. Only among male Stelco workers was there a small majority in favour of giving men priority for jobs. As one male steelworker insisted: "Between a single mother with kids and a guy supporting a family, I would take the guy first."

Women's employment typically had a significant effect on the views of both spouses. Among Hamilton couples generally, over 60 percent of employed women and of men with employed spouses supported women's equal right to paid employment in times of high unemployment. Both Hamilton women presently working exclusively as homemakers and men with homemaker spouses were about equally divided on the issue. Male Stelco workers and their spouses exhibited fairly similar differences by employment status of the woman. The employed wives of Stelco workers showed a virtually identical pattern of majority support to Hamilton working women in general. Conversely, definite majorities of both male steelworkers with homemaker wives and their wives themselves expressed agreement with men's priority for jobs. Perhaps most notably, male Stelco workers with employed wives remained about equally divided, and therefore less moved by their wives' employment than Hamilton men in general to support women's equal right to jobs. However, the general pattern in Table

Table 1
In Times of High Unemployment, Men Should Have Priority for Jobs

Hamilton Households

	Men with Employed Spouses	Men with Homemaker Spouses	All Men	Employed Women	Homemaker Women	All Women
% disagree	69	41	58	63	48	54
% agree	24	47	33	34	45	40
% can't say	7	12	9	3	7	6
N	238	153	390	164	238	403

Steelworker Households

	Men with Employed Spouses	Men with Homemaker Spouses	All Men	Employed Women	Homemaker Women	All Women
% disagree	50	35	43	60	37	50
% agree	45	60	52	37	56	45
% can't say	5	5	5	3	7	5
N	106	76	182	106	76	182

Table 2
The Proportion of Women in Traditionally Male Occupations Should be Increased Through Special Training and Hiring Initiatives

Hamilton Households

	Men with Employed Spouses	Men with Homemaker Spouses	All Men	Employed Women	Homemaker Women	All Women
% agree	47	49	48	65	52	58
% disagree	41	41	41	26	35	31
% can't say	13	10	12	9	13	11
N	238	153	390	164	238	403

Steelworker Households

	Men with Employed Spouses	Men with Homemaker Spouses	All Men	Employed Women	Homemaker Women	All Women
% agree	42	47	44	60	53	57
% disagree	56	48	53	37	39	38
% can't say	2	5	3	3	8	5
N	106	76	182	106	76	182

1 supports the not surprising conclusion of several earlier studies that people in both middle-class and working-class households with wives in paid employment are more likely to reject the male-breadwinner norm (cf. Huber and Spitze 1983; Ferree 1983; Anderson and Cook 1985; Smith 1985; Black and Creese 1986). Also, as in earlier studies, significant correlations of youthfulness and higher educational attainment with more egalitarian views on women's employment rights have been found both for men and women, whether the wife is employed or not.

On the issue of affirmative action in traditionally male jobs, the overall pattern of responses was again similar, as Table 2 indicates. Most notably, the majority of women in all categories — including Stelco homemaker wives — were likely to support such affirmative-action practices, while men in general remained more divided and a small majority of male Stelco workers expressed opposition.

While these Hamilton survey results are consistent with a general trend of declining support for male-breadwinner power, they also confirm that at least some aspects of the male-breadwinner norm remain accepted in some form by the majority of Stelco workers as well as by many of their wives. The results further confirm that many male Stelco workers with employed wives continue to defend male-breadwinner power, even if their wives disagree.

Our in-depth interviews with Stelco workers and their spouses offer further insight into the complexities and dynamics of the current renegotiation of these features of breadwinner power and, by implication, of gender identities in general. The other side of the argument that certain occupations, such as steelmaking, are only for men is the insistence that men must be breadwinners. So, while there is rarely any overt denial of women's right to paid work, an underlying identification of breadwinner status with men's work remains strong among many male steelworkers. While some men actively supported the efforts of the women to get hired at Stelco and welcomed them when they succeeded (and the

union formally and practically gave full support to the campaign), many men insisted that steelmaking, especially given the dirty, dangerous, and heavy work at Stelco, must be men's work:

> It was meant to be a man's job, working in a steel factory.

> It's not for women. There's a lot of heavy work. . . . I feel that Stelco should be for men . . . I feel the steel industry is just for men.

The notion of steelmaking as essentially men's work is not merely a simplistic assertion of male chauvinism, but is typically bound to the men's deeper sense of responsibility to provide for their families. Both the wages earned and the very sacrifice and strength required to do the work offer a basic self-esteem and self-worth. The wage packet is seen as conferring breadwinner power and status and confirming that the man has fulfilled his obligation as family provider. The male-breadwinner ideal may have been expressed baldly:

> Like I believe a man is the breadwinner, you know. He supports his wife and kids. That's just the way it is. And that's the way it should be. Men earn the money.

Or with some qualifications:

> People have their rights. But I also believe that a man is the breadwinner and that the woman should stay home. . . . My wife went out to work for six weeks one time in a restaurant, 'cuz she wanted to get out of the house. And I said okay, but that was therapy, it was not to make money or anything like that. She went out and done her thing, and then she came back. And I don't need my wife to work. If I can't support her, there's something wrong.

But, in virtually every case, the steelworker's male identity appeared to be integrally tied to his perceived capacity to bring home a "decent" or "living" wage.

Homemaker wives of steelworkers most frequently expressed the concomitant belief that women's place is in the home: "I think a mother should be home with her children. It's better for them, isn't it." But some homemaker wives' comments reflected both an awareness of the centrality of their own domestic work to the reproduction of their husband's labour power, and an assertion of their own continuing right to seek paid work:

> I make sure he goes to work happy and in a good mood every day. So he is going into his workplace not thinking about things. He can go and put his mind into his job, not worry about what is worrying at home. . . . I gave up my job when we got married, but that was a mutual agreement. I didn't do it for him. He didn't make me quit my job, you know. I could probably go back to work somehow.

Homemaker wives of steelworkers frequently reiterated versions of the male-breadwinner norm, but those who supported women working in steel typically did so on the same basis as they supported their husbands working there, the wage packet:

> It's the best money that women can earn. My husband heard stories from the guys in the plant before the women came in about the women during the war and they were really something. I think women should get those jobs if they can. The pay is really good. My girlfriend is working at Dofasco and she really likes it.

Employed wives frequently showed both a deeper appreciation of the negative side of male breadwinners' responsibility and a determination to maintain their own employment, albeit generally in low-paid or part-time jobs:

> The man might think it's terrible because he has to go to work every day. He can't afford to take a day off. The way society has put it, the man is the breadwinner in the family.

And that must be a lot of stress on you, like thinking — "I have to go to work, I have no choice, I have to work full-time. If I don't work full-time, then we don't get our money and we don't survive". . . . I never thought of staying home for long. I really enjoy getting out. And I think as soon as you lose your workplace friends, you become all your husband's friends kind of thing. And you don't have that other outlet who understand how you think . . . or you could talk about that, and laugh about — there's just the whole different feel, that's all.

Steelworkers' wives, whether employed or full-time homemakers, tended to be quite pragmatic about the possibility of women's employment at Stelco, not articulating any notion that the work is too much for women:

> I think it's great if women can handle the work.

> If they do their job . . . why not?

The employed wives of steelworkers in general expressed support for women steelworkers, and some also saw benefits to male entry into female job ghettos:

> I think the Women Into Stelco Campaign was a good idea. I feel work should be shared, no matter, anywhere. We've just hired our first male nurse. Some said there was just no way that there'd ever be men in our workplace. It's good, because they're stronger and a lot of those patients are just dead weight, you know. . . . Surely if they got through nursing school, they're just as smart as we are. It's just so silly. So, really, I can't see that it would be any problem down at the steel mill. If there's girls that can do the work, why not?

Women steelworkers noted the extensive resistance to their presence and explained it in terms of masculine ideologies:

> I think a lot of the men were threatened . . . here was a woman coming along who said she could do it just as well as they could.

Despite the common tendency for male steel-workers to construe their gender identities through their perceptions of their jobs as tough and dangerous, the presence of committed, full-time women steelworkers through the divisions of the Hilton Works began seriously to erode the basis of the masculinist ideology of steelwork.

The women recognized the masculine shop-floor culture and argued that men felt very threatened when women entered those previously all-male terrains. In particular, they suggested that men were embarrassed to have their shop-floor cultural practices made public to women:

It is like a sub-culture at Stelco. . . . The men at Stelco whose every second word is fuck . . . you meet them on the street with their families and a bad word would never cross their lips. . . . Some of us women who lived in Hamilton and maybe had their wives for neighbours saw the other side and I think that was a threat to some of them.

For them it's like having two personalities. Like Jekyll and Hyde sort of thing . . . At work they swear, they throw their garbage on the floor. I'm sure they don't do that at home. . . . They're like kids at work . . . and I could just see them go home and be you know, straight and narrow, very serious with their wives, and as soon as they get to work it's crazy . . . .Some of them just cannot handle women being in their line of work.

They also noted that the presence of women challenged and undermined the basic premises of the male-breadwinner ideology and the sex/gender division of labour itself:

The man goes out and does the job, it doesn't matter how he does it, he's got to make a lot of money and the women stay home and take care of the children. . . . It's a very nice, well-ordered life and we were changing that order. Not only were we working with them, many of us were also going home and doing what their wives were doing as well and it was very difficult for some of them.

In fact, the challenge to the masculine ideology of work potentially reveals the actual oppressive character of that work. Occasionally, the words of the men themselves offered a glimmer of insight into the way in which concepts of masculinity at the workplace hinder a clear critique of the work itself. In defending the principle that steelmaking is men's work and unsuitable for women, one man implied that there are problems with anyone doing the work:

It's dirty, heavy, it's no climate for a woman. The men's world is a little rougher than the women's. Physically a man is in better shape. Men are more mechanically minded. . . . There is nothing wrong with women, it's just that sometimes with heavy work . . . Everywhere you find place for some women, could be as strong as men, you know. But if you take the overall picture, muscularity has always been the man's. It doesn't mean that he has more brains because that is not true, but muscularity. I think that women should be outside. It is no place for women. I hate it.

Women steelworkers have most clearly perceived the limits of the masculinist ideology of steel work: "I've never seen a job that I couldn't do or any other women couldn't do. Men will say this is no place for a woman, but it's not really good for men either."

Some men who defended women's general employment rights displayed ambivalence about them as steelworkers either because their capabilities may be more limited or on the basis that they are taking jobs away from men:

Philosophically, I have to agree that [women] have the same right in the marketplace as I do. . . . In an environment like Stelco, I agree she has the right to be there, but in a life-threatening situation I wouldn't want my life being dependent on how she is going to react to that situation at that time, and we do get into some precarious positions. . . . If you were to carry it a step farther, if you are going to allow them into the marketplace, you are going to have to at some time or other approach the subject of them in positions of supervision, and how well a female supervisor on a bull gang would go I really wouldn't even like to speculate. But we can't promote them all to the main office and we can't keep them all at the lower end.

Other men expressed more direct antagonism to women steelworkers, arguing that they posed a direct threat to men's breadwinner power:

> There were a lot of men who could do these jobs. We've had quite a few cases of women who have gone to Stelco to work whose husbands work there. There were a lot of men who have families who got laid off. That's what most guys object to — I was laid off, she's taking over my job. They were making $500 to $600 a week. You lose your house, you lose your car, you lose your wife. . . .

Some of the women steelworkers noted that men were opposed to hiring women because so many men were unemployed: "They figured it was a man's job, a man's world, and there are a lot of unemployed men still out there."

Steelworkers and their spouses were very aware of actual or threatened unemployment. At the time of the study, about 5000 Stelco production workers had been let go and many more had received layoff notices. As many other workplaces in Hamilton were also laying off, most Hamilton residents had close contact with someone unemployed (Webber 1986). This fear and the realistic assessment of the basic injustice of wealth engendered in many a strong sense that it is unfair that some households have two "good incomes" while others have none. A male steelworker explained:

> What really bothers me is where there are two breadwinners. That's not fair. I don't care who the breadwinner is, the man or the woman, but there shouldn't be two breadwinners in some families when some people have no jobs. I know everyone wants to get ahead, but it's not fair when some have no jobs.

While the vast majority were unable to think about this in class terms, not able to make the leap to criticizing the existence of the real inequalities of wealth (Livingstone and Mangan, forthcoming), they found it hard to break with the notion of one primary breadwinner. Most acknowledged circumstances in which the woman might well be the breadwinner but still felt that ideally the man should be. They could also accept circumstances in which both men and women were employed but the woman had a conventional (lower paid) "woman's job." However, they were strongly hostile to households in which both partners in a couple were employed in "good" paying jobs. A male steelworker insisted:

> If she has to go out and work, then she should be the breadwinner and the man should stay home. I feel there should only be one in the family, because there's so many people out of work right now.

For many women and men who accepted the idea of the male-breadwinner norm, the employment of women at Stelco could be tolerated only if those women were required by necessity to take on the breadwinner role themselves. Unmarried women or women with husbands who were unemployed were acceptable, women married to employed men, especially those employed at Stelco or at equally well-paying jobs, were not:

> If a woman has a family to support and she wants some place where she is going to make some decent money, then she has got every right to be at Stelco that I do.

Other men were more ambivalent about the issue:

> Well, of course there are so many different things to look at today because with single parenthood, some of these women doing jobs, you know. But sometimes I see women going in, taking jobs away from a family man or something like that. But I don't feel no animosity towards them . . . I guess everybody wants a job. The way it is today, it's hard to

survive unless you have got a job. So I don't
know, I wouldn't say it's good and I wouldn't
say it's bad. I just have a middle-of-the-road
feeling about it.

Because so many male steelworkers were
outright antagonistic to or at best ambivalent
about the employment of women in the plant,
the women who started at Stelco were, at least
initially, greeted with considerable resistance.
As a result of the campaign and because there
were so few women, each was highly noticeable in her work site. Most of them described
being tested by male co-workers. Several, especially those who had led the campaign, were
harassed both by fellow workers and by fore-
men (Gray 1984; 1986). They felt management was not seriously committed to gender
equality in hiring. Despite this, most expressed satisfaction with their jobs and said
that after a few months they ceased to be perceived merely as women intruders and became
Stelco workers like everyone else (Luxton
forthcoming).

As one man described his observations of
that process:

> I would be working say in the open hearth
> and they would be there working. I found
> eventually they just seemed to fall in with the
> flow with the guys. You had to be kind of,
> you know, I wouldn't say hard-nosed, except
> the camaraderie or the language or whatever
> maybe. Don't let it bother you to work with
> a woman, so I had no problems with it, you
> know. . . . There was one lady in yard serv-
> ices, to me she was just like a typical guy. She
> went out and drank with the guys. She didn't
> seem any different to what a guy was. If you
> went out and everybody was swearing, than
> she would go along with the flow. But she
> wasn't a bad person all the same.

The actual experience of working closely
with women was the most effective antidote
to male scepticism about women's capacity to
do the work:

> As far as I'm concerned, you are a person.
> If you want to do the job, you do the job.

I will train you and that is it. . . . They gave
me one woman that gave the company trouble.
They were looking for ways to fire her. We
trained her and the foreman used to come out
every day hollering "Where the hell is she?"
I said to the foreman, she is not giving me
any trouble. She is doing one hell of a job.
And then they gave her a lay-off paper. The
day that she went, I said, "You know, you have
been one of the best skillmen, ever." She just
looked at me.

> One woman that worked in our department
> was good and better than some of the young
> fellows. She had the right personality and the
> right character to fit into our department. . . .
> She knew her job. It took her a while but she
> knew her job. I have no qualms about working
> with a woman like that.

The recognition that women can actually
do most of the work (cf. Deaux and Ullman
1983) has encouraged some male steelworkers, particularly those with employed
wives and more secure jobs, to express explicit
support for the principle of gender equality
even in Stelco:

> My wife works in a factory. . . . I had a woman
> on my crew. I don't think she made any dif-
> ference. I think it's *natural*. I think what we've
> done in the last 40 years is unnatural, in the
> fact that it was an all-male environment. Steel
> making is not, doesn't require a great amount
> of brawn. It's pretty well a push-button busi-
> ness now.

> Me, I don't care if it is a man or a woman.
> Black, white, purple, it don't matter to me,
> you know . . . I am not prejudiced about any-
> thing. There is only one thing. If she cannot
> do the job, then I think there should be some-
> thing done about it, because then it's not fair.

Concluding Remarks

Our findings show that male steelworkers,
who are widely regarded as occupying one of
the strongest bastions of working-class mas-

culinist ideology, strongly supported a general rhetoric of gender equality, as well as giving formal support through their union to the campaign to hire women. Some of these men were fully committed to women's equality. However, many men continued to believe that steelmaking should be men's work and that men should be primary breadwinners. Those male steelworkers who were more ambivalent about asserting the validity of the male-breadwinner norm, and those who, despite massive layoffs in Stelco, expressed support for women's equal right to scarce jobs, tended to be men who had had direct experiences of women's employment. Either their wives had significant employment experience or they themselves had worked with women. Among the wives of steelworkers, their own employment experiences obviously sharply affected their adherence to male-breadwinner ideologies, but even a majority of full-time housewives expressed general support for women working in traditional male jobs, like steel. Clearly, the male-breadwinner norm as a basis of gender identity is undergoing modifications in steelworker families, as well as in Canadian society generally. Such changes in gender consciousness are occurring primarily in response to the growing importance of married women as essential wage-earners, but are also stimulated by the women's movement (in this case the explicitly feminist Women Back Into Stelco campaign).

These findings are suggestive in several ways. They indicate that a strong adherence to a hegemonic masculinist ideology — to the male-breadwinner norm and the assumption that steelmaking is men's work — can inhibit the development of oppositional working-class consciousness in settings that are usually presumed to be most conducive to such development. Many other factors besides production relations per se, particularly household relations and gender, race, ethnicity, and age, shape people's consciousness. Further analyses of class and gender consciousness need to account for the complex interplay of various formative experiences rather than assume the determining force of one.

Our study further suggests that claims for a widespread "women's consciousness" do not appear to be very useful at the level of particular household and workplace analyses. At this level, there appears to be very little shared consciousness; instead, the range and variation of gender consciousness, for both women and men, requires explanation. This case study confirms the usefulness of recent Marxist–feminist perspectives, which recognize that class and gender relations are constituted through practices in at least two primary spheres of activity, paid workplaces and households.

Finally, the study also shows that, despite the discernible impact of feminism on Canadian trade-union practices (Maroney 1983) including steelworkers Local 1005 at Stelco, the language forms and prevalent social practices of the steel mill shop-floor culture clearly remain assertively masculine. Gender-based power asymmetries and the male gender consciousness that accompanies them are still strongly entrenched.

Women may have demonstrated that steelmaking is not exclusively men's work, but the majority of male steelworkers remain sceptical. With the massive layoffs in steel, almost all the women have been laid off from Stelco, thus the challenge to traditions of masculine shop-floor culture has been, for the moment, aborted. However, while the majority of men in steel still defend their right to employment before women, asserting the primacy of the male-breadwinner norm over women's full equality, there is clearly a growing tension between that ideology and women's increasing demonstration of their employment capabilities even in the most exclusive male preserves.

Notes

1. "Sex" and "gender" are terms central to this literature but enormous confusion surrounds their current usage. "Sex" refers first of all to the biological characteristics that distinguish females and

males — genital structure, hormonal proportions, the capacity to bear children or lack thereof, etc. The term "gender" was introduced to refer to the attributes and behaviours surrounding sex that are clearly social rather than biological. This very useful distinction has increasingly been obscured by an all-too-frequent conflation of the two terms. So, for example, the York guidelines for curricula vitae ask for gender, to which the obvious answer can only be "feminine with masculine tendencies on Monday mornings." In this paper we use "sex" to refer to those characteristics clearly attributable to biology, and "gender" to those that are clearly sociological. As the boundaries between the two are contentious and as the two usually interact where both are probably operative, we follow Gayle Rubin (1975) and refer to sex/gender. When referring to the literature, we use the terminology of that literature.

2. See Barrett (1980), Anderson (1983), Eisenstein (1984), and Maroney and Luxton (1987b). Connell (1985, 261) has aptly characterized the scope of these present studies of gender relations as "a network of insights and arguments about . . . the social subordination of women, and the cultural practices that sustain it; the politics of sexual object-choice, and particularly the oppression of homosexual people; the sexual division of labour; the formation of character and motive, so far as they are organized as femininity and masculinity; the role of the body in social relations, expecially the politics of childbirth; and the nature and strategies of sexual liberation movements."

3. As Weigert, Teitge, and Teitge (1986, 68–69) point out, gender identity (internalized sociocultural meanings and expectations accompanying the normal sense of maleness or femaleness), sex identity (based on biological criteria of genetic and physiological classifications), and sexual identity (in terms of preference for sexual activity with a particular gender) are often conflated in the general literature; all three interactively influence the individual's personal identification with self and others.

4. For a fuller critical review of this tendency, see Connell (1985).

5. For an excellent critical review of the literature on women's consciousness, see Lynne Marks (1987). We are also grateful for her important work theorizing the concept of women's culture (personal communication).

6. For more detailed discussion of these aspects, see for example Mann (1973), and Livingstone (1976, 1985).

7. This set of beliefs corresp[onds] eral ideology. Liberalism, an[d] feminism, has a major contr[a] On the one hand, liberalism [] opportunity for all, treating b[] as potentially equal individual[s] liberal theory supports a sex-[] bour in which men should b[e] ......ners for women who should be dependent wives and mothers. This contradiction has proved very difficult for liberalism. An early proponent of liberal feminism, John Stuart Mill, resolved it by insisting that women could do anything they wanted, but the vast majority would (should) desire to be dependent wives and mothers.

8. However, recent ethnographic studies of the experiences and perceptions of ruling-class and working-class boys and girls in school and family settings (Connell et al. 1982; Anyon 1984; Russell 1987; Valli 1987) show how this stereotype at the root of gender consciousness continues to be reproduced and modified in the "next generation," despite dramatic changes in women's work.

9. In our 1983 random sample of steelworkers, fewer than 2 percent were women. Fewer than 2 percent of male steelworkers and no stewards were born outside European or North American locations. One steward was a Canadian Indian; other respondents may, of course, have been black or some other visible nonwhite. All of the men steelworkers and their wives who were interviewed in the followup study were white. All of the women steelworkers interviewed were white.

10. It is interesting that most studies of masculine ideology at work are of working-class jobs; there are few, if any, of professional occupations. The closest are Kanter (1977), Lafontaine (1983), and Patterson and Engelberg (1978). More comparable work is necessary on proprietary-class and professional- and managerial-class occupations in which the incumbents typically exercise more discretionary control over subsequent conditions of entry and exit and thereby the continuing creation of workplace culture.

11. All statistical differences reported in the text are significant at least at the .05 level of confidence.

Works Cited

Abu-Lughad, Lila. 1985. "Community of Secrets: the Separate World of Bedouin women." *Signs* 10 (Summer): 637–57.

...son, Kristi, and Elizabeth A. Cook. 1985. "Women, Work and Political Attitudes." *American Journal of Political Science* 29(3): 606–25.

Anderson, M.L. 1983. *Thinking About Women: Sociological and Feminist Perspectives*. New York: Macmillan.

Anthias, F., and N. Yuval-Davis. 1983. "Contextualizing Feminism — Gender, Ethnic and Class Divisions." *Feminist Review* 15 (November): 62–75.

Anyon, Jean. 1984. "Intersections of Gender and Class: Accommodation and Resistance by Working-Class and Affluent Females to Contradictory Sex Role Ideologies." *Journal of Education* 166(1): 25–48.

Archer, John, and Barbara Lloyd. 1984. *Sex and Gender*. New York: Cambridge University Press.

Armstrong, Pat. 1984. *Labour Pains: Women's Work in Crisis*. Toronto: Women's Press.

Barrett, M. 1980. *Women's Oppression Today*. London: Verso.

Barrett, Michele, and Mary McIntosh. 1982. *The Anti-Social Family*. London: Verso.

Bartky, S. 1975. "Toward a Phenomenology of Feminist Consciousness." *Social Theory and Practice* 3(4): 425–39.

Bashevkin, Sylvia B. 1984. "Social Feminism and the Study of American Public Opinion." *International Journal of Women's Studies* 7(1): 47–56.

Bem, S.L. 1981. "Gender Schema Theory: A Cognitive Account of Sex Typing." *Psychological Review* 88: 354–64.

Benson, Susan. 1983. "The Customer Ain't God: The Work Culture of Department Store Saleswomen 1890–1940." *Working Class America*. Eds. Michael Frisch and Daniel Walkowitz. Urbana: University of Illinois Press. 185–211.

Black, D., and G. Creese. 1986. "Class, Gender and Politics in Canada." Unpublished paper, Department of Sociology, Carleton University, Ottawa.

Boyd, Monica. 1984. *Canadian Attitudes Toward Women: Thirty Years of Change*. Ottawa: Minister of Supply and Services.

Brittan, A., and M. Maynard. 1985. *Sexism, Racism and Oppression*. Oxford: Basil Blackwell.

Brod, H., ed. 1987. *The Making of Maculinities: The New Men's Studies*. Beverly Hills: Sage.

Buchbinder, Howard. 1987. "Male Heterosexuality: The Socialized Penis Revisited." *Who's on Top: The Politics of Heterosexuality*. Eds. H. Buchbinder, V. Burstyn, D. Forbes, and M. Steadman. Toronto: Garamond. 63–82.

Cameron, Ardis. 1985. "Bread and Roses Revisited: Women's Culture and Working Class Activism in the Lawrence Strike of 1912." *Women, Work and Protest: A Century of US Women's Labor History*. Ed. Ruth Milkman. Boston: Routledge and Kegan Paul. 42–81.

Caplan, Temma. 1982. "Female Consciousness and Collective Action: The Case of Barcelona 1910–1918." *Signs* 7(3): 545–66.

Carrigan, T., R.W. Connell, and J. Lee. 1985. "Toward a New Sociology of Masculinity." *Theory and Society* 14: 551–604.

Chafetz, Janet Saltzman. 1984. *Sex and Advantage: A Comparative Macro-Structural Theory of Sex Stratification*. Totowa, NJ: Rowman and Allanheld.

Cockburn, Cynthia. 1983. *Brothers; Male Dominance and Technological Change*. London: Pluto.

———. 1985. *Machinery of Dominance: Women, Men and Technical Know-How*. London: Pluto.

Connell, R.W. 1985. "Theorizing Gender." *Sociology* 19(2): 260–72.

Connell, R.W., et al. 1982. *Making the Difference: Schools, Families and Social Division*. Sydney: Allen and Unwin.

Corman, J. 1988. "Employment and Household Constraints on the Number of Social Ties." Paper presented at Canadian Sociology and Anthropology Meetings, University of Windsor, June.

Costello, Cynthia B. 1985. "WEA're Worth It! Work Culture and Conflict at the Wisconsin Education Association Insurance Trust." *Feminist Studies* 11(3): 496–518.

Cott, Nancy. 1977. *The Bonds of Womanhood: "Women's Sphere" in New England 1780–1835*. New Haven.

Daly, Mary. 1978. *Gynaecology, the Metaethics of Radical Feminism*. Boston: Beacon.

Davidoff, L., and C. Hall. 1987. *Family Fortunes: Men and Women of the English Middle Class 1780–1850*. London: Hutchison.

Davis, Angela. 1981. *Women, Race and Class*. London: Women's Press.

Deaux, K., and J. Ullman. 1983. *Women of Steel: Female Blue-Collar Workers in the Basic Steel Industry*. New York: Praeger.

de Beauvoir, S. 1949 (1972) *The Second Sex*. Harmondsworth: Penguin.

Delphy, C. 1979. *The Main Enemy*. London: Women's Research and Resource Centre.

Dixon, Marlene. 1983. *The Future of Women*. San Francisco: Synthesis.

Downing, Nancy E., and Dristin L. Roush. 1985. "From Passive Acceptance to Active Commitment: A Model of Feminist Identity Development for Women." *Counselling Psychologist* 13(4): 695–709.

Eason, J., D. Field, and J. Santucci. 1983. "Working Steel." *Hard Earned Wages: Women Fighting for Better Work*. Ed. Jennifer Penney. Toronto: Women's Educational Press. 191–218.

Eisenstein, H. 1984. *Contemporary Feminist Thought*. London: Allen and Unwin.

Eisenstein, Sarah. 1983. *Give Us Bread But Give Us Roses: Working Women's Consciousness in the United States 1890-to the First World War*. London: Routledge and Kegan Paul.

Emmison, M. 1985. "Class Images of 'the Economy': Opposition and Ideological Incorporation Within Working Class Consciousness." *Sociology* 19(1): 19–38.

Ferree, Myra Marx. 1983. "The Women's Movement in the Working Class." *Sex Roles* 9(4): 493–505.

Figueira-McDonough, Josefina. 1985. "Gender, Race and Class: Differences in Levels of Feminist Orientation." *The Journal of Applied Behavioral Science* 21(2): 121–42.

Firestone, S. 1971. *The Dialectic of Sex*. New York: Bantam.

Game, A., and R. Pringle. 1983. *Gender at Work*. Sydney: Allen and Unwin.

Gerson, Kathleen. 1985. *Hard Choices: How Women Decide about Work, Career, and Motherhood*. Berkeley: University of California Press.

Gibbs, Margaret S. 1985. "The Instrumental-Expressive Dimension Revisited." *Academic Psychology Bulletin* 7(2): 145–55.

Giordano, P.C., and S.A. Cernkovich. 1979. "On Complicating the Relationships between Liberation and Delinquency." *Social Problems* 26: 467–81.

Goldberg, Roberta. 1984. "The Determination of Consciousness Through Gender, Family, and Work Experience." *The Social Science Journal* 21(4): 75–85.

Gottfried, Heidi, and D. Fasenfest. 1984. "Gender and Class Formation: Female Clerical Workers." *Review of Radical Political Economy* 16(1): 89–103.

Gramsci, A. 1971. *Selections from the Prison Notebooks*. New York: International.

Gray, Stan. 1984. "Sharing the Shop Floor." *Canadian Dimension* 18(2): 17–32.

———. 1986. "Fight to Survive — the Case of Bonita Clark." *Canadian Dimension* 20(3): 15–20.

Green, P. 1979. "The Feminist Consciousness." *Sociological Quarterly* 20(Summer): 359–74.

Gurin, P., H. Miller, and G. Gurin. 1980. "Stratum Identification and Consciousness." *Social Psychology Quarterly* 43: 30–47.

Gurin, Patricia. 1985. "Women's Gender Consciousness." *The Public Opinion Quarterly* 49(2): 143–63.

Hraba, Joseph, and Paul Yarborough. 1983. "Gender Consciousness and Class Action for Women: a Comparison of Black and White Female Adolescents." *Youth and Society* 15(2): 115–31.

Huber, Joan, and Glenna Spitze. 1983. *Sex Stratification: Children, Houseworks and Jobs*. New York: Academic.

Hunt, Pauline. 1980. *Gender and Class Consiousness*. London: Macmillan.

Jaggar, Alison. 1983. *Feminist Politics and Human Nature*. New York: Rowman and Allanheld.

Kanter, Rosabeth. 1977. *Men and Women of the Corporation*. New York: Basic.

Kasper, A.S. 1986. "Consciousness Re-evaluated: Interpretive Theory and Feminist Scholarship." *Sociological Inquiry* 65(1): 30–49.

Katznelson, I., and A. Zolberg, eds. 1986. *Working Class Formation*. Princeton: Princeton University Press.

Kaufman, M., ed. 1987. *Beyond Patriarchy: Essay by Men on Pleasure, Power, and Change*. Toronto: Oxford University Press.

Komarovsky, M. 1946. "Cultural Contradictions and Sex Roles." *American Journal of Sociology* 52: 184–89.

Lafontaine, Edward. 1983. "Forms of False Consciousness Among Professional Women." *Humbolt Journal of Social Relations* 10(2): 26–46.

Lamphere, Louise. 1985. "Bringing the Family to Work: Women's Culture on the Shop Floor." *Feminist Studies* 11(3): 519–40.

Lerner, Gerda. 1986. *The Creation of Patriarchy*. London: Oxford.

Lippert, J. 1977. "Sexuality as Consumption." *For Men Against Sexism*. Ed. J. Snodgrass. Albion, CA: Times Change. 207–13.

Livingstone, D.W. 1976. "On Hegemony in Corporate Capitalist States." *Sociological Inquiry* 46(3–4): 235–50.

———. 1985. *Social Crisis and Schooling*. Toronto: Garamond Press.

Livingstone, D.W., and J.M. Mangan. Forthcoming. "Class, Gender and Expanded Class Consciousness in Steeltown." *Research in Inequality and Social Conflict*. Eds. M. Dobkowski and I. Wallimann. Greenwich: JAI Press.

Luxton, Meg. 1987. "Thinking about the Future." *Family Matters: Sociology and Contemporary Ca-*

nadian Families. Eds. K. Anderson et al. Toronto: Methuen. 237–60.

———. Forthcoming. "Getting to Work: The Challenge of the Women Back into Stelco Campaign."

Luxton, Meg, D.W. Livingstone, and W. Seccombe. 1982. "Steelworker Families: Workplace, Household and Community in Hamilton." A Research Proposal to the SSHRC

Mann, M. 1973. *Consciousness and Action Among the Western Working Class.* London: Macmillan.

Mansbridge, Jane. 1986. *Why We Lost the ERA.* Chicago: University of Chicago Press.

Marks, Lynne. 1987. "Can Women Have a Culture and Consciousness Just Like the Working Class and If Not, Why Not?" Unpublished paper, Department of History, York University.

Maroney, H.J. 1983. "Feminism at Work." *New Left Review* 141(September-October): 51–71.

Maroney, H.J., and Meg Luxton. 1987a. "From Feminism and Political Economy to Feminist Political Economy." *Feminism and Political Economy.* Eds. Maroney and Luxton. Toronto: Methuen. 5–28.

———. 1987b. *Feminism and Political Economy: Women's Work, Women's Struggle.* Toronto: Methuen.

Mason, K., and L. Bumpass. 1975. "U.S. Women's Sex Role Ideology, 1970." *American Journal of Sociology* 80: 1212–19.

Mead, M. 1950. *Male and Female.* London: Gollancz.

Meissner, Martin. 1986. "The Reproduction of Women's Domination in Organizational Communication." *Organization-Communication: Emerging Perspectives I.* Ed. L. Thayer. Norwood: Ablex.

Mitchell, J. 1966. "Women: The Longest Revolution." *New Left Review.* 40: (November-December).

———. 1971. *Women's Estate.* Harmondsworth: Penguin.

Mitchell, Juliet, and Ann Oakley, eds. 1986. *What Is Feminism: A Re-examination.* New York: Pantheon.

Morgan, Robin. 1984. *Sisterhood Is Global: the International Women's Movement Anthology.* Garden City, NY: Anchor.

Murphy, Yolanda, and Robert Murphy. 1974. *Women of the Forest.* New York: Columbia University Press.

O'Brien, M. 1981. *The Politics of Reproduction.* London: Routledge and Kegan Paul.

Parsons, T., and R.F. Bales. 1953. *Family, Socialization and Interaction Process.* London: Routledge and Kegan Paul.

Patterson, Michele, and Laurie Engelberg. 1978. "Women in Male Dominated Professions." *Women Working: Theories and Facts in Perspective.* Eds. A. Stromberg and S. Harkess. Palo Alto, CA: Mayfield. 266–92.

Percival, Terrance Q., and Elizabeth F. Percival. 1986. "The Oppositional Structure of Implicit Theories of Masculinity and Femininity, Identity and Attitudes Toward Women." *Atlantis* 11(2): 47–58.

Petchesky, Rosalind. 1984. *Abortion and Woman's Choice: The State, Sexuality, and Reproductive Freedom.* New York: Longman.

Pettigrew, Joyce. 1981. "Reminiscences of Fieldwork among the Sikhs." *Doing Feminist Research.* Ed. Helen Roberts. London: Routledge and Kegan Paul. 62–81.

Pollert, Anna. 1981. *Girls, Wives, Factory Lives.* London: Macmillan.

———. 1983. "Women, Gender Relations and Wage Labour." *Gender, Class and Work.* Eds. Eva Gamarnikow et al. London: Heinemann. 96–114.

Porter, Marilyn. 1983. *Home, Work and Class Consciousness.* Manchester: Manchester University Press.

Rapp, Rayna. 1978. "Family and Class in Contemporary America: Notes Toward and Understanding of Ideology." *Science and Society* 42(3): 278–300.

Reid, Angus. 1987. *Canadian's Views of the Role of Women in Society.* Winnipeg: Angus Reid Associates, January 24.

Ross, E. 1983. "Survival Networks: Woman's Neighbourhood Sharing in London." *History Workshop Journal* 15. 4–27.

Rowbotham, S. 1974. *Woman's Consciousness, Man's World.* Harmondsworth: Penguin.

Rubin, G. 1975. "The Traffic in Women: Notes on the 'Political Economy' of Sex." *Toward an Anthropology of Women.* Ed. R. Reiter. New York: Monthly Review. 157–210.

Ruch, Libby, O. 1984. "Dimensionality of the Bem Sex Role Inventory: A Multidimensional Analysis." *Sex Roles* 10(1–2): 99–117.

Russell, S. 1987. "The Hidden Curriculum of School: Reproducing Gender and Class Hierarchies." *Feminism and Political Economy.* Eds. H.J. Maroney and M. Luxton. Toronto: Methuen. 229–46.

Seccombe, Wally. 1980. "Domestic Labour and the Working Class Household." *Hidden in the Household.* Ed. B. Fox. Toronto: Women's Educational Press. 25–99.

Shulman, A.K. 1980. "Gender and Power: Gender Bases of Radical Feminism." *Signs* 5(Summer): 590–604.

Simpson, J., and E. Mutran. 1981. "Women's Social Consciousness: Sex or Worker Identity." *Research in the Sociology of Work I.* Eds. R.L. Simpson and I.H. Simpson. Greenwich, CT: JAI. 335–50.

Smith, D.E. 1978. "A Peculiar Eclipsing: Women's Exclusion from Man's Culture." *Women's Studies International Quarterly* 1: 281–95.

Smith, M.D., and L.J. Fisher. 1982. "Sex Role Attitudes and Social Class: A Reanalysis and Clarification." *Journal of Comparative Family Studies* (Spring): 77–88.

Smith, Tom. 1985. "Working Wives and Women's Rights: The Connection Between the Employment Status of Wives and the Feminist Attitudes of Husbands." *Sex Roles* 12(5–6): 501–8.

Smith-Rosenberg, Carol. 1980. "Politics and History in Women's Culture." *Feminist Studies* 6(1): 55–64.

Spence, J.T., and R.L. Helmreich. 1978. *Masculinity and Femininity: Their Psychological Dimensions, Correlates and Antecedents.* Austin, TX: University of Texas Press.

Stanley, Liz, and Sue Wise. 1983. *Breaking Out: Feminist Consciousness and Feminist Research.* London: RKP.

Stewart, Katie. 1981. "The Marriage of Capitalist and Patriarchal Ideologies: Meanings of Male Bonding and Male Ranking in U.S. Culture." *Women and Revolution.* Ed. L. Sargent. Montreal: Black Rose. 269–311.

Stimpson, Catharine R. 1984. "Women as Knowers." *Feminist Visions: Toward a Transformation of the Liberal Arts Curriculum.* Eds. D. Fowlkes and C. McClure. University, AL: University of Alabama Press. 15–24.

Thompson, Edward H., et al. 1985. "Attitudes Toward the Male Role and Their Correlates." *Sex Roles* 13(7–8): 413–27.

Thornton, G., D. Alwin, and D. Camburn. 1983. "Causes and Consequences of Sex-Role Attitudes and Attitude Change." *American Sociological Review* 48: 211–17.

Thornton, M. 1980. "Work and Consciousness." *Work and Inequality II.* Eds. P. Boreham and G. Dow. London: Macmillan. 198–229.

Tiano, S., and Bracken, K. 1984. "Ideology on the Line: A Typology for the Analysis of Assembly Line Workers' Images of Class and Gender Relations." *Quarterly Journal of Ideology* 8(4): 60–71.

Tolson, A. 1977. *The Limits of Masculinity.* London: Tavistock.

Turnbull, C. 1981. "MBUTI Womanhood." *Woman, the Gatherer.* Ed. F. Dahlberg. New Haven: York University Press. 205–19.

Valli, Linda. 1987. *Becoming Clerical Workers.* London: Routledge and Kegan Paul.

Vogel, L. 1986. "Feminist Scholarship: The Impact of Marxism." *The Left Academy 3.* Eds. B. Ollman and E. Vernoff. New York: Praeger. 1–34.

Webber, M.J. 1986. "Regional Production and the Production of Regions: The Case of Steeltown." *Production Work, Territory: The Geographical Anatomy of Industrial Capitalism.* Eds. M.J. Scott and M. Sturper. Boston: Allen and Unwin. 197–224.

Weigert, A.J., J. Smith Teitge, and D.W. Teitge. 1986. *Society and Identity: Toward a Sociological Psychology.* New York: Cambridge University Press.

Werner, Paul D., and Georgina W. La Russa. 1985. "Persistence and Change in Sex-Role Stereotypes." *Sex Roles* 12(9–10): 1089–100.

Westwood, Sallie. 1984. *All Day Every Day: Factory and Family in the Making of Women's Lives.* London: Pluto.

Willis, P. 1979. "Shop-Floor Culture, Masculinity and the Wage Form." *Working Class Culture: Studies in History and Theory.* Eds. J. Clarke et al. London: Hutchinson. 185–98.

Wilson, M., and R. Sennott. 1984. "Means of Knowing in the Neutralization of Women's Consciousness." *Quarterly Journal of Ideology* 8(4): 12–18.

Winter, M.F., and E.F. Robert. 1980. "Male Dominance, Late Capitalis, and the Growth of Instrumental Reason." *Berkeley Journal of Sociology* 24–25: 249–80.

Part Six

PROCREATION AND PARENTHOOD

• • •

God, what a lot we hear about unhappy marriages, and how little we
hear about unhappy sons and
daughters.
Robertson Davies, *Leaven of Malice*
(1954)

The family's functional contributions to society involve not only the procreation of children but also their social placement and upbringing. Our pronatalist values are such that
it is generally assumed that everyone, or almost everyone, will want to have children,
and will actually have them. The universality
of the parenthood mandate also implicitly assumes that everyone has both the motivation
and the capacity to assume parenthood roles.
An array of supporting assumptions are also
found just below the surface. We assume that
the actions of parents will have real consequences for their children, not only for their
present happiness or lack of it, but also in
the long range for their ultimate development
and adjustment. We assume that children
should be raised by both parents, although
the mother–child bond is typically considered
to be more central and more important than
the father–child bond. We assume, moreover,
a benevolent model of parenthood in which
children are valued for their own sake, and
are protected and nurtured in supportive
ways. When we actually begin to look closely
at the parent–child relationship, we find these
"obvious" premises called into question.

When considering how many children they
want to have, a young couple must now consider that the most usual circumstance will
be for both the husband–father and the
wife–mother to work for most of their mar-

ried lives. The wife must ask herself: "How
many children can I cope with while also coping with a job?" He must ask himself: "How
many children can I cope with while my wife
is working?" The trend toward low fertility,
which begins with the redefinition of parenthood as optional, is reinforced by high rates
of female labour-force participation.

Another factor to take into account is the
incidence of broken homes. A wife–mother
now knows, whether or not she cares to admit
it, that divorce is a clear and present danger;
it happens to about one out of three Canadian
couples, and she sees it happening all around
her. She also knows that, in the event of a
divorce, the most usual outcome will be for
her to keep her children, to be entirely responsible for their care, and to be partly if
not entirely responsible for their support. It
cannot be taken for granted that a husband–father will remain in the household and
participate in childrearing.

Therefore, the young husband or wife who
is considering the query: "How many children
do I want to have?" must also consider these
realities and simultaneously consider the
question: "How many children could I cope
with if I had to manage on my own?" The
prospect of being a single parent with one or
two children is considerably less daunting
than the prospect of being a single parent with
three or four.

About the Articles

Little attention is generally paid to the qualifications of persons to perform the parenthood role. Until recently, this issue arose only in the evaluation of persons seeking to adopt children. The increase in divorce has made it necessary to evaluate the relative capacity of mothers and fathers to care for their children and, in the event of divorce, assume custody. Steinhauer provides some criteria for assessing parenting capacity. His discussion is motivated by issues of custody, but his guidelines regarding quality of attachment, responsiveness, acceptance, and transmission of values pose questions that are as valid for teenagers contemplating their first pregnancy as for gay couples contemplating adoption.

The value assigned to the motherhood role has also led to a tendency to blame mothers for any or all of their children's shortcomings. Caplan and Hall-McCorquodale illustrate this systematic bias and offer recommendations for making our assessments of cause and effect in the parent–child relationship more objective and less biased.

While most persons may prefer to raise children in the context of a stable husband–wife family, this is by no means the only circumstance for successful parenting. The concern with lone parents must be viewed in the perspective that, for most persons, being a lone parent is an episode in life rather than a permanent situation. Moore reviews the circumstances that determine the length of time women spend as lone parents.

Although divorce is often a stressful experience, the long-range consequences for parents and children are not always negative. Tuzlak and Hillock conducted interviews with 57 divorced mothers in Toronto and found that, under some circumstances, both mothers and their children function well. Theoretical perspectives that predict negative effects of separation and divorce should be reviewed to reflect changing social realities and the possibility of positive effects.

Our increasing awareness of the dark side of husband–wife relationships that involve domestic violence is paralleled by a comparable increase in our awareness of the dark side in parent–child relationships. Parenting in dysfunctional families may involve physical and/or psychological abuse and neglect. In recent years, we have also become increasingly aware of problems involving sexual abuse, usually but not always involving fathers and daughters. Bagley describes available Canadian data on the incidence and prevalence of this problem, and on some of its long-term effects on mental health.

Further Readings

Caplan, Paula J., et al. 1984. "Toronto Multiagency Child Abuse Research Project: The Abused and the Abuser." *Child Abuse and Neglect* 8: 343–51.

McGillivray, Ann. 1985. "Transracial Adoption and the Status Indian Child." *Canadian Journal of Family Law* 4: 437–67.

Michales, Gerald Y., and Wendy A. Goldberg. 1988. *The Transition to Parenthood: Current Theory and Research*. Cambridge: Cambridge University Press.

Veevers, Jean E. 1980. *Childless by Choice*. Toronto: Butterworths.

Williams, Tannis MacBeth. 1987. "Transition to Motherhood: A Longitudinal Study." *Mental Infant Health Journal* 8: 251–65.

ASSESSING FOR PARENTING CAPACITY*

Paul D. Steinhauer

Developmental prerequisites are reviewed, and guidelines for assessing parents' current ability to provide them are presented. Problems at the interface of the mental-health, child-welfare, and family-court systems are discussed, and a framework for minimizing errors in the assessment of parenting capacity is suggested.

This paper is concerned with the central dilemma faced by child-welfare agencies and family courts, that of when to remove children permanently from their natural families. It is a dilemma because failure to remove a child promptly from a sufficiently pathogenic family can lead to serious and lasting damage, while removal that is premature or based on insufficient information will violate parental rights while, possibly, proving no less damaging to the child in the long run (Tooley 1978). This paper, which is intended as a guide to gathering and assessing the information needed for appropriate decision making, consists of three major sections. The first section attempts to define children's basic developmental needs. The second deals with assessing parents' ability to meet these needs. The third addresses the question of prediction of parenting capacity.

Children's Developmental Needs

All children need a family that is both caring and able to provide the quality and continuity

Source: *American Journal of Orthopsychiatry* 53(4): 468–81. Copyright © 1983 American Orthopsychiatric Association, Inc. Reprinted with permission.

*A revised version of a paper presented to the Ontario Family Court Clinic Conference, May 1981.

of parenting that will foster optimal development. Four dimensions of quality in the parent–child relationship — quality of attachment; ability of parents to perceive and respond to the needs of the child; ability to transmit the values of the culture; and parental rejection, both overt and covert — will be examined, as will the issue of continuity.

Quality of Attachment

The infant's first basic need, a prerequisite for normal development, is for a secure attachment to a primary caregiver, usually but not necessarily the mother. Attachment refers to the bond of caring and craving that ties the child and caregiver to each other. Once formed, the attachment persists, even in the absence of the primary caregiver. Children may form multiple attachments, but the strongest and most significant is usually the attachment to the parents (Ainsworth 1967). This is true, and perhaps even intensified, where children are raised by a homemaker or in day care. The strength of an attachment depends less on time spent together than on the quality of parental involvement and responsiveness to the child. A secure attachment is crucial to the development of trust, the capacity for intimacy, and the formation of self-esteem (Derdeyn 1977; Tizard 1977; Tizard and Hodges 1978; Tizard and Rees 1974; Tizard and Tizard 1975). It also plays a key role in the process of socialization, which prepares children to give up what is, to them, perfectly acceptable behaviour in order to safeguard an attachment (Steinhauer 1980a). A secure attachment will encourage the young child to form secondary attachments to others and to modify undesirable behaviour to please others.

Separation of children from attachment figures — especially those adults whom Goldstein, Freud, and Solnit (1973) have termed the "psychological parents" — precipitates a separation reaction. Some children are more vulnerable to risk than others for various reasons, including their basic temperament (Lander et al. 1978; Madison and Schapiro 1970); degree of prior disturbance in child and family, as well as sex of the child or of a disturbed parent (Orvaschel et al. 1979); the environment before and after separation, and others (Rutter 1979).

Generally speaking, children with anxious and avoidant attachments have more difficulty tolerating separation (Ainsworth 1969; Bowlby 1969). Nevertheless, consistently abusive or neglectful parents may leave no alternative to removing the child and trying to minimize the risks. Rutter (1960) has shown that such children fare better in an adequate substitute family than when left in chronically inadequate biological families. There is danger in taking children into care, even from such families, but the risk of leaving them exposed to chronically inadequate parenting is even greater. Tizard (1977) has shown that repeatedly shuffling children back and forth from home to foster home plays havoc with their emotional development by repeatedly interfering with attachment (Cooper 1978; Goldstein, Freud, and Solnit 1973, 1979). Thus, the earlier one can identify families unable to provide a secure attachment and meet their children's emotional needs, the sooner one can protect children by placing them permanently in adequate substitute families.

Parental Responsiveness

As well as providing a secure attachment, parents need to be able to perceive accurately and respond appropriately to their child's needs. Significant mental retardation, severe depression, and acute or chronic schizophrenia may impair parents' ability to perceive children's needs (Anthony 1970; Chandler 1978; McLean 1976; Roth 1972; Salomon 1981; Speers and Lansing 1965). Parents so psychologically immature or so preoccupied with their own needs that these consistently eclipse those of their children are likely to undermine children's development (Anthony 1970; Roth 1972; Salomon 1981; Speers and Lansing 1965). As children grow older, their needs change. Appropriate parenting demands that parents perceive this and modify their management in response to these changes. The same devotion that helps meet an infant's need for attachment can lead to overprotection, infantilization, and interference with normal individuation if the parents cannot attenuate their involvement to allow the child scope for independent behaviour. Parents whose internalized conflicts from their own pasts lead them to misperceive their child's behaviour — like the mother who considers her three-week-old girl spoiled because she cries, or the mother of a four-week-old who interprets his colic as proof of wilful disobedience and provocation — will likely have trouble responding appropriately to that behaviour.

While mental retardation, depression, and schizophrenia have been suggested as potentially undermining parenting capacity, none of these, in itself, proves an inability to parent. A psychiatric diagnosis is only relevant to parenting capacity insofar as it affects that parent's ability to meet a child's needs. This can only be determined when one knows the nature, extent, and duration of the parental condition; the type of parental behaviour when affected; whether or not there are remissions; how both parents respond during both remissions and exacerbations; the child's age; the extent of the child's needs and ability to understand the behaviour and unresponsiveness of the parent; and the availability of other family members to compensate for the indisposed parent's incapacity by supporting the child in the face of bizarre or unresponsive behaviour. Anthony (1970) has suggested that children cope better with bizarre psychotic behaviour (especially if their reality testing is confirmed by other family members) than they can with either symbiotic and enmeshed or autistic and disengaged behaviour. Thus, severe and chronic depression, insofar as it diminishes parental responsiveness, can prove more damaging and depriving than some forms of schizophrenia. Anthony also distinguished the child who is expected to confirm to the psychotic parent's expectations from others who, while still participating in the delusion, are capable of a double reality-testing through which they escape from the parent's delusional system when away from the parent. In such cases, whether the other parent supports the spouse's delusional system or the child's reality-testing is crucial. Anthony (1970) and Rutter (1971, 1978a) have demonstrated how much a healthy spouse can compensate for the disturbing behaviour of a psychotic parent.

The influence of specific conditions on parenting capacity may be highlighted by considering the likely effect of parenting by a homosexual. In an excellent review, Leverette (n.d.) concluded that while lack of long-term studies makes definite prediction impossible, expert opinion (Green 1979; Kaplan 1979; Marmor 1977; Money 1977) holds that the quality of the relationship with and care of the child are probably more important than the parent's sexual orientation. Green's short-term study (1979) agreed that a child is better off with a loving and competent homosexual parent than with an uncaring, rejecting, or uninterested heterosexual parent.

Mention should be made here of a category of parents who, having been deprived or abused as children, can only accept their children as long as they provide the gratification and sense of adequacy that the parents never experienced when they were young. Such a parent–child relationship is vulnerable, indeed, to abuse (Galdston 1965; Ilfiend 1970; Lystad 1975; Silver, Dublin, and Lourie 1969; Steele and Pollock 1968; Wasserman 1967; Wiltse 1979).

Transmission of Values

From about the time of the child's first birthday, parents' words and deeds are likely to influence the child's perceptions of good and bad, right and wrong (Steinhauer 1980a). Ideally, before adolescence, children will internalize concepts of right and wrong modelled primarily on those of the parents, and will have developed sufficient impulse control to allow them to meet those standards. These personal standards and values will be revised during adolescence as teenagers compare their family's values with those of their peers. But the child who enters adolescence without some internalized values and capacity to bind tension — that is, lacking the ability to contain the urge to act first and ask questions later — will likely have continuing difficulty respecting the rights of others and living in harmony with society. What aspects of parenting contribute to the development of these capacities?

First, the parental values must fit with those of the culture. If, for example, parents belong to a subgroup whose values are incompatible with those of the larger culture, their child may be acculturated to the family but not to the broader community. (For example, a child whose parents and relatives have been in open conflict with the law may be particularly prone to delinquency.) A more complex problem occurs in the children of recent immigrants. Immigrant parents often try to impose on their children the values of the old country, while the children, rejecting these as foreign, strive to adopt the attitudes and behaviour they are exposed to at school. (Examples would be the daughter of a Portuguese or Greek family who refuses to be chaperoned and demands the freedom to date typical American teenagers; the Latvian or Orthodox Jew who marries outside the ethnic group; or the use of physical punishment by West Indian parents.) The values of the parents' culture are not necessarily deviant, but they differ from North American norms. The clash of cultures often leads to extreme family conflict that, if sufficiently violent, sometimes spills over into the community. How far should the community accept behaviour that is deviant by mainstream standards but known to be appropriate in the immigrant culture? How does society balance respect for the family's cultural traditions and its right to freedom from societal interference against its duty to provide protection when legitimately needed by youngsters caught between two cultures?

If parents are to transmit values to their children, they must be consistent in their teaching and expectations. Effective socialization requires minimal discrepancy between stated values and observable parental behaviour; much internalization of values results from identification with parental behaviour (i.e., role modelling), and children are more likely to identify with what parents do than what they say. Parents will distort the values of the child who is the object of their own antisocial impulses, especially when these contravene their stated expectations (Green 1979). Unless treatment alleviates the need of such parents to act out through the child, or the child is protected by separation from the parents, the parents' projection onto the child of unrecognized parental psychopathology may, in time, become a self-fulfilled prophecy (Green 1979; Tizard and Hodges 1978). Finally, the parents must be regularly available — physically and emotionally — to meet the child's needs, to serve as identification figures or role models, and to enforce the expectations referred to above. Youngsters only learn to control their impulses and bind tension with continual parental availability and follow-through; without it, they remain essentially unsocialized.

Rejection, Overt and Covert

Severe and chronic rejection commonly distorts emotional and personality development. This is easily recognized when overt, or when neglect or abuse is obvious, but is harder to demonstrate when covert or masked by extreme indulgence and overprotection of the child. Parents often repress or try to conceal their rejection to avoid stigma or guilt. Some who enter into recurrent battles for custody or access remain uninterested, neglectful, or abusive, even when they win. The road to many a child's psychological hell is paved by naïve acceptance of verbal statements of parents' good intentions despite a mountain of behavioural evidence to the contrary.

Continuity of Relationship

Children need a continuous relationship with their primary attachment figures, the psychological parents who must meet their biological and psychological needs (Goldstein, Freud, and Solnit 1973, 1979). Most children's biological parents rapidly become their psychological parents as attachment proceeds, but for the infant raised in foster care, the foster parents are likely to assume this role. Once such a child is mature enough to experience separation anxiety — around eight months — any separation from the foster parents, even for reunion with the biological parents, now psychological strangers, may initiate a separation reaction.

As long as the psychological parents are meeting a child's developmental needs, the continuity of their relationship deserves society's protection. The claim of psychological attachment should have primacy in our courts over blood claims, if children's interests are to be served and unnecessary damage avoided (Goldstein, Freud, and Solnit 1973, 1979). Yet, judges too often allow parents custody or access as a biological right, unaware that psychological abandonment has already occurred. Child-welfare agencies may also violate the principle of continuity by separating children from foster parents to whom they are securely attached on the questionable grounds that they are better served by placing them for adoption; in other words, exposing them to yet another unnecessary separation (Goldstein, Freud, and Solnit 1973, 1979). The literature on planned permanent foster care vis-à-vis adoption is far from conclusive (Cooper 1978; Derdyn 1977; Madison and Schapiro 1970; Tizard 1977; Wiltse 1979). There is a major need for controlled studies comparing the stability, long-term benefits, selective use, and risk of each of these forms of long-term placement with regard to breakdown rates and results achieved.

Children between six months and four years are particularly vulnerable to separation because of their time sense and their inability to exist in an emotional vacuum (Goldstein, Freud, and Solnit 1973, 1979). At this age, dependency is maximal, while the capacity to mourn successfully the feelings stirred up by separation is particularly limited (Furman 1974). Toddlers have little ability to tolerate anxiety without having to repress it, and can rarely conceptualize and articulate their feelings to allow concerned adults to provide the assistance they need to mourn successfully (Goldstein, Freud, and Solnit 1973). Generally speaking, the more continuity is disrupted, be it through multiple moves or through being left too long in limbo while wardship and future plans are being contested, the greater the risk of severe and lasting personality damage (Derdyn 1977; Freud 1960; Goldstein, Freud, and Solnit 1973, 1979; Madison & Schapiro 1970; Pike 1976; Steinhauer 1980b; Tizard 1977; Wiltse 1979). Many juvenile court judges, lawyers, and even child-welfare workers still do not fully appreciate how damaging it is for children to be left in limbo while their case is adjourned again and again to suit the convenience of the parents or their lawyers.

Assessing Parental Ability

There are basically two tools one can use to assess parenting capacity. The first is a proper history of the child's development and of the parent–child relationship. The second is an assessment of the child in the context of the family; this involves several components, including:

- a developmental assessment of the child;
- a psychiatric assessment of the child's current mental status;
- a systematic assessment of the current family situation, particularly of the parents' ability to meet the child's needs; and
- further assessment of either or both parents, if indicated.

History

To assess parenting capacity, a systematic history of the child's development, focussing on parent–child relationships and parental attitudes toward the child, should be the starting point. Did the child result from a planned pregnancy? What were each parent's reactions both during pregnancy and following the birth? An ongoing chronological record of the child's physical, cognitive, emotional, and social development should give particular attention to the following:

- any emotional, behavioural, language, or academic problems noted; parental attitudes toward the child in general and any problems noted in particular; the reasons for and apparent effects of disruptions in continuity of the parent–child relationship;
- a history suggestive of failed or insecure attachment, including: persistent detachment, distancing, and isolation; constant attention-seeking, and multiple shallow relationships with failure to distinguish between casual acquaintances and long-term caregivers; multiple separations; parental violence, antisocial behaviour, excessive harshness, or rigidity; overindulgence and permissiveness combined with a lack of appropriate expectations;
- a detailed description of any psychiatric or major social problems affecting the parent or other family members, including the psychiatric diagnosis, if any; the severity and duration of the illness; and the nature and outcome of treatment attempts;
- a verification of information obtained from the parents, to be obtained with their knowledge and consent. Should they refuse

consent, their reasons should be explored and noted, as should previous attempts at intervention, for each of which one would explore: the reasons for the intervention; the referral source; the response to the referral; whether each referral was followed through; the number of involvements in some form of remediation; the nature and duration of each attempted intervention;

• the family's perception of each therapeutic involvement, including: the number and frequency of the sessions; the purpose of the sessions; whether or not they were considered helpful, and why. One would assess the family's level of involvement in each intervention, looking for evidence of whether an alliance between family and worker has been achieved. The reason for the termination — which might range from no further need, to an inability to obtain co-operation — should be noted. A unilateral decision to terminate should be recorded, along with how directly the family stated its reasons for terminating prior to withdrawal. If there were several therapeutic involvements, one should determine how the parents evaluated each, and the concrete results (e.g., measurably improved functioning) that each produced.

A therapeutic failure might result from inadequate treatment rather than from failure by the client to utilize a reasonable intervention. An inadequate intervention is suggested by: irregularly scheduled or frequently cancelled sessions; failure of the worker to deal with obvious but potentially contentious issues; frequent changes of worker; repeated complaints and client discontent, whether or not these appear to be legitimate, as even a questionable criticism would indicate perceived dissatisfaction.

One should also attempt to determine and record the highest level of functioning achieved by child and family over the past year and over the past five years. Doing so forces one not just to compare current and past functioning, but to document otherwise vague statements as to how much, or little, improvement has occurred.

Colleagues have confirmed the author's impression that courts tend to undervalue the importance of history on the grounds that historical data are often unreliable, since they are frequently obtained from unwilling, hostile, or manipulative clients who are involved with the agency only under duress. Workers' testimony is further undermined by the ambiguous nature of the child-welfare agency's involvement with its clients. The same worker assigned to "help" can, at any point, unilaterally decide to use information volunteered or observed during the helping process as evidence against that family in court. Presumably for this reason, lawyers frequently advise clients to avoid co-operating with child-welfare agencies.

Certainly for some clients, especially those who rely heavily on paranoid defences and on splitting (though not all parents who use these defences are incompetent), the worker's double role will make it harder to assess accurately or achieve a meaningful therapeutic involvement. This again underlines the importance of obtaining corroborating information from secondary sources (day-care centres, schools, etc.) whenever possible. Yet in spite of the rich potential for mistrust inherent in the double role of the child-welfare worker, many families still form an alliance with their worker. One should not dismiss a family's inability to work with a child-welfare agency as a normal and inevitable response to that agency's potential use of authority, since the inability to trust or form a therapeutic alliance often involves the character and defensive style of the parents. Many parents repeatedly consult clinics or professionals for assessment, but avoid treatment. If they do temporarily enter treatment, they defensively ignore any input that questions or contradicts their own views in order to maintain their precarious psychological equilibrium. It is not just welfare agencies with whom these families cannot get along. Many have a long history of difficulty with school principals, psychiatrists, other social agencies, neighbours, extended family, police, etc. Despite the strain placed on both client and agency by the child-welfare worker's double role, the more evidence there is of inability to involve that family in a therapeutic alliance, the less likely that family is to be accessible to change. Despite their initial and understandable suspicion, many families can, in time, recognize that the agency may be as determined as they are to avoid taking a child into care. Especially when the family's defensive style has repeatedly constituted an impenetrable barrier against the formation of a working alliance, the chance of future intervention effecting substantial change is slight.

Psychological Assessment

An adequate assessment includes relatively passive observation as well as a more active, direct gathering of information not spontaneously revealed (e.g., fantasy material or how a child responds when the parents set limits). Active intervention allows the examiner to test out statements made or impressions and hypotheses derived from observations. The greater the opportunity for lengthy and repeated observation, the likelier one is to arrive at valid conclusions about the family. There is considerable risk in making authoritative statements based on only a few minute's observation. Highly anxious children are likely to appear quite different on a second visit, when the examiner is no longer a total stranger and the children know they will return home after the interview.

During the assessment, the child's physical, intellectual, cognitive, emotional, and social development are compared with norms for the age. While a developmental delay is not in itself a sign of inadequate parenting, significant developmental delays, particularly if associated with other signs of a disturbed parent–child relationship, are at least suggestive, especially if there is clear evidence of normal intelligence. On the other hand, positive change in developmental level is one of the best indicators that a substitute or improved family environment is meeting a child's needs.

The examiner observes how child and parents relate to each other during the assessment. Here again, the interpretation of observed behaviour depends on age-appropriate norms. For example, separation anxiety is normal for a toddler, while a total absence of stranger anxiety or a pattern of relating to strangers as if they were familiar acquaintances or preferred to the parents, strongly suggests a disturbance in attachment behaviour. For the older child, however, the situation is reversed; stranger anxiety suggests disturbance while the absence of it is more age-appropriate.

In observing parents with children, one notes the nature and extent of their relatedness. Do they ignore each other? Does either constantly and obtrusively demand the other's attention? To what extent do they talk, listen, and make eye contact? Do parents seem intuitively empathic (i.e., tuned in and appropriately responsive) to the child's verbal or behavioural requests for attention, or do they appear distracted, distant, or harsh in response to such cues? Or is their need to control or express affection so intrusive that they cannot allow the child to explore freely or to withdraw from contact periodically? Are the parents' expectations reasonable? Do they limit inappropriate behaviour, or pretend to ignore it? If asked to set appropriate limits, can they do so effectively yet without excessive harshness? If one comments on clearly observable behaviour, can the parents acknowledge it and modify it if indicated? Can the parents discuss how they feel about the assessment, reflect on the interaction between themselves and the child and on the observation of the examiner? Does their relationship suggest to the examiner a base on which to build a potential therapeutic alliance?

Many children cannot directly express much of what they feel, especially if they have been threatened or told not to do so. Others feel disloyal or guilty saying anything that reflects badly on a parent, or that could lead to their removal from even a highly destructive family. Children, especially those who have been deprived or abused, often reveal through their play and fantasy much that they could never express directly. Drawings, doll or puppet play, and dreams may yield a more accurate picture of how the child feels about biological and foster families than would the child's responses to direct questioning. While it would be rash to conclude from a single episode of puppet play that parents were abusive or unresponsive, a repetition of the same theme expressed by the child in a variety of activities should merit attention. This is illustrated in the following case vignette:

Carol, age five, came to her foster home when she was two years old. She was then far behind in all areas of development, and extremely withdrawn and mistrustful of others, especially of men. Over the past three years, it had been agreed that she would remain in her foster home, but would visit her biological parents every other week. Recently, in view of the dramatic social and psychological gains she had made, the child-welfare agency sought psychiatric consultation with respect to the merits of a plan to remove her from her foster home and place her on adoption, a plan with which Carol had stated she agreed.

Carol's fantasy and play suggested that, in spite of her improved functioning, memories of past distress and confusion persisted, though she handled these without allowing serious disruption of current functioning and behaviour. In her puppet play, a little girl was left crying while one set of parents fought violently, only to be rescued and comforted by another set, presumably the foster parents. She described herself as having two mothers and two fathers, and stated that soon she would be adopted and would then have three mothers and three fathers. Thus, adoption to Carol meant adding yet another set of parents, not separating from those already in her life. This preoccupation with family relationships spilled over into her "three wishes," in which she wondered what had happened to a cat's kittens, and speculated on the relationship between a puppy and its mother. Finally, when asked to draw a picture of her family, she very carefully drew just one little girl.

A psychological examination, especially one including projective tests administered by a psychologist skilled in interpreting projective techniques, could provide another independent assessment that might either support or contradict hypotheses as to the true nature of the child's thoughts, feelings, and fantasies. Although hypotheses drawn from puppet play and drawings alone would be inconclusive, data of this sort can richly contribute to the total picture. It would be even more misguided to rely exclusively on how a child responds to direct questions about the relationship with the parents, either in a clinic, in open court, or in chambers. What a child wants and what a child needs may be very different. Failure to recognize this and to separate wants from needs frequently contributes to well-meaning but destructive planning. In assessing for parenting capacity, one learns more by combining an assessment of the child with an observation and assessment of the family than from either component of the assessment alone. A well-documented history is often more helpful and reliable in assessing parenting capacity than even the most meticulous psychiatric or psychological assessment.

In-patient assessments allow trained staff to observe children's interactions with other children, with staff, and with their families. They provide a more extensive and potentially more reliable picture of child and family than that obtained in a one-shot assessment. Differences in behaviour in the absence of the parents may suggest how much of the child's symptoms are reactive to the family situation rather than evidence of an internalized disorder. Prolonged observation may indicate whether all siblings are equally at risk, or why this particular child has developed symptoms such as soft neurological signs, evidence of sadomasochistic behaviour, etc. Through an extended assessment of the family's defensiveness and their accessibility to involvement, confrontation, suggestions, and other forms of therapeutic input, one can test the family's accessibility to intervention. Such short-term admissions can offer a cooling-off period, and a chance to help child and parents learn and practise new ways of binding tension and of understanding and relating to each other. Although such admissions are often accepted only under external pressure, some families are able to co-operate and learn from them; others, especially those relying heavily on paranoid and splitting defences, never overcome their distrust enough to form a working alliance with milieu staff.

Biological parents, however neglectful, rejecting, or abusive, are usually hard hit by any decision to terminate their rights and take their child into care. Wherever possible, this hurt should be minimized by allowing them some participation in the decision. It is not unusual for biological parents to withdraw their opposition to permanent wardship if they know that the agency recognizes they care about their child and that, by supporting the child's coming into care, they are helping to provide developmental assistance that they could not deliver on their own. They are particularly likely to co-operate if they sense that the agency is nonjudgmental, and that it recognizes and will protect their continuing importance to the child through access with or without ongoing supervision (Steinhauer 1977).

Predicting Parenting Capacity

It is the position of many child-welfare workers, and of the present author, that courts generally underestimate the validity of evidence presented by social workers. Frequently, a social agency has worked with a family for years and has amassed a wealth of historical data, often supported by independent secondary sources, that strongly suggest an intractable pattern of inadequate parenting. Nevertheless, judges often give less credence to such evidence than to the testimony of psychologists or psychiatrists. There seems to be a bias, largely unacknowledged, among the courts against longitudinal (i.e., historical) data provided by a caseworker as opposed to cross-sectional (i.e., current assessment) data of a psychologist or psychiatrist. It is incumbent upon all mental-health professionals to

help overcome this bias. Psychologists and psychiatrists must resist playing the game of providing assessments to satisfy the court in cases where ample historical evidence is available from the professional staff of an appropriate social agency. Social workers, for their part, must learn to provide testimony in the form that is most useful and persuasive to the courts. Material that is significant for casework may not be relevant to the issues being decided by the court. Workers must learn to select and focus their knowledge to meet the needs of the court; both fact and opinion may be relevant, but the evidence on which professional opinions are based should be set forth clearly and succinctly. Similarly, the court should be informed of any alternative conclusions or recommendations that were considered, and the rationale for their rejection in favour of the opinion presented.

Except for that minority of cases in which the signs of severe and repeated physical abuse are obvious, we must rely less on such hard evidence as broken bones, bruises, etc., than on the picture, developed cautiously and with painstaking regard for supportive detail, of a pattern of ongoing interaction between parents and children considered at risk. This will emerge mainly from the history, augmented by psychiatric and psychological assessments performed at various points along the way. This process should lead to the assignment of cases into one of three categories.

Group A

The child's development is not, and never has been, seriously at risk. The parents are adequately meeting the child's needs. Either no further intervention is needed, or the question of whether or not to seek further intervention should be left to the family.

Group B

The child's current adjustment and developmental status suggest serious problems, although until recently the parenting seemed adequate and development seemed satisfactory. Given prompt and adequate intervention, the prognosis for these parents again meeting their child's needs so that development can proceed is reasonably good. Cases in this group would generally conform to the following profile:

- evidence of basically sound child development, with minimal developmental interference on the part of the parents;
- recent onset of problem, leading to decompensation in the family's functioning and the parents' ability to meet the child's developmental needs;
- absence of a chronic parental psychiatric diagnosis that is untreatable or that has a markedly poor prognosis;
- evidence of co-operation and openness (i.e., willingness of parents to discuss events and feelings even when these might reflect badly upon themselves, and to consider the examiner's observations and suggestions) and a history of being able to seek, accept, and benefit from help for family problems;
- ability of parents to accept significant responsibility for their contribution to the development of the problem or their past failures to deal with it;
- family members have maintained adequate relationships with extended family, neighbours, or community agencies from whom they can accept advice and support.

The more of these factors that are present, the greater the likelihood that an adequate therapeutic intervention can significantly improve parenting capacity.

Group C

The child's development and adjustment currently show and have long demonstrated significant impairment. The parents have long seemed unable to meet this child's (or these children's) developmental needs, and there is little to suggest that this is likely to change

significantly, even given adequate treatment. Cases in this group would generally fit the following profile:

- evidence of widespread disturbances in physical, cognitive, language, academic, emotional, or social development;
- problems in development and adjustment have been present for years;
- one or both parents suffer from a psychiatric illness that significantly affects their parental ability and carries a poor prognosis;
- past attempts to provide help have consistently failed. Parents lack co-operation and openness, and resist involvement in the therapeutic process;
- parents cannot accept even partial responsibility for the genesis and maintenance of the problem, or for their failure to benefit from past treatment;
- the family is isolated from and unable to accept help or emotional support from friends, neighbours, extended family, or appropriate mental-health professionals.

The more of these factors one sees, the less the likelihood that therapeutic intervention can significantly improve parenting capacity.

Conclusion

This paper began with a review of our current knowledge of children's basic developmental needs. The subsequent discussion of the assessment of parenting capacity consists more of opinion than established fact, albeit carefully considered opinion based on what little is available in the literature and on the author's 20 years of experience as a practising child psychiatrist consulting several child-welfare agencies. Apart from certain circumscribed areas such as child abuse, autism, children of psychotic parents, etc., there is almost nothing in the literature that draws together and integrates what is known to develop general guidelines for assessing parenting capacity. Until controlled and systematic follow-up data on this topic are available, we must continue to determine what is least detrimental for each individual child, delaying decisions (and thus leaving children in limbo) until evidence for removal is overwhelming — or deciding to act, often on the basis of a continuing pattern, even in the absence of specific incidents of extreme neglect or abuse. In the absence of such systematic research, the final section of this paper, containing "prognostic profiles," is intended as a guide to assessing parenting capacity. When carefully applied by experienced clinicians, these profiles may constitute a useful framework for gathering and organizing the information needed for sound assessment. Although this framework is suggested as clinically relevant and as having heuristic value, even the best guidelines cannot predict the future of an individual child with complete accuracy. We are always dealing in calculated risks. The framework proposed here is intended to decrease as much as possible the truly horrendous risks that are involved when deciding whether or not to terminate parental rights.

Works Cited

Ainsworth, M. 1967. *Infancy in Uganda: Infant Care and the Growth of Attachment*. Baltimore: Johns Hopkins University Press.

———. 1969. "Object Relations, Dependency and Attachment: A Theoretical Review of the Infant-Mother Relationship." *Child Development* 40: 969–1025.

Anthony, E. 1970. "The Influence of Maternal Psychosis on Children: *folie à deux*." *Parenthood: Its Psychology and Psychopathology*. Eds. E. Anthony and T. Benedek. Boston: Little, Brown. 571–98.

Anthony, E., C. Koupernik and C. Chiland, eds. 1978. *Vulnerable Children*. Vol. 4 of *A Child and His Family*. New York: John Wiley.

Bowlby, J. 1969. *Attachment*. Vol. 1 of *Attachment and Loss*. New York: Basic.

Chandler, M. 1978. "Role-taking, Referential Communication and Egocentric Intrusion in Mother–Child Interactions of Children Vulnerable to Risk of Parental Psychosis." Anthony, Koupernik, and Chiland.

Cooper, J. 1978 [...] *rent Issues in F[...] tional Childre[...]*

Derdyn, A. 197[...] Care Placem[...] Abused Chil[...] *psychiatry* 47([...]

Epstein, R. 197[...] *Street* (June): [...]

Freud, A. 1960 [...] paper". *Psyc[...]* 53–62.

Furman, E. 1974. *A Child's Parent Dies*. New Haven, CT: Yale University Press.

Galdston, R. 1965. "Observations on Children Who Have Been Physically Abused and Their Parents." *American Journal of Psychiatry* 122(4): 440–43.

Goldstein, J., A. Freud, and A. Solnit, 1973. *Beyond the Best Interests of the Child*. New York: Free Press.

Goldstein, J., A. Freud, and A. Solnit. 1979. *Before the Best Interests of the Child*. New York: Free Press.

Green, R. 1979. Quoted in Epstein. 1979.

Harris, B. 1977. "Lesbian Mother Child Custody: Legal and Psychiatric Aspects." *Bulletin of the American Academy of Psychiatric Law* 5(1): 75–89.

Ilfiend, F., Jr. 1970. "Environmental Theories of Violence." *Violence and the Struggle for Existence*. Eds. D. Danfield, M. Gilula, and F. Ochberg. Boston: Little, Brown. 79–95.

Kaplan, H. 1979. Quoted in Epstein. 1979.

Lander, H., et al 1978. "A Measure of Vulnerability to Risk of Parental Psychosis." Anthony, Koupernik, and Chiland.

Leverette, J. n.d. "Custody Determination and the Homosexual Parent." Unpublished paper.

Lystad, M. 1975. "Violence at Home: a Review of the Literature." *American Journal of Orthopsychiatry* 45(3): 328–45.

Madison, B., and M. Schapiro 1970. "Permanent and Long-Term Foster Care as a Planned service." *Child Welfare* 49(3): 131–36.

Marmor, J. 1977. Quoted in Harris. 1977.

McLean, P. 1976. "Parental Depression: Incompatible with Effective Parenting." *Behavior Modification Approaches to Parenting*. Eds. E. Mash, L. Handy, and L. Hamerlynck. New York: Brunner/Mazel.

Money, J. 1977. Quoted in Harris. 1977.

Orvaschel, H., et al. 1979. "The Children of Psychiatrically Disturbed Parents: Difference as a

Sex of the Sick Parent." *Archives*
chiatry 36: 691-95.

76. "Permanent Planning for Foster
n: the Oregon Project." *Children Today*
22-25.

, E. 1972. "A Psychodynamic Model of the
Mother of the Autistic Child." *Smith College Studies in Social Work* 43(3).

Rutter, M. 1960. "Maternal Deprivation Reconsidered." *Journal of Psychosomatic Research* 16: 241-250.

———. 1971. "Parent-Child Separation: Psychological Effect on the Children." *Journal of Child Psychology and Psychiatry* 12: 233-60.

———. 1978a. "Early Sources of Security and Competence." *Human Growth and Development*, Eds. J. Beuner and A. Garton. London: Oxford University Press. 33-61.

———. 1978b. "Family, Area and School Influences in the Genesis of Conduct Disorders." *Aggression and Antisocial Behavior in Childhood and Adolescence*. Eds. L. Hersov, M. Berger, and D. Shaffer. Oxford: Pergamon.

———. 1979. "Maternal Deprivation, 1972-1978: New Findings, New Concepts, New Approaches." *Child Development* 50: 283-305.

Salomon, E. 1981. "Characteristics of Parents of Atypical and Autistic Children: Implications for Treatment." *Smith College Studies in Social Work* 51(2): 73-94.

Silver, L., C. Dublin, and R. Lourie. 1969. "Does Violence Breed Violence? Contributions from a Study of the Child Abuse Syndrome." *American Journal of Psychiatry*. 126(3): 152-55.

Speers, B., and C. Lansing. 1965. *Group Therapy in Childhood Psychosis*. Chapel Hill: University of North Carolina Press.

Steele, B., and C. Pollock, 1968. "A Psychiatric Study of Parents Who Abuse Infants and Small Children." *The Battered Child*, Eds. R. Helfer and C. Kempe. Chicago: University of Chicago Press. 48-85.

Steinhauer, P. 1977. "Sharing a Child with His Parents." Presented to the United Foster Parents of Erie County, Buffalo, NY (May).

———. 1980a. "Development in Infancy and Childhood." *A Method of Psychiatry*. Eds. Greben et al. Philadelphia: Lea and Febiger.

———. 1980b. "Permanency Planning: Prescription for Continuity or Chaos?" Presented to the American Orthopsychiatric Association, Toronto. 9-32.

Tizard, B. 1977. *Adoption: A Second Chance*. London: Open Books.

Tizard, B., and J. Hodges, 1978. "The effect of early institutional rearing on the development of eight-year-old children." *Journal of Child Psychology and Psychiatry* 19: 98-118.

Tizard, B., and J. Rees, 1974. "A Comparison of the Effects of Adoption, Restoration to the Natural Mother, and Continued Institutionalization on the Cognitive Development of Four-Year-Old Children." *Child Development* 45: 92-99.

Tizard, B., and J. Tizard 1975. "The Social Development of Two-Year-Old Children." *Journal of Child Psychology and Psychiatry* 16: 61-74.

Tooley, K. 1978. "Irreconcilable Differences Between Parent and Child: a Case Report of Interactional Pathology." *American Journal of Orthopsychiatry* 48(4): 703-16.

Wasserman, S. 1967. "The Abused Parent of the Abused Child." *Children* 14(5): 175.

Wiltse, K. 1979. "Foster Care in the 1970's: A Decade of Change." *Children Today* (May-June): 10-14.

THE SCAPEGOATING OF MOTHERS: A CALL FOR CHANGE*

Paula J. Caplan
Ian Hall-McCorquodale

Despite the gains achieved through the efforts of the women's movement during the past 15 years, the practice by many clinicians and members of the helping professions of blaming mothers for whatever goes wrong with their children continues to be a serious and pervasive problem. The results of our quantitative investigation of mother-blaming in major clinical journals have been published previously (Caplan and Hall-McCorquodale 1985). In that article, the extensiveness of the phenomenon is documented in quantitative terms, and the results are deeply disturbing. In order fully to appreciate the seriousness of the practice, however, and to assess what can be done to stop mother-blaming, some illustrations are useful. Consider the following: "To meet Johnny's mother is to understand his problem" (letter from school guidance counsellor, cited by Chess [1982, 95]). In a syndicated newspaper column, the following was reported:

> A 79-year-old ham radio operator was found unconscious on the floor of his workshop. Wired to his penis was a radio transmitter which had a morse code key. The wiring had electrical clips that hooked into a rheostat. This was set at 12 volts which is about the voltage of mid-to-large size American car bat-

teries. In addition the device was wired to an earphone jack on the radio. (Gifford-Jones 1981, D1)

Mitchell (1968) has described 21 similar situations: men inserting into the openings of their penises safety pins, bobby pins, pieces of coat hangers, pencils, pens, candles, straws, cuticle knives, and so on. Mitchell suggested that many of these patients suffered from overcontrolling mothers.

Before beginning our research on mother-blaming, we had suspected that even the types of information given about mothers would differ from descriptions of fathers. That suspicion was indeed borne out by our documentation. For instance, at the beginning of a case history (Nielsen et al. 1970), the following was noted:

> The father, a bricklayer, was 35 yrs old when the patient was born. He is healthy. The mother was 33 yrs old when the patient was born; she is "nervous." (p. 116)

The father was described in terms of his occupation, his age, and a positive statement about his (apparently physical) health; the mother was described in terms of her age and a negative comment about her emotional functioning. Later in that article, the authors wrote that the father hit the child and was very dominating, and that the patient cried every time he talked about his father and feared that his father did not love him. One can only speculate about why, if the father treated his disturbed son in this way, he was

Source: *American Journal of Orthopsychiatry* 55(4): 610–13. Copyright © 1985 American Orthopsychiatric Association, Inc. Reprinted with permission.

*Presented at the Institute of (and sponsored by) the Canadian Psychological Association Section on Women and Psychology, Winnipeg, June 1983, and in part at University of Toronto Department of Psychiatric Research Day, September 1983.

described at the start of the case history only in terms of his occupation and his physical health, whereas the mother was described only as "nervous." After three case histories, the most vivid by far being the one described above, the authors reached the following conclusion: "Mothers of patients with Klinefelter's syndrome are often overprotective or anxious. . . . The behavior disturbance may start at the age of 4–5 if their mothers do not protect them or take care of them" (p. 117). Such a conclusion is particularly intriguing in that the mothers in the case histories were not described as overprotective and anxious, and the only serious psychopathology noted for any parent was that of the father just described.

In the case of school phobia (Smith and Sharpe 1970), the authors wrote: "It was evident that Billy's mother was allowing reinforcement of his school avoidance behaviors by permitting him to watch television during the day and to stay up all night" (pp. 240–41). In this case the father was described as having an ideal relationship with his son. Furthermore, since the father was a farmer, he presumably worked near home during the day and did not work at night. One might wonder where he was when the mother was permitting Billy to watch television all day and stay up all night. The authors did not address this question.

Even in some articles in which the mother is not blamed, the father's possible contribution to the problem is never considered. In a study of violation of rules in a women's prison (Snortum, Hannum, and Mills 1970), four variables found to be correlated with rule violation were related to the women's perceptions of their mothers and two to their perceptions of their fathers, but only those related to their mothers were described as having done the damage. Somewhat similarly, in a study of arson (Hill et al. 1982), the only significant correlation between a family-history item and the offspring's arson was the father's drinking — but it was never mentioned in the article's discussion section.

The article that may have required the authors to stretch the farthest in order to blame the mothers dealt with the offspring of men who had served in the Canadian armed forces and been kept in prisoner-of-war camps for 44 months (Sigal 1976). Some of the offspring were found to have emotional disturbances, which the authors explained as follows: The men go off to work full of anxiety, pain and a sense of depletion; when they are at home, their lack of involvement with the family is striking; their wives' performance of their mothering functions is disturbed by this, and that is what upsets the children.

Thus, despite work by such writers as Lamb (1982), who stressed the importance of the infant's attachments to *both* parents even within the first six months of life, too many clinicians still clearly hold mothers responsible for making or breaking their children. Even when the term "parents" is used in discussing the children's pathology, often only the mothers are noted in descriptions of interactions and illustrations of problems.

Why does mother-blaming persist? And what can be done to stop it? Ruddick (1980) has suggested that mother-blaming is a consequence of the unequal distribution of power in society between females and males:

> Almost everywhere the practices of mothering take place in societies in which women of all classes are less able than men of their class to determine the conditions in which their children grow. Throughout history, most women have mothered in conditions of military and social violence, as well as economic deprivation, governed by men whose policies they could neither shape nor control. . . . A child's rageful disappointment in its powerless mother, combined with resentment and fear of her powerful will, may account for the matriphobia so widespread in our society as to seem normal. (p. 355)

The fact that psychologists and psychiatrists have so intensively studied *disturbed* children rather than *healthy* ones and discussed the causes of disturbance but not of health has further aggravated the problem.

Because mother-blaming, despite the efforts of women's rights advocates, continues to pervade the clinical literature, several recommendations can be made for clinical writers and for journal editors and their reviewers. These recommendations are important because, as Chess (1982) has written:

> It is our responsibility, as mental health professionals dealing with troubled children and their families, to gather all the relevant information, to study it carefully, and then to make our evaluations. It is the height of irresponsibility to start with the assumption that the mother is at fault (no matter how elegantly such a "blame the mother" ideology is phrased), to shape the facts to fit this ideology, and then to act accordingly. (p. 107)

Recommendations

• Whenever possible, emphasis on *mother*-infant and *mother*-child interaction should be changed to interaction between *parent* and child. Unless the data clearly warrant an emphasis on the mother's role, possible effects of the father's or other caretaker's behaviour — or absence — having been ruled out, emphasis on the mother is unwarranted. It should be kept in mind that ruling out the influence of other adults' behaviour or absence is exceedingly difficult to justify, and only rarely in the articles we examined (Caplan and Hall-McCorquodale 1985) were any such attempts even made.

• As Konstantareas et al. (1983) suggested, the effects of the child's own innate and developing characteristics must be taken into account before mothers are simply blamed for what goes wrong.

• Social practices that classify the responsibility for childrearing as the mother's province can *only* perpetuate mother-blaming; while these practices continue, fathers' absences or actions will not tend to be interpreted

as causing the child's problems (Caplan and Hall-McCorquodale 1985). Such interpretations by clinicians, researchers, and other mental-health professionals strengthen the notion that the problems are the mother's fault, and the vicious cycle continues. If it is usually the mothers who are *there* to do the childrearing (or to see that it is done), provide the history, and be the subjects of study by mental-health professionals (whether or not these mothers also have paid employment; whether or not a father or father–substitute is anywhere nearby), all material on which to base cause-and-effect theories about children's psychopathology will come from mothers' lives. In this connection, Churven (1978) has found that fathers are more reluctant than are mothers to participate in interviews. Therefore, what the father did, did not do, or might have done if things had been different, to prevent, reduce, exacerbate, or create his child's problems will not be known and will rarely be considered.

• As long as mothers are held to be primarily responsible for their children's emotional adjustment, a dangerous source of intense anxiety, self-deprecation, and fear will be brought to the relationships many mothers have with their infants. For many women, the pervasiveness of mother-blaming means that, when they give birth to or adopt a baby, they put themselves in a spotlight where, should anything go wrong, they will almost surely be accused. In view of this, it is perhaps remarkable that any mothers can relax. There are very few jobs in which one individual will be blamed for anything that goes wrong, and fewer still in which what can go wrong, and the feeling of being blamed, are so devastating. It is time to listen to the plea of Robertson Davies's (1981) character Simon Darcourt in his novel *The Rebel Angels*:

> I'm sick to death of people squealing about their mothers. Everybody has to have a mother, and not everybody is going to draw the Grand Prize — whatever that may be. What's a perfect mother? We hear too much

about loving mothers making homosexuals, and neglectful mothers making crooks, and commonplace mothers stifling intelligence. The whole mother business needs radical re-examination.

Works Cited

Caplan, P., and I. Hall-McCorquodale. 1985. "Mother-blaming in Major Clinical Journals." *American Journal of Orthopsychiatry* 55: 345–53.

Chess, S. 1982. "The 'Blame the Mother' Ideology." *International Journal of Mental Health* 11: 95–107.

Churven, P. 1978. "Families: Parental Attitudes to Family Assessment in a Child Psychiatry Setting." *Journal of Child Psychology and Psychiatry* 19: 33–41.

Davies, R. 1981. *The Rebel Angels*. Toronto: Macmillan.

Gifford-Jones, W. 1981. "The Doctor Game." *The* (Edmonton, Alberta) *Journal* (Nov. 4): D1.

Hill, R., et al. 1982. "Is Arson an Aggressive Act or a Property Offence? A Controlled Study of Psychiatric Referrals." *Canadian Journal of Psychiatry* 27: 648–54.

Konstantareas, M., et al. 1983. "Mothers of Autistic Children: Are They the 'Unacknowledged Victims'?" Presented to the Canadian Psychological Association, Winnipeg.

Lamb, M. 1982. "Paternal Influences on Early Socio-emotional Development." *Journal of Child Psychology and Psychiatry* 23: 185–90.

Mitchell, W. 1968. "Self-Insertion of Urethral Foreign Bodies" *Psychiatric Quarterly* 42: 479–86.

Nielsen, J., et al. 1970. "Klinefelter's Syndrome in Children." *Journal of Child Psychology and Psychiatry* 11: 109–19.

Ruddick, S. 1980. "Maternal Thinking." *Feminist Studies* 6: 354–80.

Sigal, J. 1976. "Effects of Paternal Exposure to Prolonged Stress on the Mental Health of the Spouse and Children." *Canadian Psychiatric Association Journal* 21(3): 169–72.

Smith, R., and Sharpe, T. 1970. "Treatment of a School Phobia with Implosive Therapy." *Journal of Consulting and Clinical Psychology* 35(2): 239–42.

Snortum, J., T. Hannum, and D. Mills. 1970. "The Relationship of Self-Concept and Parent Image to Rule Violation in a Women's Prison." *Journal of Clinical Psychology* 26(3): 284–87.

HOW LONG ALONE? THE DURATION OF FEMALE LONE PARENTHOOD IN CANADA

Maureen Moore

Statistical portrayals of lone parents and their families have largely been drawn from single time-point sources, such as the Census and some surveys. These statistics reveal current patterns that can be accumulated and compared over time. We know from the Census that in 1986 there were approximately 850 000 lone parents, most (82 percent) of them women. We know that the number of these families has been increasing over a period of years, faster than husband–wife families. We also know that although many lone parents work, they are statistically more economically disadvantaged than other families, partly because of the absence of a second earner.

Underlying these aggregate patterns and trends are individual flows in and out of lone parenting. Rather than being a permanent status, as single time-point estimates often suggest, lone parenting is usually episodic. This is a dimension that can only be seen by analyzing the family pasts of living women (because women comprise the majority of lone parents) through a retrospective survey.

Statistics Canada's Family History Survey asked about 7000 women across Canada between ages 18 and 65, about marriages, common law partnerships, divorces, deaths of spouses, and adopted children or children they had given birth to, and raised until, for

some, the point of leaving home. It thus provides all documentation necessary to reconstruct past marital and childbearing histories of women and to identify the number and duration of lone-parenting spells.

One important insight is that lone parenthood is more pervasive than current statistics indicate. About 500 000 women were lone parents in 1984, but another 900 000 had passed through this status. Most (84 percent) of these women, by the survey date, had married for the first or second time, or had begun to live with a common law spouse, while the others remained alone with their children until they had all left home. For 12 percent, ended episodes were rather brief — less than 6 months — but among an equal proportion they lasted more than 10 years. The average length was 4.6 years. Women become lone parents in a variety of ways and at different stages in their life cycles.

Lone Parenting Due to Widowhood

Widowhood tends to occur in the middle to late years of the life cycle: widowed lone parenting begins at 41.8 years of age on average. It more often befalls women because men have higher mortality rates, a tendency accentuated by age differences at marriage. Widowed lone parents have lower probabilities of union entry and are more likely than other lone parents to reach the "empty nest" without a marital or common law partner. In 1984, there were about 127 000 widowed

Source: *Canadian Social Trends* (Autumn 1988): Catalogue 11-008. Reprinted with permission from Canadian Social Trends 1988 Autumn. pp 40-2.

lone parents, who had spent an average 8.8 years in this state. Another 113 000 had changed their status by the survey date, after an average of 6.2 years. Of these, 40 percent had become empty-nesters.

Looking back from 1984, episodes of widowed lone parenting tend to span a fairly recent period of improved health, prosperity, and longer life expectancy. Experiences from the first part of the century, when more husbands were claimed by disease, accidents, and war, are not well represented. Yet 70 to 75 percent of lone parents were widowed in 1931, compared to only 28 percent in 1981. That the 1931 level of lone-parent families among all families (14 percent) has yet to be surpassed indicates the extent of these losses. By comparison, 13 percent of all families in 1986 were lone-parent families.

Although widowhood was the likeliest cause of lone parenthood in the first half of this century, demographers speculate that separation of spouses was more prevalent than the statistics show. In "Irish divorce" during the Depression, men left their families for work, solace, and escape, and war in the following decade separated soldiers from their families. Amid postwar prosperity and into the mid-1960s, widowhood remained the most frequent cause of lone parenthood, but marriage was on firmer ground. This was a time of family expansion: more than 8 million children were born, more than since the turn of the century. As a proportion of all families, the percentage of lone-parent families was about half the 1931 level for most of this period.

These outwardly stable family patterns were interrupted when marital separation and divorce began to increase, around the time the first unified federal divorce legislation was introduced in 1968. Divorce has been rising ever since. Separation and divorce are now the most common paths to lone parenthood, more often for women, who retain sole custody of children in 77 percent of divorce awards, and physical custody in more than 80 percent.

Approximately 697 000 women have been divorced parents, including 394 000 whose spells had ended, after an average length of 5.3 years. Relatively more women born between 1935 and 1944 and aged 40–49 at the time of the survey became divorced mothers than any other cohort (group of people born at the same time): 15 percent of these women became divorced mothers compared to 8 percent of women aged 50–65.

Separation, usually followed by divorce, tends to occur earlier in life than widowhood. According to Family History Survey data, separated/divorced women begin to raise children alone at an average age of 31.6. At this age, children would tend to be younger, yet the labour-force participation of female lone parents rises between the ages of 30 and 45 (peaking at 80 percent in the 40-44 year age group). Exits from lone parenthood for divorced women tend to occur after 5 to 6 years on average, most often through remarriage or common-law union entry. This movement has resulted in the growth of "reconstituted" families.

It is not known what ceiling the divorce rate will reach before it starts to abate. The probability of becoming a lone parent for the first time by the age of 25 is higher for women born in the 1950s than it was for women born in the 1940s, but, by 1984, some of these women had not yet been married.

Increases in Ex-nuptial Births

Probabilities are higher in younger cohorts, largely because of the growth in "out-of-wedlock" or "ex-nuptial" births. The annual number of these births has more than quadrupled since 1951 to a 1985 level of 59 600. Not only have there been more women exposed to the risk of single parenthood (baby-boom women entering early adulthood), but there has also been a gradual acceptance of these families. About 460 000 Canadian women of all ages have had ex-nuptial babies whom they raised, for some time, alone. As expected, only a small proportion (17 percent) were lone mothers at the time of the survey. Ended episodes lasted an average of 3.5 years, the majority with the formation of a first union. Unfortunately, the sample is too small to examine differences in duration by cohort, although one might expect the duration to have lengthened over time with the rise in average age at first marriage.

Ex-nuptial births are not new. Six percent of all women born between 1919 and 1935 (the parents of the 1950s baby boom, aged 50-65 in 1984) had ex-nuptial babies whom they did not give up for adoption; women born between 1935 and 1944 had a rate of 7 percent. Given the social mores of that era, it is likely that these births would have precipitated marriages fairly soon.

Single women become lone mothers at 20.6 years of age on average. They are the most likely of all lone parents to be living in their parental home or to have support of older adults. Births at this age, however, tend to block chances for further education and vocational training, which bring more financial freedom in the long run. Among women (living in families) who had children when younger than 20, only 15 percent attained post-secondary education, compared to about 40 percent whose first child came at the age of 25 or later. Of all women who were ever ex-nuptial mothers, only 10 percent had their first birth after 25 years of age.

Most single mothers form unions some time after the births of their children, but there is evidence of greater union instability, more likely to occur if the union was formed as a result of the pregnancy, or at too young an age. Family History Survey data show that about three in ten women who were single mothers went on to a second lone-parent experience as separated mothers.

From a reconstruction of past movements and events, we are brought to the present. Latest estimates show increases in both divorce and ex-nuptial births, with widowhood becoming a less important determinant. The long-term effects of these changes, particularly on children, are only beginning to be grasped. In 1986, about 1.2 million children (14 percent of all children under the age of 25) were part of lone-parent families. At a bottom average duration of 5.5 years, this represents a third of their childhood. We should not overstate the prevalence of lone parenting. About 82 percent of Canadian women of all ages had been leading "conventional" family lives up to the point of the survey. A substantial number of these women, however, had yet to pass a full course of the risks.

Average duration of Ended and Continuing Lone-Parent Episodes of Women Aged 18–65, by Originating Event, 1984

Originating Event	Episode Ended		Episode Continuing		Total	
	Average Duration (Years)	Number of Women (000s)	Average Duration (Years)	Number of Women (000s)	Average Duration (Years)	Number of Women (000s)
Out-of-Wedlock Birth	3.5	384	8.9	77	4.4	460
Separation/Divorce	5.3	394	6.0	303	5.6	697
Widowhood	6.2	113	8.8	127	7.5	239
Total	4.6	890	7.1	506	5.5	1 396

Reprinted from: Maureen Moore, "Female Lone Parenthood: The Duration of Episodes," *Canadian Social Trends*, Catalogue 11–008, Autumn 1988.

Summary Statistics for Lone-Parent Episodes of Women Aged 18–65, by Originating Event, 1984

	Out-of-Wedlock Birth	Separation/ Divorce	Widowhood	Total
Number (000s)	460	697	239	1396
Average age at onset (years)	20.6	31.6	41.8	29.7
Average duration (years)	4.4	5.6	7.5	5.5
Percent of episodes ended at survey date (%)	83	57	47	64
Percent of ended episodes due to formation of new union (%)	97	77	59	84

Reprinted from: Maureen Moore, "Female Lone Parenthood: The Duration of Episodes," *Canadian Social Trends*, Catalogue 11-008, Autumn 1988.

SINGLE MOTHERS AND THEIR CHILDREN AFTER DIVORCE: A STUDY OF THOSE "WHO MAKE IT"

Aysan Tuzlak
David W. Hillock

Introduction

During the past two decades, soaring divorce rates have increasingly concerned social scholars, policy makers, and lay persons alike. Even though 330.2 of every 1000 marriages in Canada end in divorce, this figure still trails far behind those for Sweden (540.5), the United States (505), Denmark (454.5), and Australia (430.6) (Statistics Canada 1980, 32, Table 21). One reason why the Canadian figures are alarming is that, traditionally, Canada has had one of the lowest divorce rates among Western nations (Elkin 1964). Since the 1968 Divorce Law Reform Act, divorce rates have sextupled, leading to the realization that divorce is no longer a "south of the border" affliction, but is quickly becoming a Canadian way of life.

A direct consequence of soaring divorce rates is an increasing number of children who lead at least a proportion of their dependent years in single-parent homes. According to recent findings, approximately 23 percent of divorcing couples have one, 21 percent have two, and an additional 8 percent have three or more dependent children (Statistics Canada 1980). From these figures, it can be concluded that at least 60 000 Canadian children every year experience divorce first hand. These figures do not include children from

desertions, informal separations (which may or may not lead to a legal divorce), annulments, and common law breakups, and therefore underestimate the actual number of children who remain in single-parent families.

Canadian courts, in spite of emphasizing the "best interests of the child" in awarding custody, still show a positive bias toward the mother. Regardless of the sex of the parent who petitions for divorce, the majority of children remain under the custody of the female parent. In 1980, 78 percent of the mothers and 16 percent of the fathers obtained custody of their child(ren) (calculated from Statistics Canada 1980, 24, Table 15). Therefore, this study will focus on the adjustment of female-headed families after separation or divorce.

Aside from the functioning of the female parent, this study explores the effects of separation and divorce on the children of mother-led families in four areas: school adjustment, relationships with peers, and relationships with the custodial and non-custodial parents. In addition, the sex of the child will be considered as a factor in terms of overall adjustment. Since the study is exploratory, specific hypotheses were not formulated, but previous research suggested that the adjustment of children would be a function of the custodial parents' adjustment and economic standing rather than a direct result of separation or divorce per se (e.g., Ambert and Baker 1984; Pett 1982a, 1982b).

Source: Conciliation Courts Review 24 (1986): 79–89. Reprinted with permission.

Theoretical Perspective

Although numerous theories that contribute to the understanding of possible effects of marital breakdown on parents and their children have been developed, the structural functional approach is one of the most frequently used. In general, this approach predicts the undesirable consequences of separation and divorce.

Structural functionalists look on the family as one of the central institutions within the larger society. Their approach emphasizes the functions of the family within society (such as the regulation of sexual activity, reproduction, socialization of the young, protection, etc.), and focusses on the functions of the family members within the family unit itself (such as the division of labour in terms of the instrumental and affectional leadership). Structural change within the family is thus perceived as problematic not only for members of the family but also for the equilibrium of the society at large. Advocates of this approach (e.g., Glasser and Navarre 1965) argue that family disruption is devastating for the members (especially the children) in at least four fundamental areas.

1. *Task Structure.* According to Glasser and Navarre, "providing for the physical, emotional, and social needs of all the family members is a full-time job for two adults" (p. 100). Since females in general are less prepared for well-paying, prestigious jobs and since they are also the ones who most frequently retain custody of the children, the lowered socioeconomic standard of the one-parent (especially female-headed) families will bear serious consequences for the adjustment of the children.

2. *Communication Structure.* Again, in this approach, parents are seen as the transmitters of the norms and values of the society to the children while simultaneously representing them in the adult world. The absence of a parent will likely create a void in the dual transmitting function of the remaining, overburdened parent, since his (or most likely her) participation will be limited in the adult world and thus lead to a structural distortion in the child(ren)'s development.

3. *Power Structure.* In the one-parent family, children will perceive power as personal rather than consensual. The nondemocratic way in which decisions are made and implemented may create a rigid conceptualization of power in the children's minds with no leeway for mediation and may, therefore, adversely affect their development. For the remaining parent, making decisions on all aspects of daily living is also perceived as an insurmountable task.

4. *Affectional Structure.* Finally, one-parent families are perceived as conducive to intense relationships between children and the remaining parent, who is more than likely to be overburdened by constant emotional demands of children without a safe outlet for his or her own needs. Also, it is suggested that in this emotionally charged atmosphere, the probability of a certain family member becoming a scapegoat is heightened.

The numerous critiques of the structural functional models will only be briefly introduced here (e.g., Baker 1984; Clayton 1975; Eshleman and Clarke 1978; Goode 1982; Lamanna and Riedmann 1985; Sprey 1969). These criticisms centre around the "taken for granted" functionality of one specific form of family (intact) and on the perception that alternative forms are deviations or oddities. Social systems, unlike physiological systems, do not have a norm from which deviations can be easily measured and are not based on cooperation, equilibrium seeking, and consensus throughout their existence. By designating one form as "desirable," functionalists imply that they perceive all other forms as harmful to themselves as well as to the society at large. The important point to be made is that the structural functional models, which have affected our perception of marital breakdown for decades, predict negative effects of divorce and separation on children of *both* sexes as well as on the adults.

Review of the Literature

Studies assessing the effects of divorce on children abound in the United States but are relatively few in Canada. However, the findings from both sources are often contradictory and a large number of studies are plagued by the researcher's methodological weaknesses and disciplinary biases (for an in-depth discussion, see Ambert 1980). Most researchers start with the a priori assumption that divorce has disruptive effects on children. Therefore, the studies that show negative effects (e.g., Ambert and Saucier 1984; Burgess 1970; Glasser and Navarre 1965; Gould 1968; Mueller and Pope 1977; Pitts 1964) are not surprising. More clinically oriented scholars begin with even less optimism and often start with children (or adults) who have been brought to the attention of (or sought help from) mental-health facilities. These researchers have found children of divorce to be susceptible to a variety of problems, such as depression (McDermott 1970; Wallerstein and Kelly 1980), antisocial behaviour and delinquency (Glueck and Glueck 1951; Whitehead 1979), low self-esteem and feelings of rejection (Despert 1962; Kaplan and Pokorny 1971; McDermott 1968; Wallerstein and Kelly 1975, 1976), sexual misconduct (Hetherington 1972; Landis 1960, 1963), and lowered academic aspirations (Wallerstein and Kelly 1976).

Only a few unpublished studies have found that divorce has no detrimental effects on children or that the initial effects are often not long lasting (Gardner 1974; Nye 1957; Wallerstein and Kelly 1980). Kurdek and Siesky (1980), after in-depth interviews with custodial parents and children of divorce, concluded that children acquired strengths and responsibilities in the course of adjusting to divorce. This conclusion highlights our contention that divorce need not be a traumatic experience for all children (p. 99). Both Colletta (1983) and Ambert (1980) assert that the negative effects are often a function of the economic difficulties that female lone parents experience and are not caused by divorce per se. This assertion appears to be supported by Pett (1982a, 1982b), who observed that economic factors directly affect the parents' social adjustment and (through their impact on the custodial parent) indirectly affect the children's social adjustment.

Bernard and Nesbitt (1981), in assessing the effects of divorce on children, conclude that divorce is "an unreliable predictor of mental illness, achievement, delinquency, and emotional predispositions" (p. 40). In addition, they suggest that a "large majority of children of divorce continue to function, engage in healthy interpersonal relationships, and succeed in school" (p. 40).

Aside from the debate concerning the effects of divorce and separation on children, there is controversy over sex differences in terms of effects. Examining families in which one parent had a psychiatric disorder, Rutter (1970) found that "discord and disruption in the home were consistently and strongly associated with antisocial disorder in boys, but not in girls" (p. 169). The author claims that this observation also holds true in marital disruption since " 'broken homes' were associated with antisocial disorder in boys, but not girls" (p. 169). Discussing civilian reactions to air raids, mortality following bereavement, and studies of foster children, Rutter (1970) suggests that boys (and men) are "more vulnerable" (p. 175) and favours the argument that girls' disorders may have a genetic component whereas boys' disorders are predominantly a function of environmental factors.

Kalter (1977) found that boys living in single-parent homes as well as boys in reconstituted families show more aggression and problems with the law than do boys from intact families. However, girls living in single-parent or reconstituted families were observed to have a wider range of problems such as aggression, sexual promiscuity, drug use, and problems with school performance.

In a recent article, Francke (1984a) claims that "boys tend to take the failure of their parents' marriages harder than girls, take longer to adjust, and show far more disruptions in behaviour" (p. 166).

Whitehead (1979) suggests that one reason studies (particularly those finding that boys experience more negative effects,) have shown sex differences, is that the behaviour of males is different from females. Whitehead's (1979) findings indicate that male children of divorced couples tend to act out, whereas female children withdraw. Teachers and physicians, for example, are more inclined to identify boys as disturbed. Aside from suggesting the reasons for observed sex differences, Whitehead (1979) argues that children of divorce fare better than children who remain in families experiencing continuous marital discord.

Since most of our understanding of the process and effects of divorce is based on studies that use negatively skewed samples (those who seek help from mental-health agencies, those who are in counselling, children having problems at school or with the law, etc.), our overall perception remains gloomy. The current study, unlike many others, addressed female parents who were not associated with mental-health agencies or social services.

Methodology

The current study used a "snowball" sampling technique. Students who were taking courses at Glendon College (York University) and their friends were interviewed. The sample consisted of 57 mothers who were either separated or divorced for at least one year and who had retained custody of their child(ren). Participants were assured of their anonymity both at the beginning and at the end of the interviews.

A questionnaire was developed that covered an array of topics found to be problematic for single mothers and their children after a separation or divorce. Apart from demographic questions, a series of questions was asked about (1) the socioeconomic changes that had taken place since the separation, (2) the emotional aura of the splitup, (3) responsibility and blame processes, (4) the perceived contribution of different factors to the breakup, (5) the emotional and financial support, (5) the division of assets, and (6) the perceived effects of the breakup on children's school performance and relationship with parents and peers. The majority of the questions were designed as closed format, on a five-point Likert-type scale. The participants were encouraged to elaborate on the questions that required a yes/no answer. The last four questions were open-ended. The interviews lasted between 45 and 60 minutes. This paper deals only with the closed-format questions.

Description of Sample

Subjects

The subjects' mean age at the time of the interviews was 37.9 years and at the time of separation had been 31.1 years. On average, the couples had been married for 9.5 years and separated for an average of 6.8 years.

Almost one-half (43.8 percent) of the subjects had some university education or a university degree. An additional 22.9 percent had completed courses or obtained a certificate from a community college, while 31.6 percent of the subjects had at least attended or completed high school. Just one subject had only completed elementary school.

In terms of employment, 57.9 percent of the subjects had full-time jobs, 12.3 percent were employed part-time, and the remainder (29.8 percent) stated no employment.

Of the 57 women, 35.1 percent defined their marital status as separated, 33.3 percent as divorced, 14 percent as remarried, and 12.2 percent as living common law. Three subjects (5.3 percent) had reconstituted their original marriages.

Ex-Partners

The general characteristics of the ex-partners as stated by the subjects of the study are as follows. The average age of the ex-partner at the time of the study was 41 years and at the time of the separation had been 34.3 years.

Of the ex-partners, 38.6 percent had either attended university or completed a degree, while an additional 19.3 percent had taken courses or obtained a certificate from a community college. One-third of the ex-spouses had attended or completed high school while the remaining 8.8 percent had attended or completed elementary school.

The marital status of the ex-spouses at the time of the study was reported to be 33.9 percent separated, 17.9 percent divorced, 30 percent remarried, and 12.5 percent living common law. Some respondents did not know the current marital status of their ex-partners.

Children

From the dissolved relationships, there were 96 dependent children (50 females and 46 males) who were under the care of their mothers (an average of 1.7 children per mother). Three of the mothers had children from more recent relationships (two males and four females), but these children were excluded from the analysis. Of the 57 women interviewed, 43.8 percent had one child, 45.6 percent two, 8.7 percent three, and 1.7 percent (one subject) had four children. The mean age of the children ($N = 93$) was 8.24 years.

As can be seen from the above sample characteristics, the subjects approximate the "average Canadian divorce profile." However, some characteristics are contrary to the general Canadian averages.

First, in terms of the couples themselves, we can see that the males are 3.2 years older than their wives at marriage. This is slightly higher than the current 2.6 years difference for all Canada (Statistics Canada 1980, 2, Table 1).

The differences between our respondents and their ex-partners in terms of present marital status, employment, and education are as follows. In our sample, the separated and common law categories for both sexes were almost identical, but the divorced and remarried categories were very different. While almost twice as many females as males reported to be divorced (33 percent versus 17 percent), twice as many males were reported to be remarried (30 percent versus 14 percent). The tendency of divorced males to remarry is also reflected in Canadian statistics (Statistics Canada 1980, 6–8, Table 4).

Another area where our sample differed from the Canadian population is employment status. Whereas 51.6 percent of the adult female population in Canada work (Armstrong 1984, 202), our sample's labour participation was higher (57.9 percent full-time and 12.3 percent part-time). The deviation of the employment status of the ex-partners from the Canadian statistics is more pronounced. All ex-spouses were claimed to have full-time jobs while the male participation rate in the labour force is 76.9 percent (Armstrong 1984, 202).

Finally, in their level of education the ex-partners and the subjects not only differed from each other but also differed from the Canadian averages. In our sample, the females have slightly more university education (43.8 percent versus 38.6 percent) and community-college experience (22.9 percent versus 19.3 percent) than the males. Hiller (1976, 63) reports that 9.8 percent of the Canadian population over 15 years of age have university education or a university degree while 43.8 percent of our sample fell into this category. This difference is probably an artifact of the employed sampling technique, since most of the subjects came from a university setting.

In relation to the children, it was previously stated that there were 1.7 children per mother, which is almost twice the Canadian average for divorcing couples. In 1980, the mean number of dependent children per divorced families in Canada was .96 (Statistics Canada

1980, 26, Table 17). However, since .96 children per family includes all divorces, approximately half of which do not involve children, our sample approximates the divorcing couples who do have children.

In sum, then, it appears that our sample fits reasonably well into the Canadian profile of single mothers with dependent children except for educational attainment and employment status, which have been attributed to the employed sampling technique.

Results

The following results pertain to the process of marital breakdown and the subsequent changes that took place in the single parents' and their children's lives.

In this study, 48 percent of the subjects claimed that they had initiated the separation whereas 37.5 percent said that the separation process was initiated by the ex-partner. The remainder (14.2 percent) stated that the separation was a mutual decision. Although most women reported to have initiated the separation themselves, a large percentage (57.9 percent) thought that their ex-spouses' actions were responsible for the breakdown of their marriages. Only 22.8 percent claimed that the responsibility was theirs and an additional 10.5 percent perceived the responsibility for the breakdown as mutual. A few women (8.7 percent) blamed a third party.

Regardless of who had initiated the separation and who was responsible for the breakdown, two thirds (66.6 percent) of the respondents recalled that the separation process was either negative or very negative. Only six women (10.5 percent) stated that the separation had taken place in a positive atmosphere.

Among the causes for marital breakdown, extramarital relationships (43.1 percent), extended family obligations (36.8 percent), sexual problems (19.3 percent), occupational problems (working late, etc.: 14 percent), social problems (choice of friends, frequency of social gatherings, etc.: 14 percent), differences in child-rearing (14 percent), and financial problems (8.7 percent) were considered most crucial. During the breakup, 10.5 percent of the women claimed that they had received emotional support from their children, 31.5 percent from their family and 33.3 percent from friends. The number of women who sought help from self-help groups or professionals was small (3.5 and 7 percent, respectively).

As far as financial help at the time of separation was concerned, 57.9 percent said that ex-partners helped, whereas financial support from family (36.8 percent), government agencies (includes scholarships: 31.5 percent), or friends (8.7 percent) was lower. Of the 57 subjects, 31.5 percent claimed a *rise* in their standard of living after the separation and 33.3 percent claimed no change. The remaining women (35 percent) mentioned a slight decline in their standard of living following the separation.

Currently, the majority of the women perceived the ex-partners' contribution to the upbringing of their children as much less than desirable. In fact, 49.1 percent claimed very little or no financial contribution, 68.5 percent claimed no contribution in terms of the educational development of their children. Over half of the subjects (59.6 percent) claimed no help from ex-partners for children's leisure and recreational needs and 81.7 percent claimed no contribution from the ex-partners to children's emotional needs and development. In spite of the perceived lack of involvement of the majority of fathers, only 21 percent of the women claimed that the separation process had had any negative effects on their children. Interestingly, 57.9 percent stated that their children would not have been any different if they had remained in the intact family. One-fifth (21 percent) of the women felt that the calm atmosphere after the separation was actually beneficial for the children, while 50 percent claimed that they had become more tolerant toward their children after the separation (only 5.5 percent reported a decline). Children's performance at school, relationships with peers, mother, and father since the separation are depicted in Table 1.

Table I

Mothers' Ratings of Children on Four Scales

Scale	School	Peers	Mother	Father
Better*	13%	9%	40%	23%
	11	8	36	20
Same	67%	82%	43%	37%
	57	72	38	32
Worse	20%	9%	17%	40%
	17	8	15	35
Totals	100%	100%	100%	100%
	85	88	89	87

*Items are condensed from a five-point scale.

As Table 1 indicates, the vast majority (67 percent) of mothers perceived no change in their children's school performance or their relationship with peers (82 percent) after the separation. In fact, 13 percent of the mothers claimed that the children improved in their school work and 9 percent claimed that the children's relationship with their peers improved following the separation. Only 20 percent of the mothers felt that their children's school work declined and 9 percent stated that their relationship with their peers was not as good. As far as the post-separation relationship with the parents is concerned, 43 percent of the women said that their relationship with their children stayed the same and 37 percent of the women claimed that the children's relationship with the father showed no change. An additional 40 percent of the women claimed a better relationship with their children since the separation, while 23 percent of the women perceived that the children had better relationships with their fathers. Only 17 percent of the women felt that the relationship with their children was not as good as before the separation. Forty percent of the women perceived a deterioration of the relationship between the children and their fathers. On a five-point scale, the mother's ratings of the children's current relationship with the mother and the father are significantly different (correlated $t(86) = 3.702$, $p < .001$ two-tailed).

The data were analyzed for sex differences. As far as the school performance was concerned, there were no differences ($M = 3.143$ for both groups). In terms of peer relations and relationship with the father and mother, there were slight differences between the two sexes, but none of these differences reached a level of significance (Peer: $t(86) = -.553$, $p < .20$; Father: $t(85) = -1.245$, $p < .20$; Mother: $t(87) = -.621$, $p < .20$).

Discussion

The 57 women interviewed for this study were those who had kept their children after a separation.

An important aspect of this study that should be addressed here is that the subjects of the study were highly educated women, the majority of whom were able to retain their standard of living after a separation. In this sense, the sample of the study deviates from the general population of female-headed families, most of which subsist close to or below the poverty line. Therefore, although the results of the study are not generalizable to all female-headed families, this deviation makes the current results intriguing in themselves.

In the present study, almost half of the subjects (48.2 percent) claimed that they initiated the separation while the majority (57.9 percent) were certain that the ex-partners were responsible for the breakdown of the marriage. In this regard, our findings closely paralleled earlier observations (Ambert 1980; Ambert and Baker 1984; Goode 1956). One explanation of this phenomenon was provided by Goode (1956) almost three decades ago. He stated, "in our society the husband more frequently than the wife will engage in behaviour whose function, if not intent, whose result, if not aim, is to force the other spouse to ask for the divorce first" (p. 135). Our study seems to support Goode's (1956) assertion.

In terms of the stated causes of the breakdown, it was found, in a majority of cases, that more extramarital relations (42.1 percent) and extended family obligations (36.8 percent) were salient. Earlier studies had indicated economic problems to be one of the chief factors in marital dissolution (Blood and Wolfe 1960). In Ambert's (1980) terms, "poverty can, directly or insidiously, attack family life and either destroy relationships or prevent them from ever taking a strong hold" (p. 70). In the current study, very few women (8.7 percent) mentioned financial problems among the causes for their marriage breakdown. This is not surprising, because the subjects were able to avoid a decline in their standard of living after the separation. Our sample appears to represent only a privileged minority of the mostly impoverished female-headed families.

One theme that emerged from the interviews was the lack of involvement of the ex-partners with the upbringing of the children. In fact, 49.1 percent of the women claimed that the fathers' monetary contribution was very little or none at all, whereas a larger percentage (68.5 percent) complained about the fathers' lack of involvement with the children's educational development. The concern expressed by the majority of women (81.7 percent) was the fathers' passivity in terms of the children's emotional needs. In spite of these problems, the mothers still were confident of their children's well-being within the female-headed family environment. As Ambert (1980) argues "when economic conditions are more favourable . . . [the mother's] relationship with her children is likely to be close and rewarding" (p. 147). Referring to women similar to the subjects of this study, Ambert (1980) suggests that "women who have children and are very involved in their work may find, after divorce, that they have more time to devote to both as well as to themselves" (p. 149). The reported increase in tolerance here may therefore be just another implication of the increased time for self and children in this specific group.

The children of the present sample of women seem to have adjusted well after the separation and divorce. Very few mothers reported a decline in their school performance (20 percent), relations with peers (9 percent) or in the mother–child relationship (17 percent). Our findings suggest that 80 percent or more of the children are functioning just as well or better than during the pre-separation period. The only area that seems to deteriorate is the children's relationship with their fathers (40 percent). This may result from, for example, problems with access, distance between the fathers' and the children's residences, the new relationships and commitments of over 40 percent of the fathers, and from the unfulfilling and artificial environments in which the fathers have an opportunity to see their children (Epstein 1974; Wallerstein and Kelly 1980). On the other hand, it may simply be due to the bias of the mother's perception. We must point out, however, that the majority of children seem to retain meaningful relationships with their mothers. As Pett (1982a) argues, the most important factor in children's post-divorce adjustment may be the positive relationship with the custodial parent; this may well explain the lack of problems of the children of our subjects.

An interesting finding of the current study was the lack of differences between the male and female children with regard to post-divorce school performance, peer relations, and relations with both the custodial and non-custodial parents. This finding seems to contradict earlier findings by Rutter (1970), Wolkind and Rutter (1973), Francke (1983a, 1983b), and Biller (1970) that show significantly more negative effects of divorce on boys. Whitehead (1979), questioning the link between parental discord and maladjustment in male children, concludes that girls and boys are equally likely to be negatively affected by separation and divorce, although the effects take the form of antisocial behaviour in boys and withdrawal in girls. In the present study, although no direct questions about antisocial behaviour or withdrawal were asked, no mothers mentioned such behaviour during open-ended questions or during their ratings on school performance and relationship with peers, mother, and father. The ratings were primarily "the same" or "better."

Summary and Conclusions

Using the snowball sampling technique previously described, 57 women from the Metropolitan Toronto area who were separated or divorced for at least one year and had custody of their child(ren) were interviewed. The findings indicated that the 96 children of the subjects were functioning well in their school and had good relationships with their peers and their mothers. A little less than half of the mothers reported a decline in their children's relationship with the father. Contrary to earlier findings, there were no significant differences between the female and male children in any of the four categories of interest.

Before we can discuss the overall implications of the current observations, we should emphasize some of the difficulties in making generalizations. For example, the subjects of the current study did not experience a sharp decline in their standard of living after the marital breakdown.

Furthermore, the current results are based solely on the mothers' perceptions and recollections. Of course, it would have been more desirable if the fathers, school teachers, and especially the children themselves were also included in the study to paint a more accurate picture. Because, in our study, these additional sources of information are not present, the lack of negative effects and the lack of sex differences must be evaluated with caution.

On the other hand, what adds considerable confidence to our results is the earlier finding that parents and children significantly agree with one another in their responses pertaining to the lack of sex differences (Pett 1982a). If this is the case, our finding of "no significance" is significant indeed.

The often-observed negative effects of separation and divorce by both clinically oriented and systems-oriented researchers have helped to preserve the myth that "divorce has inordinate powers to hurt people regardless of the

mental health and maturity of the adults and children involved" (Bernard and Nesbitt 1981, 40). No statistics are available on the men and women who remain in undesirable unions to protect their children from the well-popularized negative effects of marital breakdown; nevertheless, there is evidence that remaining in unhappy but intact homes is more destructive to a child than living with a single parent (Whitehead 1979). Also, there are no available statistics on children who are brought up without behavioural and/or emotional problems by capable lone parents. Faced with the negative expectations of the structural-functional or clinical approaches, we often seek (and find) adverse effects of separation on adults as well as on children. In this way, we reinforce the status quo, under which the intact nuclear family is considered the most desirable family structure.

According to the structuralist approach, the absence of a parent is expected to have a shattering effect on children. The absence of one parent (usually the father), is perceived as disrupting the task, power, affection, and communication structures of the system, and having severe consequences for its functioning. What the systems approach seems to ignore is that some intact families are non-functional, and that lone-parent families are also systems with established adaptation, goal attainment, integration, and pattern-maintenance strategies. Although the transition from the former to the latter may be difficult, the outcome will undoubtedly depend on who the male, the female, and the children are, regardless of the type of system. Some new systems can and do become as strong or stronger than their "intact" predecessors.

The present sample of well-functioning female-headed families is an example to the point. The findings, indicating that divorce and separation need not be traumatic, support earlier findings by Kurdek and Siesky (1980), Pett (1982a), Bernard and Nesbitt (1981), and Desimone-Luis, O'Mahoney, and Hunt (1979). Theoretical orientations that fail to take into account the economic characteristics surrounding divorce often confuse the effects of sheer deprivation (which might be just as devastating for intact families) with the psychological effects of the breakup. Such perspectives also directly or indirectly help preserve the status quo under which the intact family (no matter how flimsy) is revered while ever-growing numbers of single-parent homes are viewed with suspicion, if not fear. New theories need to be developed to predict and explain the effects of separation and divorce and to reflect the quickly changing social realities.

Far ahead of her time, Mead once said:

As things are, we insist that the most flimsy, ill conceived and unsuitable mating be treated as a sanctified lifelong choice. At the same time, we insist that every divorce, however much it is dictated by every consideration for the welfare of parents and children, be regarded as a failure and be listed as an index of social disorder along with suicide, homicide, narcotic addition, alcoholism and crime. By insisting upon these views of divorce, we debar ourselves from developing appropriate institutions for protecting children from an unrealistic dependence on a situation of lifelong marriage between their parents. (qtd. Bohannan 1971, 124)

Although these words were written more than half a century ago, we still emphasize the negative effects of divorce. We reinforce this emphasis in our observations of people who have trouble coping. A more positive approach will expand our understanding of single-parent families by concentrating not only on those who face problems, but also on those who function well. Only through such a shift in our thinking will we gain a deeper understanding of a phenomenon that is here to stay and devise strategies that will increase the proportion of those "who make it." For example, young children can be taught that traditional marriages are not the only acceptable form of meaningful relationships; marriages rarely parallel the fairy tales in which people live "happily ever after." Both boys and girls can be socialized to seek self-fulfilment without lifelong dependence on a significant other,

and to pursue interests, higher education, and occupational skills that will protect them from economic, psychological, or social devastation if their family situation drastically changes. This refocussing should also take place in court practices, where the care of children will be perceived as an equally shared responsibility of both parents, not as something contingent on the continuation of the intact family or on the assignment of custody, by default, to the female parent.

The suggested changes can only occur if we conquer the "divorceaphobia" that exists in our society and give due attention (and respect) to those "who make it."

Works Cited

Ambert, A. 1980. *Divorce in Canada.* Toronto: Academic.

Ambert, A., and Baker, M. 1984 "Marriage Dissolution: Structural and Ideological Changes." *The Family, Changing Trends in Canada.* Ed. M. Baker. Toronto: McGraw-Hill Ryerson. 85–103.

Ambert, A., and J. Saucier. 1984. "Adolescents' Academic Success and Aspirations by Parental Marital Status." *The Canadian Review of Sociology and Anthropology* 21(1): 62–74.

Armstrong, P. 1984. *Labour Pains: Women's Work in Crisis.* Toronto: Women's Press.

Baker, M. 1984. *The Family: Changing Trends in Canada.* Toronto: McGraw-Hill Ryerson.

Bernard, J.M., and S. Nesbitt. 1981. "Divorce: An Unreliable Predictor of Children's Emotional Predispositions." *Journal of Divorce* 4: 31–42.

Biller, H.B. 1970. "Father Absence and the Personality Development of the Male Child." *Developmental Psychology* 2: 181–201.

Blood, R.O., Jr., and D.M. Wolfe. 1960. *Husbands and Wives.* New York: Free Press.

Bohannan, P. 1971. "The Six Stations of Divorce." *Divorce and After.* Ed. P. Bohannan. New York: Doubleday.

Burgess, J.K. 1970. "The Single-Parent Family: A Social and Sociological Problem." *The Family Coordinator* 19: 137–44.

Clayton, R.R. 1975. *The Family, Marriage and Social Change.* Lexington, MA: Heath.

Colletta, N.D. 1983. "Stressful Lives: The Situation of Divorced Mothers and Their Children." *Journal of Divorce* 6(3): 19–31.

Desimone-Luis, J., K. O'Mahoney, and D. Hunt. 1979. "Children of Separation and Divorce: Factors Influencing Adjustment." *Journal of Divorce* 3: 37–41.

Despert, L. 1962. *Children of Divorce.* New York: Dolphin Books/Doubleday.

Elkin, F. 1964. *The Family in Canada.* Ottawa: Vanier Institute of the Family.

Epstein, J. 1974. *Divorced in America.* New York: Dutton.

Eshelman, J.R., and J.N. Clarke. 1978. *Intimacy, Commitments and Marriage: Development of Relationships.* Boston: Allyn and Bacon.

Francke, L.B. 1984a. "The Sons of Divorce." *Annual Edition: Marriage and Family 84/85.* Eds. O. Pocs and R.H. Walsh. Guilford, CT: Dushkin.

—— 1984b. "Children of Divorce." *Annual Edition: Marriage and Family 84/85.* Eds. O. Pocs and R.H. Walsh. Guilford, CT: Dushkin.

Gardner, R.A. 1974. "Psychological Aspects of Divorce." *American Handbook of Psychiatry.* 2d ed. Vol. 1. Ed. S. Ariel. New York: Basic.

Glasser, P., and E. Navarre. 1965. "Structural Problems of the One-Parent Family." *Journal of Social Issues* 21: 98–109.

Glueck, S., and E. Glueck. 1951. *Unraveling Juvenile Delinquency.* Cambridge, MA: Harvard University Press.

Goode, W.J. 1956. *After Divorce.* Glencoe, IL: Free Press.

—— 1982. *The Family.* 2d ed. Englewood Cliffs, NJ: Prentice-Hall.

Gould, E. 1968. "The Single-Parent Family Benefits in Parents Without Partners." *Journal of Marriage and the Family* 30: 666–71.

Hetherington, E.M. 1972. "Effects of Father Absence on Personality Development in Adolescent Daughters. *Developmental Psychology* 7: 313–26.

Hiller, H.H. 1976. *Canadian Society: A Sociological Analysis.* Englewood Cliffs, NJ: Prentice-Hall.

Kalter, N. 1977. "Children of Divorce in an Outpatient Psychiatric Population." *American Journal of Orthopsychiatry* 47: 40–51.

Kaplan, H.B., and A.D. Pokorny. 1971. "Self-Derogation and Childhood Broken Home." *Journal of Marriage and the Family* 33: 328–50.

Kurdek, L.A., and A.E. Siesky. 1980. "Effects of Divorce on Children: The Relationship Between Parent and Child Perspectives." *Journal of Divorce* 4(2): 85–99.

Lamanna, M.A., and A. Riedmann, 1985. *Marriages and Families.* 2d ed. Belmont, CA: Wadsworth.

Landis, J.T. 1960. "The Trauma of Children When Parents Divorce." *Marriage and Family Living* 22: 7–13.

—— 1963. "Dating Maturation of Children from Happy and Unhappy Marriages." *Marriage and Family Living* 25: 351–53.

McDermott, J.F. 1968. "Parental Divorce in Early Childhood." *American Journal of Psychiatry* 124: 1424–32.

—— 1970. "Divorce and Its Psychiatric Sequalae in Children." *Archives of General Psychiatry* 23: 421–28.

Mueller, C.W., and H. Pope. 1977. "Marital Instability: A Study of Its Transmission Between Generations." *Journal of Marriage and the Family* 39: 83–92.

Nye, F.I. 1957. "Child Adjustment in Broken and in Unhappy Unbroken Homes." *Marriage and Family Living* 19: 356–61.

Pett, M.G. 1982a. "Correlates of Children's Social Adjustment Following Divorce." *Journal of Divorce* 5(4): 25–39.

—— 1982b. "Predictors of Satisfactory Social Adjustment of Divorced Single Parents." *Journal of Divorce* 5(3): 1–17.

Pitts, J.R. 1964. "The Structural Functional Approach." *Handbook of Marriage and the Family.* Ed. E.T. Christensen. Skokie, IL: Rand McNally. 51–124.

Rutter, M. 1970. "Sex Differences in Children's Responses to Family Stress." *The Child in His Family.* Eds. E.J. Anthony and C. Koupernik. New York: Wiley-Interscience.

Sprey, J. 1969. "The Family as a System in Conflict. *Journal of Marriage and the Family* 31 (November): 699–706.

Statistics Canada. 1980. *Vital Statistics. Vol. 2: Marriages and Divorces.* Catalogue 84–205. Ottawa: Statistics Canada.

Wallerstein, J., and J. Kelly. 1975. "The Effects of Parental Divorce: Experiences of the Preschool Child." *Journal of Child Psychiatry* 14: 600–16.

—— 1976. "The Effects of Parental Divorce: Experiences of the Child in Later Latency." *Journal of Child Psychiatry* 14: 256–69.

—— 1980. *Surviving the Breakup: How Children and Parents Cope with Divorce.* New York: Basic.

Whitehead, L. 1979. "Sex Differences in Children's Responses to Family Stress: A Reexamination." *Journal of Child Psychology and Psychiatry.* 20(3): 247–54.

Wolkind, S., and M. Rutter. 1973. "Children Who have Been 'In Care': An Epidemiological Survey." *Journal of Child Psychiatry* 14: 97–105.

MENTAL HEALTH AND THE IN-FAMILY SEXUAL ABUSE OF CHILDREN AND ADOLESCENTS

Chris Bagley

The author addresses basic issues in the sexual abuse of children within the family. Sexual abuse is distinguished from incest. The cultural roots of sexual abuse are discussed, and insights of the feminist model are applied. Various limited studies of incidence and prevalence are reviewed with a view to estimating possible rates of abuse in Canada. Studies linking early sexual abuse with a range of serious physical and psychosocial sequelae are reviewed. The author discusses treatment models and the goals of treatment, and argues strongly for improved services to the affected population and for a fundamental value change in society that will eliminate the sexual victimization of children.

Basic Issues in Child Sexual Abuse

Definitions

Although the term "incest" is persistently used to describe sexual assaults on children within the family, incest and child sexual abuse are not synonymous. Incest is a concept that should be defined in anthropological or sociobiological terms. It concerns the aversion toward and the rules and taboos concerning continued sexual relations between closely related people that are likely to result in pregnancy and an alternative family (Bagley 1969; Van Den Berghe 1983). Incest always concerns sexually mature individuals, usually in

Source: *Canada's Mental Health* 32 (1984): 17–23. Reprinted with permission of the Minister of Supply and Services Canada.

a consensual union. The large majority of cases of child sexual abuse do not fulfil these conditions, but involve the sexual coercion and domination of young children of either sex by adults (Meiselman 1978; Schlesinger 1982). Sexual abuse of children is usually the act of someone known to the victim, most probably a family member (Goodwin, McCarthy, and DiVasto 1981). However, stepfathers or cohabiters are more likely than biological fathers to assault children in the home. Legally, incest involves having sexual intercourse with a close relative; however, many sexual assaults on children, whether by relatives or by nonrelatives, stop short of actual intercourse. This does not usually make the psychological trauma of the assault any less serious (Herman and Hirschman 1981).

Cultural Issues and Values

Another problem concerns the incest taboo itself: since sexual assaults on children are widespread, either the taboo is being frequently violated, or else the idea of incest applies to a different category of adult relationships. The latter is a much more plausible hypothesis. Florence Rush, in her historical review of the "best kept secret" (1980), produces a mass of evidence to show that the sexual exploitation of children has been an integral but undiscussed aspect of Western culture for many centuries. The sexual concern of males with deflowering the purity and innocence of childhood led to the obsession

314

of many Victorian males with the exploitation of children, a passion that has borne fruit in the modern obsession with nymphets and child pornography. So-called sexual emancipation, Rush argues, has led to the male fantasy of a utopia in which "men will never be burdened by emotional traumas, venereal disease, pregnancy, commitments, responsibilities, charges of rape, statutory rape or child molestation as the consequence of their sexual behaviour."

Sexual abuse of children takes many forms, and is certainly not confined to the intercourse defined by the incest statute. Sexual abuse can range from the sexualization of children for commercial purposes (in advertisements or mass media), to the exploitation of children through pornography, and to various kinds of sexual assault ranging from exposure and manual interference to the grossest forms of sexual assault on prepubertal children. The feminist view, which I accept, is that this sexual exploitation of children, especially within the family context, is made possible by a deep-rooted value climate that allows males to regard females, (especially powerless females), as suitable objects for all kinds of exploitation.

Adults who sexually assault children, including their own, are frequently described in the literature as inadequate personalities who have created or are experiencing disordered marital relationships, and who often use alcohol (Frude 1982). These clinical profiles don't contradict the argument that child sexual assault is caused, fundamentally, by a value principle that underpins the exploitation of all children. The argument asserts that weak and relatively powerless males use children (usually, but not always, female children) not only for sexual gratification, but also for the exercise of power and status (Peters 1976).

Incidence and Prevalence

The available evidence suggests that the true incidence of child sexual assault within a family context is unknown, but that the phenomenon has almost certainly involved a significant minority of all children — perhaps as many as 10 percent. Sarafino estimated in 1979 that a total of 336 200 sexual offences of all kinds were committed against children in the United States each year (1979). This figure, based on agency reports, is almost certainly an underestimate; other figures put the figure at between 5 and 15 percent of the child population (Finkelhor 1978).

Finkelhor (1979a) surveyed a population of college students in the United States, and found that 19 percent of the women and 9 percent of the men had been sexually assaulted by the age of 16. Girls from lower-income families were more likely to have been assaulted, as were girls from socially isolated backgrounds and those from family situations in which the natural mother was absent. Eleven percent of the women in this survey had been assaulted when under age 12 by someone aged 18 or over, usually someone within their intimate social network. Finkelhor concluded that

these figures confirm the growing suspicion that sexual victimization of children is very widespread. They also show that it is very much a family problem. If we were to extrapolate on the basis of this data, something we are not really entitled to do, given the limitations of the sample, we would estimate that about 9 percent of all women are sexually victimized by a relative, and about one and a half percent are involved in father–daughter sex.

One of the limitations of these estimates, which Finkelhor acknowledges, is that children from low-income families (considered a high-risk group) are less likely to become college students. In addition, a frequent result of child sexual assault in the family is disorganized behaviour, including dropping out of school; this also makes college attendance less likely. These two factors, which would tend to lower the rate of reported sexual abuse in the college-student sample, suggest that Finkelhor's estimates for the general population may, in fact, be underestimates.

Another type of study — a nonrandom survey of a large female population in North America — provided a different perspective (Wolfe 1981). In 1980, 106 000 female readers of the large-circulation magazine *Cosmopolitan* returned a postal questionnaire to the magazine. Of the self-selected respondents, 11 percent had experienced sexual relations with a relative when a child: 5 percent reported brother–sister relations, 3 percent father–daughter, and a further 6 percent reported sexual assault by an uncle, grandparent, or other relative. Rape, threats, and coercion were frequently featured in these reports, and only sex between siblings close in age was subjectively reported to have no harmful psychological sequelae for the girl. Often the trauma reported was severe and long-lasting. This interesting survey cannot give accurate estimates for the population at large, but it does confirm the widespread nature of the problem and the trauma that the assault frequently entails for the female victim.

Two estimates of the prevalence of the sexual abuse of children are available from random samples of U.S. adult populations. Finkelhor surveyed 521 adult men and women in the Boston area: 12 percent (15 percent of the women and 6 percent of the men) had suffered sexual abuse as children or adolescents, both within and outside the family (Finkelhor 1982). Using somewhat different definitions, Russell surveyed 930 adult women in San Francisco (1983). Sixteen percent of her respondents reported at least one sexual assault within the family before the age of 18; 12 percent reported at least one such experience before they were 14. Only 2 percent of these within-family sexual assaults on children were reported to the authorities. Fathers (including stepfathers) and uncles were the most likely to commit serious assaults on children (including forced intercourse). Russell reports a prevalence of father–daughter sex relations that is five times Finkelhor's estimate. Generalized to the total U.S. adult population, Russell's figures would suggest that at least three million American women may be suffering from the long-term effects

of earlier sexual abuse by fathers, stepfathers, or other male relatives.

A number of unpublished Canadian studies, including surveys of high-school populations, were available to the Badgley Committee on Sexual Offences Against Children and Youth (1982). My own estimate for Canada (which will not necessarily agree with the Badgley Commission estimate) is that at least 5 percent of all females will, by their sixteenth birthday, have experienced traumatic sexual assault within a family context. I estimate, based on this 5 percent incidence figure (which I consider conservative) and on the available data on the average length of time over which assaults continue, that the average proportion of children in elementary and junior high school currently being assaulted (within the past week) is 0.75 percent or about seven or eight per 1000. Every elementary school in Canada will, on the most conservative estimate, have two or three students who are currently being sexually assaulted within their families. In addition, about five times this number (an increasing number as the average age of the students increases) will still be suffering trauma as a result of past sexual abuse. None of the individuals in this estimate will have received any assistance from formal helping agencies for the sexual abuse or for its long-term effects.

The legacy of this trauma stays with an individual for a lifetime, and the extrapolation of this 5 percent estimate to the female population in Canada produces the staggering estimate that over half a million women are probably suffering impaired mental health associated with the long-term psychological legacies of childhood sexual assault. Given the apparent scale of the phenomenon, there is certainly some logic in the feminist complaint that the sexual assault of female children is an important aspect of the socialization of women for passivity and of personality problems associated with or leading to subordination (Tsai, Felman-Summers, and Edgar 1979).

The most frequent evidence on the amount and the harmfulness of child sexual abuse comes from the surveys of patient, client, and agency populations. A number of workers (Meiselman, Renvoize, Forward, and others) were motivated to research the subject when they realized that a large number of their female patients in unselected clinical populations had experienced sexual assault as children, and that those assaults were often causally related to later clinical problems (Meiselman 1978; Schlesinger 1982). Other surveys of runaway teenagers (Schultz 1980), young drug users (Denward and Densen-Gerber 1975), and young prostitutes (James and Meyerding 1977) have indicated that at least half of these female populations have been victims of child sexual assault. Furthermore, there is clear evidence from systematic clinical studies that these assaults have an important causal relationship with later disturbed behaviour (Anderson 1982; Bagley 1983a).

The Reporting of Sexual Abuse

An important issue is whether the actual incidence of child sexual assault is increasing, or whether both cultural values and professional practice are changing in ways that make it easier for victims to report abuse. Clearly, 1978 was a key year for professional understanding of the problem of child sexual abuse, with a "knowledge explosion" of books and monographs bringing an enlightened focus to understanding the problem, its consequences, and its treatment (Bagley 1982a). Previously, reports on the topic had been sparse, and were often biased. They suggested that the incidence of sexual assault on children was low; that such assaults were the result of family dysfunctions in which mothers held a large share of blame; that often the victims of such assault were not harmed or traumatized; and that often the child victims themselves played a seductive role, leading on the weak but sexually frustrated male. It is astonishing, in retrospect, that the professional community should have accepted such myths and distortions so passively; this should remind us that current practice and concepts in other areas of child welfare may be similarly biased. On this model, then, the great increase in agency reports of child sexual abuse (Finkelhor 1981) is an indication that victims are now more likely to perceive that such assaults are wrong, that complaining to people outside the family is legitimate, and that such complaints will bring meaningful help.

This may be an overly optimistic view, however. The supreme authority of the family over children is still widely stressed, and in the private domain of family socialization a child may have no alternative but to believe the adult male who tells the child that conformity to sexual domination is necessary along with the other conformities required of children.

The coerced silence of the child victim is frequently described in case materials (Butler 1978). This silence is one of the many factors that devastate the self-esteem of the victim and make later revelation so difficult. Until recently, a child who managed to reveal the assault to outsiders was not believed; this is probably still the case in many traditional communities. If the child was believed, she or he was stigmatized and the offence itself ignored. For help-seeking to occur, the child has to be assured that the threats against disclosure are unrealistic or empty, and that professionals such as teachers, ministers, police, crisis workers, and social workers will be both sympathetic and effective in bringing help. All of these ideal conditions are frequently not met (Skolseg 1983).

Although it is easier now for women and children to escape from physically and sexually abusive males, alternative sociological forces also make it likely that the amount of sexual abuse of children within families could be increasing (Finkelhor 1980). First, the eroticization of childhood by adults in the 1970s, largely for commercial purposes, may have accentuated a focus on children as suitable victims for sexual assault. Family changes may also be important. David Finkelhor points out that the presence of an unrelated adult male in a household is a special risk factor for children in terms of sexual assault, and such "blended" families are increasing as divorce and remarriage rates increase. Another potent factor is the development in the 1960s and

1970s of an ideology emphasizing the rights of individuals to sexual fulfilment. Whether or not rates are rising, the fundamental problem, Finkelhor argues, remains one of masculine sexuality and the power and dominance that men still exercise in sexual relationships. The development of the sexual "freedoms" of the 1960s and 1970s has, as Florence Rush (1980) points out, operated to the advantage of males rather than females, and has led to the development of an ideology asserting that all kinds of sexual fulfilment, including sex with children, are legitimate. If sexual abuse of children is ultimately to diminish, profound value changes must take place in the whole area of relationships between men and women.

The Short-Term and Long-Term Effects of Child Sexual Abuse

There is no good epidemiological evidence on the short- and long-term physical, psychological, and behavioural sequelae of earlier child sexual abuse in adolescents and young adults. The estimates from nonrandom adult populations suggest, however, that at least a minority of victims carry profound problems into adulthood. Studies of clinical populations suggest that sexual abuse has many profoundly adverse consequences. Especially in the immediate aftermath of the assault, children suffer a wide range of psychological and physical traumas. These short- and long-term sequelae have profound implications for the whole of the child-care and child-welfare system, and make child sexual abuse an overwhelmingly serious problem. For at least a minority of the victims, profound and permanent personality damage results. This damage can be reversed only by skilled, intensive, and prolonged individual and group therapy. Unless treated adequately, this personality damage has lifelong consequences (Forward and Buck 1978).

Hill (1982), in a review of literature on sequelae up to 1980, lists the following immediate traumas to child victims:

- physical traumas, including vaginal and anal lacerations;
- infections and venereal disease;
- associated physical abuse, including bruises and burns;
- pregnancy and menstrual disorders;
- sleeping and eating problems, bedwetting, thumb-sucking, night terrors;
- depression, loss of self-esteem, and withdrawal from peers;
- learning disabilities or developmental delays;
- running away, drug and alcohol use, subsequent juvenile prostitution;
- a pervasive sense of anxiety, fear, and terror;
- confusion and guilt surrounding secrecy;
- anger and aggression directed at siblings and at the nonviolating parent.

The harmful sequelae of child sexual abuse and its links to other kinds of behavioural problems are illustrated in a study by Silbert and Piven (1981) that is quite typical in terms of both its methodology and its findings. Silbert surveyed 200 street prostitutes in San Francisco. Seventy percent of the women she located were under 21, and 96 percent were runaways when they began prostituting, usually as juveniles. The results, Silbert reports,

are alarming, and contradict commonly held viewpoints on prostitution from many aspects. The excessive victimization, physical and sexual abuse, and learned helplessness, coupled with the young ages and disturbed backgrounds of the women, produce a distressing portrait of women trapped in a lifestyle they do not want, and yet feel unable to leave. Sixty percent of the subjects were the victims of juvenile sexual exploitation, and most subjects started running away from home as a result of sexual, physical or emotional abuse. Once in the streets, they were victimized by both customers and pimps: they were beaten, raped, robbed and abused . . .

The majority of the girls came from middle-class families with a formal religious atmosphere. This was no protection against sexual exploitation of the children by fathers or step-fathers. Seventy percent of the abused girls suffered repeated sexual assault by the same family member, often for a period of years. Almost all of these child victims lost their virginity as a result of the abuse, but they were trapped in their male-dominated households, and could escape only by running away. Once in the streets, the obvious means of survival was through prostitution. The majority of respondents who had been sexually assaulted within their families felt that their drift into prostitution was directly related to the earlier sexual assault.

Our own review of the monograph and journal literature on child sexual abuse in the period 1978 to 1982 (Bagley 1982a, 1983b) has identified the following sequelae of earlier sexual abuse in adolescents and adults:

- suicidal gestures and attempts (probably in about 5 percent of all sexually abused girls);
- long-term personality problems, including guilt, anxiety, fears, depression, and permanent impairment of self-image (probably in a majority of female victims);
- more acute personality sequelae, including chronic psychosis, self-mutilation, induced obesity, anorexia, hysterical seizures, and a chronically self-punitive lifestyle, in a reaction to acute feelings of guilt and self-disgust (probably in about 5 percent of sexually abused girls);
- running away from home, or removal by judicial and child-welfare authorities who were unaware of or indifferent to the sexual abuse (probably in about 20 percent of female victims);
- prostitution or sexually dominated or exploited lifestyle (probably in about 5 percent of female victims);
- withdrawal, coldness, frigidity, or lack of trust in psychosexual relationships (probably in about 5 to 10 percent of female victims);
- aggression, aggressive personality disorder, and chronic delinquency (in about 5 percent of victims);

- drug and alcohol abuse leading to chronic addiction and health impairment (in about 5 percent of victims).

Many of these adverse sequelae are linked or overlapping; however, I estimate, both from research reports and from clinical practice, that at least 25 percent of girls who are sexually abused within their families have serious long-term problems of adjustment and behaviour, while a further 25 percent have at least some chronic personality problems. The first, most seriously disturbed, group features prominently in caseloads of disturbed, drifting, runaway adolescents; however, this fact is not well understood by workers in this field, who continue to treat only the symptoms of the abuse syndrome, often in a superficial or indeed punitive way.

Finkelhor (1979b) argues that sexual relations between adults and children are wrong because children cannot give informed consent, and that arguments against such sexual relationships on empirical grounds have the inherent weakness that, if no harmful outcome can be identified, then the relationships are, *ipso facto*, permissible. There are difficulties with Finkelhor's approach, however. There is a considerable and persuasive literature on children's rights, maintaining that children do have a legal and moral right to give informed consent at an early age in relation to, for example, medical and surgical intervention. By the same token, children have the right to refuse interventions and acts that they regard as unpleasant or demeaning (Cohen 1980). Given the possibility of informed choice, the vast majority of children will, I believe, refuse the sexual advances of adults. The ultimate argument against the sexual exploitation of children by adults is that in at least half of the cases, and perhaps in more than half, long-term and perhaps permanent impairment of mental health will result. In advance, there is no way of telling with any certainty which type of child will be the most damaged: the age of the child, the type of assault, and the length of time over which the assaults take place do not seem to be good predictors of adult psychosocial outcome. However, the degree of force and coercion used, with threats to ensure silence and continued compliance, appears to be particularly related to long-term harm, especially when the abuser is a previously trusted authority figure such as a father (Finkelhor 1979a).

Sexual assault within a family violates a child's safety needs, which in Maslow's important developmental model (1973) are fundamental needs for a child. The violation of these safety needs in the family, which provides total safety for most children, imposes on the child a situation of lonely terror in which she is forced to deceive her mother and engage in sexual practices that she may find stimulating but simultaneously disgusting. The long-term effect of this self-disgust is a continued self-hatred and self-devaluation, and an acute difficulty in many aspects of human relationships. The reaction for any individual will, of course, vary according to the pre-existing personality, temperament, and vulnerability of the child; all too often, however, the victimized child is one who has poor self-esteem to begin with and who accepts the abuse as just one more demeaning burden that adults impose on children. According to Linda Sandford (1980), such a child tells herself:

> I don't like this, but what do I know? I'm never right about anything. . . . I know if I tell anyone about this, they'll get mad at me for making trouble. . . . Nobody else likes me, not in the whole world, except for this person, so I'll do what he says.

Children with poor ego strength and impaired self-concept are probably most likely to be victims and are easy to coerce into silence. Children in psychologically open families are likely to have both a close relationship with their mother and the ego-strength to resist seductive approaches from an adult male, as well as the ability to reveal such abuse immediately (Adams and Fay 1981; Justice and Justice 1979).

Treatment Models

The sexual abuse of children often causes profound and long-lasting damage, so clearly treatment has to be intensive and prolonged if profound traumas are to be reversed. Two major treatment programs led by Suzanne Sgroi (1982) and Hank Giarretto (1982b) have recently published clinical handbooks giving detailed accounts for innovative practitioners. The reader is advised to consult these handbooks, since a detailed account of intensive treatment models cannot be given here.

Practitioners in this field need to be mature, skilled, well-educated people, who have come to terms with their own sexuality and their feelings toward the sexual exploitation of children. Former victims of abuse who have been through extensive healing programs are particularly valuable as resource people in running self-help groups since they, of all people, can understand the meaning of abuse and empathize with victims. In Giarretto's program, victims ("Sons and Daughters United") and parents, including offenders ("Parents United"), form an important part of an integrated treatment model (Linedecker 1981: see this text re intervention and therapy with male victims). The overall approach to treatment has a number of fundamental tasks:

• To understand and try to change the values of the community, of individuals, and of professionals concerning the sexual abuse of children.
• Once abuse has been revealed, to work toward an integrated response to the concerns of interested parties — the sexually abused child, child-protection workers, sex-crimes investigators, Crown prosecutors, and specialized therapists. The result should be a plan of action that serves the fundamental interests of the child or adolescent victim.
• To engage in a prolonged and intensive treatment program involving victim, siblings, mother, and father with associated self-help groups.

- To undertake the treatment of adult former victims still suffering long-term effects of earlier sexual abuse.
- To undertake preventive education with young children to enable them to understand the sexually abusive approaches of others; to give them a healthy self-concept that will enable them to resist these approaches; and to assure them that responsible adults will listen and take appropriate protective action when they complain of abuse.

The need for community education to achieve value changes is clear when we understand the traditional reaction to sexual abuse of a child. Even if the child is able to construct a cognitive and moral framework that allows her to understand that the abusive adult behaviour is wrong and can be resisted, she has to complain to a parent, teacher, minister, relative, or counsellor. This person must first of all believe her; in the past, many abused children were put down and dubbed as liars. Then the adult has to listen sympathetically, and finally take effective action that will end the abuse in a way that does not further damage the child's self-esteem. These expectations were in the past unlikely to be fulfilled: even when she was believed, a girl was unlikely to obtain effective help. Usually the abuse could only be stopped when she was removed from the house to a children's shelter. Here, in a setting identified with juvenile delinquents and runaways, the victim's concept of herself as a bad or wicked person was likely to be further reinforced.

Value change is crucial if child victims are to receive active, integrated, effective help. In this changed model, the offender should be removed from the home, not the victim. Sometimes the teenage girl herself will ask to spend a period with a relative or in a foster home; this wish should be respected. All action taken at the point of disclosure should involve the fullest integration of different services (e.g., child-welfare workers, special therapy teams, police, and prosecutors). In most jurisdictions, reporting of child abuse

to the director of child welfare is, in theory at least, mandatory, and at that point police should also be informed. However, in all of the actions taken by workers of various kinds there should be one underlying principle or goal: all actions should serve the best interests of a damaged, unhappy, traumatized young person, and the goal of all actions should be to enable the girl to recover her sense of dignity, self-respect and self-esteem (Giarretto 1982b). For the adaptation of this approach to meet the needs of a Canadian community, see Anderson and Mayes (1982).

Failure to Meet the Victim's Needs

In most Canadian cities, adequate co-ordination of services for sexually abused children does not yet exist. Child-welfare or child-protection workers who are unprepared and untrained for such work can still act with panic, embarrassment, or even denial, remove the child from the home, and leave things at that. The child is "punished," but receives no therapy related to the sexual abuse. Judith Herman reports the case of a girl removed from home after reporting sexual assault:

> The director of the institution where I was placed had been trained as a counsellor. What I resent about her now is that I lived there for four years, and even though she knew what had happened, she never once took me aside and said, "Would you like to talk about it?" From age fourteen to eighteen I had nobody to help me work out my feelings. I cried myself to sleep every night. (1981)

Herman's case is an example drawn from the 1970s. The following case, from a large western Canadian city in the mid-1980s, illustrates how far attitudes and treatments have to go:

> Margaret, living in a one-parent family, was a lonely, isolated child. She had few friends, and wasn't close to her mother. When she was

eleven, a neighbour and family friend sexually assaulted and finally raped her over a period of months. This precipitated a crisis of withdrawal, moodiness, crying, and wandering from home, but she was not able at that time to reveal the sexual abuse. Her exasperated mother sent her to stay with her father in another province for a time. In that man's house she was further sexually abused. On return to her mother she was again in conflict with her mother, and finally took off at the age of 13. She was soon recruited on the streets by a leading pimp, and for two years she was a very high-priced juvenile prostitute. She gained nothing from this experience except grief and further self-disgust. She was admitted to hospital after a drug overdose, and then went to a group home as a temporary ward of the province. In the group home, she was able to reveal for the first time the earlier sexual assaults on her by her father and by the family friend. The only person she felt able to talk to was a sympathetic but untrained aide in the group home. The so-called professionals in the home, as well as her social worker, agreed to "let sleeping dogs lie," hoping that she had blanked out her traumatic past. She entered a very withdrawn phase, and her reluctance to talk about things again was taken as an acquiescence in this denial. As one of her workers put it, "Even if we wanted to refer her for therapy, there's nowhere in this city we could send her." Margaret was returned to her mother, since the province no longer held any legal responsibility for her, now she was 16. It is not clear what happened between her and her mother, but after two months she was admitted to hospital after a serious suicide attempt. She has been diagnosed as borderline psychotic, and in her acutely withdrawn and depressed state has been, at the age of 16, in a mental hospital for the past two months. She is being treated with psychotropic drugs, and still no one has offered her any therapeutic program that might exorcise this terrible ghost from her past. She remains in a permanent state of self-disgust. The best she can achieve is a state of numbness, and detachment from herself, "like when I was doing tricks. I used

to pretend I was on the wall like a fly or a bird, and then I would fly away into the sky."

An Integrated Approach

How could this disastrous outcome for Margaret have been prevented? In an ideal community, she would have known about the nature of sexual abuse, and would have been able if not to resist the initial threats and coercion then at least to report the abuse promptly, with the confidence that speedy and effective action would be taken. That action would have removed the source of the abuse, but would not have required her to endure gruelling cross-examination in court. A humane approach used in some judicial systems is to permit a social worker who has interviewed the child to give evidence in court as a proxy for the victim.

Let's suppose Margaret had been able to reveal the second incident of abuse, when she was 13, to someone like a teacher. In an integrated treatment system, a protection worker would have been informed immediately and would have ensured the girl's safety needs by removing the offender from the house. In a community model, such as the one developed by Giarretto in San Jose, prosecutors would build on community sentiment supporting an integrated treatment program. In the face of such pressure, the offender would likely plead guilty in return for a suspended sentence. An intensive program of therapy would then begin, involving first of all individual treatment of the victim, with the following aims:

• Validating the child's experience and the resulting feelings as important and not atypical. Confused feelings of hatred toward those whom we are supposed to love are normal in such a situation.
• Alleviating the child's guilt feelings: victims frequently hold themselves responsible for the abuse, and their guilt is intensified on disclosure and the ensuing family disruption.

• Exploration of the child's feelings toward individual family members, particularly ambiguous feelings toward mother and siblings.
• Exploration of the child's perception of feelings of other family members toward her. The initial goal is to concentrate on increasing self-awareness and self-esteem in the victim, before she joins groups of victims and/or begins joint sessions with her mother.

The mother, the forgotten person in the treatment process, also needs counselling. She needs to know the course treatment will take and its implications; she needs to ventilate and explore her feelings; and she needs to unburden her feelings of guilt and shame. Her own childhood history and feelings about sexuality need to be explored, too, before she can play an active part in treatment and self-help groups.

The adult male must be helped to accept responsibility for the sexual abuse, not only in a legal sense, but also in an emotional and moral sense. To achieve this, the focus must be on the personality, feelings, and childhood of the offender rather than on the offence itself. This is an essential prerequisite for dyadic counselling in which adult and victim will eventually talk to each other frankly: the offender tells the victim why he abused her, and accepts that the responsibility is entirely his. The child herself, in being able to forgive the adult family member, has then reached an important stage in recovering self-respect and divesting herself of hatred, both external and internal. Other important dyads include mother–victim and mother–father. Family therapy in a group is not an integral part of this process; traditionally family therapy that includes both offender and victim from the outset has been singularly unsuccessful in meeting the victim's needs (Giarretto 1982a). However, group treatment of victims alone can be highly effective (Forward and Buck 1978).

Finally, the two self-help groups, Parents United and Daughters and Sons United, provide an important point of community contact and community education, as well as continued peer support for victims. They represent an important long-term component of treatment.

A single case of sexual abuse will occupy many hours of the time of several therapists, whose work must be co-ordinated with the activities of other professionals, such as protection workers and police. This poses a dilemma for child-welfare agencies and their budgets. Treating victims in a way that can restore adequate mental health is complex and expensive, and requires considerable reorientation of roles, values, resources, and practice. Social-service delivery systems have been extremely reluctant to countenance such changes. It can be argued that expenditure of time, energy, and resources now will save a great deal in the long run by reducing the need to institutionalize victims, and will help to restore mental health to the existing victims. However, such arguments have failed to convince child-welfare authorities of the need for or the possibilities of change. Unfortunately, in times of restraint, welfare bureaucracies are rarely open to appeals or arguments even on grounds of cost benefits, efficiency, rationality, or humanity.

A major thrust is therefore necessary to bring about value changes that will not only reorder services and expenditures for the treatment of victims in the short run but will also, in the long run, prevent the sexual abuse of children. One way of helping this happen is through educational programs that tell children what sexual abuse is, how to resist it, and how to report it; operating concurrently with such programs would be a widely publicized "open line" that victims could ring to get help about sexual abuse.

In the face of professional weakness, lassitude, and denial, the initiative has to be taken by victims themselves. A growing movement of private agencies using Giarretto's humanistic models and methods has given rise to dynamic and effective self-help groups of former victims. In time, these volunteer groups can offer their own open line, and can bring increasing pressure for change on intransigent social-service delivery systems (Bagley 1982b). In Calgary, Giarretto's approach has been adapted by Anderson and Mayes to suit local needs.

An immediate practical concern regarding adequate referral and treatment is that all those who have contact with young people in a professional or volunteer capacity be aware of the possibility that sexual abuse underlies current distress or disturbed behaviour. In every such case the question "Are you currently being abused by anyone?" should be asked. For most young people the question will be meaningless, but for a critical minority the answer will be crucially important.

Conclusions and Summary

Sexual abuse of children in a family context is much more widespread than was previously thought; moreover, such abuse frequently has devastating consequences for victims. Indeed, it can permanently impair mental health and adjustment if treatment is absent or inadequate.

Family sexual abuse of children should be clearly distinguished from incest, which involves adults rather than children. Sexual abuse is supported by a deep-rooted value principle that allows the exploitation of weak and powerless people, particularly female children. Socialization for sexual subordination in childhood is an aspect of the general subordination of women. This general value principle allows ego-weak men semblances of power that they exercise over the most vulnerable members of their families with relative impunity. Fundamental changes in societal values are essential to enable victims to reveal abuse and to obtain effective help from adults; such value changes are also essential if educational programs to prevent sexual abuse of children are to develop effectively. We have argued that child-welfare authorities are generally cautious and conservative in this area. Former victims themselves must therefore lead a community-based movement for the development of open and comprehensive counselling and help services that can reach all those currently being abused and assist former victims who suffer impaired mental health as a result of earlier abuse.

Works Cited

Adams, C., and J. Fay. 1981. *No More Secrets: Protecting your Child From Sexual Assault.* San Luis Obispo, CA: Impact.

Anderson, C., and P. Mayes. 1982. "Treating Family Sexual Abuse: The Humanistic Approach." *Journal of Child Care* 2: 31-47.

Anderson, L. 1982. "Notes on the Linkage Between the Sexually Abused Child and the Suicidal Adolescent." *Journal of Adolescence* 5. 157-62.

Badgley, R., 1982. Committee on Sexual Offenses Against Children and Youth. Personal communication. Toronto, June.

Bagley, C., 1969. "Incest Behaviour and Incest Taboo," *Social Problems* 16: 505-19.

———. 1982a. "Child Sexual Abuse and Childhood Sexuality: A Review of the Monograph Literature 1978 to 1982." *Journal of Child Care* 2: 100-21.

———. 1982b. "The Gentle Revolution." *Starting Over: Newsletter of Sons and Daughters United.* Calgary Chapter (P.O. Box 1161, Station J., Calgary, Alberta, 403-242-8529)(April).

———. 1983a. "Adult Mental Health Sequels of Family Child Sexual Abuse." Paper given to Annual Meeting of the American Association for the Study of Social Problems. Detroit (September).

———. 1983b. "Child Sexual Abuse: Annotated Bibliography of the Journal Literature, 1978 to 1982." *Journal of Child Care* 4.

Butler, S. 1978. *Conspiracy of Silence: The Trauma of Incest.* San Francisco: New Glide.

Cohen, H. 1980. *Equal Rights for Children.* New York: Littlefield Adams.

Denward, J., and J. Densen-Gerber. 1975. "Incest as a Causative Factor in Antisocial Behavior: An Exploratory Study." *Contemporary Drug Problems* 4: 323-40.

Finkelhor, D. 1978. "Sexual Victimization of Children in a Normal Population." Paper given to Second International Congress on Child Abuse and Neglect, London (September).

———. 1979a. *Sexually Victimized Children.* New York: Free Press.

——. 1979b. "What's Wrong with Sex Between Adults and Children? Ethics and the Problem of Sexual Abuse." *American Journal of Orthopsychiatry* 49: 692–97.

——. 1980. "Risk Factors in the Sexual Victimization of Youth." *Child Abuse and Neglect* 4: 265–73.

——. 1981. "Sexual Abuse: a Sociological Perspective." Paper given to Third International Congress of Child Abuse and Neglect, Amsterdam (April).

——. 1982. *Child Sexual Abuse in a Sample of Boston Families.* Document No. US188 of the Family Violence Research Program. University of New Hampshire.

Forward, S., and C. Buck. 1978. *Betrayal of Innocence: Incest and Its Devastations.* Toronto: Macmillan.

Frude, N. 1982. "The Sexual Nature of Sexual Abuse: a Review of the Literature." *Child Abuse and Neglect* 6: 211–23.

Giarretto, H. 1982a. "A Comprehensive Child Sexual Abuse Treatment Program." *Child Abuse and Neglect* 6: 263–78.

——. 1982b. *Integrated Treatment of Child Sexual Abuse: A Treatment and Training Manual.* Palo Alto, CA: Science and Behavior.

Goodwin, J., T. McCarthy, and P. DiVasto. 1981. "Prior Incest in Mothers of Abused Children." *Child Abuse and Neglect* 5: 87–95.

Herman, J. and L. Hirschman. 1981. *Father-Daughter Incest.* Cambridge, MA: Harvard University Press.

Hill, S. 1982. "Child Sexual Abuse: Selected Issues." M.S.W. Thesis, University of Calgary.

James, J., and J. Meyerding. 1977. "Early Sexual Experience and Prostitution." *American Journal of Psychiatry* 134: 1381–85.

Justice, B., and R. Justice. 1979. *The Broken Taboo: Sex in the Family.* New York: Human Sciences.

Linedecker, C. 1981. *Children in Chains.* New York: Everest House.

Maslow, A. 1973. *Dominance, Self-Esteem and Self-Actualization.* Monterey, CA: Brooks/Cole.

Meiselman, K. 1978. *Incest.* San Francisco: Jossey-Bass.

Peters, J. 1976. "Children Who Are Victims of Sexual Assault and the Psychology of Offenders." *American Journal of Psychotherapy* 30: 398–421.

Rush, F. 1980. *The Best Kept Secret: Sexual Abuse of Children.* New York: McGraw-Hill.

Russell, D. 1983. "The Incidence and Prevalence of Intrafamilial and Extrafamilial Sexual Abuse of Female Children." *Child Abuse and Neglect* 7: 133–46.

Sandford, L. 1980. *The Silent Children: A Parent's Guide to the Prevention of Child Sexual Abuse.* New York: Anchor.

Sarafino, E. 1979. "An Estimate of Nationwide Incidence of Sexual Offenses Against Children." *Child Welfare* 58: 127–34.

Schlesinger, B. 1982. *Sexual Abuse of Children.* Toronto: University of Toronto Press.

Schultz, L., ed. 1980. *The Sexual Victimology of Youth.* Springfield, IL: Charles C. Thomas.

Sgroi, S., ed. 1982. *Handbook of Clinical Intervention in Child Sexual Abuse.* Lexington, MA: Lexington.

Silbert, M., and A. Piven. 1981. "Sexual Abuse as an Antecedent to Prostitution." *Child Abuse and Neglect* 5: 407–11.

Skolseg, P. 1983. "Social Service Coordination of Treatment of Victims of Child Sexual Abuse." *Child Welfare Forum* 2.

Tsai, M., S. Feldman-Summers, and M. Edgar. 1979. "Childhood Molestation: Variables Related to Differential Impacts on Psychosexual Functioning in Adult Women." *Journal of Abnormal Psychology* 88: 407–17.

Van Den Berghe, P. 1983. "Human Inbreeding Avoidance: Culture in Nature." *Behavioral and Brain Sciences* 6: 91–123.

Wolfe, L. 1981. *The Cosmo Report.* New York: Arbor House.

Part Seven

FAMILY ISSUES OF THE MIDDLE-AGED AND THE ELDERLY

◆ ◆ ◆

The Knights had been married nearly sixteen years. They considered themselves solidly united. Like many people no longer in love, they cemented their relationship with opinions, pet prejudices, secret meanings, a private vocabulary that enabled them to exchange glances over a dinner table and made them feel a shade superior to the world outside the house.

Mavis Gallant, *My Heart Is Broken* (1964)

The experience of family life is not constant over the life course. When we compare the circumstances of young adults with those of their parents or of their grandparents, we have to take into account at least two separate dimensions of difference between generations. Some differences are *quantitative* — that is, they are differences in degree. A person of 70 has had five decades of adult experience, whereas the person of 40 has only had two. In addition, however, there is a less obvious difference that has been termed the *cohort effect*. Persons of a given cohort — that is, persons who were all born at the same time — may have had experiences that were not shared with other cohorts. Such *qualitative* differences in experience are differences in kind, rather than differences in degree.

To see what this means in everyday life in the 1990s, let us briefly consider some of the life experiences of three ages of people in later life. In 1990, a person who is 80 years old was born in 1910 and would have been a teen-ager during the Roaring Twenties. A person aged 60 was born in 1930 and would have been a teenager during the boom following World War II. In contrast, a person aged 40 was born in 1950 and would have been a teenager in the 1960s, a revolutionary time of counterculture and innovation. When we try to isolate the effects of ageing by comparing persons in their eighties with those in their sixties or their forties, we can account for quantitative differences in years of experience, but we cannot control the qualitative differences in the nature of those experiences. All of our generalizations about ageing and the aged need to keep in mind the important caveat of the cohort effect.

The cohort effect is especially critical in considering a society that is not stable and is experiencing rapid social and technological changes. How rapid is rapid? As an illustration, consider the following letter written by a senior citizen and addressed: "For All Who Were Born Before 1945":

We were born before television, before valium, before polio shots, frozen foods, Xerox, plastic, contact lenses, frisbees, and the pill. We were before credit cards, split levels, split atoms, laser beams, microwaves, and ballpoint pens. Before panty hose, dishwashers, clothes dryers, electric blankets, air conditioners, drip dry clothes and before man walked on the moon. . . . We were before househusbands, gay rights, computer dating, dual careers, and commuter marriages. We were before day-care centres, group therapy, and nursing homes. We never heard of FM radio, tape decks, electronic typewriters, artificial hearts, word processors, yogurt, and guys wearing earrings. For us, time sharing meant togetherness, not condominiums. A chip was a piece of wood. Hardware meant hardware and software wasn't even a word. . . . In our day, grass was mowed, Coke was a cold drink, and pot was something you cooked in. Rock music was grandma's lullaby and aids were helpers in the principal's office. We were certainly not before the difference between the sexes was discovered, but we were surely before the sex change. We made do with what we had; and we were the last generation dumb enough to think that you had to be married to have a baby. (Farrell 1987)

About the Articles

The family circumstances of the elderly are essentially different for men than for women, in that most older men are married, whereas most older women are on their own. Dulude elaborates on this substantial difference, and on its implications for the social, financial, and medical problems that may be associated with advancing age.

Family ties in later life may include not only relationships with one's mate and one's children, but also with grandchildren. As life expectancy increases, it is increasingly likely that children will know their grandparents, and that relationships with them may continue into the adult years. Wilcoxon points out how

grandparents may be significant others for their grandchildren and may function as an important family resource.

The filial obligations of children to their parents are not clearly spelled out in our society. Bengston and de Terre discuss the impact that changing demographic facts have on intergenerational interaction, and examine the conflicting needs of the elderly both to remain independent as long as possible and to find the assistance and support they eventually may need.

When an elderly person does need family care, the person most likely to provide it is not a son, but a daughter or a daughter-in-law. Aronson discusses the role of the female caregiver as another example of unpaid labour in the family, and explores the dilemma of middle-aged women who are often caught between the demands of their children and the demands of their ageing parents. The projected increase in the elderly population will lead to a demand for more and more caregiving services. These new demands will require new social policies to distribute the burden more equitably between men and women and between the private resources of the family and the public resources of the community.

Further Readings

Blau, Theodore H. 1984. "An Evaluative Study of the Role of Grandparent in the Best Interests of the Child." *American Journal of Family Therapy* 12: 46–50.

Connidis, Ingrid. 1989. *Family Ties and Aging.* Toronto: Butterworths.

Gee, Ellen M., and Meredith Kimball. 1987. *Women and Aging.* Toronto: Butterworths.

Marshall, Victor W. 1987. *Aging in Canada: Social Perspectives.* Markham, ON: Fitzhenry and Whiteside.

Northcott, Herbert C. 1984. "Widowhood and Remarriage Trends in Canada 1956 to 1981." *Canadian Journal on Aging* 3: 63–77.

Novak, Mark. 1988. *Aging and Society: A Canadian Perspective*. Scarborough, ON: Nelson Canada.

Ramirez-Barranti, Crystal C. 1985. "The Grandparent/Grandchild Relationship: Family Resource in an Era of Voluntary Bonds." *Family Relations* 34: 343–52.

Rodgers, Roy H., and Gail Witney. 1981. "The Family Cycle in Twentieth Century Canada." *Journal of Marriage and the Family* 43: 727–40.

Rosenthal, Carolyn J. 1983. "Aging, Ethnicity and the Family: Beyond the Modernization Thesis." *Canadian Ethnic Studies* 15: 1–16.

)LD: MEN IN COUPLES AND
_ONE

The ultimate irony, for women, is that after a lifetime of having a multitude of mythical qualities and failings attributed to them because of their sex, they are suddenly told that after a certain age these differences between the sexes no longer exists. American activist Tish Sommers (1976) protested against this final injustice:

> Curious how we lose our sex when we reach 65! Not just sexuality, or sexiness, but more basic than that. We even lose our gender. No longer are we older women and men, but we suddenly join a new category — senior citizens (or old folks, or the elderly). New bureaucracies are concerned with our welfare, new laws cover our rights (such as they are), and new councils make recommendations to an unresponsive government.
>
> Most statistics lump us together, male and female . . . masking tremendous differences between the sexes, and above all obscuring how much aging is a woman's issue. (p. 13)

One of the most striking aspects of ageing is the growing predominance of women in the older population. While older males outnumbered females in the first half of this century, this has since reversed; by the time of the 1981 census, 57 percent of Canadians aged 65 and over were women. This imbalance in favour of women is greatest in the oldest age groups: there were 124 females per 100 males aged 65 to 79, and 187 women per 100 men

in the 80-and-over group (Statistics Canada 1985, Table 2; Government of Canada 1983, 20).

Projections for the future indicate that the gap in life expectancy will persist, but will get smaller as more women adopt the bad health habits of men. Most important among these is smoking, which some studies hold responsible for 75 percent or more of the difference in longevity between women and men (Gee 1984, 10–13; Miller and Gernstein, 349–55). In spite of this, Statistics Canada predicts that by the year 2001 there will be 134 females per 100 males in the 65 to 79 age group, and women aged 80 and over will outnumber their male counterparts by more than two to one (Government of Canada 1983, 20).

But numbers alone do not explain why ageing is a woman's issue. The most tragic fact of life for old women is that the blessing of their superior longevity too often turns out to be a curse. Instead of more twilight years of fulfilment and serenity, it brings to many of them a decade or more of loneliness, ill health, and poverty. This is obvious when the day-to-day lives of elderly women and men are compared.

Relationships

The most obvious difference in lifestyle between the sexes in old age is that the majority of the males live with their wives while most female seniors do not have a spouse. This seems strange at first, since it takes both a

Source: *Women and Men: Interdisciplinary Readings on Gender* (Markham, ON: Fitzhenry and Whiteside, Ltd., 1987): 323–39. Greta H. Nemiroff (editor). Reprinted by permission of the author.

Table 1
Marital Status of People Aged 65 and Over in Canada, 1983

Age	Married (%)		Widowed and Divorced (%)		Never Married (%)	
	Men	Women	Men	Women	Men	Women
65–69	83	58	10	34	7	8
70–74	79	46	13	45	8	9
75–79	73	32	18	58	9	10
80+	57	15	34	75	9	10
Total						
65+	76	40	16	51	8	9

Source: Statistics Canada, unpublished preliminary post-censal estimates for 1983.

woman and a man to make a couple, but it is less surprising when we remember that a typical bride marries a man who is older than she and who has a shorter life expectancy than she does. As a result, many male pensioners are married to women under the age of 65, and most women can expect to become widowed.

As Table 1 demonstrates, this discrepancy in marital status is very large and accentuates with age: among Canadians aged 65 to 69, more than 80 percent of the men are married compared to less than 60 percent of the women; for those aged 80 and above, still over half of the males have a spouse compared to only 15 percent of the women. As the proportions of elderly men who are married and of elderly women who are widowed have both been increasing over the years, this gap is expected to get even larger in the future.

Before much research on these subjects was undertaken, it was widely believed that both sexes suffered a dramatic loss when they became old. Men had to give up their jobs, which had been their major source of identity and social status, and women lost their husbands who provided them with their principal life roles (Posner [1977] 1980, [47] 80–87). This was later denied by elderly people themselves, who reported that the death of a spouse was the single most critical experience of a person's life, requiring most changes and adjustment (Matthews 1982, 227). Retire-

ment is felt to be much less disruptive, being ranked twenty-eighth out of 34 life events (with divorce ranking seventeenth).

The other obstacle to the neat retirement/widowhood parallel is that more and more women must go through both. In 1984, 41 percent of all married Canadian women aged 45 to 64 had a job outside their homes (Statistics Canada 1984a, Table 58). The traditional view that retirement was less difficult and more "natural" for women has also been largely debunked (Atchley and Corbett 1977; see also Szinovacz 1982).

First, a job may be just as important for a woman as for a man. She is just as likely to be committed to it. Retirement could therefore result in "withdrawal symptoms" for women as well as for men.

Second, the assumption that women can easily refocus to "in-home" roles ignores the fact that it was because of the loss of such roles in middle age that they initially became involved in jobs. Most women at retirement have no children living at home and 30 percent are widows. . . .

Third, because they have gotten a late career start, their retirement is likely to come before their job goals are achieved.

Another element that probably contributes to the distress of older widows is that post-retirement marriages tend to be happier than most. Little is known about the reasons for this, but it has been surmised that: (1) if a marriage lasts long enough, the spouses stand a better chance of resolving their differences; and (2) older people are marriage survivors, with less successful couples having split up along the way (Abu-Laban 1980, 126–27). In any case, older couples do more things together than younger spouses and are less restricted by traditional sex roles — for example, older husbands are more likely than younger ones to participate in homemaking tasks.

Obviously, the closer the spouses were before one of them died, the harsher the transition to widowhood. Many who went through this experience report that it left them shattered (Evans 1971, 149): "I was conscious of my hands dangling uselessly by my sides. I was a person with no job to do, no place to fill, no function in life." It may be just as well that fewer men become widowed because they seem to have more difficulty in adapting to this role. For one thing, widowers are less likely to have close friends than widows (Strain and Chappell 1982). For another, at least some of these men are unable to cook and clean for themselves and cannot afford to pay someone else to perform these services (Berardo 1967). These factors may explain why the suicide rate of elderly men who live alone is much higher than that of everyone else in the same age group (Jarvis and Boldt 1980).

At the other emotional extreme, widowers have a much greater chance of getting remarried than widows. Given the fact that unmarried women aged 65 and over outnumber unmarried men by more than three to one,[1] the chances of a widow finding another husband are only slightly better than those of winning the lottery. Should these women — oh! horror — have relationships with noticeably younger men, they will run head on against our society's double standard of ageing. Susan Sontag (1972, 38) wrote that:

The convention that wives should be younger than their husbands powerfully enforces the "minority" status of women, since being senior in age always carries with it, in any relationship, a certain amount of power and authority. There are no laws on the matter, of course. The convention is obeyed because to do otherwise makes one feel as if one is doing something ugly or in bad taste.

Widows are also hampered from engaging in relationships with men by the myth saying that older women are no longer interested in sex. Masters and Johnson (1966, 247) laid this to rest once and for all in 1966, when they wrote that "there is no limit drawn by the advancing years to female sexuality." According to an analysis of a national American survey on sexuality (Tavris 1977, 62):

Although the stereotype of sexless older people possibly comforts those who have no partners, and possibly reassures those who never liked sex in the first place . . . the fact is that sexual response continues long into old age for many people. . . .

Members of both sexes may lose sexual desire, but this is generally a result of lower expectations, boring sexual routine, or lack of a partner — not inevitably of the lesser capacities of the body.

The author ended by quoting the following opinion offered by a female respondent to the survey (Tavris 1977, 65): "I am 60 years old and they say you never get too old to enjoy sex. I know, because once I asked my Grandma when you stop liking it and she was 80. She said, 'Child, you'll have to ask someone older than me.'"

None of the above comments should be interpreted to mean that the majority of widows lead isolated lives and never talk to anyone. For one thing, some widowed women enjoy the greater freedom and independence they experience following the death of their spouses (Lopata 1973, 88). For another, even though almost half of spouseless elderly women live alone, a third are living with their children or other family members (Fletcher and Stone 1986, 36). Studies also show that the majority of widows have extensive social networks or relatives and acquaintances whom they see or talk to frequently (Lopata 1979). Younger widows have a harder time, since they are often made unwelcome in social circles where most people still come in twos.

Contrary to rumours that children are abandoning their old parents, most elderly mothers report seeing them at least once a week. This is not necessarily a blessing, however, since the frequency of contact with their children makes little difference to old people's feelings of loneliness and life satisfaction (Arling 1976, 757–68). In other words, old widows who hardly ever see or hear from their children are not necessarily less happy than those who see them every day.

On second thought, this is not so outlandish. Although parents and children are usually closer to each other than strangers, they have little in common and do not normally make good companions. The same is *not* true of relationships with other family members, friends, and neighbours, who are much more likely to be equals and to share common interests and goals. Older women who were never married have an advantage in that respect, since they have long ago gotten used to making friends outside their immediate family circles (Norris 1980).

Health

Numerous studies have concluded that health is the single most important factor determining whether old women and men are happy and satisfied with their lives (Riddick 1982, 45–59). Part of the reason for this may be that healthy elderly people who see many of their contemporaries becoming ill or disabled feel happy that they have themselves been spared. Even more likely, bad health is a strong spoiler that can drastically reduce people's activities and make them miserable.

The truth about old people's health is that it deteriorates with age. When a representative sample of Ontario senior citizens was asked whether their health prevented them from accomplishing a list of common daily tasks, it was found that only 16 percent of those aged 65 to 74 could not do heavy housework, which was the most strenuous of the tasks listed (Seniors Secretariat 1985, 34). This compared with 26 percent of those aged 75 to 84, and 54 percent of those who were 85 years old and above. In addition, women were more likely than men of the same age to report their health as being poor.

Although elderly women are only one-fifth as likely to commit suicide as men, (Jarvis and Boldt 1980, 147), a greater proportion of them than of men suffer from depression and anxiety (Gold 1984, 33). The classic doctors' response to such complaints is to hand out tons of tranquillizers and sleeping pills. A Saskatchewan survey found that 55 percent of women aged 50 and over and 43 percent of the men had doctors' prescriptions for drugs affecting the nervous system (Harding 1978). Overall, a phenomenal 77 percent of women aged 65 and over take some type of drug, compared with 66 percent of their male counterparts (Statistics Canada 1985, Table 17).

All this would seem to indicate that women's longer lives are often bought at the price of years of unhappy discomfort. In hard numbers, it has been calculated that although women's life expectancy at birth is 7.5 years longer than that of men, their disability-free life expectancy is only 3.6 years longer. For those who survive until the age of 65, the average life expectancy of women is 4.3 years longer, but the difference in disability-free time is only 1.7 years (Statistics Canada 1985, 79).

Very little is known of the reasons why older women enjoy poorer health than older men. This is consistent with the general low priority and underfunding of all areas of medical research that concern the problems of women, and older women in particular. Dr. Robert Butler, an eminent U.S. gerontologist, has accused the medical establishment of being ageist and sexist. "All too often a woman's health problems are written off in terms of her being pre-menopausal, menopausal, post-menopausal — or, ultimately, senile

(Burwell 1981, 242). Some male gerontologists have even suggested that increased efforts to improve the health of older women might be undesirable, and that "an equally appropriate action might be to examine why women live so long, and remove the factors that lead to this persistence" (Borgatta and Loeb 1981).

One urgent area of research relates to whether older men's better health status is due to their being able to rely on high-quality home services and care. Most senior men have built-in housekeepers and nurses — their wives. By contrast, most old women who become sick and frail have no live-in companions and must fend for themselves. In the absence of adequate government-sponsored supports such as visiting nurses, professional homemakers, and meals-on-wheels services, most widows must do without minimal comforts or must turn for help to the second most important caregivers in families, their daughters.

The plight of these daughters, who have been called "the women in the middle" and "the sandwich generation" is expected to worsen as the very old become a larger proportion of our population. Support for caregiving daughters and wives was the main theme of the first national convention of the Older Women's League in the United States in 1983 (Keeney 1983, 23).

> Women spoke of having to give up salaried jobs to spend as many as 20 years caring full-time for incapacitated spouses or parents. "In that time, you become a forgotten woman . . . You can rarely leave the house, and no one comes to visit you because it's too depressing."

The main demand issuing from the conference was for respite care legislation that would allocate state funds for temporary services. These services would "include adult day-care centres, and an arrangement where caregivers would get a week, a weekend, or even a few hours' relief" (p. 23). Even higher on the list for both caregivers and care receivers are: (1)

complete, well-integrated free or low-cost services allowing seniors to live on their own as long as possible; and (2) "good-quality institutions that aren't looked at with fear and trepidation" (Burwell 1981, 248).

Unless these recommendations are implemented, it is feared that incidents of violence against the elderly might reach epidemic proportions. "Granny-bashing," as its name implies, is largely directed against women (Schlesinger 1984). Its typical victims are old, confused, and physically disabled parents living with their children. The abuses reported range from insults to financial extortions to blows severe enough to cause death. Relatively few cases of this exist today, but there is every reason to believe that the situation will degenerate if the government does not step up its involvement in order to ease the burden of old people's families.

The trend now is in the opposite direction. Spurred by growing deficits, governments are deaf to the results of many surveys showing that most senior citizens of both sexes do *not* want to move in with their children or depend on them for essential services (Ciffin, Martin, and Talbot 1977, 65). Instead, they want more formal assistance to help them live independently in their own homes as long as possible. When this is no longer feasible, more than 80 percent prefer life in an institution within a short distance of their families rather than moving in with their children. Women are even more adamant than men on this, with 85 percent of those questioned voicing that opinion (Connidis 1983). This is confirmed by figures showing that old people who live with their children or other relatives are older, sicker, and poorer than other seniors — they are the ones who are least likely to have a choice (Statistics Canada 1984b; Béland 1984)

Good institutions for incapacitated old people are presently in very short supply. A *Globe and Mail* survey of Ontario nursing homes (Jefferson and Rowan 1981) found that most of them had waiting lists. On quality, the investigating journalists concluded that: "Of the 50 nursing homes we visited, there were six where we would have been quite happy to leave a friend or relative, and 15 where we would not have wanted to leave anybody. The remaining homes did not strike us as either particularly good or bad."

Since more than three-quarters of nursing home residents are female, most of them in their late seventies and eighties,[2] it is women who are the most frequent losers in life's last game of chance, nursing-home roulette.

Money

After ten years or so of intense pension reform debates in Canada, one of the few things on which all its participants agree is that too many Canadian women spend their last years in poverty. The figures are distressingly eloquent: in 1983, 31 percent of women aged 65 and over had incomes below Statistics Canada's poverty lines. The comparable figure for men was a much lower 17 percent.[3]

When marital status and age are taken into account, much larger differences between the sexes appear. Table 2 indicates that seniors who live in families, meaning most of the men, actually experience a drop in their pov-

erty rate (from 10.3 percent to 8.7 percent) as they get older, possibly because the younger group includes many who are married to nonpensioner wives.[4] By contrast, the category of people living alone or with nonrelatives, where most women are found, experiences a huge increase in poverty with advancing age. At 70 years old and over, a phenomenally high 63.5 percent of unattached women live in poverty.

The cause of this huge gap in the living standards of the elderly men and women is that Canada's pension system was designed by men to benefit men. This was not done out of spite against women, but out of the traditional belief that the world is composed of only two categories of people: full-time participants in the labour market (husbands and fathers), and the people they support (women and children). If you provide adequate pensions to the first group, it was felt, the second group would automatically be taken care of (National Council of Welfare 1979, 25–27).

The problem is that in the real world, people do not fit in such convenient categories. About 10 percent of women never marry, more than half of those who do marry become

---

Table 2
Incidence of Poverty Among People Aged 65 and Over, Canada, 1982

Living Arrangement	Percentage in Poverty	
	Families Headed by Males	Families Headed by Females
Living with Spouse or Relatives:		
Age 65–69	10.3	23.5
Age 70+	8.7	23.0
	Men	Women
Living Alone or with Nonfamily:		
Age 65–69	34.7	50.6
Age 70+	47.3	63.5

Source: Unpublished data from Statistics Canada.

widowed at some point, and the rate of marriage dissolution through divorce and separation is growing by leaps and bounds. As a result, the National Council of Welfare estimated, fully three-quarters of all women end up having to support themselves and, increasingly, their children as well (Dulude 1981). Since very few of these "unprotected" women had lifelong full-time jobs giving them access to good pension plans and allowing them to accumulate substantial savings, it is inevitable that most of them will end up poor when they are old.

What does it mean to be old and poor? It means having to sell your home when your husband dies, because you need the money to live and cannot afford to hire people to do such jobs as cleaning the gutters, shovelling snow, and fixing the roof. Because the area where you have lived for a long time has few apartments for rent, especially suitable for seniors (no steep stairs, low cupboards, close to the stores), you will probably have to move closer to the city centre, leaving many of your friends behind and losing most of the familiar signposts of your existence.

Being poor also means that you cannot afford a car or taxis and become more dependent on public transportation. Seniors often complain about train and bus services that are less frequent when they need them most, in the evenings and on Sunday. They also have problems with physical design on most public transport facilities. As one old woman put it, one-and-a-half foot high bus steps are simply not designed for human beings, let alone for old ladies with stiff joints (Dulude 1978, 79). After a while, it becomes simpler to stay home, and even trips to the doctor become major expeditions.

Most important perhaps, having no money for extras prevents you from buying the services you desperately require when you become older and frailer. Not for you the two- or three-times-a-week housekeeper to help with the shopping and the house-cleaning chores. Nor can you afford a private nurse to care for you, thereby delaying the time when you have to go to a hospital or a nursing home. One of the most common health hazards for old women is broken bones suffered while working in their homes.

At the very least, being poor prevents elderly women from leading a full life. Lack of money is one of the main reasons they give when they are asked why they do not see more people, entertain friends, and engage in activities they would normally enjoy (Seniors Secretariat 1985, 26). It is no wonder that the lives of so many old women come to revolve almost entirely around their television sets and their telephones.

At its worst, having too little money forces you to live like this woman whose plight is described in a National Council of Welfare report (National Council of Welfare 1979, 12–13):

"If you're really interested," said 67-year-old Mary S., "I'll tell you what it's like being an old woman alone who's only got the government pension to live on. . . . It's wearing out your second-hand shoes going from one store to another trying to find the cheapest cuts of meat. It's hating having to buy toilet tissue or soap or toothpaste, because you can't eat it. It's picking the marked-down fruits and vegetables from the half-rotting stuff in the back of the stores that used to be given away to farmers to feed their animals. It's hunting the thrift shops and Salvation Army stores for half-decent clothes."

"Emergencies come up; grandchildren have birthdays; clothes wear out; cleaning products run out; bus rates go up. How do we manage? We pay our rent and utilities and we eat less.

"We live in fear. Fear of the future, of more illness, less money, less pride. Fear that the cheque won't arrive and we won't be able to work our way through the red tape in time to pay our rent. Fear that we will run out of food before the next cheque comes in.

"So, fear holds you in line. It is our punishment for getting old and sick."

What Should Be Done

It has often been said that people age and die as they have lived. The facts of ageing for typical men and women — the men living quite comfortably in their own homes until their death with their loving mates by their bed-sides, the women condemned to a penny-pinching existence alone in small apartments before their last move to a nursing home — bear this out. Just as women are second-class citizens throughout their lives, they are also second-class senior citizens at the end of it.

The implication is that it is not a simple matter to give women equality in their old age. It requires nothing less than a complete overhaul of the dependency system on which the relationship between the sexes is based now. This does not necessarily mean that women must become more like men — in-deed, men's lower life expectancy and their lesser ability to cope as widowers reveal im-portant flaws — but that the life choices women make should maximize rather than di-minish their self-reliance.

The first prerequisite to achieving inde-pendence is a truly free choice of lifestyle un-hampered by myths about ideal feminine roles and career choices. As long as girls' ambitions are systematically dampened and they are led to believe that the most crucial activity of their existence is to find Mr. Right, they will continue to shy away from more profitable professional pursuits and to invest the bulk of their energies in their emotional lives. The idea is not to transform all women into the male ideal of the workaholic robot, but to fos-ter the growth of their intellectual side and thereby discourage them from putting all their eggs in the increasingly fragile marriage basket.

Unfortunately, a fundamental change of this sort cannot be achieved through govern-ment policy or legislation. It requires a mas-sive change in attitudes, especially among par-ents who are the main source of models for their children. The good news in that respect is that married women's entry in huge numbers in the labour market in the last dec-ades has shattered the myth that women's only role is that of wife, mother, and holy keeper of the home. Economic growth has had a great deal to do with this development, which was also stimulated by skyrocketing di-vorce rates that made it clear that a woman

without a paid job is only a man away from the welfare roll.

The bad news is that the jobs these women took were the worst ones around. Most fe-male earners are still segregated in low-paying, nonunionized, dead-end occupations (Arm-strong and Armstrong 1978). Even worse, married women with paid jobs continue to do all the child-care and homemaking tasks in their homes (Meissner et al. 1975; Clark and Harvey 1976). The message daughters now get is that a woman must have a job, as insurance if nothing else, but that it must not be so demanding as to interfere with her homemaking role. Outside of some rarefied yuppie circles, the idea that husbands should share the child-care and housekeeping tasks has not yet caught on.

Faced with these obstacles, the women's movement developed alternative strategies. First, it pressed for the upgrading of tradi-tionally female jobs through the introduction of laws requiring the payment of equal wages for work of equal value. By making it possible to compare different occupations, for example those of female secretaries and male mainte-nance staff, these laws raise women's wages and prevent systematic exploitation of female employees. Most provinces have yet to im-plement such legislation.

Second, most women's organizations rec-ommended important changes to Canada's pension system to give female employees more opportunities to save for their old age. The most important of these proposals calls for an expansion of the Canada and Quebec pension plans, which are the only retirement programs in which all women with earnings participate. Noting that the present retirement benefits paid by these programs only equal 25 percent of average lifetime earnings, which is much too low, women's groups are asking for these payments to be doubled (National Action Committee on the Status of Women 1983, 10–11). If this were implemented, it would improve the financial situation of eld-erly men as well, since many of them do not enjoy adequate pension coverage now.

The other side of the coin consists of in-creasing the financial security of women who work only or mainly in their homes. Examples of ways in which this could be done include: (1) the equal ownership and control by both spouses of all the assets they acquire during their life together (Dulude 1984); (2) the equal splitting of pension credits between the spouses for the time they are married (National Action Committee on the Status of Women 1983, 12–13); and (3) the direct coverage of full- and part-time homemakers under the Canada and Quebec pension plans (National Action Committee on the Status of Women 1983, 13–17; Canada Pension Plan Advisory Committee 1983). To this day, none of these recommendations has been fully implemented anywhere in Canada.

While each of these measures would bring some women closer to a more economically secure old age, none would strike at the crucial problems of loneliness and the lack of role that so many women feel after the death of their lifetime companion. Part of these problems results from the difference in age and life expectancy between the spouses, and part from the lack of integration of old people in the mainstream of our society.

As we saw earlier, a large proportion of the life-expectancy difference between the sexes is attributable to lifestyle factors that are likely to diminish, but not disappear, as time goes by. Assuming that some difference will persist because of the physiological superiority of women, one may ask whether it might not be appropriate to launch a campaign to discourage young women from marrying older men.

When the author tried to do this in a modest way recently by asking a predominantly female high-school class why almost all of them preferred older boyfriends, she met with an unanimous answer: girls like older boys, they said, because they are more "solid" and more capable of being "leaned on." When the author challenged this and ventured to suggest a relationship with an equal might be more desirable for both sexes, she got blank stares and no response.

A preliminary conclusion to be drawn from this episode is that sexism is even more deeply ingrained in young girls than was ever suspected. Not only are men told that younger women are preferable because they are more graceful, pliant, and easier to influence, but girls internalize this prejudice themselves by seeking mates who will have a built-in advantage over them.

This age factor is even more evident in second and third marriages because men are still operating under the same youth-is-beauty-is-desirable assumption. As a result, many lonely women in their thirties, forties, and older desperately cling to the remnants of their youth to attract men of their own age and more. Susan Sontag (1972, 38) deplored this and urged an end to this disgraceful race with time:

> Each time a woman lies about her age she becomes an accomplice in her own underdevelopment as a human being.
>
> Women have another option. They can aspire to be wise, not merely nice, to be competent, not merely helpful; to be strong, not merely graceful; to be ambitious for themselves, not merely for themselves in relation to men and children. They can let themselves age naturally and without embarrassment, actively protesting and disobeying the conventions that stem from this society's double standard about aging. Instead of being girls, girls as long as possible, who then age humiliatingly into middle-aged women and then obscenely into old women, they can become women much earlier — and remain active adults, enjoying the long career of which women are capable far longer.
>
> Women should allow their faces to show the lives they have lived. Women should tell the truth.

Because of the way our society is organized, older women without mates are also very often women without roles. Survey reports show that both elderly women and men would like to play a more active role in society, would like to do more to help other people (Seniors Secretariat 1985, 17–18). This need is not met by the New Horizons program, which is the main federal source of funds for seniors' activities in Canada. New Horizons pays no salaries to its elderly participants, and most of the projects it funds are leisure-oriented. In 1984–85, only 6 percent of the activities it subsidized involved giving direct assistance to other people.[5]

Gerontologist Alex Comfort disagrees (1976, 6) that leisure activities do much good to the elderly, and believes instead that working is the best way of keeping loneliness and unhappiness at bay:

> I am frankly disturbed by the emphasis on leisure as the prescribed state of later life. Leisure is a con. It should occupy an occasional afternoon, not twenty years. . . .
>
> Old citizens have as much right as the young, if not more, to sit on the porch or be hippies. But both those are in my sense occupations: they have goals, and even secession from the world is part of the world. And they rest upon choice, not rejection by society.
>
> Leisure in our culture means not doing what you choose, but activity which is by definition goalless and irrelevant, and our emphasis on it childrenizes older people.

Examples of the types of government initiatives that could answer this need include the American Foster Grandparent Program, which pays a modest stipend to low-income people over the age of 60 who participate in projects that help children with special problems. As well as being beneficial to thousands of retarded, disabled, or emotionally disturbed preschoolers, it was found that the program increased the life expectancy of its "grandparents" (Saltz 1977, 126–32). Other services that presently exist only on a sporadic and unpaid basis in Canada — often sponsored by local YWCAs — are Widow-to-Widow programs that seek out recently widowed women, through obituaries among other means, and offer them help in coping with the range of emotional, financial, and other difficulties they encounter at that time.

These and many other useful programs could give isolated and bored elderly women

and men a new purpose in life and a way of supplementing their meagre incomes. They would also contribute to making seniors better integrated and more valued members of our society. The importance of adopting such an attitude was best expressed in a presentation made to the U.S. Council on the Aging in 1975 (U.S. Federal Council on the Aging 1976, 51):

> We can no longer ignore the economic plight of the older woman. We have three choices: (1) let her slowly starve, (2) provide her increasingly expensive, inadequate welfare services; or (3) help her to remain an independent, contributing member of society.
>
> We can give her a fish and feed her for day. . . . Or we can teach her to fish and she will feed herself, and perhaps some others too.

Notes

1. Statistics Canada, unpublished preliminary post-censal estimates for 1983.
2. Statistics Canada, unpublished data from the 1975 survey of nursing homes.
3. Calculated from Statistics Canada (1983, Table 1).
4. Table 2, unpublished data from Statistics Canada, compares date from the 1982 Survey of Consumer Finances to Statistics Canada's low-income cut-offs as recalculated in 1978. Note that the category called "Families Headed by Males" cannot be compared to the one entitled "Families Headed by Fer━━━ ━━━━━━ ━━━━━━ Canada uses the sexist practi━
ples ir
5. U
rizons

Wo

Abu
  Li
  Vi
  an
Arli
  F
  M

Du
on
visory
━━━. 19
Mind. Cana
of Women.
━━━. 1984. Love
Advisory Council o
Evans, Jocelyn. 1971. Li
Dying: A Personal Memoir
Cited in Matthews 1980, 14

Armstrong, Pat, and Hugh Armstrong. 1978. *The Double Ghetto: Canadian Women and Their Segregated Work.* Toronto: McClelland and Stewart.

Atchley, Robert C., and Sherry L. Corbett. 1977. "Older Women and Jobs." *Looking Ahead: A Woman's Guide to the Problems and Joys of Growing Older.* Eds. Lillian Troll et al. Englewood Cliffs, NJ: Prentice-Hall.

Béland, François. 1984. "The Family and Adults 65 Years of Age and Over: Co-residency and Availability of Help." *Canadian Review of Sociology and Anthropology* 21: 302–17.

Berardo, Felix M. 1967. "Social Adaptation to Widowhood Among a Rural-Urban Aged Population." *Washington Agricultural Experimental Station Bulletin* 689 (Dec.). Cited in Abu-Laban 1980, 129.

Borgatta, E.F., and M.B. Loeb. 1981. "Toward a Policy for Retired Persons: Reflections on Welfare and Taxation." *Aging and Retirement: Prospects, Planning and Policy.* Eds. N.G. McCluskey and E.F. Borgatta. Beverly Hills: Sage.

Burwell, Elinor J. 1981. "Discussion of Neena L. Chappell's Paper on the Future Impact to the Changing Status of Women." *Canada's Changing Age Structure: Implications for the Future.* Ed. Gloria M. Gutman. Vancouver: SFU Publications.

Canada Pension Plan Advisory Committee. 1983. *More Effective Participation of Homemakers in the Canada Pension Plan.*

Ciffin, S., J. Martin, and C. Talbot. 1977. *Retirement in Canada.* Vol. II: *Social and Economic Concerns.* Ottawa: Health and Welfare Canada, Department of Policy Research and Long-Range Planning.

Clark, S., and A.S. Harvey. 1976. "The Sexual Division of Labour: The Use of Time." *Atlantis* 2: 46–66.

Comfort, Alex. 1976. "Age Prejudice in America." *Social Policy* (Nov.-Dec.).

Connidis, Ingrid. 1983. "Living Arrangements Choices of Older Residents: Assessing Quantitative Results with Qualitative Data." *Canadian Review of Sociology* 8: 359–75.

[J]ude, Louise. 1978. *Women and Aging: A Report [on t]he Rest of Our Lives.* Ottawa: Canadian Advisory Council on the Status of Women.

[19]81. *Pension Reform With Women in [Cana]dian Advisory Council on the Status*

Marriage and Money. Canadian [on] the Status of Women.

[Li]ving With a Man Who Is New York: Taplinger.

Fletcher, Susan, and Leroy O. Stone. 1986. *The Living Arrangements of Canada's Older Women.* Statistics Canada. Catalogue 86–503.

Gee, Ellen M. 1984. "Mortality and Gender." *Canadian Woman Studies* 5: 10–13 (special issue on ageing).

Gold, Dolores. 1984. "Sex Differences in the Experience of Aging." *Canadian Woman Studies* 5: 3.

Government of Canada. 1983. *Fact Book on Aging in Canada.* Ottawa: Supply and Services Canada.

Harding, J. 1978. *A Socio-Demographic Profile of People Prescribed Mood-Modifiers in Saskatchewan.* Regina: Alcoholism Commission of Saskatchewan, Research Division.

Jarvis, George K., and Menno Boldt. 1980. "Suicide in Later Years." *Essence* 4: 145–58.

Jefferson, James, and Mary Kate Rowan. 1981. "You Adjust . . . It's Like the Army." *Globe and Mail* (March 17).

Keeney, Jill Johnson. 1983. "Care-Givers: Top Issue for Older Women." *Ms* (March).

Lopata, Helena Z. 1973. *Widowhood in an American City.* Cambridge, MA: Schenkman.

———. 1979. *Women as Widows: Support Systems.* New York: Elsevier Holland.

Masters, William H., and Virginia E. Johnson. 1966. *Human Sexual Response.* Boston: Little, Brown.

Matthews, Anne Martin. 1980. "Women and Widowhood." *Aging in Canada.* Ed. Victor W. Marshall. Markham, ON: Fitzhenry and Whiteside. 227.

———. "Review Essay — Canadian Research on Women as Widows: A Comparative Analysis of the State of the Art." *Resources for Feminist Research* (special issue on ageing) 11: 2.

Meissner, M., E.W. Humphreys, S.M. Meis, and W.J. Scheu. 1975. "No Exit for Wives: Sexual Division of Labour and the Cumulation of Household Demands." *Canadian Review of Sociology and Anthropology* 12: 424–39, Part 1.

Miller, G.H., and Dean R. Gernstein. "The Life Expectancy of Nonsmoking Men and Women." *Public Health Reports of the U.S. Department of Health and Human Services* 98: 4.

National Action Committee on the Status of Women. 1983. *Pension Reform: What Women Want.*

National Council of Welfare. 1979. *Women and Poverty.* Ottawa: Supply and Services Canada.

Norris, Joan E. 1980. "The Social Adjustment of Single and Widowed Older Women." *Essence* 4: 135–44.

Posner, Judith. [1977] 1980. "Old and Female:

The Double Whammy," *Essence* 2: 1. Reprinted in *Aging in Canada*. Ed. Victor W. Marshall. Markham, ON: Fitzhenry and Whiteside.

Riddick, Carol Cutler. 1982. "Life Satisfaction among Aging Women: A Causal Model." *Women's Retirement*. Ed. M. Szinovacz. Beverly Hills: Sage.

Saltz, Rosalyn. 1977. "Fostergrandparenting: A Unique Child-Care Service." *Looking Ahead: A Woman's Guide to the Problems and Joys of Growing Older*. Eds. Lillian Troll et al. Englewood Cliffs, NJ: Prentice-Hall.

Schlesinger, Rachel Aber. 1984. "Granny-Bashing: An Introduction to the Problem." *Canadian Woman Studies* 5: 56–59.

Seniors Secretariat. Secretariat for Social Development of Ontario, and United Senior Citizens of Ontario. 1985. *Elderly Residents in Ontario: An Overview* (May).

Sommers, Tish. 1976. "Ageing is a Woman's Issue." *Response* (March): 12–15.

Sontag, Susan. 1972. "The Double Standard of Aging." *Saturday Review* (Sept. 23).

Statistics Canada. 1983. *Income Distributions by Size in Canada*. Catalogue 13–207. Ottawa: Supply and Services Canada.

———. 1984a. *The Labour Force*. Catalogue 71–001. (Dec.). Ottawa: Supply and Services Canada.

———. 1984b. *Living Alone*. Catalogue 99–934. Ottawa: Supply and Services Canada.

———. 1985. *Women in Canada: A Statistical Report*. Catalogue 89–503E. Ottawa: Supply and Services Canada.

Strain, Laural A., and Neena L. Chappell. 1982. "Confidants: Do They Make a Difference in Quality of Life?" *Research on Aging* 4: 479–502.

Szinovacz, Maximiliane. 1982. "Introduction: Research on Women's Retirement." *Women's Retirement*. Ed. M. Szinovacz. Beverly Hills: Sage.

Tavris, Carol. 1977. "The Sexual Lives of Women Over 60." *Ms* (July).

U.S. Federal Council on the Aging. 1976. *Commitment to a Better Life: National Policy Concerns for Older Women*.

GRANDPARENTS AND GRANDCHILDREN: AN OFTEN-NEGLECTED RELATIONSHIP BETWEEN SIGNIFICANT OTHERS

S. Allen Wilcoxon

The author discusses the grandparent–grandchild relationship and its implications for counselling activities. The historical and contemporary role expectations of grandparents and grandchildren, the reciprocal significance of this relationship, and ways to use the relationship in counselling services and programming in various settings are reviewed.

Counsellors have become increasingly aware of the conceptual and applied literature depicting the family as an organized, predictable system of members with unique patterns for relating to one another. This systemic perspective seems to have fostered an appreciation for the complexity of intergenerational relationships that affect contemporary family life. Much of the contemporary family literature, however, has focussed on the nuclear family, with little mention of "the grandparent generation." Boszormenyi-Nagy and Spark (1973) noted that to view the nuclear family apart from its ancestral past is to ignore an integral aspect of the family's present life. Similarly, Bowen (1978) asserted that the influences from previous generations are of equal, and in some cases greater, importance than nuclear family life for understanding difficulties manifested in the lives of contemporary family members.

Source: *Journal of Counseling and Development* 65 (1987): 289-90. © American Association for Counseling and Development. Reprinted with permission.

Developmental writers have asserted that the grandparent–grandchild relationship has the potential for affecting the development of children in a way that cannot be duplicated in any other relationship (Baranowski 1982; Kalish and Knudston 1976). In this regard, Peck (1978) noted that the relationship may positively affect grandchildren in that "those who are loved usually develop into loving people who, in turn, make positive contributions to society" (p. 168).

The stereotypical view of grandparents might include the perception of feeble widows or widowers with limited access to family and friends. Although this is true for an unfortunate number of grandparents, most are physically capable, mobile, healthy, and socially active (Kivnick 1982). Shanas (1983) noted that four-fifths of all elderly citizens (i.e., 65 years of age and older) lived independently in a community setting and that many grandparents lived near their children and grandchildren, affording frequent opportunities for interactions.

A review of the contemporary professional literature suggests that relationships with grandparents are a frequently neglected aspect of family life with a variety of potential implications for counselling activities. Such activities could be therapeutic, developmental, educational, or preventive in nature, depending on opportunities for interactions and the creativity of the counsellor. In this article, I examine selected contemporary information concerning the grandparent–grandchild relationship and its significance for counselling services. Specific emphasis is placed on the significance of the grandparent–grandchild relationship for children and adolescents at critical stages of development, the importance of the grandparent status for ageing adults, and the potential for this relationship to affect attitudes of middle-generation adults.

The Significant Grandparent

Contemporary research has been revealing regarding changes in grandparent roles. Traditional role assumptions for grandparents have fostered the idea of the domineering, controlling family matriarch or patriarch. Neugarten and Weinstein (1964) noted that this relationship historically has featured dictatorial authority and power. According to Barranti (1985), striking changes have evolved concerning the perceived and ascribed roles of grandparents. Kivnick (1982) wrote that contemporary grandparents seem to view their roles as being less associated with power and more associated with indulgence, warmth, and pleasure without responsibility. Kornhaber and Woodward (1981) reported that contemporary grandparents seem to have been ascribed multidimensional roles. Specifically, these authors identified the following roles for contemporary grandparents:

- historian — a link with the cultural and familial past;
- role model — an example of older adulthood;
- mentor — a wise adult experienced in life transitions;
- wizard — a master of story-telling to foster imagination and creativity; and
- nurturer–greatparent — an ultimate support person for familial crises and transitions.

Research efforts have focussed recently on the significance of the grandparent–grandchild relationship in affecting child development. Kalish and Knudston (1976) noted that the

intergenerational link with grandparents may be crucial in resolving crises regarding ego development and subsequent risk taking by children and adolescents. Baranowski (1982) surmised that developmental crises of childhood and adolescence revolve around establishing one's own unique identity in the context of continuity from one's ancestral past. In a much bolder statement, Kornhaber and Woodward (1981) observed that "the complete emotional well-being of children requires that they have a direct, and not merely derived, link with their grandparents" (p. 163). (I question this "requirement" because many grandchildren may not have such opportunities, but they develop into happy, productive citizens. The emphasis on the enhancing quality of positive grandparent–grandchild relationships, however, seems to be more realistic.)

The contemporary literature further suggests that the grandparent–grandchild relationship is significant in terms of meeting the developmental and nurturing needs of grandchildren. This relationship seems also to be of significance for therapeutic efforts with grandchildren or families of adults in crises.

The Significant Grandchild

The grandparent–grandchild relationship is not simply a one-way street for nurturing and otherwise meeting important needs of grandchildren. The systemic perspective advances the notion of reciprocal satisfaction of needs between family members. Kivnick (1982) proposed a compensation–deprivation model to describe grandparents' desires for grandparent status. The enhanced esteem of grandparent status and its associated role privileges seem to hold great promise for prospective grandparents facing demoralizing physical, social, and material losses in older years (Barranti 1985).

From this perspective, Englund's (1983) distinctions between *parentage* and *parenting* seem to be particularly pertinent for the grandparent–grandchild relationship. Parentage is related to the social–familial status of

Parentage — biorelationship / parenting
Parenting — responsibility

being a parent (or grandparent) within the family system, whereas parenting is associated with the responsibilities of setting limits, making decisions, and attending to similar childrearing duties. In light of Kivnick's compensation–deprivation model and the prevalent notion of contemporary grandparents preferring "pleasure without responsibilities," it may be that prospective grandparents desire the status of grandparentage but have relatively little interest in grandparenting. Prospective grandparents may also exert pressure on childless, middle-generation adults, which may promote resentment or anger in the subsequent grandparent–grandchild relationship.

Recent studies have focussed on the perceived significance of the grandparent–grandchild relationship for grandchildren entering young adulthood. Barranti (1985) noted that, although many grandchildren ascribed significance to this relationship during their earlier years, the grandparent–grandchild relationship decreased in significance during their late adolescence and early adulthood. A corresponding decrease in the perceived significance of this relationship has not been reported by ageing grandparents. Although this change in the grandparent–grandchild relationship may not negate the gains in self-esteem and morale associated with grandparenting status, it is possible that such changes could affect the attitudes and emotions of older grandparents.

Implications for Counselling

Counselling interventions focussed on grandparent–grandchild relationships have received increasing emphasis over the past two decades. Hill et al. (1970) contended that a thorough social history for children must include data concerning relationships with grandparents. In this way, the professional can collect information such as the nature of the relationship between parents and grandparents, relationships with extended family members, the level of familial involvement with grandparents (i.e., emotionally close or emotionally distant), favouritism in grandparent–grandchild relationships, and changes in family life across time.

The grandparent–grandchild relationship may often be a key issue that affects difficulties in discordant families. Bowen (1978) noted that a cross-generation coalition (i.e., grandparent–grandchild relationship) may often result in a middle-generation parent being excluded from positive emotional exchanges. He further observed that such a configuration could promote negative feelings by the parent directed toward both the grandparent and the grandchild. Williamson (1981) observed that this pattern can affect the ego strength of middle-generation adults by forcing them to remain in a subordinate posture with their parents. He further suggested that overcoming this subordinate status is a necessary aspect of adult development. Framo (1981) wrote that failure to resolve difficulties with one's parents could be replicated in relationships with one's children and spouse, thereby perpetuating a negative self-concept as well as strained familial relationships.

Counselling activities tailored to emphasize the significance of the grandparent–grandchild relationship could include a variety of modalities in a number of service settings, including the following:

- a "Grandparents Day" emphasis in schools;
- workshops and seminars for "expectant grandparents";
- "Grandchildren Days" for grandparents in day treatment programs;
- "Adopt-a-Grandparent" activities supported by various community- or school-service groups;
- three-generation family therapy for discordant families;
- support group activities specifically designed for grandparents; and
- grandparents as supportive adjuncts in counselling services for children and middle-generation adults experiencing traumas such as terminal illness and divorce.

The decline in mortality rates seems to be a statistic with implications for the grandparent–grandchild relationship. Simply stated, the average life expectancy for adults has increased appreciably because of advances in medical technology and health awareness. Barranti (1985) observed that this change may affect contemporary grandparent–grandchild relationships in that adults are becoming grandparents at earlier ages while retaining their roles as grandchildren for a longer period of time. Barranti further speculated that today's children may be grandparents for up to half of their lives. In the light of this prediction as well as other contemporary information noted in the professional literature, it seems that counsellors should consider the significance of the grandparent–grandchild relationship in their intervention, programming, educational, and research efforts and activities. Otherwise, the grandparent–grandchild relationship may remain an often neglected relationship between *significant* significant others.

Works Cited

Baranowski, M.D. 1982. "Grandparent–Adolescent Relations: Beyond the Nuclear Family." *Adolescence* 17: 575-84.

Barranti, C.C.R. 1985. "The Grandparent–Grandchild Relationship: Family Resource in an Era of Voluntary Bonds." *Family Relations* 34: 343-52.

Boszormenyi-Nagy, I., and G. Spark. 1973. *Invisible Loyalties*. New York: Harper and Row.

Bowen, M. 1978. *Family Therapy in Clinical Practice*. New York: Jason Aronson.

Englund, C.L. 1983. "Parenting and Parentage: Distinct Aspects of Children's Importance." *Family Relations* 32: 21-28.

Framo, J.L. 1981. "The Integration of Marital Therapy with Sessions with Family of Origin." *Handbook of Family Therapy*. Eds. A.S. Gurman and D.P. Kniskern. New York: Brunner/Mazel. 133-58.

Hill, R., N. Foote, J. Aldous, R. Carlson, and R. MacDonald. 1970. *Family Development in Three Generations*. Cambridge, MA: Schenkman.

Kalish, R., and F.W. Knudston. 1976. ment Versus Disengagement: A Lifespan ceptualization." *Human Development* 171–82.

Kivnick, H.Q. 1982. "Grandparenthood: An Overview of Meaning and Mental Health." *Gerontologist* 22: 59-66.

Kornhaber, A., and K.L. Woodward. 1981. *Grandparents/Grandchildren: The Vital Connection*. Garden City, NY: Anchor Press/Doubleday.

Neugarten, B., and K. Weinstein. 1964. "The Changing American Grandparents." *Journal of Marriage and the Family* 26: 199-204.

Peck, S. 1978. *The Road Less Traveled*. New York: Simon and Schuster.

Shanas, E. 1983. "Old Parents and Middle-Aged Children: The Four- and Five-generation Family." *Journal of Geriatric Psychiatry* 17: 7-19.

Williamson, D.S. 1981. "Personal Authority Via Termination of the Intergenerational Hierarchical Boundary: A "New" Stage in the Family Life Cycle." *Journal of Marital and Family Therapy* 7: 441-52.

The mass media continually publicize deficiencies in family support for the aged. Although most of these deficiencies are not substantiated by contemporary research, dramatic social changes have occurred that have implications for the family context of older people. While increases in life expectancy result in greater numbers of grandparents and great-grandparents than ever before, lower fertility places a greater burden on fewer lineal descendants for their care. Most older people prefer to remain independent from children whenever possible; at the same time, patterns of visiting, exchange of assistance, support, and intergenerational agreement appear high. Practitioners working with families should point out that norms appropriate to earlier historical periods may have changed; in particular, idealized images of family life in the mythical past are dysfunctional, both to the parent-caring middle-aged and to the professional.

Of the many contemporary myths concerning family relations, none may be so pervasive as that of older persons abandoned by their families. There is a widespread belief that ageing individuals no longer can rely on their families for assistance, honour, and support in meeting the vicissitudes of old age. Comparison is frequently made to the situation in earlier historical periods or to other "traditional"

Source: *Marriage and Family Review* 2 (1980): 51–76. Copyright © The Haworth Press, Inc., 10 Alice Street, Binghamton, N.Y. 13904-1580. Reprinted with permission.

Preparation of this paper was supported in part by Grant No. 90-A-1297 from the Administration on Aging (Stephen McConnell, Principal Investigator) and by training grant No. AG-0037-03 from the National Institute on Aging (K. Warner Schaie, Program Director).

cultures where older family members were far more revered and supported than today.

Current research on the family, while reflecting some rather striking social changes over the past decade, lends little support to the stereotype of isolated, lonely older persons bereft of family (Shanas 1979; Shanas and Sussman 1979; Sussman 1976). Indeed, recent sociohistorical research suggests that intergenerational relations a century or more ago were not as harmonious, nor was contact as frequent, as nostalgia has made them appear (Anderson 1977; Hareven 1978). Moreover, contemporary data indicate high rates of interaction, mutual support, and affection between older family members and their kin (Bengtson and Treas 1980; Shanas 1979).

There are, however, a number of problems regarding family relations and ageing that have significant consequences for practitioners and policy makers. In this review, we wish to emphasize the changing social context of family relations that gives rise to these problems. We wish also to note the necessity for both macrosocial (societal) and microsocial (individual) perspectives in addressing the problems and resources that the family represents for the older person.

Social Change and the Family: Demographic Changes

One of the most striking changes of the twentieth century concerns demographic shifts that have increased the number and proportion of old people in our population. At the same time, decreases in mortality rates have widened the sex differential in mortality and contributed to the presence of more four- and five-generation families. Paradoxically, these changes have also reduced the number of family members available for the older individual today, as is discussed below.

Seven major trends should be observed. First, starting around 1850, improvements occurred in *life expectancy*, with dramatic changes taking place between 1900 and 1950 (Rao 1973). In 1900, average life expectancy was 49.2 years. This figure increased to 69.5 years by 1955, and to 71.9 years by 1974 (U.S. Bureau of the Census 1976). Reduction of childhood mortality, made possible by improvements in sanitation and conquest of the so-called children's diseases, allowed for longer life expectancy at all other life stages. In 1900, 33 percent of the population lived to age 65 or better. By 1974, over half of all Americans born survived to this age.

Declines in mortality have affected a second and related phenomenon — that is, the increase in the *sex mortality differential* (SMD) for the same period. The SMD, which refers to the difference in male–female life expectancy at birth, was 2.9 years in 1900. By 1974, it had increased to 7.7 years (U.S. Bureau of the Census 1976, 26).

Medical technology has raised the SMD by helping to decrease maternal mortality and by improving the detection and treatment of cancer in the female reproductive organs (Retherford 1975). The differential has also been raised by the increase in cigarette smoking in our society during this century, because more men than women smoke. While increased smoking on the part of women has narrowed this gap somewhat, continuing sex differences are predicted. Racial differences also operate; the average life expectancy of nonwhite persons is less than that for whites, but in 1974, the relative difference in death rates between the sexes was greater for whites than for nonwhites.

A third change results both from improvements in life expectancy and from the increased SMD. Today, there is greater probability that the surviving member of the oldest

generation of a family will be a *female over the age of 75.* This occurrence is an outgrowth of the reduction in age-specific death rates for women, along with the tendency for females in our society to marry men older than themselves.

Each of these phenomena, particularly longer life expectancy, leads to a fourth issue. Today there is an *increased likelihood that the youngest generation will have a grandparent*, particularly a grandmother, around for the greater portion of his or her lifetime than ever before. Historians and demographers agree that the emergence of the three-generation family is mainly a twentieth-century phenomenon, because high mortality rates made the overlap of three generations demographically unlikely in the past. Furthermore, the growth of three-generation families during this century, has been accompanied by the growth of four-generation families.

The growing population of multigenerational families has led to a fifth change, a *decrease in the number of younger relatives* for older family members. Between 1890 and 1930, the available number of relatives for the elderly was fairly constant, with increases in joint survivorship of couples (Kobrin 1976). Recently, some cohort-specific effects may be witnessed in the present population of individuals reaching old age. The unprecedented low fertility of women who postponed or skipped marriage and childbearing during the Depression of the 1930s has been an object of discussion by several demographers (Glick 1975; Kobrin 1976; Treas 1977). The effects of this low birth rate are now being experienced by that cohort of mothers who bore the smallest number of children ever recorded up until that time. Kobrin observes that the generation of daughters (i.e., women aged 35–44) relative to their widowed mothers has shifted from approximately 2.8 daughters per mother before 1930 to approximately 1.2 daughters per mother, according to recent census data. Thus, younger generations have a greater number of older relatives than ever before. With the exception of the 1947–57 birth cohort, the decline in the birth rate has led to the opposite experience for the elderly. The implications of this change become salient in our discussion of intergenerational relations.

A sixth change, *expansion of women's roles beyond family responsibility*, may also be observed. In the past, the events of the female life cycle tended to be patterned exclusively after the family cycle: childbearing and child-rearing during the earlier years; the care of older parents in the middle age. Greater fertility control, earlier age at first marriage and birth of first child, smaller family size, longer postparental period, and longer life expectancy these patterns. Van Dusen and Sheldon (1976) note that these changes, along with shifts in ideology about the role of women, suggest a trend in which marriage and family life is no longer an exclusive preoccupation for many women.

The major change in nonfamilial activity for women has occurred in rates of labour-force participation. Between 1950 and 1973, the overall labour-force participation of women rose by one-third. This increase was accompanied by a shift in the modal characteristics of the employed women from young and single to middle-aged and married. The largest rise in women's labour-force participation between 1947 and 1969 occurred for women between the ages of 45 and 54; in that group, the proportion employed increased from 33 percent to 54 percent (Troll 1971). Closely following this group were females ages 55 to 64, whose level of employment rose from 24 percent to 43 percent during the same time period. During the 1960s, more women aged 40 and over were employed than were younger females.

The implications of increased nonfamilial activity by women are central to any discussion about relations with ageing parents. For one thing, women have been described as the chief "kinkeepers" in the family, and are more likely to be turned to by older parents, particularly a widowed mother (Adams 1968; Lopata 1973). In 1977, 39 percent of married women with preschool children were in the labour force (U.S. Department of Labour 1979). Treas (1977) notes that the increase

in employment by these younger females suggests that if women have less time for the care of their own young children, they will also be less available for the care of any ageing parents or relatives.

Seventh, *new institutions have emerged and modified families' responsibility for their ageing members*. In previous centuries, economic support occurred primarily within families. The growth of subsidized education for the young, as well as federal old age, survivors, and disability insurance (OASDI) for the older worker, has led to society-wide transfers now taking place between nonrelated age cohorts. Social Security income maintenance programs have taken over major support of the elderly.

In keeping with these changes, new bonds of intermediary linkage to bureaucracies providing this support appear to have emerged for the younger relatives of ageing individuals (Anderson 1977; Munnichs 1977; Streib 1977; Sussman 1976, 1977). Sussman (1976) describes this relatively recent role for families on behalf of elderly members. Children and other relatives in the family network are able to mediate on behalf of the aged in the latter's attempts to obtain services from human-service organizations, as well as to provide information about housing, pension eligibility, and other entitlements. In future, the movement away from economic support of the elderly by their families is expected to continue. Other forms of help, however, will probably persist.

The effort of establishing linkages to government and other bureaucratic structures is not without its effect on the quality of intergenerational relationships. Historical evidence suggests that the direct support of the elderly by their younger kin frequently occurred under constraint of local Poor Laws, and not without tension and resentment (Anderson 1977). The creation of the pension system for the aged has been cited as an important factor in the reduction of such tensions, because cash resources are now brought to the family by the older individual. Similarly, the older person's ability to contribute makes his or her presence in the family more desirable. Thus, as Sussman (1979) suggests, the quality of the relationship between older individuals and their families may be different in a society in which the younger generation has responsibility for direct support of the elderly from that in a society in which the government offers financial and other human service support.

Family Structure

Recent studies of family life have examined the relationship between social change in the larger social structure and such features as family composition and living arrangements (Bengtson and Treas 1980; Berkner 1972; Goode 1963; Katz 1975; Laslett 1976; Little and Laslett 1977). The traditional image in our culture is one of an extended family household composed of a "friendly assortment of related people of all ages" (Bane 1976, 37).

Goode (1963) has conceptualized this description as "the classical family of western nostalgia": "It is a pretty picture of life down on grandma's farm. There are lots of happy children and many kinfolk live together in a large rambling house. Everyone works hard . . . and in general the household is economically self-sufficient" (p. 10). According to this nostalgic view, the elderly fared well both in society and in the family group. To be old was to be revered, and to hold a secure place in the everyday life of the family.

When compared to this historical ideal, modern society appears less positive. The family of today is seen as bereft next to these overflowing households of the past. The elderly, in particular, are seen as victims of these changes. Younger family members ostensibly have abandoned older relatives to public institutions, supposedly indifferent to their plight. Does current research uphold this view?

Family Composition

Laslett (1976) studied mean household size in 100 communities in England between 1574 and 1821 from census data, birth, marriage, and death records, and from personal documents. His findings suggest that the most common family form was nuclear, and that the average number of persons in the household was slightly under five. Bane (1976) notes that during the colonial period in America, family size was somewhat larger than what Laslett found in England. In America, the average household size declined from 5.6 persons in 1850 to 4.1 in 1930 (Bane 1976, 39). Bane attributes this decrease mainly to the effects of industrialization and urbanization, where children's economic contribution to the family is of less value than in an agricultural setting. In 1977, the average family in America had 3.39 members; this represented a drop from 3.61 persons per household in 1970 (U.S. Bureau of the Census, 1978). The decrease in household size has largely resulted from lower birth rates, but family dissolution through separation or divorce has also contributed to the change.

In samples of the elderly in the United States, Great Britain, and Denmark, Shanas et al. (1968) found family composition reflected three trends: higher rates of marriage, earlier age at first marriage, and earlier age of childbearing. The effects of these phenomena are twofold. First, the greater proportion of the population who marry at least once during their lifetime reduces the number of spinsters acting as "maiden aunts" for the family. Traditionally, these women have been more likely to take in ageing parents or a widowed mother (Treas 1977). Second, the earlier age of marriage and childbearing has shortened the span of time between generations. The more frequent occurrence of four-generation families is in part a result of four generations being born during almost the same period of time that it took three generations earlier this century.

In the three-nation study (Shanas et al. 1968; Shanas 1978) 40 percent of the population aged 65 and over were widowed, separated, or divorced. Widowhood was by far the most common status for women. In the United States, 52 percent of females over age 65 were widowed, as opposed to only 17 percent of the men. Similarly, 76 percent of the men, as opposed to 38 percent of the women, were married. These data are comparable to findings from other studies. The older single male is more th·n six times more likely to wed or re-wed than the unattached female of the same age (Treas and VanHilst 1976).

In Shanas's 1975 study, four out of five older respondents reported one or more surviving children. Four out of five of those with children also had grandchildren. About one-fourth were great-grandparents. Of respondents over the age of 80, three-fourths had great-grandchildren.

Living Arrangements

The family of earlier times has also been scrutinized by historians and demographers with regard to living arrangements. Reconstructions of the past point to a different picture of residence patterns than our cultural ideology suggests. The stereotype of three generations living harmoniously under one roof has been refuted on demographic grounds alone. Before the twentieth century, life expectancy did not permit the overlap of three generations for very many years after a young couple married and started their own family (Berkner 1972; Laslett 1976). Furthermore, household-reconstruction techniques reveal that even when they survived, most of the elderly did not live with offspring (Laslett 1976).

Demographic shifts have consequences for the living arrangements of older family members. The growth of one-person households, which represented 5 percent of all household types in the United States in 1900 and 9 percent of all households in 1950, doubled to 18 percent in 1973 (Kobrin 1976). Most of these households are maintained by women, the majority of whom are age 55 and older (U.S. Bureau of the Census 1978). The increase in this type of living arrangement also reflects both the preference and the ability of the older woman to maintain her own residence, even when widowed. Most older people state they prefer to live in their own homes and not with relatives (Shanas 1979). This is especially true for married

couples. Today, increased availability of pensions and other retirement benefits make separate residence economically feasible.

Historically, the three-generation family has always comprised less than 10 percent of all families in those societies we know about. In Laslett's English study, 6 percent of all households were composed of three generations (p. 153). If other persons than the nuclear family were present, they were more likely to be servants or lodgers than relatives. In 1960, 5 percent of American families had three or more generations living together (Carter and Glick 1976, 159). In 1970, this figure was 7 percent (Bane 1976, 39). Thus, this figure has remained relatively stable over several centuries.

Lopata (1973) indicates that when families do share living quarters with relatives, this may reflect a crisis situation rather than preference. Lack of sufficient funds to live alone, poor health, or death of a spouse were reasons given in her study for intergenerational cohabitation. Furthermore, the sharing of living quarters was seen as a temporary, rather than as a permanent arrangement. Carter and Glick (1976) indicate that the age of the family members, income level, race, and ethnic background all serve as intervening variables leading to shared housing. Co-residence is more likely to occur when the household head is very young or very old, when income level is low, and where the older family member is nonwhite.

When the elderly do live with a child, it is usually with a daughter (Lopata 1973; Shanas et al. 1968). Preference for residence with unmarried rather than married offspring also exists: in the cross-national study, Stehouwer (1968) found that 15 percent of single persons over 65 lived with an unmarried child. Two percent lived with offspring who were married. More older people of minority ethnic status live with children than do whites of similar age (Bengtson, Kasschau, and Ragan 1977). Family structure and composition are important determinants of the nearness of kin for older people. One study (Shanas et al. 1968) found that more married than widowed persons lived far from their nearest child. Among widowed, separated, or divorced elderly, 88 percent lived within one hour's travelling time of their nearest child, while slightly fewer (82 percent) of the married lived within this distance. Similarly, Lopata (1973) found the modal time-distance of adult children from their mother was within one hour.

In summary, recent macrosocial changes — demographic, economic, and normative — have influenced the family life of older members in several ways. Most older people today are members of three-generation families, and almost half of them live to become great-grandparents. Although life expectancy has increased for both men and women, the increasing sex–mortality differential results in most of the very old being female. This trend, coupled with the fact that most husbands are older than wives at marriage, means that the most common marital status of the older individual is widowhood. Most of the elderly have surviving children and grandchildren, and some have great-grandchildren. The elderly prefer to live in their own homes, and most aged persons are able to maintain such living arrangements, unless decreased physical mobility, impaired health, financial strain, or an unforeseen crisis necessitates other arrangements. Although the elderly like to live separately, they prefer to reside near their offspring.

Family Solidarity

Surprisingly few empirical studies on intergenerational relations have explored the ways in which older family members spend time with, assist, feel about, and agree with other kin members. These behaviours can be conceptualized as expressions of family solidarity. There are three major dimensions along which this construct may be operationalized:

1. *associational solidarity*, which includes activities and interaction among family members;

2. *affectual solidarity*, which refers to sentiments and feelings occurring between family members; and

3. *consensual solidarity*, or the agreement on life values and norms or standards of behaviour (Bengtson, Olander, and Haddad 1976).

Problems of measurement in these and other dimensions of kinship interaction among the aged have been reviewed elsewhere (Bengtson and Schrader 1980), along with a listing of 21 batteries of questions that were used in earlier research.

Associational Solidarity

In our discussion of the activities in which family members engage, we will focus on two broad areas. The first, involving type and frequency of contacts among generations, has been studied by Litwak (1960), Sussman (1965), Rosow (1967), Shanas et al. (1968), Adams (1968), Hill et al. (1970), and Troll (1971). The second area is the exchange of assistance and support between immediate and more distant family.

Contact: Type and Frequency

Sussman (1965) reviewed the literature on kin relations published before the mid-1960s. He found strong support for the existence of ongoing contact between adult children and their parents, such as the sharing of social activities, and the exchange of both material and nonmaterial aid. Litwak (1960) has described interfamilial relations in our society that do not rely solely on geographic and occupational proximity for their existence, as a "modified extended family" arrangement. Sussman and Slater (1963) found a continuum of family types ranging from highly integrated kin networks to those that were isolated from the larger family group (see also Hill et al. 1970; Stehouwer 1968).

In a three-generation study, Hill et al. (1970) found that social class was related to the amount of intergenerational visiting in which family members engaged. Working-class men had more intergenerational contact than did white-collar men. Sussman (1965) notes that married daughters seem to have closer ties to parents than do married sons. Data from these studies support the finding that daughters, more than sons, have been the major "kinkeepers" in both type and frequency of contact with older parents, as is the consensus in the literature.

Exchange of Assistance and Support

The exchange of assistance and support between older persons and their children has been a topic of much research on intergenerational relations (Adams 1968; Hill et al. 1970; Kreps 1965; Lopata 1973; Rosow 1967; Shanas et al. 1968; Sussman 1965; Troll 1971). Troll notes two general patterns of economic assistance: one type of flow from old to young, and a second kind, which flows in both directions from the middle generation. These patterns are modified by such variables as sex of offspring, child's life circumstances, and social class of parent or child.

Hill et al. (1970) found that in a crisis situation all three generations chose kin as their preferred source of help. The middle generations gave help the most frequently, married children received help most frequently, and the grandparent generation was least active in both the giving and receiving of help. Furthermore, exchanges of help among these three generations were greater than exchanges among all other sources of help.

A lack of specific information regarding intergenerational financial assistance has been noted by Sussman (1965). The total amount of money given within a specified period of time has not been examined, nor has the ratio of earned income to dispersed income received systematic study. While Kreps (1965, 1977) has observed that *inter*generational support of the elderly now takes place on a society-wide, or income-transfer basis, the extent and meaning of *intra*familial assistance still warrants attention. Such information is essential in understanding the kinds of behaviours that link members of a family together.

Affectual Solidarity

Affectual integration or solidarity has been described as "mutual positive sentiment among group members and their self expressions of love, respect, appreciation, and recognition for one another" (Nye and Rushing 1969). Similar notions are suggested by "empathy" and "unconditional positive regard," as described by Carl Rogers (1961). Another psychological construct related to solidarity is emotional dependence or interdependence. Measures of solidarity also include their polar opposites, such as lack of solidarity or conflict between generations.

Positive Feelings

Bengtson and Black (1973) observe that the level of affectual solidarity in a relationship is difficult to operationalize, or even conceptualize, and thus has not been adequately researched. Using a three-generation sample, they attempted first to construct theoretically and then to operationalize measures of family solidarity. They found seven dimensions of solidarity based on their subjects' reports of feeling toward their parent or child: (1) degree of understanding; (2) trust; (3) fairness; (4) respect; (5) the affection that was perceived as characterizing the relationship; (6) the quality of communication; and (7) general statements about getting along and feeling of closeness of the relationship. They note that intergenerational relationships are dyadic; hence, they measured their subjects' perceptions of the other's feelings toward him or her, as well as their feelings for the other person.

The data showed the lowest measure of solidarity occurring in the youngest group, i.e., among those individuals who are least independent of their parents. The researchers observed that a young adult child's perception of solidarity with his parents seems to increase as he moves further into an adult's social position. Furthermore, when full adult status is achieved, the level of solidarity expressed appears similar to that felt by his parents toward their own elderly parents.

The relationship between feelings of closeness to the parent and similarity in values was examined by Adams (1968). In his sample, 65 percent of his young adult respondents indicated close and affectionate ties with their parents. Of this group, a majority (54 percent) tended to have similar values and interests. Of the group that characterized their relationship with their parents as distant, 74 percent held different values from their parents. Adams observed no correlation between affection or similarity in values and simple frequency of interaction. Sex and social-class differences appeared in the data. Adult mothers and daughters were likely to agree on values and interests, to the degree that these focussed on home and children. However, the effects of earlier socialization on affectional ties could override such consensus. A daughter's feelings of closeness to her father were associated with her father's occupational position; the son's closeness of relationship with his mother varied positively with *his* occupational status. In interpreting these differences, Adams notes the effects of differential socialization. The role of each parent is influenced by occupational level, and is later reflected in affectional as well as consensual variation when the child becomes an adult. The effects of early socialization appear to be inseparable from and interwoven with adolescent aspirations and goals, the occupational choices of the young adult, and the quality of later relationships with the family.

Dependence

Rosow (1967) studied the emotional dependence of older people on their children. One aspect of this research examined whether dependence on offspring increased as the parent grew older. The researchers hypothesized that emotional dependence of the elderly would increase with age. High role loss, such as death of spouse or retirement, was thought to intensify the dependence of older parents upon their adult offspring. The findings from this study revealed that social role loss was not systemically associated with emotional dependence of the aged on their families. Instead, dependence was seen as a stable ongoing psychological characteristic, basically unrelated to variation by age or sex, and unaffected by objective change. Rosow concluded that there are emotionally dependent personality types rather than increased emotional dependence based on the social position of the elderly.

Goldfarb (1965, 1969) also suggests that dependence is a psychological or continuous characteristic rather than the result of developmental change. He has constructed two typologies: the nondependent and the dependent personality. Personalities, their subtypes, and social characteristics are described and associated with each of these general types. In Goldfarb's theory, the earlier life of the individual is important; adaptive patterns learned in infancy and early childhood lay a foundation for successful coping and the development of social skills, or of crippling feelings of inadequacy and fear. Either personality type may be socioculturally reinforced as the person matures. Goldfarb's concept of dependence among elderly persons deals with the overt expressions of behaviours and attitudes that have always been a part of the individual. Thus, new behaviours may be expressed in old age, but the underlying needs and motivations reflect a "lifelong feeling of helplessness and dependency" (p. 1).

Friction Between Generations

Four decades ago, Davis (1940) suggested several variables most likely to be central to conflict between generations: (1) age difference between parents and children; (2) the effects of advancing age on the rate of socialization process; and (3) physiological, psychological, or social differences implied by belonging to different generations. Many variables were found to be related to an increase in conflict between generations. Among the most important factors was the rate of social change in the society at large. Such change contributed to shifts in socialization practices between generations. What was thought to be essential for successful childrearing by one generation of parents might become obsolete or even be considered harmful by a younger cohort of parents. Under these conditions, a certain amount of intergenerational friction would seem inevitable.

Family relationships involving older persons reflect change both in the individual and in the family over time. Peterson (1968) notes that "much of the difficulty between middle-aged persons and their parents is the final statement of their failure to work our closeness earlier in life." Similarly, Steinman (1979) states that transitions and changes in family life, such as the loss of a spouse and its subsequent effects on intrafamilial relations, may reactivate earlier, unresolved conflicts between parents and adult children.

There is relatively little empirical research on parent–child relations over the whole life cycle, especially after adolescence. In the data that are available, events transpiring at earlier stages of the relationship are linked to the quality of interaction that occurs when parents reach old age. For example, Streib and Thompson (1959) cite the work of Smith et al. (1958), who studied cohabiting three-generation families in urban and in small rural areas. The researchers found a greater likelihood of positive adjustment by the older family member in those households where their children reported a very close relationship with their parents when they were teenagers, as compared with individuals whose children felt less close to them during adolescence. The current status of relationships of the elderly with younger family members may be conceptualized as the outcome of an ongoing panorama of events and interactions (Elder 1978).

Consensual Solidarity

As has been previously discussed, in the perception of many respondents, independent living and noninterference appear to be the two major hallmarks of successful intergenerational relationship. Beyond these general norms are other, more specific expectations for behaviour.

Hill et al. (1970) found support for three prevalent norms in family life in his three-generation study: (1) reciprocity; (2) "noblesse oblige"; and (3) filial responsibility. The norm of reciprocity constrains both the giver and the receiver in any exchange of aid among members of an extended family. Non-reciprocated giving was correlated with high interaction with kin; on the other hand, non-reciprocity in receiving seemed to lead to breakdown or lessening of activities with kin. "Noblesse oblige" implies that more advantaged members of a family are obligated to help their less fortunate relatives in their hour of need. Filial responsibility refers to the responsibility of children for their parents. Differences in agreement with these norms by generations were not reported in this study.

Conflicting evidence exists in the literature on filial responsibility (or filial maturity, as it is sometimes called). Bleckner (1965) discusses this behaviour as another stage of the development sequence, occurring after genital maturity, but before one's own old age. Here the adult child turns to his parent

> no longer as a child, but a mature adult with a new role and a different love, seeing him for the first time as an individual with his own rights, needs, limitations, and a life history that, to a large extent, made him the person he is long before his child existed. (p. 58)

This perspective grows out of emotional maturity and independence on the part of the child, rather than on guilt or unfinished emancipation from the parent. Filial maturity provides for its own gratification; it should prepare the offspring for his or her own old age through identification with the aged parent. Bleckner is careful to differentiate the filial role, which refers to being depended on by the parents, from role reversal, where the child takes a parenting role toward an older or incapacitated parent.

Bleckner's suggestion is theoretical, not empirical. Data from actual studies, both current and historical, suggest that feelings of duty and obligation are more characteristic than motives of self-gratification and fulfilment for adult children who assist their elderly parents (Adams 1968; Anderson 1977; Berkner 1972; Steinman 1979). Adams discusses "obligatory motivation" in kin affairs. In his data, women expressed stronger feelings of obligation toward their parents than did men. This was especially true if their parents lived nearby. The perceived degree of closeness in the relationship between the adult daughter and either parent did not appear to affect these feelings. When a mother was widowed, however, more sons than daughters felt a sense of obligation toward her. Adams also found feelings of obligation toward older parents more characteristic of working-class than of middle-class respondents.

Seelbach and Sawer (1977) found levels of filial responsibility expectancy negatively related to parental morale. That is, the higher the level of filial responsibility expectancy, the lower the morale of the older family member. This relationship was upheld for males, for younger respondents, for married respondents, and in particular, for blacks. These findings suggest that extended family norms may be incompatible with and even dysfunctional within an urban–industrial society. Seelbach and Sawer further state that older persons whose norms about family life include expectations of obligation and duty among family members may be at odds with their offsprings' expectations. Such discrepancies point to conflict, rather than to compatibility in older parent-adult child relations.

Sussman (1976) and Kreps (1965, 1977) cite ways in which the bureaucracy has replaced the family in assuming traditional responsibility for elderly kin. As discussed previously, families, rather than directly providing for their older members, act as facilitators or links to bureaucratic information and entitlement. Social-security legislation, enacted during the 1930s, has made possible increasing financial and residential independence for the elderly. Normative support for this independence appears to exist among both younger and older adults (Sussman 1976). Norms today support independence, residentially, financially, and with respect to involvement in the private affairs of another's household. Strong feelings of filial responsibility, especially when held by the older person, appear correlated with low morale and suggest discrepancies in expectation between the two generations.

Implications for Practice and Research

Our review has suggested that the family context for older persons has changed considerably in past decades and is inextricably woven with the macrosocial trends that characterize the larger society. Yet older people continue to be tied to their families. The clinical practitioner or social-policy analyst would be well advised to remember both factors — changes in social context and the continued importance of families — in addressing the family life of older people considering, the myths and inaccuracies that are currently evident (Shanas 1979).

Life-Cycle Education

Many of the social and psychological issues that occur in families with ageing members can be appraised in the light of their relatively recent occurrence in human history. Both the ageing of our population and the increased expectation of survival are twentieth-century phenomena. Reductions in fertility and mortality rates have led to a larger proportion of old persons in our populations than ever before (Hauser 1976) and to the possibility of three- or four-generation families for almost everyone in our society. This radical demographic change in such a short period of time does not, however, raise the consciousness of all those who are affected.

Butler (1975) observes that systematic scientific investigation on the consequences of medical technology for human living is nonexistent. He argues for the allocation of research moneys to the study of the social, economic, demographic, and personal effects of scientific breakthroughs. He argues further that additional funds should be set aside to educate the public about new developments and their possible effects on individuals' lives, and describes such a strategy as "a social form of preventive medicine" (p. 358).

Instead of being an experience of disruption and crisis, change can be anticipated and planned for. For example, the literature suggests that women who anticipate widowhood and "rehearse" for that role fare better when it actually occurs than those who do not (Glick, Parkes, and Weiss 1974). Preparation for old age in other spheres of living may enhance coping capacities for this stage of the life cycle by anticipating modal changes associated with old age (Hagestad 1980).

Adult-education courses on planning for retirement or death have already begun to appear in many communities. Butler (1975) argues that education should be a lifelong phenomenon, rather than an activity of youth. Education for social utilization (i.e., life cycle education) may be an effective medium for teaching psychological, familial, and other tasks that relate to particular processes and stages of life, such as growing old.

Education and consciousness-raising are also desirable to help dismantle what Laslett (1976) calls "the world we have lost" syndrome. In this review, we have presented data that demythologizes the past from the idyllic cast of Goode's "classical family of western nostalgia." The dissemination of this new information to the public is important, because much misinformation about the past is held by policy makers and clinical practitioners as well as by family members themselves. Loosening the bonds of the mythical past permits a more creative search for solutions to the problems of growing old in today's society. Didactic information, offered in an educational setting, may effectively accomplish this task.

Mental Health and Ageing

The Well-Being of the Elderly

What is the relationship between family cohesion on the one hand and the well-being of the older family member on the other? Although mental-health practitioners often assume a direct linkage, the evidence is contradictory.

One stream of evidence indicates that the emotional health of the elderly is quite independent of family life (Carp 1967; Johnson and Bursk 1977; Johnson 1978; Rosow 1967). Rosow's (1967) study on age-segregated housing indicates a positive relationship between age-concentration of older individuals in a local environment and the tendency for these individuals to exhibit higher morale and better integration. Physical health has also been cited as a major influence in emotional well-being (Johnson and Bursk 1977; Johnson 1978; Kutner 1956; Spreitzer and Snyder 1974). Gubrium observes that good health enables the individual to have mobility. Spreitzer and Snyder found self-perceived health and economic sufficiency to be the strongest predictors of life-satisfaction in their study. Johnson and Bursk (1977) found that health and attitude toward ageing were important correlates of the affective quality of the relationship the elderly had with their adult children.

Of all the environmental resources, financial solvency or socioeconomic status in general has been cited most frequently as having an impact on morale or well-being (Kutner et al. 1956; Lowenthal et al. 1967; Spreitzer and Snyder 1974). Kutner et al. hypothesizes that high socioeconomic standing may provide an opportunity for optimism and a sense of well-being through cultural achievement, social position, and other material benefits that may offset some of the debilitating conditions of the later years. Low status alone served as a depressant, but when coupled with poor health, the outlook became grim. Similarly, Morgan's (1976) analysis of widowhood found that health, finances, and other situational factors influence morale. Family interaction was only one of several variables involved.

The other viewpoint reflected in the research literature does involve the family with the emotional well-being of the elderly. Here, the mental health needs of the older person cannot be separated from the family in which they are members. In this position, family relationships are seen as dyadic, or even triadic, and involve both the middle and younger generations. Goldfarb (1965) observes that the increase in three- and four-generation families in our population both complicates intrafamily interaction and presents a new source of problems in family relationships. Guilt, feelings of obligation, and a torn sense of loyalties may affect the in-between, middle-aged generation.

Back (1977) observes that in modern society the family is mainly an area for emotional relationships. Historical data suggest that economic necessity and local Poor Law regulations often forced older family members to reside with their offspring when there was no way for them to maintain independent living arrangements. Constraint, not choice, brought the two generations together, and this obligation to assist older parents was more often than not a source of intergenerational tension. The quality of family relationships was secondary to survival under conditions of economic scarcity.

Kreps (1977) suggests that, as other organizations assume financial responsibility for ageing adults, intergenerational strain resulting from the economic burden of the elderly on their children should decrease. Such change would permit family relationships in the later years to be based on shared interests, affection, and emotional support, rather than on the old bonds of duty and obligation. Shanas and Sussman (1977) also make this observation.

Strategies for Intervention

Various strategies for clinical intervention have been suggested to assist the family in coping with the presence of an older member or to resolve unfinished business from previous intrapsychic on interpersonal conflict. Individual, conjoint, and group counselling have been cited as techniques to enhance both individual and family coping patterns when there is an elderly family member. Goldfarb (1969) describes a model for the therapist and the dependent, elderly patient where a supportive relationship, not unlike the early parent–child relationship, is formed. Here, the patient is allowed to become the child, and in this relationship may experience enough feeling of emotional security to try out new expressions of dependent behaviour. The basic personality of the person is not altered, but is shifted to less offensive types of need expression that are less alienating to others.

Although problems requiring professional assistance may arise for the older individual, several researchers recommend the provision of services to other members of the family (Peterson 1974; Pollock 1975; Schwartz 1977; Sparks 1974; Steinman 1979).

Pollock's (1975) model offers counselling to younger family members, even when the presenting problem may concern the aged individual. Often the older person is not directly involved in the counselling process. This strategy is particularly effective for families with a senile, extremely depressed, or otherwise disturbed elderly member. The children of these persons are frequently overcome with resentment, exasperation, and guilt about their reactions to their parent's behaviour. This type of therapy provides support for personal growth and satisfaction, as well as the lessening of guilt feelings toward the older parent in the middle-aged child. Schwartz (1977) and Steinman (1979) likewise recommend supportive counselling to the middle generations. Sparks (1974) advocates the inclusion of the oldest generation in counselling sought by families with marital problems or parent–child conflicts. Often, the patterns that adults have learned in their own parental families may be reflected in relationships with their spouse or children. By including their parents in the therapeutic process, new insights about dysfunctional behaviour learned earlier in life may be uncovered and can shed light on present difficulties. Unfinished parent–child issues from the adult child's past may also be amenable to resolution in this therapeutic context.

Family problems are not the only difficulties in the lives of older adults that may require professional help. Financial and legal matters as well as housing and medical needs, may all lead elderly individuals to seek counselling. When life transitions such as retirement are the reason for requesting help, Peterson (1974) suggests including the spouse in the sessions. The short-term effects of retirement or preretirement counselling are often too tangential to make a major impact by themselves. The presence of a spouse serves as an additional resource to aid the retiree in his adjustment.

Needed Research

The mediating role of the family on behalf of its older member should be the subject of much future research. The development of skill and knowledge for dealing with bureaucracies is one outcome of socialization. Previous family membership in associations or organizations develops competence in the ability to mediate as an advocate or ombudsman on behalf of the older, or any, family member (Sussman 1977).

Several experiments have been carried out with regard to family caretaking of an older relative (Sussman 1977; Rosenmayr 1977). These involve direct compensatory payment to family members who are willing to provide care to the aged person, as a supplement to or in combination with compensation provided by other community agencies also involved with the elderly individual. Rosenmayr notes that for a family member to be able to help an older person, that helper must be supported by other institutions and must receive monetary, psychological, and normative support for his or her caregiving activities.

The importance of cash allowances paid relatives caring for older adults has already been correlated with the willingness of the caretaker to take the older individual into his or her home. Sussman's (1977) research point to the possibility of moving the aged person back to the household and local community if adequate compensation and supportive services are provided. Followup studies are needed to further specify the conditions under which such arrangements might work and be mutually beneficial for all generations.

The field of family research is ripe for an exploration of the positive dynamics in family life. Identification of processes characteristic of so-called healthy families has occupied only a small proportion of studies (Hagestad 1980). To date, much of the study of the family has been rooted in a medical (or clinical)

model, constructed by marriage and family counsellors who came into contact with troubled families (Skolnick 1978). Similarly, the field of social gerontology was first identified as the scientific study of ageing as a social problem, since concern with the personal difficulties of those in their later years was the first to be earmarked for research (Maddox and Wiley 1976).

Models for optimal functioning of all generations in the family have yet to be specified. Not be overlooked in such models should be the needs of all generations, particularly the youngest members of the family, since Hagestad (1980) suggests that some of the antecedents of excessive and inappropriate dependency in old age are inadequate nurture and attention and past neglect of dependency needs in childhood.

It should be obvious that the well-being of an older family member is related to his or her individual history as a child, spouse, and parent. This, however, is often easy to overlook. Both the family of origin and the family of procreation need to be studied, in addition to the larger sociohistorical context, for their impact on elderly individuals. The ordering of importance of these life experiences also deserves attention, so that family research and therapeutic intervention may address and treat the most relevant issues of family life (Shanas and Sussman 1979).

Works Cited

Adams, B.N. 1968. *Kinship in an Urban Setting*. Chicago: Markham.

Anderson, M. 1977. "The Impact on the Family Relationships of the Elderly of Changes since Victorian Times in Governmental Income-Maintenance Provision." Shanas and Sussman 1977, 36–59.

Back, K.W. 1977. "Social Systems and Social Facts." Shanas and Sussman 1977, 196–203.

Bane, M.J. 1976. *Here to Stay*. New York: Basic.

Bengtson, V.L., and K.D. Black. 1973. "Solidarity Between Parents and Children: Four Perspectives on Theory Development." Paper presented at the Annual Meeting of the National Council on Family Relations, Theory Development Workshop.

Bengtson, V.L., E.B. Olander, and A.A. Haddad. 1976. "The 'Generation Gap' and Aging Family Members: Toward a Conceptual Model." *Time, Roles and Self in Old Age*. Ed. J.B. Gubrium. New York: Human Sciences.

Bengtson, V.L., P.L. Kasschau, and P.K. Ragan. 1977. "The Impact of Social Structure on the Aging Individual." *Handbook of the Psychology of Aging*. Eds. J. Birren and K.W. Schaie. New York: Van Nostrand Reinhold.

Bengtson, V.L., and J. Treas. 1980. "Intergenerational Relations and Mental Health." *Handbook of Mental Health and Aging*. Eds. R.B. Sloan and J.E. Birren. Englewood Cliffs, NJ: Prentice-Hall.

Berkner, L. 1972. "The Stem Family and the Development Cycle of the Peasant Household: An 18th-Century Austrian Example." *American Historical Review* 77: 398–418.

Binstock, R., and E. Shanas, eds. 1976. *Handbook of Aging and the Social Sciences*. New York: Van Nostrand Reinhold.

Black, K.D., and V.L. Bengtson. 1973. "The Measurement of Solidarity: An Intergenerational Analysis." Paper presented at the Annual Meeting of the American Psychological Association, Montreal (August).

Bleckner, M. 1965. "Social Work and Family Relationships in Later Life with Some Thoughts on Filial Maturity." Shanas and Streib.

Butler, R. 1975. *Why Survive? Being Old in America*. New York: Harper and Row.

Carp, F.M. 1967. "The Impact of the Environment of Old People." *The Gerontologist* 7: 106–8, 135.

Carter, H., and P.C. Glick. 1976. *Marriage and Divorce: A Social and Economic Study*. Cambridge, MA: Harvard University Press.

Davis, K. 1940. "The Sociology of Parent-Youth Conflict." *American Sociological Review* 4: 523–35.

Elder, G.H., Jr. 1978. "Family History and the Life Course." *Journal of Family History* 2: 279–304.

Glick, P.C., C.M. Parkes, and R.S. Weiss. 1975. *The First Year of Bereavement*. New York: John Wiley and Sons.

Goldfarb, A.I. 1965. "Psychodynamics and the Three-Generation Family." Shanas and Streib.

———. 1969. "The Psychodynamics of Dependency and the Search for Aid." *The Dependencies of Old People*. Ed. R.A. Kalish. Ann Arbor: Institute of Gerontology, University of Michigan.

Goode, W. 1963. *World Revolution and Family Patterns*. New York: Free Press.

Hagestad, G.O. 1980. "Problems and Promises in the Social Psychology of Intergenerational Relations." *Aging, Stability and Change in the Family*.

Ed. R.

Haraven, Life Cour New

Hauser, ulat

Hill, Ger Co

Johns sh dr

Katz West: ramily Century City. Cambridge, MA: Harvard University Press.

Kerckhoff, A. 1965. "Nuclear and Extended Family Relationships: A Normative and Behavioral Analysis." Shanas and Streib.

Kobrin, F. 1976. "The Fall in Household Size and the Rise of the Primary Individual in the United States." *Demography* 13: 127–38.

Kreps, J. 1965. "The Economics of Intergenerational Relationships." Shanas and Streib.

———. 1976. "The Economy and the Aged." Binstock and Shanas, 272–85.

———. 1977. "Intergenerational Transfers and the Bureaucracy." Shanas and Sussman 1977, 21–35.

Kutner, B., D. Fanshel, A.M. Togo & T.S. Langner. 1956. *Five Hundred Over Sixty*. New York: Russell Sage.

Laslett, P. 1976. "Societal Development and Aging." Binstock and Shanas.

Little, M., and B. Laslett. 1977. "Adolescence in Historical Perspective: The Decline of Boarding in 19th Century Los Angeles." Mimeo.

Litwak, E. 1960. "Occupational Mobility and Extended Family Cohesion." *American Sociological Review* 25: 9–21.

Lopata, H.Z. 1973. *Widowhood in an American City*. Cambridge: Schenkman.

Lowenthal, M.F., P.L. Berkman & Associates. 1967. *Aging and Mental Disorder in San Francisco: A Social Psychiatric Study*. San Francisco: Jossey-Bass, Inc., Publishers.

Maddox, G., and J. Wiley. 1976. "Scope, Concepts and Methods in the Study of Aging." Binstock and Shanas, 3–34.

Morgan, L. 1976. "A Re-examination of Widowhood and Morale." *Journal of Gerontology* 31: 687–95.

Munnichs, J.M.A. 1977. "Linkages of Old People with Their Families and Bureaucracy in a Wel-

360   FAMILY ISSUES OF THE MID

fare State, the Nether-
man 1977, 92–116.
Nye, F., and W. Ru
Measurement B
Eds. J. Had
Peacock.
Peterson, J
New Y

ands." Shanas and Suss-

shing. 1969. "Toward Family
esearch." *Marriage and Family*.
en and E. Borgotta. Itasca, IL:

1968. *Married Love in the Middle Years*.
ork: Association Press.

. 1974. "Therapeutic Intervention in Mar-
l and Family Problems of Aging Persons."
*Professional Obligations and Approaches to the
Aged*. Eds. A.N. Schwartz and I.N. Mensh.
Springfield: Charles C. Thomas.

Pollock, S. 1975. "A Model for Indirect Therapy
with the Elderly." Paper presented at the Tenth
International Congress of Gerontology,
Jerusalem.

Rao, S.L.N. 1973. "On Long-Term Mortality
Trends in the United States, 1850-1968."
Demography 10: 405-19.

Retherford, R.D. 1975. *The Changing Sex Differential in Mortality*. Westport, CT: Greenwood.

Rogers, C. 1961. *On Becoming a Person*. Boston:
Houghton Mifflin.

Rosenmayr, L. 1977. "The Family — A Source
of Hope for the Elderly." Shanas and Sussman
1977, 132-57.

Rosow, I. 1967. *Social Integration of the Aged*. New
York: Free Press.

Schwartz, A.N. 1977. *Survival Handbook for Children of Aging Parents*. Chicago: Follett.

Seelbach, Wayne C. and William J. Sawer 1977.
"Filial responsibility, expectations, and morale
among aged parents," *The Gerontologist* 17:
492-9.

Shanas, E. 1978. Final Report. National Survey of
the Aged. A Report to the Administration on
Aging.

———. 1979. "Social Myth as Hypothesis: The
Case of the Family Relations of Old People."
The Gerontologist 19:3-9.

Shanas, E., et al., eds. 1968. *Old People in Three
Industrial Societies*. London: Routledge and
Kegan Paul.

Shanas, E., and G.F. Streib, eds. 1965. *Social Structure and the Family*. Englewood Cliffs, NJ:
Prentice-Hall.

Shanas, E., and M.B. Sussman, eds. 1977. *Family,
Bureaucracy, and the Elderly*. Durham, NC: Duke
University Press.

———. 1979. "The Family in Later Life: Social
Structure and Social Policy." Paper prepared for
a meeting on Stability and Change in the Family,
Committee on Aging, National Research Council, Annapolis, Maryland (March 22-24).

Skolnick, A. 1978. *The Intimate Environment*. 2d
ed. Boston: Little, Brown.

Sparks, G.M. 1974. "Grandparents and Intergenerational Family Therapy." *Family Process* 13:
225-37.

Spreitzer, E., and E.E. Snyder. 1974. "Correlates
of Life Satisfaction Among the Aged." *Journal
of Gerontology* 29: 454-58.

Stehouwer, J. 1968. "The Household and Family
Relations of Old People." Shanas et al.,
117-226.

Steinman, L.A. 1979. Reactivated Conflict with
Aging Parents." *Aging parents*. Ed. P.K. Ragan.
Los Angeles: University of Southern California
Press.

Streib, G.F. 1977. "Bureaucracies and Families:
Common Themes and Directions for Further
Study." Shanas and Sussman 1977, 204-14.

Streib, G.F., and W. Thompson. 1959. "The Older
Person in a Family Context." *Handbook of Social
Gerontology*. Ed. C. Tibbetts. Chicago: Univer-
sity of Chicago Press. 447-88.

Sussman, M.B. 1965. "Relationships of Adult
Children with Their parents in the United
States." Shanas and Streib.

———. 1976. "The Family Life of Old People."
Binstock and Shanas, 218-43.

———. 1977. "Family, Bureaucracy, and the Elderly Individual: An Organizational Linkage Perspective." Shanas and Sussman 1977, 2-20.

Treas, J. 1977. "Family Support Systems for the
Aged: Some Social and Demographic Considerations." *The Gerontologist* 17: 486-91.

Treas, J., & A. VanHilst. 1976. "Marriage and
Remarriage Rates among Older Americans." *The
Gerontologist* 16: 132-36.

Troll, L. 1971. "The Family of Later Life: A Decade Review." *Journal of Marriage and the Family*
33: 263-90.

U.S. Bureau of the Census. 1976. *Demographic Aspects of Aging and the Older Population in the
United States*. *Current Population Report Series PC-
23, No. 59*. Washington: USGPO.

———. 1978. "Household and Family Characteristics: March 1977." *Current Population Report
Series P-20, No. 326*. Washington: USGPO.

U.S. Department of Labor. 1979. *Handbook of
Labor Statistics 1978*. Washington: USGPO.

Van Dusen, R., and E. Sheldon. 1976. "The
Changing Status of American Women: A Life
Cycle Perspective." *American Psychologist* 31:
106-16.

FAMILY CARE OF THE ELDERLY: UNDERLYING ASSUMPTIONS AND THEIR CONSEQUENCES*

Jane Aronson

Through a review of the literature, this article explores the debate between the traditional perspective that conceives it as natural that families take care of those of their elderly members who are frail or in need and an emerging critique of this view. The critique exposes the invisible divisions of caring work between men and women and between public and private arenas, and challenges the comfortable imagery of "family care." The implications of this analysis for the future are considered, both for constructive changes in social policies and for the reformation of assumptions on which research and practice with the frail elderly and their families are based.

Until recently, it has been considered normal that families take care of those of their elderly members who are frail or in need of help. This accepted view is expressed in the cluster of social policies that affect the elderly and their families, and is implicit in the practices of those professional groups (nurses, social workers, doctors, etc.) that implement these policies. For example, the availability of younger family members is considered an im-

Source: *Canadian Journal on Aging* 4 (1985): 115–25. Reprinted with permission.

*The work reported here was supported in part by the National Health and Development Programme through a National Health Fellowship to the author. I would like to express my appreciation to Dr. Margrit Eichler for her encouragement in the initial preparation of this paper. Some of the preliminary ideas were generated as part of a project in the Social Work Department at Mt. Sinai Hospital that was assisted by the Laidlaw Foundation; both are gratefully acknowledged.

portant ingredient in everyday decisions regarding entitlement to homemaker service or priority for nursing-home admission.

Now, however, a developing perspective challenges this view, questions the assumptions that it makes about the family, and exposes its implications for old people, for different family members, and for services provided by the state. It demonstrates the socially constructed nature of what has been perceived as an obvious way to care for the elderly by highlighting the invisible divisions of caring work between men and women and between the public and private arenas.

The debate between these two perspectives occurs in the context of important demographic and social changes that make care of the elderly a matter of current concern. Like most industrialized countries, Canada is experiencing a population ageing, and a number of features of this process will have implications for health and social policies. The population aged over 65 is projected to increase substantially and, within that cohort, the proportion of people over 75 years of age will rise sharply. From 3.2 percent (747 000) of the total population in 1976, it is projected that the over-75 age group will constitute 5.2 percent (1 621 000) in 2001 and 8.3 percent (3 408 000) in 2051 (Denton and Spencer 1980). Increased numbers in this latter group are especially important, because they tend to experience multiple health problems and shrinking social ties, making heavy demands on health and social services. Accompanying these demographic trends, there are a number of social changes in process that will likely reduce the availability of caregivers in the middle age ranges: the trend toward smaller family size; women's increased participation in the paid labour force; and changes in the form of the family, especially increases in rates of divorce and remarriage (Bengtson and Treas 1980).

Alongside these changes in families and in the demographic balance of the population, we are witnessing efforts to cut public expenditures. Albeit with qualitative differences, these processes are being experienced in Canada, the United Kingdom, and the United States, which are the sources of literature to be discussed in this paper. From the United States, Minkler (1983) warns of the dangers of blaming and scapegoating the aged and notes that "when the economy is perceived in terms of scarcity, social problems are redefined in ways that permit contracted, less costly approaches to their solution" (p. 158). Government statements in all countries foreshadow continuing cuts in public spending on social welfare and, simultaneously, the family is exhorted to shoulder its responsibilities and take care of its own. Family care of the elderly is portrayed as a cheap and attractive solution. Given this pressing context, it seems especially important to clarify and make explicit the way that the care of the elderly is now shared, both between the family and the state and within the family.

The purpose of this paper is to review the literature on family care of the elderly, looking particularly at the differences between what I shall refer to as the "mainstream" literature that has tended to take the family for granted, and the emerging critique that is attempting to disentangle its largely implicit assumptions and their consequences. The literature reviewed includes sociological and gerontological sources, as well as professional writing on services to the elderly. There is relatively little Canadian work in this area; where available it will be included, but much of the material originates in Britain and the United States. In conclusion, some consideration will be given to the future, particularly to the implications for constructive changes in social policies.

Some key points drawn from the emerging critique of family care of the elderly will be used to organize the literature reviewed. This critique has its origins, for the most part, in studies of social policy in Britain. Building on the revealing analyses of unpaid housework that began in the late 1960s, it draws attention to the links between state intervention in the care of the elderly and individuals' experience of giving and receiving care. The emerging analysis has a broad scope and, at its core, it appreciates the ideology that has invisibly suffused the notion of caring in the family. Caring has been associated with women and has been seen in a psychological focus rather than as an expression of political and economic relations. This limited vision has been powerfully reinforced by prevailing culture and ideology, including the state and social policies. Four particular elements of this developing critique seem to offer a useful framework for looking at care of the elderly by the family:

1. the sexual division of care within the family;
2. the relationship of unpaid labour within the family to women's position in the labour market;
3. old people's experience of being cared for by the family; and,
4. historical analyses of the nature of family care in the past.

The literature will be organized under these four headings, the first two being, perhaps, the most central. Under each, the developing critical ideas will be discussed briefly and compared with research and theory drawn from relevant sociological, gerontological, and professional literature that represents developments in those fields. Eichler's (1983) conceptualization of four biases commonly found in the study of families (monolithic, conservative, sexist, and microstructural) will also be used as an analytical tool to sharpen the evaluation of this material.

The Sexual Division of Family Care

Critics of conventional approaches to family care have demanded clarification of the meaning of the term in practice. Finch and Groves (1980) refer to the warm imagery of "family care" and "community care" and suggest that they are fictional:

> the provision of primary care falls not upon "the community" but upon identifiable groups and individuals, in a way which is not necessarily equitable. Indeed, this can best be expressed in terms of a double equation — that in practice community care equals care by the family, and in practice care by the family equals care by women. (p. 404)

They go on to cite British studies documenting the likelihood that many women, as wives, daughters, and daughters-in-law, will at some time in their lives care for elderly relatives. The before-mentioned ideology of women's caring function and primary commitment to the domestic sphere, comes into play here. Again based on British data, Land (1978) notes that, unlike women, men are not expected to look after themselves, or, even less, to care for frail or disabled relatives. There are exceptions to this: most commonly, elderly husbands who look after infirm wives. Given women's longer life expectancy and tendency to marry men older then themselves, however, intergenerational caring is seldom provided by men. A recent British publication, in accenting the sexual division of family care, points out that

> the notion of "family care" often assumes a particular model of family life which includes all or many of the following characteristics: an elderly person either living with or near their family; a stable "nuclear" family; and an able-bodied woman at home supported financially by her husband at work. (Family Policy Studies Centre 1984, 17)

This assumption exhibits what Eichler terms the monolithic bias; it ignores the reality of the diverse family forms that now exist. In fact, significant numbers of women are facing the multiple demands of holding down jobs, looking after children, and caring for elderly relatives. One Canadian article addresses these issues critically (Neysmith 1981), but I have been unable to locate any Canadian studies of the extent of women's work in caring for old people.

Against this background, it is striking to find that in much of the mainstream literature on family care, the sex of the principal caregiver is never identified. The family is treated as the smallest unit of analysis and the differential distribution and meaning of caring between family members are simply ignored. Writing over ten years ago, Isaacs, Livingstone, and Neville (1972) expressed both the powerful ideology that associates women with caring and an apparent ambivalence about stating that most of the domestic caring of old people falls to women:

> No one could work with the relatives of the geriatric patients of Glasgow, as we did, without developing a profound admiration for their devotion and self-sacrifice, and their willing acceptance of a gigantic burden. . . . But still one can ask whether the Health Service of a highly taxed Welfare State should have to depend so much on its unsung heroes and heroines, the middle-aged and elderly housewives. (p. 70)

Failure to consider the sex of caregivers as a variable of interest did not stop ten years ago; it continues in recent contributions to major journals (for example Béland 1984; Johnson and Catalano 1983; Kraus 1984; Shanas 1979). In the United States, Brody (1981, 1983) has offered an important corrective to this pattern. She describes a prototype of family caregivers — "Women in the Middle": "such women are in middle age, in the middle from a generational standpoint, and in the middle in that the demands of their various roles compete for their time and energy" (p. 471). Scholars like Brody are beginning to develop empirical descriptions of women's views about caring work. Alongside this type of research, the more theoretically oriented criticism of the social and sexual division of caring is also becoming more acute. The challenge that lies ahead is to link these two levels of analysis, and explore how the ideology of family care is translated into the everyday experience of the frail elderly and the family members that care for them.

The Relationship of Unpaid Labour Within the Family to Women's Position in the Labour Market

Consideration of the sexual division of unpaid labour within the family is inseparable from the consideration of men's and women's position in the labour market. Land writes:

> It is important for us to recognize that, if we ascribe to women the primary responsibility for providing domestic services for other members of the family, their daily lives are structured in a way which profoundly affects their opportunities in the wider society in general and the labour market in particular. (1978, 259)

She goes on to argue that patriarchal values have sustained a pattern whereby men's primary commitment is to the labour market, while women are relegated to a position of dependence in the domestic arena. That some women may want to stay in paid employment because of financial need is hardly considered, much less that they may be motivated to work, as men are, by enjoyment of work's challenge and social meaning. Eichler (1984) traces the process by which this interconnection between paid and unpaid labour emerged and attained visibility in the analysis of housework — a debate that paved the way for consideration of women's unpaid caring for infirm and disabled family members. Since is does not involve market costs, the value of women's unpaid care of the elderly and other dependent groups has been invisible. Because

it does not appear in any public accounting or marketplace, it is, in effect, treated as free and without value. However, if the socially constructed distinction between economic "production" and "dependence" is unmasked, its worth and social usefulness can no longer be overlooked. As Rimmer (1983) observes of community-care policies, "such policies often appear low cost in public expenditure terms because they both fail to recognize *all* the costs of care and, as a matter of policy, fail to compensate one of the main groups of carers — married women" (p. 131). Based on this analysis, there have been some attempts to assess the real costs of caring for elderly family members (Nissel and Bonnerjea 1982). Besides the financial losses incurred, Finch and Groves (1980) also consider the opportunities to accumulate pension benefits or equity that are forgone. This latter point, they suggest, can make a woman's decision not to work or to give up work to care for an elderly relative "a prelude to poverty in old age for the carer" (p. 507). The spectre of entrapment and dependence from generation to generation that this last description raises is appalling in its injustice.

The insights generated by this structural analysis of women's caring apparently have not, for the most part, filtered into the mainstream literature on family care of the elderly. Much of the work simply does not address the real value of care or women's disadvantaged position in the labour market; in fact, two studies quite explicitly reinforced their dependent status. In concluding their study of geriatric patients in Glasgow, Isaacs, Livingstone, and Neville make it very clear that the primary commitment of women is to their families and that they should have no expectation that other family members, namely husbands, should share the responsibility for care of an elderly relative. Recognizing the stress and fatigue that caring for a sick old person can produce, they suggest

> that one of the more effective methods of keeping a daughter from being overwhelmed by strain is to encourage her to go out to part-

time employment. This might involve having a home help to look after the patient while the daughter worked to earn the money to pay for the home help. (1972, 102)

In a more recent study in the United States, Cicirelli (1983) conveys similar judgments about the sometimes weak justification for women to undertake paid work rather than care for an elderly relative at home. He compared the amounts of help provided to elderly parents by children with intact and those with disrupted marriages, and proceeded to rank order the strength of their justifications for choosing paid work over unpaid caring. Sole-support women were judged to have a reasonable case and women in marriages to have a poor case, while men were exempted from consideration altogether as they are "under greater pressure (than women) to perform and achieve in order to maintain and advance in their jobs" (p. 623).

While these two cases may be extreme in their conservatism, much of the literature on family care reflects a microstructural bias (Eichler 1983) that does not easily incorporate the broader analysis of women's oppression. A good deal of the literature in the professional journals reflects this tendency and, presumably, is based on the socialization of doctors, social workers, etc., that emphasizes the individual case rather than the collective experience of problems. A number of studies produced good descriptions of caregivers' sense of stress and burden but closed with very limited suggestions for change, often emphasizing psychological and emotional adjustments (Cicirelli 1983; Johnson and Catalano 1983; Hill 1984; Jones and Vetter 1984). While there may be a place for research with this focus, a greater balance between microstructural and macrostructural analysis would be desirable.

Old People's Experience of Being Cared for in the Family

While much of the critique of family care has been concerned with exposing the indirect and direct costs borne by women, some studies are beginning to focus on care from the perspective of old people. Walker (1983) notes how little we know about old people's views, but points out the high degree of dependence that can characterize the relations of old people with their children. Opportunities for equalizing such relationships by means of reciprocal exchanges diminish with the elderly person's infirmity and need. In a qualitative study of old women, Matthews (1979) refers to her respondents' "lack of power in the sacred institution" (p. 135). She suggests that emphasis on the family as the normal, even correct source of support of the elderly enhances their dependence:

The data indicate that the extended family structure is intact, but that the quality of the relationship is affected adversely by the low status of old women who have a weak power base from which to be treated as equals. They are dependent on the relationship because in their eyes they have no one else to whom to turn for "moral support." (p. 134)

A few studies of elderly people's relationships with friends and peers are responding to this theme. In her introduction to just such a study conducted in Winnipeg, Chappell (1983) suggests that relations with nonfamily age peers have been neglected in the gerontological community's preoccupation with family ties. She hypothesizes that relationships between elderly peers are characterized by a greater potential for sharing and exchange by virtue of such common experiences and concerns as retirement, widowhood, physical limitations, shared generational experiences, and adjustment to impending death. Chappell's ability to weigh the effects of these phenomena is limited somewhat by their reduction to fairly crude measures of interaction and satisfaction but, nonetheless, she found a high degree of satisfaction with peer relationships in her sample and concludes:

Since friendship rests on mutual choice and need, it sustains a person's sense of usefulness and self-esteem more effectively than family relationships with their obligatory character. Friendship, because of its voluntary nature, may result in greater communications and intimacy. (p. 96)

Development of research in this area and consideration of its implications for living arrangements and social programs will be valuable (Bengtson and Treas 1980). As yet, however, it is in its early stages and, in the mainstream literature, goes against the tide of preoccupation with the family as the source of support for old people. A particularly clear example of the pursuit of this preoccupation is the work in the sociological and gerontological literature that attempts to measure old people's morale or life satisfaction and relate it to their interaction with family members (Lee and Ellithorpe 1982). The expectation is that the greater the interaction, the higher the morale and, despite repeated failures to establish this association, the work goes on. The possibility that the family, as presently formulated, is not always the only or most effective form of support is often not countenanced or explored.

Historical Analysis of Families' Care of Elderly Kin

The last element to be considered here in the developing critique of family care is the accuracy of our understanding of the past and its impact on the present. In the current debate, it is sometimes suggested, especially in political contexts and in the media, that there was a golden age when the family willingly integrated and sheltered its infirm members. This golden age is contrasted with the present, when, it is suggested, the family is disintegrating and shirking its responsibilities to kin. This portrayal of the present family achieved enough currency to prompt some studies investigating whether "families still care." They were uniformly unsuccessful in finding evi-

dence of willingly shirked responsibilities or neglected elders (Shanas 1979).

The contributions of some historians have been most important in clarifying the image of families in the past. Based on United States data, Hareven (1981) states emphatically that "the historical evidence regarding family relations of older people contradicts any myth about a golden age in the family relations of the aged in the past" (p. 163). From different demographic and social contexts, Synge (1980) draws similar conclusions from nineteenth-century Ontario, and Anderson (1977) from data on Victorian England. All three describe the precariousness of support for old people, economic ties, hardships, and the uncertainties that characterized and disrupted relations between kin. Anderson carefully marshals data to consider the impact of the introduction of old-age pensions in 1909 on relationships between the aged and their families. Contrary to the current popular portrayal, he concludes that, rather than undermining families' interest in their elderly members, pensions served to support their efforts and to reduce the rate of institutionalization. Making a forceful link between the readings of the past and interpretations of the present, Hareven (1981) disentangles accurate history from political expedience and dominant ideology about the family and cautions us that

it would be a mistake, therefore, to leave kin to take care of their own at a time when the chances for people to do so are considerably diminishing. Nor should the historical evidence about the continuity in kin relations be misused in support of proposals to return welfare responsibilities from the public sector to the family without basic additional supports. An examination of the historical patterns reveals the high price that kin had to pay in order to assist each other in the absence of other forms of societal support. The historical precedent thus offers a warning against romanticizing kin relations. (p. 162)

Policies and Practices Related to Family Care of the Elderly

A superficial survey of government policies that concern themselves directly with the care of old people by their families suggests very little state involvement. In Canada, the only explicit provision in the area of family care is an income-tax provision that permits people to claim a tax deduction for the care of an infirm relative. However, armed with the critical perspective discussed above, attention must be drawn to the effect of an absence of government involvement. Absence of public provision of care requires the presence of private provision. Walker (1983) suggests that, in the guise of nonintervention, the state exerts a profound influence on the way old people are cared for and the way that their caretakers, largely women, are not compensated for their work. He observes that "the state occupies a dual role in relation to community care: it may provide direct support where this is absolutely necessary, but its main concern is to ensure the continuance of the prime responsibility of the family for the support and care of its own members" (p. 121). In Canada, it is evident that government policies indirectly related to family care of the elderly provide minimal levels of support and services. For example, income-maintenance programs (old-age pensions, and guaranteed income supplement) are set so low that many old people live in poverty with few or no choices about how to obtain care that they might need. Furthermore, key elements of health and social services — home care and residential care — are, with regional variations, acknowledged to be quite inadequate to meet present needs. A recent federal government publication (Government of Canada 1982) mirrors this kind of ambiguity about the social division of care. It vacillates between an emphasis on individual and family responsibilities, recognition of social changes affecting families and the aged, and an assertion of the properly limited role of government in the private domain of the family.

Some excerpts from a section of the report reveal this ambiguity and obfuscation:

> The general expectation on the part of society is that individuals should function as independently as possible and assume overall responsibility for their own well-being, and that of their families. . . . Over time the idea that governments, on behalf of the people, should assume responsibilities which previously were considered to belong to individuals and families has taken root. . . . Thus a sharing between the individual and the state has become accepted. The line of demarcation is, however, not sharply defined; it could shift with changing economics and social conditions. (pp. 137–38)

In this context of state nonintervention or minimal provision for the maintenance of old people, the way in which the limited benefits and services that are available are allocated becomes crucial. In their everyday practice with old people and their families, health and social-service professionals apply eligibility criteria and make discretionary decisions that determine who will assume care for the dependent elderly. In effect, through their aggregated practices, they draw the "line of demarcation" referred to in the federal report.

To be most useful, future work on the care of the elderly in Canada will require analysis at a macro level of social policies affecting the elderly and their families, together with analysis of policy implementation at the micro level, where service providers and old people actually meet.

Policy Changes: Visions for the Future

The challenge for the future is to produce both improved conditions for the elderly and a more equitable sharing of caring responsibilities between men and women and between the public and private domains. From the literature reviewed here, it is clear that what is required is not simply a quantitative increase in resources devoted to the care of the elderly, but also a qualitative reformulation of the assumptions underlying the way that care is valued and resources distributed.

With regard to just such a reformulation of the value of care, it is proposed that those providing care be properly compensated for their work in terms of wages and pension benefits. A system of payment could be devised under which elderly people in need of care would receive either money or vouchers to purchase services. For the old person, such a system would create real choices and independence and assurance of a decent minimum level of care. Much of the literature limits its recommendations to these kinds of changes, but those developing the most critical structural analysis stress that changes in the family arena can only be successful if accompanied by changes in the labour market. In describing their "alternative" scenario, Finch and Groves (1980) capture these ideas well:

> It is clear that major policy and legislative changes in the field of employment are called for. There are no simple answers here, but it seems crucial to find ways of reformulating traditional expectations about working life and current employment practices to provide for men and women who wish to provide care, without irreparably damaging their future work prospects. At the present time, the notion of full-time work, continuous over the adult life span, is central to the notion of the "good employee" and is crucially related to appointments, job security, promotions, and pensions. The development of part-time work, job-sharing, periods of "caring" leave and other similar arrangements appear to have something to commend them. (p. 513)

These proposals could do much to rectify the sexual division of caring work that has disadvantaged women so extremely. With regard to the social division of care, the critique of present patterns demands that the state be committed to a quantitatively larger share of the support of the frail elderly. Adequate income maintenance and increased provision of health and social services are needed. People require different degrees of care in different environments as they age; this should be recognized in a range of services and facilities beyond the usual home care–institution dichotomy.

An analysis of the boundary between public and private responsibility also prompts qualitative reformulation of policy and practice, and exposes some of the conventional assumptions and vocabulary of services and research related to the care of the elderly. As noted earlier, terms like "community" care and "family" care tend to mask the fact that care in the private arena is provided largely by female family members. Optimistic references to "informal caring networks" and "social networks" of friends and neighbours as potential care providers bear little relationship to this reality. They do, however, provide seductively simple pretexts for leaving care in the private domain (Allan 1983). In their everyday practice with increasingly scarce resources, professionals find themselves constantly evaluating need and setting priorities for service. The unambiguous acknowledgement of this work as a form of rationing resources clears the way for debate and for a study of the way these resources are distributed. Distribution becomes, correctly, a political and economic question, rather than either a professional dilemma or an implicit discretionary process.

These broad proposals and ideas seem constructive and reasonable. However, the present climate of cuts in public expenditures and strengthening conservatism suggest a bleak prospect for anything but piecemeal implementation. Right-wing ideology perpetuates a romanticized view of family life that shores up the present highly skewed division of responsibility for the care of dependent groups between the state and the family. Some observers note, with concern, the tendency to set the needs of dependent groups against each other, rather than questioning the distribution of income in society more broadly (Silverstone and Burack-Weiss 1983). While there are enormous differences between social-welfare policies in the United States and Canada, the trends south of the border should make us vigilant, especially as we hear increased suggestions for dismantling what were previously considered principal elements of health and welfare provision in Canada.

Set against this discouraging political context, however, some trends point toward future progressive changes in social policies. Recent studies exploring attitudes toward family responsibility for the care of the elderly suggest cohort differences in expectations about filial obligations and egalitarian gender roles (Brody et al. 1983; West, Illsley, and Kelman 1984). Persistent attitudes of the kind identified would certainly run counter to cuts in public-service provision or care arrangements that reinforce women's economic dependence.

To summarize, the emerging critique of arrangements for the care of the elderly effectively uncovers and challenges some of the assumptions and consequences of the conventional, largely unquestioned use of the term "family care." In particular, it calls attention to the resulting distribution of responsibility for caring work that is heavily skewed to the private rather than the public sphere and toward women rather than men. Consideration of the consequences of this pattern at all levels in the process — the state, service providers, family members, and old people — makes possible real debate about both the fairness of current patterns of provision and possible alternatives. Empirical studies grounded in the challenging conceptual insights that the critique offers can inform the debate and ensure that it remains vigorous and open.

Works Cited

Allan, G. 1983. "Informal Networks of Care: Issues Raised by Barclay." *British Journal of Social Work* 13: 417–33.

Anderson, M. 1977. "The Impact on the Family Relationships of the Elderly of Changes Since Victorian Times in Governmental Income-Maintenance Provision. *and the Elderly*. Eds. E. S Durham, NC: Duke Un

Béland, F. 1984. "The Fa of Age and Over: Co-J of Help." *Canadian* thropology 21(3): 302–1

Bengtson, V.L., and J. Treas. 1980. "The Family Context of Mental Health and Aging. *Handbook of Mental Health and Aging*. Eds. J.E. Birren and R.B. Sloane. Englewood Cliffs, NJ: Prentice-Hall.

Brody, E.M. 1981. "'Women in the Middle' and Family Help to Older People." *Gerontologist* 21(5): 471–80.

Brody, E.M., P.T. Johnsen, M.C. Fukomer, and A.M. Lany. 1983. "Women's Changing Roles and Help to Elderly Parents: Attitudes of Three Generations of Women." *Journal of Gerontology* 38(5): 597–607.

Brody, S., S. Poulshock, and C.F. Masciocchi. 1978. "The Family Caring Unit: A Major Consideration in the Long-Term Support System." *Gerontologist* 18(60): 556–61.

Chappell, N.L. 1983. "Informal Support Networks Among the Elderly." *Research on Aging* 5(1): 77–99.

Cicirelli, V.G. 1983. "A Comparison of Helping Behaviour to Elderly Parents of Adult Children with Intact and Disrupted Marriages." *Gerontologist* 23(6): 619–25.

Denton, F., and B. Spencer. 1980. "Canada's Population and Labour Force: Past, Present and Future." Marshall, 10–26.

Eichler, M. 1983. *Families in Canada Today: Recent Changes and Their Policy Consequences*. Toronto: Gage.

———. 1984. "The Connection Between Paid and Unpaid Labour and its Implication for Creating Equality for Women in Employment." Paper prepared for the Royal Commission of Inquiry on Equality in Employment.

Family Policy Studies Centre. 1984. *The Forgotten Army: Family Care and Elderly People*. London: Family Policy Studies Centre.

Finch, J., and D. Groves. 1980. "Community Care and the Family: A Case for Equal Opportunities?" *Journal of Social Policy* 9(4): 487–514.

———, eds. 1983. *A Labour of Love: Women, Work and Caring*. London: Routledge and Kegan Paul.

Government of Canada. 1982. "Balancing Personal Independence, Interdependence and Public Responsibility." *Canadian Governmental Report on Aging*. Ottawa: Ministry of Supply and Services.

n, T.K. 1981. "Historical Changes in the ming of Family Transitions: Their Impact on Generational Relations." *Aging: Stability and Change in the Family*. Eds. R.W. Fogel et al. New York: Academic. 143–68.

Hill, C.J. 1984. "Caring for an Elderly Relative." *Canada's Mental Health* 21(1): 13–16.

Isaacs, B., M. Livingstone, and Y. Neville. 1972. *Survival of the Unfittest: A Study of Geriatric Patients in Glasgow*. London: Routledge and Kegan Paul.

Johnson, C.L., and D.J. Catalano. 1983. "A Longitudinal Study of Family Supports to Impaired Elderly." *Gerontologist* 23(6): 612–18.

Jones, D.A., and N.J. Vetter. 1984. "A Survey of Those Who Care for the Elderly at Home: Their Problems and Needs." *Social Science and Medicine* 19(5): 511–14.

Kraus, A.S. 1984. "The Burden of Care for Families of Elderly Persons with Dementia." *Canadian Journal on Aging* 3(1): 45–51.

Land, H. 1978. "Who Cares For the Family?" *Journal of Social Policy* 7(3): 357–84.

Lee, G., and E. Ellithorpe. 1982. "Intergenerational Exchange and Subjective Well-being Among the Elderly." *Journal of Marriage and Family* 44(1): 217–24.

Marshall, V.W., ed. 1980. *Aging in Canada: Social Perspectives*. Markham, ON: Fitzhenry and Whiteside.

Matthews, S.H. 1979. *The Social World of Old Women: Management of Self Identify*. Beverly Hills: Sage.

Minkler, M. 1983. "Blaming the Aged Victim: The Politics of Scapegoating in Times of Fiscal Conservatism." *International Journal of Health Services* 13(1): 155–68.

Neysmith, S.M. 1981. "Parental Care: Another Female Family Function?" *Canadian Journal of Social Work Education* 7(2): 55–63.

Nissel, M., and L. Bonnerjea. 1982. *Family Care of the Handicapped Elderly: Who Pays?* London: Policy Studies Institute.

Rimmer, L. 1983. "The Economics of Work and Caring." Finch and Groves 1983, 131–47.

Shanas, E. 1979. "The Family as a Social Support System in Old Age." *Gerontologist* 19(2): 169–74.

Silverstone, B., and A. Burack-Weiss. 1983. *Social Work Practice with the Frail Elderly and Their Families*. Springfield, IL: Charles C. Thomas.

Synge, J. 1980. "Work and Family Support Patterns of the Aged in the Early Twentieth Century." Marshall, 135–44.

Walker, A. 1983. "Care for Elderly People: A Conflict Between Women and the State." Finch and Groves 1983, 106–28.

West, P., R. Illsley, and H. Kelman. 1984. "Public Preferences for the Care of Dependency Groups." *Social Science and Medicine* 18(4): 287–95.

Part Eight

SERIAL MONOGAMY: DIVORCE AND REMARRIAGE

◆ ◆ ◆

Happy families are all alike; every unhappy family is unhappy in its own way.

Leo Tolstoi, *Anna Karenina* (1876)

The divorce rate in Canada is relatively high, and is likely to remain so. When we consider the lifetime experience of all married persons, at least one-quarter and perhaps as many as one-third will experience at least one divorce. Many factors have contributed to this phenomenon, not the least of which is the simple fact that husbands and wives are living longer than they did in the recent past. Relatively few people are widowed in youth or in middle age. The longer duration of marriage creates more years that are "at risk" for separation or divorce.

It is a sociological and psychological rule to decry the divorce experience as a traumatic event and define it as a major crisis for the couple themselves and for whatever children may be involved. These assertions are routinely followed by the observation that, when comparisons are made between separated or divorced persons and their married counterparts, the formerly married almost always exhibit a higher incidence of psychological disturbances, ranging from relatively minor psychosomatic complaints such as loneliness or depression to major problems such as alcoholism, psychotic breaks, or suicide attempts. We cannot argue with the observation that divorce is *often* a traumatic event, or with the observation that divorced persons *often* seem to be less well-adjusted than their married counterparts. We do, however, suggest

that divorce is not *always* traumatic, and that persons who get unmarried are not *always* psychologically damaged by their experiences. It must be remembered that at least half of the people involved in divorce actions actively sought a divorce with the implicit assumption that reclaiming a single status would enhance the quality of their life experience. The continued and growing popularity of divorce-seeking indicates that not all of them can have been mistaken. One facet of the divorce process that has been neglected is the possibility that the experience will be considered an achievement rather than a failure, and will be considered a source of joy or other positive emotions rather than of despair (Veevers 1990). Divorce may be characterized by positive as well as negative experiences, and may be defined as a chance for growth and an opportunity for constructive change.

For some persons, the divorce option does not signify a decline in the importance of the family as much as an unwillingness to tolerate unhappy circumstances. Berger and Kellner make this point when they observe: "Typically, individuals in our society do not divorce because marriage has become unimportant to them, but because it has become so important that they have no tolerance for the less than completely successful arrangement they have contracted with the particular individual in question" (this volume, p. 00).

About the Articles

When a couple divorce, the subjective experience of the wife may be quite different from that of her husband. Baker points out that our empirical knowledge of divorce is influenced, and sometimes biased, by our failure to explore male–female differences in the divorce experience, and by disparities in Canadian and American approaches. She argues that an integration of critical and feminist perspectives with conventional mainstream sociology would provide a more comprehensive and balanced approach.

Remarriages between divorced persons may create a complex binuclear family that involves two households organized around divorced parents. Rodgers and Conrad explore the complexity of courtship under a variety of circumstances of custody and co-parenting.

In the recent past, the "doctrine of tender years" supported the supposition that children, especially young children, needed to stay with their mother and were better off with her than with their father. The new legal perspective begins with two different suppositions: first, that custody should be decided "in the best interests of the child"; and second, that those best interests often involve continued contact with both parents. Green explores the dimensions of the emerging trend toward joint custody after divorce, outlines some of the major problems associated with it, and suggests some solutions.

The early concepts of divorce involved an adversary system, with an innocent party against a guilty party, and with outcomes to be resolved in terms of which one deserved to gain the most benefit. The modern concept of divorce as marriage breakdown views divorce as a problem to be solved rather than as a case to be won. Landau shows how mediation by an impartial professional can resolve some disputes about custody and access in a nonadversarial way, achieving an equitable and voluntary agreement that may mitigate some of the potentially destructive aspects of the divorce process.

Further Readings

Adams, O.B., and D.N. Nagnur. 1988. *Marriage, Divorce and Mortality: A Life Table Analysis for Canada and Regions.* Catalogue 84-536E. Ottawa: Statistics Canada, Health Division, Social and Economic Studies Division.

Ahrons, Constance R., and Roy H. Rodgers. 1987. *Divorced Families: A Multidisciplinary Developmental View.* New York: W.W. Norton.

Irving, Howard H., Michael Benjamin, and Nicholas Trocme. 1984. "Shared Parenting: An Empirical Analysis Utilizing a Large Data Base." *Family Process* 23: 561–69.

McKie, D.C., B. Prentice, and P. Reed. 1983. *Divorce: Law and the Family in Canada.* Catalogue 89-502E. Ottawa: Statistics Canada.

Morrison, Katalin, and Airdrie Thompson-Guppy. 1985. "Cinderella's Stepmother Syndrome." *Canadian Journal of Psychiatry* 30: 521–29.

Payne, Julien. 1986. "Future Prospects of Family Conflict Resolution in Canada." *Conciliation Courts Review* 24: 51–70.

Pike, Robert. 1975. "Legal Access and the Incidence of Divorce in Canada: A Socio-Historical Analysis." *Canadian Review of Sociology and Anthropology* 12: 115–33.

Robinson, Barrie W., and Wayne W. McVey, Jr. 1985. "The Relative Contributions of Death and Divorce to Marital Dissolution in Canada and the United States." *Journal of Comparative Family Studies* 16: 93–109.

Sloss, Elizabeth, ed. 1985. *Family Law in Canada: New Directions.* Ottawa: Canadian Advisory Council on the Status of Women.

Veevers, Jean E. 1990. "Traumas Versus Strens: A Paradigm of Positive Versus Negative Divorce Outcomes." *Journal of Divorce*, forthcoming.

HIS AND HER DIVORCE RESEARCH: NEW THEORETICAL DIRECTIONS IN CANADIAN AND AMERICAN RESEARCH

Maureen Baker

Although Canadian divorce rates have been steadily rising over the past few decades, Canadian sociologists have not devoted much time or attention to marriage dissolution as a research topic. In comparison, the United States has experienced much higher rates of marriage dissolution and, perhaps for this reason, a burgeoning field of research has developed on separation and divorce. In fact, a specialty journal (the *Journal of Divorce*) was started in 1976 to publish the increasing number of articles in this field.

Because of the paucity of published journal articles in Canada on separation and divorce, one could easily get the impression that no research is being done. Undoubtedly, as noted above, one of the reasons for the near absence of articles on separation and divorce in Canadian journals is the lower rate of divorce in Canada. Another may be the small number of journals and the lack of enthusiasm within mainstream sociology for family studies. In an analysis of articles published in the *Canadian Review of Sociology and Anthropology* (CRSA) from 1971 to 1980, Grayson and Magill (1980) found that relatively few articles on the family have been accepted. Although this may reflect the fact that the *Journal of Comparative Family Studies* publishes some of the sociology articles that might be published in the CRSA, some of the best articles by Canadian authors go to the *Journal of Marriage*

and the Family, or other American specialty journals.

Through a critical review of Canadian research on separation and divorce and a brief comparison with publishing trends on this topic in American journals, we have identified a new feminist approach to the study of marriage dissolution. This new approach not only highlights the importance of sex as a variable mediating the divorce process, but also emphasizes the sexual inequality in the labour market, an opportunity structure for remarriage that favours men, a continuing double standard, and traditional custody patterns.

In nonfeminist studies, husbands and wives are assumed to view their family experience in similar ways and to experience similar problems in adjusting to divorce. Using a conflict approach or exchange theory, feminist researchers have provided considerable evidence that men and women experience separation and divorce differently. The notion of the family as an egalitarian unit has been questioned. Also, the idea that we can study marriage and the family while ignoring the legal, social, and economic structures of the larger society has been rejected.

In this paper, we argue that research on separation and divorce *is* being carried out, but for various reasons is not appearing in Canadian sociology or family journals. Using research on marriage dissolution as an example of research that is in touch with present family changes, we argue that the Canadian journals are presenting a very conservative and unrealistic image of the field. At the same time, the

Source: *Journal of Comparative Family Studies* 15(1984): 17–28. Reprinted with permission.

American journals are publishing far more material on separation and divorce that is leading to important insights into the nature of the divorce experience. Most of the new critical research that focusses on power differentials and sex differences in Canada is being done by women, while most of the published articles are authored by men. This reflects on increasing polarization in Canada within the field of family sociology.

Canadian Research on Marriage Dissolution

Few sociologists other than Ambert (1980) have published books on separation and divorce research. The *Journal of Comparative Family Studies* has published most of the research, but in articles of varying quality. The *Canadian Journal of Sociology* has accepted only one article on divorce or separation since its beginning in 1975. And the *Canadian Review of Sociology and Anthropology* has accepted only four in the past twelve years. Despite the fact that a large number of women specialize in the field of marriage and the family, only one of these articles on separation and divorce was authored by a woman.

Most of the articles in the Canadian journals have concentrated on demographic statistics and their correlates with divorce rates. (We will discuss each article separately, but only those articles written by Canadian-based authors will be mentioned.) For example, Palmer (1971) outlined the correlates of high divorce rates and reasons for divorce, basing her conclusions on interviews with divorcing couples in southwestern Ontario. Kuzel and Krishnan (1973) examined remarriage after divorce and widowhood, calculating Canadian remarriage probabilities based on age and sex. Pike (1975) analyzed the historical incidence of divorce in Canada, concluding that rising divorce rates are related to increased court facilities and liberalized laws. Peters (1976a) presented a demographic profile of divorce, listing social and economic

conditions that correlated with high divorce rates. McVey and Robinson (1981) provided statistics showing age and regional variations in separation and divorce rates in Canada. And Davids (1982) analyzed statistical data on the extent of divorce among Jews in Canada. The majority of the above articles deal with statistical correlates of divorce and make little attempt to analyze the experience of separated and divorced people.

Several articles examine kinship structure and divorce. Heinrich (1972) argued that divorce could be viewed as integrative in Eskimo society, because the Eskimo tend to retain those ties of affinity created by marriage after divorce, and extend their wide circle of kin and extrakin relationships through remarriage. Weissleder (1974a) argued from anthropological data in Ethiopia that divorce is affected by similar structural processes as marriage and should not be viewed as the result of personal or psychological motives.

In his theoretical article based in part on the same data (1974b), Weissleder suggested that rising rates of divorce and changing family composition are more related to changes in household technology and the labour-force participation of women than to any personal failures or feelings of discontent. Women's labour in the household is no longer needed, and "released time permits thoughts of career ambitions. . . . Individuals, male and female, are transformed into independently viable beings who can accomplish all the tasks needed to sustain a culturally acceptable existence" (p. 216). Unlike the authors of the previously mentioned articles, Weissleder takes into consideration the changing technological, economic, and social patterns in explaining marriage dissolution.

In 1970, Schlesinger published an exploratory study of remarriage among 90 divorced men and women. Focussing on personal adjustment to remarriage, he pointed out a number of sex differences in the divorce and remarriage experience. For example, he found that more women than men experience a lowering of self-esteem and status in their community after divorce. Although this difference is mentioned, it is not pursued, because Schlesinger implied that the adjustment process is very similar for both sexes. Peters (1976b) also made this assumption in his study of mate selection and marital experiences in first and second marriages.

Most of the sociological articles assume that factors affecting marriage and divorce impinge on men and women equally. This is one aspect of what Eichler (1981) refers to as "the inadequacy of the monolithic model of the family." Many of the studies do not consider sex to be an important independent variable in affecting the postmarital experiences. Other studies mention sex as a variable, but do not follow up the implications of their data. For example, Kuzel and Krishnan (1973) analyzed remarriage probabilities from 1961 to 1966 in Canada. Some of their most outstanding findings related to the much higher remarriage probabilities for men after both divorce and widowhood. This held true for all age groups, but particularly after the age of thirty. This differential is not as great in the United States, they tell us. Kuzel and Krishnan (1973) concluded that the remarriage chances of Canadian women are increasing for females 35 and above, but *decreasing* for females under 35 years. Their comment on this conclusion seems unusually naive: "These results are rather surprising. With the present state of our knowledge, we are unable to account for these declining probabilities of remarriage for young females" (p. 220). Kuzel and Krishnan leave the discussion of sex differences at this point to concentrate on an explanation of American–Canadian differences in divorce and remarriage rates. Their article concludes as follows:

• Remarriage rates are changing.
• The changes are more favourable to men.
• Higher remarriage rates for women are anticipated in the future, as divorce rates soar. Since women are more likely than men to remarry formerly married people, high divorce rates should improve women's chances of remarriage.

Basing their article entirely on statistical remarriage probabilities, the authors do not draw on other sociological material to explain the sex differences that appear in their data. For example, they make no reference to the rising rates of labour-force participation among women that reduce the economic necessity for remarriage. They also ignore Bernard's work (1972), which suggests that men benefit more from the institution of marriage and are more likely to see it as a desired option. Not only are ideological reasons for low remarriage rates omitted, but also a discussion of the age-gradient. Women are choosing from a declining pool of older men, and therefore have fewer structural opportunities to reenter marriage.

McVey and Robinson (1981) have recently published the only article on separation and divorce ever published by the *Canadian Journal of Sociology* in its seven years of existence. Their article argues that we cannot rely on divorce rates as the chief indicator of marital disruption, since the proportion of separated people is equal to or exceeds the divorced in every five-year age category. This information is presented as a "new insight" (according to the article title). The fact that there are more separated and divorced females than males in the Canadian population is mentioned, but explained in two sentences. Men have higher remarriage rates and tend to underreport their separated status. No further explanation of these sex differences occurs. However, the authors take pains to expand on provincial age variations in statistics on separation and divorce, combining males and females. This methodological decision is unmerited when we consider that in 1976 there were almost 10 000 more separated women and 11 000 more divorced women than men in the city of Toronto alone (Statistics Canada 1976). McVey and Robinson made the decision virtually to ignore sex as an important variable, and focus instead on age and regional differences.

Hobart (1975) published an enlightening study of behaviour and attitudes toward the division of matrimonial property in Alberta couples. A considerable amount of disagreement became apparent between husbands and wives on the hypothetical division of matrimonial property, especially among city dwellers. Generally, he found that women tended to be more egalitarian than men. Couples with an employed wife in a high-status occupation both tended to be more egalitarian than couples with a housewife. However, mothers who were financially dependent on their husbands tended to adopt a perspective that Hobart calls "distinctively male": that most of the matrimonial property belongs to the husband, since his earnings paid for it. A surprisingly large minority of housewives were ignorant of their husbands' financial assets. In particular, older women who were not gainfully employed, farmers' wives, those with little education, and those from low-income families lacked knowledge of their husbands' financial status. Hobart refers to this situation as "vulnerable ignorance." But he also identifies another group of young, well-educated wives who were gainfully employed, but were also ignorant of their husbands' stocks, bonds, or pension plans. Although he suggests that this may be a result of retaining separate bank accounts and separate lives, he states that his data do not indicate this. Hobart ends his article with a feminist statement: "we must anticipate that until 'women's lib' perspectives become more accepted among men there will be increasing difference of opinion, and perhaps increasing conflict, when couples go through divorce and have to confront these issues" (p. 452). This article stands alone in that the author does not make the assumption, as others have, that husbands and wives always form an ideological unit. He implies that they have different interests in the division of matrimonial property, with women developing more egalitarian attitudes than their husbands. He also suggests that this will lead to future conflict if men do not become more egalitarian.

Unlike Hobart and Weissleder, most Canadian authors discuss the family in a social, political, and economic vacuum. They tend to ignore economic changes, such as women's increasing labour-force participation. Most of them are oblivious to women's lower wages in the labour force, to women's financial dependence on their men, to double standards of sexuality, and to the implications of women's close connection with children. In other words, most articles imply that men and women are affected in similar ways by structural constraints.

American Research on Marriage Dissolution

Comparing the Canadian studies to research published in the American journals is a difficult task because of the sheer volume of American material. In the 1970 Decade Review in the *Journal of Marriage and the Family*, research and theoretical writings on the family from the 1960s revealed that only demographic and personality factors related to marital stability were included (Hicks and Platt 1970). In the 1980 review, some generalizations were made on the nature of research and theoretical writings on divorce, desertion, and remarriage (Price-Bonham and Balswick 1980). First, the literature is interdisciplinary and tends to focus on divorced women and their children. Some of the conclusions suggest that divorce rates have been high among women experiencing premarital pregnancy, childless women (Bumpass and Sweet 1972), women who have received education beyond the bachelor's level (Houseknecht and Spanier 1976); and women with high employment earnings (Ross and Sawhill 1975; Hannan, Tuma, and Groeneveld 1977). However, few authors discuss *why* these factors lead to high divorce rates. The education, employment, and income factors are the opposite correlations to those shown for men. This fact is often passed over or rapidly explained.

Scanzoni (1972) created an explanation for rising rates of divorce by using exchange theory in terms of bargaining power between spouses. As the woman's access to resources and power increases, a more egalitarian relationship is created. All issues become open to bargaining, and if not successfully resolved, could lead to divorce. A similar theory is presented in Huber and Spitze's article (1980) on considering divorce. They suggest that employed wives with young children in situations where the husband is minimally involved in the family and housework are most likely to consider divorce as an option. Presumably, these women feel that they are no longer financially dependent on their husbands and while they have taken on the new role of breadwinner, their husbands have not increased their contributions to the household.

In the American literature on divorce, there is also considerable research on postmarital adjustment. Again, the focus remains on women and children, who most often come before social-welfare agencies and are viewed as "needy." The problems of single-parenting have been discussed in detail, but usually from the women's point of view. Relatively few studies have been published on single fathers, and while most authors suggest that the difficulties of males and females in this situation are similar, several authors have found that men are more sympathetically viewed by relatives and neighbours and therefore receive more assistance as single fathers (Brandwein, Brown, and Fox 1974). Some recognition that men's average incomes tend to be much larger than women's and that men suffer fewer financial constraints is beginning to appear in the American literature.

A controversy remains on the differences in the impact of divorce and separation on men and women. Several studies have outlined the high rates of postmarital stress, accidents, suicide, and death for men, and the lower rates for women (Glick and Carter 1970; Gove 1972). At the same time, however, women seem to experience a more negative economic impact (Brandwein, Brown, and Fox 1974), have little time for social life because of retaining custody of the children (Raschke 1977), seldom receive the support payments granted by the court after one year of separation (Brandwein, Brown, and Fox 1974), and experience problems in dating and

finding new heterosexual relationships (Raschke 1977). The fact that men are more likely to remarry than women implies either a greater opportunity structure for remarriage or a greater desire to remain within the institution of marriage.

Only a few studies *highlight* sex differences in postmarital experiences. For example, Brandwein, Brown, and Fox (1974) indicated that single fathers with custody are viewed differently from single mothers. Raschke (1977) pointed out some negative consequences of custody for women, and also found that gainful employment for women is related to better postmarital adjustment. Smith (1979) concluded that alimony continues women's dependence on men. The role of women's liberation ideology as an adaptive coping mechanism has been explored in several articles (Brown, Perry, and Harbury 1977; Granvold, Pedler, and Scheillie 1979; Kessler 1975).

The American divorce literature of the 1970s generally concludes that there is a lack of clearly defined institutional norms relating to separation and divorce, although divorce and remarriage "are beginning to develop identifiable patterns of regularity" (Price-Bonham and Balswick 1980). Perhaps this means that social scientists have done enough research to identify patterns in postmarital behaviour. However, the research still tends to focus on women and on clinical populations. Lack of longitudinal studies means that we have little empirical evidence of the ways in which people cope with divorce after two or three years. Similarly, most of the studies relate to divorce rather than separation. Consequently, we lack data on those who do not seek legal dissolution of their marriages. Nor do we have any research on divorce in the later years. Most studies concentrate on people of childbearing age, because marital dissolution is seen as most socially consequential in its effect on children. However, despite these criticisms, the American research goes beyond the simple analysis of divorce rates on which the Canadian research has focussed. Some American studies have highlighted the differences in power and vested interests between the sexes, presenting a less positive image of the nuclear family than the one presented in Canadian journals.

A Feminist Perspective on the Family

In North America, the discipline of sociology has been numerically dominated by males. Therefore, not surprisingly, most of the journal articles on family sociology have been authored by men. However, as a growing number of women enter the discipline at the lower ranks, the focus of research seems to be changing to incorporate a feminist perspective on the family. This perspective assumes that the interests of men and women sometimes differ, that sexual inequality is pervasive in our society, that negotiation and power struggles are a part of interpersonal relations in the family, and that women's role is still viewed as basically a domestic one despite the changes in women's labour-force participation. Traditional family structures and laws are seen to be beneficial for the smooth functioning of capitalist society and for men, but not always to be conducive to equality for women.

This new focus on the political economy of the family has not pervaded the divorce literature, either in Canada or in the United States. But some researchers are beginning to look beyond the micro analysis of family interaction to how the capitalist economy, social-welfare decisions, labour-market opportunities, and ideologies of acceptable adult roles affect postmarital behaviour. For example, over the past few years several conference presentations in Canada have used this approach in making observations about life after marriage. Research on battered women (Miller and Felt 1979) and on transition houses for women (Brookes 1981) has discovered that increasing numbers of women are leaving the institution of marriage because of high levels of family violence. New ways of dealing with these "refugees from the family" are being created through women organizing to help other women. MacDonnell

(1980) presented her research on married and unmarried mothers and their children, highlighting increasing rates of illegitimacy and marital dissolution and the inadequate financial resources of unmarried mothers. Baker (1981a, 1981b) presented research findings on support networks and marriage dissolution, focussing on the different ways in which men and women experience divorce and on women's role in providing assistance to both sexes after separation. Ambert (1981) discussed the remarriage behaviour of two different income groups of women. Steele (1981) presented her own video of a welfare mother's experiences in coping with agencies, with her own family, and with regulations that were designed to keep her in a dependent role. However, this research has three things in common: it is done by women, it has been presented to largely female audiences, and it is unpublished.

Polarization of the Sexes in Family Research

If we assume that people's life experiences affect their research interests, it is not surprising that most research on family conflict and marital dissolution is being done by women. Women (along with children) are the usual victims of family violence. Women are also the initiators of separation and divorce (Baker 1980; Ambert 1980). The correlation between high education for women and high divorce rates means that academic women are often personally involved in marriage dissolution. As early as 1964, Bernard pointed out the higher divorce rates for female university professors in comparison to male professors. If we also accept Bernard's 1972 thesis that marriage as an institution is more beneficial to men, then female sociologists may feel more marginal to the institution of the family and more critical of it.

The 1981 annual meeting of the Canadian Sociology and Anthropology Association illustrated the division in family sociology in Canada. In one session, which dealt with marriage dissolution and remarriage, papers were presented by four women sociologists. The general session on the family (which was organized by a man) contained a paper on premarital cohabitation (presented by a man) and a paper on the family lives of employed women in India (presented by a woman). Papers on women and domestic labour tended to be presented in "women's studies" sessions by women and attended by a largely female audience. A session entitled "conceptualizing motherhood" also consisted of three female participants and drew upon feminist theory. The session on family theory contained two men and one woman, and the woman presented a critical analysis of family research and theory (Eichler 1981).

Many of the researchers using a critical approach to the family or analyzing the political economy of the family are women. But many of these do not view themselves as "family sociologists." These "refugees from family sociology" have left the substantive area — which tends to be stagnating theoretically — for the developing field of women's studies. But by doing this, they have implied that men have not been interested in these new theories and that women need female solidarity to pursue research on women. Since women's studies are dominated by women, both numerically and in terms of theoretical approaches, men are reluctant to participate. Research and theoretical papers tend to be presented in conference sessions to essentially female audiences, who are "talking to themselves" or "preaching to the converted." These feminist papers are often received enthusiastically by an audience that has not found this material in published sources. Thus, the most innovative research often becomes "ghettoized."

While more family studies classes at the university level are being taught by women sociologists using a feminist perspective, most of the journals in Canada continue to publish more traditional material. The increasing participation of women in the labour force, the changing power structure in the family, men's resistance to women's equality, higher rates of separation and divorce, greater numbers of single-parent families, changing kin relations, and an increasing disillusionment on the part of middle-class educated women with marriage are barely mentioned in the published journal articles of this discipline in Canada. Although passing reference is made to some of these changes, few go beyond a superficial analysis of these trends. The segregation mentioned above for conferences apparently also applies to journal articles. Men publish in sociology and family journals and women publish in women's studies journals that tend to be granted lower status in academic circles.

The trend toward segregated journals is far more apparent in Canada than in the United States. A feminist perspective is present in some of the articles in the *Journal of Marriage and the Family* and in the *Journal of Divorce*. Although many of the authors using this perspective are women, men also incorporate feminist ideas into their articles. But in Canada there seems to be a "his" and "hers" family sociology that is creating an unhealthy division within the field. If much recent research on the family is omitted from mainstream sociology, then other sociologists are left with the impression that nothing new is happening in the field. In fact, researchers are finding a more favourable climate in social work and women's studies than in mainstream sociology. Lack of contact between social workers and sociologists as well as between feminists and traditionalists within sociology creates a segregated substantive area.

The solution to this problem of segregation is not to create a new feminist family journal. This would just further ghettoize those academics who pursue this sort of research. Rather, integration of varying theoretical perspectives would be more fruitful both for the discipline and for the careers of those moving away from mainstream family studies. If efforts were made to bridge the gap, the field of family sociology would blossom and become much more attractive to the many young scholars who are presently studying the institution under some other name than "sociology of the family."

Works Cited

Ambert, Anne-Marie. 1980. *Divorce in Canada*. Toronto: Academic.

———. 1981. "Behavioural Differences Towards Remarriage Between Financially Secure and Financially Insecure Women." Presented to the Annual Meetings of the Canadian Sociology and Anthropology Association, Halifax, May.

Baker, Maureen. 1980. "Support Networks and Marriage Dissolution." Unpublished Report. Toronto: Faculty of Social Work.

———. 1981a. "The Personal and Support Networks of the Separated and Divorced." Presented to the Annual Meetings of the Canadian Sociology and Anthropology Association, Halifax, May.

———. 1981b. "Women Helping Women: The Transition from Separation to Divorce." Presented to the Annual Meetings of the Canadian Research Institute for the Advancement of Women, Halifax, November.

Bernard, Jessie. 1964. *Academic Women*. University Park, PA: Pennsylvania. State University Press.

———. 1972. *The Future of Marriage*. New York: Bantam.

Brandwein, R.A., C.A. Brown, and E.M. Fox. 1974. "Women and Children Last: the Social Situation of Divorced Mothers and Their Families." *Journal of Marriage and the Family* 35: 498–514.

Brookes, Anne-Louise. 1981. "Women in Transition: Process and Change in a New Political Structure." Presented to the Annual Meetings of the Canadian Research Institute for the Advancement of Women, Halifax, November.

Brown, P., L. Perry, and E. Harburg. 1977. "Sex Role Attitudes and Psychological Outcomes for Black and White Women Experiencing Marital Dissolution." *Journal of Marriage and the Family* 39 (August): 549–61.

Bumpass, L. and J. Sweet. 1972. "Differentials in Marital Instability: 1970." *American Sociological Review* 37: 754–56.

Davids, Leo. 1982. "Divorce and Remarriage Among Canadian Jews." *Journal of Comparative Family Studies* 13(1): 37–47.

Eichler, Margrit. 1981. "The Inadequacy of the Monolithic Model of the Family" *Canadian Journal of Sociology* 6 (3): 367–88.

Glick, P.C., and Carter, H. 1970. *Marriage and Divorce: A Social and Economic Study*. Cambridge, MA: Harvard University Press.

Gove, W.R. 1972. "The Relationship Between Sex Roles, Marital Status, and Mental Illness." *Social Forces* 51: 31–44.

Granvold, D.K., L.M. Pedler, and S.G. Scheillie. 1979. "A Study of Sex Role Expectancy and Female Post Divorce Adjustment." *Journal of Divorce*, 2 (Summer): 383–94.

Grayson, J. Paul, and Dennis W. Magill. 1980. "One Step Forward, Two Steps Sideways: Sociology and Anthropology in Canada." Prepared for the Canadian Sociology and Anthropology Association, May.

Hannan, M., N. Tuma, and L.P. Groeneveld. 1977. "Income and Marital Events: Evidence from an Income Maintenance Experiment." *American Journal of Sociology* 82: 1186–1211.

Heinrich, Albert. 1972. "Divorce as an Integrative Social Factor Among Eskimos." *Journal of Comparative Family Studies* 3(2): 265–72.

Hicks, M.W., and M. Platt. 1970. "Marital Happiness and Stability: a Review of Research in the Sixties." *Journal of Marriage and the Family* 32 (November): 553–74.

Hobart, Charles W. 1975. "Ownership of Matrimonial Property: A Study of Practices and Attitudes." *Canadian Review of Sociology and Anthropology* 12 (4) Part 1: 440–52.

Houseknecht, S.K., and G.B. Spanier. 1976. "Marital Disruption and Higher Education Among Women in the United States." Paper presented at the Conference on Women in Midlife Crisis. Ithaca, NY, October.

Huber, Joan, and Glenna Spitze. 1980. "Considering Divorce: An Expansion of Becker's Theory of Marital Instability." *American Journal of Sociology* 86 (1): 75–89.

Kessler, S. 1975. *The American Way of Divorce: Prescriptions for Change*. Chicago: Nelson-Hall.

Kuzel, Paul, and P. Krishnan. 1973. "Changing Patterns of Remarriage in Canada 1961–1966." *Journal of Comparative Family Studies* 4(2): 215–24.

MacDonnell, Susan. 1980. "Single Mothers and Their Children." Presented to Annual Meeting of Atlantic Association of Anthropologists and Sociologists (Welfare Research). Sydney, NS, March.

McVey, Wayne W. Jr., and Barry, W. Robinson. 1981. "Separation in Canada: New Insights Concerning Marital Dissolution." *The Canadian Journal of Sociology* 6 (3): 353–66.

Miller, Anne, and Lawrence Felt. 1979. "Battered Women: Myths, Realities and New Directions for Future Research." Paper presented to the Association of Anthropologists and Sociologists, Halifax, March.

Palmer, Sally, E. 1971. "Reasons for Marriage Breakdown: A Case Study in South-Western Ontario." *Journal of Comparative Family Studies* 2 (August): 251–62.

Peters, John, F. 1976a. "Divorce in Canada: A Demographic Profile". *Journal of Comparative Family Studies* 7(2): 335–49.

———. 1976b. "A Comparison of Male Selection and Marriage in the First and Second Marriages in a Selected Sample of the Remarried Divorced." *Journal of Comparative Family Studies* 7(3): 483–90.

Pike, Robert. 1975. "Legal Access to the Incidence of Divorce in Canada: a Sociohistorical Analysis." *Canadian Review of Sociology and Anthropology* 12 (2) 1975: 115–33.

Price-Bonham, Sharon, and Jack O. Balswick. 1980. "The Non-Institutions: Divorce, Desertion, and Remarriage." *Journal of Marriage and the Family* 42 (4): 959–72.

Raschke, Helen J. 1977. "The Role of Social Participation in Postseparation and Postdivorce Adjustment." *Journal of Divorce* 1 (Winter): 129–39.

Ross, H.L., and I.V. Sawhill. 1975. *Time in Transition: The Growth of Families Headed by Women.* Washington, DC: Urban Institute.

Scanzoni, John. 1972. *Sexual Bargaining: Power Politics in American Marriage.* Englewood Cliffs, NJ: Prentice-Hall.

Schlesinger, Benjamin. 1970. "Remarriage as Family Reorganization for Divorced Persons — A Canadian Study." *Journal of Comparative Family Studies* 1(1): 101–18.

Smith, J.S. 1979. "Alimony for Men — the Changing Law." *Florida State University Law Review* 7 (Fall): 687–700.

Statistics Canada. 1976. *Demographic Characteristics, Marital Status.* Catalogue 92-824. Ottawa: Supply and Services Canada.

Steele, Lisa. 1981. "Women in Crisis: Creating Video Dramatizations." Presented to the Canadian Research Institute for the Advancement of Women Annual Meetings, Halifax, November.

Weissleder, W. 1974a. "Amhara Marriage: The Stability of Divorce." *Canadian Review of Sociology and Anthropology* 11 (1): 67–85.

———. 1974b. "No-Illusion Marriage and No-Fault Divorce." *Canadian Review of Sociology and Anthropology* 11 (3): 214–29.

COURTSHIP FOR REMARRIAGE: INFLUENCES ON FAMILY REORGANIZATION AFTER DIVORCE*

Roy H. Rodgers
Linda M. Conrad

Courtship for remarriage has not been a major topic for either empirical research or theorizing. This article presents a theoretical approach to the specific issue of the impact of courtship for remarriage on postmarital family reorganization, based on existing theory and research. Several propositions for empirical testing derived from the theoretical argument are presented and discussed in relation to each of five subsystems within the reorganizing postmarital family system.

A survey of recent courtship literature indicates a bias in this field toward studying young, heterosexual, never-married persons. In addition, the emphasis has been on identifying factors that influence courtship behaviour and progress, such as couple similarity, peer and parental approval, and family background variables (Adams 1979; Booth, Brinkerhoff, and White 1984: Hill, Rubin, and Peplau 1976). Courtship in the population of older, divorced women and men has only recently come to the attention of some investigators (Peters 1976). Most of this research focuses on the remarried state, ignoring the courtship process leading up to remarriage (cf. Walker et al. 1979, for an annotated bibliography). When the question of courtship

for remarriage is addressed, the emphasis is on courtship as a dependent variable. As such, demographic variables (Goode 1956; Spanier and Glick 1980), past marital history (Hunt 1966), and current family circumstance (Bernard 1956; Weiss 1979) are cited as important factors influencing the courtship process.

In contrast, the following discussion represents an attempt to treat courtship for remarriage as an independent variable. The dependent variable of interest will be the level of family reorganization after divorce. The dearth of empirical studies dealing with courtship for remarriage, let alone treating courtship as an independent variable, has made it necessary to draw almost exclusively from research on remarried families.

The substitution of remarriage literature for more direct studies on courtship is justified on at least two accounts. First, potential mates of formerly married persons are often introduced to other family members only after there is some assurance of a commitment between the courters (Weiss 1979). A commitment between the courters is likely to result in family members acting and reacting towards the situation more as if it were a remarriage than a dating relationship. Second, divorced courting partners often take on the roles of husband and wife in relating to one another (Bernard 1956; Hunt 1966). To the extent that they interact like husband and wife, their courtship behaviour can be expected to be similar to the interaction that

Source: *Journal of Marriage and the Family,* 48 (1986): 767–75. Copyright © 1986 by the National Council on Family Relations, 3938 Central Ave. N.E., Minneapolis, MN 55421. Reprinted with permission.

*The authors acknowledge the helpful comments on Constance R. Ahrons and the anonymous reviewers of earlier drafts of this article.

will occur in remarriage. There are, of course, important differences between courtship for remarriage and actual remarriage, and these differences will be kept in mind when characteristics of remarriage are substituted for the independent variable, courtship.

Binuclear-Family Relationship Theory

Recent investigations into the nature of ongoing relationships following separation or divorce (Ahrons 1979, 1980a, 1980c; Hetherington, Cox, and Cox 1978; Wallerstein and Kelly 1979) provide the conceptual and empirical background to discuss the dependent variable, level of family reorganization after divorce. Ahrons (1979) points out that marital disruption changes the family system from a nuclear to a binuclear system. The binuclear system contains two households organized around the divorced parents. (The two households need not be equal with respect to physical qualities nor in their importance or influence on children, although this is sometimes the case.) In moving toward binuclearity, family members must establish new patterns of relating — a task Ahrons (1980a) has termed systemic reorganization. In addition to this task, a new family identity needs to be established to reflect the reality of a divorced family system. The new family identity, together with the altered patterns of relating, help define the level of binuclear family reorganization.

Courtship is characterized by behaviours that move two people toward increased "intimacy, interdependence, and commitment" (King and Christensen 1983). For young, never-married persons the process is well defined by established norms (Aldous 1978; Broderick and Smith 1979). These norms help guide not only the behaviour of the courting couple but also that of the couple's friends and families. The couple spend increasing amounts of time in exclusive interactions, while at the same time friends and family members limit their demands on the couple's time and energy. Strong marriage and family norms help predict that parents and peers will approve of, and actively assist, the courtship (assuming certain conditions are met — for example, the timing is "right" and the chosen mate is acceptable: Aldous 1978). In contrast, the absence of institutionalized norms for courtship among formerly married persons makes predicting outcomes for this population more difficult (cf. Cherlin 1978, and Price-Bonham and Balswick 1980, for discussions of the noninstitutionalized nature of separation, divorce, and remarriage). Factors peculiar to the couple and their relationship to others assume primary importance. Bernard (1956), and later Hunt (1966) noted the differences between the courtships of the never-married and the divorced. These differences include the manner in which the couple make public their commitment to one another, the speed at which the courtship progresses toward marriage, and the timing of specific courting behaviours such as sexual intimacy.

The differences in courtship of formerly married couples is partly a result of prior experiences in intimate relationships, the lack of norms governing appropriate behaviours for the divorced or separated, and, not insignificantly, the influence of parents, children, and the ex-spouse (Bernard 1956). Just as parents, children, and an ex-spouse can affect the nature of the courtship process for divorced men and women, the courtship of these formerly married persons can have an impact on the members of the divorced family system. The question then becomes one of how courtship for remarriage influences the relationships being re-formed in divorced families.

Postmarital-Family Reorganization Theory

A theoretical framework in which to view the influences of courtship for remarriage on the divorced family system is provided in recent work by Rodgers. His propositional theory of postmarital family reorganization will be used to guide a discussion of some of the available research on courtship and remarriage. First, an overview of the main points of the theory is warranted (Rodgers 1986; Ahrons and Rodgers, forthcoming).

The postmarital family, like the nuclear family, is treated in the theory as a social system. Several features of systems theory make it useful to employ this term when discussing postdivorce families, particularly with respect to the influences of courtship on family reorganization. As a system the family maintains boundaries that distinguish it from other social groupings. Boundaries define who belongs to a given system and what functions will be performed in that system. The boundaries are permeable to varying degrees to allow the family and its members to interact with other systems. The family system is made up of a number of subsystems — the spousal subsystem, the parent–child(ren) subsystem, the sibling subsystem, and the extended-family subsystem are the most immediately obvious. In binuclear family systems, several new subsystems result from the expansion of the basic nuclear-family system. Four that are of importance in the discussion to follow are the noncustodial parent–child, custodial parent–child, the non-coparenting, and the co-parenting subsystems. As with the family unit, subsystems have boundaries that are to some degree permeable, thus permitting exchanges across systems.

Another relevant feature of systems thinking is the concept of interdependence. Interdependence means that a change in any part of the system will have an impact on the entire system. The extent to which a change affects the whole system depends on the degree of boundary permeability. If the boundaries around a particular system are not well defined in terms of membership and function, it is possible that even minor changes would have far-reaching consequences. Well-defined, distinct boundaries, on the other hand, may limit the impact of a change. (The

idea of boundary clarity, as defined by Minuchin 1974, 53–54, is related to the concept of permeability. Boundary clarity varies from very rigid — low permeability, or disengaged, to very diffuse — high permeability, or enmeshed.)

In addition to viewing the postdivorce family as a system, Rodgers brings together four extant theoretical orientations in his handling of family reorganization. The most relevant to the present discussion are Ahrons's conceptualization of the binuclear family (1979, 1980a, 1980c) and McCubbin and Patterson's work on family-stress theory (1983). The concept of binuclearity was mentioned earlier. Family-stress theory provides a vehicle for identifying the impact of stressors and crises in the system, as well as for predicting the family's ability to cope with them.

In its simplest form, the McCubbin and Patterson model relates the presence of a stressor to the existence of resources and the family definition of the situation to predict the level of crisis and subsequent adaptation. The major advantage of the model is that it views the coping and adaptation responses of the family as a process taking place over time. Two phases, adjustment and adaptation, are identified in this coping process. The adaptation phase is further divided into a restructuring level and a consolidation level.

In the adjustment phase of the coping process, a stressor is introduced into the family system where prior strains and hardships may already be present. These demands are matched with existing resources and the family definition of the situation to provide some level of resistance to the stressor becoming a crisis.[1]

Families try to cope with the stressor by avoidance, elimination, or assimilation. If the impact of prior strains and the hardships that the stressor may produce are not too great — and existing resources and the definition and appraisal of the situation are satisfactory — the family may resist a crisis. Their adjustment may lie somewhere between "maladjustment" and "bonadjustment" — with maladjustment, of course, leading into crisis.

Should the stressor develop into a crisis, the family would move into the restructuring level of the adaptation phase. At this level of adaptation, other stressors may be introduced into the system, and new resources identified to assist in the coping process. The family may return to the level of crisis and begin again if they cannot handle the load added by the pileup of other stressors experienced. If the resources are inadequate, if they cannot reach and implement mutually acceptable solutions to their situation and/or if the maintenance of the system fails, the family remains in crisis. They must continue their attempts to restructure, or, having consumed their energy in coping, they may enter an organization state of exhaustion.

If the family is successful in its restructuring, the final coping response is to consolidate at the new level of family reorganization. Refinement in the use of available resources and the further development of shared definitions and problem solutions allow them to reach a new condition of "maladaptation/bonadaptation" that may be more or less effective than the one that existed prior to the onset of the stressor. Of course, it is possible that the family is unable to meet its demands with available resources, in which case it may re-enter the restructuring level or fall once more into crisis or, possibly, into a state of exhaustion.

In the discussion to follow, courtship for remarriage may be viewed as a stressor that has an impact on the binuclear family reorganization process. Whether the stressor becomes a crisis, of course, depends on the system's ability to cope with the impact of the stressor.

Applications of the Theory to Remarriage Courtship

In setting forth his model of the separation, divorce, and remarriage process, Rodgers attempted to follow the strategies of Burr et al. (1979, 8–9) for developing propositional theory. This approach involves six steps:

1. conceptual clarification of the major dependent variable to be explained;
2. review of theories pertaining to the phenomenon of interest capable of being rendered context-free;
3. formulation of a limited number of general context-free propositions;
4. deduction of context-specific propositions at lower orders of abstraction;
5. scanning of research for empirical support, if any, for the deduced propositions; and
6. incorporating all of these propositions into an accounting model format.

Rodgers does not claim that all that is called for in this list has been accomplished in his work at its current level of development. However, his ultimate objective is to develop a theory that generally meets these criteria. The discussion to follow is intended as a contribution to this propositional theory-building process, specifically to steps 4 and 5.

One can view the postdivorce family as a system in which members are involved in a process of restructuring family relationships in an effort to cope with the stresses and demands accompanying the termination of the marriage. In a nuclear family, relationships evolve over time. A common residence provides a setting for family interactions, and well-established norms define appropriate behaviours for these interactions. Divorce shatters this routine by changing the temporal and spatial arrangement of family members (Walker and Messinger 1979) and altering the expectations for how members should relate to one another. During the restructuring of family relationships after divorce, changes in any part of the family system will to varying degrees affect each of the subsystems. Courtship for remarriage of one or both of the ex-spouses is one action that may have far-reaching consequences for the system as a whole. The impact of the courtship process on the various subsystems will depend in part on the timing of its introduction into the reorganizing system.

The Noncustodial Parent–Child Subsystem

After a divorce, family members must establish new patterns of interacting with one another. As with a nuclear family, patterns of interaction in a divorced system differ depending on which two (or more) members are involved in the interaction. (Cf. Ahrons 1980b, 1981, 1983; Bowman and Ahrons 1985; and Ahrons and Wallisch 1986, for extensive discussions of the postdivorce parenting relationship.) The subsystem for which the re-establishment of a relationship probably requires the greatest effort is the noncustodial parent–child subsystem. In the absence of physical proximity, and with legal restrictions on contact, as well as those imposed by the ex-spouse, the noncustodial parent must consciously plan interactions with his or her child (Walker and Messinger 1979). As a result, noncustodial parent–child subsystems are extremely varied in their quality and strength and in the nature of their interactions (Keshet 1980).

Assuming it takes time to establish new patterns of interacting within the subsystem, the early introduction of a stepparent figure by way of the courtship of the *custodial* parent could retard development of the relationship between noncustodial parent and child. Loyalty issues may be raised by the introduction of a new member into the divorced family system (McGoldrick and Carter 1980), and noncustodial parents may become anxious about the possibility of a relationship developing between the child and the custodial parent's new partner. This may be especially true if the noncustodial parent–child subsystem has not solidified (Keshet 1980). Alternatively, the new partner may pressure the custodial parent to limit access to the noncustodial parent, as is sometimes the case in remarriages (Weiss 1979). Should this happen, the noncustodial parent may react either by withdrawing from the subsystem or by fighting for the right to access.

The courtship of the noncustodial parent is also likely to have an impact on the developing relationship in the noncustodial parent–child subsystem. One possible outcome is that the parent may partially withdraw from the noncustodial parent–child system. Contact with a nonresident child is sometimes irregular, and visitation is often out of the control of the noncustodial parent. In contrast, interaction with a new dating partner is more in the divorced parent's control and has the potential to offer a continuously available source of emotional intimacy, which is no longer the case with the nonresident child. Provided with a reliable source of emotional support from a new partner, the noncustodial parent may be less motivated to develop new patterns of interacting with his or her child (Keshet 1980).

If the noncustodial parent–child subsystem has developed new rituals and provides a well-defined environment for its actors, the introduction of a courting partner by either ex-spouse should have limited impact on the subsystem. In fact, it is possible that such a unified subsystem will create problems for the integration of a courting partner into the divorced family system (Keshet 1980). At the same time, it must be recognized that the introduction of a new partner into the parent's life does upset the stability to which both the parent and child have become accustomed.

The preceding discussion can be summarized in propositional statements P1 and P2 (Table 1). We would expect, on the basis of McCubbin and Patterson's formulation, that the degree of stress introduced by the remarriage courtship process could result in crisis in the noncustodial parent–child subsystem if the coping resources available are inadequate.

The Custodial Parent–Child Subsystem

Another parent–child subsystem in the divorced system is that of the custodial parent and child. This subsystem, like the noncustodial parent–child subsystem, is faced with the task of redefining some of its patterns of interacting. According to research by Hetherington, Cox, and Cox (1978), the process of establishing new rituals and routines takes

Table I
Derived Propositions: Noncustodial and Custodial Parent–Child Subsystems

Number	Propositions
P1.	The earlier that courtship for remarriage is introduced after divorce in a divorced-family system, the greater the degree of disruption in the establishment of new patterns for interacting in the noncustodial or custodial parent–child subsystem, regardless of whether it is the noncustodial or custodial parent who is courting.
P2.	The ease of integration of a new partner into the divorced-family system is negatively related to the unity of the noncustodial parent–child subsystem. This relationship is probably stronger when the new partner is the romantic interest of the noncustodial parent.
P3.	The earlier that courtship for remarriage is introduced in a divorced-family system, the greater the degree of disruption in the establishment of new patterns of interacting in the custodial parent–child subsystem, particularly when the courtship involves the custodial parent.
P4.	The courtship of the noncustodial parent, in the absence of courtship for the custodial parent, is positively related to the degree of conflict between the ex-spouses.
P5.	The courtship of the noncustodial parent, in the absence of courtship for the custodial parent, is positively related to attempts by the custodial parent to interfere with the relationship between the noncustodial parent and the child.
P6.	The more the custodial parent's new partner displaces the child as a source of emotional support for the parent, the greater the probability of a negative reaction of the child to the new partner.
P7.	The more the custodial parent's new partner displaces the child as a source of emotional support for the parent, the greater the level of problems that are likely to arise in the custodial parent–child relationship.
P8.	The more the custodial parent's new partner relieves the child of the burden of extra reponsibilities resulting from the divorce, the greater the probability of the child reacting favourably to the new partner.
P9.	The more the custodial parent's new partner relieves the child of the burden of extra responsibilities resulting from the divorce, the lower the probability of problems arising in the custodial parent–child relationship.
P10.	The more the custodial parent attempts to interfere with the relationship between the noncustodial parent and the child, the lower the quality of the custodial parent–child subsystem.

several years. However, once new patterns are in place, the custodial parent–child unit looks very different from the former parent–child subsystem of the nuclear family (Keshet 1980). Children are likely to play a larger role in family life, share greater intimacy with the parent, and have a more equal relationship to the parent than is true of intact families.

The introduction of a courting partner into the divorced system is expected to influence developments taking place between the custodial parent and child. Because the custodial parent and child share a common residence, the child is usually quite aware of the parent's courtship. This awareness is heightened by the fact that the custodial parent and his or her new partner assume marriage-like roles in relating to one another. As a consequence, the new partner is very visible in the child's life. The courter displaces the child as the primary source of emotional support to the parent, and the child loses his or her recently acquired "special" status. The child may resent the loss (Weiss 1979) and his or her relationship with the custodial parent may be adversely affected. Alternatively, the child may be relieved of the burden of increased responsibilities that often accompany living in a divorced family system (Hunt 1966; Weiss 1979). To the degree the child feels relieved of added responsibilities because of the presence of the courter, the relationship between the custodial parent and child may not be adversely affected.

The custodial parent–child subsystem can be affected by the courtship of the noncustodial parent. The impact of the noncustodial parent's courtship is likely to be felt through the reactions of the custodial parent. Hetherington, Cox, and Cox (1978) found that the remarriage of one of the ex-spouses tended to activate old conflicts for the spouse who was not remarrying. In the case where the custodial parent (in this case the female) was not remarrying, financial issues and feelings of jealousy were often raised. A possible consequence of any conflict between ex-spouses is the limiting of child access by the custodial parent. Although intended to punish the noncustodial parent, this action could also have a damaging effect on the relationship between the custodial parent and his or her child. The child may resent his or her parent directing anger at the noncustodial parent, and loyalty conflicts could result (McGoldrick and Carter 1980).

In summary, propositional statements P3–P10 (Table 1) are offered. Once again, the coping resources of the binuclear family will determine whether crisis results from the introduction of the stressor of remarriage courtship.

The Non-coparenting Subsystem

In terminating the spousal subsystem after divorce, the former spouses often continue some form of interaction not related to parenting. The boundaries between this non-coparenting subsystem and the coparenting unit must be well defined if the couple is to be successful in continuing parenting responsibilities (Ahrons 1980c). If the two systems are not clearly differentiated, then a change in one will have immediate impact on the other. If the boundaries between the two subsystems are clear and their functions kept separate, the impact of changes across their borders will be minimized. The importance of role clarity in these two systems is highlighted by the courtship behaviour of one, or both, of the ex-spouses. As noted above, a remarriage (and presumably also courtship for remarriage) can activate emotional jealousies and conflicts (Hetherington, Cox, and Cox 1978) between ex-spouses. If boundaries between the non-coparental and coparental subsystems are not distinct, it is possible for jealousies and conflicts originating in the non-coparenting subsystem to spill over into the coparental domain (cf. P5). If this should happen, stress may be created in the parent-child subsystems as a result of tensions between the former spouses in their interactions as coparents. The concept of clarity in coparental and non-coparental roles is important, then, in understanding other aspects of remarriage courtship.

The ongoing non-coparental relationship itself will be affected if either one of the ex-spouses introduces a new romantic interest into the divorced system. As we have already seen, one way courtship may have an impact on this subsystem is to create conflict and jealousy between the ex-spouses. Hetherington, Cox, and Cox (1978) found this to be especially true when the ex-husband was the one remarrying. In the case of an ex-wife remarrying, men were less upset, possibly for financial reasons, or because of their relative lack of emotionality. Weiss (1979) notes that the ex-husband sometimes makes changes in maintenance payments in response to his ex-wife's dating behaviour.

There are alternative possibilities as well. Keshet (1980) finds that remarriage causes a further "distancing" between ex-spouses in their non-coparental relationship by forcing the nonmarrying spouse to become more autonomous. The distancing that occurs after the remarriage of one of the spouses may also be a reaction to the final destruction of a lingering fantasy of reconciliation (Weiss 1979). Another reason for attenuation in the non-coparenting relationship may be that the spouse who was responsible for ending the marriage feels relieved when the other spouse establishes a new relationship (Keshet 1980). Finally, if both spouses establish new relationships, it appears that the intensity of their non-coparental relationship is attenuated (Hetherington, Cox, and Cox 1978). Thus, a number of factors that operate in the relationship between courtship for remarriage and the functioning of the non-coparental subsystem may lead to crisis in binuclear family reorganization — a fact reflected in the propositions P11–P18 (Table 2).

The Coparenting Subsystem

The coparenting relationship between ex-spouses is expected to be affected by the courtship process to the extent that the boundaries around this subsystem are not well defined. If conflict spills over from the non-coparental subsystem, the coparenting relationship may deteriorate. It is possible that the result would be one parent undermining the work of the other parent with respect to childrearing (Weiss 1979). Conflict over the new relationship, however, need not be the issue. Keshet (1980) suggests that the coparenting relationship can be complicated by the mere presence of a new partner if the non-custodial parent resists having possibly to deal with that new partner when arranging visitation with his or her child. Alternatively, the courtship of the custodial parent may cause the noncustodial parent to increase his or her

---

Table 2
Derived Propositions: Non-coparenting and Coparenting Subsystems

Number	Proposition
P11.	Courtship for remarriage of the ex-husband is positively related to the degree of conflict in the non-coparental subsystem of the divorced family. This relationship is intensified if the ex-husband was the initiator of the divorce and is reduced if the ex-wife was the initiator of the divorce.
P12.	Courtship for remarriage of the ex-wife is negatively related to the degree of conflict in the non-coparental subsystem of the divorced family. This relationship may be reversed if the ex-husband uses the courtship of the ex-wife as an opportunity to revise the financial support that he provides.
P13.	Courtship for remarriage by one ex-spouse is positively related to increased autonomy in the noncourting spouse.
P14.	The greater the autonomy on the part of the non-courting ex-spouse, the greater the probability of distancing in the non-coparenting relationship.
P15.	Courtship for remarriage by one ex-spouse is positively related to destruction of fantasies about reconciliation by the noncourting ex-spouse.
P16.	The more that the remarriage courtship of one ex-spouse results in the destruction of fantasies about reconciliation by the noncourting ex-spouse, the greater the distancing in the non-coparenting relationship.
P17.	Courtship for remarriage by the noninitiating ex-spouse is positively related to a feeling of relief by the initiating ex-spouse.
P18.	Courtship for remarriage, when both spouses are involved in new relationships, is positively related to an attenuation of the non-coparenting relationship.
P19.	The more the noncustodial parent is required to relate to the new courtship partner in visitation arrangements with the child, the lower the quality of the coparenting relationship.
P20.	The more either parent feels the need to compete with the courter for his or her child's affection, the lower the quality of the coparenting relationship.
P21.	The more that either parent wishes to have increased time available to spend with a new courtship partner, the lower the quality of the coparenting relationship.

demands for access to the child in response to increased competition for the child's affection (Keshet 1980). A final possibility is that both parents would seek to decrease their commitment as coparents in order to have more time to spend developing the relationship with their new partner.

Propositions P19–P21 (Table 2) reflect the further potential for crisis in this subsystem arising from the stressor of remarriage courtship.

The Extended-Family Subsystem

An area that has recently sparked the attention of researchers is the effect of marital disruption on the relationships in the extended family (Ahrons and Bowman 1982; Kalish and Visher 1982; Mead 1970). Some of this research has looked specifically at remarriage and the role it plays in determining intergenerational patterns of relating (Furstenberg 1981). Although courtship for remarriage is probably not identical to the remarried state with respect to extended kin, it may be possible to isolate variables from the available research that would be applicable to the discussion of courtship influences on family reorganization.

Following a divorce, contact with relatives by marriage is generally reduced, while interaction with blood relatives may be heightened (Furstenberg 1981). Mead notes, however, that many divorced mothers make a special effort to maintain their children's relationships with the paternal grandparents. In turn, many paternal grandparents "jealously protect the 'rights' and 'privileges' that the son–father has relinquished or been deprived of" (1970, 110). She goes on to say that this grandparental behaviour is accentuated when the mother remarries. Other researchers have noted the relative advantage that the custodial parent's kin seem to have over the kin of the noncustodial parent in terms of maintaining contact with children of the divorce (Ahrons and Bowman 1982). This latter research suggests there may be a loss of kin ties to both

the children and noncustodial family following a divorce. When a remarriage occurs, children from the divorced system are provided with new kin ties to "replace those lost through divorce" (Cherlin 1981, 84). Assuming there is a limited amount of time in which to engage in kin contacts, the new relationships established through the remarriage may take priority over the contacts with kin of the noncustodial parent (especially for geographically distant kin). Donald Anspach (1976) found that remarriage kin relationships were at least as important as consanguine kinships; this suggests that if contact with any kin is discontinued, it is likely to be that of the ex-spouse. Furstenberg (1981) notes that the gains and losses of extended kinships may differ considerably for joint-custody arrangements.

Our society both accepts and encourages the establishment of ties with kin of a remarriage (Furstenberg 1981). Acceptance of the new partner's kin probably aids in the integration of the stepparent into the family. Consequently, an effort will usually be made to establish contacts with that kin group. If this process occurs before the remarriage, that is, during courtship, then propositions P22–P25 (Table 3) may be expected to hold. The coping resources of the binuclear family are once again put to the test in reducing the potential for crisis.

Conclusion

The propositional statements and discussion have centred on the impact of courtship on each of several subsystems within the divorced-family system. The relationships stated have been quite general, partly because of the paucity of supporting research and partly because of the complexity of identifying relevant variables. It is not the act of courting per se that is relevant, but rather the implications that the courtship has for the divorced-family system.

The introduction of a courting relationship into the reorganizing-family system may be

Table 3
Derived Propositions: Extended-Family Subsystem

Number	Proposition
P22.	Courtship for remarriage is positively related to contact of the parent–child subsystem with kin of the new partner. This relationship is stronger for the custodial parent–child subsystem than it is for the noncustodial parent–child subsystem. It is further directly affected in the noncustodial parent–child subsystem by the degree of contact between the noncustodial parent and the child.
P23.	Courtship for remarriage is negatively related to contact of the parent–child subsystem with kin of the former partner. This relationship is stronger for the noncustodial-parent subsystem than it is for the custodial-parent subsystem and refers to contacts initiated by the parent.
P24.	Courtship for remarriage of the noncustodial parent is positively related to an increase in that parent's contact with kin of the new partner and negatively related to contact with kin of the ex-spouse.
P25.	Courtship for remarriage is positively related to attempts by kin of the noncustodial parent to maintain contact with the child(ren). This relationship is stronger when the courtship for remarriage involves the custodial parent. It is even stronger if the courting custodial parent is the mother.

seen as an additional stressor with which the family must deal, or it may be viewed as a resource. Depending on which definition it is given by those involved, the consequences will be very different for the system as a whole. Different members may give the situation quite different definitions; in this case the system will eventually have to come to some agreement about its meaning. On the other hand, coming to agreement on a meaning that makes reorganization difficult also introduces stress and potential crisis.

Certainly the courting parent's self-esteem is enhanced by his or her new relationship, and this is likely to have positive consequences for the parent–child subsystem (Bernard 1956). Financial assistance is often provided through the courter (typically a male courter) giving much-needed help to a custodial parent who may be on a limited income (Weiss 1979). The potential is also present for the courter to assist in child care and relieve the custodial parent of the burden of being the primary caregiver.

In contrast, the courtship process can bring with it many stressors that, added to existing stressors, could push members of the divorced family system into crisis. Uncertainty

about whether to remarry because of past experiences can cause emotional advances and withdrawals during the courting process. If the custodial parent is involved in the courtship, the added responsibility of finding a good stepparent for his or her children may cause some agonizing last-minute evaluations of the new partner (Walker and Messinger 1979). New partners enter a system with an established history (Keshet 1980), and there are no guidelines for how they should fit in. Consequently, there may be several false starts in attempting to build relationships with the parent, his or her children, and possibly his or her ex-spouse (Bernard 1956). The nature of the divorced family as a system suggests that the impact of a change brought on by courtship for remarriage can be far-reaching.

It appears the key in determining what influence courtship for remarriage may have on the divorced-family system lies in identifying what meaning courtship has for the system's members. Another essential requirement is to identify the point at which the courtship enters into the family coping process following marital disruption. While it is beyond the scope of this article, analysis in future studies should also consider how other variables at the individual, family, and societal level may modify and elaborate the propositions set forth here. Some of these variables include family composition (number, age, and gender of children), social and psychological characteristics of the family and of individuals involved (socioeconomic status, ethnic status, personality characteristics, marital history, divorce history, and the like), and the level and character of the involvement of the legal system and other social agencies in the reorganizing family system. Direct research on courtship for remarriage, guided by theoretically derived propositions, appears to hold promise for unraveling the mysteries of how postmarital intimate relationships affect the level of postmarital-family reorganization.

Note

1. A stressor is a life event or transition "which produces, or has the potential of producing, change in the family social system" (McCubbin and Patterson 1983, 8). A crisis "is characterized by the family's inability to restore stability and by the continuous pressure to make changes in the family structure and patterns of interaction. . . . Stress may never reach crisis proportions if the family is able to use existing resources and define the situation so as to resist systemic change and maintain family stability" (p. 10).

Works Cited

Adams, Bert N. 1979. "Mate Selection in the United States: A Theoretical Summarization." Burr et al. 259-67.

Ahrons, Constance R. 1979. "The Binuclear Family: Two Households, One Family." *Alternative Lifestyles* 2: 499-515.

———. 1980a. "Divorce: A Crisis of Family Transition and change." *Family Relations* 29: 533-40.

———. 1980b. "Joint Custody Arrangements in the Postdivorce Family." *Journal of Divorce* 3: 189-205.

———. 1980c. "Redefining the Divorced Family: A Conceptual Framework for Postdivorce Family Systems Reorganization." *Social Work* 25: 437-41.

———. 1981. "The Continuing Coparental Relationship between Divorced Spouses." *American Journal of Orthopsychiatry* 5: 415-28.

———. 1983. "Predictors of Paternal Involvement Postdivorce: Mothers' and Fathers' Perceptions." *Journal of Divorce* 6: 55-69.

Ahrons, Constance R., and Madonna E. Bowman. 1982. "Changes in Family Relationships Following Divorce of Adult Child: Grandmother's Perceptions." *Journal of Divorce* 6: 49-68.

Ahrons, Constance R., and Roy H. Rodgers. Forthcoming. *Divorced Families.* New York: W.W. Norton.

Ahrons, Constance R., and Lynne S. Wallisch. 1986. "The Relationship Between Spouses." *Intimate Relationships: Development, Dynamics, and Deterioration.* Eds. Steve Duck and Daniel Perlman. Beverly Hills, CA: Sage. 269-96.

Aldous, Joan. 1978. *Family Careers.* New York: John Wiley and Sons.

Anspach, Donald F. 1976. "Kinship and Divorce." *Journal of Marriage and the Family* 38: 323-30.

Bernard, Jessie. 1956. *Remarriage.* New York: Dryden.

Booth, Alan, David B. Brinkerhoff, and Lynn K. White. 1984. "The Impact of Parental Divorce on Courtship." *Journal of Marriage and the Family* 46: 85-94.

Bowman, Madonna E., and Constance R. Ahrons. 1985. "Impact of Legal Custody Status on Fathers' Parenting Postdivorce." *Journal of Marriage and the Family* 47: 481-88.

Broderick, Carlfred, and James Smith. 1979. "The General Systems Approach to the Family." Burr et al. 1979. 112-29.

Burr, Wesley R., et al. eds. 1979. *Contemporary Theories about the Family.* Vol. 1. New York: Free Press.

Cherlin, Andrew. 1978. "Remarriage as an Incomplete Institution." *American Journal of Sociology* 84: 634-50.

Cherlin, Andrew. 1981. *Marriage, Divorce, and Remarriage.* Cambridge, MA: Harvard University Press.

Furstenberg, Frank F., Jr. 1981. "Remarriage and Intergenerational Relations." *Aging: Stability and Change in the Family.* Eds. R.W. Fogel et al. New York: Academic. 115-42.

Goode, William J. 1956. *After Divorce.* Glencoe, IL: Free Press.

Hetherington, Eileen Mavis, Martha Cox, and Roger Cox. 1978. "The Aftermath of Divorce." *Mother-Child, Father-Child Relationships.* Eds. J.H. Stevens, Jr., and M. Matthews. Washington, DC: NAEYC. 149-76.

Hill, Charles, Zick Rubin, and Letitia Peplau. 1976. "Breakups Before Marriage: The End of 103 Affairs." *Journal of Social Issues* 32: 147–68.

Hunt, Morton M. 1966. *The World of the Formerly Married*. New York: McGraw-Hill.

Kalish, Richard A., and Emily Visher. 1982. "Grandparents of Divorce and Remarriage." *Journal of Divorce* 6: 127–40.

Keshet, Jamie Kelem. 1980. "From Separation to Stepfamily: A Sub-system Analysis." *Journal of Family Issues* 1: 517–32.

King, Charles E., and Andrew Christensen. 1983. "The Relationship Events Scale: A Guttman Scaling of Progress in Courtship." *Journal of Marriage and the Family* 45: 671–78.

McCubbin, Hamilton I., and Joan M. Patterson. 1983. "The Family Stress Process: The Double ABCX Model of Adjustment and Adaptation." *Social Stress and the Family: Advances and Developments in Family Stress Theory and Research*. Eds. Hamilton I. McCubbin, Marvin B. Sussman, and Joan M. Patterson. New York: Haworth. 7–37.

McGoldrick, Monica, and Elizabeth A. Carter. 1980. "Forming a Remarried Family." *The Family Life Cycle: A Framework for Family Therapy*. Eds. Elizabeth A. Carter and Monica McGoldrick. New York: Gardner. 265–94.

Mead, Margaret. 1970. "Anomalies in American Post-Divorce Relationships." *Divorce and After*. Ed. Paul Bohannan. Garden City, NY: Doubleday. 97–112.

Minuchin, Salvador. 1974. *Families and Family Therapy*. Cambridge, MA: Harvard University Press.

Peters, John F. 1976. "A Comparison of Mate Selection and Marriage in the First and Second Marriages in a Selected Sample of the Remarried Divorced." *Journal of Comparative Family Studies* 7: 483–90.

Price-Bonham, Sharon, and Jack O. Balswick. 1980. "The Noninstitutions: Divorce, Desertion, and Remarriage." *Journal of Marriage and the Family* 42: 959–72.

Rodgers, Roy H. 1986. "Post-Marital Reorganization of Family Relationships: A Propositional Theory." *Intimate Relationships: Development, Dynamics, and Deterioration*. Eds. Steve Duck and Daniel Perlman. Beverly Hills, CA: Sage. 239–68.

Spanier, Graham B., and Paul C. Glick. 1980. "Paths to Remarriage." *Journal of Divorce* 3: 283–98.

Walker, Kenneth N., and Lillian Messinger. 1979. "Remarriage After Divorce: Dissolution and Reconstruction of Family Bounda[ries]. [Family Process] 18: 185–92.

Walker, Libby, et al. 1979. "An Ann[otated] [Bib]liography of the Remarried, the Living [together] and Their Children." *Family Process* 193–212.

Wallerstein, Judy S., and Joan B. Kelly. 1979. "Children and Divorce: A Review." *Social Work* 24: 468–75.

Weiss, Robert S. 1979. *Going It Alone*. New York: Basic.

DY AND THE EMERGING
FAMILY*

Childrearing patterns are changing in North American families. Traditionally, the mother shouldered the major childrearing responsibilities while the father functioned primarily as the breadwinner. Insofar as the father had any clearly defined parental role, it was that of emergency disciplinarian and occasional "good-time Charlie." Good old Dad did not change diapers, feed infants, cook, or do any of "those" things. Even with two adults living in the home, the traditional family was, functionally speaking, a single-parent family.

An increasing number of fathers are now becoming active parents, and relishing the role. In the long run, a stronger and healthier two-parent family unit will undoubtedly emerge. In the short run, however, the change has brought problems. For both economic and social reasons, the emerging two-parent family also tends to be a two-career family. While this brings important benefits, it also brings new tensions. Combining full-time employment and full-time parenting can be a tremendous strain, one that, if not properly handled, can contribute to marital breakdown.

When the two-parent family does break down, estranged parents soon discover that our legal system has not kept pace with social change. Family law in most American states, and throughout Canada, is still based on the single-parent concept. Moreover, the single parent is usually assumed to be the mother.

The province of Saskatchewan even has a law entitled the Deserted Wives' and Children's Maintenance Act (not "spouses," only "wives"). Only four American states make joint custody the "presumptive disposition" for children of divorce. No Canadian province does (Japenga 1980, V:1–3; Poll 1981).

Eventually this will change. The head of the American Bar Association's Special Committee on Joint Custody has observed: "Legally, it's terrifying for a lot of lawyers and judges, but by the end of the 1980s it will be the rule rather than the exception" (Whicher 1979). The change may or may not happen that fast. Meanwhile, however, many children now being raised in two-parent families will, because of marital breakdown, be processed through a legal system still geared to the single-parent concept. Many are already undergoing this experience. To the families of these children, this is not a theoretical issue. It is an immediate and painful reality.

The Biases of the Existing Legal Vocabulary

Even a casual glance at the existing legal vocabulary shows something of the problem. Traditionally, one parent gets "custody," the other gets "access." The very word "access," used in this way, implies an inequality between the parents. It strips one parent of any responsibility or authority. Moreover, it makes the child into a form of property. ("Hey, Mom, can I have access to the car tonight?")

*The author acknowledges the assistance of David Geary.

Source: *Conciliation Courts Review*, 21, no. 1 (1983): 65–75. Reprinted by permission of the Association of Family and Conciliation Courts.

From the child's perspective, "access" is not something the parent needs, but something the child needs. Yet, when both parents have been performing caretaking and nurturing roles and developing strong emotional bonds with the child, it is difficult to say that the child needs greater "access" to one parent than to the other. Moreover, from the child's point of view, "access" implies not only a need to spend time with both parents, but a need to maintain the child–parent relationship with both. That relationship can only be truly maintained if both parents have responsibility and authority. As the director of the Family Relations Division for one Connecticut jurisdiction has observed, "in a majority of cases both parents are considered capable custodians and . . . the children in many such situations reveal attachment to both parents and a need for the *guidance and supervision* of each parent." (Salius 1979, B16: emphasis added). From a child-centred perspective, "access" implies not sole custody but joint custody.

In short, the legal vocabulary is not child-centred with respect to two-parent families. Another indication of this is found in the word "visiting." Traditionally, along with "custody" for one parent and "access" for the other, comes the notion that the child "lives" with one parent while the other has "visiting" rights. Again, the very word implies an inequality between the parents. When the two-parent family breaks down, however, available literature suggests that both parents usually provide a complete home environment for the child, including bedroom, clothes, books, toys, records, and so on. Moreover, the child usually spends a substantial amount of time, often averaging two nights a week or more, in each house (e.g., Roman and Haddad 1978, 123–48; Woolley 1979, 102–12; Galper 1980, 31–52). In such cases, the child has not one but two homes.

Behind the conventional vocabulary lurks the conventional wisdom that every child needs "a stable home." Indeed, every child needs at least one stable home. However, when the child has been raised by two par-

ents, and has developed strong emotional bonds with both, stability means preserving both those bonds intact. This means providing a stable home, a "live-in" relationship, with each parent.

Misusing King Solomon

Those resistant to the idea of two stable homes tend to argue that "two homes equal no home," and that unless the child spends a clear preponderance of time in one home, the child will be "torn in half." The highly coloured phrase "torn in half" evokes the biblical story of King Solomon's Wisdom; yet it completely misses the point of the story. The purpose of the King's strategy, in proposing that the infant be cut in half, was to expose the fact that one claimant was a real parent, the other a spurious parent. King Solomon, in short, was dealing with a one-parent situation.

Had he been dealing with a two-parent situation, the whole story would have been different. Had he suggested cutting the infant in half, genuine parents would both obviously have offered to give the child up. Then what? Indeed, had King Solomon been dealing with two genuine parents, joint custody might have become the norm thousands of years ago. As it stands, however, the story makes no sense when applied to a two-parent situation. It tells us nothing about what makes the child of a two-parent family feel "torn apart."

In fact, there is no statistical evidence whatsoever to support the claim that having two stable homes tears children apart. On the contrary, researchers who have worked extensively in the field report that what really tears children apart is the conflict between their parents. If the parents are at peace, the children are more likely to do well. If the parents are at war, the children are more likely to suffer.[1]

This does not mean that living arrangements are irrelevant. They are very important. A child who has strong bonds with both parents does not wish to be deprived of either.

If anything, it is the attempt to weaken one of those bonds that can truly cause the child to feel "torn apart." Preserving both bonds helps keep the child intact. As one researcher puts it, "When parents separate, this divides a child's loyalty. In order for the child *not* to feel 'torn' or to develop a disturbing inner conflict, he should have as much chance as possible to see both parents" (Ramos 1979, 145; cf. Woolley 1979, 24).

Available evidence suggests that children adapt much better to two homes than to being forcibly torn away from one parent. In their California study, Wallerstein and Kelly found that when children lived with only one parent, even when visits by the other parent were "at a level deemed 'reasonable,' . . . there was great dissatisfaction. . . . Aside from pleas to reunite their parents, the most pressing demand children brought to counselling was for more visiting." Roman and Haddad report similar findings. They quote one joint custody father as saying: "I think it is certainly more damaging for a child to have only minimal contact with one absent parent than it is to have two sets of clothes, books, and toys." Another father told them: "My kids don't visit, they *live* here, it's much more natural. The *other* way is unrealistic. *It* puts unrealistic pressure on parent and child to compress everything into five or six hours. I've seen it — the fathers walk the children in the park like dogs."

Living in two stable homes, moreover, is likely to decrease the problem of loyalty conflict. Woolley summarizes her findings thus:

Provided that each parent honours the other's right and responsibility to care for the youngsters, the question of divided loyalties simply doesn't come up; because each home is recognized as valid by both adults and children, there need be no conflict. Among the children I talked with or have read the comments of, having two separate homes is no problem. It is well established, understood, and accepted that each parent has authority in and over his or her home, and that they take turns or share in such things as teacher–parent conferences,

disciplinary problems, and outside activities and recreations.

This question of divided loyalties is much more likely to be present in the sole custody situation. (Woolley 1979, 199; cf. Wallerstein and Kelly 1980, 134; Roman and Haddad 1978, 119, 127)[2]

Postmarital conflict often includes one or both parents attempting to weaken the child's bond with the other. In such conflict, demands for unequal living arrangements can play a strategic role. Because the goal of weakening a child–parent bond is not a praiseworthy one, parents pursuing such a strategy are usually reluctant to admit, even to themselves, that this is what they are doing. Instead they rationalize the strategy. Wallerstein and Kelly describe "embittered-chaotic" parents who adopt a strategy of weakening the child's bond with the former spouse. "The intent, vigorously denied, of such embittered-chaotic mothers was to punish the father by destroying the father-child relationship."

When pressed, however, such parents are unable to present evidence that equal living arrangements are harmful to the child, since no such evidence exists. They also tend to resist the conclusion that it is the parental conflict itself that is damaging to the child. This is understandable, since it is their own demands for an unequal relationship that create the conflict. Such rationalization and resistance, however, only serve to perpetuate the conflict, thereby further damaging the child (Wallerstein and Kelly 1980, 134).

Time-Sharing and Custody: Which Comes First?

One of the least understood problems facing divorced families is the relationship between time-sharing and custody. Traditionally, custody decisions have been made first, and time-sharing arrangements have followed therefrom. Only recently have courts and family service workers begun to realize that it should be the other way around. In terms of the day-to-day practicalities of living arrangements, time-sharing is the most important issue with which former spouses must deal. Indeed, many if not most custody disputes come down to disputes over time-sharing. Logically, the time-sharing arrangements that should be made first, and then custody should be treated as a means of implementing those arrangements.

In the emerging two-parent family, postmarital stability with both parents generally implies at least roughly equal time. Moreover, the child's schedule should be arranged so as to maximize stability. Galper presents various schedules already in use. The point of each is to preserve the bonds with both parents (Galper 1980, 34–36, 91–92).

Equal living arrangements need not be identical living arrangements. The child's clothes, furnishings, books, toys, records, and so on will vary from one home to the other. Nor are equal living arrangements likely to spawn a destructive competition to purchase the child's favour. On the contrary, parental inequality is far more likely to result in such a competition, with one parent attempting to compensate for a reduced position while the other attempts to protect a privileged position. By contrast, parental equality frees the parents from the need to compete, and allows them to be more child-centred. Children with two stable homes quickly come to accept that in their two homes they have "some things the same, and some things different" (Galper 1980, 72–72; Woolley 1979, 199).[3]

While custody should logically be a means of implementing time-sharing arrangements most harmoniously, this does not mean it has no other function. Custody conveys both responsibility and authority. In postmarital situations, however, the demand for sole custody is often much more than a demand for sole responsibility and authority with respect to the child. It is a demand for power over the former spouse. Here traditional practice is especially unsuited to the two-parent family. With two actively involved parents, perpetuating a lopsided power relationship not only undercuts parental equality; it can be a powerful stimulus to conflict.

At this point, conventional vocabulary offers an apparent escape hatch. It is found in the word "reasonable." Sole custody and unequal living arrangements are all right for the two-parent family (or so the argument goes), so long as the noncustodial parent has "reasonable access" or "reasonable visiting rights." Yet what seems "reasonable" to one person often seems totally "unreasonable" to another. The mere insertion of a word does not automatically resolve the conflict. Indeed, it may postpone or even prevent a resolution, since, especially in the case of the two-parent family, it rests on unwarranted and dangerous assumptions.

Does Sole Custody Resolve Conflicts?

The first assumption is that sole custody is an effective means of conflict resolution. Here we confront a fundamental confusion in conventional legal thought. The purpose of custody is not to resolve parental conflicts; it is to ensure that someone is responsible for the child. Just as every child needs at least one stable home, so every child needs at least one responsible custodian. Yet, when both parents have been exercising responsibility and authority, and suddenly only one of them is permitted to do so, the result can be a disaster.

The assumption behind granting sole custody in a two-parent situation is that one parent will eventually have to submit to the other. Yet, with two actively involved and strongly committed parents, sole custody may simply set up a pattern of dictatorship and resistance. This may result in ongoing conflict and a "revolving door" situation in which the parents are constantly in and out of court, each claiming to be the more "reasonable." Again, such ongoing conflict does not benefit the child.

Researchers have not generally found that sole custody can turn an assertive noncustodial parent into a submissive one. As Roman and Haddad observe, "to the contrary, under sole custody we do not see that conflict is minimized. If anything, sole custody exacerbates parental conflict and the children are often used by the mother as a club." This accords with the findings of Woolley and Galper (Roman and Haddad 1978, 117; Woolley 1979, 141–42; Galper 1980, 184–88).

A second assumption, a corollary to the first, is that the court order will finally "settle" things. That is, the court order is itself a means of conflict resolution. Yet no court order, however detailed, can anticipate all situations. Indeed, the very inclusion of the word "reasonable" invites differing interpretations. Thus, without ever violating the court order, the noncustodial parent can continue to resist the sole authority of the custodial parent. Again the result may be an increase rather than a decrease in conflict. Wallerstein and Kelly point out: "There is also much evidence that such custody and visitation struggles, usually requiring several years to settle in court, have no end. They continue on within the family after the legal intervention has ended and are frequently back into court again within a year of what was to be the 'final' judgement." Recent studies indicate that joint custody awards return to court "less frequently than contested sole custody and visitation awards" (1980, 30; cf. Ernst and Altis 1981, 675). [4]

A third unsupported assumption, a corollary to the other two, is that people who cannot live together cannot co-operate after separating. That is, estranged parents cannot be "reasonable" with each other, therefore one of them must have final authority, tempered by the assurance that such authority will somehow be exercised in a "reasonable" way. Even though they cannot both be "reasonable" when sharing authority, one of them will be "reasonable" when monopolizing authority.

The assumption is not only illogical; it ignores the question of why parents cannot co-operate. In fact, parents frequently separate for reasons that have little or nothing to do with childrearing. With two-parent families in particular, the main source of postmarital conflict may be the inequality itself. Courts are constantly facing parents coming back to argue about distribution of the child's time. In such situations, the supposed solution is often the source of the problem. The most "reasonable" course may be to avoid creating the inequality in the first place.

Again recent research is instructive. Roman and Haddad note that "it is not uncommon for joint custody parents to frankly admit their antipathy toward one another but, at the same time, to maintain that they do not intend to harm their children just because they might like to harm one another." Here parental conflict also overlaps with the issue of parental role-modelling. A key strength of the emerging two-parent family is that it gives the child two active, wholesome role models. Parental equality in the postmarital period allows both parents to continue as role models, each within a stable home environment. By reducing conflict, equality also makes it less likely that the child will experience two role models who are constantly at war. Roman and Haddad found it "overwhelmingly the case that joint-custody couples show reduced conflict and their children are quite well adjusted." This accords with the findings of Abarbanel, Nehls, Woolley, and Galper. Inequality, by contrast, promotes conflict, making it more likely that the parents will be in a constant state of tension, and thus less able to set an example of "reasonableness." (Roman and Haddad 1978, 116; Abarbanel 1979, C17; Nehls 1979, C37; Woolley 1979, 199–207; Galper 1980, 187; and Poll 1981, 56).

In the case of the two-parent family, then, the conventional solution of "reasonable" sole custody can be seen to rest upon unwarranted and dangerous assumptions. The conventional solution, in short, is not a solution at all. Indeed, it is unwarranted to assume that the courts can actually impose a lasting solution. Perhaps all they can do is to provide incentives to greater or lesser co-operation.

How Current Practice Rewards Noncooperation

Here conventional wisdom is most tragically counterproductive. It is frequently argued that joint custody cannot work in contested cases. That is, joint custody cannot be imposed unless both parents agree.[5] But if one parent has a strong expectation of receiving sole custody, this very attitude gives that parent an overwhelming incentive to object to joint custody. It encourages that parent to say, in effect, "We can't co-operate; therefore I have to have total power." Indeed, it encourages that parent to be as uncompromising and unco-operative as possible, simply to prove the point. Conventional wisdom thus encourages greater conflict in two ways. It encourages the very inequality that is the source of conflict, and encourages one parent to behave in a way that makes imposition of the inequality more likely. In short, it rewards noncooperation.

In discussing joint custody, family court counsellors readily admit that they never see the uncontested cases, since these do not come to court. This only underlines the fact that when courts deny joint custody because of a parental objection, and in particular when they impose sole custody on a two-parent family, they are basing their decisions on the issue of parental conflict rather than on the child's relationship to the individual parents. When it is considered how counterproductive such efforts at conflict resolution usually are, it is hard to see how they could be less child-centred.[6]

This is especially true where objections to joint custody have nothing to do with the child. With separation and divorce often comes an emotional need to absolve oneself of blame for the marital breakdown. Demanding sole custody can be a way of justifying one's own behaviour while blaming the other parent. As Benedek and Benedek (1978) point out: "*Motives for seeking custody* may be conscious or unconscious, mixed, vague, even irrational. A parent may seek custody . . . to vindicate himself, or to emerge as a 'winner,'

or to make his spouse out as the 'bad guy" (p. 398). Wallerstein and Kelly (1980) found that "the embittered-chaotic parent was significantly more likely to turn to the court than his less angry counterparts. The desperate need to salvage shattered self-esteem and wreak vengeance on the offending spouse was most often an underlying motive for such battles, now given status and legitimacy by court ritual" (p. 30).

By contrast, acceptance of joint custody implicitly relieves one's spouse of blame. This may be motivation enough to prompt an objection to joint custody. However, if joint custody can be undermined by any objection at all, it does not matter that the objection is unrelated to the child. The court may not intend to award custody of a child as compensation for perceived marital injury; yet this may nonetheless be the unintended result. In such cases, the child is actually being used as a pawn.[7]

Most important, current practice fails to take into account the effect of the custody order itself on the child's life. Wallerstein and Kelly observe: "The structure itself sets the broad limits for what transpires between parent and child during the years that follow" (1980, 121). In the same vein, Stack points out: "It is plausible that the welfare of children of divorced parents is more dependent upon the effect of a custody decision on the ongoing relationships between the parents and the possibility for ongoing relationships between parents and children than on a final decision that can effectively terminate the relationship between the noncustodial parent and the child" (1976, 511). By objecting to joint custody, even for trivial reasons, an uncooperative parent can nonetheless adversely effect the child's entire future.

Behind all this, however, still lurks the fear that co-operation cannot be imposed, and that joint custody is therefore an invitation to perpetual conflict. Again the problem may lie in overestimating the actual power of the courts. Perhaps the issue is not one of imposing co-operation, but of providing less incentive to noncooperation. The former may well be beyond the power of the courts; the latter is certainly within their purview. Moreover, it must always be kept in mind that acquiescence may be no easier to impose than co-operation.

The "Catch-22" Objection to Joint Custody

Even so, many courts remain reluctant to depart from conventional practice. Despite growing evidence of its unsuitability to two-parent families, they prefer to adhere to such practice, at least until some other jurisdiction has taken the risk of "innovation." This means, however, that the reluctant court never accumulates new evidence within its own jurisdiction. In essence, it sets up a "catch-22" with respect to joint custody, saying in effect: "We never award joint custody in contested cases because we don't know if it will work; and we don't know if it will work because we never award joint custody in contested cases."

Not all courts are equally reluctant. Galper tells how, partly on the basis of her testimony, a Pennsylvania judge broke new ground in his jurisdiction by ordering joint custody over the objection of one parent. In an appendix to Galper's book (1980, 182, 185), lawyer Lynne Gold-Bikin notes that she has had "a number of clients who have joint custody — some have worked it out between themselves, while others have had it imposed by a wise judiciary." More recently, in a landmark Canadian case, the Manitoba Court of Appeal upheld an order for joint legal custody and divided physical custody despite the objection of the mother.[8] Significantly, the Court stated with respect to joint legal custody, not that the parents were already co-operating, but that they seemed "able to co-operate." Such instances, however, are still far rarer than the "catch-22" approach.

Again, the effect of the "catch-22" approach can only be to encourage noncooperation on the part of a parent who expects to receive sole custody. In such circumstances, a stand-pat approach may be far riskier than cautious "innovation." Indeed, from the child's perspective, the real "innovation" may lie in being torn away from one parent. As Galper suggests, "Having two homes allows for *more* continuity in the child's relationships with his parents" (1980, 88: emphasis in original).

Does Joint Custody Require More Interparent Contact Than Sole Custody?

One objection often raised concerning joint custody is that it forces former spouses to have much greater contact than does sole custody. As one sceptical mother put it, "It's too much like being married." Where time-sharing has been worked out before the custody decision, however, this objection is largely obviated. As long as the child's schedule is clear and consistent, there is no need for constant negotiation. This underlines the importance of arranging time-sharing first and custody afterwards.

As in sole-custody families, joint-custody parents must still be in contact in case of emergencies, or to discuss health and school problems and the like. Such contacts, however, are far easier once conflicts over time-sharing have been eliminated. Decisions as to where the child goes to school can be made annually (and in most cases even less frequently), through mediation or arbitration if necessary.

Most important, on a day-to-day basis, joint-custody parents tend to lead separate lives and make separate decisions just as do sole-custody parents. Especially where both former spouses have been actively parenting since the child's birth, and have set up complete, independent, and stable home environments for the child, day-to-day contact between parents becomes unnecessary.

Nor must former spouses necessarily feel cordial toward each other. As Galper points out:

I know many people who have divorced, can't stand each other, and manage to work out joint custody. What they have learned is that it is in their children's best interests for them to get out of the way and allow their children to be close to the other parent. If they can't talk to each other enough to work that out, they can use friends, relatives, or lawyers. Interaction can be minimal and on a specific schedule. A child's relationship is too important — precious really — to be dictated by whether or not those parents can maintain a civil relationship with one another. (1980, 187)[9]

The key lies in the structuring of the situation. The clearer the structure, the less chance there is for built-in conflict. A well-structured parental equality provides a much firmer basis for allowing former spouses to "let go" of each other than does an unequal, relatively unstructured arrangement. If anything, it is the demand for unequal time and sole custody that may signal an unacknowledged wish to retain power over a former spouse and thereby perpetuate an emotional relationship after the marriage has ended.

Are Children Luggage?

At this point, proponents of sole custody invariably fall back on one argument. Supposing one parent wishes to relocate: would not joint custody deny that parent's right to freedom of movement? Again we see how non-child-centred conventional wisdom really is. Certainly both parents should be free to live where they choose. The child, however, is not part of either's luggage. A child-centred approach would suggest that the paramount right is the child's right to an ongoing, nurturing relationship with both parents. Under joint custody, if either parent wishes to relocate, both parents have an obligation to work out an arrangement that preserves the child's bonds with each. This can be done through arbitration if necessary. Joint custody, in short, makes it less likely that the child's bond with one parent will simply be disregarded.

In Canada, the courts are more frequently upholding joint custody awards, even where the parents have chosen to live thousands of miles apart.[10]

Sole custody, by contrast, has a distinct disadvantage in such situations. If tension between estranged parents becomes sufficiently high, sole custody makes it easier for the custodial parent to relocate as a way of fleeing the tension. While superficially attractive, in the case of a two-parent family this may be a tragically false solution. It not only forcibly uproots the child in the short run, but may set the stage for a backlash against the custodial parent in the long run. Moreover, if the noncustodial parent is likewise able to relocate, the conflict may merely be transferred to a new locale, where family, friends, and other support figures are not readily available. Joint custody does not give either parent judicial incentive to pursue such a course of action (Galper 1980, 116–18; Woolley 1979, 203–205).[11]

Should Children Be Forced to Take Sides?

The key is to keep all arrangements as child-centred as possible. Here again parental equality has a distinct advantage over inequality. One of the most destructive aspects of post-marital discord is that it can force the child to take sides, even though this is the last thing the child wishes to do. When parental inequality is imposed, sooner or later the child becomes aware of it, and begins to question it. If the inequality has engendered conflict, as it is likely to do in a two-parent situation, the child almost invariably becomes enmeshed in it.

Predictably, the custodial parent will view the child's involvement as a passing stage that the child will leave behind, provided that the noncustodial parent does not encourage or perpetuate the conflict. In two-parent situations, however, it cannot be assumed that the noncustodial parent will give up that easily. Available evidence suggests that such conflicts can go on for years, and that children become more torn apart as they get older. Just as the literature indicates that children go on trying to reunite their parents for years, long after both parents have lost interest, so it indicates that the child's need for two close relationships may persist regardless of anything the parents do or do not do.

Here Wallerstein and Kelly furnish important evidence. They found that many children "formed strong, and often long-lasting, alignments with one parent against the other. . . . The life span of these alignments appeared related to custodial arrangements." At the same time, "Within the postdivorce family, the relationship between the child and both original parents did not diminish in emotional importance to the child over the five years. . . . It has been, in fact, strikingly apparent through the years that whether or not the children maintained frequent or infrequent contact with the noncustodial parent, the children would have considered the term 'one parent family' a misnomer. Their self-images were firmly tied to their relationship with both parents and they thought of themselves as children with two parents who had elected to go their separate ways" (1980, 77–78, 307).

In this regard the child of divorce faces an especially cruel dilemma. If the conflict persists, the child is forced to take sides. If one parent gives up and eventually fades away, the child may feel betrayed, disillusioned, and abandoned. The long-term result may be an adult behaviour pattern in which personal relationships consist of a desperate attempt to recapture the lost parent figure. Only through ongoing parental equality is the child spared the destructive consequences of either an unwanted choice or an equally unwanted abandonment.

Again Wallerstein and Kelly provide key evidence. After five years, 39 percent of the children in their study felt "rejected and unloved" by the father. "Furthermore," they add, "there is evidence in our findings, that lacking legal rights to share in decisions about major aspects of their children's lives, many noncustodial parents withdrew from their children in grief and frustration. Their with-drawal was experienced by the children as a rejection and was detrimental in its impact" (1980, 211, 310).[12]

Allowing Children to Choose Both Parents

There is general agreement in the literature that children should not become unnecessarily involved in the custody process. The reason for this is that the children are best spared the burden of making a choice. Yet, this premise is rarely carried to its logical conclusion. Most children would indeed prefer not to choose between their parents. Stated positively, most would choose both parents if they could. Yet the present system is set up so as to deny most children this option. As Woolley points out:

Recent studies with infants indicate that, given the opportunity for close contact, very young babies recognize and respond to mother *and* father more or less equally. Certainly the idea that small children relate better to the mother than to the father appears to be a reflection of our cultural practice rather than any innate preference. . . . Yet our present system of child custody completely overlooks the fact that the children have already established complex and vital bonds with *each* parent.

For children old enough to articulate their feelings, a key issue may be whether or not they have clearly internalized the concept of two homes. This can only be determined, however, by being sensitive to the child's own statements. (Woolley 1979, 23).[13]

This, in turn, raises the issue of how the child's views are to be ascertained. It need not involve subjecting the child to cross-examination on the witness stand. Nor need it even involve interviewing the child in the judge's chambers, though that would probably be less stressful to the child. It may merely mean taking account of the child's statements as expressed during the custody investigation, or hearing the parents' statements as to the child's views, provided both parents agree as to the authenticity of such statements. The key point, however, is that since postmarital parental equality is the one solution that allows the child to choose both parents without taking sides against either, every effort should be made to ascertain the child's genuine feelings in the matter.

Evidence suggests, moreover, that children tend to be quite straightforward in such matters. Abarbanel quotes a young child's view of living in two houses: "That's fair because mommy and daddy love them" (qtd. Roman and Haddad 1978, 141). Woolley quotes an 11-year-old who told her, "Thank goodness my parents love me enough to let me love both of them" (1979, 28). And Roman and Haddad quote one teenager as saying, "The best thing of all is we haven't had to choose between our parents, but have a real everyday life with each of them" (1978, 70).[14]

Recent Developments

Times are slowly changing. Most existing legislation still both assumes and reinforces the idea of postmarital parental conflict. Thus a 1970 Michigan law refers to the "love, affection and other emotional ties existing between *competing* parties and the child" (Ramos 1979, 37: emphasis added). Even so, more and more legislative assemblies are at least considering establishing a presumption in favor of joint custody. The California amendment, which became effective on January 1, 1980, establishes a conditional presumption in that direction, and also declares that "it is the public policy of this state to assure minor children of close and continuing contact with both parents after the parents have separated or dissolved their marriage" (Poll 1981, 57–58). The literature on joint custody has grown enormously in recent years. In addition, in such decisions as the Manitoba case of *Fontaine v. Fontaine*,[15] the courts are now refusing to reward noncooperation, and are beginning to move beyond the "catch-22" objection to joint-custody.[16]

That further legislative change will eventually be forthcoming seems clear. In the interim, as various cases in both Canada and the United States indicate, most courts have the authority to act even in the absence of explicit joint-custody legislation. What is needed, in advance of such legislation, is a change in attitude, a questioning of old biases and assumptions, and in particular an ability to think not in terms of "access" or "visiting" but in terms of time-sharing between two stable homes.

Above all, what is needed is a willingness to entertain the two-parent concept as worthy of encouragement in the postmarital period. Parental inequality, based on unequal time-sharing and sole custody, is profoundly dissonant with that concept. Parental equality, including equal time-sharing and joint custody, is profoundly in harmony with it.

Notes

1. For criticism of the idea of two stable homes, see Westman (1979, B40); Ramos (1979, 90); Law Reform Commission of Saskatchewan (1979, 41). An older, much-criticized work by Goldstein, Freud, and Solnit, *Beyond the Best Interests of the Child* (1973) does not even address the issue of two homes. The authors simply assume one psychological parent and one home, and indeed argue (p. 38) that "the noncustodial parent should have

5. This argument is made by Salius (1979, B17), Ramos (1979, 94–95), Ernst and Altis (1981, 674), and the Saskatchewan Law Reform Commission (1979, 46). It is challenged by Galper (1980, 184–85) and by Stack (1976, 515).

6. Interviews with family court counsellors, Unified Family Court, Saskatoon, Saksatchewan, January-April 1982. See also Woolley (1979, 141); Elkin (1977, 55); Gaddis (1978).

7. See also the Saskatchewan Law Reform Commission Report (1979, 8): "At present, children are all too often pawns in the matrimonial war between their parents." However, the authors overlook parental equality as a possible solution.

8. *Fontaine v. Fontaine* (1980), 18 R.F.L. (2d) 239 (Man. C.A.).

9. This was confirmed in interviews with sole-custody and joint-custody parents, Saskatoon, Saskatchewan, January–June, 1982.

10. For recent Canadian decisions, see *Groom v. Groom and Monty* (1979), 10 R.F.L. (2d) 257 and *Berard v. Berard* (1979) 10 R.F.L. (2d) 371.

11. For material indicating that joint custody also eases the transition to remarriage for parents and children alike, see Greif and Simring (1982).

12. See also Woolley, (1979, 25); Hetherington (1974); and Hetherington, Cox and Cox (1977). For the story of one father's protracted (and ultimately successful) fight to maintain contact with his children, see Peacock (1982).

13. See also Lamb (1977).

14. For further data on children's own views, see Watson (1981, 478).

15. See note 8 above.

16. An excellent review of recent custody literature is provided in Folberg and Graham (1981, 71–122).

Works Cited

barbanel, Alice. 1979. "Shared Parenting After paration and Divorce: A Study of Joint Cus-" Milne.

Richard S., and Elissa P. Benedek. 1978. and the Divorce Court Worker." ts Help Their Children Ed. Eugene ork: Brunner, Mazel.

"Postdivorce Counseling in " Journal of Divorce 1(1).

h Altis. 1981 "Joint Cus- Not By Law But By : 669–77.

Fineberg, Anita. 1979 "Joint Custody of Infants: Breakthrough or Fad?" *Canadian Journal of Family Law* 2: 417–54.

Folberg, H. Jay, and Marva Graham. 1981. "Joint Custody of Children Following Divorce." *Family Law: An Interdisciplinary Perspective* Ed. Howard H. Irving. Toronto: Carswell.

Gaddis, Stephen M. 1978 "Joint Custody of Children: A Divorce Decision-Making Alternative." *Conciliation Courts Review* 16(1): 19.

Galper, Miriam. 1980. *Joint Custody and Co-Parenting: Sharing Your Child Equally.* Philadelphia: Running Press.

Goldstein, Joseph, Anna Freud, and Albert J. Solnit. 1973. *Beyond the Best Interests of the Child.* New York: Free Press.

Greif, Judith. 1979a. "Fathers, Children, and Joint Custody." *American Journal of Orthopsychiatry* 49 (April): 311–19.

———. 1979b. "Joint Custody: A Sociological Study," *Trial* 15 (May): 32–65.

Greif, Judith, and Sue Klavans Simring. 1982. "Remarriage and Joint Custody." *Conciliation Courts Review* 20(1): 9–14.

Hetherington, E. Mavis. 1974. "Girls Without Fathers." *Psychology Today* (June).

Hetherington, E. Mavis, Martha Cox and Roger Cox. 1977. "Divorced Fathers." *Psychology Today* (April).

Japenga, Ann. 1980. "Joint Custody Bill: Family Balancing Act." *Los Angeles Times* (June 9).

Lamb, Michael. 1977. "Father-Infant and Mother-Infant Interaction in the First Year of Life." *Child Development* 48(1): 167–81.

Law Reform Commission of Saskatchewan. 1979. *Tentative Proposals for Custody Law Reform. Part I: Substantive Law.* Saskatoon: Law Reform Commission.

Milne, Ann, ed. 1979. *Joint Custody: A Handbook for Judges, Lawyers, and Counsellors.* Fort Lauderdale: Association of Family and Conciliation Courts.

Nehls, Nadine M. 1979. "Joint Custody of Children: A Descriptive Study." Milne.

Peacock, Donald. 1982. *Listen To Their Tears.* Vancouver: Douglas and McIntyre.

Poll, Edward. 1981. "The Evolution of Joint Custody." *Conciliation Courts Review* 19(2): 53–59.

Ramos, Suzanne. 1979. *The Complete Book of Child Custody.* New York: G.P. Putnam's Sons.

Ricci, Isolina. 1976. "Dispelling the Stereotype of the 'Broken Home'." *Conciliation Courts Review* 12(2).

Roman, Mel, and William Haddad. 1978. *The Disposable Parent: The Case for Joint Custody*. New York: Holt, Rinehart and Winston.

Salfi, Dominick, and Nina Cassady. 1982. "Who Owns This Child? Shared Parenting Before and After Divorce." *Conciliation Courts Review* 20(1).

Salius, Anthony. 1979. "Joint Custody." Milne.

Stack, Carol B. 1976. "Who Owns the Child? Divorce and Child Custody Decisions in Middle-Class Families." *Social Problems* 23(4): 505–15.

Wallerstein, Judith, and Joan Berlin Kelly. 1980. *Surviving the Breakup: How Children and Parents Cope With Divorce*. New York: Basic.

Watson, Mary Ann. 1981. "Custody Alternatives: Defining the Best Interests of the Children." *Family Relations* 30 (July): 474–79.

Westman, Jack. 1979. "Joint Custody from the Child's Point of View." Milne..

Woolley, Persia. 1979. *The Custody Handbook*. New York: Summit.

ΛN OPTION FOR
ΛMILIES

Background

Over the past decade, many judges, lawyers, mental-health professionals, and disputing spouses have become disillusioned with the adversarial approach to resolving family disputes. Unlike other civil-litigation cases, in which the disputants go their separate ways after an adversarial court battle, parents must continue to co-operate in the interests of their children for years following the court proceeding. Recent research has shown that children are the innocent victims of family breakdown, and the more intense the parental conflict following separation, the more likely that the children will be torn apart by a conflict of loyalties over their parents (Wallerstein 1985, 116). Also, the more adversarial the struggle to end the marriage, the more difficult it is for parents to work co-operatively in the future (Folberg and Taylor 1984; also see Irving and Benjamin 1987, particularly Chapter 10, "Shared Parenting: Evidence and Implications," 193).

Mediation is a method of dispute resolution which has as its objective a co-operative, voluntary and equitable outcome to a conflict. Agreement is reached by the parties themselves with the assistance of an impartial professional. The emphasis on improved communication and co-operation between the parties is attractive to the legal profession, the mental-health profession, and parents because a mediated solution is likely to be honoured

Source: *Advocate Quarterly* Vol 9. No. 1 (February 1988): Reprinted with the permission of the author and Canada Law Books Inc., Aurora, Ontario.

(Pearson and Thoennes 1985, 451), tension between the parties usually diminishes, and the children benefit from a more meaningful relationship with both parents (Kelly 1987; also see Wallerstein and Kelly 1980). Over the past several years mediation has attracted considerable interest as an alternative to litigation, particularly for disputes involving children. Recently, Mr. Justice Zuber examined the court structure in Ontario (Zuber 1987) and recommended the use of mediation for resolving a wide range of legal disputes, particularly for conflicts arising out of marriage breakdown.

Before we can discuss meaningfully the process or procedures used in mediation it is important to consider the historical context for dealing with family law disputes, the perceived problems with the approach of the past, and then how and why mediation emerged as an alternative approach for assisting separated spouses.

Family Law: Toward a Nonadversarial Approach

The history of family law for the past century reflects an enormous social change; a change in our traditions, our values, and our cultural mores. As our assumptions about the family, the permanence of marriage and the role of mothers and fathers change, so do the laws and the legal procedures for handling family problems.

In the past, the primary social objective of family law was to preserve marriage and, therefore, divorce was either prohibited or socially shunned. Until recently, divorce was granted only on fault-oriented grounds. For example, in Canada, until 1968, virtually the only ground for divorce was adultery. The courts showed their disapproval of marriage breakdown by inflicting a punitive consequence on the party who was guilty of destroying the marriage. The guilty party was usually denied custody of the children and received limited or no access. In addition, the criteria for obtaining support or custody of the children were not based on present-day concepts of fairness and equity, but rather were tied in with moralistic judgments and judicial restribution. If the "guilty party" were a man, he would usually be obligated to pay support indefinitely, regardless of the wife's needs; a wife who committed a single act of adultery could lose support for life.

Because of the very serious consequences of divorce both in the courts and in terms of society's reaction, family law cases were handled in an intensely adversarial manner. The objective of each lawyer was to present his client as morally pure and blameless, while alleging immoral conduct by the other spouse. Private detectives and lawyers were the principal beneficiaries of the highly polarized morality plays that were staged in the courtroom.

Present-day family laws reflect the change in social attitudes to marriage breakdown. In the first place, the law no longer provides strong protection for marriage or a bulwark against divorce — but rather reflects the concept that adults should be free to choose whether or not to remain in the marital union (Divorce Act 1985). Fault is no longer a necessary ingredient for being granted a divorce and support and custody are no longer used as part of the social sanction against divorce.

Today the laws are far less arbitrary and reflect such concepts of equity and fairness as "marriage is a social and economic partnership." This means that the economic product of the marriage should be shared between the spouses at the time of breakdown. Custody decisions are based on the needs or best interests of children and economic support is

determined on the basis of financial need and ability to pay, with conduct explicitly excluded as a criterion.

With the change from a moralistic, fault-finding approach to a less judgmental legal framework, the procedures in family law cases have also shifted considerably. Today, the emphasis is on negotiation, pretrial conferences, mediation of matrimonial disputes, and other techniques designed to assist couples to reach an early resolution of the issues in dispute. Particularly where children are involved, the courts and the legislatures now seem to understand that, while the spousal relationship may come to an end, the need to continue in a co-operative framework for the sake of children may continue for many years. An adversarial procedure leads to bitterness and hostility and undermines the necessary co-operation required for parenting.

Clinical research has demonstrated the need for parents to co-operate in the interests of their children and it has also demonstrated that divorce is a complex clinical problem with individuals going through stages that are somewhat similar to a grieving process (Kübler-Ross 1975; also see Wallerstein 1983, 230). The research of Drs. Wallerstein and Kelly (Wallerstein and Kelly 1980, footnote 4) that followed 60 families over a ten-year period documents the long-term emotional repercussions on both parents and children. Litigation exacerbates and prolongs the emotional strain on all parties and, therefore, nonadversarial alternatives are being encouraged to limit the harmful emotional consequences of marriage breakdown.

Further impetus for changing the procedure in family law cases has come from the enormous increase in the number of divorces in recent years, the backlog of cases in the courts, the escalating expense of family law litigation, as well as the tremendous increase in the number of children affected by marriage breakdown. It is estimated that approximately 1.5 million children in the United States each year experience separation. To deal with the problem, a number of jurisdictions in the United States, for example, California, Michigan, Utah, and Maine, have reduced trial lists by requiring at least one meeting with a mediator prior to litigating custody and access issues. In Canada, mediation can be ordered or arranged on consent in most provinces and, in the family courts of Winnipeg and Edmonton, couples routinely attend at least one mediation session prior to litigating custody and access issues.

In summary, the chief precursors to mediation include the shift from fault-oriented to no-fault divorce, the greater increase in numbers of people divorcing, the exorbitant costs of a divorce, the emotional strain for both adults and children, and the long delays in the court process that keep people's lives in limbo for several years prior to litigating their family law matters.

Legislation

Recent legislative amendments, both provincial and federal, have stimulated the use of mediation in family law cases. This legislation has served to heighten awareness among both lawyers and the general public as to the availability of mediation as an option to be considered prior to resorting to litigation. Set out below are some examples of both federal and provincial legislation with respect to mediation.

Federal Legislation

The Divorce Act, 1985, s.c. 1986, c. 4
Section 9(2) requires lawyers to advise their clients to consider mediating any issues in dispute (including custody and child and spousal support) prior to litigating these issues. Lawyers must also inform clients about mediation services that are available in the community. Every lawyer assisting a client to commence a divorce proceeding must sign an affidavit certifying that he or she has carried out the obligations set out in s. 9.

Ontario Legislation

The Children's Law Reform Act, R.S.O. 1980, c. 68
Section 31 (enacted 1982, c. 20, s. 1) permits the courts to order mediation at the request of the parties to resolve custody and access disputes. The mediator must consent to being appointed and must agree to file a report with the court within a time period specified by the court.

Before beginning the mediation, the parties must decide whether they wish "open mediation" or "closed mediation." The difference between open mediation and closed mediation arises in cases where the parties fail to reach agreement. In closed mediation, if the parties fail to reach agreement on one or more issues, the mediator can state only that the parties failed to reach agreement on one or more issues. If the parties elect open mediation and they fail to reach agreement on one or more issues, the mediator may file a full report on the mediation, including anything that the mediator considers relevant to the issues being mediated. In both open and closed mediation, if the parties succeed in reaching an agreement, the mediator prepares a report setting out the agreement reached.

The mediator is required to file his or her report with the clerk or registrar of the court and give a copy of the report to each of the parties and to counsel, if any, representing the child.

If the parties have agreed to closed mediation, then evidence of anything said or any admission or communication made in the course of the mediation is not admissible in any proceeding except with the consent of all parties to the proceeding in which the mediation order was made. It should be noted that the statutory obligation to report cases of child abuse (pursuant to s. 68 of the Child and Family Services Act, 1984, S.O. 1984, c. 55) would supersede the statutory privilege under s. 31 of the Children's Law Reform Act.

The court must require the parties to pay the fees and expenses of the mediator and must set out in the order the proportions to be paid by each party.

Family Law Act, 1986, S.O. 1986, c. 4

Section 3 permits the court to order mediation on the consent of the parties for resolving disputes involving property division, child and spousal support, and custody of and access to children. The provisions of this statute are similar to the court-ordered mediation under s. 31 of the Children's Law Reform Act, as described above. This statute expands the scope of mediation beyond custody and access issues and envisions what has been called "comprehensive mediation," that is, the mediation of both financial matters and issues related to children.

Rules of the Unified Family Court

Rules 20 and 21 of the Rules of Practice and Procedure, R.R.O. 1980, Reg. 939, governing the Unified Family Court in Hamilton, provide that, as soon as reasonably possible after proceedings have been commenced, the presiding judge shall inquire whether or not there have been attempts made to resolve or narrow the issues in dispute. In order to resolve or narrow the issues, the judge, at any stage in the proceeding, may convene a meeting of the parties with the judge or with a person designated by the court for this purpose.

The person before whom a meeting is convened is required to present to the parties, for their approval in writing, a memorandum setting out the matters agreed upon by the parties at their meeting. The person shall file the memorandum with the court unless the parties file a consent to a final order that disposes of all issues. That is, the court may order the parties to attend either a pretrial conference or a meeting with a mediator and the purpose of the meeting is to arrive at a settlement or to narrow the issues in dispute.

Manitoba Legislation

The Queen's Bench Act, R.S.M. 1970, c. C280, s. 52(4) (rep. and sub. 1984–85, c. 3, s. 3),

permits the judge or master of the Manitoba Court of Queen's Bench (Family Division), at any stage of the proceedings to refer any of the issues in dispute to a conciliation officer or to any other person agreed to and engaged by the parties.

The conciliation officer is required to attempt to resolve the issues in dispute but, where he or she concludes that a settlement cannot be reached, he or she reports to the court that the case is ready for trial.

In Manitoba, the legislation provides for closed mediation unless the parties otherwise consent. It appears that legislation in Manitoba does not permit the conciliation officer to submit a report, even in cases where a settlement is reached unless the parties consent to such a report being prepared and submitted to the court.

British Columbia Legislation

The Family Relations Act, R.S.B.C. 1979, c. 121, s. 3, permits the court to appoint a family court counsellor for the purpose of resolving family law issues that are in dispute.

The family court counsellor is authorized under the legislation to offer the parties to the dispute any advice and guidance that he believes will assist in resolving the dispute.

As with the Manitoba legislation, the Family Relations Act protects information from disclosure in mediation cases unless the parties consent otherwise.

In Ontario, Manitoba, and British Columbia, where matters are not resolved prior to trial, either through mediation or negotiations, the judge may order an assessment or family investigation to determine the best interests of children in cases where custody of or access to children is disputed. Custody assessments can be ordered whether or not the parties consent and negative inferences may be drawn if the parties refuse to participate. The assessor's report must be submitted to court and an order can be made requiring the parties to pay the fees and expenses of the assessor, in such proportions as the court sees fit.

The Mediation Process: Objectives

Private Ordering

Mediation is a process whereby an impartial professional, usually a mental-health professional, but sometimes a lawyer, helps the parties negotiate a voluntary settlement of the issues in dispute. The mediator does not act on behalf of either party and does not impose a settlement but rather acts as an impartial facilitator, an educator, and a communicator who helps parties clarify issues, identify and deal with feelings, and generate options in order to arrive at a mutually acceptable settlement without the need for an adversarial court battle. The objective, particularly in custody and access mediation, is to find a solution that is in the best interests of the children and within the capabilities of the parents. The emphasis is on private ordering through a co-operative process, not on winning or losing.

In litigation, decision-making is delegated to an external authority, namely a judge. Judges are finders of fact and function at their best when their judgments are based on factual or legal disputes. However, family law matters are not primarily factual or legal in nature. On the contrary, most family law conflicts centre around feelings such as lost self-esteem, anger, betrayal, and disappointed expectations. These are not the types of issues that lend themselves to judicial decision-making. Research has shown that when parties take responsibility for negotiating their own settlement, there is likely to be greater compliance, a reduction in tension and a reduction in frequency of relitigation (Pearson and Theonnes 1985, footnote 3; also Irving and Benjamin 1987, footnote 2, particularly Chapter 12).

Lasting Agreement

A key difference between family law disputes and other types of disputes is that parties to the former type will continue to have an ongoing relationship even after a settlement is reached or a court order made. This is particularly true where children are involved. For this reason, the important goal is not merely to reach a settlement, but rather to reach a settlement that lasts. To achieve this goal, the mediator tries to ensure that the settlement is fair to both parties, and that the significant needs and concerns have been addressed in the process. Mediation is often described as interest-based negotiation (Fisher and Ury 1981).

In addition, successful mediation usually incorporates a mechanism for change so that any agreement can be adapted flexibly to changes in life circumstances such as the remarriage or relocation of a parent, or changes in the children's needs as they grow older. A lasting solution must also take into account the external pressures on the parties from, for example, new partners, extended family members, financial factors, work situations, and the expectations of their solicitors. The interests of all those affected are more easily addressed in mediation than in litigation.

The adversarial system has very different objectives, procedures, and usually long-term effects when compared to mediation. In the adversarial system, the lawyer is a partisan combatant and is under no obligation to present information or to consider the interests of anyone other than the client who retains him. The effect on others, such as children or grandparents, and the effect on the long-term relationship between the parties is not the concern of the lawyer. The lawyer's only focus is on obtaining the best result in court.

Education Regarding the Effects of Separation and Divorce

A third objective of custody mediation is to educate parents about the effects of separation and divorce on their children. Research has shown that, at the time of separation or divorce, most parents are so caught up in their own loss of self-esteem, grief, and anger that it is difficult for them to focus on the needs of their children and maintain an adequate standard of parenting. This diminished parenting capacity comes at a time when the children need their parents the most (Wallerstein 1986; also see Ricci 1981).

In addition to their own psychological trauma, parents often lack adequate information as to how their children are likely to react or how they should respond when making parenting decisions. The lack of communication between the parents at this point often creates additional confusion and uncertainty for the children and maximizes the possibility of distrust, suspicion, and increased hostility among family members.

The mediator can assist parents by providing information about child development and the usual responses of children to separation and divorce at different ages. The mediator acts as an important role model by describing the children's needs and behaviour in a non-judgemental way, avoiding the assignment of blame. In mediation, the parents are encouraged to discuss concerns with respect to the children and arrive at a constructive solution, rather than blame the other parent for behaviour problems that the children may display (Landau, Bartoletti, and Mesbur 1987; also see Goldstein 1982).

As a result, parents are more likely to adopt a co-operative approach to parenting, which includes the sharing of important information with respect to the children, consulting each other with respect to discipline problems, health care, and emotional needs, and participating in parenting responsibilities such as taking the children to doctors' appointments and to recreational activities. In mediation, the focus is on improving the quality of parenting by encouraging parents to respond constructively to their children's needs rather than destructively to their own needs. This educative function and co-operative approach are clearly missing from litigation which seems to fuel a desire for revenge and to exacerbate a climate of mistrust.

Improved Communication Between Parents

A fourth objective of mediation is to improve the parents' ability to communicate about parenting issues so that they can resolve issues more successfully on their own in the future. During the process, the mediator encourages parents to adopt more appropriate techniques such as effective listening skills, asking for clarification (rather than making personal attacks), making positive self-statements about desired future behaviour (rather than blaming the other parent for past behaviour), and recognizing and encouraging co-operative behaviour in the other parent.

In an adversarial process, clients are usually advised not to speak directly to each other but rather to communicate through their lawyers. This tends to widen the gulf between the parties and to make ongoing communication about parenting issues more difficult. Following a trial, parties tend to be even more polarized and communication may be permanently disrupted, a result that has long-term negative consequences for children.

Encouraging Behavioural Changes

One of the most significant aspects of mediation, in contrast to litigation, is that it is future-oriented. Where litigation attempts to reach a just result based on the merits of past behaviour, mediation focusses on each party's willingness to make commitments about changing behaviour in the future. Mediation focusses on what parties would like to have happen, and what they are willing to do now and in the future to achieve that result. Custody litigation requires that parents focus on each other's weaknesses, whereas mediation attempts to identify and encourage strengths that are relevant to parenting. It is this fundamental difference in outlook that makes mediation particularly appropriate where parties have to maintain a relationship following the court proceeding.

The Present Status of Mediation in Canada

Most provinces now have a professional mediation association and in addition, Family Mediation Canada, a federal organization has been in existence since 1984. In Ontario, the Ontario Association for Family Mediation (OAFM) was created in 1982 and presently has a membership of over 480 individuals including lawyers, mental-health professionals, and judges.

OAFM has been working toward several major goals. First, the association has been taking the steps necessary to establish mediation as a profession. In 1986, a Code of Professional Conduct was adopted and all members now subscribe to this code (Ontario Association for Family Mediation 1987). More recently, Standards of Practice, including criteria for a Practicing Mediator category of membership, were adopted by the board of directors. For example, those wishing to qualify as practising mediators in OAFM must now complete a 40-hour training program and meet certain professional qualifications. The association is developing education standards for training mediators, and several experienced mediators offer training programs on a regular basis.

A second major goal of OAFM is increasing awareness of mediation as an alternative method of dispute resolution. A brochure explaining the concept of mediation and a Directory of Services with information about mediators and mediation facilities across the province are available for distribution. Educational meetings are held several times each year, and an ongoing dialogue with legislators and government officials has been established.

The third goal has been the expansion of mediation to other parts of Ontario and across Canada. The association has encouraged membership outside of Toronto and an Ottawa region has been formed. In addition, in 1987, the Ontario Association formed an affiliation with the federal organization, Family Mediation Canada (FMC), to ensure a strong national voice with respect to divorce legislation and mediation policy and to provide a forum for sharing information about such issues as training, ethics, provincial standards of practice, legislative reform, rules of court, procedure, and research.

Over the past few years, an increasing number of lawyers across Canada have entered the practice of mediation. On October 24, 1986, the Law Society of Upper Canada issued a communiqué (Law Society of Upper Canada 1986) establishing guidelines for lawyers acting as mediators in family law disputes. These guidelines form a code of conduct for lawyers, and clarify the boundary lines between the role of the lawyer acting as counsel for one of the parties and the role of the mediator providing an impartial service to both parties. Several other provinces, including British Columbia and Saskatchewan, have recently developed guidelines for their lawyers who wish to practise as mediators.

In summary, much of the structure required for the development of mediation as a profession is now in place. There is still much to be done, however, particularly in the area of training and certification.

The Future of Mediation in Ontario

Over the past ten years it has become clear that an increasing number of clients and their solicitors are selecting mediation as the preferred approach for resolving family law disputes, particularly those involving children. This trend will likely continue in the future and is likely to receive increased support from legislators and the judiciary. At this point it is important to increase the awareness of judges, lawyers, and the general public about the availability of mediation services and how mediation may be helpful. Research is needed to refine our knowledge about the use of mediation for resolving different types of issues with clients from different socioeconomic and cultural backgrounds.

At the present time, the Law Society of Upper Canada along with the Federal Department of Justice, the Ontario Ministry of the

Attorney General and the Laidlaw Foundation have funded a study of the cost benefits and social benefits of mediation for legally aided clients. Results of this study are now in the process of being analyzed. The results of research to date are encouraging but there is still much to be learned. A number of studies have been completed examining the Conciliation Services at 311 Jarvis St. in Toronto, the Frontenac Project in Kingston, and the Conciliation Service at the Unified Family Court in Hamilton.

The Zuber Inquiry Report, entitled *The Report of the Ontario Courts Inquiry*, was released in August 1987, and sets the stage for the future of mediation in Ontario. This report strongly encouraged the use of alternative methods of dispute resolution such as pretrial conferences, mediation, and arbitration for both civil and criminal disputes but emphasizes that mediation is particularly important in family law cases. Mr. Justice Zuber recommended that mediation be encouraged at two stages, namely, prior to litigation and after the commencement of proceedings. With respect to prelitigation mediation, Mr. Justice Zuber recommended

> that the rules respecting matrimonial cases be amended to provide that, prior to the commencement of an application, either spouse may request mediation and that, upon receipt of such a request, mediation service will be offered to the parties. (Zuber 1987, footnote 5 at 212)

If a spouse refuses to attend mediation following a request, Mr. Justice Zuber recommended that there be no sanction. However, this would be an indication that court action was required.

Once litigation has commenced, Mr. Justice Zuber recommended that mediation occur in the context of a system of mandatory pretrials. According to Zuber, J.A., pretrials should be compulsory and should occur at an early stage following the commencement of proceedings. A conciliatory pretrial would be most appropriate for disputes involving children where the parties must continue to interact following the legal resolution of their dispute. He stated that

> disputes involving the custody of and access to children are difficult, sensitive and emotional and are best resolved in an atmosphere of moderation and conciliation. In such an atmosphere, there is at least the possibility of leading the parties to an agreement. Such an agreement is usually superior to an externally imposed solution. It is more likely to be honoured and less likely to produce continuing friction. It bears repeating that the adversary method is a poor way to resolve any matrimonial dispute and is the worst way to resolve the issues of custody and access.
>
> The power given to the judge (rule 21) [of the Unified Family Court rules] enables the judge to refer the parties to a mediator. However, in busy courts, it will be more efficient if this function is performed by someone else.
>
> The mediator or mediation services can be built in to the court system or be performed by an outside agency. The determination of which mechanism is best should be left to the regional Courts Management Committees. (Zuber 1987, 211)

Mr. Justice Zuber has set out a model that could include mediation by a judge as part of the pretrial or mediation through a court-based service or a contract with an outside agency or a referral to a private mediator.

It should be noted that most of the recommendations contained in the Zuber Report with respect to mediation are already possible under existing legislation. What is different is the strong endorsement given by Zuber, J.A., for the use of mediation at an early stage i proceedings.

Conclusion

Mediation is being utilized m frequently in family law disp it is increasingly importan yers to become famili process and with their respective roles in the process. Judges and lawyers would benefit from training in mediation skills for cases in which they act as mediators. This is one of the recommendations made by Mr. Justice Zuber. In addition, it will be important for the judiciary to learn to identify at an early stage those cases that are appropriate for referral to other professionals.

Lawyers have a very significant role to play in the mediation process. As the Codes of Professional Conduct for OAFM and FMC indicate, mediators are obligated to refer the parties for independent legal advice at any point in the mediation process, but certainly prior to signing an agreement. In addition, lawyers have an important role in ensuring that there is full disclosure of all relevant material for the issues being mediated. For example, mediators usually refer the parties to independent lawyers for assistance in completing the financial information forms. In addition, lawyers have a role in negotiating or, if necessary, litigating issues that are not referred to mediation or that are not resolved in the mediation process. Research has shown that when lawyers are supportive of mediation, the mediation is more likely to succeed (Pearson, Thoennes, and Vanderkooi, 1982). Mediation presents a good opportunity for a co-operative partnership between lawyers, mediators, and the judiciary in which each group can contribute its specific skills in the most useful way to help families facing separation and divorce.

Kelly, J.B. 1987. "Mediated and Adversarial Divorce: Comparisons of Client Perceptions and Satisfaction." Paper presented at the American Psychological Association Annual Meeting, New York, August.

Kübler-Ross, E. 1975. *Death: The Final Stage of Growth.* Englewood Cliffs, NJ: Prentice-Hall.

Landau, B.L., M. Bartoletti, and R. Mesbur. 1987. *Family Mediation Handbook.* Toronto: Butterworths.

Law Society of Upper Canada. 1986. *Communiqué.* October 24.

Ontario Association for Family Mediation. 1987. *Code of Professional Conduct* (revised). June 5.

Pearson, J., and N. Thoennes. 1985. "Divorce Mediation: An Overview of Research Results." 19 Col. J.L. & Soc. Prob. 451.

Pearson, J., N. Thoennes, and L. Vanderkooi. 1982. "The Decision to Mediate: Profiles of Individuals who Accept and Reject the Opportunity to Mediate Contested Child Custody and Visitation Issues." *Therapists, Lawyers and Divorcing Spouses* 17.

Ricci, I. 1981. *Mom's House, Dad's House.* New York: Macmillan.

Wallerstein, J.S. 1983. "Children of Divorce: The Psychological Tasks of the Child." *American Journal of Orthopsychiatry* 53: 230.

———. 1985. "The Long Over-burdened Child: Some Long-term Consequences of Divorce." *Social Work* 116–123.

———. 1986. "Women After Divorce: Preliminary Report from a Ten Year Follow-Up." *American Journal of Orthopsychiatry* 56: 65.

Wallerstein, J.S., and J.B. Kelly. 1980. *Surviving the Breakup: How Children and Parents Cope with Divorce.* New York: Basic.

Zuber, The Honourable Mr. Justice. 1987. *Report of the Ontario Courts Inquiry.* Toronto: Queen's Printer for Ontario.

Part Nine

FAMILIES, SOCIAL POLICIES, AND THE STATE

• • •

We all know how Adam said to Eve: "My dear, we live in a period of transition."
Vida D. Scudder, *The Privilege of Age*
(1939)

In social systems that are characterized by *familism*, the family unit takes precedence over the individual. Teaching a child how to be part of his or her nuclear family involves instruction in the nature of the child's duty, and the extent of obligations to his or her kin. Having *filial piety* — that is, having respect for one's parents and honouring them — is a primary virtue. There is an emphasis on recognizing one's duty, and on one's willingness to perform it even if it means some sacrifice of one's own immediate needs or wants. In one sense, *the individual exists for the family.*

An *individualistic* system — that is, one in which the needs and wants of the individual person are of primary importance — is antithetical to a familistic system. The self-actualization of the person, and the maximization of growth and personal happiness, are primary goals. In one sense, *the family exists for the individual.* People get married and/or have children in anticipation that it will maximize their own personal adjustment; they stay married and/or remain with their children with the same ends in mind. Rather than the suppression of self that is the emphasis of familism, individualism stresses personal fulfilment.

A familistic family system is not necessarily any better or worse than an individualistic system, but it is different. Moreover, in the period of transition from one way of thinking to the other, family members may experience considerable confusion in balancing what they feel they "should" do and what they have a "right" to do in terms of their own personal happiness. The familistic system is undoubtedly more stable: however, that stability is often bought at considerable cost to individual contentment.

A familistic system involves an implicit assumption that there is one "right" way for families to be structured and one "right" timetable for their pattern of life events to unfold. Variations from this structure or from the orderly sequence of events in the timetable are considered by definition to be abnormalities, and therefore problems. The "solution" to these problems is to change the deviant behaviour to conform with the dominant model. Thus, if the dominant model specifies that everyone should marry when they grow up, and then have children, the "problem" persons are those who marry too soon or who do not marry at all, as well as those who have children without being married, or who marry without having children.

The social reality in Canada today is that there is not *one* way of organizing families, but a variety of ways. Moreover, each of these alternative ways of living appears to be satisfactory for some persons at some time in their lives. Rather than trying to make all families conform to a single standard and considering them to be "deviant" if they do not, it makes much more sense to recognize a *pluralism* in family forms. From this perspective, the only families that would be considered intrinsically problematic are those that violate some other principle of behaviour — as, for example, the family that includes victims of incest or violence. There is an increasingly wide definition of the arrangements that can be considered to be family or at least family-like relationships. Furthermore, there is an increasing emphasis on the rights of individuals. This process may alter or even reverse the expected balance of power between men and women, parents and children, and young adults and the elderly.

About the Articles

The process and pace of social change are not uniform in all segments of society. As a result, real changes in the family often occur before appropriate changes in laws and policies can keep pace. Eichler describes the policies that are congruent with what she calls the "old" family model in contrast to the "new," and outlines the modifications that are needed to correct the mismatch of current family realities with current family policies.

One solution to the problems faced by working wives who face a "double shift" is to increase the support given to daycare services. Prentice observes how the daycare issue has been transformed from a peripheral issue for feminists to a "mainstream" issue with wide political consequences. This process is an excellent example of the transformation of a situation from a "private trouble" to be resolved at the individual level into a "public issue," which is a legitimate focus of concern for the whole community.

A general social trend has been toward the protection of children. Thomlison and Foote show how the balance has shifted away from a focus on the rights of parents toward a recognition of the rights of children and youth to a wider variety of protections and safeguards.

In the more developed nations, the widespread and seemingly irreversible decline in birth rates has had many consequences, one of which is a dearth of children for adoption. The dilemma faced by involuntarily childless couples may create what Prichard suggests is a market for babies. While his approach is in some ways analogous to Jonathan Swift's satirical "Modest Proposal," the issues he raises are real enough, and the problems discussed are of ongoing concern not only to childless couples but to anyone concerned with the future of procreation.

Further Readings

Boyer, J. Patrick (Chairman). 1985. *Equality for All: Report of the Parliamentary Committee on Equality Rights.* Issue No. 29. Ottawa: Queen's Printer, House of Commons.

da Costa, Derek Mendes. 1978. "Domestic Contracts in Ontario," *Canadian Journal of Family Law* 1: 232–53.

Eichler, Margrit. 1988. *Families in Canada Today: Recent Changes and Their Policy Consequences.* Toronto: Gage.

Luxton, Meg. 1987. "Thinking About the Future." *Family Matters: Sociology and Contemporary Canadian Families.* Eds. Karen L. Anderson et al. Toronto: Methuen. 237–60.

Popenoe, David. 1987. "Beyond the Nuclear Family: A Statistical Portrait of the Changing Family in Sweden." *Journal of Marriage and the Family* 49: 173–83.

FAMILY POLICY IN CANADA: FROM WHERE TO WHERE?

Margrit Eichler

Introduction

Families in Canada have always displayed some variability. In societies in which we find important social changes, these changes inevitably have some effect on families, for the simple reason that people are affected by such changes and that these same people are likely to live in families. Families in Canada have, therefore, never been static structures, and they have never been all of the same kind (Nett 1981). The nuclear family in which father, mother, their own biological children, and nobody else lived happily together has always largely been a myth; families were not necessarily happy just because they lived under the same roof, and there have always been family disruptions for reasons of death and desertion, as well as migration because of economic necessity.[1]

Nevertheless, there are times in which changes are particularly marked, and in which one pattern is being visibly replaced by another. First, I will argue that we are currently living in such a period, where one type of family is being replaced by another, without the process having been completed. Second, I will briefly describe some of the prominent features of contemporary Canadian families. I will construct a model of what I call the "old" family, which represents a simplified theoretical construction of what was. Similarly, I will construct a model of the "new" family, which

is a simplified hypothetical construction of where I see us, as a society, moving, and will locate our contemporary families somewhere between these two poles.

Third, I will examine social policies that are appropriate for the "old" model of the family, and those that are appropriate for the "new" model of the family, and note the fit (or lack of fit) between the micro levels and macro levels. Last, I will briefly discuss some of these considerations for law.

Descriptions of Contemporary Families in Canada

Recently, there have been some major changes in Canadian households and families that can be addressed under the headings of (1) demographic changes, (2) changes in the nature of economic co-operation, (3) changes in awareness with respect to family violence, and (4) consequences of (1) and (2).

Demographic Changes

One of the most striking changes we can observe is the decrease in fertility. Canadian women have fewer children than ever before. While in 1960 the average number of children per woman was about 3.9, by 1985 it had sunk to fewer than 1.7 (Eichler 1988). That is, fertility has decreased by more than half in a quarter-century.

Life expectancy, by contrast, has risen constantly. For a male born in Canada in 1931, the life expectancy at birth was 60 years, and for a female born in that year, it was 62.1

Source: *Justice Beyond Orwell*. Canadian Institute for the Administration of Justice. (Montreal: Les éditions Yvon Blais. 1985). 385–404. Revised for this volume. 1989. Reprinted with permission from Rosalie S. Abella and Melvin Rothman (editors).

,ears. For a male born in Canada in 1976, the life expectancy is 69.6 years, and for a female born in that year it is 76.9 years (Statistics Canada 1979). Barring unforeseen disasters of a national scope, one would expect the life expectancy to continue to rise in the future. This means that there will be more older people around who will eventually need to be taken care of, and fewer younger people to provide this care. In terms of family relationships, this means that there are likely to be more grandparents alive during the youth and young adulthood of their grandchildren, and fewer grandchildren per grandparent.

The divorce rate has increased steadily and consistently over the past decades, rising from a rate of 39.1 in 1960, which represents 6980 divorces in that year in Canada, to a rate of 308.8 in 1986, which represents 78 160 divorces (Statistics Canada 1989). This steep increase follows a small decline during the years 1983-85 (Eichler 1988) probably due to the speculation around the introduction of the new divorce law. The new divorce law took force in July 1986, and divorces went up. Indications are that for the time being the divorce rate will continue to climb.

Due to the great increase in divorce, there has been a great increase in remarriages. In 1986, 30 percent of all marriages contracted in that year involved at least one previously married partner, compared to 12.3 percent of all marriages in 1967 (Statistics Canada 1989).

The great bulk of that increase is due to divorced rather than widowed persons remarrying; indeed, the proportion of widowed people remarrying has consistently declined, no doubt due to the increased life expectancy. One would expect this trend to continue for as long as the divorce rate remains high or increases.

Further, there has been a large (although inconsistent) increase in the percentage of births to unmarried mothers. While in 1960 only 4.3 percent of all children were born to unmarried women, representing 20 413 children, the percentage has risen to 18.7 percent

in 1986, representing 68 308 children (Statistics Canada 1989).[2]

One consequence of the increase in divorce and in the births to unmarried women is that the proportion of children living in one-parent households has increased. Approximately 17 percent of all families with children consisted of one-parent households in 1981, mostly headed by women (Economic Council of Canada 1983). About 40 percent of these female-headed families were poor in 1986 (National Council of Welfare 1988).

Changes in Economic Co-operation

In the past, women dropped out of the labour force when they married. In the 1960s, the prevalent pattern was that they remained in the labour force after marriage until the birth of the first child, at which time they dropped out of the labour force, sometimes to return after the last child had entered school (Ostry 1968).

The labour-force participation of married women has increased consistently (Eichler 1988), and today the majority of Canadian wives are in the paid labour force. We have thus crossed a threshold (around 1980) that changed the majority pattern for husband–wife families from a breadwinner family to a two-earner family.

A corollary of this change is that the majority of Canadian children now have a mother who is in the paid labour force, although wives and mothers are, of course, not an identical group (Eichler 1988).

Changes in Awareness of Family Violence

Until quite recently, violence within families was effectively hidden. It is only since the mid-1970s that some consistent scholarly and public attention has been focussed on this problem. As a consequence, we have no reliable information about the incidence of family violence in the past, and very little information about its incidence and nature in the present. Therefore, statements about changes in any type of familial violence are impossible, because there is no basis against which to assess contemporary information, even to the degree that it exists.

The editors of one of the most recent comprehensive American books on family violence conclude:

> the family is the predominant setting for every form of physical violence from slaps to torture and murder. In fact, some form of physical violence in the life cycle of family members is so likely that it can be said to be almost universal. . . . If this is indeed the case, then violence is as typical of family relationships as is love. (Hotaling and Strauss 1980, 4)

There is no reason to suspect that Canada would fare any better in a representative study of violence within families. One often-cited estimate is that 10 percent of all Canadian wives (legal or common law) are being battered by their husbands (MacLeod 1980).

Furthermore, the Committee on Sexual Offences Against Children and Youths found in a National Population Survey that 30.4 percent of all males and 53.9 percent of all females reported that they had been victims of sexual offences ranging from unwanted exposure to a sexual attack during their childhood. Looking only at the most serious form of assault — namely, whether anyone had ever tried to have sex with them or had forcibly sexually assaulted them — the committee found that 22.1 percent of the women and 10.6 percent of the men had experienced this form of assault (Committee on Sexual Offences Against Children and Youths 1984).

The committee concluded in terms of changes in incidence as follows:

> The best evidence available . . . suggests that the volume of these crimes in relation to population growth has remained at a relatively constant level for some time. In this respect, the major change that appears to have occurred is not so much an alteration in the incidence of these offences, but the fact that Ca-

nadians as a whole are becoming more aware of a deeply rooted problem whose dimensions have not significantly shifted in recent decades. (p. 185)

Finally, the committee found that well over half of all actual assaults occurred in the homes of victims or suspects, and that the majority of the assailants were already known to and possibly trusted by the assaulted victims; this placed the problem well inside the circle of the family.

Consequences of Demographic Changes and Changes in Economic Co-operation

Because of the earlier-noted increases in divorce, unmarried motherhood, and remarriage, we find an increasing gulf between marital and spousal roles. This shows itself in the high proportion of households in which dependent children live with only one of the their biological parents, while the other biological parent is living in another household. Moreover, either one or both biological parents may have remarried a spouse who thus becomes a wife or husband but not a biological mother or father to the children involved. Whether or not the stepparent is experienced as a social parent by the children concerned seems to vary greatly from family to family (Gross 1985).

It is not the fact of stepparenting that is startlingly new, but the scope of the phenomenon, as well as the continuing existence (and often involvement) of the non-coresidential parent in the parenting process.

To state the same facts differently, another consequence of these same factors is a large (and increasing) incongruity between household and family membership. In other words, the members of one household do not necessarily have the same family members. Imagine the case of a family with two children, in which the husband and wife (who are father and mother to the children) divorce; the father maintains contact with his children through visiting arrangements, while the mother has custody and the children reside with her. In that case, the mother and the children form one household, and for the mother, they form her family, while the children have family members in two households, namely their own and their father's.

Now let us assume that the father marries another woman who brings a child from a previous union into this marriage, and that eventually the father and his new wife have another child together. The children of the first family now have a half-sibling and a step-sibling, as well as potentially a stepmother in their father's household; however, the child whom the father's second wife brought into her marriage also maintains contact with his father. This example can be continued by assuming that the first wife also remarries a man with or without children, that the previous partner of the second wife of the original children's father has remarried, and so on. It is, however, sufficient to illustrate the point that household and family membership is no longer necessarily congruent, and that, as a consequence, members of one household may have different family members.

This opens up new sets of relationships that were previously less common and creates problems in relationships that also were previously less common. Parents of adult children who marry a partner who brings a child into this marriage may find themselves in a quasi- or step-grandparental relationship to this child, and children who are not biologically related may nevertheless be step-siblings and share half-siblings. On the other hand, parents of adult children who have lost custody of their children may have difficulty maintaining contact with their grandchildren, if the custodial parent does not wish for such contact.

As a consequence of the changed pattern of economic co-operation, a shift has occurred from the breadwinner couple to the two-earner couple as the norm, the full-time mother has become a minority phenomenon, and the majority of Canadian children experience some form of shared child care.

Finally, we note that a large proportion of women and children are living in poverty. This can be attributed to a number of factors. First, there is a high proportion of one-parent households, as noted above, and many of these households are living in or near poverty, especially if the head is female (as is the case in the vast majority of one-parent households). Second, women generally have lower-paying jobs than men and maintenance payments are generally exceedingly low, not reflecting the real costs of providing for a child, let along for child care (Dulude 1984). Furthermore, child-related benefits are low by comparative international standards (Kamerman and Kahn 1978, 1981) and our social-welfare legislation actively discourages the changeover from a poor female-headed household on social assistance to a husband-wife family with somewhat higher resources (Eichler 1984).

To sum up, Canadian families today are characterized by a wide degree of differences in terms of composition, structure, type of economic co-operation (or lack thereof), with quite divergent consequences for different families. There are one-parent and two-parent households, husband-wife households in which the partners are not joint parents to all or some children involved, an increasing separation between marital and spousal roles, and increasing incongruity between family and household memberships. A majority of wives are in the labour force, making the husband-wife breadwinner family a minority, while we find an increase in the proportion of one-parent households. Most Canadian children today do not have a full-time mother at home and therefore experience some form of shared child care. Only a small minority of these children find places in a licensed, supervised day-care setting. The majority are cared for in unlicensed, unsupervised settings, where the care ranges from excellent to appalling (Eichler 1988; Canadian Advisory Council on the Status of Women [CASW] 1986).

Finally a large number of women and children find themselves in or near poverty.

Canada is not alone in experiencing these trends. At least some of them seem to be connected with the process of industrialization, since we find similarities in familial structures in all highly industrialized countries. The demographic changes noted in Canada can also be observed in other highly industrialized countries, as well as a trend for women (and therefore presumably wives and mothers) to participate in the paid labour force in large numbers. Overall, we can also observe a large discrepancy between household and family membership, as suggested by internationally high divorce and/or illegitimacy rates. Interestingly, these trends are observable in all highly industrialized countries, regardless of political regime — that is, they are found in Eastern Europe as well as in Western Europe, North America, Japan, New Zealand, and Australia (Eichler 1984; Inkeles 1980).

Clearly, then, we are in a period of considerable social change as far as familial structures are concerned. It now becomes important to identify the direction of the ongoing changes, especially if we wish to assess the adequacy of policies affecting families, now and in the future.

The "Old" and "New" Model of the Family

Mary Ann Glendon (1980) has argued that we are currently in a period of "unsettled assumptions" about marriage. She suggests that we are moving toward a "new marriage" complemented by a "new property," both of which result from a complex shift in the relative importance of family, work, and government as status determinants and sources of support. She characterizes the "new marriage, American Style," as having

> two earners, mutually dependent on their combined sources of income, the wife earning less than the husband. The wife's earning, though low, seem, together with her earning potential, to be a major factor that makes it easier for husbands as well as wives to depart

from a marriage. . . . Since three out of four divorced persons remarry, the new marriage is often a subsequent marriage. . . . Thus, one can fairly say that in the United States, there is now a fundamental right to marry, and marry and marry. (p. 62–63)

Building on this analysis, I will develop models of the "old family" and of the "new family" (rather than the "new marriage") since, as far as social policies are concerned, the entire family (including the children) must be considered. If the above summary of recent trends is correct, and if there is indeed a growing dissociation between marital and parental roles, this situation must be systematically integrated into any consideration of the adequacies of social policies.

With the models of the "old" and "new" families, I will develop models of social policies that correspond to the "old" and the "new" families at the macro level. In developing these models, we must assume that behaviours at the micro level and assumptions about these behaviours as displayed in policies at the macro level are congruent. This will allow us to place current familial styles of behaviour somewhere on a continuum between "old" and "new" families, and to assess the degree of congruence of current social policies in view of the placement of contemporary Canadian families on the old–new continuum.

The Model of the "Old Family"

I will structure the discussion in terms of four dimensions: ideology, economy (in terms of responsibility and dependency), household composition and management, and personal care.

Ideologically, the old family is characterized by a very strong sex-role differentiation that affects all other dimensions. The roles of wives and husbands, fathers and mothers, are clearly distinguished and largely nonoverlapping. This is manifested in the assignment of economic responsibility and household management as well as in the responsibility for

Table 1
"Old Family" Model

Ideology	Sex-role differentiation
Economic responsibility	Husbands/fathers as breadwinners, wives as secondary earners or non-earners
Economic dependency	Wives/children as dependents of husbands/fathers
Household composition	Assumption of congruence between household and family membership; the nuclear family seen as normative; wives equated with mothers, husbands equated with fathers
Household management	Wives/mothers as full-time or part-time homemakers with sole responsibility for household management; husbands/fathers not responsible for household management; unclear distinction between spousal and parental obligations
Personal care	Mothers/wives/adult daughters/(-in-law) responsible for provision of care for children and adults; fathers/husbands/sons/(-in-law) not responsible for provision of care for children and adults

personal care. The father/husband is seen as responsible for the economic well-being of the entire family, while the mother/wife is seen as responsible for the physical, emotional, and overall well-being of family members. This includes providing care to family members in need of care, including sometimes aged parents. By corollary, the father/husband is not seen as responsible, except in economic terms, for providing care to family members in need of care, while the mother/wife is not seen as responsible for the economic well-being of the family.

In this model, the wife and children are conceptualized as economic dependants of the husband/father, and the work that wives perform within the household as full-time or part-time homemakers is necessarily invisible with respect to its economic value (Eichler 1985). If wives or mothers are in the labour force, their paid work is supplementary to their homemaking functions and their earnings are seen as of secondary importance.

As far as household composition is concerned, the nuclear family, consisting of a husband, wife, and their biological children (and nobody else), is seen as normative. As a consequence, household and family memberships are treated as congruent. Further,

there is an unclear division between spousal and parental obligations; as a consequence, wives are equated with mothers, and husbands are equated with fathers, while parents who do not reside with their children are treated as non-parents. The model of the "old family" is summarized in Table 1.

The Model of the "New Family"

By contrast with the "old family," the "new family" is premised on the notion of sex equality rather than sex-role differentiation. This applies to all dimensions of interaction. Consequently, the roles of husbands and wives, mothers and fathers are not differentiated on the basis of sex but on the basis of individual factors, and they overlap to a high degree. Household management as well as economic responsibilities are shared by husband and wife. Both father and mother are seen as responsible for the economic, physical, emotional, and overall well-being of the various family members.

Children are seen as the economic dependants of both mother and father, and both wife and husband are full-time participants in the labour force and are, in addition, responsible for the housework.

Table 2
"New Family" Model

Ideology	Sex equality
Economic responsibility	Husbands and wives (fathers and mothers) are both earners, equally responsible for their own support and that of the children
Economic dependency	Children are dependants of their mothers and fathers
Household composition	No assumption of congruence between household and family members; a variety of family types acknowledged and accepted; wives not unquestioningly equated with mothers, nor husbands with fathers
Household management	Shared responsibility between husband and wife; clear distinction between spousal and parental obligations
Personal care	Mothers/fathers, wives/husbands, daughters/sons, daughters-in-law/sons-in-law equally responsible for provision of care for family members in need of care to the degree that this can be combined with full-time paid work

Male relatives are co-responsible with female relatives for the care of family members in need of care.

As far as household composition is concerned, a variety of structures are recognized as constituting the different types of families. A potential incongruity between spousal and parental roles due to unmarried motherhood, divorce, remarriage and other factors is acknowledged and accepted. Consequently, there is a clear distinction between spousal and parental obligations, since husbands are not necessarily equated with fathers, wives are not necessarily equated with mothers, and non-coresidential parents are recognized as such.

The model of the "new family" is summarized in Table 2.

Social Policies Appropriate for the "New" and "Old" Families

In this section, we will consider each characteristic of the "new" and the "old" families and consider what type of social (including economic) policy would be appropriate to each model. To do this, we must shift our attention from the micro level to the macro

level and consequently translate some of the dimensions employed at the micro level to those appropriate for the macro level.

The ideological dimension remains as it is, but the economic dimension, which was split into responsibility and dependency for the microlevel, needs to be split into labour-market policies, the tax structure, and other government transfers to consider some of the implications of the old and new models of the family. Household composition remains as a dimension, and personal care translates into social services. Household management (that is, unpaid housework) is integrated into labour-market policies, the tax structure, other government transfer programs, and social services.

In the following section, I will consider which social policies are logically congruent with the "old and the "new" models of the family.

Policies Congruent with the "Old Family"

As far as the ideological dimension is concerned, policies must obviously be based on the notion of sex-role differentiation to match the "old" model of the family. This means that for the purpose of labour-market policies, men are treated as the primary earners, and women as the secondary earners or non-earners. Since women are seen as solely responsible for household management, it follows that men, whether they do or do not have a family, are seen as completely unencumbered by family responsibilities. Conversely, all women with families are seen as encumbered by familial responsibilities, or, if without family, as potentially encumbered, depending on their age and other characteristics (such as their assessed likelihood to get married or to have a child). Only if, in the eyes of an employer, a woman is highly unlikely ever to acquire a family of her own, could she possibly be considered as a worker of equal value to a male worker. Since, however, this woman does not have dependants, she requires a lower wage than a comparable male worker.

The tax structure will, logically, provide some tax relief (for example, a spousal exemption) to the man who has dependants (such as a wife and children).

Other government programs will provide replacement income in case of the incapacity or absence of a male breadwinner. Social-assistance programs, for example, will provide financial assistance to mothers with dependent children but without a male to depend on, but will withdraw such assistance when a man who is theoretically capable of earning an income assumes some aspects of a husband role. Since husbands are equated with fathers, this a logical policy to pursue. By contrast, if a wife's earnings cease, this loss of income will not entitle the family to a replacement income.

Conversely, when a wife/mother is incapable of providing care to family members for reasons of incapacity or absence, the state will provide replacement service. For example, when a wife or mother is unable to do housework due to a serious and prolonged illness, the provincial hospital insurance plan may provide a substitute homemaker; it will not do so, however, when a man cannot do housework because he is incapacitated or absent,

regardless of whether he did so before he became incapacitated.

As far as household composition is concerned, the assumption underlying policies is that membership in a household is identical with family membership, and, conversely, that there are no nuclear-family relationships or importance between households. There is little concern, then, with enforcing the economic responsibility of parents (predominantly fathers) toward their dependent children if they no longer (or never did) reside with them, for whatever reason.

With respect to social services, women are assumed to be available for the care of family members in need of care, whether these women do or do not have paid employment (which is always of secondary importance compared to their family responsibilities, while the reverse is true for men). Accordingly, there is no societal reason for providing child care for husband-wife families, since the wife is (or if she is not, she should be) available for looking after the children; nor is there much concern with providing care for people needing it who have mothers, wives, adult daughters, or daughters-in-law nearby.

The policies appropriate for the old model of the family are summarized in Table 3.

Policies Congruent with the "New Family"

If policies appropriate for the old family — "old policies," so to speak — are premised on the notion of sex differentiation in the ideological dimension, policies appropriate for the new family — "new policies" — must be premised on the notion of sex equality. From this, a large number of consequences flow for all other social policies.

With respect to the economy, and for purposes of labour-market policy, women and men are treated equally as primary earners, and all employment programs are equally targeted toward women and men. There is no wage differential on the basis of sex, and employers as well as labour law recognize that the vast majority of workers — male and fe-

Table 3
Policies Appropriate for the "Old Family" Model

Ideology	Sex-role differentiation
Economy:	
labour-market policy	Men seen as primary earners, women as secondary earners or non-earners; preference is therefore given to men over women in all employment programs; women are treated as labour-force reserve; a large wage-differential by sex; employers and labour law regulations treat male workers as unencumbered by family responsibilities, and female workers as encumbered or potentially encumbered
Tax structure	Provides relief to male earners with dependants (i.e., wife and/or children)
Other government transfers	Provide replacement income in case of absence of male breadwinner (or presence but incapacity to earn income); provide replacement care in case of incapacity or absence of wife/mother
Household composition	For the purposes of eligibility to benefits, household membership is equated with family membership, and eligibility is determined on basis of family need rather than individual entitlement; rights and obligations of non-coresidential parents are not enforced
Social services	No universal day care, universal relief for adult family members in need of care, institutionalized right to care for temporarily sick family members on the part of workers

male — have some familial relationships and therefore some responsibility toward their family members. There is no difference on the basis of sex in the way in which these familial responsibilities are recognized and accepted.

The tax structure provides relief to parents with respect to the costs attached to rearing children, but adults are not conceptualized as dependants of other adults.

Other government transfers provide replacement income and replacement care in case of incapacity or absence of one parent (either mother or father).

For the purposes of government programs, variability in family structures is recognized and accepted. In other words, household membership is not automatically equated with family membership, and ongoing parental responsibilities of non-coresidential parents are continuously enforced.

As far as social services are concerned, it is recognized that it is, in principle, impossible for any person to be responsible for his or her own economic welfare and hold a full-time paid job while at the same time being responsible for a person in need of care on a full-time basis, such as a dependent child or an adult in need of care. Therefore, there is a network of social services that provides care for children as well as for adults in need of care. Alternatively, there is a wage replacement system to reimburse adults who care for other people, including their own family members, for their losses in income. Labour law recognizes the right of paid workers to some paid time off for family responsibility, just as we now recognize the right to paid statutory holidays, vacation, and sick leave.

The policies appropriate for the new model of the family are summarized in Table 4.

Table 4
Policies Appropriate for the "New Family" Model

Ideology	Sex equality
Economy: labour-market policy	Women and men seen as primary wage earners; all employment programs equally targeted to female and male workers; no wage differential by sex; family responsibilities of male and female workers equally recognized and accepted
Tax structure	Provides relief to parents
Other government transfers	Provide replacement income and replacement care in case of absence or inability of one parent
Household composition	Eligibility for benefits is based on individual entitlement rather than family status; household and family memberships are not equated, unless, in fact, congruent; rights and obligations of non-coresidential parents are enforced
Social services	Wide network of social services for child care and adults in need of care and/or a wage-replacement system for people caring full-time for family members

Placement of Contemporary Families and Policies on the Old–New Continuum

In Canada today, it becomes obvious that at the micro level we have moved a fair distance towards the "new family." Sex equality as an ideology is more often accepted than not, more wives are earning money than are completely economically dependent on their husbands, family laws have been amended to make both parents responsible for the economic well-being of their children as well as for their care and other housework, a variety of family types coexist (although they are not always acknowledged or socially accepted), and the increase in remarriages has generated some awareness that spousal and parental obligations must be distinguished, especially when dealing with the aftermath of divorce. We do no really know to what degree male relatives are involved in the care of their family members who are in need of care.

Nevertheless, it would be quite incorrect to say that as a society we have generally adopted the "new family" as the model of the family. We are, at present, clearly in a transitional stage. This expresses itself in two different ways. First, a substantial proportion of the population (particularly its middle-aged and older segments), were brought up while the "old model" was the accepted model of the family. These people presently must cope with circumstances that have changed. Even if they themselves eventually adopt a new style of life, part of their history will remain tied up with the old model. For example, if a wife takes on full-time paid employment after she has been a homemaker for twenty years, she will never make up the loss in seniority and pay that is attributable to the time she worked as an unpaid homemaker.

Second, some people still choose to follow a modified version of the old model of the family in their own behaviour. Although the majority of mothers work for pay, substantial numbers drop out of the labour force when their first child is born. Presumably, these people will eventually find themselves in a situation similar to that presently encountered by middle-aged or older women who have conformed to the old model of the family.

Because of this second group of relatively young people, we will remain in a transitional stage for a least another thirty years. Even when these women return to the labour force, most of them will not be able to make up in areas such as career progress, acquisition of seniority, or income potential for the years they worked without pay in their homes.

To the degree that women are less likely to be full-time members of the paid labour force, it makes sense for them to provide more of the care for family members, thereby continuing sex-role differentiation in the personal-care dimension.

Nevertheless, we seem to be well on our way toward the new model of the family at the micro level.

When we turn to social policies, a totally different picture emerges. Our present policies are, in general, more congruent with the old model of the family than with the new model.

Although more women than ever before are currently in the paid labour force, sex segregation of occupations has not decreased in the recent past, but may even have increased (Economic Council of Canada 1983; Abella 1984).

The wage differential between the sexes continues to be large. While there is a very limited (by international standards) acceptance of female family responsibilities, there is hardly any recognition of male family responsibilities, although paternity leaves can be obtained in some professions by male employees.[3] Parental leaves are, of course, only one component of recognizing the family responsibilities of workers. A statutory right to time off in case of illness of family members is crucial. Generally, it is not available to either male or female employees at present in Canada, although such provisions do exist in other countries.

The tax structure provides some relief to parents, but also to breadwinners with dependants (the spousal exemption). Our social-assistance programs tend largely to be premised on the notion of the "old family." Eligibility to benefits is partly premised on family membership and partly on individual entitlement; in general, it is fair to say that the rights and obligations of non-coresidential

parents (usually parents without custody) are inconsistently enforced (Dulude 1984).

Social services provide no wide public network for child care or for adults in need of care. For instance, only a small minority of our children are cared for in public day-care settings, and the majority are in ad hoc private-care situations. This presents a serious problem. Our family structure has been changing quite rapidly, but our social policies are "out of whack" because they have not changed at the same speed.

One of the many consequences of the mismatch between the "new family" and "old policies" is the increasing incidence of poverty among women and children that was noted in the first section of this paper. Many efforts to reform the family law can, in fact, be understood as an attempt to remedy this situation by sharing assets between ex-spouses more equally. In the last section of this paper, then, I will briefly consider some of the legal implications of the above discussion.

Legal Implications of the Move Toward the New Family

Before the latest spate of revisions of the various family laws that started with the enactment of the Ontario Family Law Reform Act in 1978, family law tended to be firmly based on the model of the old family. Laws were, as a rule, premised on the assumption of sex-role differentiation, the breadwinning role of the father, the homemaking role of the mother, female responsibility for the provision of care, and congruence between household and family membership. This assumption was, perhaps, most clearly exemplified in the notion of illegitimacy.

With the new legislation, the law has moved quite decisively in the direction of adopting the premises of the new family model. In practice, however, we are faced with some significant problems, because we are at present in a transitional period. Ex-wives and their children tend to fall into poverty on divorce, while ex-husbands tend to be better off economically after divorce (Weitzman 1985; Eichler 1988).

While many other issues can be traced back to this basic disjunction between how people actually live together and how economic and social policies assume they live together, much concern has been focussed on the ex-wives and their children. Major efforts to improve their situation include a push for complete sharing of all assets (including business assets) between ex-spouses.

There are, I propose, several problems with a full community-of-property regime that applies to everybody. If the foregoing analysis is correct, the major problem is located at the level of economic and social policies, not primarily at the level of family law. Legal reformers might therefore profitably shift their attention to developing and implementing legal measures to improve the economic position of *all* women. Further, we must devise legal obligations and entitlements for men to discharge their part of familial responsibilities, so that the burden (and joy) of caring for others can, in fact, be shared between women and men. While this is clearly the long-range goal, there will be many casualties, because the present transition period will last for a long time yet. For women who entered marriages under the old terms, assuming they would be economically provided for, a community-of-property regime would certainly be appropriate.

Nevertheless, a compulsory community-of-property regime for everybody would, in principle, reward women on the basis of their husband's economic contributions, not on the basis of their own work. In this situation, under the euphemism of "partnership," women would continue to be treated as their husbands' dependants. By contrast, I would argue that some women should get *all* the property (for instance, if they have raised children and also had a paying job), while other women who have not raised children or cared for adults who are unable to care for themselves and who have not had a paying job do not, perhaps, deserve half of all the property accumulated by the husband. And what do we do with wives who have supported husbands, done all or most of the housework, and cared for others? Will they have to split their property with a man who has not contributed his share?

To me, it seems somewhat ironic to argue for any one property regime for all families at the exact time when we are faced with a wide diversity of family types that will inevitably be with us for a long time to come. It also seems ironic to me to argue for ex-wives primarily on the basis of their spousal role, rather than on their parental as well as their spousal roles, given that we are faced with an increasing dissociation between spousal and parental roles. In other words, the contributions of women as wives and as mothers should be separately assessed, just as the contributions of men as husbands and as fathers should be separately assessed. If a woman has been carrying the parenting role for the father as well as for herself, this should be acknowledged in property settlements.

Nevertheless, economic equality for women will not come about by reforming the family law — it will come about by reforming labour law, revising our tax structure, and reshaping our economy. That is not to say that further reform of family law in unimportant, but merely to point out that it must not be seen as solving some problems that are beyond its purview. People who do socially useful work in their homes must be rewarded for this work socially, not privately; raising children must be seen as a social contribution, not only as a private contribution; and men and women must equally share family responsibilities in spite of their paid work, just as women must have the same access to jobs and the benefits attached to them as men have (Eichler 1985). Once we achieve these goals, ex-wives will not be so poor, and children will not sink into poverty merely because their parents divorce or were never married in the first place.

Notes

1. For American data, see Bane (1979). For a historical Canadian example, see Hareven (1978). See also Pike (1975).

2. For comparative data on illegitimacy rates, divorce rates, and labour-force participation rates of women, see Eichler (1984). For comparative rates of fertility and other factors, see Inkeles (1980).

3. The recent revisions of the Unemployment Insurance Act have increased the likelihood that new fathers will have access to parental leaves.

Works Cited

Abella, R.S. 1984. *Equality in Employment. A Royal Commission Report.* Ottawa: Minister of Supply and Services.

Bane, Mary Jo. 1979. "Marital Disruption and the Lives of Children." *Divorce and Separation: Context, Causes and Consequences.* Eds. George Levinger and Oliver C. Moles. New York: Basic. 276–86.

Canadian Advisory Council on the Status of Women. 1986. *Report of the Task Force on Child Care.* Ottawa: Minister of Supply and Services.

Committee on Sexual Offences Against Children and Youths. 1984. *Sexual Offences Against Children.* Canada: Minister of Justice and Attorney General of Canada, Minister of National Health and Welfare. 185.

Dulude, Louise. 1984. *Love, Marriage and Money . . . An Analysis of Financial Relations Between Spouses.* Ottawa: Canadian Advisory Council on the Status of Women.

Economic Council of Canada. 1983. *On the Mend: Twentieth Annual Review.* Ottawa: Minister of Supply and Services.

Eichler, Margrit. 1984. "The Familism–Individualism Flip-Flop and Its Implications for Economic and Social Welfare Policies." *Social Change and Family Policies.* XXth International CFR Seminar, Key Papers, part 2. Melbourne, Australia Institute of Family Studies and ISA International Sociological Association (CFR Committee on Family Research). 431–72.

———. 1985. "The Connection Between Paid and Unpaid Labor and Its Implication for Creating Equality for Women in Employment." *Research Studies of the Commission of Equality in Employment.* Ed. Rosalie S. Abella. Ottawa: Minister of Supply and Services. 537–46.

———. 1988. *Families in Canada Today. Recent Changes and their Policy Consequences.* 2d rev. ed. Toronto: Gage.

Glendon, Mary Ann. 1980. "New Marriage and the New Property." *Marriage and Cohabitation in Contemporary Societies. Areas of Legal, Social*

and *Ethical Change. An International and Interdisciplinary Study.* Eds. John M. Eekelaar and Sanford N. Katz. Toronto: Butterworths. 59–70.

Gross, P. 1985. "Kinship Structures in Remarriage Families." Unpublished Ph.D. thesis. University of Toronto, Department of Sociology.

Hareven, Tamara K. 1978. "The Dynamics of Kin in an Industrial Community." *The American Journal of Sociology* 84: 5151–82.

Hotaling, Gerald T., and Murray A. Strauss. 1980. "Culture, Social Organization and Irony in the Study of Family Violence." *The Social Causes of Husband–Wife Violence.* Eds. Murray A. Strauss and Gerald T. Hotaling. Minneapolis: University of Minnesota Press. 4.

Inkeles, Alex. 1980. "Modernization and Family Patterns: A Test of Convergence Theory." *Family History.* Vol. 1, No. 6 in *Conspectus of History.* Eds. Dwight W. Hoover and John T.A. Koumoulides. Muncie, IN: Dept. of History, Ball State University.

Kamerman, Sheila B., and Alfred J. Kahn. 1978. *Family Policy. Government and Families in Fourteen Countries.* New York: Columbia University Press.

———. 1981. *Child Care, Family Benefits, and Working Parents. A Study in Comparative Policy.* New York: Columbia University Press.

MacLeod, Linda. 1980. *Wife Battering in Canada: The Vicious Circle.* Ottawa: Canadian Advisory Council on the Status of Women, Minister of Supply and Services.

National Council of Welfare. 1988. *Poverty Profile 1988.* Ottawa: Minister of Supply and Services

Source: *Resources for Feminist Research* 17(1) with permission.

ica[...]
egy i[...]
respond[...]
stitutionaliz[...]
the state. One[...]
streaming" with[...]
there are still many[...]
movement, the critic[...]
manded transformed rela[...]

THE "MAINSTREAMING" OF DAY CARE

Susan Prentice

During the last federal election, viewers of the televised debate sponsored by the National Action Committee on the Status of Women (NAC) were privy to an astonishing event: the leaders of all three political parties declared their support for child care. In retrospect, we can see how the attention paid to the issue during the 1984 election reflects the current process of institutionalization of child care in and by the state. In a span of little over a decade, child care has moved from being a radical and militant demand of feminists and socialists to a legitimate issue on the social-policy agenda of the state.

At the level of both the Ontario and federal governments, the child-care movement has seen the state adopt some of its most fundamental demands. The state has indicated its willingness to expand services, to increase funding to ensure access for low-income parents, and to redress the exploitative wages of day-care workers. The child-care movement perceives these concrete and financially significant initiatives by the state as victories. Yet, a number of the initiatives contradict the movement's original demands for state support for child care.

The child-care movement has made significant changes in its political analysis and strategy [over] the past decade. These changes both [led] to, and are a reflection of, the [institutionaliz]ation of child care at the level of [the state. One] consequence of this is a "main[streaming" with]in the movement. Although [there are many] different voices within the [movement, it is a genera]l perspective that de[scribes its posi]tions through the so-

[...88): 59–63. Reprinted

cialization of child care in the 1970s is now barely a whisper.[1]

As a member of the day-care community, I want to encourage discussion and debate on the contradictions of recent child-care policy and organizing by the movement. We need to explore the implications of engaging in the social-policy process of the state. Such debate on the current contradictions of our demands and government policy is *not* to imply that the movement should retreat from engaging with, and making demands on the state. Instead, we intend to use our experience to clarify our struggle and to strengthen our position in the ongoing process of defining our needs and making our demands.

Child care is not unique in this process of being taken up by the government; other feminist issues have been similarly institutionalized. To some degree, this is a consequence of feminist demands for reforms by the state; but to a greater degree, the current focus by feminists on the policy process can be attributed to the institutionalization of feminism by the state. Child-care advocates, perhaps more than other feminist organizers, have made the decision to engage with the social policy process as their strategy. To understand this requires an analysis of both the movement's policy engagement and state responses to it.

The State and the Institutionalization of Child Care

In recent years, the state has declared its support for child care through changes in its rhetoric, policy, and funding, as well as through its relationship to child-care advocates.

Changes in the state's rhetoric have been dramatic. Bureaucrats and elected officials have made clear statements about the state's commitment to child care, and indicated their alignment with the child-care movement. For example, in his address to the Ontario Coalition for Better Day Care 1987 Conference, Minister of Community and Social Services John Sweeney discussed the "partnership" between the day-care movement and his ministry, noting that "in many ways, you in the Coalition for Better Day Care have in mind much the same goals that we in the MCSS are working towards (Ontario Coalition for Better Day Care 1986, 13).[2] At the municipal level, the report of the Metropolitan Toronto Daycare Planning Task Force argues that Metro should "work co-operatively with the [day care] community" to enhance child-care services as a part of its "advocacy activities." (1986, 11, 14).

In addition to changing its rhetoric, the state has also begun to develop ways to engage child-care activists in the social policy process of the state. One way of doing this has been through funding child-care groups; another has been to develop processes to involve advocates directly in government policy-making within the state. In Ontario, child-care advocates now hold day-care development jobs with boards of education and municipal and provincial governments. The distinction between child-care advocates and bureaucrats is a fine one as advocates work both directly and indirectly as government consultants and researchers.

Child-care policy has become a priority on the government agenda at the municipal, provincial, and federal levels. Municipal governments, particularly the government of Metropolitan Toronto, have pushed the province of Ontario for greater support for child care, and the province has pushed the federal government for greater resources. One example of this is the recent struggle by John Sweeney to win increased federal support for Ontario's child-care services from federal Minister of Health and Welfare Jack Epp. In Ontario and elsewhere, existing services have been ex-

panded. Furthermore, the government has initiated pilot projects for "flexible and innovative services" and resource centres. These new and expanded services are indications of increased government attention to child care.

Despite the obvious benefits of this institutionalization of child care, we are increasingly aware of the contradictory nature of many of these new policies. Ontario's direct grants, and proposals to change federal funding arrangements are two examples that most clearly illuminate the limits of state support for child care.

In 1979, Action Day Care — realizing that massive child-care expansion would require capital and operating resources beyond the limits of individual families and communities — began calling for state financing of child care through a provincial direct operating grant. At the municipal level, this organizing strategy was successful. In 1984, the City of Toronto established a three-year, $3 million direct grant program to raise worker wages in nonprofit programs. Child-care advocates continued to maintain their strategy of demanding a provincial direct grant. In 1987, the provincial government announced it was undertaking broad initiatives to support child care in Ontario: one feature of the New Directions policy (which will infuse the Ontario child-care system with $325 million annually by 1990) is a direct operating grant. The province's direct grant, however, will be available to existing commercial as well as to nonprofit programs.

Direct grants were demanded by the child-care movement as a way to break out of the user-fee catch-22, in which parents' fees had to rise if day-care workers' wages were to increase. Direct grants were seen as one step in the direction of complete public funding of child care. While Ontario's direct grant will have the intended effect of raising workers' wages without raising parents' fees, it will also have serious unintended consequences.

When commercial day-care centres receive ongoing operating funding, their profitability is greatly enhanced. This lucrative environment for day care results in the massive expansion of commercial services. Such is the case in Alberta, where nearly three out of four day-care centre spaces are profit-making; the province vies with Newfoundland for the dubious distinction of being the Canadian province with the highest percentage of commercial child care. The situation in Alberta is directly attributable to a policy that made both commercial and nonprofit programs eligible for a direct operating grant. Ontario's direct grant may similarly invite the expansion of commercial care, despite a "grandfather" clause designated to restrict the grant to existing commercial centres.

Profit-making day care is doubly troublesome: as well as providing lower quality of care along every index possible (worker wages, parental satisfaction, staff training, turnover rates, etc.), it also prompts the growth of a politically powerful free-enterprise day-care lobby. Commercial operators historically have worked to downgrade government standards and regulations to increase their profitability. The free-enterprise lobby has been effective in keeping a regressive pressure on standards in the United States, and was pivotal in a key struggle in Ontario in 1974 over the "Birch proposals."

The direct grant is therefore contradictory on two counts. Although advocates and the press in Ontario have hailed direct grants as an indication of the strength and success of the day-care movement, as well as an indication of the state's commitment to child care, this policy reflects serious contradictions within the state on the issue of child care. While the manifest purpose of the direct grant is to support child care, it actually undermines the demands of child-care activists. Further, it is also an example of how a strategy of the day-care movement — an organizing demand — can hold negative as well as positive implications for child care.

Advocates are caught in a similarly contradictory position with respect to proposed changes to federal funding. The Canada Assistance Plan (CAP), established in 1966, has provided the main support for the development of child care. This plan is Canada's major piece of federal welfare legislation, and establishes federal–provincial cost sharing of eligible services. Although CAP was not designed to fund a child-care system, day-care services are funded through it. There is no ceiling on the federal child-care contribution: the federal government is required to match provincial expenditures on eligible services. Day-care advocates have raised strong objections to funding child care through CAP, arguing that welfare funding perpetuates inadequate and stigmatized child care.

Early this year, the Mulroney government proposed ending child-care funding under CAP and replacing it with a new Child Care Act and changes to the tax system as part of a seven-year, $5.4 billion child-care package.[3] Total expenditures proposed under the Child Care Act will be capped, whereas spending under the previous Canada Assistance Plan was unlimited. In the long run, the closed funding proposed by the national strategy will potentially reduce child-care dollars. Further, the federal strategy places an increased reliance on funding child care through indirect spending on the tax system, offering parents an increased deduction for child-care expenses. Through the tax system, the federal government has chosen to focus on fee-paying parents over direct public funding to create a child-care system. Arguments against using tax dollars are widespread and familiar: they benefit high-income over low-income earners, they do not distinguish between regulated child care and unregulated babysitting, they require parents to pay cash up front, they do nothing to increase the supply of service, etc. The child-care movement, which has for years objected to CAP's welfare orientation, may now be in the paradoxical position of defending CAP against the proposed "progressive" Child Care Act.

The state's position, both federally and provincially, is contradictory. Its policy initiatives are designed to support child care, and appear to be responses to child-care advocates. While ostensibly aligning with the child-care movement, the government is actually developing services that contradict the movement's goals. For example, the avowed support of Ontario's New Direction policy for nonprofit care is contradicted by its willingness to give direct operating funds to commercial programs. Notwithstanding its rhetoric, the federal government's move to replace the welfare funding of child care with a new act has more to do with the control and restructuring of welfare programs than supporting child care.

The "Mainstreaming" of the Child-Care Movement

The child-care movement's analysis and strategy have also changed since the beginning of the decade. Throughout the mid- and late-1970s, organizations such as the Day Care Organizing Committee and later the Day Care Reform Action Alliance promoted "free" child care. However, during this period there was political tension between differing factions; between demands for a mass, government-funded and (possibly) government-run child-care system that emphasized universal access, and demands for what O'Brien-Stenfels calls a "utopian" system, most often parent/worker cooperatives, that emphasized issues of service delivery.[4]

By the early 1980s, advocates who demanded government-financed child care emerged in leadership roles through groups such as Action Day Care (ADC), the Ontario Coalition for Better Day Care, and later (and more unevenly) the Canadian Day Care Advocacy Association.

Action Day Care led a campaign to popularize the idea of "universally accessible" child care as a more politically strategic (although not less radical) demand than "free" child care. This strategy was introduced into the newly emerging Ontario Coalition for Better Day Care by activists from Action Day Care. One participant in this process, a member of both ADC and the Ontario Coalition, remembers that "to get the support of the social service organization, the group

dropped the demand for free universal day care and substituted the more nebulous phrase "universally accessible" (Colley 1982, 310).

"Universally accessible" day care incorporated a notion of being free, yet it also had the advantage of association with other "universal" programs such as health care, pensions, and education, all of which have distinct limits in their application. But universal care was congruent with socialist assumptions about the impact of class on accessibility; it was assumed to be less class-biased than the utopian parent co-operative that was supported by mainly white, educated, middle-class, urban, and politically sophisticated parents and workers. The 1982 national day-care conference in Winnipeg saw the culmination of the "universal access" intervention. Resolution after resolution reflected a commitment to a universal, as opposed to a targeted, child-care system. Delegates who had formed a Universal Access Caucus and arrived with "Universal Care" buttons won the plenary handily. The popularization of "universal access" as opposed to "free" within the child-care movement had been achieved.

At the same time as demands for "reasonable" child-care policy were advanced by the child-care movement, the state began to make some concessions to the advocates' position. As the state took steps to place child care on the political agenda, advocates grew excited about the possibility of winning real victories in the short term (Ontario Coalition for Better Day Care 1987). They stepped up pressure on the government for increased resources as the latter appeared willing to expand services and to address questions of accessibility, affordability, and underfunding.

In the 1980s, the struggle between the child-care movement and the state has been increasingly played out in the social-policy process where child-care advocates have been increasingly visible. Changes in the government, as well as an increased receptivity to government within the child-care movement, have resulted in a new and more collaborative relationship. Since the early 1980s, child-care groups have been increasingly (although inadequately) funded by the state. They have thus been able to employ staff, establish offices, and produce high-quality policy materials. In Ontario, advocates now participate in a range of municipal and provincial advisory groups, task forces, and other consultative bodies. They have informal yet influential relationships with senior bureaucrats in departments such as Ontario's Ministry of Community and Social Services, and Health and Welfare Canada.

One significant outcome of this changing relationship between the movement and the state has been that the movement has effectively "shaped" its demands in the familiar and nonchallenging language of "service to families" and "women's right to work," and away from the politics of gender and class relations. Because social policy is predicated on normative construction of "the family," "mothering," and the sexual division of labour, neither class nor gender are recognized by the state in its response to the child-care problem. The state identifies neither the organization of private capital nor the construction of the "normal" eight-hour working day; neither the division of public and private nor the gendered division of labour between women and men in households; not even the construction of women as the primary caregivers of children. Instead, in the language of social policy, child care is "needed" because of mothers' labour-force participation.

Advocates have challenged some of the assumptions of social policy. By extending the idea of "the family," the day-care movement has exposed contradictions within state policy. Through adroit manipulation, a conservative notion of family is turned back on itself and used to justify a call for extended child care. Advocates argue that child care actually strengthens "the family" by supporting its members. The popularization of the idea of "universal" child care (however interpreted) extends the idea of social responsibility for children in much the same way that the fight for universal health care and education transformed social expectations. Yet, the language

of liberal social policy cannot challenge the free-market assumptions of child care, nor can it comment on the most basic dynamics of patriarchal capitalism. Despite latitude for rework or stretching the language and concepts of state policy, the terrain of social policy is mediated by the state in the interests of dominant groups and it is difficult for child care advocates to make more than minor adjustments. The institutionalization of child care by the state was partly legitimized by this shift in the strategy of child-care advocates.

Changes in the structure of the child-care movement have also contributed to a decrease in the militancy that marked earlier moments. Since 1980, child-care advocates have steadily built coalitions, weighing the strength of broadly based organizations (even if sometimes paper tigers) against smaller, less politically muscled groups. While coalitions offer an important opportunity for different groups to work together in solidarity, they also frequently require a moderation of political demands to maintain this solidarity. The erosion of the demand for "free" day care described above is one example. Another is the fact that broader politics of feminism receives less attention than policy development and implementation. An analysis of gender inequality and the sexual division of care has nearly disappeared from arguments about the social context of child care. A clear example was provided by the April 1988 Canadian Day Care Advocacy Association Conference (the first national conference since 1982). Speakers at the opening session of the conference stressed that "children are our most valuable resource." Of four opening statements to the conference, only one was organized around an explicit attention to feminism.

The changing strategy and structure of the child-care movement has contributed to its "mainstreaming." The mainstreaming of day care has had the result of moderating the demands and practice of the child-care movement. The trade-off for the policies that have been won as child care has become institutionalized is an increasingly commodious daycare system and the abandonment by the child-care movement of the critical demand for transformed relations. While expanded child-care services will improve many women's lives and make their paid labour more possible, it leaves gender relations within nuclear families unchanged, does not challenge the social definition of woman as mother, and does nothing to reorganize the seemingly unbreakable chasm of "public" and "private" realms and responsibilities.

Commodified Child Care

To a certain degree, child-care politics in the late 1980s can be understood as the result of the commodification of child care both by the state and (in part) by the child-care movement itself. The process of commodification has been an increasingly important issue for political theorists: Nancy Hartsock's work may be the best known and most concise feminist comment on the debate (Hartsock 1985).

Hartsock uses a complex interrogation of epistemology, using Sohn-Rethel's work, to explore the dimension of market exchange (Sohn-Rethel 1978). Hartsock and Sohn-Rethel isolate three key features as the defining characteristics of commodity exchange; the opposition of use from value (and the associated opposition of quality from quantity), the opposition of people who participate in the exchange (what Sohn-Rethel calls "practical solipsism"), and exchange abstraction (a refinement of what Marx called "commodity fetishism"). Hartsock warns that "adopting the market model involves one in a logic of domination that carries a variety of anti-social consequences. . . . The deep problem is the theorization of social life in any of the terms provided by the commodity form" (1983, 101).

While day care may seem very far from an epistemological discussion of exchange abstraction, it is, in fact, deeply implicated in it. Child care has been constructed as a commodity by the state through social policy and service. Just as health care has been objectified

and quantified as a question of "beds," child care has been reduced from a set of social relations to a question of day-care "spaces." This construction is very close to the "exchange abstraction" identified by Hartsock and Sohn-Rethel.

Political and strategic resolutions to the quantity/quality see-saw have been endlessly negotiated and renegotiated among child-care activists. In a user-fee system of care, there are objective conflicts of interests between the users of care (parents and children) and the providers of care (owners, operators, and often day-care workers). This conflict between participants — Sohn-Rethel's "practical solipsism" — is enhanced in commercial care, where the dynamics of profit mark the opposition even more strongly. When the issue of care is turned into a question of quantity, this fundamental opposition is obscured and the state and the free-enterprise day-care lobby can declare their alignments with the child-care movement. This was the case last summer when the Association of Day Care Operators of Ontario, the commercial owners' lobby group, proclaimed itself part of "the day-care movement" and praised the province's initiatives, even as it lobbied to extend the eligibility of commercial programs for the direct grant.

In the objectified language of social policy, quality of care is merely a technocratic manipulation of the professional standards of early childhood education. When the objective of child care is the safeguarding of children for 40 hours a week while their mothers work, the relations sustained and created by care are inconsequential when compared to the successful provision of adequate "spaces." A system of child care, theorized, organized, and implemented in the terms of care-as-commodity, could provide universal access to service. Such child care would extend the options of children and parents, yet would deliver service in ways that did not challenge the assumptions of social policy. G. Leslie warns that this kind of child care would "represent just another incursion of the state into private life" (1978, 37).

The state is more receptive to demands for commodified service than to demands for transformative care. When the day-care movement enters the social policy arena without explicitly challenging the assumptions of commodified care, it is construed as a supporter, albeit a reluctant one, of this kind of care. Through this engagement with the state, the day-care movement comes very close to demanding care in the commodified terms of state policy. Increasingly throughout the 1980s, the day-care movement has edged closer to making demands that implicitly legitimate the state's institutionalization of child care, in ways more recognizable as care-as-commodity than care-as-social-relations.

In contrast, at different moments the day-care movement has hinted at the transformative possibilities of noncommodified care. In the early 1970s, it was posed as a question:

How can we have babies in a society that makes babies burdens to everyone, particularly to women, and at the same time not lose our ability to work effectively to destroy this inhumane system? If we do not come to grips with this question now, we will either spend childless lives or suddenly find ourselves entrapped by motherhood and depoliticized as a result. (Killian 1972, 93)

The 1970s conception of noncommodified care — mainly restricted to the idea of parent co-operatives — was often vague and romantic. At its core, however, was a desire for noncommodified, community-based care. It was sometimes called care "by and for the community." Parents who had had good experiences with co-operative day-care centres were its most enthusiastic proponents. One father identified that, in community care, "the potential for a centre for growth and support not only for children but for parents, is one of the most fantastic aspects . . . a kind of *praxis*" (Foster 1972, 105–6). An American summary provides a glimpse of the potential of noncommodified care:

Childcare is not an isolated phenomenon. . . . Good childcare is a foundation upon which people can continue to re-make and build anew their own neighborhood and local community. In the process of organizing themselves around a human need — free, community-controlled childcare — parents, teachers and children can grasp their right to organize around their human needs: good health, good housing, good work, good public education and recreation and a good environment. (Sassen and Avrin 1974, 43)

There are real and troubling class and race biases in many forms of community-based care (particularly parent co-operatives) as commentators, often former participants, have identified (Cameron and Pike 1972). Despite these contradictions, co-operative childcare programs struggled to challenge the social relations between men and women, adults/parents and children, and the relationship of individuals to the community. There may be many ways to imagine noncommodified services; parent co-operatives are only one model. While undertheorized, politically fraught, and all too often an ultimate failure, co-operative child care was an attempt to transcend care-as-commodity. This critique needs to be extended and placed centrally on the agenda of the current day-care movement.

Currently, the contemporary day-care movement's attention to noncommodified care is contained within its demands for non-profit care with parent boards of directors. Yet, even this limited notion of community control may be growing increasingly unpopular in the day-care movement, if the events of the 1988 Canadian Day Care Advocacy Association (CDCAA) Conference are any indication. During the conference, the Ontario caucus prepared resolutions to take to the plenary. An amendment to include "community-based" in a motion reiterating support for "universally accessible, publicly-funded, high quality, non-profit, comprehensive care" was proposed. The caucus defeated the amendment, while the chair commented reassuringly that the CDCAA calls for "Boards of Directors composed of at least 51 percent parents." "Representative boards" are quite different from explicitly noncommodified, community-based care.

Many advocates argue that a system of universal child care must in fact abandon community control to ensure a mass-service provision. I believe this position is both politically pessimistic and dangerous. The child-care movement must extend its demands beyond the call for universal access to include the transformative possibilities of noncommodified care. The task calls for debates on various models of service delivery. Undertaking this project is an intensely political necessity. As feminists and child-care advocates, we need services that do more than simply permit women to work. We need to redistribute the labour of reproduction in ways that challenge current social relations and the interests that dominate them.

Future Organizing

It is important to point out that the fight to win the present demands of the child-care movement is still an enormous struggle. Demands for any type of socialized-care program — even in the commodified terms that state policy promotes — is still a struggle in an increasingly conservative climate. In the era of the free-trade agreement and the Meech Lake accord, there is much to be said for (and much hard labour involved in) simply preventing cutbacks and erosion to existing services. A defensive fight to protect existing policies against a federal government intent on moving to the right is still a progressive one.

Yet it appears that the struggle for child care has moved to a new stage. The child-care movement has successfully convinced the government to initiate policies and programs to increase state support for child care. Now that the state has undertaken to implement service, the movement needs to reconsider its analysis and strategy to address the institutionalization of child care. I have argued that an analysis of the commodification of care is

critical to this project. Without this reconsideration, the child-care movement may find itself in the peculiar situation of "winning" a widely accessible but commodified system of child care. Having "won" its battle, the "successful" child-care movement will be faced with a certain *crise d'existence*.

There are many lessons for feminist organizing to be drawn from an analysis of the institutionalization of child care within the state and the mainstreaming of the day-care movement. The first relates to the question of strategy. The day-care example indicates that participation in the policy-making process may have unintended consequences for social movements. As feminists and activists, we must develop tactics that challenge the power of the state to define and limit the terms of our demands, and to moderate our politics and strategy.

The second point is that we need stronger feminist analysis before we can predict the results of political practice with any certainty. Especially, we need a sophisticated and perceptive theory about the enormous power of the state to blunt, incorporate, and absorb political challenge. This theorization can best be done through historically specific analysis of our struggles with and against the state.

And finally, on a different plane, the day-care example points out the weakness and ambivalence of feminist theory and action around family and child policy and issues of care. A long-standing and understandable legacy of mistrust and anger at women's subordination within the family, and a belief in the need to smash the sexual division of the labour of social care, have not come together in anything resembling a comfortable or intellectually coherent position. The labour of caring for children and for family remains an often unexamined practice of many women's lives, despite an imprecise feminist demand that this work should be shared equally between men and women. We need to be able to theorize about and organize around the social relations that spring from the realities of being bodied: these include birth and care for those who are very young, sick, differently abled and aged, as well as otherwise needy. Without this, feminism will be unable to address dilemmas of care and will effectively concede issues of family and care to the right.

Notes

1. For a discussion of the transformative possibilities of socialized care, see Killian (1969); Leslie (1978); and Sassen and Avrin (1974).
2. In 1987, the Coalition changed its name to the Ontario Coalition for Better Child Care.
3. At the time of writing, the final figure on federal spending was under negotiation between the federal and provincial governments. The final figure proposed in 1988 was $6.4 billion. On April 27, 1989, Finance Minister Michael Wilson cancelled Bill C-144.
4. For a discussion of the different perspectives of child care, including the "utopian" position, see O'Brien-Stenfels (1973).

Works Cited

Cameron, B., and C. Pike. 1972. "Childcare in a Class Society." *Women Unite.* Toronto: Women's Press.

Colley, S. 1982. "Free Universal Daycare: The OFL Takes a Stand." *Union Sisters.* Eds. L. Briskin and L. Yantz. Toronto: Women's Press.

Foster, J. 1972. "Sussex Day Care." *Women Unite.* Toronto: Women's Press.

Hartsock, N. 1985. *Money, Sex and Power: Towards a Feminist Historical Materialism.* Boston: Northeastern University Press.

Killian, M. 1972. "Children Are Only Littler People . . . Or the Louis Riel University Family Coop. Vancouver."*Women Unite.* Toronto: Women's Press. 1972.

Leslie, G. 1978. "Childrearing as Social Responsibility." *Good Daycare.* Ed. K. Gallagher Ross. Toronto: Women's Press.

Metropolitan Toronto Daycare Planning Task Force 1986. *Blueprint for Childcare Services: Realistic Responses to the Need* (November 17).

O'Brien-Stenfels, M. 1973. *Who's Minding the Children? The History and Politics of Childcare in America.* New York: Simon and Schuster.

Ontario Coalition for Better Day Care. 1986. *Conference Proceedings* (December).

————. 1987. *Newsletter* (January).

Sassen, G. and C. Avrin. 1974. "Corporate Child Care." *Second Wave* 3(3).

Sohn-Rethel, A. 1978. *Intellectual and Manual Labour: A Critique of Epistemology.* Atlantic Highlands, NJ: Humanities.

CHILDREN AND THE LAW IN CANA THE SHIFTING BALANCE OF CHILDREN'S, PARENTS', AND THE STATE'S RIGHTS

Ray J. Thomlison
Catherine E. Foote

Introduction

Canada's laws regarding children and families can be examined on the basis of the balance they strike among the rights and obligations of the child, the family, and the state. In the past, legislation and policies have traditionally adopted what may be called a paternalistic and reactive stance toward ensuring the well-being of Canadian children. The emphasis has been on apportioning power over children between parental figures and the state, and on weighing family (parental) autonomy versus state intrusion into the family. Government intervention has generally followed a residual or safety-net model, in which the authorities react to rescue or protect children, and only after specified problems have occurred in the families. A shift, however, is apparently beginning in the field of Canadian child and family law. The earlier focus on parental and state rights is now being tempered with a growing concern for the rights of the children themselves; this movement may lead to laws and policies that are more proactive or preventive.

Following a brief description of the historical context of current child and family law in Canada, this paper outlines the important principles that underlie the legislation and reflect the continuing attempt to balance conflicting rights. The body of the paper provides two examples of attempted balance: the first from the field of "child protection," and the second from the field of what used to be termed "juvenile delinquents," now referred to as "young offenders." The paper closes with an indication of future directions for the shifting balance of the child's, the family's, and the state's rights within the process of seeking the welfare of Canada's children.

The Social, Legal, and Historical Context

Canada's government is constituted on three levels: a central federal authority for the nation as a whole, ten provinces and two territories, and numerous municipalities. In this federal system, legislative power is distributed between the central or national body and the regional bodies. The British North America Act of 1867 (later to form the substance of the Constitution Act, 1982) first legislated the division of powers between the federal Parliament and the provincial legislatures.

Because family law was not considered a distinct area of law in 1867, no allocation of legislative jurisdiction over family law as such was undertaken in the British North America

Source: *Journal of Comparative Family Studies* 18(1987): 231–45. Reprinted with permission.

Act (Hogg 1981). Although no explicit reference was made in that act to constitutional authority over families and children per se, such references have been taken to be implied in particular clauses. Also, given the breadth and pervasiveness of family matters in society, it appears that the intent was not to concentrate a comprehensive authority in one legislative body. For example, in section 91 (subsections 26 and 27), the federal government was given exclusive legislative competence regarding marriage and divorce and regarding criminal law, while in section 92 (subsections 12 and 13), provincial governments were assigned exclusive jurisdiction over the solemnization of marriage and over property and civil rights.

Thus, the federal Parliament has been able to legislate on children's issues that are ancillary to marriage and divorce (such as custody and financial support after marriage breakdown), as well as on criminal matters pertaining to children (for example, neglect, rape and sexual assault, incest, sexual abuse, juveniles who break the law). Parliament also oversees native children, citizenship, and many financial support programs that benefit children. Provincial governments have placed most of their ability to pass child-oriented legislation under the auspices of their power over property and civil rights, and the ordering of private relations. Thus, provinces legislate matters such as illegitimacy and affiliation, succession and names, guardianship, adoption, consent, child protection, education, other child-welfare concerns, and custody, access, and maintenance. These last three are within provincial jurisdiction if not ancillary to divorce.

In fact, the provinces predominate in Canada in the legislative field of meeting children's needs. Considering the combination of the constitutional allocation of powers, quantity of legislation, administration of services, administration of courts, and division of financial responsibility, it is clear that provincial governments control the preponderance of provisions made for children in this country (Canadian Council on Children and Youth 1978; Hogg 1981). Dominance does not imply homogeneity, however. One important indicator of heterogeneity is the fact that Quebec's provincial justice system is governed by a Civil Code based on continental European traditions, while the other provinces and the territories (and indeed the federal government) rely on the British common law system of precedents and case law once they are outside statute law.

Canada is a relatively heterogeneous nation: the provinces and territories have marked regional distinctions, with significant geographic, linguistic, cultural, and economic differences. In fact, each province or territory may be more homogeneous within itself than is the country as a whole (Hogg 1981). The lack of uniformity in laws across the country (despite efforts in a number of substantive areas to co-ordinate legislation interprovincially) reflects these regional discrepancies. An advantage of such a federal rather than unitary system is that the regions can function as "sociolegal laboratories." Individual provinces or territories can try out, and perhaps find acceptance, for new laws and policies that might be too radical for the nation overall, and regions can then learn from one another (Hogg 1981).

Specific legislation to address the matters of children and the family in Canada was enacted in the last two decades of the 1800s, and was consolidated in the early decades of the 1900s. These developments were greatly influenced by reforms in British laws and courts. But Canadian legislation then stagnated until the 1960s, at which time the field became quite active once again with a general "renaissance" in family law (Bala and Clarke 1981).

The Philosophy Underlying Current Laws and Policies

In Canada in the past, little of the philosophy and values underlying policy regarding children was formally and explicitly articulated in the law. New legislation, however, attempts to enshrine the following beliefs:

- The family is the basic unit of society and the most fundamental setting for the nurturing of and caring of children.
- As the best environment in which children can be raised (since the family is the best social structure for meeting the needs of children, and the potential of children is thereby best realized within the family), the family ought to bear the primary responsibility in society for the care and support of dependent minors.
- In return for this duty, the privacy of the family ought to be recognized and the integrity of the family supported.
- The state should intervene legally to disrupt a family on the basis of consent, or if involuntarily, only in exceptional circumstances.
- Society needs to provide some way of safeguarding the rights and entitlements of those who are not capable of doing so for themselves (such as children), and of protecting dependants who are at risk.
- Children have interests and needs as separate individuals, which may come into conflict with the interests and needs of parents, other adults, and the state (Canadian Council on Children and Youth 1978; Legal Education Society of Alberta 1985).

Beliefs and assumptions such as these appear to derive from the interplay of four major concepts that have directed the form of child-oriented law in Canada.

First, the principle of *patria potestas*, or the power of the father, indicates that the authority and autonomy of the family (traditionally vested in the father) ought to take priority in the question of child rearing. The parent (father) has a prima facie right to custody (care and control) of the child. The state should not intervene in the family except under extraordinary circumstances.

Second, with the principle of *parens patriae*, or the state as parent substituting for or acting in lieu of the parent, the state is sanctioned to intervene in the family when a member cannot safeguard his or her own interests. Because of its interest in preserving future generations of workers and citizens, the state has

the power and the obligation to assert guardianship and care over persons who are disabled or cannot take care of themselves. Although the parent still has the primary obligation to meet the child's needs, the state has the authority to limit parental power over children or to compel parents to carry out their duties and obligations toward their children, in order to protect children who are not able to ensure that their own needs are met.

Third, the "best interest of the child" principle implies that the welfare of the child is to be the paramount consideration in the law and its administration. State intervention can be justified here if it proposes to realize the child's best interests, if judicial and administrative decision making are based on the maximization of the welfare and well-being of the child. The state can interfere with parental rights if such interference can be cast as being in the best interests of the child.

All three of these principles impose adults on children and assert the general authority of a parental figure, whether in the form of an actual parent/guardian or a representative of the state, over the child. The assumption is that children are incomplete and not competent to know, decide, and safeguard their own interests. They are dependent and need care; adults are obliged to assume responsibility for them.

The fourth principle, namely the "child as a person before the law," differs in its attempt to de-emphasize the power of adults over children. It stresses instead the child's status as a separate, individual citizen, entitled to all the rights afforded to any citizen who comes into contact with the law. As persons in their own right, children would, for example, be entitled to independent legal representation and to be a party to any legal actions that pertain to them.

Children in Need of Protection

The General Concept of Child Protection

The potential conflict between, and the attendant need for a balance of, the rights and obligations of parents, children, and the state are perhaps best demonstrated in the field of child-protection legislation. As the state has shown itself increasingly willing to become directly involved in supervising family relationships, there has developed in accompaniment an increasing interest in the rights of family members (Bala, Liles, and Thomson 1982). Various laws refer to the conditions under which the state will become active in caring for a child. Each province and territory has legislation that assigns the government-mandated authority to intervene in a family when a child is defined as being in need of the state's protection.

If a child is reported to be neglected, abused, or exploited, he/she can be removed from the home ("apprehended") by officials acting under provincial-government legislation. The case will be heard by a judge, who will decide whether the child is "in need of protection" and what disposition ought to follow from that finding. The laws invoked in this child protection process constitute a guarantee of parental rights, a trend toward a concern with children's rights, and a statement of the state's authority to intervene in what are ordinarily private family affairs. In other words, the rights of the child, parents, and state must all be accounted for. Children have a right to be protected from harm, parents have a right to custody of their children which must be protected if the state is trying to apprehend, and such apprehension is a drastic but necessary power of the state (Sammon 1985).

Parents are bound by positive duties to actively meet the needs of, care for, protect, and financially maintain their children; the younger the child, the greater may be the obligations. Parental rights, however, such as the right to decide what is best for the child and the right to impose reasonable discipline for the purpose of correcting and training a child, countervail these duties and obligations (Dickens 1978).

The rights of the parents to full custody, care, and control of their children, unless some significant matter renders them unfit,

implies minimal state interference with the family's entitlement both to privacy and to choice of a variety of lifestyles and child-rearing methods. Parental autonomy (the exercise of rights generally free from state intrusion) exists within the following areas: possession and services of the child; visiting the child; consenting to marriage and adoption; appointing guardians; and determining education, religion, discipline, medical treatment, name, nationality, and domicile.

The assumption is that parents are responsible for and capable of deciding what is best for their children; they know how to raise their children and ought to be allowed to do so freely as they see fit. Furthermore, it is assumed that the interests of parent and child coincide or at least do not conflict, and that the parent will make decisions that operate to achieve the best interests of the child. As a consequence, the child should remain in his or her own home, with removal generally perceived to be the last resort only when serious problems occur (that is, only in extraordinary circumstances of parental failure to meet the child's needs). Legislation attempts to safeguard the rights of parents to order their own family affairs, free from unnecessary state intrusion.

On the other hand, children should not be seen as merely dependent, incompetent, passive possessions of their parents, but rather as persons with their own rights, who happen to be in the state of childhood. Despite the fact that they are dependent and do have a limited capacity or development compared to adults, children should nevertheless have their separate interests and entitlements recognized and protected, probably with special provisions that acknowledge the particular characteristics of childhood. Although it is first the role of parents to protect the best interests of children, and only secondarily the state's, some parents may not be able to see or serve children's interests as separate and different from their own (Steinhauer 1982). Children ought to be entitled not only to state intervention on their behalf after a problem has occurred, but also to state support and prevention efforts before drastic problems arise to harm them. Overall, ensuring the best interests, welfare, protection, and well-being of the child should be paramount.

Legal provisions exist for the government to be involved in guaranteeing protection of and proper care for children. It is believed that the state has an interest in and the right to protect children and promote their welfare, even if this implies a limitation on the interests and rights of parents. Indeed, the state is perceived to have a duty to intrude when a dependant is at risk. At this time, the state's role in this field tends to be envisioned as one emphasizing broad authority for compulsory intervention to protect children at risk when parents have been defined as unfit, or when care is deemed inadequate (usually by the dominant cultural expectations). Under the federal Criminal Code, parents or guardians can be charged with failure to provide the necessities of life to their children, and other sections of the Code mandate criminal charges for injuries against children such as assault, bodily harm, and sexual offences. Under provincial child-welfare statutes, children defined as being in need of protection are assisted by the state.

Most child-protection legislation is currently phrased in terms of negative statements about children's needs and of negative standards for parental behaviour: what parents must not do to the children who are in their care and control. The laws express a minimum standard of child care in a negative manner, so that a parent who is perceived to fall below the standard is liable to such involuntary government intervention as apprehension of the child and the pressing of criminal charges against the parent.

Legislation in Canada is only beginning to focus on positive standards and goals for childrearing, to state what parents ought to be doing for children, and to reflect an explicit concern with children's needs rather than just parental unfitness. Laws are starting to incorporate the needs of children as affirmative rights expressed by positive standards, and not just to assert negative standards of minimum care (Royal Commission on Family and Children's Law 1975).

What parents ought not to be doing for their children is only one part of a total stipulation of minimum child-care standards. The focus can be on the behaviour of parents and on the needs of children. Standards that contain both negative and positive elements provide for involuntary intervention as well as support, prevention, and voluntary involvement by the government. Children can require assistance rather than protection, and perhaps should not have to suffer some harm before action can be taken on their behalf. Several jurisdictions in Canada are examining the possibility of mandating not just protection in law, but also prevention and offers of support and assistance in the home (Cruickshank 1978; Robertshaw 1980). Aid to families as reflected in law can be more supportive, voluntary, and culturally appropriate than is presently the case.

Family law, and child welfare law in particular, have the dual and perhaps conflicting purposes of supporting families while at the same time protecting individuals who are at risk within those families (Thomson and Barnhorst 1982). The first purpose desires to respect family authority and autonomy through minimal government intervention (and may be most protective of parents), but the second appears to call for greater state intervention (and may be more protective of children). Contradictory principles are operating in which the state is to protect parents' rights (parents are responsible for raising and caring for their children, so children are in some sense the property of their parents), and at the same time to protect children's interests (children are citizens in their own rights) (Djao 1983). A number of approaches in the justice system try to balance the amount and direction of intervention in the family.

The Child-Protection Delivery System

When government intervention is deemed necessary by child-welfare officials, the family is entitled to have its case heard quickly by an independent, impartial third party, usually a judge in a court of law, who will decide whether or not a child is in fact in need of protection and how the case ought to be dealt with. The bases for such adjudication and disposition are essentially vague in the law. Since judicial and administrative discretion often threaten family autonomy by allowing unfettered possibilities for intervention, the criteria for decision making are being made more clear, specific, and narrow, more procedural safeguards are being developed, and bases for quick action or response are being promoted. The traditional assumption that government workers necessarily provide benevolent, effective services and act in the best interests of the child (which in turn led to the assumption that there existed little need to limit the workers' discretion) is being questioned. More precise and restrictive grounds are being proposed for such discretionary processes as apprehension, court adjournment, defining a child as "in need of protection," disposition and placement, and care review.

Earlier criteria for adjudicating whether a child is in need of protection have been too broad and vague. Laws have contained a continuum ranging from more "passive" forms of deprivation (for example, omissions leading to neglect, such as failure to provide for needs in general, failure to provide medical treatment, abandonment, emotional deprivation, and failure to ameliorate a handicapping condition), to more "active" forms of ill-treatment (for example, commission of abuse that is physical, sexual, nutritional, and/or emotional in character); juvenile delinquents or young offenders are included in these laws. Defining something like abuse is particularly difficult in a society that still sanctions in law the use of corporal punishment by parents, teachers, and other persons in loco parentis; there remains an acceptance in some legislation of the use on a child of "reasonable force under the circumstances" for purposes of "correction." Mandatory reporting schemes and central registries regarding neglected and abused children are now largely recognized as necessary in Canada, even though their components, purposes, and effectiveness are sometimes questioned.

The disposition continuum from a supervision order through temporary wardship to permanent or Crown wardship (with or without the child's access to the parents) has relied heavily on the best interests or welfare-of-the-child principle. If intervention is called for, there is now an interest in using some version of a "least restrictive/drastic/disruptive available alternative" principle to choose the most appropriate course of action, in an effort to maximize the use of families and to keep families together, or at least in contact if apprehension does occur. In general, removal of a child from his or her own home is seen as the most drastic, and therefore the least desirable, solution, and only as the last resort in the most severe cases. The belief is that children are normally better off with their own families than living in some sort of substitute family.

Children's Rights Within Child-Protection Hearings

Child-protection hearings tend to reflect the belief that family matters are private and of concern only to the litigants: parents have rights to privacy regarding their conduct toward their children. The hearings are usually closed and held in camera, with no publishing of identifying information (Robertshaw 1980). Such hearings usually take the form of a judicial inquiry or trial within an adversarial system, in which the child is not typically a party to the action. Children do have the right to be a party in civil litigation such as torts, contracts, and estates. A child can sue in these actions by his or her "next friend" or can be defended by a guardian *ad litem* (for example, in either case, by his or her parent or guardian). If there is no parent or guardian, or a conflict of interest exists between the child and the parent or guardian, the court can appoint some other person to act for the child (for example, an "Official

Guardian" from the provincial government) under statute law or under *parens patriae*.

Within child-welfare or child-protection actions, however, the child who is the subject of the protection application is generally not a party to the action as a right. In effect, the child is not a "person" under the law. The child certainly has an interest in, and will be affected by, the outcome of the proceeding, but is not usually a party to the hearing per se. Thus, he or she is not entitled on the basis of natural justice to, for example, separate legal representation or counsel, to be notified or present, to give evidence, to call witnesses, to cross-examine, to make submissions, or to appeal. Only the parents and the government authorities have status as parties according to statute.

When parents and the state are in conflict over the child and the state is claiming parental unfitness, it is assumed that the state authorities can fully represent the interests of the child, since they have the same interests as the child (that is, his or her "best interests"). The state is in the best position to put forward the child's welfare, so there is no need for the child to be a party to the specific action or to have rights to party status in general. The authorities are by definition the "next friend" of the child. The law currently reflects this paternalistic assumption that the government authorities necessarily know and act in the best interests of the child when the parents have failed to so act (Robertshaw 1980; Royal Commission on Family and Children's Law 1975).

Although awareness of children's rights is on the increase, such rights are still largely discretionary and not automatic at this time. Affirmative legal rights of children are just now being expressed and enforced through legislation that states entitlements, means of enforcement, and remedies (Leon 1978). This securing of rights tends so far to concentrate on legal representation of children as the best guarantee (Leon 1978). For example, several provinces have begun to introduce schemes for separate legal counsel for children in at least some types of child-protection cases.

Canada has not had the deeply entrenched civil-liberties tradition that one finds in such countries as the United States, where child advocacy is much more prevalent and there has been a greater emphasis on the civil rights of children (Berkeley, Gaffield, and West 1977–78). The Canadian belief still tends to be that parents or guardians have the primary responsibility to ensure children's rights, with the state playing a secondary role in the matter. Canada's founding legislation, the British North America Act of 1867, was not based on the American individualistic liberal premises of "life, liberty, and the pursuit of happiness." Instead it stressed the more conservative principles of "peace, order, and good government" (Berkeley et al. 1977-78).

Youth in Conflict with the Law

In the past, child welfare law in Canada has tended to operate on the basis of a residual, problem-centred model, in which the state intervenes only after a family has failed, in order to correct specific problems (Armitage 1975; Djao 1983). A trend away from a reliance on punitive and adversarial approaches toward an inclusion of remedial and supportive ideas can now be discerned (Sammon 1985). This same trend is not as apparent in the field of children or youth who come into conflict with the law: those who used to be called "juvenile delinquents" and are now termed "young offenders." This field does permit, however, another perspective on the balance of parents', children's, and the state's rights.

The "child-saving" social-reform movement in Canada at the turn of this century arose with the discovery of urban social problems. It differentiated children and adults, imposing a dependent status on the former and designating them as requiring protection, help, guidance, and supervision. Children's crime and delinquency were perceived as social diseases arising from the urbanized, industrialized environment of the day, and as such, it was thought that they ought to be amenable to treatment. Children needed to be saved or rescued from the undesirable and harmful aspects of their lives. The philosophy was that a child should be dealt with not as a "criminal" or "offender" needing punishment, but rather as someone who is found to be guilty of the offence of "delinquency," and therefore is a "juvenile delinquent" requiring supervision, guidance, assistance, discipline, and correction. While children are capable of committing criminal acts, they are nevertheless different from adults in their understanding of and responses to those acts, and therefore ought to be treated differently once apprehended.

By defining children as necessarily dependent, it was possible to assert that they need to be protected by external parental figures, and thus to render their lives vulnerable to intervention. Juveniles were to be shielded from the evils of the adult criminal law system and spared the full impact of criminal law, by having a separate juvenile justice system created that would emphasize not punishment but diversion and rehabilitation within a treatment-oriented setting. It was deemed acceptable to deny certain substantive rights and procedural safeguards to juveniles to expedite their special handling in this new separate system: the concern was more with treatment at disposition and less with rights at adjudication (Bala, Liles, and Thomson 1982; Leon 1977-78). The juvenile system would emphasize prevention of delinquent and criminal behaviours, protection of the community through rehabilitation of the child offender, best interests of the child, diversion, and probation as a form of support to the child in the home.

The Juvenile Delinquents Act of 1908 in Canada codified these beliefs. The statute was federal since it was Parliament that had been given exclusive legislative power over criminal law by the British North America Act. By focussing on the need to protect, help, and treat troubled children, minimal attention had to be paid to building such things as rights and accountability into the system, to criteria of due process, natural justice, and fair and equal

consideration before the law. Special courts, procedures, dispositions, and institutions were devised, with both adjudication and disposition together intended to function as part of the treatment of the delinquent. The trial was meant to be part of the treatment, in which strict adherence to ordinary court processes might be of detriment to a child (Leon 1977-78).

The intervention net cast by this system, however, was wider than just commission of crimes according to adult criminal law standards (Bala, Liles, and Thomson 1982). The Juvenile Delinquents Act included not only all criminal offences according to the adult standards of the federal Criminal Code. It also incorporated violations of other federal laws and of provincial and municipal statutes, as well as "sexual immorality or any similar form of vice," and any other act that would cause the child to be committed to an industrial school or juvenile reformatory.

Thus, the Juvenile Delinquents Act subsumed a number of what are termed "status offences," acts that would be offences only for children, and not for adults if the latter engaged in the same behaviour; no "crime" has been committed according to adult standards, but the behaviour is deemed unacceptable for a minor. With these, the state was able to intervene for reasons or causes unique to a particular status, namely childhood, and the label of "offence" would be applied only to actions of those persons who occupy a childhood status. Such offences included the use of liquor and tobacco, driving and curfew violations, truancy, and sexual immorality.

The children's rights movement more than half a century later, beginning in the 1960s, was willing to compromise much of the special protective treatment earlier afforded juvenile offenders, with provision of greater explicit rights and safeguards to them (Bala, Liles, and Thomson 1982). The thesis was that child-saving had led to many perhaps unintended but nevertheless undesirable outcomes, and it was now time to recognize and ensure children's rights and freedoms. Special (that is, differential) handling under the rhetoric of "help" or "treatment" had allowed great discretion in the system, which was then subject to abuse. Designating juveniles as dependent meant that others must know what is in their best interests, and ought to protect juveniles as dependents, not permitting them their legal rights.

The Juvenile Delinquents Act had remained in force and essentially unchanged since its passage in 1908. In 1982, Royal Assent was given to a new Young Offenders Act; it was proclaimed to be in force in 1984 for children under 16 years of age, and then in 1985 the act was extended to all those under 18 years. It asserted that society has a right to be protected from criminal acts regardless of the age of the perpetrator, and young people were now to be held more responsible for their behaviour, although still not totally accountable given the assumption that they have not yet reached full maturity.

Under the old child-saving approach, criminal or delinquent behaviour was the child's response to negative external forces affecting him or her but beyond his or her control. Thus, juveniles could not really be held responsible for their actions. This assumption rendered juveniles vulnerable to the intrusive and interventionist "saving of delinquents." Within the new approach, juveniles are held more responsible, so can have less intervention imposed on them. Juveniles are to have guaranteed, through special safeguards, the same rights as adults to due process, natural justice, and fair and equal treatment before the law.

The Young Offenders Act retains the concept of a separate, provincially administered justice system for children and youth. It does, however, alter the ages of the offences to which the Juvenile Delinquents Act referred. The minimum age of criminal responsibility was seven under the old act, but the new Young Offenders Act is only concerned with children 12 years of age and older. Those seven- to twelve-year-olds formerly subject to the federal provisions of the Juvenile Delin-

quents Act now come under the jurisdiction of provincial (usually child-welfare) laws.

The Young Offenders Act is limited to the breaking of federal laws alone; provincial and municipal violations and status offences are now excluded from federal jurisdiction and concern. The new act no longer extends the reach of criminal law practices into provincial statutes and municipal by-laws or ordinances, and the former Juvenile Delinquents Act offences regarding such matters as sexual immorality and vice are omitted as well. This move has permitted a clearer distinction between child-welfare and criminal jurisdictions.

The Juvenile Delinquents Act was fundamentally a piece of morality-based social-welfare legislation, relying on the *parens patriae* powers of the state to intervene broadly with what was assumed to be benevolent (and quite unfettered) discretion (Catton 1981). The goal then was treatment, but the stance of the new Young Offenders Act is more punitive and custodial. The shift from the label "delinquent" to one of "offender" reveals the philosophical change toward a responsibility/accountability model. Public protection receives greater emphasis, as do the rights of the children who are in conflict with the law.

Conclusion: Future Directions

As indicated in the preceding descriptions of the fields of child protection and youth in conflict with the law, there now exists in Canada some movement toward including the rights of children as a third variable in the traditional equation that was meant to balance only state and parental rights. This movement is reflected in other areas of child and family law as well. For example, most jurisdictions have omitted the distinction between legitimate (born inside of wedlock) and illegitimate (born outside of wedlock) children. Many also recognize some rights and obligations for common law spouses regarding their children, and under most legislation children are entitled to support from and access to both parents. Within the field of adoption, a growing commitment can be found to disclosure of identifying information for adult adoptees, and to intra- (rather than trans-) racial adoptions for placements that are more culturally appropriate for children.

This latter trend is particularly important for Canada's native children, who have typically been a major casualty of our child-welfare system. They are greatly overrepresented in that system, especially within the "in-care" population. Less than 5 percent of the total child population of Canada is native, but across the country, more than 25 percent of children in care are natives. In the western provinces and the territories where Indian, Métis, and Inuit concentrations are higher, the figure rises to over 50 percent. Phrased in another way, 1.35 percent of all Canadian children are in government care, but more than 3.5 percent of all native children are in care. The child-welfare system is generally agreed to have served native children and their families poorly. Efforts are now being made in some areas of the country to relinquish control of child-welfare services to the native communities themselves, as a way of recognizing the children's rights to be raised within their own culture and in a manner that may better promote their well-being.

As a final example, the proclamation in 1982 of the Constitution Act (to replace the British North America Act of 1867) included a Canadian Charter of Rights and Freedoms. The Charter provides for a number of fundamental freedoms and for the right to life, liberty, and the security of the person, as well as rights not to be arbitrarily detained or imprisoned and not to be subjected to cruel and unusual treatment or punishment. It also specifies that every individual is equal before the law and has the right to equal protection and benefit of the law. It is important to note for the purposes of this paper that such equality is assured regardless of age. The new Charter is another indicator that, in a variety of ways, Canada has recently begun to moderate

its earlier emphasis on adult (parent and state) rights with a consideration for children's rights as well.

Works Cited

Armitage, A. 1975. *Social Welfare in Canada*. Toronto: McClelland and Stewart.

Bala, N.C., and K.L. Clarke. 1981. *The Child and the Law*. Toronto: McGraw-Hill Ryerson.

Bala, N., H. Liles, and Judge G. Thomson. 1982. *Canadian Children's Law*. Toronto: Butterworths.

Berkeley, H., C. Gaffield, and G. West. 1977–78. "Children's Rights in the Canadian Context." *Interchange* 8 (182):1–4.

Canadian Council on Children and Youth. 1978. *Admittance Restricted: The Child as Citizen in Canada*. Ottawa: Canadian Council on Children and Youth.

Catton, K. 1981. "Children in the Courts: A Selected Empirical Review." *Family Law: An Interdisciplinary Perspective*. Ed. Howard H. Irving. Toronto: Carswell. 185–215.

Cruickshank, D.A. 1978. "Court Avoidance in Child Neglect Cases." *The Child and the Courts*. Eds. Ian F.G. Baxter and Mary A. Eberts. Toronto: Carswell. 203–27.

Dickens, B.M. 1978. "Legal Responses to Child Abuse in Canada." *Canadian Journal of Family Law* 1: 87–125.

Djao, A.W. 1983. *Inequality and Social Policy*. Toronto: John Wiley and Sons.

Hogg, P.W. 1981. *Family Law in a Federal System*. Number WS-2 of Family Law and Social Policy Workshop Series. Toronto: Faculty of Law, University of Toronto.

Legal Education Society of Alberta. 1985. *The New Child Welfare Act*. Edmonton: Legal Education Society of Alberta.

Leon, J.S. 1977–78. "New and Old Themes in Canadian Juvenile Justice: The Origins of Delinquency Legislation and the Prospects for Recognition of Children's Rights." *Interchange* 8 (1&2): 151–75.

———. 1978. *Legal Representation of Children in Selected Court Proceedings: The Capacity of Children to Retain Legal Counsel*. Child in the City Report Number 1. Toronto: Child in the City Programme and Centre for Urban and Community Studies, University of Toronto.

Robertshaw, C. 1980. *Outline of Key Legislative Issues Relating to Child Abuse*. Discussion paper, Child Abuse Study. Ottawa: Social Service Programs Branch, Department of National Health and Welfare.

Royal Commission on Family and Children's Law. 1975. *Children's Rights*. Fifth Report of the Royal Commission on Family and Children's Law. Part III. Victoria: Queen's Printer.

Sammon, W.J. 1985. *Advocacy in Child Welfare Cases*. Toronto: Carswell.

Steinhauer, P. 1982. *The Courts from the Children's Perspective*. Number WS-7, Family Law and Social Policy Workshop Series. Toronto: Faculty of Law, University of Toronto.

Thomson, Judge G., and R. Barnhorst. 1982. *Policy and Practice in the Child Welfare Area*. Number WS-6, Family Law and Social Policy Workshop Series. Toronto: Faculty of Law, University of Toronto.

ET FOR BABIES?*

ard

Introduction

The market is perhaps the most commonly used mechanism for allocating scarce resources. As an allocative mechanism it has many attractive features that permit it to predominate over other systems such as bureaucracies, regulatory agencies, lotteries, juries, queues, and the like. But, despite its predominance, the market is far from universal in its use. As a result, an important aspect of economic analysis is to examine the characteristics of situations in which the market is not used as the primary allocative device in order to illuminate the limits and implications of the market as an allocative mechanism.

This paper addresses that task in the context of family law. In particular, I examine the reasons why we are reluctant to use a market mechanism in place of existing bureaucratic procedures for the adoption of newborn babies. The purpose of the essay is to understand the limits of the market rather than to promote its use. However, I pursue the topic by first detailing the affirmative case for a market in babies and then examining its deficiencies. My intention is to use the specific

Source: *University of Toronto Law Journal.* 34 (1984): 341–57. Reprinted with permission of the University of Toronto Press.

*This essay was inspired by the provocative argument in favour of a market for babies that was presented in Landes and Posner (1978, 323). That article includes many of the facts and arguments relied on in this essay. In teaching a course in Economic Analysis of Law, I often used the article by Landes and Posner as a basis of a discussion of the limits of markets and the use of market notions in analyzing law. Since this essay draws heavily on those class discussions, it includes the comments of numerous students as well as my own thoughts. In addition, I have benefited from the comments of Bernard Dickens, Jack Knetsch, John Palmer, Michael Trebilcock, Cindy Blakely, and participants in the Law and Economics Workshops at the University of Western Ontario and the University of Toronto.

case as a vehicle for a more general understanding of the limits of market mechanisms and concepts in family law and related areas, thus contributing perspective to this symposium issue on the economic analysis of family law.

In proceeding in this way I run the risk of being misunderstood as advocating a market mechanism for allocating newborn babies. The opposite is true. My primary motivation is writing this essay has been a desire to reconcile my intuitive opposition to such a system (opposition that I assume is widely, if not universally, shared) with the analytical methods of economic analysis of law. Indeed, the purpose runs deeper, extending to the vitality of economic analysis of law. For, if economic analysis is to remain a vital and creative role within legal scholarship, its limits must be explored as vigorously as its strengths.

It should also be clear from this statement of purpose that I have no direct interest in criticizing the performance of social workers and other personnel working within the existing system of adoption. While comparison of the existing system and a possible market mechanism inevitably involves some unflattering comments on the former, these are directed not at the participants in the system but rather at the inherent limits of an administrative procedure for allocating babies.

The remainder of the essay consists of four parts. First, a brief review of the current adoption system and the resulting baby shortage is presented. Second, an alternative, market-based mechanism is sketched and its likely effects are suggested. Third, in the most substantial part of the paper, the primary objections that might be made to such a mechanism are listed, categorized, and evaluated. Finally, in the fourth and concluding part, this assessment of a possible market for babies is related back to the central purpose of the paper: an enhanced understanding of the limits of markets.

The Present Situation

The results of the existing regulatory system that governs the allocation and adoption of newborn children are in many respects tragic. At present, in Canada and the United States, many people unable to have children naturally want to adopt, but there are far too few newborn children to meeting the demand; accordingly, many couples are deprived of the privileges and joys of childrearing. In addition, the existing regulatory procedures allocating these scarce newborns subject childless couples to very substantial costs.

The evidence of the tragedy is ubiquitous. Local, national, and international observations confirm the point. For example, in at least one region in Southern Ontario the local Children's Aid Society has simply closed its intake desk because there is already such a backlog of approved applicant couples that it would be useless to process any further applications. In Metropolitan Toronto, there is an enormous disparity between the number of couples seeking to adopt a child and the available supply. The current situation in Toronto involves a minimum wait of one and a half to two years for a childless couple after they first contact the Children's Aid Society. Furthermore, although some couples do receive a child within two years, many wait much longer. In other parts of the province, the wait is now approximately ten years. Similarly, in 1980 in Vancouver there were 30 newborn children available for adoption, while 1000 couples were approved and ready to receive an adopted child.[1]

The evidence of the tragedy can also be found in increasing evidence of black market activity in the sale of babies. News reports from Vancouver,[2] Toronto,[3] and the United States (Louenheim 1977) are unanimous in reporting increasing black-market activity characterized by very high prices for newborns (as much as $40 000), but continued interest on the part of childless couples. However, these reports also suggest that most of the economic rewards derived from these transactions are being gathered by the physicians and the lawyers involved in arranging them, and not by the mothers who bear the children.

The reasons for the shortage are simple. The supply of newborns has decreased dramatically, primarily as a result of the increased availability of contraceptive devices and legal abortions. A statistic indicative of the change in availability of newborns can be found in Metropolitan Toronto. In 1969, the Protestant Children's Aid Society placed approximately 1000 children, while in 1979 it placed only 179 children of which only 71 were less than one year old.

The consequences of this very substantial undersupply of adoptable babies are varied. The primary effect is that many couples who desire children are left childless. While accurate statistical information is not available, it has been estimated that up to 6 percent of couples who desire children are unable to have them naturally (Landes and Posner 1978). Given the existing short supply of babies, the magnitude of the social tragedy from the perspective of childless couples is readily apparent. The other consequences are somewhat less obvious. Childless couples are tempted to use fertility drugs and other fertility-increasing treatments that necessarily increase the risk of children being born with various kinds of infirmities. Couples are also tempted to have children naturally, even in circumstances where genetic counselling indicates they should not, since the alternative of adoption is so unavailable. On the supply side, there is no incentive for mothers to give up their newborns, because at present those who do so are not remunerated in any way for their children. As a result, the decision that the child is unwanted is often delayed for a year or two until the opportunities for and desirability of adoption are substantially decreased. Furthermore, the pregnant woman who plans to give up her child has no economic incentive to care for her child while it is in uterus since no reward is paid for producing a well-cared-for child. Thus, injury-reducing abstinence such as forgoing smoking and drinking is not economically encouraged by the present system.

In Ontario, the present scheme of regulation is created by the Child Welfare Act.[4] This statute creates a virtual monopoly in the adoption business for certain licensed agencies, although it does permit individually licensed adoptions under restrictive conditions. Under the statute, the Children's Aid Societies, which are the primary agencies charged with adoption regulation, must screen and approve prospective adopting couples. Once a couple is approved, they join a queue formed at a central registry in each geographic district in the province. When a newborn becomes available, three couples who might be appropriate parents for the child are selected administratively. Then the social worker assigned to each couple engages in an advocacy process within the agency to determine which of the three couples should succeed. As a general rule, there is an attempt to match the educational backgrounds and economic circumstances of the couples and the natural mother. In addition, subject to the best interests of the child, an attempt is made to respect the desires of the natural mother as to the type of home environment she wishes for her child.[5]

One's ability to qualify or even be screened by a Children's Aid Society is determined by the geographic location of one's residence. Thus, in order to qualify for Metropolitan Toronto's Children's Aid Society, a couple must maintain a residence in Metropolitan Toronto. Since some districts in Ontario have considerably shorter waiting lists than others, an incentive is created to maintain a second residence in a district with a shorter list merely to qualify for an adoption. It has thus been reported that couples from districts out-side Toronto where the intakes are closed or very limited maintain apartments for a period of years in Toronto in order to qualify for Metro's Children's Aid Society.

In addition to creating this regulatory scheme, section 67 of the Child Welfare Act provides that "no person, whether before or after the birth of a child, shall make, give or receive or agree to make, give or receive a payment or reward for or in consideration of or in relation to" an adoption or proposed adoption. As a result, market transactions in babies are strictly prohibited.

Similar administration and regulatory schemes are in place across Canada. Their details vary substantially, but their essential characteristic — administrative allocation — remains constant. A clear alternative would be a market-oriented system in which babies would be allocated to couples, based on the prices the couples were prepared to pay. In the section that follows, the possible advantages of such a mechanism are set out.

The Market Mechanism

At first blush the market mechanism might seem to be considerably more attractive than the existing regulatory scheme in that it appears to be able to make most people better off. The reasons are numerous.

First, one would anticipate an increase in the quantity of babies supplied in order to meet the demand. This would eliminate the present queue and satisfy the desires of virtually all the childless couples left unsatisfied by the present system and shortage. Women would engage in the production of children for adoption, responding to the financial incentives of the marketplace.

Second, one would anticipate that the market would lead to the realization of comparative productive advantages in that the supply of newborns would be undertaken by those best able to produce, satisfying the needs of those unable to have children and providing a realistic alternative for those for whom childbirth is possible but genetically unwise. Furthermore, one might anticipate some substitution of producers with relatively low opportunity costs for those with high opportunity costs. That is, persons for whom pregnancy comes only at the cost of substantial disruption of their other activities (for example, employment) might well decline to carry a child, opting to purchase a baby from a substitute carrier whose opportunity costs would be lower. This effect would be limited, of course, by the extent to which mothers derived positive utility (and paid maternity leaves) from carrying their own children and by the extent to which parents preferred natural to purchased children.

Third, one would anticipate that the market would generate information about the pedigrees of newborns that would permit the matching of couples' desires and the newborns' attributes. One would anticipate that there would be an incentive to disclose the quality of the newborns and that information-certification procedures and agencies would develop to enhance the information market.

Fourth, one would expect the newborns to be of a higher quality than the existing newborns available for adoption. The promise of remuneration for prospective mothers would lead to an incentive for the appropriate care of children in utero since a warranty of such behaviour would attract a positive reward in the marketplace. In addition, one would anticipate that prospective mothers would exercise greater care in the selection of their sexual mates since the quality of the mate would also influence the price to be obtained upon birth.

Fifth, one would expect an extremely competitive market structure. There would be extremely low entry barriers; a very large number of producers, both actual and potential; slight economies of scale; and enormous difficulties in cartelization. While there might be some brand-name identification over time, one would not anticipate that this would lead to significant barriers to entry.

Sixth, the market process would provide an incentive for parents to correct errors in judgement and shortcomings in contraceptive devices since they would be in a position to sell the child for a positive reward rather than simply give it away. This should reduce the number of foster children, because the market for newborns would create an incentive to make the disposal at the time of birth. At the same time, however, reducing the cost of errors in judgement and inadequate contraceptive techniques and devices might lead to a corresponding decrease in the care exercised by sexually active friends and couples.

Seventh, one would expect the market to produce the children at a relatively low cost — certainly at a cost much below the existing black-market prices. The market would be free from the costs of hiding transactions from law-enforcement officials, from substantial legal penalties, and from the fraudulent practices that at present permeate the black market. Furthermore, one would anticipate that the suppliers of the children would get a substantial portion of the economic return and that lawyers and physicians would be in a less strong position to take advantage of their clients and patients. With respect to price, one would anticipate that it would approximate the opportunity cost of a woman's time during pregnancy. It should be stressed that this need not by any means equal the amount of compensation that a person would earn in other market activities for the full nine months, since pregnancy is far from totally disabling. Therefore, it would not be surprising if a price as low as $3000 to $5000 per child were common in some segments of the market.

Eighth, the market could develop various efficiency-enhancing mechanisms. In particular, one might anticipate that a futures market would develop in which children in utero could be traded, permitting the reallocation of the risks inherent in childbirth so as to better reflect the various tastes for risks of different participants in the market. Furthermore, one might imagine that market intermediaries might form to hold portfolios of children in utero, thus diversifying and reducing the nonsystematic risk.

Ninth, on the distributive side, the market would be likely to display qualities considerably more attractive than the existing system. One would expect that the producers would be persons with relatively low opportunity costs who at present have very limited opportunities for income-earning activities. This would present a new source of productive activity at a reasonable level of reward. Furthermore, one could anticipate that this would result in some shift of wealth away from the purchasers of babies to the producers, who would presumably be from less-advantaged circumstances. In addition, the distributive effects of devoting some of the economic returns to the mothers and taking it away from those at present able to exploit the illegality of the black market would surely be attractive.

The Objections

In sum, quite a robust case for the market can be made. It would appear to work well. It would satisfy a lot of unsatisfied people, have attractive distributive results, and increase the degree of individual freedom and choice in the adoption process as the monopolistic regulatory powers at present enjoyed by the Children's Aid Societies would be eliminated.

Despite the attractions, and despite the inadequacies of the present system, most would find the prospect of a market for babies to be grotesque. Indeed, the mere description has a ring of parody to it as the incongruity of market notions and babies jars the reader. Somewhere within most of us there is at least an intuitive reaction that there is something indecent about the prospect of a market for babies.[6] The prospect of prices, contracts, advertising, credit, discounts, specials, and all the other attributes of consumer transactions seems disquieting. But, when asked for an explanation for this reaction, can one do better than simply assert its unacceptability? In what follows, I consider a number of possible objections.

There are three categories of objections to relying on a market mechanism. The first might be termed market-failure concerns. Here the argument meets the proposal on its own terms, not objecting to the market in principle but stressing that the market would not work well in this particular context. The second category of objections concedes that the market would work essentially as I have suggested, but that, as a market mechanism, it would possess one or more objectionable characteristics that cause us to reject the mechanism as a whole. The third category of objections attacks the entire proposal, not just its market aspects, arguing that it fails in its essential conception.

Market Failure Objections

The first line of reaction to the proposal for a baby market is to meet it on its own terms. That is, a critic might ask whether or not this is a situation in which the market would in fact produce optimal results even if the other categories of objections canvassed below are found unpersuasive. A number of doubts might be raised.

First, there is the problem that "good" babies may drive out the "bad." At present, given the shortage of babies, childless couples are prepared to adopt children who are available although, in the eyes of the adopting parents, less than perfect. If the market proposal were adopted, the supply of children with highly desired characteristics would increase and the demand for other children would diminish. This would presumably increase the number of unadopted children suffering from retardation, birth defects, and other undesired characteristics who would subsequently become foster-children. This would presumably reduce the level of welfare of both these children and society in general and must be counted as a substantial negative effect of the market proposal.

Second, there may be some significant information imperfections in the proposed market. While the market mechanism would encourage the disclosure of information concerning the newborns, there would, of course, be an incentive for mothers to disclose the good information and withhold the bad. To the extent that lies and inadequate disclosure cannot be discovered until after the transaction has taken place, a "market for lemons" problem may arise. In some ways this is analogous to concerns about the commercialization of blood donations (Akerlof 1970). It is alleged that a market mechanism for blood donation increases the percentage of donors carrying hepatitis, because the donors have a positive incentive to conceal their knowledge that they have had the disease; this incentive is not present in a system of collection based on gifts. However, it must be recognized that the continued existence of this phenomenon depends on the absence of a relatively low-cost means of screening potential donors for hepatitis. Similarly, the extent to which the "lemon" phenomenon would infect the baby market depends on the possibility and cost of tests designed to verify pedigree information proferred by the mother. Furthermore, since the purchase of a baby is a much more substantial purchase than the purchase of pint of blood, the costs that a prospective purchaser would rationally be prepared to bear in screening the donor would be proportionately increased. Thus, while there is undoubtedly a potential problem of information deficiency, its magnitude may not be overwhelming and may diminish with further scientific and technological advances.

A third concern with the market solution may be that it would generate a higher total population since one would anticipate there would be some increase in the supply of newborns. It might be argued that this population increase is an externality that individual market decisions would fail to recognize, leading to what in social terms may be an oversupply of babies. While it is certainly true that the population should increase with the adoption of this proposal, it is enormously difficult to judge whether this is a good or bad thing, and, even if it is a bad thing, whether that is cause to reject the proposal. If there is a concern with the total level of baby production, there is a wide range of existing social policies that create financial incentives and disincentives for the production of children. It would seem more appropriate to control the overall level of population through these mechanisms rather than through depriving some small segment of the community of the ability to experience the joys of raising a family. If society must bear a burden with respect to the control of population, it would seem only just that this burden be spread relatively equally across the population.

The fourth concern relates to the possibility that this scheme might permit or indeed encourage genetic breeding; people would be able to "order" the baby they desire as opposed to merely relying on the genetic lottery that natural parents face. While hypothetically plausible, it does not seem probable in reality that there would be serious breeding effects. While some couples may favour blue-eyed, blond-haired boys and others dark-haired girls, no one set of tastes is likely to dominate, for the same reason that no particular colour or make of car seems to capture universal approval. As with other commodities, one would anticipate a full range of tastes with respect to children's characteristics. So, while there should be a better matching of couples' preferences with the children they would actually receive through the market, the total distribution of children by type should remain relatively unchanged.

A fifth concern expressed by some critics is that permitting a market in newborns might also encourage a market in "used" children as people would be tempted to "trade in" unsatisfactory children and "trade up" by purchasing a newborn. If the state did not regulate obligations with regard to child support, this concern would no doubt be realized. However, under the market for babies proposal, once a couple has purchased a child they could be required to assume the same obligations, liabilities, and responsibilities that accrue to couples who now adopt children or have children naturally. To the extent there is a trade-in phenomenon at present, it would be continued, but it seems unlikely that it would be substantially increased. Indeed, if this were thought to be a serious social problem, one might deny entry to the market to any couple who traded in their child so as to eliminate that couple's access to the market for a second purchase.

Objections in Principle

Distributive Concerns

A common critique of market-oriented solutions relates to their distributive consequences. That is, the typical critic will concede that the market would be efficient, but then will point out that its impact on the distribution of wealth would be so unacceptable that the efficiency advantages should fade into insignificance. In essence, the distributive consequences are said to be so strong as to dominate any possible efficiency gains. Is that concern well founded with respect to a proposal for a market for babies? Some might argue that the effect of such a market would be that some people would be so impoverished by having paid for their baby that they would be unable to provide sufficiently high-quality care for the child. This seems implausible. It would appear to assume an extremely high price for children, an assumption which would ignore the realities of the low opportunity cost of likely mothers. Furthermore, it ignores the costs incurred by persons attempting to manipulate the existing regulatory system, whether by maintaining a second residence or by spending money to impress social workers as to their ability to provide a comfortable home environment for the child. In addition, it ignores the cost of childbirth that all natural parents go through. The opportunity costs incurred by most natural parents would not be substantially less than the market price I would anticipate for a child under the market system. In sum, this concern built around the cost of the child seems unpersuasive.

An alternative formulation of the distributive concern is that the rich would get all the "good" babies. In response, it should first be noticed that the objection seems to assume that this does not happen already, thus ignoring the reality that one's income and wealth are generally thought by adoption agencies to be important variables in determining one's suitability for parenthood. The objection also seems to ignore the prospect of an increased supply of "good" babies that one would anticipate under the market system. That is, if supply were held fixed, the concern might be persuasive in that the rich would presumably be better able to pay in order to satisfy their desires for children with characteristics found most desirable by adopting parents. However, under the market system, the supply of such children would presumably be dramatically increased, leaving the rich with what they want but also leaving many others fully satisfied. Again, the objection seems unpersuasive.

Any arguments as to the distributive effects of the proposal must also be counterbalanced by the distributive effect identified earlier of a shift in rents to the suppliers of children — that is, to mothers, who would be drawn from a generally poorer class and away from the crooks, shady lawyers, shady physicians, and others who at present trade on the tragedy of the existing regulatory failure and the fears of pregnant women.

One way of testing whether the issue of the distributive impact of the market proposal goes to the core of one's objection to it is to ask whether one would feel better about the proposal if the market were made wealth neutral as opposed to wealth sensitive (Calabresi and Bobbitt 1978, 98–103). If not, then distributive arguments are probably not the central source of one's intuitive opposition to the proposal.

Cost of Costing

Another principled objection to the market focuses on one of its inevitable aspects: the creation of prices (Calabresi and Bobbitt 1978, 32). The concern is that a market for babies would generate negative secondary consequences because a market mechanism by definition generates explicit prices. In particular, the pricing of babies might violate two principles, each of which we hold dear. The first is that life is infinitely valuable — "a pearl beyond price." With prices of $3000 per baby, the reality of the limited price of life (at least at the point of creation) and the ideal of the infinitely valuable would contrast starkly. The second principle is that all lives are equally valuable. With higher prices for white than nonwhite children, and higher prices for healthy than sick children, and other similar forms of price differentials, the reality and the ideal would again clash.

The concern here is real but difficult to evaluate. It is but one example of a much more general problem of public policy. Whenever life is at stake, the difficulties of pricing and of costing must be faced. Thus, whether it is the standard of care in tort law, the design of a Pinto, highway design, or medical research, one cannot avoid implicitly or explicitly dealing with the price of life. Perhaps it is the degree of explicitness that would be inherent in this scheme that gives rise to the vigour of the opposition. It may also be that the differences in prices would correspond with differences that we strive particularly hard to overcome by means of other social policies. That is, to the extent that differences in price fell along racial grounds, to adopt a policy of a market for babies would be directly contradictory to the wide range of social policies designed to minimize discrimination on racial grounds.

Commodification

While related to the previous concern regarding the costs of costing, the concern here is that trading in certain commodities degrades the commodities themselves (Kelman 1979b). That is, certain things should be above the hustle and bustle of the marketplace so as to preserve their dignity; this leads to the conclusion that trading in such commodities is inherently bad. That is, by creating a market one would commodify something — life — that should not be treated as a commodity. Put even more strongly, the concern is that

the special value we attribute to children depends in part on the fact that they cannot be traded. Thus, trafficking in lives becomes presumptively bad. There is a dynamic dimension to this concern as well, because trading activity would alter our views regarding the nature of the commodity at stake, reducing over time our aversion to engaging in this form of trade.

Again, the difficulty in evaluating this concern is that it is hard to know which goods fall within this category of goods that should not be commodified. Trading in babies is not directly analogous to slavery. Is it more closely analogous to long-term contracts for services? If so, why do we not have the same sense of concern about the multi-year contracts of professional athletes as we do about a market for babies?

In addition, in the midst of whatever reactions one has along this line or some of the earlier lines of objection, it is important that they not be treated in isolation from some of the compensating effects of the market proposal. That is, unless these concerns are made absolutes they must be considered in the context of a probable substantial reduction in the number of abortions performed and of the very substantial increase in happiness for previously childless couples. How these compensating effects should be weighed in the balance is unclear, but, absent the most extreme forms of rejection of the utilitarian calculus, some consideration must be given to them.

Oppression

Put bluntly, the proposal for a market for babies smacks of slavery. More broadly, the concern is that such a scheme would oppressively and involuntarily relegate poor women to an occupation that we do not wish to promote (or to be seen to promote) and that would deprive the participants of their dignity. This concern may be similar to concerns about prostitution, wet nurses, and markets for blood. However, it is not entirely clear what makes this matter oppressive when other lines of poorly paid work are seen to be less so. If the concern is simply that wages will be low, regulatory intervention is possible. If the concern is that this type of production takes advantage of the women's low opportunity cost, the response must be to recognize the truth of that proposition but to ask how this differs from any other situation of employing someone with a low opportunity cost.[7] If it is a concern for the nature of the work, what is it about childbearing that makes it somehow dishonourable when done for money but most honourable when done for other reasons? Why does paying for childbirth or engaging in childbearing for the sake of money convert a dignified activity into a despised one? The answer must lie in one of the other concerns (for example, commodification) rather than in oppression per se. That is, we may object to the commodification of sex (prostitution), blood donation, or mothers' milk production (wet nurses) not only because of the low opportunity cost, but because of the combining of low opportunity cost with an opportunity to engage in market activity in an area where commodification itself is objectionable.

At the same time, it is not entirely clear what the focus of concern is in this respect. Some would argue that it is women who are being oppressed, but others might argue that it is the newborns who are being oppressed. One way to test this proposition might be to ask whether the concern would be the same if the market were in test-tube babies, so as to relieve any concern about a class of women being oppressed. If the concern remains, it seems that is must be broader than merely the oppression of women.

The Absence of a Relationship Between Willingness to Pay and Quality of Parent

Another line of attack on the proposal would be to point out that, while willingness to pay for a commodity may be the best measure of desire, people may desire children for the wrong reasons. That is, someone may wish to acquire a child for the purpose of beating or otherwise abusing it, rather than loving it or caring for it. This is no doubt true, but again does it go to the heart of the problem?

Presumably the same perverted desires motivate people to give birth naturally. In Canadian society, we do not require an ex ante check on the reasons for having natural children, and thus one must question why ex ante review of suitability for parenting should be required under the market scheme. However, even if some ex ante scheme is desired (as it is under the existing regulatory mechanism), it is, of course, not inconsistent with having a market scheme of allocation. That is, it would be quite simple to require anyone wishing to make a bid in the baby market first to obtain a parenting certificate from some regulatory agency. This licence would be granted or denied on the basis of whether or not one met the minimum necessary qualifications for parenting. There would be no limit on the number of certificates granted. If this step were adopted, it is difficult to see how the divergences of willingness to pay and quality of parent would be any more extreme under the market for babies proposal than under the existing regulatory mechanism.

Misconception Objections

The first category of objections focussed on market failure and the second on principled objections to the use of the market in the context. The third category, while related to the second, attacks the proposal as being wrong in its very conception of the problem. This objection can be stated in three ways.

The Improper Object
The market-for-babies proposal would meet what is at present the unmet demand of childless couples who wish to adopt a child and are unable to do so as a result of the insufficient supply of children. A critic might suggest that the proposal is directed toward a social end that is misconceived from the start. That is, it can be argued that the purpose of the existing process is not to meet the desires of childless couples for children, but rather to take care of a limited number of unwanted

newborns, with the merely incidental side effect of bringing great joy and happiness to childless couples. Under the latter formulation, the number of couples satisfied or left dissatisfied is largely irrelevant to our judgement about the allocative mechanism, since it is assumed that the function of the system is to distribute those babies that are produced as a by-product of the existing sexual and marital activities and rules. The success of the mechanism should therefore be judged in terms of the welfare of the unwanted newborns, not that of childless couples. Furthermore, any system that would increase the supply of children requiring adoption would be directly counterproductive in terms of the objective of designing a system solely for distribution of unwanted babies.

This line of argument is compelling if it is accepted that no weight should be given to the preferences of childless couples. How such a judgement could be taken, though, is somewhat more problematic; it is not at all clear what value is being preserved or promoted by denying this fundamental happiness to the large number of couples left childless under the existing scheme. If it were possible to identify that value, perhaps all the other concerns about the market solution might be derived from it.

The Second-Best Argument

Another response to the market for babies proposal is to acknowledge that, although it would be better than the existing situation, it would not be the best possible mechanism. That is, alternatives such as banning abortion or prohibiting contraceptive devices might be better responses in that they would increase the supply of babies. Or it might be argued that leaving the supply fixed and instituting a pure lottery would be better than the existing distribution mechanism. Or indeed, it might be argued that an alternative source of supply — foreign babies from third-world countries with excess newborns — might represent a better and distributively more attractive source of babies. All these possibilities have merit. However, none of them seems to go to the heart of the matter — that is, why the market itself is seen to be so objectionable. That is, most people's reaction to the market-for-babies proposal is that it is bad *per se*, not bad relative to alternative mechanisms. The interesting question remains why the market is seen to be bad *per se*.

Jonathan Swift's "Modest Proposal"

Swift's satirical solution to the problem of starvation in Ireland may be thought to be analogous to the market-for-babies proposal.[8] We need only read Swift's proposal to be confident of its unacceptability; it is a classic satire. Thus, if the analogy is compelling, one must dismiss a market for babies with similar dispatch. However, to draw the analogy between the two proposals one must find the essence of each to be the *marketing* of babies, thus giving less weight to the distinction between killing and giving life to babies. To me, this is not an entirely satisfactory characterization of the two proposals. It fails to distinguish between the giving of life and the taking of life. That is, the Swift proposal depends on terminating a life after its successful creation. That would appear to be so fundamentally in contradiction with the right to life, which is accepted by essentially everyone to be above any utilitarian calculus, that any set of potential benefits becomes irrelevant to the merits of the proposal. However, in the case of a market for babies there is no deprivation of life but rather the creation of new life, and it is only possible objections to this creation of new life that must be offset against the obvious benefits of the scheme. At this point it is more difficult to identify any absolute right equivalent to that of preserving life that would be violated by creating more life.

Conclusion

I end where I started, focussing on the limits of markets by asking whether these objections to a market for babies are persuasive. To the extent that they are, they may help define the limits of markets in other situations requiring an allocative device.

The need for a coherent appreciation of the limits of market-based allocative mechanisms is enhanced at a time when we are being inundated by signs of the increased commercialization of activities closely related to a market for babies. Campus-newspaper advertisements seek sperm donors: "Semen will be used for artificial insemination for couples who cannot have children due to male infertility. Men of all backgrounds are needed and in particular of Chinese, Japanese, Black and East Indian backgrounds. Donors . . . will be paid for their involvement."[9] A couple having a child but wanting a new car are reported to have traded in their baby for a used Corvette.[10] News reports tell of surrogate mothers who charge a fee for carrying a child for a couple who are not otherwise able to produce their own child but who desire the injection of at least the husband's genes: "[Through] Surrogate Parenting Associates, Inc. . . . an infertile couple and their surrogate can be matched for a fee of between $15,000 and $20,000 which covers payment to the surrogate as well as medical, incidental, and legal fees" (Hammond 1981). Speculation is common that the near future holds promise of commercial banks for sperm, body parts, and other life-creating products.[11]

In many of these situations, a market mechanism may offer the promise of increased supply. For example, kidneys, livers, hearts, and other body parts would no doubt be far more available — at a price — if financial rewards could be paid to the donors. But, despite this promise of supply, the predominant reaction is to resist and to look for alternatives. This common pattern of resistance surely reflects concerns of the kind identified in this essay. At the same time, I believe that these concerns should be understood as to some extent contingent upon cultural and social values that themselves change over time. Transitions in these values can and do occur, responding to a complex shifting social consensus.

We may well be in just such a period of transition to a society in which the objections to the baby market will lose much of their force. Such a transition was experienced in the late nineteenth century with respect to life insurance, which was thought for a time to represent a form of trafficking in and valuing of lives (Zelizer 1979, 62-63, cited in Gordon 1980, 912). Whether the same transition is about to occur with respect to the market for babies, semen, surrogate mothers, body parts, and the like may well depend in part on the strength, coherence, and nature of the objections to the market-for-babies proposal and the extent to which we can identify them and commit ourselves to the preservation of the values that inform them.

Notes

1. *Province* [Vancouver], April 7, 1980.
2. Ibid.
3. *Sunday Star* [Toronto], April 6, 1980.
4. R.S.O. 1980, c. 66.
5. While I am not familiar with solid evidence on this point, anecdotal evidence suggests that this consideration further diminishes any arguments that to vary the existing scheme of distributing babies would necessarily be counter to the child's best interests. In one case I am familiar with, the choice of the successful adopting family was made on the basis that the natural mother wished for an outdoor style of life for her child and the adopting family had submitted a photograph of the parents posing with a canoe.
6. The proposal for a market for babies has even provoked academic emotion. For example, see Kelman (1979b, 688, n.51): "As always, Posner poses as the tough rationalist fending off sissified moralists; his rationalism, though is spotty, incomplete, and misleading. He thus manages to be both irrational and immoral, which may have been his aim in this little parody of Jonathan Swift's 'Modest Proposal'."
7. See the discussion in Kelman (1979a, 769 at 788 ff.), citing Nozick (1969).
8. A colleague, E. Weinrib, and Kelman (1979b) have both suggested the analogy.
9. *Varsity* [Toronto], March 9, 1981.
10. *Star* [Toronto], September 5, 1980.

11. At present, in Ontario, section 10 of the Human Tissue Gift Act prohibits commercial trafficking in human tissues and body parts. Interestingly, the prohibition arguably does not include either sperm or children.

Works Cited

Akerlof, George A. 1970. "The Market for 'Lemons': Quality, Uncertainty and the Market Mechanism." *Queen's Journal of Economics* 84: 488-50.

Calabresi, Guido, and Philip Bobbitt. 1978. *Tragic Choices*. New York: Norton.

Gordon, Robert W. 1980. "Review of *Tort Law in America: An Intellectual History*, by G. Edward White." *Harvard Law Review* 94: 903-10.

Hammond, Michael. 1981. "Mothers and Child." *Quest* 10: 67-8, 70.

Kelman, Mark. 1979a. "Choice and Utility." *Wisconsin Law Review* 1979: 769-97.

———. 1979b. "Consumption Theory, Production Theory and Ideology in the Coase Theorem," *Southern California Law Review* 52: 669-98.

Landes, Elizabeth M., and Richard A. Posner. 1978. "The Economic of the Baby Shortage." *Journal of Legal Studies* 7: 323-48.

Louenheim, Barbara. 1977. "Innocents, Inc.," *Student Lawyer* 6: 23-4, 45.

Nozick, A. 1969. "Coercion." *Philosophy, Science and Method*. Morgenbesser et al. eds. New York: St. Martin's. 440-72.

Zelizer, V.A.R. 1979. *Morals and Markets: The Development of Life Insurance in the United States*. New York: Columbia University Press.

Part Ten

EVOLUTION, REVOLUTION, AND THE FUTURE OF THE FAMILY

• • •

No mariner ever enters upon a more unchartered sea than does the average human being born in the twentieth century. Our ancestors knew their way from birth through eternity; we are puzzled by the day after tomorrow.

Walter Lippmann, *The Readers Digest* (1962)

Some kinds of family changes can be seen as the logical outcome of a continuation of current trends. They evolve gradually from pre-existing conditions and represent *quantitative* changes — a difference of degree. Other changes, however, can be termed revolutionary; they represent an abrupt jump-shift from existing circumstances. Their unexpected newness leads to family variations that are *qualitative* changes — a difference in kind. At least three new factors are in the process of revolutionizing the Canadian family: first, the impact of the new birth-control technology; second, the recognition of the homosexual way of life as a legitimate alternative lifestyle; and third, the spectre of AIDS. Speculations about the future are always hazardous, but they are especially hazardous in these areas, because there are no relevant precedents for what is most likely to occur. What we can say with confidence is that these developments will make a real difference to family systems during the next decade.

Until the recent past, the process of "having" children usually involved the birth of a child after its mother had conceived it during intercourse with her husband. Occasionally, the child was conceived by another couple during intercourse and the family unit was created by a process of adoption. The first innovation in this sequence was the use of artificial insemination. This was followed in rapid succession by fetal sex preselection, *in vitro* (test-tube) fertilization, embryo transfers, frozen embryos, and surrogate motherhood. The process of "having" a child may now involve three persons and/or couples: the genetic parents who supply the egg and sperm; the birth parents (that is, the "incubator" mother who carries the baby to term and her husband, if any); and finally the social parents who assume the social roles of father and mother. The relationships of these persons to "their" baby and to each other have yet to be delineated. However these issues are resolved, they will certainly demand a redefinition of the rights and obligations of parents and children.

At present, Canadian law defines a "marriage" as a union between a man and a woman. By definition, therefore, a stable gay couple who have made a permanent commitment to live together and function as a couple cannot be considered to be married, even

463

though in social terms they form a unit that is the equivalent of a spousal union. One issue that is currently before the courts is the extent to which gay unions can or should be considered "as if" they were marriages, in the same way that common law unions are often treated "as if" they were legal marriages. As long as gays can form only informal unions, they are excused from many of the obligations of the married state. Unfortunately, however, this policy also excludes them from the protection that may be offered to husbands and wives.

A recent Gallup poll revealed that half the population considered AIDS to be Canada's most urgent health problem, and were concerned it might become an epidemic. In Montreal, 20 percent of respondents reported that, because of the risk of AIDS, they had either changed their behaviour or were seriously thinking of doing so (Gallup Canada 1988f). Nationally, one person in eight saw AIDS as a reason to modify behaviour; this proportion will doubtless increase as the problem becomes more acute, and as public-education campaigns become more extensive.

About the Articles

The norms that define family membership and kinship evolved when the process of reproduction involved only two persons: a biological father who inseminated a biological mother to create a child equally related to both of them. In recent years, the new biotechnology of birth has provided a wide range of alternative strategies that can lead to the birth of a baby. The many options now available were originally developed to help otherwise infertile couples to achieve the birth of their own child. However, as the biotechnology of birth improves, it will doubtless by used by many individuals or couples who wish to achieve better control over the birth process. Overall reviews the major procedures and devices now being used, and speculates on their ultimate consequences for future families.

Homosexual families have somewhat different potential problems than do other families. Agbayewa discusses how the social role of father may be fulfilled by lesbian couples with children. In a similar vein, Stein points out the need for therapists to be aware of issues unique to homosexual family forms.

A decade ago, family sociologists would confidently have predicted that the norms of sexual permissiveness established in the 1970s would continue to flourish and would come to be endorsed by increasing proportions of the population. Today, it is clear that the spectre of AIDS will dramatically modify those liberal projections. Much of the social import of virginity was directly related to the perennial threat of illicit pregnancy. This consideration, which had been a major bulwark of the traditional double standard, became increasingly obsolete with the introduction of effective contraception. With the potential spread of AIDS to the heterosexual community, however, virginity may again become a socially significant characteristic. Moreover, since AIDS is an "equal-opportunity disease," limiting the number of one's sexual partners may become as important for males as for females. Strike presents data on the incidence of AIDS in Canada. Finally, Macklin discusses the many implications of the AIDS epidemic for Canadian and American families, both now and in the future.

Works Cited

Gallup Canada, Inc. 1988f. "Many Canadians Concerned About Possible AIDS Epidemic," *The Gallup Report*. August 25.

Further Readings

Arditti, Rita, Renate Duelli Klein, and Shelley Minden (eds.) 1984. *Test-Tube Women: What Future for Motherhood?* London: Pandora Press.

Bayles, Michael D. 1984. *Reproductive Ethics.* Englewood Cliffs, NJ: Prentice-Hall.

Brodribb, Somer. 1984. "Reproductive Technologies, Masculine Dominance and the Canadian State". *Occasional Papers in Social Policy Analysis*. Toronto, Ontario: Ontario Institute for Studies in Education.

Macklin, Eleanor D., and Roger H. Rubin, eds. 1983. *Contemporary Families and Alternative Lifestyles: Handbook on Research and Theory*. Beverly Hills, CA: Sage.

Patton, Cindy. 1986. *Sex and Germs: The Politics of AIDS*. Montreal: Black Rose.

Singer, Peter, and Deane Wells. 1984. *The Reproduction Revolution: New Ways of Making Babies*. Oxford: Oxford University Press.

Sommerville, Margaret A. 1982. "Birth Technology, Parenting and 'Deviance'." *International Journal of Law and Psychiatry* 5: 123–53.

Steadman, Jennifer H., and Gillian T. McCloskey. 1987. "The Prospect of Surrogate Mothering: Clinical Concerns." *Canadian Journal of Psychiatry* 32: 545–50.

Walters, William, and Peter Singer (eds.) 1982. *Test-Tube Babies: A Guide to Moral Questions, Present Techniques and Future Possibilities*. Melbourne: Oxford University Press.

[REPRODU]CTIVE TECHNOLOGY AND [FUTU]RE OF THE FAMILY

Introduction

This article examines some of the ways in which recent developments in the technology of reproduction may affect the kinds of relationships that now exist primarily within the so-called nuclear family. I am concerned with how these new relationships between men and women and between parents and children may change what we are able to be and do and become, as children, as parents, and as spouses.

Reproductive technology is burgeoning, and so is discussion about it by sociologists, legal experts, feminists, and philosophers. Many — but especially doctors, lawyers, and scientists — are willing to sing the praises of reproductive technology, yet they seldom stop to consider its implications for our future. The general rule appears to be: what can be done should be done; if it is possible to manipulate human reproduction, then human reproduction should be manipulated. In contrast to this approach, I argue that we must consider carefully what may be the potential effects of reproductive technology on human relationships.

Some forms of reproductive technology are already very familiar. Today contraception, abortion, and often birth involve the use of some form of reproductive technology. But,

Source: *Women and Men: Interdisciplinary Readings on Gender.* (Markham, ON: Fitzhenry and Whiteside, Ltd., 1987), 245–62. Reprinted with permission of Greta H. Nemiroff (editor).

in this article, I shall discuss several procedures and devices that have been developed much more recently: fetal sex preselection, prenatal diagnosis and surgery, in vitro fertilization and embryo transfer, and surrogate motherhood. I will briefly describe each of them, and suggest what implications each has for the future of the family.

There are two general themes that unify this discussion. The first concerns reproductive freedom and choice. I argue that new reproductive technology has a paradoxical effect on reproductive freedom, particularly on the reproductive freedom of women: on the one hand, it appears to enhance our capacity to make choices, but on the other hand, a closer examination suggests that there are many ways in which reproductive technology may serve to reduce the reproductive choices we can make.

The second theme concerns the tendency toward the commodification[1] of human beings and the introduction of certain sorts of economic considerations into social relationships. Children, in particular, are commodified by reproductive technology, which permits them to be treated in some respects as consumer goods that can be made to order and purchased on the open market. A child becomes a product with an exchange value, a luxury item that one might or might not want or need. At the same time, reproductive technology permits men to become primarily the consumers of reproductive services and reproductive products. Finally, reproductive technology also transforms women into reproductive consumers, but, more directly and more significantly, it makes women the suppliers of reproductive services and products. Thus, the economic relationships of buying, selling, and leasing are transforming traditional family alliances.

Fetal Sex PreSelection

The term "fetal sex preselection" refers to various means that have been proposed for the purpose of determining, at the time of conception, the sex of the fetus.[2] A variety of techniques for sex preselection have been experimentally tested (Hanmer 1981, 175; Nentwig 1981; Hoskins and Holmes 1984; Largey 1978; Glass 1982, 113–29). Most promising among them are methods that involve separating X-bearing and Y-bearing sperm by means of filtering or centrifugation. The woman is then artificially inseminated with a sperm sample containing a significant concentration of the type of sperm that will produce a child of the desired sex. Thus, the woman's chances of conceiving a child of the "right" sex are increased, although success is by no means guaranteed.

At least two important questions about the use of fetal sex preselection could be raised: first, are individuals ever justified in making use of preselection techniques to determine the sex of their children? If so, when and why are they so justified, and if not, why are they not justified (Powledge 1981; Bayles 1984, 33–36)? Second, what sort of social policy about research into, and development and availability of, sex preselection should we have (Etzioni 1968; Lappé and Steinfels 1974; Postgate 1973; Westoff and Rindfuss 1974)? I will concentrate mainly on the second of these.

To reflect on the issue, it is necessary to consider, first, the possible effects of the use of fetal sex preselection. At the moment, these effects are chiefly a matter of speculation. But we do know that there is a world-wide preference for male offspring over female off-

spring. Study after study has shown that this preference is held by men even more strongly than by women; that if a couple is to have only one child, they prefer a boy; that people want their first-born to be a boy; and that, if they want an odd number of children (three, five, etc.), they want more boys than girls (Williamson 1976a, 1976b; Pebly and Westoff 1982). In the light of this well-documented preference for male offspring, it seems likely that widespread use of sex preselection techniques would result in a change in the sex ratio: that is, far more males than females would be born. Would this mean that, because of our fewer numbers, women would be more cherished and valued (Keyfiitz 1983, xii; Williamson 1983)? Or would it mean even greater restrictions on and control over women, to "safeguard" our scarce sexual and reproductive services (Postgate 1973, 16)? Would the use of fetal sex preselection produce a decrease in population, since people would get exactly the kinds of children they want (Meier 1968; Postgate 1973, 14)? Or would it mean an increase in crime, violence, and war (since men are primarily responsible for these) (Etzioni 1968, 1109; Rowland 1984)? Would human freedom expand or diminish?

At least superficially, it looks as if the use of fetal sex preselection would increase our reproductive choices and control. But we must consider who makes the choices and who is in control. Fetal sex preselection enables people to act on their biases against females. Who would make that choice? Would it be women, who often express no preference of their own for the sex of their offspring,[3] but may tend to want a male child for the sake of their husbands? Would it be men, who may make the choice for male offspring, perhaps with the goal of obtaining a son to carry on their name?

Or, in impoverished countries, and in those subject to stringent state control, would the choice of fetal sex be imposed by governments anxious to set limits on the numbers and kinds of children produced by their citizens? Several social scientists advocate the widespread use of fetal sex preselection because they believe it will reduce the population explosion. This would occur, it is claimed, because parents would no longer need to have "just one more child" to obtain a child of the desired sex. More radically, it has also been proposed that the use of sex-preselection techniques (inevitably resulting in the birth of far more boys than girls) would reduce the population because there would be so many fewer women to bear children (Postgate 1973, 14). In this scenario, the price of fetal sex preselection is state control of reproduction, and, perhaps, considerable sacrifice of individual autonomy.

We must also consider the possible effects of this technique on the children themselves. On the one hand, it has been argued that the use of fetal sex preselection would produce happier families (Powledge 1981, 202): the parents get the kind of children they want; the children, whether boys or girls, are wanted as boys or girls. On the other hand, it has also been suggested that the use of fetal sex preselection would exaggerate existing gender roles: parents who want a son so much that they use sex-preselection methods to obtain one would expect that son to act like a "real boy," and pre-selected daughters might be expected to be "little ladies" (Lappé and Steinfels 1974, 2).

These stereotypes could be further exacerbated by the fact that sex preference is related to desired birth order: particularly in North America, people usually prefer a son first, then a daughter (Westoff and Rindfuss 1974, 635). But studies have consistently found certain important differences between first- and second-born children, regardless of their sex. In terms of ability and academic and professional success, first-borns are overrepresented (Williamson 1976a, 859). Second-born children, however, are likely to be socially adept and popular (Forer 1977). Thus the use of sex-preselection techniques could confirm existing stereotypes about the sexes and relegate women to "second class" status, because they would be denied the advantages of being the first-born (Williamson 1976a, 860; Rowland

1984, 361–62). On this view, gender stereotyping of children would be increased, to the detriment of their freedom to develop.

The use of fetal sex preselection also exemplifies the tendency toward the commodification of children. While apparently being valued for their own sake, through fetal sex preselection, children are treated as a type of consumer good. The parents — perhaps most often the father — pay their money and take their choice: instead of being stuck with whatever nature brings, they purchase the type of child they want. But unfortunately, unlike some other forms of technology, the use of fetal sex preselection does not permit unsatisfied parents to return a defective product. Assuming, as I think we must, that technology would not be fail-safe, we might wonder about the fate of those children — primarily females — who would be the "wrong" sex (Hoskins and Holmes 1984, 238). The use of fetal sex preselection appears to imply that children are wanted, not for their own sake, for their own individual characters and abilities, but rather for the sake of the gender they represent.

Prenatal Diagnosis and Fetal Surgery

This tendency toward the commodification of children is even more evident in the use of prenatal diagnosis and fetal surgery.

Prenatal diagnosis involves the use of such procedures as ultrasound tests, chorionic villi sampling, and amniocentesis. These techniques permit the acquisition of a great deal of information about possible structural and chromosomal defects in the fetus, as well as its sex. In an ultrasound test, high-frequency sound waves are projected into the woman's uterus, and the waves reflected back are resolved visually to allow the fetus to be "seen" on a display screen (Lippman 1985, 3). In chorionic villi sampling, a tube is inserted through the vagina and cervix to the placenta, from which a small amount of tissue is removed. The tissue can be examined for evidence of fetal defects. This test can be performed as early as eight or nine weeks into the pregnancy, but it is not yet widely available in Canada (Lippman 1985, 3–4, 14). On the other hand, amniocentesis is easily available. It involves the insertion of a needle through the woman's abdomen and into the amniotic fluid that surrounds the developing fetus. Fluid containing cells from the fetus is removed and can then be examined in the laboratory. However, amniocentesis cannot be performed before about 16 weeks into the pregnancy, and, unlike chorionic villi sampling, a further two or three weeks are necessary to wait for the results of the analysis of the fluid (Lippman 1985, 1–2).

In the context of prenatal diagnosis, it is assumed that a fetus found to be defective will be aborted. The use of chorionic villi sampling permits an early abortion, in the first trimester of pregnancy, but a verdict of fetal defects detected through amniocentesis results in a very late abortion, at about five or six months' gestation.

In addition to diagnostic tests of the fetus, fetal surgery is also being developed (Ruddick and Wilcox 1982, 32; Hubbard 1982). This involves cutting open the woman's uterus during the pregnancy, temporarily removing the fetus, correcting a defect (such as a block in the urinary system), and then replacing the fetus in the uterus to enable the pregnancy to continue to term.

In general, once again, these technologies appear to enable us to obtain the kind of child we want, by repairing correctable defects and eliminating fetuses with noncorrectable handicaps. Yet, this very factor may contribute to the growing tendency to treat the child as a material commodity, a consumer good to be purchased by means of money and medical technology. Prenatal diagnosis and fetal surgery permit us to make more and more detailed specifications of the type of child we want. The techniques encourage us to raise our standards for what are considered to be acceptable offspring. The development of these tests means that men and women become the consumers of special reproductive services designed to enhance the quality of the child–product. Although there can be no

doubt that they permit the birth of more and more healthy babies, some ethicists and some handicapped persons themselves (Saxton 1984) fear that the widespread use of prenatal diagnosis and fetal surgery will mean that in the future any children born with handicaps will tend to be regarded as unfortunate mistakes who should have been eliminated before birth.

These technologies also appear to increase our information and choice about reproduction. However, some recent writers have also challenged this assumption. Some forms of prenatal testing are not always easily available. For example, in Canada, chorionic villi sampling is so far available only to women who are enrolled in a scientific trial of the technique (Lippman 1985, 14). On the other hand, other diagnostic procedures, such as ultrasound, are now so routine that women do not have the opportunity and the right to refuse them — in spite of the fact that the long-term effects of ultrasound are not yet known (Lippman 1985, 12–14). It is taken for granted that the pregnant woman will submit to an ultrasound test twice in her pregnancy and that, if she is 35 or over, she will undergo amniocentesis. And then, if the fetus is found to be defective (to have, for example, Down's Syndrome), can she freely choose to continue the pregnancy if she so desires, or is pressure exerted on her to have an abortion (Rothman 1984)? In this context, the autonomy of the woman is not increased but decreased.

Another problem attendant upon prenatal testing and surgery is that these processes draw more and more attention to the status and well-being of the fetus, and tend to treat the woman as no more than a sort of carrier or environment for it (Ruddick and Wilcox 1982, 12; Hubbard 1982). This sets the stage for what some legal experts see as a potential conflict between the alleged rights of the fetus and the rights of the pregnant woman (Gallagher 1984, 65, 66, 134, 135; Ruddick and Wilcox 1982, 11; Hubbard 1982; Robertson 1983a; Rodgers-Magnet 1985).

This conflict has already manifested itself in at least two areas. In the United States, there have been landmark cases in which a caesarean section has been ordered to be performed on an unwilling woman for the sake of the supposed well-being of her fetus, as determined by still-fallible prenatal tests. In those cases, the courts found that the safety of the fetus took priority over the autonomy and reproductive control of the mother (Gallagher 1984, 66; Annas 1982, 16, 17, 45). In Canada, certain cases have found that a child was the victim of prenatal abuse as a result of the mother's use of alcohol or drugs (Proudfoot 1983; Gentles 1983, 24–25). These findings, while they seem to give greater and greater protection to the fetus (and I do regard that as a desirable goal) may also provide a sturdy background for the erosion of maternal freedoms.

Some writers have wondered, then, whether the growing concern for the welfare of the fetus can be considered to be consistent with our current regulation of abortion. On the one hand, the abortion law, both here and in the United States, permits the killing of the fetus under specified conditions. On the other hand, more and more steps are being taken in other circumstances to safeguard the health of the fetus. Are these tendencies compatible with each other? Is it consistent to attempt to protect the health of the fetus at various stages of its existence, and yet also to sustain the mother's right to terminate its existence (Gentles 1983, 19–29; Keyserlingk 1983)?

These questions suggest that in evaluating the implications of prenatal diagnosis and fetal surgery we should be assessing the relative claims of fetal rights and women's autonomy. Reproductive technology encourages physicians and scientists to see the pregnant woman as an adversary of the fetus (Gallagher 1984, 134; Gentles 1983, 23; Robertson 1983a, 443). The possibility exists that proposals to require certain restrictions on the mother's behaviour, in the interests of allegedly protecting fetal life and well-being, could be the result of the growing technological focus on the state of the fetus (Annas 1982,

45; Robertson 1983a, 443–44; Keyserlingk 1982; Shaw 1984). In the future, we should therefore consider whether these technologies actually increase our reproductive control and choice, or whether in fact they subtly detract from the freedom of pregnant women (Leeton, Trounson, and Wood 1982, 2–10).

In Vitro Fertilization

The technology of in vitro fertilization (IVF) must be evaluated in conjunction with embryo transfer and the storage of frozen embryos. In IVF, a woman is treated with hormones that stimulate her to produce several ova (eggs) simultaneously. Under general anaesthesia, these ova are removed from her body. A sperm sample is obtained from her partner and is added to the ova in a petri dish. It is hoped that at least one and possibly more than one fertilized egg will be produced. The fertilized eggs are permitted to develop to the eight- or sixteen-cell stage; they are then transferred to the woman's uterus. Sometimes not all of the fertilized eggs are implanted; they can be frozen for possible use at a later date.

The main rationale for the use of IVF and embryo transfer is the treatment of infertility — ordinarily, the treatment of infertility in the woman. In the typical case, the woman produces ova, but they are unable to reach the uterus because her fallopian tubes are blocked. When surgery to open the tubes is unsuccessful, her only hope for a pregnancy lies in the IVF technique. Less frequently, the procedure can also be used for one type of male infertility. In this case, the man produces sperm, but in insufficient quantities and concentrations to permit fertilization of the ovum in vivo, that is, within the woman's body. It is thought that in this instance the artificial environment of IVF permits fertilization to take place more easily than it would within the environment of the woman's body (Edwards 1983, 95).

Like the other technologies discussed so far, IVF and embryo transfer appear to expand human control over reproduction, by enabling childless individuals to reproduce. And there can be no doubt about the very real grief experienced by many infertile couples (Menning 1984, 17-19; Coman 1983; Greer 1984, 46-47; Taymor 1978, 94-96; Edwards and Steptoe 1980, 121; Bainbridge 1982). Once again, however, it is necessary to look a little more closely at what the technology really accomplishes, and at who is in control of it.

This technology is not, first of all, available on demand. Specific criteria are used by the medical profession to determine who will have access to it. In most writings on infertility, the impression given is that infertility is only significant and worth treating in persons who are heterosexual and married, and have a so-called stable relationship with their partners (Kass 1971, 1972; Acosta and Garcia 1984). Thus, women who are single and/or lesbian, for example, and in some cases those who are judged by the physician not to have the appropriate potential for parenting, often do not have access to these forms of reproductive technology (Arditti, Klein, and Minden 1984, 5; Rothman 1982; Brodribb 1984, 15-16). It seems that the way in which IVF and embryo transfer are made available serves to reinforce the traditional connection between motherhood and marriage, and the dependence of women on men.

Furthermore, for couples who are judged to be eligible for the procedure it is not an unmixed blessing. The process of extracting ova involves rather painful surgery. If it is not successful, the woman may have to undergo the surgery more than once. Moreover, at most Canadian clinics, the woman has no choice as to whether or not all of the fertilized eggs will be implanted in her. Thus, despite the increased probability of multiple birth, if the clinic's policy is to transfer them all, then regardless of what the woman thinks of the prospect of giving birth to twins or triplets or quadruplets, they are all transferred (Brodribb 1984, 16).

It should be noted that in such countries as Britain, the United States, and Australia,

the fate of so-called spare embryos — those produced by means of IVF and not subsequently transferred to the mother's uterus — is a hotly debated moral issue. Should spare embryos be discarded, or frozen for possible future use (Annas 1984, 50-52; Grobstein 1982, 5-6; Great Britain 1984, 55-69)? The attitude toward this appears to depend mainly on one's beliefs about the personhood of the embryo.[4] But there may be other reasons for being concerned about issues pertaining to the so-called spare embryo. The fact that embryos can be frozen for future use emphasizes the fact that the procedure of IVF permits women to become suppliers of reproductive products (Annas 1984, 51-52).

There is already a century-long social history of men supplying sperm, for a price, for the purpose of artificial insemination. Now technology permits women to be vendors in a comparable fashion. Women can donate or sell their ova to women who do not ovulate, or whose ova cannot be extracted from their bodies. Moreover, women can also donate or sell embryos, by means of a new process known as uterine lavage. In this procedure, the donor woman is artificially inseminated. If conception takes place, the fertilized egg travels from the fallopian tube to the uterus. Before the embryo implants in the uterine wall, it can be washed out of the uterus and recovered; it can then be transferred to the uterus of another woman who is unable to ovulate (Council for Science and Society 1984, 91). Thus women become, through reproductive technology, the suppliers of reproductive products — ova and embryos — that can be purchased by infertile individuals. The commodification of reproduction now extends to both sexes.

The embryo transfer stage, whether it follows IVF or uterine lavage, is a perilous one. Very often, a number of attempts will have to be made at transferring embryos; most failures in IVF occur at this stage (Great Britain 1984, 30). And in fact, the procedure has a rather low success rate. One Canadian clinic claims a success rate of 20 percent,[5] but that estimate seems rather optimistic; a 12 percent success rate is more usual (Leeton, Trounson, and Wood 1982, 7–8). The procedure is also quite expensive: in this context, the acquisition of a child-commodity requires an investment of several thousand dollars. The total amount depends on how many attempts must be made until either a pregnancy is achieved or the couple gives up.[6]

Finally, the idea of "giving up" is itself significant. Some writers on infertility and artificial reproduction have suggested that the development of reproductive technology has drastically changed the significance of and attitude toward infertility. While IVF appears to expand our options, it may in other ways reduce them. The use of IVF and embryo transfer may help to sustain traditional ideas about the importance to women of childbearing, because it exacerbates what has been called "the moral pressure to have children" (Laurance 1982). The infertile couple can no longer merely accept their infertility as a sort of mysterious incapacity inflicted by fate; instead they must resort to lengthy, expensive, painful, exhausting diagnostic and surgical procedures. If they fail to make full use of all that medicine offers them, then they seem to have wilfully chosen their infertility (Rothman 1984, 31–32).

I believe, therefore, that while the development of procedures such as IVF can help a very few fortunate individuals with specific sorts of infertility, it also encourages us to think of infertility as a disease, a treatable disease. It encourages us to see the infertile as persons who are handicapped and in dire need of help. Instead of assisting them to adjust to and accept the fact that they do not have a child who is genetically related to them, or, better still, instead of encouraging all of us to feel concern and responsibility for all children, it drives home the idea that a family without children is not a "real" family. It implies that an individual is not complete, not a real woman or a real man, without her or his "own," genetically related child, and that childless persons should explore all possible means of obtaining one.[7]

Surrogate Motherhood

Like IVF, surrogate motherhood is resorted to as a corrective for infertility. When a woman, for a variety of reasons, is unable to sustain a pregnancy, her husband can hire a woman to bear "his" child. There are two possible procedures here. First, if the wife produces ova, one or more of these can be extracted from her and fertilized with her partner's sperm. This would make use of the IVF technique. The embryo or embryos that are thereby produced could then be transferred to the surrogate who would gestate them and surrender the baby or babies to the couple at the end of the pregnancy.

More commonly, surrogate motherhood as it is presently practised involves not IVF but the much older process of artificial insemination of the surrogate with the sperm of the man who hires her. Conception then takes place within the surrogate's body, the pregnancy proceeds, and the woman surrenders the baby to the couple after its birth (Rassaby 1982, 97–98; Singer and Wells 1984, 107–14; Bayles 1984, 22–23; Robertson 1983b).

Thus, in the first case, the surrogate provides only her reproductive services: the use of her uterus and all of its capacities for nurturing a fetus. In the second, actual, case, the surrogate not only provides reproductive services but also supplies, in her ovum, a reproductive product: that is, one-half of the baby's genetic inheritance. So, one question that arises immediately is whether there are any important moral, psychological, or social policy differences between the two forms of surrogate motherhood. However, I think that most of the important questions about surrogate motherhood, in either form, arise in connection with its potential effect on the children that are thereby produced, and also in regard to what the practice suggests about the social position of women and about women's relationships to men.

It seems clear, first of all, that there is some potential for problems arising from surrogacy — problems that, first and foremost, can affect the well-being of the child that is produced. Because the practice of hired surrogacy is so new, no one knows yet what all of the possible effects might be on a child that has been ordered and purchased by its parents. For example, we already know that adopted children in later life very often feel a longing to search for their genetic parents; it seems possible that a child born to a surrogate might later want to seek her out.

However, other problems pertaining to surrogate motherhood are not merely hypothetical, but have actually occurred in surrogate arrangements in the United States. It is particularly clear in these contracts that once again the child is being treated as a commodity. Perhaps we should wonder generally about our social attitudes toward children if buying babies becomes a widespread and acceptable practice.

The baby produced by a surrogate is an expensive commodity: the going rate for hiring a surrogate is now from $20 000 to $25 000 (Robertson 1983b, 29). Presumably the hiring couple wants a top-quality product. As a result, some surrogate contracts even specify both that the surrogate explicitly forgo her right to choose an abortion, and also that she agree to undergo an abortion if fetal testing indicates the presence of a handicapped child (Dranoff 1984, 26; Helm et al. 1985). But what happens if the baby is born with a defect anyway, or is not of the sex for which the couple was hoping? Does the commissioning couple have to accept damaged goods? What is the fate of a child for whom no one wants to take responsibility?[8] Or perhaps the mother produces not one baby but two. In a way, the commissioning couple seem to get double their money's worth. Are they entitled to both children? What if they only want one? A more serious possibility is that the baby is born dead. Has the mother then fulfilled her responsibility; is she entitled to payment?

One of the most serious complications that has so far arisen with some frequency in surrogate arrangements is that some mothers are unwilling to surrender the child after it is born (Rassaby 1982, 101–102; Singer and Wells 1984, 120–21). The other side of the coin is that some couples have been known to change their minds about taking the baby they have ordered, if their circumstances change dramatically: if, for example, one of them dies, or the marriage breaks down.[9] If the surrogate also does not want the baby, it again becomes an unwanted child.

More subtle, perhaps, but just as important, are the questions that the practice of surrogate motherhood raises about the position of women in society and about women's relationships to men and to their offspring.

First, the existence of surrogate emphasizes that we can now clearly distinguish between different forms of motherhood and fatherhood (Rothman 1982, 154, 156, 158). Thanks to reproductive technology, a baby could, potentially, have five different parents: its genetic mother and genetic father, who supply the ovum and the sperm; its carrying mother, who gestates the embryo produced by the union of ovum and sperm; and finally its social mother and father, the individuals who rear the child produced by the carrying mother.

The possibility of making these distinctions also permits the development of a distinctly commercialized form of reproductive labour. Medical and legal writers, as well as the surrogates themselves, tend to see surrogacy as a type of job (Munro 1985). But if it is a job, it is a most peculiar one. The incumbent is required to be on duty 24 hours a day. The pay is very low, far below the present minimum wage: even though the hiring couple may pay $20 000, the surrogate receives only about $10 000 of that; the rest goes for lawyers' fees, medical expenses, psychological and physical tests, and travel expenses (Munro 1985). It is also a job that can drastically reduce the surrogate's personal autonomy. Often, surrogacy contracts will include provisions that severely limit what the woman eats and drinks, the timing of her sexual activities, her leisure pursuits and physical activities, and her use of medical services, including her right to an abortion (Dranoff 1984, 26; Mady 1981, 332–38).

I think it is important to ask whether in fact this is the sort of "job" we would value and would want to encourage for women. Would you want your daughter or sister to take up a "career" as a surrogate mother? Should surrogacy be presented by vocational counsellors as a new job option? Is this the sort of thing you would want to put on your curriculum vitae or résumé?[10] Surely the answer to each of these questions is no. From the point of view of the women involved (whatever its benefits for those who are infertile), surrogacy does not seem to be the sort of practice we would want to encourage, at least in its commercialized form.

Surrogate motherhood represents the final step in the commodification of reproductive relationships. Some feminist writers, in fact, have compared it to prostitution. A prostitute sells her sexual services; a surrogate mother sells her reproductive services (Dworkin 1983, 174–88). In the latter context, the consumer of the services is, usually, a man, not a woman: the surrogacy contract is ordinarily an agreement between the surrogate and the man who hires her; the infertile wife is a legal nonentity for the purposes of the arrangement (Ince 1984). And the lawyer who recruits surrogates and negotiates the contract with the hiring couple is very like a pimp, for he derives great economic benefit from handling the sale of reproductive services.

I want to emphasize here that in comparing surrogate mothers to prostitutes, I am not condemning the women who make money in these ways. Instead, I am concerned about the sort of social system in which women see their future only in terms of selling their reproductive capacities. The women who now seek work as surrogate mothers are often poor and uneducated (Parker 1983). For them, surrogacy may appear to be a sort of last resort, when more lucrative and prestigious forms of employment are unobtainable. In becoming surrogates, they take on work that denies their individuality, that values them only to the extent that they are successful and healthy reproductive machines. In that respect, surro-

gate mothers are interchangeable and anonymous (Dworkin 1983, 182). Although the hiring father has the freedom to choose which woman he wants to bear his child (Munro 1985), the surrogate herself has little choice in the matter, especially if she is recruited through a surrogacy agency, such as those that operate in the United States.

Thus, once again, although the practice of surrogate motherhood appears to increase our reproductive freedom by allowing some infertile women and the men to whom they are married (at least those who are wealthy) to acquire a baby, in fact in other respects, in its highly commercialized form, it diminishes at least some women's reproductive freedom and control. For, as the popular press has so aptly suggested, surrogacy amounts to no more than a depersonalized rent-a-womb arrangement.

Conclusion

Much more could be said about the impact of reproductive technology on the future of the family. But even a brief examination suggests that this technology raises serious questions with regard to the commodification of reproduction and reproductive relationships within the family, and the scope and meaning of reproductive freedom and choice, particularly for women.

New reproductive technology generates many conflicts and contradictions. It has the potential to be both an asset and a liability for the future of human relationships. Perhaps the main source of this ambiguity is the question of power that it raises. If women and men, both as individuals and as members of the groups, share control over reproductive technology, it may be put to uses that benefit us all. But as now seems to be the case, most people are able to exert very little control over research into and the development and applications of reproductive technology,[11] then it may be a real threat to our hopes for a humane future.

Notes

1. I use the term in the Marxist sense. See, e.g., Engels (1970, 580).

2. I will exclude from consideration the topic of postconception fetal sex selection, which involves the discovery of the sex of the fetus through the process of amniocentesis or chorionic biopsy, and subsequent abortion if the fetus should turn out to be of the "wrong" sex. See Roggencamp (1984) for discussion of a specific case.

3 In the United States, women are likely to say that they want a balance in the sex of their offspring. See Pebley and Westoff (1982, 178).

4. There is an enormous amount of philosophical discussion of this issue, usually in connection with the abortion debate. For a discussion of the issue in the context of IVF, see Johnstone, Kuhse and Singer (1982).

5. Personal communication from Dr. Murray Kroach, LIFE program, Toronto East General Hospital, Toronto, Ontario, March 22, 1985.

6. For example, the LIFE program at the Toronto East General Hospital charges $1500 per attempt at embryo transfer. However, that amount is described as a "bargain" compared to the costs at some clinics in the United States, which charge $5500 on average per cycle. (Dr. Murray Kroach, personal communication, March 22, 1985.)

7. These ideas are given dramatic expression throughout Edwards' and Steptoe's *A Matter of Life*, which narrates the full history of the production of the first "test-tube baby," Louise Joy Brown.

8. The result of the surrogacy arrangement in 1981 between Judy Stiver and Alexander Malahoff was a baby with microcephaly, who was wanted by neither of the parties to the contract (Singer and Wells, 118-19).

9. For example, in the Stiver/Malahoff case, Malahoff's marriage to his infertile wife ended before Stiver's baby was born.

10. I owe this suggestion to Lorraine Code.

11. This is a major theme of Brodribb's paper.

Works Cited

Acosta, Anibal A. and Jairo E. Garcia. 1984. "Extracorporeal Fertilization and Embryo Transfer." Aiman 217.

Aiman, James, ed. 1984. *Infertility: Diagnosis and Management* New York: Springer-Verlag.

Annas, George A[...] Most Unkindes[...] *Report* 12 (June[...]

———. 1984. "[...] tecting Embryo[...] *The Hastings C[...]

Arditti, Rita, Re[...] Minden, eds. 1[...] *ture for Motherh[...]

Bainbridge, Isabe[...] The Experience[...] ton 119-27.

Bayles, Michael M. 1984. *Reproductive Ethics.* Englewood Cliffs, NJ: Prentice-Hall.

Bennett, Neil G., ed. 1983. *Sex Selection of Children.* New York: Academic.

Brodribb, Somer. 1984. "Reproductive Technologies, Masculine Dominance and the Canadian State." *Occasional Papers in Social Policy Analysis No. 5.* Toronto: Ontario Institute for Studies in Education.

Coman, Carolyn. 1983. "Trying (and Trying and Trying) to Get Pregnant." *Ms.* (May). 21-24.

Council for Science and Society. 1984. *Human Procreation: Ethical Aspects of the New Techniques.* Oxford: Oxford University Press.

Cragg, Wesley, ed. 1983. *Contemporary Moral Issues.* Toronto: McGraw-Hill Ryerson.

Dranoff, Linda Silver. 1984. "Ask a Lawyer." *Chatelaine* (January): 26.

Dworkin, Andrea. 1983. *Right-Wing Women.* New York: Perigee.

Edwards, R.G. 1983. "The Current Clinical and Ethical Situations of Human Conception in Vitro." *Developments in Human Reproduction and Their Eugenic, Ethical Implications.* Ed. C.O. Carter. New York: Academic.

Edwards, Robert, and Patrick Steptoe. 1980. *A Matter of Life: The Story of a Medical Breakthrough.* London: Hutchinson.

Engels, Frederick. 1970. "The Origin of the Family, Private Property and the State." *Karl Marx and Frederick Engels: Selected Work.* Moscow: Progress.

Etzioni, Amitai. 1968. "Sex Control, Science and Society." *Science.* 161(3846): 1107-12.

Forer, Lucille, with Henry Still. 1977. *The Birth Order Factor.* New York: Pocket.

Gallagher, Janet. 1984. "The Fetus and the Law: Whose Life is it Anyway?" *Ms.* (September): 66, 134-35.

Gentles, Ian. 1983. "The Unborn Child in Civil and Criminal Law." Cragg 24-29.

H. 1982. *Getting Pregnant in the Advances in Infertility Treatment and lection.* Berkeley, CA: University of California Press.

Britain. Department of Health and Social Security. 1984. "Report of the Committee of Inquiry into Human Fertilisation and Embryology." Command Paper 9314 (July).

Greer, Germaine. 1984. *Sex and Destiny: The Politics of Human Fertility.* London: Secker and Warburg.

Grobstein, Clifford. 1982. "The Moral Uses of 'Spare' Embryos." *The Hastings Center Report.* 12 (June).

Hanmer, Jalna. 1981. "Sex Predetermination, Artificial Insemination and the Maintenance of Male-Dominated Culture." *Women, Health and Reproduction.* Ed. Helen Roberts. London: Routledge and Kegan Paul.

Helm, Sarah, et al. 1985. "Nothing Left to Chance in 'Rent-A-Womb' Agreements." *Toronto Star* (January 13).

Holmes, Helen B., Betty B. Hoskins, and Michael Gross, eds. 1981. *The Custom-Made Child? Women-Centred Perspectives.* Clifton, NJ: Humana.

Hoskins, Betty B., and Helen Bequart Holmes. 1984. "Technology and Prenatal Femicide." Arditti 238–41.

Hubbard, Ruth. 1982. "The Fetus as Patient." *Ms.* (October): 32.

Ince, Susan. 1984. "Inside the Surrogate Industry." Arditti 101–102.

Johnstone, Brian, Helga Kuhse, and Peter Singer. "The Moral Status of the Embryo: Two Viewpoints." Leeton 49–63.

Kass, Leon R. 1971. "Babies by Means of In Vitro Fertilization: Unethical Experiments on the Unborn?" *The New England Journal of Medicine* 285 (November 18): 1176–77.

———. 1972. "Making Babies — The New Biology and the 'Old' Morality." *The Public Interest* 26 (Winter): 20.

Keyfitz, Nathan. 1983. "Foreword." Bennett xii.

Keyserlingk, Edward W. 1983. "Balancing Prenatal Care and Abortion." Cragg, 29–37.

———. 1982. "The Unborn Child's Right to Prenatal Care (Part 1)." *Health Law in Canada.* 3(1): 10–12.

Lappé, Marc, and Peter Steinfels. 1974. "Choosing the Sex of Our Children." *The Hastings Center Report* 4 (February): 1–4.

Largey, Gale. 1978. "Reproductive Technologies: Sex Selection." *Encyclopedia of Bioethics* Ed.

Warren T. Reich. New York: The Free Press. 1439–41.

Laurance, Jeremy. 1982. "The Moral Pressure to Have Children." *New Society.* 5 (August): 216–18.

Leeton, John F., Alan O. Trouson, and Carl Wood. 1982. "IVF and ET: What It Is and How It Works." *Test-Tube Babies: A Guide to Moral Questions, Present Techniques and Future Possibilities.* Melbourne: Oxford University Press.

Lippman, Abby. 1985. "Access to Pre-Natal Screening Services and Trials: Who Decides?" Paper delivered at the Policy Workshop on Medical Control: Pregnancy Issues. Sixth Annual Biennial Conference of the National Association of Women and the Law. Ottawa (February 22).

Mady, Theresa M. 1981. "Surrogate Mothers: The Legal Issues." *American Journal of Law and Medicine.* 7 (Fall): 332–38.

Meier, Richard L. 1968. "Sex Determination and Other Innovation." *Population in Perspective.* Ed. Louise B. Young. New York: Oxford University Press. 410.

Menning, Barbara Eck. 1984. "The Psychology of Infertility." Aiman 17–29.

Munro, Margaret. 1985. " 'Rent-a-Womb' Trade Thriving Across Canada–U.S. Border." *The Montreal Gazette* (January 21): D-11.

Nentwig, Ruth M. 1981. "Technical Aspects of Sex Preselection." Holmes 181–86.

Parker, Philip J. 1983. "Motivation of Surrogate Mothers: Initial Findings." *American Journal of Psychiatry* 140 (January): 117–18.

Pebly, Anne R., and Charles L. Westoff. 1982. "Women's Sex Preferences in the United States: 1970 to 1975." *Demography* 19 (May): 177–89.

Postgate, John. 1973. "Bat's Chance in Hell." *New Scientist.* 58 (April): 12–16.

Powledge, Tabitha M. 1981. "Unnatural Selection: On Choosing Children's Sex." Holmes 193–99.

Proudfoot, Madame Justice. 1983. "Judgement Respecting Female Infant 'D.J.'" Cragg 16–18.

Rassaby, Alan A. 1982. "Surrogate Motherhood: The Position and Problems of Substitutes." Leeton 101–102.

Robertson, John A. 1983a. "Procreative Liberty and the Control of Conception, Pregnancy, and Childbirth." *Virginia Law Review* 69 (April): 437–50.

———. 1983b. "Surrogate Mothers: Not So Novel After All." *The Hastings Center Report.* 13 (October): 28–34.

Rodgers-Magnet, Sandra. 1985. "Foetal Rights and Maternal Rights: Is There a Conflict?" Paper delivered at the Policy Workshop on Medical Control: Pregnancy Issues. Sixth Annual Biennial Conference of the National Association of Women and the Law. Ottawa (February 22).

Roggencamp, Viola. 1984. "Abortion of a Special Kind: Male Sex Selection in India." Arditti 266–77.

Rothman, Barbara Katz. 1982. "How Science Is Redefining Parenthood." *Ms.* (July/August). 156.

———. 1984. "The Meanings of Choice in Reproductive Technology." Arditti 31–32.

Rowland, Robyn. 1984. "Reproductive Technologies: The Final Solution to the Woman Questions?" Arditti 361–62.

Ruddick, William, and William Wilcox. 1982. "Operating on the Fetus." *The Hastings Center Report.* 12 (October): 32.

Saxton, Martha. 1984. "Born and Unborn: The Implications of Reproductive Technologies for People with Disabilities." Arditti 298–312.

Shaw, Margery W. 1984. "Conditional Prospective Rights of the Fetus." *The Journal of Legal Medicine* 5(1): 83–89.

Singer, Peter and Deane Wells. 1984. *The Reproductive Revolution: New Ways of Making Babies.* Oxford: Oxford University Press.

Taymor, Melvin L. 1978. *Infertility.* New York: Grune and Stratton.

Westoff, Charles F., and Ronald R. Rindfuss. 1974. "Sex Preselection in the United States: Some Implications." *Science* 184 (May 10): 633–36.

Williamson, Nancy E. 1983. "Parental Sex Preferences and Sex Selection." Bennett 142.

———. 1976a. "Sex Preferences, Sex Control and the Status of Women." *Signs* 1: 847–62.

———. 1976b. *Sons or Daughters: A Cross-Cultural Survey of Parental Preferences.* Beverly Hills, CA: Sage.

S IN THE NEWER FAMILY FORMS:
R FEMALE?*

M. Oluwafemi Agbayewa

**Current social trends have produced signifi-
cant changes in the family system, with the
emergence of newer family forms — single-
parent and homosexual families. The author
used the example of a six-year-old boy in a
female homosexual family to discuss the theories of sex-role development. The literature
on father-absence and the converging roles of
father and mother, men and women, were reviewed with suggestions that women may
function as fathers in the newer family forms.
Longitudinal studies of children in these
newer family forms are needed to define the
implications of these social changes for
personality-development theories and mental-
health care delivery.**

The last 30 years have witnessed certain social
changes that have great impact for the practice
of psychiatry. These changes have led to al-
terations in social roles and functions, especially in the social system called the family.
An attempt to understand a specific aspect
of these changes, that is, children raised by
homosexual couples, will be explored in this
paper.

Evolving family patterns reflect social
changes such as industrialization, urbanization, advancing education, and changing roles
of females and children, culminating with the
emergence of the nuclear family (Taeuber

1969). A variant of the nuclear family is the
single-parent family which is associated with
increasing freedom of choice and the reintro-
duction of women into the labour force (Tavuchis 1969). This has led to the increased
ability of women to provide materially for
themselves and their children, more confidence in risking divorce or marriage, and opting out of marriage rather than spend a lifetime in subjugation and misery. There is
currently one divorce to every three marriages
in Canada (Statistics Canada 1983); more
than one out of every seven families and over
90 percent of all one-parent families are
headed by women while fewer than 10 percent
of divorced fathers have custody of their children in the United States (Bilge and Kaufman
1983). Thus, there is a trend toward increasing father-absent families within society, with
mother-absence being much less frequent.

The 1970s saw the increasing rejection of
traditional family forms, particularly by those
in homosexual relationships. Many homosexuals have children from previous heterosexual
relationships of whom they increasingly obtain legal custody (Riddle 1977; Bell and
Weinberg 1978). Those previously unin-
volved in heterosexual relationships or with
no children from such relationships may
adopt, or become pregnant through artificial
insemination (Lego 1981). Very little is
known of the development of children who
live with their homosexual parents, and less
still when the custodial parent cohabits with
a homosexual "spouse." To anticipate the implications of these new family types on child
development, we need to focus on an obvious

Source: *Canadian Journal of Psychiatry* 29 (1984): 402–406. Reprinted
with permission.

*I wish to acknowledge the assistance of the Women's Issues Group,
Health Sciences Centre, Winnipeg, and P. Leichner, M.D., for their
suggestions, and M. Penner for her secretarial assistance.

aspect of personality development that would be affected — that is, sex-role development.

Theoretical Review

Factors determining sex-role development in children continue to be controversial. However, three theoretical approaches are generally espoused: biological, social-learning, and cognitive developmental theories. The biological theories posit that sex hormones, which may have an early differentiating function in terms of propensity for aggression, may also lay the groundwork for other more complex sex roles. Much of the socialization experience of children is considered to be preparation for their participation in the reproductive system — that is, continuity of the species. The reproductive system leads to disparities in the life plans of men and women by virtue of anatomical differences. This is evidenced by the Freudian psychoanalytic theory of psychosexual development. Biological differences between the sexes play a major role in the oedipal conflict, the resolution of which calls for identification with same-sex parents (Brenner 1974; Weitz 1977). It could be assumed from this theory that the absence of same-sex parents would lead to impaired identification, and thus impaired development or absence of same-sex role characteristics.

The social-learning theories of sex-role development propose that the family provides the child with the closest and most prolonged models of adult life and sex roles, with lifelong influence on the child. Extrafamilial models are provided by peers and other adults. Roles played by children are differentially reinforced within both the home and the society, with behaviours reinforced in any child depending on the culturally sanctioned roles for that sex. Bandura (1965) showed that imitative aggressiveness, which was observed more in boys than girls, occurred equally in both sexes when positive incentives were introduced. It would also seem that modelling is enhanced not so much by the sex of the model, but by the emotional bond that exists. This is supported by studies that found both boys and girls more similar to their mothers than to their fathers on personality measures (Friese et al. 1978; Hetherington and Frankie 1967), and Byrne (1972) found a significant correlation between mothers and children of both sexes for authoritarianism. It could, however, be argued that the choice of model is determined by a child's gender identity. For instance, Kohlberg (1966) postulates that the child makes an unalterable cognitive categorization of himself or herself as boy or girl (gender identity); this judgement then organizes the subsequent development of behaviours (sex role).

Kohlberg's cognitive developmental theory of sex-role acquisition describes three major cognitive steps in the development of sex role:

1. The child develops an awareness of two separate and different sexes (including his or her own sex) — that is, gender identity. This is usually established at about two to four years of age.
2. Development of a system of values for various behaviours and attitudes: differential valuing and differential modelling. The child imitates sex-appropriate behaviours, avoids sex-inappropriate behaviours and objects, and models same-sex individuals.
3. Development of emotional attachment and identification with same-sex parent. The child continues to be influenced by outside forces such as peers, teachers, extended-family members, and heroes.

The cognitive developmental theory combines aspects of both the biological and social learning theories. In a different context, Money, Hampson, and Hampson (1957) came to similar conclusions in their studies of hermaphrodites. They observed that a person's gender role and orientation become established, beginning at a very early age, as that person becomes acquainted with and deciphers a continuous multiplicity of signs that point in the direction of his being a boy or her being a girl. The above theories imply the necessity of same-sexed parents for a normal development of at least certain personality characteristics such as sex role. There is, however, some role for cultural values and extra-familial same-sex individuals in the child's development.

The case of a six-year-old boy from one of the newer family forms is presented to facilitate a review of the limitations of present theories as they apply to such families, and the implications that these family forms have for psychiatric theory and practice in the future.

Case Description

Martin is a six-year-old boy referred to the clinic by his mother with the following complaints: sexual preoccupation, such as peering into mother's room at night; "spying" on mother and girlfriend in the bath; fondling his genitals; constantly disagreeing with his mother; kicking and locking up his cat; lying and fighting. All these complaints dated back several months. He seems happier when mother is out; likes to play and be with mother's live-in girlfriend (Ms G.) whom he calls "Daddy." He wants Ms G. to play ball games with him and to take him out. Ms G.'s attempts to convince him that she is not his father are often countered by Martin's request that she should be his father, or at least be his friend if not father. Mother tried unsuccessfully to discourage this relationship. Some of the attempts to convince him that Ms G. is not his father include pointing out the differences between a man and a woman, and, on the basis of this, categorizing Ms G. as a woman who cannot be a father. Martin is able to identify Ms G. as a woman like his mother, but still regards her as father. He calls the mother "Mom" and realizes that he lived with a father before, who is a man. Now, he says that Ms G. is his new father.

This is Martin's first contact with any mental-health professional. The parents separated when Martin was 2½ years old. Martin lived with his father and grandparents until age five, when his father remarried and his mother assumed custody. At the point of contact, Martin was in a kindergarten (preschool)

where an assessment by the school psychologist did not find any abnormalities in his intellectual functioning, conduct, and peer relationships. He was initially aggressive at school, but had improved to "co-operative and friendly" by the teacher's assessment.

Pregnancy was full-term Caesarean delivery following a prolonged labour. Although the father physically assaulted the mother throughout pregnancy, there was no evidence of malformation at birth. Martin was a quiet baby whose development up to contact was normal, with no significant history of past or present physical illness. His biological sex, and sex-role identity are male at this point. These are inferred from examination of the external genitalia, vocational aspirations to be a truck driver, favourite toys and games that include racing cars, and peer group composition of predominantly boys; roles played in fantasy games are male and he drew a boy first in the draw-a-person test (Green 1978; Giddings and Halverson 1981).

Martin's mother is 25 years old and, with the 25-year-old girlfriend, lives a rather socially isolated life within the community. She was married to Martin's father for a total of about three years before separation and then divorced three years ago. She describes him as often unemployed, selfish, uncaring, and physically aggressive and abusive. She felt unloved by her parents, physically abused by her mother, and neglected by her father. Although aware of her homosexual preferences prior to marriage, she was non-practising because of lack of opportunity. Following her separation from the husband, she had a few unrewarding homosexual relationships before meeting and falling in love with her current girlfriend. They have stayed together for over two years now. Mother was jealous of the son's relationship with Ms G., found it intolerable, and did everything to interrupt any interactions between them. She was unable to understand that Martin's sexual preoccupation was age appropriate and saw him as a male, and thus threatening. It also became clear that what Martin wanted from Ms. G. was a father–son relationship. He seemed to have re-created a complete family with Ms G.

in the role of father — that is, mother's spouse. Therapy that included all three members of this reconstituted family focussed on mother's feelings toward Martin, especially those displaced from ex-husband onto Martin.

Gender identity determined by both biological characteristics and assignation was established earlier in life, and thus normal in Martin. Extra-familial socialization in peer-group culture, social environment, and symbolic world such as television characters (Friese et al. 1978) probably contributed to his masculine sex-role development. Martin could have developed his own system of values with differential valuing of his own sex and thus attributes behaviour generally attributable to that sex (sex role). This cognitive process could have occurred prior to his stay with homosexual parents, but is maintained. However, the abstract concept of sex roles is not established until 11 years of age, since the development of Piagetian formal operation is necessary for the linkage of sex roles with social systems, work, and family roles. Martin, while able to identify the different sexes and even at a concrete level to differentiate certain traditional roles, is unable to formally differentiate traditional and culturally determined family roles of the sexes. His age and behaviours (such as sexual preoccupation) suggest intensification of oedipal conflicts, probably because of sexual activities by mother and her girlfriend. To resolve these conflicts, Martin has identified with mother's "spouse," whom he has labelled "father," although he recognizes her as a woman. Being mother's spouse, Ms G. fulfils some criteria for father and is thus an available choice for the needed psychological father.

Discussion

Fox (1970) sees the family less as a unit but more as a field of action where various bonds operate for various purposes. It is the purpose that determines which bonds will be forged, strengthened, or ignored. This basic unit consists of the mother-and-child dyad, to which males could be peripheral. In this case, it

seemed that for Martin to adequately resolve the age-appropriate conflicts, he needed to identify with "mother's spouse" — that is, father. How often are such conflicts adequately resolved within father-absent families?

Schlesinger (1970) noted that children of one-parent families are confused about the absent parent and experience school and health difficulties; many of them feel humiliated at being abandoned by their parent. Benedek (1970) suggested that there are crucial phases of development for the child in relationship with the father. These are supported by findings of significantly fewer masculine self-concepts in boys under the age of six in father-absent families and the importance of the father for girls' personality development (Benedek 1970; Hetherington 1966; Biller and Bahm 1971; Biller and Weiss 1970). Most studies of father-absent families occurred in the 1950s and 1960s, before the full impact of social changes, such as increasing choices, desires, and opportunities for independence among women, could be felt. Results from these studies are nonconclusive, but it could be inferred that, in the absence of any other family dysfunctions, the boy from a father-absent family is not psychologically inferior to his father-present counterparts (McCord, McCord, and Thurber 1962; Biller 1968, 1976; Sprey 1970). Moreover, the studied characteristics such as aggressiveness and dependence are stereotypes that may not be universal discriminants of the sexes (Vroegh 1968; Ellis and Bentler 1973).

We must differentially consider the sex of cohabiting homosexual parents in assessing the implications for their children's development. We do not have enough experience yet to conclude the effects on the children of living with these parents. Preliminary reports so far suggest that these children are essentially no different from other children (Green 1978; Weeks, Derdeyn, and Langman 1975) and that homosexual parents can be good role models for children (Riddle 1977, 1978; Miller 1979; Bozett 1980). In considering how homosexual parents can meet the roles of father and mother, it should be noted that the role of father now approximates that of mother, in that it is less authoritarian, more permissive, and places less emphasis on the father–son work relationship. (Benedek 1970). Anthropological studies report societies with female husbands (exclusive of coitus) (O'Brien 1977) and no fear of maladjustment in the children of these families. Oboler (1980) reported a culture in which children have little contact with the fathers, while the female fathers possess all the characteristics of the male fathers; Biller and Bahm (1971) documented the importance of maternal factors in the development of masculinity in male father-absent boys. Father–husband characteristics include being strong, active, and providing for a wife and children with unquestioned authority (Benedek 1970). These androgynous characteristics, according to the above reports and research in this area, may be found in both males and females (Riddle 1978; Berzins, Welling, and Wetter 1978). The effects of sexual disturbances on family life reported by Nichtern (1977), and the difficulties in children of single parents observed by Schlesinger (1970) are not unique to children of these new family forms, but also occur in dysfunctional families of heterosexual parents.

Bilge and Kaufman (1983) have suggested that "it is not family form, but the support system and methods of socialization that have the greater impact on children". Solnit (1976) anticipated this when he commented that new forms, variations of family structure, and functions are to be expected. They can be viewed as efforts to humanize and enhance our development and survival, as long as the continuity of affectionate bonds and exclusive intimacies are keystones to these new forms. At the point of contact, the boy in the example given above had symptoms that were resolved by family therapy. What should the long-term management approach be? How does one explain the circumscribed neglect of reality, that is, calling a woman father? How will the emergence of newer family forms, especially those in which homosexual partners assume parenting roles, affect the development of children? Does normal development require a male father and a female mother with

certain specified traditional characteristics or are these roles interchangeable? Is there any need for specialized services to this group of children and their families (Mayadas and Duehn 1976)? Tentative answers to these questions could be inferred from the above review, but definite answers can come only from longitudinal studies of the newer family forms (single parent–male/female, and homosexual parents–male/female).

The importance of such studies is underlined by the fact that one-fifth of all lesbians and one-tenth of gay men are parents (Bell and Weinberg 1978), with single-parent families increasing. The changes in traditional sex roles and the emergence of new family forms in society have major implications for psychiatric practice and theory in the future.

Works Cited

Bandura, A. 1965. "Influence of Models' Reinforcement Contingencies on the Acquisition of Imitative Responses." *Journal of Personality and Social Psychology* 1: 589–95.

Bell, A.P., and M. Weinberg. 1978. *Homosexualities: a Study of Human Diversity*. New York: Simon and Schuster.

Benedek, T. 1970. "Fatherhood and Providing." *Parenthood: Its Psychology and Psychopathology*. Eds. E.J. Anthony and T. Benedek. Boston: Little, Brown 167–83.

Berzins, J., M. Welling, and R. Wetter. 1978. "A New Measure of Psychological Androgyny Based on the Personality Research Form." *Journal of Consultative Clinical Psychology* 46: 126–28.

Bilge, B. and G. Kaufman. 1983. "Children of Divorce and One Parent Families: Cross-Cultural Perspectives." *Family Relations* 32: 59–71.

Biller, H.B. 1968. "A Note on Father Absence and Masculine Development in Lower Class Negro and White Boys." *Child Development* 39: 1003–6.

———. 1976. "The Father–Child Relationship: Some Crucial Issues. *The Family — Can It Be Saved?* Eds. V. Vaughan and T. Brazelton. Chicago: Year Book Medical. 69–76.

Biller, H.B., and R.M. Bahm. 1971. "Father Absence, Perceived Maternal Behavior and Masculinity of Self-Concept Among Junior High School Boys." *Developmental Psychology* 4: 178–81.

Biller, H.B., and S.D. Weiss. 1970. "The Father-Daughter Relationship and the Personality Development of the Female." *Journal of Genetic Psychology* 116: 79-93.

Bozett, F. 1980. "Gay Fathers: How and Why They Disclose the Homosexuality to Their Children." *Family Relations* 29: 173-79.

Brenner, C. 1974. *An Elementary Textbook of Psychoanalysis*. Revised ed. New York: International Universities.

Byrne, D. 1973. "Parental Antecedents of Authoritarianism." *Journal of Personality and Social Psychology* 26 (1): 65-76.

Ellis, L.J., and P.M. Bentler. 1973. "Traditional Sex-Determined Role Standards and Sex Stereotypes." *Journal of Personality and Social Psychology* 25 (1): 28-34.

Fox, R. 1970. "Comparative Family Patterns." *The Family and Its Future*. Ed. K. Elliott. London: J. and A. Churchill. 1-12.

Friese, H., et al. 1978. *Women and Sex Roles: a Social Psychological Perspective*. New York: W.W. Norton.

Giddings, M., and C.F. Halverson. 1981. "Young Children's Use of Toys in Home Environments." *Family Relations* 30: 69-74.

Green, R. 1978. "Sexual Identity of 37 Children Raised by Homosexual or Transsexual Parents." *American Journal of Psychiatry* 135: 692-97.

Hetherington, E.M. 1966. "Effects of Paternal Absence on Sex-Typed Behavior in Negro and White Preadolescent Males." *Journal of Personal and Social Psychology* 4: 87-91.

Kohlberg, L. 1966. "A Cognitive Development Analysis of Children's Sex Role Concepts and Attitudes." *The Development of Sex Differences*. Stanford, CA: Stanford University Press. 82-173.

Lego, S. 1981. "Beginning Resolution of the Oedipal Conflict in a Lesbian About to Become a "Parent" to a Son." *Perspective in Psychiatric Care* 19: 107-11.

Mayadas, N., and W. Duehn. 1976. "Children in Gay Families: An Investigation of Services. *The Homosexual Counselling Journal* 3: 70-83.

McCord, J., W. McCord, and E. Thurber. 1962. "Some Effects of Paternal Absence on Male Children." *Journal of Abnormal and Social Psychology* 64: 361-69.

Miller, B. 1979. "Gay Fathers and Their Children." *Family Coordinator* 28: 544-52.

Money, J., J. Hampson, and J. Hampson. 1957. "Imprinting and the Establishment of Gender Role." *Archives of Neurology and Psychiatry* 77: 333-36.

Nichtern, S. 1977. [...] on Family Life." [...] uality 11: 116-2[...]

Oboler, R. 1980. [...] Woman/Woma[...] Kenya." *Ethnol[...]

O'Brien, D. 1977 [...] Bantu Societie[...] *Cultural View.* [...] lumbia University Press.

Riddle, D. 1977. "Gay Parents and Child Custody, Issues." Unpublished manuscript.

———. 1978. "Relating to Children: Gays as Role Models." *Journal of Social Issues* 34: 38-58.

Schlesinger, B. 1970. *The One-Parent Family*. Toronto: University of Toronto Press.

Solnit, A.J. 1976. "Marriage: Changing Structure and Functions of the Family. *The Family — Can It Be Saved?* Ed. Vaughan V. Brazelton. Chicago: Year Book Medical. 231-38.

Sprey, J. 1970. "The Study of Single Parenthood: Some Methodological Considerations." Schlesinger 13-25.

Statistics Canada. 1983. *Marriages and Divorce: Vital Statistics*. Statistics Canada Publication No. 84: 205.

Taeuber, I.B. 1969. "Change and Transition in Family Structures." *The Family in Transition*. Fogarty International Center for Advanced Study in the Health Sciences. Fogarty International Center Proceeding No. 3. Bethesda MD: National Institute of Health. 35-97.

Tavuchis, N. 1969. "The Analysis of Family Roles." *The Family in Transition*. Fogarty International Center for Advanced Study in the Health Sciences. Fogarty International Center Proceeding No. 3. Bethesda MD: National Institute of Health. 12-23.

Vroegh, K. 1968. "Masculinity and Femininity in the Preschool Years." *Child Development* 39: 1253-57.

Weeks, R., A. Derdeyn, and M. Langman. 1975. "Two Cases of Children of Homosexuals." *Child Psychiatry and Human Development* 6: 26-32.

Weitz, S. 1977. *Sex Roles: Biological, Psychological and Social Foundations*. New York: Oxford University Press.

HOMOSEXUALITY AND NEW FAMILY FORMS: ISSUES IN PSYCHOTHERAPY

Terry S. Stein

To many of us today the possibilities and limitations of human intimacy within our lives and society have become profound and pressing personal and political questions. . . . For the life of us we need to know more about the possible forms of intimacy between women and women, between men and men, between the sexes, and among all the dispossessed. . . . If we want to learn what kind of society and social change might make friendliness the rule instead of the exception, the study of the history of human intimacy may help us to define, and struggle to create, that radically new and revolutionary political economy of love [Katz 1976].

Several forces have converged over the past two decades to establish homosexuality as a basis for structuring alternative lifestyles and creating new family forms. These forces include the decision by the American Psychiatric Association (APA) in 1973 to remove homosexuality from its list of diagnoses of mental disorders; the development in society of a variety of nontraditional family arrangements associated with changes in traditional gender-role requirements; and the definition and legitimation of gay male and lesbian social identities that have resulted from gay visibility and political activism. The high incidence of acquired immune deficiency syndrome (AIDS) in gay men has also contributed to a greater awareness in American society about homosexuality. While AIDS has clearly increased the level of stress experienced by gay men, both because of a greater risk of disease and because of anti-gay reactions associated with the

public's fear of AIDS, discussion about the disease and its high rate of occurrence in gay men has also served to drive homosexuality and the associated lifestyle out of the closet and into the mainstream media.

Despite greater awareness about homosexuality and the widespread development of new family forms associated with it, the fields of psychiatry and psychotherapy have not yet systematically studied the needs of the individuals in these families. This article reviews the recent literature on the topic and presents an overview of issues relevant to psychiatry and psychotherapy. In a 1979 article on therapy with the homosexual family, DiBella (1979) stated that "there are appreciable resistances to the use of family psychotherapy with homosexual families. It is evident that this situation is in opposition to the practice of good community psychiatry." There is little evidence that the resistance to working with homosexual families has diminished significantly since that time, but the needs of this population have become even more apparent in the intervening years.

Psychiatry's definition of homosexuality as a form of mental illness prior to the APA's 1973 decision to reverse this position was primarily a reflection of two factors: first, that the homosexual persons being observed shared certain group characteristics other than sexual orientation, such as having a psychiatric illness or being in special settings like prisons or the military; and second, that the researchers held a common a priori assumption that only exclusive heterosexuality can be normal. As a result of the bias introduced by these factors, little was known about the

Source: *Psychiatric Annals* 18 (1988): 12–20. Reprinted with permission.

lives of homosexual men and women in non-clinical populations. The types of family arrangements actually associated with homosexuality had not been described. In fact, many conclusions about the capacity of gay men and lesbians to participate in intimate relationships were based on extrapolations from observations of persons who were mentally ill or in stressful and aberrant settings like prisons. Within psychoanalysis and psychiatry, virtually the only interest concerning homosexuality and the family had been efforts to unravel in the family of origin an etiology for homosexuality as a mental illness, either as the outcome of a particular constellation of family relationships or as a result of specific familial factors that predisposed individuals to develop a homosexual adaptation as an adult. Bieber's (1962) well known study of the homosexual male and his family of origin is an example of this type of effort, which focussed on pathological factors in the relationships within the family of origin that were believed to cause homosexuality.

As a result of the published reports of psychoanalytic and psychiatric research that were designed to establish retrospectively a pathological childhood background for all homosexual men (partly to justify an assumption of pathology in the adult homosexual), a variety of cultural stereotypes about adult homosexual relationships were reinforced. Even now, these stereotypes — for example, that gay men cannot sustain long-term adult relationships, that gay male or lesbian relationships when they do exist simply represent attempts to mimic already distorted perceptions of male–female relationships, or that children raised by homosexual parents are somehow at greater risk for mental illness — continue to keep many psychotherapists from understanding and working with the variety of intimate relationships encountered by gay men and lesbians.

The range of topics related to homosexuality and the family is quite extensive; it includes not only those family systems in which gay men and lesbians participate as adults, but also the process of development of the child's sexual orientation within the family, heterosexual family systems in which one parent is homosexual or bisexual, and the interaction of the homosexual person with his or her family of origin during the process of coming out. These topics are beyond the scope of the current article. The focus of this paper is on homosexual families, defined as those family systems comprised of an adult intimate relationship between two gay men or two lesbians, referred to as same-sex couples, and of relationships between an adult homosexual or same-sex couple and their children.

Overview of Research

Extensive nonclinical studies of the relationships of gay men and lesbians have begun to provide us with the information necessary to appreciate the diversity of family systems and lifestyles of these individuals. Following upon earlier surveys of sexual behaviour that indicated the extent of homosexual behaviour in our society, later studies have demonstrated the wide range of types of adult relationships associated with homosexuality in twentieth-century America (Bell and Weinberg 1978; Blumstein and Schwartz 1983). Specific stages in gay male relationships, based on such factors as length of relationship and age of partners, have been outlined (McWhirter and Mattison 1984), and special issues for lesbian couples have been identified, including problems with parenting and a tendency toward psychological fusion (Hall 1978; Krestan and Bepko 1980).

An important area of interest in empirical research regarding the homosexual family has been the interaction between lesbian mothers and their children, with the factor most frequently examined being the effect of the mother's homosexuality on her children. There appear to be no significant differences between lesbian and heterosexual mothers on measurements of such variables as ratings of ideal child, maternal attitude and self-concept, sex-role behaviour, and types of general concerns (Pagelow 1980; Mucklow and

Phelan 1979; Kweskin and Cook 1982). However, lesbian mothers do perceive a greater degree of oppression than single heterosexual mothers. Many of the special issues of concern to the lesbian mother, including custody rights, kin support, and social stigmatization, are related to this perceived oppression (Lewin and Lyons 1982).

The research on gay fathers has examined characteristics of the fathers, as opposed to looking at the behaviours or perceptions of these men in relation to their parental role. One study demonstrated that gay fathers generally describe adequate and positive family backgrounds (Skeen and Robinson 1984); another study reports that gay men who are fathers versus those who are not fathers have similar degrees of masculinity as measured on the Bem Sex-Role Inventory (Robinson and Skeen 1982); and a final study examined the experiences of gay fathers who disclose their homosexuality to their children (Bozett 1980).

The effects of parental homosexuality on children have been studied extensively in lesbian mothers, but there are no parallel reports regarding gay men as fathers. This absence of research on the topic undoubtedly reflects a gender-role difference that men in general, regardless of their sexual orientation, tend to parent less than women in American society, but it may also represent a taboo against acknowledging that gay males even function as parents in our society. This taboo may result in part from a persistent myth that gay men routinely, or at least in disproportionately large numbers in comparison to heterosexual men, sexually abuse children. The research on child sexual abuse has repeatedly demonstrated that this is a myth, and that in fact, virtually all perpetrators of child sexual abuse are heterosexual men, with most instances of such abuse occurring within traditional families between older males and younger females. Nevertheless, research on the relationships between gay fathers and their children remains almost nonexistent.

Research studying the effects of lesbian mothers on their children has consistently demonstrated that there are no significant differences between children raised by lesbian and by heterosexual mothers in terms of their sexual identity, gender-role behaviours, and level or types of psychiatric disturbances. The reports by Green (1978) and Kirkpatrick (1981) and her associates are most notable in this area. Additional studies (Golombok, Spencer, and Rutter 1983; Miller, Jacobsen, and Bigner 1982) have examined a wide range of areas of possible effect of lesbian mothers on their children, including the type of household environment in which they are raised, the social and emotional aspects of the children's development, and the impact of the mother's sexual orientation on the peer relationships of the children. No significant differences have been demonstrated between these children and children raised in single-parent households by heterosexual mothers. The effects of divorce on children of lesbian mothers, special problems related to disclosure of homosexuality by mothers to their children, and the effects of absent fathers are additional concerns in such households (Hotvedt and Mandel 1982).

General studies of lesbian couples and their children have conclusively demonstrated that sexual orientation alone produces no significant differences between nontraditional and traditional families. Differences between these family types are based instead on the sex of the two partners (same-sex dyads instead of male–female dyads), the effects of stigmatization and variation in degree of disclosure related to homosexuality in contrast to heterosexuality, and the lack of role models and social support systems for nontraditional couples and families. The clinically based reports discussed in the following section provide additional insight into the special problems related to the homosexual family that may occur within psychotherapy.

Couples Therapy

Articles discussing psychotherapy of gay male and lesbian couples form the most extensive literature relevant to the topic of psychotherapy with the homosexual family. A major concern in therapy with same-sex couples is the therapist's ability to work with these couples in a nonjudgmental and accepting manner. Additionally, because most training programs for mental-health professionals do not include education about the special needs of gay people, the level of the therapist's knowledge about this population may be insufficient. The therapist who works with gay male or lesbian couples must understand the major issues these couples face and the differences between same-sex and heterosexual couples.

Many of the problems for same-sex couples relate to factors associated with being two women or two men in a relationship. These problems will be discussed below. Other issues are common for both male and female same-sex couples and can be seen as related to the homosexuality of the couple and the societal reaction to such couples. These issues include dealing with discrimination and prejudice, defining the relationship in the absence of visible role models, managing legal and business matters in the absence of relevant laws and policies, struggling with family relationships, coming out, determining the nature of sexual relationships, and deciding if and how to relate to children (Schrag 1984; Winkelpleck and Westfeld 1982).

Lesbian Couples

The largest number of articles on the topic of therapy with same-sex couples focus on the lesbian relationship. An early report on counselling with lesbian couples suggested that lesbians should be considered as "ordinary human beings with a minority (but not abnormal) sexual orientation" (Pendergrass 1975, 94). While the two case examples of lesbian couples presented support the view that such couples enact sex-role stereotyping similar to heterosexual couples, Pendergrass also suggested that many of the issues for lesbian couples are the result of negative societal attitudes toward homosexuality.

Subsequent articles about psychotherapy with lesbian couples have not shown that the stereotype of masculine–feminine role differentiation in these couples is valid. Instead, these articles have further elucidated the features of such couples that derive from the fact that the partners are both women, and have expanded the role of stigmatization in determining the nature of the problems these women experience in relationships. Two women in an intimate relationship bring with them intrapsychic and interpersonal similarities that may increase the capacity for some forms of intimacy at the same time that they create certain problems in maintaining psychological boundaries.

Problems with emotional fusion, or merger, in lesbian relationships, as well as characteristics sometimes associated with fusion, such as decreased sexual activity in lesbian as compared to gay male or heterosexual couples, have been well documented (Krestan and Bepko 1980; Roth 1984; Burch 1986; Kaufman, Harrison, and Hyde 1984), and a variety of therapeutic strategies have been described to help deal with these problems within psychotherapy. These strategies focus on increasing the amount of differentiation and individual autonomy of the two partners. Other problems identified for lesbian couples (Roth 1984) relate to sexual expression, including concern about the degree of monogamy, conflict over heterosexual behaviour, and decreased genital sexual activity; to the diminished economic and social resources associated in this society with being a woman (and additionally with being women who are not closely affiliated with men); and to differences between the partners in level of coming out and degrees of lesbian identity.

Special problems for the therapist who works with lesbian couples have also been identified (McCandish 1982). The heterosexual therapist may experience difficulty in identifying or being empathic with the degree of stigmatization and the resultant stress on the lesbian couple, or may have to struggle to overcome negative attitudes toward homosexuality and stereotypes of lesbians. Lesbian therapists, while probably less likely to experience these difficulties, may have to overcome a tendency to idealize the relationship or to become overidentified or overinvolved with the couple. The countertransference reactions of therapists working with lesbian couples parallel reactions in any therapy situation that derive from essential differences and similarities between therapists and patients.

Gay Male Couples

Very few studies have been published regarding psychotherapy with gay male couples. The paucity of research and reporting about this topic may reflect in part a limitation similar to the taboo against studying gay male fathers discussed above. Because the stereotype of the gay male suggests that he is unable to participate in intimate, long-term adult relationships, the phenomenon of gay male couples has simply not been recognized. Therefore, gay male relationships have not been studied or managed within the context of psychotherapy. In contrast to the belief that gay men do not participate in intimate relationships with each other, Weinberg and Williams (1974) found in the 1960s that 71 percent of their large sample of gay men were living with a partner. Data on the number of gay men who are also raising children, either with another adult or as single parents, are not available and would be difficult to obtain, but it is clear that a large majority of gay men are living with a partner and that undoubtedly many of these men also participate in some form of child-rearing.

McWhirter and Mattison (1984) described six developmental stages with specific characteristics through which gay male couples pass. The six stages identified are the following:

- Stage one — blending (year 1);
- Stage two — nesting (years 2 and 3);
- Stage three — maintaining (years 4 and 5);

- Stage four — building (years 6 through 10);
- Stage five — releasing (years 11 through 20);
- Stage six — renewing (beyond 20 years).

They also list typical tasks with which the men struggle during each stage: for example, equalizing the partnership in Stage one and merging of money and possessions in Stage five. These authors also identify an approach to psychotherapy with male couples that focusses on an assessment of the presenting problem and the individual characteristics of the partners, and relates these factors to phase-specific issues for the couple. Finally, they discuss the influence of other factors relevant to the problems with which male couples present to psychotherapy but not related to stages, such as the presence of antihomosexual attitudes (both within the relationship and in society), and the level of coming out of the two partners.

Forstein (1986) presents a discussion of psychotherapy with male couples that considers a variety of additional issues, including the impact of male socialization on the dynamics of pairing, the role of sexual attitudes and behaviours, and the impact of AIDS on gay men. The issue of male socialization is particularly important for gay male couples because of its influence on the capacity for intimacy. Unlike two women, who may demonstrate problems with psychological fusion, two men may have to overcome barriers to intimacy that develop as a result of socialization to be independent, or at times even defensively separate, when in relationships.

Although the impact of AIDS on gay male couples has been enormous, a full consideration of the topic is beyond the scope of this article. However, it is important to be aware that as a result of AIDS and the various AIDS-related conditions caused by infection with the human immunodeficiency virus (HIV), many gay male couples will present for therapy with the primary problem of confronting a chronic and sometimes terminal disease within the context of their relationship. These couples will be dealing not only with the same issues faced by gay men in general, but will also be confronting concerns about death and dying. Whether issues related to physical illness, death, or grieving are present for a particular couple, all gay men have been influenced by the spectre of this dreaded disease. Male couples can, therefore, be expected to present routinely with concerns related to fears of disease, to altered patterns of sexual behaviour, and to changing needs and expectations in relationships.

Forstein (1986) also examines the influence of the therapist's sex and sexual orientation on psychotherapy with gay male couples and discusses a variety of transference and countertransference issues that may develop in such work. The types of transference and countertransference reactions that occur often reflect many of the same distortions, projections, and prohibitions that occur in relation to homosexuality within the larger society. The examination of these reactions within the relatively safe environment of psychotherapy can serve as a basis for helping the male couple work through problems they encounter as a result of sharing some of the misperceptions about homosexuality and intimacy between two men. Also, therapists must work to understand the basis for their reactions to gay male couples, both in their own personalities and in society's attitudes and beliefs about these pairings.

Families with Children

The family structures in which gay men and lesbians participate are by definition different from a traditional family, because they do not include two (married) parents, one male and one female, and their children. However, many of the parents in homosexual families were married to heterosexual partners at the time they had their children, and following divorce the new family form may differ little from other single-parent or reconstituted families. In these situations, the families will need

to deal with the impact of divorce and the effects of having an absent parent. The degree to which the homosexual parent acknowledges and acts upon his or her homosexuality and the presence or absence of a same-sex partner will determine whether these families appear outwardly to be any different from heterosexual families. Homosexual parents who are completely closeted may present special issues related to the need to maintain secrecy and to a possible constriction of intimate relationships. Parents who are open about being homosexual will need to deal with their children's reactions to this situation.

Other important concerns for homosexual families who have gone through a divorce are which parent has custody of the children and the extent to which the homosexuality of a parent has been a factor in determining custody or visitation rights. Any family who has undergone a prolonged and bitter struggle in the process of divorce can be expected to suffer greater stress, and when the struggle is focussed on the homosexuality of a parent, additional stress related to stigmatization and possible discrimination usually occurs. The effects on the children in such situations can be devastating, especially if the rights of a capable parent who is loved and respected are withdrawn solely because of the parent's sexual orientation.

Newer family structures comprised of one or two adult homosexuals and their children who are not the product of heterosexual marriages are being created in increasing numbers. The largest numbers of these families consist of lesbians who have children, either following artificial insemination or in conjunction with a male. The father in these families may or may not coparent with the mother. These families differ from families that have gone through divorce in several ways, including the fact that the children have not experienced any disruption of the parental unit and that most of these children have been carefully planned for because of the need to arrange for impregnation of the mother. Smaller numbers of gay men adopt or arrange to have children. This may occur more frequently in the future, however, if existing custody, adoption, and foster-parent regulations continue to be challenged by gay-rights groups.

Early reports relevant to psychotherapy with the homosexual family focussed on possible detrimental effects of the lesbian parent on her children. However, problems in the children specifically related to the parent's sexual orientation have not been identified (Green 1978; Kirkpatrick, Smith, and Roy 1981; Weeks and Derdeyn 1975). Recently, there have been attempts to understand more fully the experience of the child in these settings and to identify the factors that might be affected as a result of the differences in these families from more traditional families (Agbayewa 1984). For example, the influence on a child's development of having two parents of the same sex is not yet understood and must be studied over time. Does one parent in such instances assume a position as mother, and one as father? If not, what are the implications for theories of child development that assume a clear role differentiation between mother and father? These and other questions remain to be answered.

The unique problems presented by the homosexual family in psychotherapy are generally related to the need to deal with reactions to homosexuality, within the family, in the extended family, and in the environment outside the home, and to factors that result from the gender arrangements in these families. These situations may create particularly strong countertransference reactions in the therapist, because of concern about the well-being of the children and difficulty in understanding the roles and communications of various family members in the absence of adequate models for these systems. In addition, there continues the considerable resistance, both within the psychotherapy professions and within the communities where psychotherapists practise, to the idea of developing specific approaches to working with homosexual families (DiBella 1979). Nevertheless, several authors have begun to discuss the spe-

cial problems of this group of psychotherapy patients with the primary focus continuing to be on those families with lesbian mothers (Hall 1978; Loulan 1986; Shernoff 1984).

In general, families with lesbian mothers struggle with the same issues as other families, but in addition have to manage problems involving coming out, discrimination, and disempowerment (as a result of both being homosexual and a woman), persistent questions about the appropriateness of being a mother, and concerns about integrating a female partner into the family. Difficulties in any of these areas may affect the degree of economic, emotional, and social support available to the mother and her children. For example, coming out to the extended family, either by choice or as a result of disclosure of the mother's homosexuality by others, may lead to loss of support from the family, disapproval, or legal confrontations regarding custody. The therapist working with these families must understand the many levels of psychological, interpersonal, economic, and legal vulnerability in these situations, and must consider not only the dynamics of the family system, but also the special needs of the lesbian and, when relevant, the particular problems of female couples.

Conclusion

The current knowledge about newer family systems that include gay men and lesbians has been discussed in terms of its application in psychotherapy with such families. Homosexual families are presented as a significant and growing segment of the population with specific concerns and needs. Many of the concerns of these families result from the need to deal with the stigmatization of and discrimination against gay men and lesbians in American society. Unique issues involve the special problems associated with the dynamics of same-sex couples in contrast to heterosexual couples and the absence of role models for these families. Many problems of homosexual families are shared with other nontraditional family forms and may include the management of divorce, the effects of an absent parent on children, and difficulties in communication. Psychotherapists must become aware of the particular transference and countertransference reactions that may arise in working with these families to be helpful to them.

Works Cited

Agbayewa, M.O. 1984. "Fathers in the Newer Family Forms: Male or Female?" *Canadian Journal of Psychiatry* 29: 402-6.

Bell, A.P., and M.S. Weinberg. 1978. *Homosexualities*. New York: Simon and Schuster.

Bieber, I., et al. 1962. *Homosexuality: A Psychoanalytic Study*. New York: Basic.

Bieber, I., H.J. Dain, and P.R. Dince. 1962. *Homosexuality*. New York: Basic.

Blumstein, P., and P. Schwartz. 1983. *American Couples*. New York: Pocket.

Bozett, F.W. 1980. "Gay Fathers: How and Why They Disclose Their Homosexuality to Their Children." *Family Relations* 29: 173-79.

Burch, B. 1986. "Psychotherapy and the Dynamics of Merger in Lesbian Couples." *Contemporary Perspectives on Psychotherapy with Lesbians and Gay Men.* eds. T. Stein and C. Cohen. New York: Plenum.

DiBella, G.A.W. 1979. "Family Psychotherapy with the Homosexual Family: A Community Psychiatry Approach to Homosexuality." *Community Mental Health* 15(1): 41-46.

Forstein, M. 1986. "Psychodynamic Psychotherapy with Gay Male Couples." *Contemporary Perspectives on Psychotherapy with Lesbians and Gay Men.* Eds. T. Stein and C. Cohen. New York: Plenum.

Golombok, S., A. Spencer, and M. Rutter. 1983. "Children in Lesbian and Single-Parent Households: Psychosexual and Psychiatric Appraisal." *Journal of Child Psychology and Psychiatry* 24: 551-72.

Green, R. 1978. "Sexual Identity of 37 Children Raised by Homosexual or Transsexual Parents." *American Journal of Psychiatry* 135: 692-97.

Hall, M. 1978. "Lesbian Families: Cultural and Clinical Issues." *Social Work* 23: 380-87.

Hotvedt, M.E., and J.B. Mandel. 1982. "Children of Lesbian Mothers." *Homosexuality: Social, Psychological and Biological Issues.* Eds. W. Paul and J. Weinrib. Beverly Hills, CA: Sage.

Katz, J. 1976. *Gay American History*. New York: T.Y. Crowell.

Kaufman, P.A., E. Harrison, and M.L. Hyde. 1984. "Distancing for Intimacy in Lesbian Relationships." *American Journal of Psychiatry* 141: 530-33.

Kirkpatrick, M., C. Smith, and R. Roy. 1981. "Lesbian Mothers and Their Children: A Comparative Survey." *American Journal of Orthopsychiatry* 51: 545-51.

Krestan, J.A., and C.S. Bepko. 1980. "The Problem of Fusion in the Lesbian Relationship." *Family Process* 19: 277-89.

Kweskin, S.L., and A.S. Cook. 1982. "Heterosexual and Homosexual Mothers' Self-Described Sex-Role Behavior and Ideal Sex-Role Behavior in Children." *Sex Roles* 8: 967-74.

Lewin, E., and T.A. Lyons. 1982. "Everything in its Place." *Homosexuality: Social, Psychological and Biological Issues.* Beverly Hills, CA: Sage.

Loulan, J. 1986. "Psychotherapy with Lesbian Mothers." *Contemporary Perspectives on Psychotherapy with Lesbians and Gay Men.* Eds. T. Stein and C. Cohen. New York: Plenum.

McCandish, B.M. 1982. "Therapeutic Issues with Lesbian Couples." *Journal of Homosexuality* 7: 71-78.

McWhirter, D.P., and A.M. Mattison. 1984. "Psychotherapy for Male Couples: An Application of Staging Theory." *Innovations in Psychotherapy with Homosexuals.* Eds. E. Hetrick and T. Stein. Washington, DC: American Psychiatric. 116-31.

Miller, J.A., R.B. Jacobsen, and J.J. Bigner. 1982. "The Child's Home Environment for Lesbian vs. Heterosexual Mothers: A Neglected Area of Research." *Journal of Homosexuality* 7: 49-56.

Mucklow, B.M., and G.K. Phelan. 1979. "Lesbian and Traditional Mothers' Responses to Adult Response to Child Behavior and Self-Concept." *Psychology Report* 44: 880-82.

Pagelow, M.D. 1980. "Heterosexual and Lesbian Single Mothers: A Comparison of Problems, Coping, and Solutions." *Journal of Homosexuality* 5: 189-204.

Pendergrass, V.E. 1975. "Marriage Counseling with Lesbian Couples." *Psychotherapy: Theory, Research, and Practice* 12: 93-96.

Robinson, B.E., and P. Skeen. 1982. "Sex-Role Orientation of Gay Fathers Versus Gay Nonfathers." *Perceptual and Motor Skills* 55: 1055-59.

Roth, S. 1984. "Psychotherapy with Lesbian Couples: The Interrelationships of Individual Issues, Female Socialization, and the Social Context." *Innovations in Psychotherapy with Homosexuals.* Eds. E. Hetrick and T. Stein. Washington, DC: American Psychiatric Association. 89–114.

Schrag, K.G. 1984. "Relationship Therapy with Same-Gender Couples." *Family Relations* 33: 283–91.

Shernoff, M.J. 1984. "Family Therapy for Lesbians and Gay Clients." *Social Work* 29: 393–96.

Skeen, P., and B.E. Robinson. 1984. "Family Backgrounds of Gay Fathers: A Descriptive Study." *Psychological Reports* 54: 999–1005.

Weeks, R.B., and A.P. Derdeyn. 1975. "Two Cases of Children of Homosexuals." *Child Psychiatry and Human Development.* 6: 26–32.

Weinberg, M.S., and C.A. Williams. 1974. *Male Homosexuals: Their Problems and Adaptations.* New York: Oxford University Press.

Winkelpleck, J.M., and J.S. Westfield. 1982. "Counseling Considerations with Gay Couples." *Personnel and Guidance Journal* 60: 294–96.

AIDS IN CANADA*

Carol Strike

Acquired immune deficiency syndrome, or AIDS, continues to represent a formidable challenge to Canadian society. AIDS is primarily a sexually transmitted disease caused by the human immunodeficiency virus (HIV). This infection may result in development of life-threatening opportunistic infections and/or malignancies. While research for a cure or vaccine is ongoing, and education programs highlighting the dangers of this disease have been developed and introduced both to the public and in schools, the total number of cases of AIDS in Canada continues to increase.

AIDS Cases and Deaths

The first AIDS case in Canada was diagnosed in 1979; by the end of 1987, a total of 1654 cases had been documented.

A record number of new AIDS cases (615) were diagnosed in Canada in 1987. In fact, this figure was over 28 percent higher than the number of new cases diagnosed the previous year. As a result, the total number of AIDS cases in Canada rose 59 percent in 1987 (see Figure 1). This overall rate of growth, however, was down from 1986, when there had been an 86 percent increase. As well, by

Source: *Canadian Social Trends*, Summer 1988. Cat. 11008E. Reproduced with permission of the Minister of Supply and Services Canada. 1989.

*All data in this article are from the Federal Centre for AIDS, a branch of Health and Welfare Canada. In September 1987, the Federal Centre for AIDS accepted a revision proposed by the U.S. Center for Disease Control and broadened the criteria for an AIDS diagnosis. The new criteria will be applied to cases not previously identified as AIDS that occurred before this date. The resulting reclassification of some of these cases as AIDS may increase the total number of reported cases of this disease. As of April 2, 1990, 3682 cases of AIDS had been reported in Canada. See figures 1 and 2.

the end of 1987, 963 people in Canada had died from AIDS.

Individuals can carry the HIV for an indefinite period without developing either the illnesses characteristic of AIDS or any of the symptoms of the infection. The Federal Centre for AIDS has estimated, for example, that about 30 000 people in Canada carry the HIV. Current evidence suggests that around 35 percent of carriers will develop AIDS within six years of infection. The Federal Centre for AIDS has projected that by the end of 1991, between 4000 and 7000 people in Canada will have been diagnosed as having AIDS.

Major Risk Factors for AIDS

The majority of AIDS patients have been homosexual or bisexual men. This group made up 80 percent of all cases through the end of 1987, as well as 84 percent of new patients in 1987.

People from countries where the HIV is widespread made up the second-largest group of AIDS patients. Through 1987, 5 percent of all cases were in this category, with most likely acquiring the infection through sexual activity.

Intravenous (IV) drug abusers made up 3 percent of the total number of AIDS cases. Of these, 2.5 percent were also homosexuals or bisexuals, while the remaining 0.6 percent were people with no other risk factor.

Recipients of blood transfusions or other blood products made up another 5 percent of all AIDS patients, while heterosexuals who contracted the HIV infection through sexual contact with someone in a high-risk group made up 2 percent of all cases. In another

3 percent of cases, risk factors were not identified.

In addition, 2 percent of AIDS patients have been children under age 15. Through 1987, 33 such cases had been reported. In 29 of these cases, transmission was from mother to fetus; the others contracted the infection through transfusions received before universal testing of blood donors was implemented.

Additional Risk Factors: Age and Sex

Men aged 20–49 make up the vast majority of AIDS patients. Through 1987, 83 percent of all those diagnosed with AIDS were men in this age range. Men aged 30–39 had the highest cumulative incidence of AIDS, with 38 cases per 100 000 men in this age group. Men aged 40–49 and 20–29 also had higher than average rates: 24 and 13 cases per 100 000 population, respectively.

Men aged 50 and over had a cumulative AIDS rate of 5 cases per 100 000 population. In no other group did the AIDS rate exceed 1.5.

The incidence of AIDS is much lower in Canada than in the United States. By the end of 1987, almost 50 000 cases had been reported in the United States. When expressed on a per-capita basis, the incidence of AIDS was more than three times higher in the United States than in Canada.

For the most part, though, AIDS patients in Canada and the United States have similar characteristics. In both countries, most patients are men between the ages of 20 and 49, with those aged 30–39 having, by far, the highest cumulative rates.

Homosexual or bisexual men also account for the majority of AIDS cases in both countries, although their share is greater in Canada (80 percent) than in the United States (65 percent). Intravenous drug abusers, including homosexual or bisexual drug abusers, make

Figure 1
Number of New Cases* of AIDS, 1982–1987

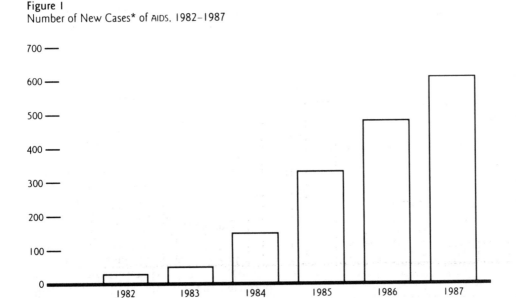

Source: Health and Welfare Canada, Federal Centre for AIDS
*Number of new cases in 1979, 1980, 1981, and 1988 were 1, 3, 6, and 767, respectively.

up a much greater proportion of AIDS victims in the United States. Through 1987, 25 percent of American AIDS patients compared with just 3 percent of those in Canada were IV drug abusers.

As in Canada, AIDS in the United States is regionally concentrated. Just two states, California and New York, account for almost half of all U.S. cases. On the other hand, the incidence of AIDS in Canada is roughly similar to that in European countries.

Most AIDS Cases in Three Provinces

AIDS cases in Canada are concentrated in three provinces — Ontario, Quebec, and British Columbia. Through 1987, these provinces, representing about 73 percent of the Canadian population, accounted for 89 percent of all AIDS cases. As well, 87 percent of new cases diagnosed in 1987 occurred in these provinces.

British Columbia had the highest cumulative rate of AIDS of any province. Through 1987, 10.9 AIDS cases had been diagnosed in British Columbia for every 100 000 residents of that province.

Quebec and Ontario also had very high cumulative AIDS rates. Through 1987, there were 7.8 AIDS cases per 100 000 population in Quebec and 6.9 in Ontario. Trends in these two provinces, however, took different directions in 1987. The number of new cases rose 46 percent in Ontario; in contrast, the number of new cases in Quebec was almost the same in 1987 as in the previous year.

With a rate of 3.9, Alberta was the only other province in which the cumulative incidence of AIDS was over 3.5 cases per 100 000 population. Prince Edward Island and the Northwest Territories both reported their first AIDS case in 1987, while the Yukon had yet to report a case through the end of 1987 (see Figure 2).

Figure 2
Total AIDS Cases per 100 000 Population,* by Province, 1979–1987

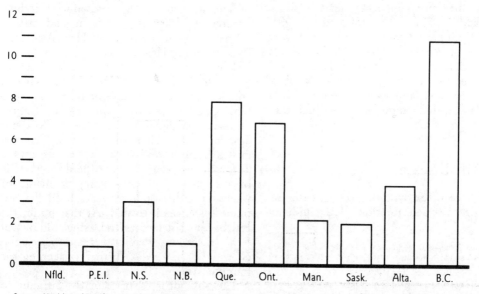

Source: Health and Welfare Canada. Federal Centre for AIDS.

*In April 1990, the total AIDS cases per 100 000 changed from a low of 2.3 in Prince Edward Island to a high of 23.3 in British Columbia.

AIDS: IMPLICATIONS FOR FAMILIES*

Eleanor D. Macklin

Over 50 000 cases of acquired immune deficiency syndrome (AIDS) have been reported to date in the United States, and between 1 million and 1.5 million persons are estimated to be infected by the human immunodeficiency virus (HIV). Facts about the disease and its epidemiology are reviewed, and the implications for families and human-service professionals are discussed.

The disease known as AIDS (acquired immune deficiency syndrome) was first diagnosed in the United States in 1981. As of January 18, 1988, 51 361 cases of AIDS had been reported in the Centers for Disease Control and 56 percent of these had already died (Centers for Disease Control 1988). It is estimated that between 1 million and 1.5 million persons in the United States are currently infected with the human immunodeficiency virus (Osborn and Brandt 1987) and by the end of 1991, 179 000 will have died because of the disease (Institute of Medicine 1986). Yet, it is only recently that family professionals have become sensitized to the profound impact of these realities on families and their members as well as on the communities in which they live.

AIDS: The Disease

AIDS is a complex syndrome of diseases resulting from a deterioration of the individ-

ual's immune system. It is associated with infection by the human immunodeficiency virus (HIV), which enters and destroys the crucial white blood cells known as T-4 lymphocytes (Institute of Medicine 1986). Because of this damage to the immune system, patients develop infections that normal immune systems are able to ward off (e.g., pneumocystis carinii pneumonia, Kaposi's sarcoma, toxoplasmosis). It is these so-called opportunistic diseases that are usually the eventual cause of death.

Clinical symptoms of HIV typically include some or all of the following: extreme fatigue, fever, night sweats, continuing bouts of diarrhea, swollen lymph nodes, unexplained weight loss, heavy and continual unexplained dry cough, thrush, purple growths on the skin or mucous membranes, unexplained bleeding, progressive shortness of breath, and varying degrees of dementia (e.g., see New York State Department of Health 1986).

The virus is particularly insidious because it is a retrovirus, which means that when it enters a cell it is capable of reprogramming that cell's DNA, so that when the cell reproduces it reproduces the virus (see Gallo 1987; Gonda 1986). Therefore, when a virus attaches itself to and penetrates a susceptible T-4 cell, the virus remains there for the life of the cell, sometimes lying dormant for weeks, months, or even years until the immune system is activated. At that point, the cell becomes a factory, releasing millions of new viruses into the bloodstream to seek and enter other T-4 cells, further weakening the immune system.

The HIV virus is particularly difficult to combat because of its capacity to change its external coat or envelope, thus producing var-

Source: *Family Relations* 37 (1988): 141–49. Copyright 1988 the National Council on Family Relations, 3989 Central Ave. N.E., Suite 550, Minneapolis, MN 55421. Reprinted by permission.

*Based on a plenary address given at the annual meeting of the National Council on Family Relations, Atlanta, GA, November 15, 1987. Appreciation is given to Sandra Caron and Richard Needle for their consultation and support.

iants and mutants of the virus that cannot be recognized by the body's antibodies. Hence, it has been difficult to produce effective vaccines. Moreover, the virus is capable of crossing the "blood-brain barrier" and invading the brain directly, resulting in debilitating neurological disease and deterioration and eluding any drug that is not also capable of penetrating the central nervous system (Osborn and Brandt 1987).

The good news is that the virus is relatively fragile and not easily transmitted. Although generally present in body fluids, the greatest concentration is in blood and semen and, to a lesser extent, in vaginal secretions. Traces have been found in urine, feces, saliva, and tears, but the concentrations appear to be too low to be contagious and the chances are very remote that the virus could be spread by even such activities as "deep kissing" (Windom and Koop 1987; see Norwood 1987 for an easy-to-read discussion of the risks of transmission associated with various forms of lovemaking).

The implications of the following facts are important:

• *Once an individual is infected with* HIV, *he or she is infected for life.* Although the person may not show any clinical symptoms for months or even years, it is estimated that at least 25–50 percent of infected persons will progress to AIDS within five to ten years after infection (Institute of Medicine 1986). Based on studies of cases infected via blood transfusion, the median time between infection with HIV and the development of clinical symptoms of AIDS is estimated to be 4.5 years (Friedland and Klein 1987). Once the infection has progressed to a point where the individual has clinical symptoms, the disease is usually fatal within two years and, to date, about 80 percent have died within three years of diagnosis (see Table 1).

Great strides have been made in developing drugs to retard the progress of the disease once an individual has been infected. Azidothymidine (AZT), which was announced in

1986, appears to prolong the lives of many who take it. But the cost is high (about $200 a week for a drug that may have to be taken every four hours for life), and there are often severe side effects such as anemia. It has been suggested that lifestyle changes designed to minimize activation of the immune system and shore up the body's resources also may have beneficial effects. Persons who are seropositive (i.e., whose blood has been found to have antibodies to HIV and who are therefore presumed to have been infected by the virus) are urged to avoid emotional stress and exposure to infection and to do whatever possible to enhance their general health and well-being (e.g., see Norwood 1987).

There is as yet little understanding of the factors that affect the progression of the disease or even the initial susceptibility to infection. The role of possible cofactors (e.g., infection by other viruses such as those associated with herpes and other sexually transmitted diseases, recreational drug usage, malnutrition, poor sanitation, general poor health) is currently being explored (e.g., Folks et al. 1987).

• *Once an individual is infected with* AIDS *he or she is capable of infecting others.* The risk of infection apparently is dependent on such factors as amount of virus in the body, nature of the contact, frequency of the contact, and susceptibility of the recipient. The virus appears to be transmitted in only three ways: (1) by direct blood to blood contact via needles that retain a residue of infected blood (as in the sharing of unclean needles and syringes by intravenous drug users) or the introduction of infected blood or blood products into the blood stream; (2) sexual behaviours that allow infected semen or vaginal fluids to enter the mucous membranes or blood system of the partner, as in anal intercourse (where there is risk of tearing the thin rectal lining) or where there are open sores, lesions, or ulcerations (as are commonly associated with various sexually transmitted diseases); or (3) from an infected mother to her infant, either during pregnancy or at time of birth or, in rare occasions,

Table 1

Cases of AIDS and Case-Fatality Rates by Half-Year of Diagnosis in United States (as of January 18, 1988)[a]

	Number of Cases	Number of Known Deaths[b]	Case-Fatality Rate in Percent
1981			
January–June	88	82	93
July–December	183	166	91
1982			
January–June	365	321	88
July–December	649	566	87
1983			
January–June	1 229	1 093	89
July–December	1 599	1 370	86
1984			
January–June	2 476	2 015	81
July–December	3 232	2 611	81
1985			
January–June	4 451	3 447	77
July–December	5 685	4 106	72
1986			
January–June	7 036	4 395	62
July–December	8 166	3 868	47
1987			
January–June	9 314	3 220	35
July–December	6 813	1 359	20
Total[c]	51 361	28 683	56

[a] See AIDS Weekly Surveillance Report 1988 (January 18). Atlanta, GA: Centers for Disease Control, 5, Table G.

[b] Reporting of deaths is incomplete.

[c] Table totals include 75 cases diagnosed prior to 1981, of which 64 are known to have died.

through nursing (e.g., see Institute of Medicine 1986; Windom and Koop 1987).

Unlike most infectious diseases (e.g., colds, flu, measles, TB), there is no evidence that the virus is transmitted by air, water, food, sneezing or coughing, sharing drinking glasses or utensils, shaking hands or hugging or casual kissing, touching an object handled or breathed on by an infected person, insect bites (see Booth 1987a, and Leishman 1987a, for detailed discussion of possible role of insects), or by living with a person with AIDS or who is seropositive (e.g., New York State Department of Health 1986). There have been

documented instances of health-care or laboratory workers who have been infected after experiencing deep punctures with needles containing infected blood or through direct exposure to highly concentrated laboratory specimens, but these are very rare and appear to involve lack of attention to proper technique (Barnes 1988; Weiss et al. 1988).

AIDS: The Epidemiology

In this country, persons with AIDS have, by and large, been homosexual or bisexual men, intravenous drug users, and the female partners of bisexuals or intravenous drug users (see Table 2). About two-thirds of all persons with AIDS are gay or bisexual men and 25 percent are intravenous drug users, with the latter group accounting for an increasing proportion of the total. While low in numbers, one of the most profoundly affected of the risk groups have been hemophiliacs, 70–80 percent of whom have been infected with HIV (Friedland and Klein 1987). It is estimated that about 12 000 persons in the United States were infected through blood transfusions prior to 1985 when a test was perfected for screening the blood-donor supply (Friedland and Klein 1987). To date, the great majority of persons with AIDS have been in New York and California, although there has been a sizeable spread to Florida, Texas, New Jersey, Illinois, Pennsylvania, Georgia, and Washington, DC, and no state has remained immune (Centers for Disease Control 1988).

Although women have been a small proportion of the total AIDS population in the United States, they are of particular concern because of the risk of infection to offspring during pregnancy or childbirth (Guinan and

Table 2
United States AIDS Cases Reported to Centers for Disease Control (as of January 18, 1988)[a,b,c]

	Males		Females		Total	
	No.	%	No.	%	No.	%
Adults						
Homosexual/Bisexual Males	32 799	70	—	—	32 799	65
IV Drug Users	6 831	15	1 877	50	8 708	17
Homosexual Males and IV Drug Users	3 796	8	—	—	3 796	8
Hemophilia/Coagulation Disorder	489	1	20	1	509	1
Heterosexual Cases[d]	938	2	1 095	29	2 033	4
Transfusion, Blood/Components	773	2	405	11	1 178	2
Undetermined[e]	1 230	3	330	9	1,560	3
Subtotal	46 856	93	3 727	7	50 583	100
Children[f]						
Hemophilia/Coagulation Disorder	39	9	3	1	42	5
Parent with/at risk of AIDS	302	72	294	82	596	77
Transfusion, Blood/Components	62	15	43	12	105	13
Undetermined[e]	18	4	17	5	35	4
Subtotal	421	54	357	46	778	100
Total	47 277	92	4 084	8	51 361	100

[a] See *AIDS Weekly Surveillance Report* 1988 (January 18). Atlanta, GA: Centers for Disease Control, p. 1, Table A.

[b] These data are provisional.

[c] Cases with more than one risk factor other than the combinations listed in the table are tabulated only in the category listed first.

[d] Includes 1156 persons (257 men, 899 women) who have had heterosexual contact with a person with AIDS or at risk for AIDS and 877 persons (681 men, 196 women) without other identified risks who were born in countries in which heterosexual transmission is believed to play a major role.

[e] Includes patients on whom risk information is incomplete (e.g., refusal to be interviewed), men reported only to have heterosexual contact with prostitute, patients still under investigation, and patients for whom no specific risk was identified.

[f] Includes all patients under 13 years of age at time of diagnosis

Hardy 1987; Stone 1987). About 80 percent of all U.S. children with AIDS have a parent who has AIDS or who is at risk for AIDS, and it is estimated that 40–50 percent of all infants born to a mother who is HIV positive will also be seropositive (Friedland and Klein 1987). Again, the factors that determine transmission of the infection are not clear, and it is possible for an uninfected infant to be born to a mother who has previously borne an infected child. Moreover, some infants are born seropositive because they received HIV antibodies from the mother but not the virus itself.

Most of the women and children with AIDS are from poor minority families with few resources and little available support. The majority of women diagnosed with AIDS have been intravenous drug users or partners of intravenous drug users, and a large number are in the New York City area. It is estimated that about 60–70 percent (or 150 000) of the intravenous drug users in New York City are infected with HIV and that 30 percent of these intravenous drug users are female (Stone 1987). Because large numbers of intravenous drug users are black or Hispanic, the majority of women with AIDS and almost 80 percent of all children with AIDS are black or Hispanic (Windom and Koop 1987). Whereas blacks and Hispanics only account for 12 and 7 percent of the U.S. population, respectively, blacks account for 25 percent of all known AIDS cases and Hispanics 14 percent (Centers for Disease Control 1988).

Although it is clear that AIDS is spreading rapidly among heterosexuals who are intravenous drug users, it is unclear how quickly it is spreading into the mainstream heterosexual population or what the probability of infection is for those sexually active heterosexuals who avoid sexual contact with members of high-risk groups (Leishman 1987b). It is estimated by the Centers for Disease Control that, whereas the pool of infected heterosexuals probably exceeds a quarter of a million people, only about 30 000 heterosexuals without identified risks already carry the infection (Boffey 1988). Since AIDS can be transmitted by both males and females and has spread rapidly in the heterosexual population of Central Africa (see Dickson 1987, and Quinn et al. 1986, for excellent reviews of AIDS in Africa), some have feared that a similar epidemic will happen here. However, the conditions in Africa may be too dissimilar to those in the United States to warrant generalization (e.g., different patterns of sexual behaviour, more sexually transmitted disease, poorer nutrition and hygiene, less well-screened blood supply, more general use of unsterile needles).

Similarly, some have feared that the prevalence rates for heterosexuals may, in time, come to mirror the current rates for homosexuals (see Stone 1987, for discussion). Just as the seropositive rate was once low for the gay community and now more than one-half of the gay community in San Francisco may carry the virus (Boffey 1988), so too there may be a gradual explosion into the heterosexual population. On the other hand, because gay men have usually had more partners and more venereal disease than heterosexuals, and because anal intercourse is a more effective route of transmission than vaginal intercourse, others argue that such fears are unrealistic.

Attempts have been made to relate rates of transmission to sex, sexual behaviour, number of partners, and duration of the partnership (see Friedland and Klein 1987, for extensive review of the literature). Male-to-male and male-to-female transmission is well documented, while the frequency of female-to-male transmission is less clear in the United States. This may be due to the fact that the latter form of transmission is less efficient (e.g., semen carries a greater quantity of the virus than do vaginal secretions). Or it may simply reflect the fact that the epidemic in the United States began in the gay and bisexual male population and among intravenous drug users, and the majority of these persons are male.

With time and an increase in the number of infected women, female-to-male transmission may become more common. There is bidirectional transmission of other sexually transmitted diseases and infection rates for men and women are equal in the Third World countries. While heterosexual transmission still accounts for a relatively small number of current U.S. cases, the proportion of cases attributable to heterosexual transmission is increasing more rapidly than for other groups and may approach 10 percent by 1991 (Friedland and Klein 1987).

Studies of long-term partners of heterosexuals infected with HIV have found a wide range in rates of seroconversion and one apparently cannot predict the probability that a partner will eventually become infected (see Stone 1987). Research to date on monogamous spouses of persons infected through blood transfusions has generally found that many more wives than husbands were seropositive. For example, in a New York City Health Department study reported by Stone (1987), of 20 husbands married to infected women, one was infected, and of 50 wives married to infected men, eight were infected. On the other hand, Stone (1987) notes that research that has followed couples over time has found that, with long-term sexual contact, women tend to transmit the disease as effectively as men. For example, he reports a study of spouses of 45 AIDS patients at the University of Miami Medical Center in which 12 of the 17 male partners and 14 of the 28 female partners had seroconverted. A possible conclusion is that women may be more at risk from casual sex than men, but that there is substantial transmission both ways for steady partners.

Effect on Families

Much of the original concern about the psychosocial aspects of AIDS focussed on the person with AIDS and on ways of providing necessary treatment and support. Only slowly did society come to recognize the implications of the disease for the many persons who were emotionally involved with the person with AIDS, such as lovers, partners or spouses, parents, siblings, children, friends, and caregivers. It is estimated that by the end of 1991, more than 270 000 persons in the United States will have been diagnosed as having AIDS (Windom and Koop 1987) and that many more will be seropositive. Multiply that number by the number of biological and functional family members that any one person with AIDS might have, and it is soon clear that a large proportion of our society will know and care about someone who is infected with HIV.

The problems that can be anticipated are by now fairly well understood (e.g., see Martelli, Peltz, and Messina 1987; Moffatt 1986; Mohr et al. 1988; Peabody 1986; Salisbury 1986; Walker 1988). Among the more obvious are the following:

Social Stigma and Isolation

Because of prejudice, homophobia, and hysteria resulting from an unrealistic fear of contamination, it is not unusual for persons known to have AIDS or to be HIV-positive to be fired from jobs; ejected from apartments; denied service by a wide variety of professionals including dentists, physicians, and funeral directors; refused admission to school; shunned by neighbours; and avoided by relatives. Professionals who work with families of persons with AIDS are familiar with the stories: the parent whose son has died who hesitates to talk about it; the lover whose partner has died who fears that no one will be willing to date him or her; a physician treating AIDS patients who learns that his or her preschooler's friends are not allowed to visit the house; and the AIDS patient who reports that the maid has refused to come to clean his or her room. Even the professional may be hesitant to take clients who have AIDS for fear of losing other clients.

Fear of Contagion

Almost everyone who has a family member with AIDS or HIV infection will experience at some point the fear of becoming infected, even knowing there is no basis for the fear. The partner may hesitate to share the same bed, relatives may hesitate to share a meal, grandmothers may hesitate to babysit, and family members in general may question how much they want to be involved. Significant relationships are often severely tested by the increased personal vulnerability that many experience and the difficulty individuals have in talking directly about these anxieties.

Fear of Infection

The person with AIDS will experience both the fear of becoming infected and the fear of infecting others. There may even be an initial hesitancy to be tested for fear of learning the results, a reluctance to get the results, a reluctance to be intimate for fear of infecting loved ones, a fear of picking up an infection which one's own damaged immune system cannot handle, a fear that the treatment for that infection will not be effective, a fear of the often painful treatments, and the inevitable fear of death and the process of dying. All of these fears inevitably reverberate throughout the family or relationship system, further stressing those relationships.

Fear of Abandonment

Many patients are plagued by the question of what will happen when he or she becomes too ill to continue to care for him or herself. Many face rejection by family and friends when the diagnosis of AIDS is revealed. For many, it is the first time that the family has been told directly that the individual is gay or bisexual or has engaged in behaviours of which they may not approve. Some family members, unable to bear the strain involved in watching a loved one deteriorate, slowly pull away in order to protect themselves. Others may have to choose between caregiving and meeting their own personal needs or the needs and demands of their own partner and

children. In some cases, the family is nonexistent or is incapable of giving the necessary care. In even the best of circumstances, there may be the unspoken fear that there is a limit to what others can handle and that everyone will gradually and quietly disappear.

Guilt

There is the guilt experienced by family members who once rejected a now dying relative because he was gay, the guilt over past behaviours that may have led to one's own infection or that of one's partner or child, the guilt for abandoning a partner because of fear of infection or not being able to handle the emotional strain, and the frequent guilt experienced by the well partner for having been spared.

Anger

There is the inevitable anger at fate for the illness, at the disease itself, at one's self for behaviours that may have led to the infection, at the partner for being sick, at the partner who may have been the source of the infection, at society for being judgmental and unsupportive, and even at the TV for reminding one that AIDS kills when one knows that continued life will depend on thinking positively.

Grief

There is the recurring grief at the impending loss as well as the grieving at the actual loss — loss of life, loss of potential, loss of health, loss of relationship, loss of normalcy. This is made even more difficult by the fact that families often do not feel free to openly discuss the death and that, in some instances, partner or child survivors may be facing the same potential death. Because the illness tends to affect young persons and individuals in their most productive years, the usual grief associated with chronic illness and death may even be intensified.

Economic Hardship

Persons with AIDS and their significant others often find themselves poverty-stricken due to loss of earning power, the high cost of treatment, and the lack of adequate financial assistance. This further erodes self-esteem and self-sufficiency and makes it difficult for individuals to maintain the independence and sense of control central to their emotional well-being (see Salisbury 1986).

Case examples of how the epidemic affects families are legion. The following are among those of which the author is aware:

• The grandmother in the inner-city slum with three grandchildren to care for, two of whom are sick with AIDS, who has already lost a daughter to AIDS due to infection by the drug-using boyfriend.

• The mother who learns of her own HIV infection only after her second child is born with AIDS, who fears the father's wrath for having infected his only son, and who worries about who will care for her children when she is gone.

• The gay couple whose parents urge the well partner to leave to protect himself (would they suggest that of a heterosexual married couple?), who fear that any physical closeness will infect the other, who struggle with whether the well partner should be tested to see if he is already infected and with how they will handle a positive or negative outcome of such testing.

• The bisexual man who has not told his wife of his lifestyle and who, when he learns that he is seropositive, agonizes over whether he has infected her, fears telling her, fears suggesting the use of a condom because she will suspect, fears not using a condom, thinks of her desire to become pregnant, and eventually distances himself to avoid dealing with all the emotional pain.

• The mother who learns simultaneously that she is seropositive and pregnant for the first time and anguishes over whether or not to have an abortion.

• The wife whose husband has had an affair and who has convinced herself that he has given her AIDS, even though she has received two negative test results.

• The student who finds a notice in a lover's desk that he has tested positive and then fears telling him, because he will know that she was snooping, and fears telling her regular boyfriend because he will be so angry at her.

• The parent who worries about teenage offspring but doesn't know how to talk to them in a way which will affect their behaviour.

What Can We Do?

Public Education

It is now clear that it will be many years before science will discover an effective vaccine or treatment. In the interim, education about the modes of transmission and safe-sex practices is the only effective avenue to prevention and the only hope for a more rational and humane response to the issues. However, to educate effectively requires a direct and explicit discussion of the very sexual practices that many find repulsive, or at least embarrassing.

Although not fail-proof, condoms have been demonstrated to be the most effective method, other than abstinence, to protect against the interchange of blood, semen, and vaginal fluids, and they are recommended as a basic safe-sex practice when engaging in fellatio and anal or vaginal penetration. The gay community in New York City and San Francisco have made significant strides in the reduction of sexually transmitted disease and in reducing the HIV seroconversion rate among gay men. This has been accomplished largely through the use of sexually explicit instruction regarding the techniques of safer sex as well as heightened motivation to change behaviours (Gay Men's Health Crisis 1987).

In spite of the above, there has been great debate about the advisability of mentioning condom use in public school sex education or of advertising condoms on public television. Even in New York State, a state that has every reason to deal as effectively and directly as possible with AIDS prevention, the decision to allow the mention of condoms beginning in the seventh grade came only after much struggle (Carmody 1987).

With a few exceptions, for example, the Assistant Secretary of Health and the Surgeon General of the U.S. Public Health Service (see U.S. Department of Health and Human Services 1986, and Windom and Koop 1987), national policy makers have not provided relevant leadership. Education Secretary Bennett, echoing the position of the Reagan administration, has consistently argued that teachers and parents should emphasize abstinence as the best safeguard against AIDS and that to promote the use of condoms suggests to teenagers that adults expect them to engage in sexual intercourse (Bennett 1987).

To many observers, this seems to ignore the fact that about 28 percent of persons aged 12 to 17 are currently sexually active, about 70 percent of teenage girls and 80 percent of teenage boys have had at least one coital experience, and an estimated five million have used intravenous drugs (Yarber 1987a). Surveys of university students suggest that even this age group lacks factual information about AIDS, believes that they personally have no reason to be concerned, and do not discuss these topics with their partners (Caron, Bertran, and McMullen 1987). Given that about one-quarter of all AIDS cases are among persons aged 20 to 29 and the incubation period of AIDS can be up to five years or more, a large proportion of current AIDS cases may have been originally infected during adolescence.

Senator Helms was able to persuade the U.S. Senate to pass (94–2) an amendment to the Labor, Health and Human Resources, and Education appropriations bill for fiscal 1988 that prohibits the Centers for Disease Control from using any of the funds to provide AIDS educational activities that "promote or encourage" homosexuality (Booth, 1987b, 1036). This is in spite of the fact that gay persons, who represent about 10 percent of the U.S. adult population, are a major risk group and in need of education and counselling regarding how to reduce that risk.

Most professionals agree that there is a need for AIDS education in the schools and colleges. The question is at what level, how explicit the information should be, and whether there should be a strong moral message regarding premarital sex and alternative lifestyles (see Yarber 1987a).

Two curricula, in particular, have received positive reviews from sex educators (Brick 1987): *Teaching AIDS: A Resource Guide on AIDS* (Quackenbush and Sargent 1986), and *AIDS: What Young Adults Should Know* (Yarber 1987b). See also *SIECUS Report*, July-August 1987, for an annotated bibliography of books, booklets, pamphlets, curricula, and audiovisuals for AIDS and safer sex education. Several books have been specifically written for family members of persons with AIDS (e.g., Martelli, Peltz, and Messina 1987; Moffatt 1986).

Voluntary, Anonymous Testing with Counselling

Since April 1985, all blood donated to U.S. blood banks has been routinely tested for antibodies to HIV by the ELISA (enzyme-linked immunosorbent assay) screening test (see Barnes 1987, and Hunter 1987 for reviews of facts and issues related to testing). If reactive (i.e., "seropositive") blood is retested by the same method and if again reactive is tested by the more complicated Western blot test. A positive test result indicates that the individual has been exposed to HIV and presumably still harbours the live virus and can transmit it to others. There is no way to know whether an HIV-positive person will eventually develop AIDS.

Because the ELISA test was designed to ensure protection of the blood supply, it frequently results in false positive results that require further confirmation. A higher percentage of these false positives will occur in the case of persons in low-risk groups where the likelihood of true positives is rare. Because the development of antibodies can require up to one to three months after infection or, on occasion, as much as six months or more, it is possible to get a false negative if the blood sample is obtained before the point of seroconversion. With a growing number of laboratories entering the market, and no federal regulation of laboratory procedures, there is an increasing problem with test inaccuracy (Barnes 1987).

The issue of testing has been particularly controversial because of the conflict between concerns for public protection and concerns for civil liberties. There have been various proposals for universal testing; for testing of all marriage-licence applicants, pregnant women, army recruits, prison inmates, hospital admissions, immigrants, patients at drug abuse and sexually transmitted disease clinics, and prostitutes; and for the tracking and testing of all partners of persons with AIDS or who are HIV positive.

In establishing a policy regarding testing, one must be very clear about the purpose of the testing. Is it to gather epidemiological data in order to establish societal infection rates and chart the course of the epidemic? To protect the public health by identifying all possible carriers of infection? To provide information to doctors so they may better treat their patients? Or to inform individuals so that they may make wise decisions with regard to their own behaviours? The danger is that the results of testing will be used, inadvertently or otherwise, to stigmatize the individual, and the reality is that universal mandatory testing of large groups of persons would be too costly and ineffective to be viable. Persons in high-risk groups, who most need to learn of their infection status, would be likely to "go underground" to avoid testing, and among low-risk groups there would be large numbers of false positives, thus arousing unnecessary and sometimes debilitating stress.

The arguments against mandatory testing of marriage-licence applicants are typical: it is estimated that it would cost $100 million annually to test the 3.8 million persons who marry each year, and there are far too few laboratories and technical staff to handle the volume with sufficient accuracy. Many of the high-risk women become pregnant while single, and so would not be reached through this process. A large proportion of marriage applicants have already been sexually active and, hence, are at risk of transmission prior to marriage. There would be insufficient staff to provide the pre- and post-test counselling necessary to help persons deal with the potentially very personal and often highly emotional implications of either a negative or a positive test result (Shernoff 1987).

Given the above realities, until such time as the availability of an effective cure makes knowledge of one's HIV status essential for health, the only viable solutions are (1) to educate all persons to routinely use safe-sex techniques unless they have been in an exclusively monogamous relationship for an extended period of time, and (2) to provide easy access to voluntary anonymous testing combined with professionally performed pre- and post-test counselling.

Currently before Congress are two bills (HR 3071 and S 1575) that would provide monies for testing and pre- and post-test counselling, with confidentiality of testing records and federal prohibitions against discrimination on the basis of antibody status or AIDS diagnosis. The House bill (HR 3071) was introduced by Waxman (D-CA) and referred to the Subcommittee on Health and the Environment (of the Energy and Commerce Committee), while the Senate bill (S 1575) was introduced by Kennedy (D-MA) and referred to the Committee on Labor and Human Resources. Testing is currently recommended for persons with a history of intravenous drug use, sexual partners of intravenous drug users, pregnant women whose history places them in a high-risk category, and persons who received transfusions of blood or blood components from

1978 to mid-1985 (Coulis and DeSiena 1987).

Integrated Family-Oriented Health Care

It is estimated that, in 1991 alone, we will need to provide health care for at least 174 000 AIDS patients at a cost of $8 billion to $10 billion. In New York City, the majority of patients are medically indigent and hospital costs average $800 per day and $60 000 a year per patient (Heagarty 1987). With the projected care needs, many health-care systems will be overwhelmed. There is an urgent need for federal funds to share in the costs of compassionate care for patients in and outside the hospital setting.

Increasingly, programs are experimenting with ways to help patients remain in their homes for the majority of the time with the help of professional caregivers, family members, and significant others (Smith 1987). A model program has been developed by St. Vincent's Hospital and Medical Center in New York City, where 30 percent of their AIDS patients are hospitalized two to seven times each year for an average of 16 days per visit, with many patients remaining in their homes 8-11 months per year (O'Brien, Oerlemans-Bunn, and Blanchfield 1987). Two-thirds of the caseload of the supportive care staff involves supervising the care of AIDS patients at home and assisting them through the repeated bouts of illness that are characteristic of the disease.

The physical and psychological effects of the disease are similar to those of any of the life-threatening catastrophic illnesses (such as cancer or end-stage renal disease). The major differences are the typical age of the patient and the social stigma and isolation that often accompany the disease. The patient may live outside the usual family unit, and the caregiving partner or friend may be young and inexperienced in dealing with death and illness, fearful of contracting the disease, and, in some cases, may develop AIDS during the course of caregiving.

The psychological concomitants of the disease can be as distressing as the physiological effects (Salisbury 1986). Persons who have progressed to full-blown AIDS typically experience the emotional stages of any dying patient: denial, anger, bargaining, depression, and acceptance. Some experience repeated anxiety over the uncertainty of the disease, with this sometimes expressed in angry outbursts at families and caregivers. Some experience mild chronic depression, with alternating waves of anger, guilt, self-pity, and anxiety. There may be gradual infection of the central nervous system leading to forgetfulness, poor concentration, confusion, and even dementia. As the disease progresses and there is persistent fatigue and a decline in physical well-being, the person will become more and more dependent on others and increasingly obsessive about the disease process. The particular individual's reaction will be strongly influenced by the reactions of significant others and the extent to which there is available emotional and social support.

Efforts should be made to help the individual participate as actively as possible in normal occupational, leisure, and social activities and to take an active role in his or her treatment by attending support groups and by learning about nutrition as well as techniques of stress management and relaxation. The goal is to maximize quality of life and to reduce fear, isolation, and helplessness.

Communities need to provide a battery of services including chronic-care facilities, home nursing services, counselling, anonymous testing, social services, and welfare assistance (e.g., see Griggs 1986). There must be help for seropositive individuals and their significant others as well as for persons in the more advanced stages of the disease. A team approach to work with the patient and the family is essential to prevent burnout. The AIDS Project at the Ackerman Institute for Family Therapy in New York City has developed a model program devoted to providing therapy for HIV-infected individuals and their families/significant others so that they can be helped to talk directly about the difficult emotional issues elicited by the illness (Mohr et al. 1988; Walker 1987; Walker 1988). The Gay Men's Health Crisis in New York City and The Shanti Project and Visiting Nurses and Hospice of San Francisco provide various models for community care (see Arno, 1986; "Reaching Out . . ." 1987).

Long-Term Implications

The National Coalition on AIDS and Families was organized in November 1987 as a working association of organizations and professionals concerned with the impact of the AIDS epidemic on families (Caron, Macklin, and Rolland 1987, 1988). It views AIDS as a major crisis facing all families and believes that persons and organizations concerned with the well-being of families must take an active role to help them prepare to deal effectively with this crisis.

The principles underlying the work of the coalition can serve as guidelines for all professionals concerned with AIDS and families:

- AIDS affects families and not just the individual that contracts the disease.
- The family plays a key role in education, prevention, and attitude change regarding AIDS.
- The family must be seen as the unit of care in the treatment of AIDS. Families need to be educated regarding this role and be provided the support services they require in order to be effective.
- The impact on the family continues beyond the illness and death of the infected member.
- Special attention must be given to the needs of low-income families and families of colour because these families suffer most severely from the AIDS epidemic.
- The impact of the AIDS epidemic on families, and the reaction of families, will vary with ethnicity, religion, race, and social class.
- Efforts must be made to reduce the stigma, discrimination, and isolation of families with an HIV-infected member.

- Preventive and educational efforts must be rational, pragmatic, and supportive of healthy sexuality.
- Decisions regarding the psychosocial aspects of prevention and treatment must be based on solid theory and research.
- Social policy regarding AIDS must recognize and respond to the strengths and needs of families.

The AIDS epidemic offers our society an opportunity and a challenge to conquer some of our most long-term and difficult social issues. To do so will require that we reach past our fears and prejudices to our most compassionate and rational selves. If we can do so, the current tragedy may have powerfully positive implications for our whole society:

- We may finally achieve federally funded health care.
- The epidemic may provide the motivation needed to develop adequate drug rehabilitation services.
- Research on the virology of AIDS may hasten the understanding of other diseases whose cure has long eluded us.
- We may finally develop effective sex education that will, in fact and not just in theory, have significant impact on attitudes and behaviours.
- We may narrow the gap between the gay and straight worlds. Already the epidemic has helped to inform the non-gay community about gay lifestyles and the dynamics of gay relationships. Efforts of such projects as Gay Men's Health Crisis and Shanti have done much to win respect for the strength and compassion of the gay community.
- The crisis may heighten the abilities and predisposition of individuals to make conscious rational decisions about their sexual lives and to effect more open, realistic communication with their sexual partners.
- Experience with the dying of so many young persons, and recognition of the inability of traditional services to deal effectively

with the present crisis, may do much to accelerate the hospice and home-care movement and help our society develop more humane approaches to the process of death.

One is reminded of the poster of a small child and the words, "I have AIDS. Please hug me. I can't make you sick" (see AIDS Hot Line for Kids). It is hopefully symbolic that, whereas the logo for the Third International Conference on AIDS (held in Washington, DC, in 1987) was a picture of the virus, the logo for the Fourth International Conference on AIDS (to be held in Stockholm, Sweden, in 1988) is of a human family: "The silhouettes of human figures — a man, woman, and child — are the most prominent feature of the design, overshadowing the virus and signalling the emergent awareness of the profoundly human issues raised by the epidemic and its impact on all humanity" (Osborn and Brandt 1987, 14).

Works Cited

Arno, P. 1986. "The Nonprofit Sector's Response to the AIDS Epidemic: Community-Based Services in San Francisco." *American Journal of Public Health* 76: 1325–30.

Barnes, D.M. 1987. "New Questions About AIDS Test Accuracy." *Science* 238: 884–85.

———. 1988. "AIDS Virus Creates Lab Risk." *Science* 239: 348–49.

Bennett, W.J. 1987. *AIDS and the Education of Our Children: A Guide for Parents and Teachers.* Washington, DC: Department of Education.

Boffey, P.M. 1988 "Spread of AIDS Abating, But Deaths Will Still Soar." *New York Times* (February 14): 1, 35.

Booth, W. 1987a. "AIDS and Insects." *Science* 237: 355–56.

———. 1987b. "Another Muzzle for AIDS Education?" *Science* 238: 1036.

Brick, P. 1987. "Curricula Reviews — AIDS: Education For Survival." *SIECUS Report* 15(6): 16-17.

Carmody, D. 1987. "Guide Approved for Curriculum in AIDS Classes." *New York Times* (October 24): 2.

Caron, S.L., R. Bertran, and T. McMullen. 1987. "AIDS and the College Student: The Need for Sex Education." *SIECUS Report* 15(6): 6-7.

Caron, S.L., E.D. Macklin, and J. Rolland. 1987. "Report on Organizational Meeting of the National Coalition on AIDS and Families." Atlanta, GA. Unpublished Proceedings. (Copy available from E. Macklin.)

———. 1988. "Report on Meeting of the Steering Committee of the National Coalition on AIDS and Families." New York (January 9). Unpublished proceedings. (Copy available from E. Macklin.)

Centers for Disease Control. 1988. *AIDS Weekly Surveillance Report* (January 18). Atlanta, GA: CDC.

Coulis, P.A., and J.J. DeSiena. 1987. "AIDS Immunodiagnosis: Questions and Answers About Screening Tests." *AIDS Patient Care* 1(June): 25-27.

Dickson, D. 1987. "Africa Begins to Face Up to AIDS." *Science* 238: 605–7.

Folks, T.M., et al. 1987. "Cytokine-Induced Expression of HIV-1 in a Chronically Infected Promonocyte Cell Line." *Science* 238: 800.

Friedland, G.H., and R.S. Klein. 1987. "Transmission of the Human Immunodeficiency Virus." *The New England Journal of Medicine* 317: 1125–35.

Gallo, R.C. 1987. "The AIDS Virus." *Scientific American* 256 (January): 45-56.

Gay Men's Health Crisis. 1987. *The Safer Sex Condom Guide for Men and Women.* New York: Gay Men's Health Crisis.

Gonda, M.A. 1986. "The Natural History of AIDS." *Natural History* 95 (May): 78–81.

Griggs, J., ed.. 1986. *AIDS: Public Policy Dimensions.* New York: United Hospital Fund of New York.

Guinan, M.E., and A. Hardy. 1987. "Epidemiology of AIDS in Women in the United States: 1981 through 1986." *Journal of American Medical Association* 257: 2039–42.

Heagarty, M.C. 1987. "AIDS: A View from the Trenches." *Issues in Science and Technology* 3(2): 111–17.

Hunter, N. 1987. "AIDS Prevention and Civil Liberties: The False Security of Mandatory Testing." *SIECUS Report* 16(7): 1–9.

Institute of Medicine, National Academy of Sciences. 1986. *Confronting AIDS: Directions for Public Health, Health Care, and Research.* Washington, DC: National Academy Press.

Leishman, K. 1987a. "AIDS and Insects." *The Atlantic Monthly* 259 (September): 56–72.

———. 1987b. "Heterosexuals and AIDS: The second stage of the epidemic." *The Atlantic Monthly* 259 (February): 39–58.

Martelli, L.J., F.D.P. Peltz, and W. Messina. 1987. *When Someone You Know Has AIDS: A Practical Guide.* New York: Crown.

Moffatt, B.C. 1986. *When Someone You Love Has AIDS: A Book of Hope for Family and Friends.* New York: Penguin.

Mohr, R., et al. 1988. "AIDS and Family Therapy." *The Family Therapy Networker* 12(1): 33–43, 81.

New York State Department of Health. 1986. *AIDS: 100 Questions and Answers.* Albany: New York State Department of Health.

Norwood, C. 1987. *Advice for Life: A Woman's Guide to AIDS Risks and Prevention. A National Women's Health Network Guide.* New York: Pantheon.

O'Brien, A.M., M. Oerlemans-Bunn, and J.C. Blanchfield. 1987. "Nursing the AIDS Patient at Home." *AIDS Patient Care* 1: 21–24.

Osborn, J.E., and E.N. Brandt. 1987. *Summary Report: III International Conference on Acquired Immunodeficiency Syndrome (AIDS) — June 1–5, 1987.* Washington, DC/Bethesda, MD: National Institutes of Health.

Peabody, B. 1986. *The Screaming Room: A Mother's Journal of her Son's Struggle with AIDS.* San Diego: Oak Tree.

Quackenbush, D., and P. Sargent. 1986. *Teaching AIDS: A Resource Guide on AIDS.* Santa Cruz, CA: Network Productions.

Quinn, T.C., et al. 1986. "AIDS in Africa: An Epidemiologic Paradigm." *Science* 234: 955–63.

"Reaching Out to Ease the Pain of Final Days." 1987. *USA Today* (September 28): 40.

Salisbury, D.M. 1986. "AIDS: Psychosocial Implications." *Journal of Psychosocial Nursing* 24 (December): 13–16.

Shernoff, M. 1987. "Pre- and Post-Test Counseling for Individuals taking the HIV Antibody Test." *SIECUS Report* 16(7): 10–11.

Smith, A.M. 1987. "Alternatives in AIDS Homecare." *AIDS Patient Care* 1 (June): 28–32.

Stone, M. 1987. "Q and A on AIDS." *New York* (March 23): 34–43.

U.S. Department of Health and Human Services. 1986. *Surgeon General's Report on Acquired Immune Deficiency Syndrome.* Washington, DC: U.S. Public Health Service.

Walker, G. 1988. [...] *Therapy Network[...]*

Walker, L.A. 198[...] ilies." *New Yo[...]* 16–22, 63, 78.

Weiss, S.H., et a[...] nodeficiency [...] Laboratory W[...]

Windom, R.E., [...] *AIDS Answers.* [...] Association.

Yarber, W.L. 1987a. "School AIDS Education: [...] itics, Issues, and Responses." *SIECUS Report* 15(6): 1–5.

———. 1987b. *AIDS: What Young Adults Should Know.* Reston, VA: American Alliance for Health, Physical Education, Recreation, and Dance.

Contributors

M. Oluwafemi Agbayewa (MB, FRCP) is Associate Professor of Psychiatry at the University of British Columbia, in Vancouver, and Head of the Department of Psychiatry at the Regional Hospital in Prince George, British Columbia.

Paul Ammons (PhD) is Associate Professor at the University of Georgia, in Athens, with a joint appointment in the School of Social Work and the Department of Child and Family Development.

Jane Aronson (PhD) is Assistant Professor of Social Work at McMaster University, in Hamilton.

Chris R. Bagley (DPhil) is Professor in the Faculty of Social Work at the University of Calgary.

Maureen Baker (PhD) is Associate Professor in the Department of Sociology at Scarborough College, University of Toronto.

Roderic P. Beaujot (PhD) is Associate Professor of Sociology at the University of Western Ontario, in London, and Director of its Centre for Canadian Population Studies.

Vern Bengston (PhD) is Professor and Director of the Gerontology Research Institute in the Andrus Gerontology Center at the University of Southern California, in Los Angeles.

Peter Berger (PhD) is University Professor and Director of the Institute for the Study of Economic Culture at Boston University.

Gary Caldwell is a researcher at the Institut québécois de recherche sur la culture in Montreal.

Paula J. Caplan (PhD) is Professor of Applied Psychology at the Ontario Institute for Studies in Education, Toronto, and head of its Community and Feminist Psychology Program.

Linda M. Conrad (MA) is currently a Research Associate with the Langley School District in Vancouver.

J.E. Cutler was a sociologist who worked and wrote early in the century, and whose work foreshadowed many of the later concerns about gender roles and family relationships.

Maria de Koninck (PhD) is Chair of Women's Studies at Laval University, in Quebec, and Professor in its Department of Social and Preventive Medicine.

Edythe de Terre (PhD), also known professionally as Edythe Krampe Adin, is a lecturer in the Sociology Department and in the Child Development Program at California State University, in Fullerton.

Louise Dulude (MLL) is a doctoral student of laws at the University of Ottawa.

Donald G. Dutton (PhD) is Professor in the Department of Psychology at the University of British Columbia, in Vancouver.

Margrit Eichler (PhD) is Professor of Sociology at the Ontario Institute for Studies in Education, in Toronto.

Catherine E. Foote (MA, MSW) is a doctoral candidate in Social Work at the University of Toronto.

Daniel Fournier (PhD) is a researcher at the Institut québécois de recherche sur la culture in Montreal.

Jane Gaskell (EdD) is Professor and Head of Social and Educational Studies at the University of British Columbia, in Vancouver.

Jay Goldstein (PhD) is Associate Professor in the Department of Sociology at the University of Manitoba, in Winnipeg.

David Green (PhD) was Professor of History at the University of Saskatchewan, in Saskatoon, and is employed in the private sector.

Ian Hall-McCorquodale (BSc) is a graduate student in psychology at the Ontario Institute for Studies in Education, Toronto.

Tim B. Heaton (PhD) is Associate Professor of Sociology at Brigham Young University, in Provo, Utah.

David W. Hillock (MSW) is a doctoral candidate in Social Work at the University of Toronto.

Clinton J. Jesser (PhD) is Professor of Sociology at Northern Illinois University, in Dekalb.

Mansfried Kellner (PhD) is Professor of Sociology at Johann Wolfgang Goethe-Universität in Frankfurt-am-Main, in West Germany.

Karen K. Kersten (PhD) is a Clinical Research Fellow at the University of Michigan, in Ann Arbor.

Lawrence K. Kersten (PhD) is Professor of Sociology at Eastern Michigan University, in Ypsilanti.

Barbara Landau (PhD, LLB, LLM) is a psychologist, mediator, family law lawyer, and a member of the Board of Directors of the Academy of Family Mediators.

D.W. Livingstone (PhD) is Professor of Sociology at the Ontario Institute for Studies in Education, in Toronto.

Eugen Lupri (PhD) is Professor of Sociology at the University of Calgary.

Meg Luxton (PhD) is Associate Professor of Social Science at Atkinson College in York University, Toronto.

Naomi B. McCormick (PhD) is Professor of Psychology at State University of New York College at Plattsburgh.

Eleanor D. Macklin (PhD) is Associate Professor and Director of the Marriage and Family Therapy Program in the Department of Child, Family and Community Studies at Syracuse University.

Kevin McQuillan (PhD) is Associate Professor of Sociology at the University of Western Ontario, in London.

Maureen Moore (BA) is a senior analyst in the Demography Division of Statistics Canada, in Ottawa.

Christine Overall (PhD) is Associate Professor of Philosophy at Queen's University, in Kingston.

Susan Prentice (MES) is a graduate student in sociology at York University, Toronto.

J. Robert S. Prichard (LLM, MBA) is President of the University of Toronto, and former Dean of Law at the University of Toronto.

Roy H. Rodgers (PhD) is Professor of Family Science at the School of Family and Nutritional Sciences at the University of British Columbia, in Vancouver.

Carol Schmid (PhD) is Professor of Sociology at Guilford Technical Institute in Jamestown, North Carolina.

Alexander Segall (PhD) is Professor of Sociology at the University of Manitoba, in Winnipeg, and a Research Associate in the Centre on Aging in Winnipeg.

Terry S. Stein (MD) is Professor of Psychiatry in the Colleges of Osteopathic Medicine and Human Medicine at Michigan State University, in East Lansing, and Director of its AIDS Education Program.

Paul D. Steinhauer (MD, FRCP) is Professor of Psychiatry at the University of Toronto, and Director of Training in its Division of Child Psychiatry. He is Senior Staff Psychiatrist at the Hospital for Sick Children, in Toronto.

Nick Stinnett (PhD) is Professor in the Department of Human Development and Family Studies at the University of Alabama, in Tuscaloosa.

Carol Strike (BA) is a staff writer for *Canadian Social Trends*, and has a continuing research interest in the study of AIDS and its social consequences.

Ray J. Thomlison (PhD) is Professor and Dean of the Faculty of Social Work at the University of Calgary.

Jan E. Trost (PhD) is Professor of Sociology at Uppsala Universitet, Sweden.

Aysan Tuzlak (PhD) is Assistant Professor in the Department of Sociology of Scarborough College, University of Toronto.

Jean E. Veevers (PhD) is Professor of Sociology at the University of Victoria.

Charles F. Westoff (PhD) is Professor of Sociology at Princeton University.

S. Allen Wilcoxon (EdD) is Associate Professor of Counselor Education at the University of Alabama, in Tuscaloosa.

Hans L. Zetterberg (PhD) was a faculty member in the Department of Sociology at Columbia University, in New York.

To the owner of this book:

We are interested in your reaction to *Continuity and Change in Marriage and Family* by Jean E. Veevers.

1. What was your reason for using this book?

   _____ university course   _____ continuing education course
   _____ college course   _____ personal interest
                                _____ other (specify)

2. In which school are you enrolled? _____

3. Approximately how much of the book did you use?

   ____ ¼   ____ ½   ____ ¾   ____ all

4. What is the best aspect of the book?

5. Have you any suggestions for improvement?

6. Is there anything that should be added?

Fold here

(fold here and tape shut)

0116870399-M8Z4X6-BR01

Heather McWhinney
Publisher, College Division
HARCOURT BRACE & COMPANY, CANADA
55 HORNER AVENUE
TORONTO, ONTARIO
M8Z 9Z9